THE BEHAVIOR OF FISH
AND OTHER AQUATIC ANIMALS

A contribution to the integration of psychological and biological approaches to behavior, this treatise synthesizes the relevant thinking in these disciplines by reporting the behavior of a selected number of fish and other aquatic animals. The contributors, representing their respective disciplines of biology and psychology, have taken special care to assure that this work will be of value to readers from either audience. Topics covered include psychosensory physiology, toxicology, and ethology.

Besides serving as an introduction and review of current theoretical and experimental work, the book provides research designs and indicates potentials for future research. It is addressed to professionals in psychology, animal behavior, ethology, zoology, marine biology, and to advanced students in these disciplines.

THE BEHAVIOR
OF FISH
AND OTHER
AQUATIC ANIMALS

CONTRIBUTORS

C. I. ABRAMSON

RICHARD R. FAY

A. M. GRANDA

WILLIAM N. HAYES

KAREN LEE HOLLIS

LEONARD C. IRELAND

JOHN W. KANWISHER

GEORGE S. LOSEY, JR.

G. C. McLEOD

H. MARCUCELLA

J. H. MAXWELL

DAVID NORTHMORE

J. BRUCE OVERMIER

FRANCES C. VOLKMANN

DEAN YAGER

THE BEHAVIOR
OF FISH
AND OTHER
AQUATIC ANIMALS

Edited by

DAVID I. MOSTOFSKY

Department of Psychology
Boston University
Boston, Massachusetts

ACADEMIC PRESS   New York   San Francisco   London   1978

A Subsidiary of Harcourt Brace Jovanovich, Publishers

ACADEMIC PRESS, INC.
111 Fifth Avenue, New York, New York 10003

United Kingdom Edition published by
ACADEMIC PRESS, INC. (LONDON) LTD.
24/28 Oval Road, London NW1 7DX

Library of Congress Cataloging in Publication Data

Main entry under title:

The Behavior of fish and other aquatic animals.

Includes bibliographies.
1. Fishes—Behavior. 2. Aquatic animals—Behavior.
I. Mostofsky, David I.
QL639.3.B43   597'.05   77-80791
ISBN 0-12-509250-4

PRINTED IN THE UNITED STATES OF AMERICA

Contents

List of Contributors   ix

Preface   xi

1   The Symbiotic Behavior of Fishes

GEORGE S. LOSEY, JR.

I.	Introduction—Modern Views of Symbioses	1
II.	Field Methods of the Marine Ethologist	2
III.	Symbioses Involving Many Species	4
IV.	Symbioses Involving a Small Number of Species	17
V.	Concluding Remarks	24
	References	27

2   Behavioral Toxicology and Teleost Fish

H. MARCUCELLA AND C. I. ABRAMSON

I.	Introduction	33
II.	Conditioning and Learning	35
III.	Behavioral Toxicity	57
IV.	Summary	70
	References	71

3   Vision in Fishes: Color and Pattern

DAVID NORTHMORE, FRANCES C. VOLKMANN, AND DEAN YAGER

I.	Introduction	79
II.	Spatial Vision	82
III.	Chromatic Vision	114
	References	129

4 The Function of the Teleost Telencephalon in Behavior: A Reinforcement Mediator

KAREN LEE HOLLIS AND J. BRUCE OVERMIER

I.	Introduction	137
II.	Analysis of the Role of the Telencephalon	148
III.	Telencephalon Ablation, Behavior, and Reinforcement	157
IV.	Comparative Psychological Research: A Comment	176
	References	188

5 Sound Detection and Sensory Coding by the Auditory Systems of Fishes

RICHARD R. FAY

I.	Introduction	197
II.	Sound Detection	198
III.	The Analysis of Auditory Information	211
IV.	Auditory Localization	219
V.	Auditory Electrophysiology	224
VI.	Conclusion	229
	References	231

6 The Behavior of Turtles in the Sea, in Freshwater, and on Land

A. M. GRANDA AND J. H. MAXWELL

I.	Introduction	237
II.	Systematics	242
III.	Sensory Systems	244
IV.	Major Behavior Patterns	251
V.	Conclusion	276
	References	276

7 Visually Guided Behavior of Turtles

WILLIAM N. HAYES AND LEONARD C. IRELAND

I.	Introduction	281
II.	The Testudinata	282
III.	Depth Perception	285
IV.	Visual Alarm Reactions	288
V.	Optokinetic Responses	292
VI.	Water-Finding Behavior	300
VII.	Migration and Homing	305
VIII.	Summary and Conclusions	313
	References	314

8 The Gas Bubble Disease of Fish

G. C. McLEOD

I.	Introduction	319
II.	Adaptation to Supersaturation	320
III.	Supersaturation: An Environmental Problem	324
IV.	Experimental Induction of Gas Bubble Disease in Adult Atlantic Menhaden	324
V.	Testing Procedure for Gas Supersaturation	328
VI.	Symptomatology of Gas Bubble Disease in Menhaden	330
VII.	The Interaction of Changing Temperatures and Supersaturation of Gases in Adult Menhaden	332
VIII.	Conclusions	334
	References	338

9 Underwater Acoustic Biotelemetry: Procedures for Obtaining Information on the Behavior and Physiology of Free-Swimming Aquatic Animals in Their Natural Environments

LEONARD C. IRELAND AND JOHN W. KANWISHER

I.	Introduction	342
II.	Sound as a Medium for Underwater Telemetry	346
III.	Biological Applications of Underwater Acoustic Telemetry	349
IV.	Construction of Telemetry Equipment and Equipping Animals with Transmitters	363
V.	Conclusions and Speculations	372
	Appendix	373
	References	375

Index

381

List of Contributors

Numbers in parentheses indicate the pages on which the author's contributions begin.

C. I. ABRAMSON (33), Department of Psychology, Boston University, Boston, Massachusetts

RICHARD R. FAY (197), Department of Surgery, Section of Otolaryngology, Bowman Gray School of Medicine, Wake Forest University, Winston-Salem, North Carolina

A. M. GRANDA (237), Institute for Neuroscience and Behavior, University of Delaware, Newark, Delaware

WILLIAM N. HAYES (281), Department of Psychology, Albion College, Albion, Michigan

KAREN LEE HOLLIS (137), Department of Psychology, University of Minnesota, Minneapolis, Minnesota

LEONARD C. IRELAND (281, 341), Department of Psychology, Oakland University, Rochester, Michigan

JOHN W. KANWISHER (341), Department of Biology, Woods Hole Oceanographic Institution, Woods Hole, Massachusetts

GEORGE S. LOSEY, JR. (1), Department of Zoology, and Hawaii Institute of Marine Biology, University of Hawaii, Honolulu, Hawaii

G. C. McLEOD (319), New England Aquarium, Central Wharf, Boston, Massachusetts

H. MARCUCELLA (33), Department of Psychology, Boston University, Boston, Massachusetts

J. H. MAXWELL (237), Institute for Neuroscience and Behavior, University of Delaware, Newark, Delaware

DAVID NORTHMORE (79), Institute for Neuroscience and Behavior, University of Delaware, Newark, Delaware

J. BRUCE OVERMIER (137), Department of Psychology, University of Minnesota, Minneapolis, Minnesota

FRANCES C. VOLKMANN (79), Clark Science Center, Smith College, Northampton, Massachusetts

DEAN YAGER (79), Department of Behavioral Sciences, State College of Optometry, State University of New York, New York, New York

Preface

The revitalized interest in marine life and aquatic animals has brought with it special opportunities for the added participation by the specialties of comparative and experimental psychology. The historical union of the biological sciences and the behavioral sciences was once restricted to matters of abstruse theory or isolated ethological phenomena. Now, advances in both disciplines have created interdependencies in a variety of research settings. Research in aquatic life provides the most recent development for extending this joint partnership. While the level of expertise in this area resides mostly in biology, at least three categories of considerations warrant a critical and careful examination of the argument for a more aggressive and informed involvement by psychology at this time. They provide the guiding spirit for this book.

The first category relates to the value which would be realized as a result of enabling essential contributions to basic science. Much of what classical biology of a century ago defined as its mandate is currently a daily preoccupation of many psychological laboratories. The fine-grain analysis of an organism's behavior, in both its natural and contrived environments, has been increasingly the focus of psychological inquiry. While biologists have refined and adapted much of chemistry and physics for their methodology and analysis, the basic scientific inquiry relating to the behavior of living organisms has been supported by psychologists concerned with learning, perception, biophysical conditioning, social behavior, emotionality, and related "psychological" aspects of the total descriptive profile. These questions take on even greater importance when the issues are raised in the context of comparisons with other species. A disproportionate emphasis by behavioral scientists in studying only selected organisms has resulted in a seriously deficient understanding of aquatic life. For the growth of psychology as a science, and for the necessary complement of the efforts of biologists, such a "knowledgeability gap" needs to be drastically and rapidly reduced.

A second concern relates to the need for supporting the emergence and development of hybrid specialties. The collaborative union among the sciences has had several noticeable effects. First, it has produced a number of disciplines or fields which are identified by their hyphenated or concatonated labels, symbolic of autonomous and viable enterprises which represent an integrated and deliberate program of codisciplinary activity. The behavioral sciences have had their share of such hyphenated unions (witness psychophysics, neuropsychology, and psychopharmacology). Other specialized interests appear on the threshold of gaining such independence and recognition (e.g., behavioral neurophysiology). Whether "behavioral biology," "behavioral ecology," or some comparable endeavor can emerge and survive in the scientific community remains to be seen. More important is the recognition of the *need to explore* joint codisciplinary research for specialized bodies of inquiry. Marine biology, marine ecology, etc., seem to be the sponsoring agents of specialization in which behavioral techniques and theory comprise a meaningful component of the system.

Finally, there is the category of application and practical utilization. One pressing concern in assessing conditions relevant to conditions of marine ecology (and ultimately relevant to any proposed innovations for management of that environment) relates to reliable measurements and to the derivation of predictive equations for the behavior of marine life under specified conditions. Some of these questions are answerable for cellular and molecular levels only. Some are solvable by techniques of chemical assay and biophysical determinations. And not least, a large measure of the final information sought will depend upon understanding the observable (albeit grosser) perceptuomotor activity of these organisms—the daily preoccupation of experimental psychology. There are two realizations of such a behavioral program. First, it enables the derivation of a systematic and programmatic determination of relevant behavior, i.e., it provides a stable set of dependent variables against which to measure a variety of "treatment effects" (akin to the objective in psychopharmacology). Second, it sets the stage for intervention and modification of the environment to assure necessary behavioral control. One can consider the specific instance of toxicity or pollutants. The hope would be that a program of behavior research would ultimately provide an assessment of the effects of such stimuli on a variety of behaviors and functioning of the organism. Also, it is reasonable to plan for a program that would ensure avoidance or compensation by the organism to offset the threat that has invaded his ecological world.

The *Zeitgeist* of such activity has brought with it the need for published materials that can responsibly depict the status quo of existing knowledge, and that can serve to educate the scientist who is desirous of an organized presentation focused on biobehavioral issues and techniques. The appearance of this volume represents the first attempt to organize the original writings of specialists concerned with a variety of these issues and techniques. It is hardly the last work; hopefully it will rather serve to provide the necessary impetus for vitalizing a most important area of inquiry.

DAVID I. MOSTOFSKY

THE BEHAVIOR
OF FISH
AND OTHER
AQUATIC ANIMALS

1

The Symbiotic Behavior of Fishes

GEORGE S. LOSEY, JR.

   I. Introduction—Modern Views of Symbioses 1
   II. Field Methods of the Marine Ethologist 2
  III. Symbioses Involving Many Species 4
      A. Interaction within Feeding Guilds 4
      B. Interaction between Feeding Guilds 11
  IV. Symbioses Involving a Small Number of Species 17
      A. Goby/Shrimp Relationships 17
      B. Anemone/Fish Associations 19
      C. Mimetic Relationships 21
   V. Concluding Remarks...................................... 24
      A. Research Guidelines in Symbiosis 24
      B. Symbiotic Guidelines for Research on Social Behavior 26
     References 27

I. INTRODUCTION—MODERN VIEWS OF SYMBIOSES

The term "symbiosis" has been variously defined in the last century since its introduction by deBary (1879). I retain the original usage of the term as meaning "living together." This forces the symbiologist to consider virtually any interspecific relationship in which the species have at least some effect on one another. Symbioses have been subdivided in a variety of ways into familiar categories such as mutualism, parasitism, commensalism, etc. (Table I). The degree of harm as opposed to benefit that is realized by the symbionts due to their association was the basis of the earliest subdivision (e.g., Allee *et al.*, 1949). Many subsequent workers have shunned the subjective criteria of "harm" and "benefit" and used more objective indicators such as population growth rate (Odum, 1959), physiological dependency (Cheng, 1967), or survival value

TABLE I
Some Methods of Categorizing Symbioses

	Commensalism	Parasitism	Mutualism	Competition
Classic	Benefit to one No effect to other	Benefit to one Harm to other	Benefit to both	Harm to both
Population growth	Increase to one No effect to other	Increase to one Decrease to other	Increase to both	Decrease to both
Physiological	Facultative metabolic Dependency of one	Obligate metabolic Dependency of one	Obligate metabolic Dependency of both	Undefined

(Losey, 1972a). All of these measures prove to be valuable at one time or another as indicators of the status of the relationship between the species and the individuals of the species.

The form and the consequences of the relationships between symbionts may be highly variable in many cases. Keys (1928) indicated that the effect of ectoparasitic isopods on fish might become important only under adverse conditions. Lincicome (1971) with endoparasites and Losey (1972a, 1974a) with cleaning symbiosis in fish have indicated how some symbioses might exist as a mutualism, commensalism, or parasitism depending upon environmental factors. The status of any symbiosis as a mutualism or parasitism results from the balance of many factors. Our understanding of symbiotic relationships can be greatly increased through study of changes in the status of the symbiosis in response to changes in environmental factors.

This chapter explores a series of symbiotic relationships in fishes that range from broad multispecific types that have little or no intimacy between symbionts to intimate mutualistic relationships. Symbioses that have only limited interest in the study of behavior are avoided. The reviews are intended to aid nonsymbiologists in the understanding of the interspecific behavior of their animals and to encourage research on fish symbioses.

II. FIELD METHODS OF THE MARINE ETHOLOGIST

Although many behavioral problems can be approached by an observer restricted to the surface of the water, compressed gas diving has greatly extended the range of problems that can be approached. The observer may remain under water for many minutes or even hours with SCUBA or rebreather gear or remain for days to weeks in a saturation diving habitat. However, aside from the increased logistic difficulty of such methods, the marine ethologist is faced with

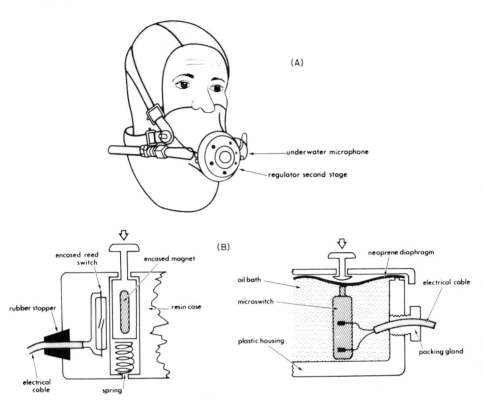

Fig. 1. "A" illustrates one type of underwater microphone for use with a tape recorder. (Drawn from advertisements by Hydro Products, a Tetratech Company, San Diego, California.) "B" gives a stylized drawing of two types of underwater keyboard switches for use with event recorders. Several such switches would be placed in each housing.

additional problems. A free swimming diver generates a variety of acoustic and visual stimuli. Exhaled air and swimming motions of a large and not entirely graceful biped appear to have a strong influence on many fishes. The use of underwater visual and acoustic blinds (Losey, 1971) or nearly bubble-free re-breather gear can help to solve these problems, but cost and logistic difficulty usually prevent their use. Underwater television can solve many of these problems (Myrberg, 1973), but it imposes similar cost and logistic problems. However, in many cases the use of television is demanded for at least some parts of the study. I have found dramatic changes in the types and numbers of fish observed on a Hawaiian reef when a diver was in the water as opposed to when only a television camera was present, and Myrberg (1973) has reviewed the value of television for the marine ethologist.

Those scientists fortunate enough to have access to an underwater television system also eliminate the problem of underwater recording of observations since standard laboratory equipment can be used during playback of video tapes. The diver is less fortunate. Most divers resort to writing slates with underwater paper or plastic. Some waterproof papers can even be used in common duplicating machines to produce standard data formats, maps, etc. (R. Nolan, University of Hawaii, personal communication). Underwater tape recorders can be used by placing a microphone inside of a full-face mask or by using a special mouthpiece that leaves the lips and teeth free to move and incorporates an underwater microphone (Fig. 1a). The tape recorder is probably the single most valuable piece of equipment for the marine ethologist. Underwater event recorders allow an even finer level of quantification in the field (Losey, 1971, 1972a, 1974a), but at present, they are not commercially available. However, a moderate amount of tooling skill can produce a waterproof switch box of reed switches, actuated by magnets, or a diaphram type of switch box (Fig. 1b). This may then be connected to a four- or eight-channel miniature event recorder in an underwater housing to form a powerful data recording tool for the diver. Miniature digital recorders may also be used but they require an interface to a computer or some mechanical data retrieval device.

Regardless of the methods and hardware employed and the handicap of operating in the foreign aquatic medium, recent years have testified to the feasibility of observational and experimental field studies of marine animals. They have proved to be of extreme value in the guidance and interpretation of more highly controlled laboratory studies. In studies of symbioses involving many species, such field observations are extremely important adjuncts to laboratory studies.

III. SYMBIOSES INVOLVING MANY SPECIES

Perhaps the broadest level of analysis of symbiotic interaction involves the temporal and spatial organization of marine reef fishes. Review of the complex predatory interactions and changeover patterns from the diurnal to nocturnal faunal elements is beyond the scope of this chapter. Hobson (1965, 1968, 1972, 1973) provides an in-depth study of these relationships. Instead this chapter will focus upon interactions within feeding guilds which have received a recent surge of attention from fish behaviorists, and upon a few more specialized relationships that cross the boundaries between feeding guilds.

A. Interaction within Feeding Guilds

1. The Guild of Benthic Herbivores

The relationships between species of herbivorous reef fishes have only recently received detailed attention and now promise to be one of the most fascinating symbioses in the reef environment. This section will outline how the social behaviors and feeding habits of many herbivorous fishes are interdependent on other sympatric members of their feeding guild.

Several types of social organizations are found among the benthic herbivorous fishes. They may be solitary home ranging, paired or in small roaming groups, form large uni- or multispecific schools, or show temporary to permanent territorial defense. Jones (1968) and Helfrich *et al.* (1968) were first to mention that the social organization of one species might result from the presence of others. They indicated that the frequent group feeding behavior of the manini (*Acanthurus triostegus*) enabled them to violate the territories of other species that were vigorously defended against individual intruders. Lorenz (1966) hypothesized that the bright colorations of many coral reef fishes served to avoid interspecific aggression. This contributed to the belief of earlier workers that cases of interspecific aggression resulted from "mistaken identity" of another species as a conspecific. Rasa (1969) indicated that the most frequent interspecific attacks of the territorial damsel fish, *Pomacentrus jenkinsi*, were directed toward the morphologically similar surgeon fish, *Ctenochaetus strigosus*.

Recent work, however, tends to refute or at least greatly modify these results. Albrecht (1969), Low (1971), Myrberg (1972), MacDonald (1973), Syrop (1974), Itzkowitz (1974), and Thresher (1974) have shown that several pomacentrid fishes which defend benthic territories and feed on benthic algae defend these territories at least somewhat selectively, usually against other benthic herbivores. In several cases the most frequent attacks were directed toward competitors with little or no morphological similarity to the territory holder. Myrberg and Thresher (1974) have suggested the concept of the serial territory wherein the boundary at

Fig. 2. The distance at which some territorial *Pomacentrus* spp. (A) might be expected to attack a carnivore, (B), an omnivore, (C), and a competitive herbivorous fish (D). The herbivore which probably competes with the territory holder is attacked at the greatest distance. See text.

which an intruder is attacked varies for different species and depends, at least partially, on the intruder's feeding habits (Fig. 2). Jones (1968) indicated the possible existence of a generic pecking order in terms of the species' relative ability to exploit and defend a food supply. This same type of interspecific hierarchy also appears to exist between certain cichlid fishes (G. W. Barlow, University of California, Berkeley, personal communication).

These studies have suggested a variety of problems in the interspecific or symbiotic behavioral ecology and ethology of fishes. I will list some of these problems below, usually with little more than superficial evidence to support their existence. Several of these relationships have also been suggested by Barlow (1974a,b) along with valuable comparisons to the cichlid fishes.

a. Aggression and Interspecific Territorial Defense. The most thoroughly documented form of interaction between herbivorous fishes is territorial defense. Species of acanthurid and pomacentrid fishes have been found to defend territories against other herbivorous fishes (e.g., Low, 1971; Barlow, 1974a). *Eupomacentrus planifrons* (Myrberg and Thresher, 1974) and probably many others express this territory by attacking other species at varying distances from the center of their feeding area: herbivores are attacked at a distant perimeter, whereas species such as carnivores may be tolerated until quite close to the center of the territory, or not attacked at all. The obvious interpretation of this territory as a protected feeding space in *Eupomacentrus jenkinsi* was supported by Syrop (1974). He found that the standing crop of filamentous algae was greater within territories of *E. jenkinsi* as opposed to surrounding unprotected areas, and that they defended larger territories on a reef that had a greater number of herbivorous competitors. He also indicated that the territory holder may maintain the standing crop of algae within the territory at the level of maximum sustainable yield.

Sale (1974) has drawn attention to the importance of interaction between herbivores that all defend territories in the same habitat. In some areas, he found that interactions between species of territorial pomacentrids may be more common than intraspecific interactions. He also found that many of these species coexist in the same microhabitat despite broad overlap in feeding habits and territorial behavior. He has suggested that the relative abundance of these species in any one area is largely determined by chance: i.e., all of the species are nearly equal in their ability to defend a space and that successful recruitment results from the "random creation of vacant living space, and . . . the uncontrolled dispersal of the pelagic larvae of all guild species" (Sale, 1974, p. 1). Coexistence of several competitive species in the same area might also be explained as an "edge effect" such that the habitat studied is intermediate between the habitats to which each species has specialized. There might as well be a ceiling effect on the degree of territoriality that is possible: All of these pomacentrids are highly aggressive in the defense of their territories. The energetic demands of more and more vigorous defense may limit these species to similar maximum levels of territorial defense. Their random dispersal of larvae and sedentary adult life could preclude any altruistic favoring of the recruitment of ones own species (see Trivers, 1971) and contribute to the maintenance of the coexistence of competitors.

In contrast to the overt competition depicted by Sale (1974), Nursall (1974a,b) and Sale (1975) have drawn attention to overlapping territories and character displacement. Herbivorous fishes of widely disparate morphology, size, and habitat utilization may share the same territories. Territory sharing has been found in blenniids (Losey, 1968) in which a smaller individual may defend a small territory within the boundaries of a superior individual of the same species. In this case, the relationship is possible due to the submissive and appeasement behavior of the subordinate individual. However, in many tropical reef fishes, such overlap within a species usually occurs when a juvenile of strikingly different coloration overlaps with an adult of its own species or where strikingly different species are involved. This supports Lorenz's (1966) view that high contrast color patterns in reef fishes serve to reduce interspecific aggression, but in light of the overwhelming evidence presented above, this view appears to be operative only when the degree of competition is reduced by a divergence of ecological requirements as well as morphological characteristics.

Investigation of the causal basis of interspecific territorial defense presents a challenge to fish behaviorists and promises to be a valuable tool in the study of territoriality and aggression (Myrberg and Thresher, 1974; Sale, 1974). Thresher (1974, and personal communication) has taken the first steps toward such analysis with revealing results. Many workers have assumed that territorial defense and aggression are identical systems. Thresher has found a seasonal correlation between measures of aggression and changes in the interspecific territorial defense perimeters in *Eupomacentrus partitus,* but a lack of correlation between these measures on a smaller time scale. While the priming or motivating effects of previous agonistic experience on the aggressive tendencies of an individual have been clearly shown in many animals, including fishes (Heiligenberg, 1965), Thresher has been unable to find such correlations between agonistic priming and interspecific territorial defense. Agonistic behavior for the defense of a food supply may well have evolved in a causal framework at least somewhat separate from intraspecific aggression in *E. partitus.* And yet, Thresher has also indicated a perplexing relationship between the presence of conspecifics and the defense of a serial territory. Individual *E. partitus* that have been isolated from conspecifics for several weeks lose all signs of the serial territory and begin to show similar territorial defenses against all other species. However, exposure to a conspecific for several days restores the former selectivity of their defense, and the serial territory is restored! Chases are again initiated against various species at species specific distances from the center of its territory. The significance of this phenomenon is presently obscure, but it clearly indicates that interspecific territorial defense and perhaps territoriality in general must be approached as a potentially unique element in the agonistic repertoire of the species.

It is also clear that such territorial defense is not merely the result of mistaken identity. The territorial animal must be responding to stimuli that separate potential competitors from other fishes. The range of effective stimuli and the ontogeny of the stimulus–response mechanisms have not been investigated, but such studies are vital to our understanding of this relationship. How broad is the potential range of stimuli that will release or can come to release the territorial response? What is the contribution of experience to the shaping and modification of the releasers of territorial defense? What is the relationship of these mechanisms to intraspecific territoriality?

Several of these questions also suggest that the functions of bright colorations in reef fishes demand further investigation. As Barlow (1974b) has suggested, Lorenz (1966) demonstrated a sharp perceptual ability in recognizing the relationship between color patterns and intense competition between tropical reef species. But whereas Lorenz presumed that this reflected a fine subdivision of the habitat and a reduction of overt competition between species, Barlow suggested that the bright colorations of many acanthurids serve as "broadcast signals," presumably as a warning of the sharp blade at the base of the tail. One should also consider the possibility that Lorenz's hypothesis of "escape from interspecific aggression" contributed strongly to the evolution of bright colorations in order to avoid interspecific attacks due to "mistaken identity." However, those species which were subjected to strong selective pressures to discriminate competitors may then have evolved other means of choosing which species to chase independent of their similarity in coloration. This hypothesis allows one to reconcile the differences between the various functions that have been suggested for poster coloration and recent studies of interspecific aggression. These questions and many others will undoubtedly demand much attention from fish behaviorists in the years to come and should provide valuable insight into the evolution of agonism.

b. Social Organization.   Social organization has been shown to respond to varying environmental conditions in animals ranging from fishes to primates. Many studies have included the density of conspecifics and sometimes relevant predators as variables which contribute to the determination of social organization. Few, however, have considered the effects of competitive species, and these studies have concentrated primarily on tropical insectivorous birds. Studies such as Moynihan (1968) have indicated the importance of the presence of competitors in the formation of mixed species flocks, but such relationships usually do not include drastic changes in the intraspecific social organization of the species.

Intraspecific and interspecific aggregations or "flocks" have been noted for many tropical herbivorous fishes (Randall, 1961; Jones, 1968; Itzkowitz, 1974; W. Bengeyfield, University of Hawaii, Dept. of Zoology, unpublished report). Barlow (1974a) has indicated a relationship between the density of competitive species and the formation of these aggregations. The common Indo–Pacific herbivore, *Acanthurus triostegus* (manini), may be found as solitary individuals or in large, roaming aggregations. Manini are frequently chased by many other reef herbivores and appear to be inferior to nearly all other herbivores on the reef in their ability to gain exclusive access to a food supply. Barlow found that where one of the manini's competitors, *A. nigrofuscus,* was lacking, manini tended to exist as solitary individuals. But in the presence of many *A. nigrofuscus,* the individual manini were excluded from their benthic food supply and formed large aggregations. These aggregations in turn invaded the territories of *A. nigrofuscus* and other herbivores which were unable to defend them effectively against so large a number of individuals. Adoption of the aggregating mode of organization functions as a counter to the ploy of territorial defense of a food supply. When aggregating, manini usually serve as a nuclear species (sensu Moynihan, 1962) for the formation of mixed species groups. They may be joined by many other species of acanthurids as well as a variety of other species. In Hawaii, many species of herbivores may serve as nuclear species for such groups including *A. nigrofuscus, A. olivaceous,* and *Scarus* spp. (Barlow, 1974a; W. Bengeyfield, unpublished report; G. Losey, personal observation). In some cases this involves a shift from a territorial mode of life to that of an aggregating species that then swims and feeds with other species that would otherwise be chased from its territory. For example, while *A. nigrofuscus* may exclude solitary manini from the bottom in some areas, other herbivores appear to exclude *A. nigrofuscus* in other areas and the *A. nigrofuscus* may then aggregate or join aggregations of manini. Complex mixed species groups may be formed in this manner that lack agonistic interactions between species except during actual feeding bouts (W. Bengeyfield, unpublished report). Itzkowitz (1974) found that herbivores such as scarids and *Acanthurus bahianus* were consistently found as "core" (nuclear) species for mixed species aggregations on Jamaican reefs. He found that some of the less numerous "associate" (attendant) species shifted their normal foraging pattern to match that of the "core" species.

The relationships between territorial and gregarious tendencies in these fishes, as well as the effects of food availability, await study. It also appears that the aggregating mode of life may be adopted due to the inability to defend a territory in some areas due to surge or tidal changes (Nursall, 1974a; G. Losey, personal observation), which may result in partial defense of a "territory" and/or aggregation as a protection against predation (see Hobson, 1968; Barlow, 1974a). Barlow (1974a) has supported the obvious adaptive value of aggregating in order to exploit a defended food supply in terms of the risk of an individual being attacked, but the actual gain of the individual in terms of food ingested as opposed to effort expended awaits investigation.

Mixed species aggregations of fishes are also of interest in their own right, particularly in comparison with mixed species flocks in birds (Moynihan, 1960, 1962, 1968; McClure, 1967; Vuilleumier, 1967; Morse, 1970; Buskirk et al., 1972). W. Bengeyfield (unpublished report) indicated that while the concepts of nuclear vs. attendant and active vs. passive species suggested for birds by Moynihan (1962) can be applied to these fishes, changes in category were common. Itzkowitz (1974) also indicated a general agreement with nuclear vs. attendant species, but he diverged somewhat from Moynihan's scheme in that he required a ''core'' species to lead the troop. This is equivalent to the nuclear passive category of Moynihan's scheme. While Moynihan (1968) indicated character convergence between species of the same mixed species flocks, such convergence is not indicated in fishes (G. Losey, personal observation). These discrepancies may well relate to the changeable nature of the social structure of many of these fishes as outlined above.

Study of mixed species aggregations in fishes is in an infantile stage of development and should occupy the efforts of behaviorists and ecologists for some time. Their studies will no doubt include both herbivorous and even predaceous fishes that have recently been found to aggregate in much the same manner as herbivores (G. Ludwig, University of Hawaii, personal communication), as well as many less active daytime aggregations of nocturnally active fishes (Itzkowitz, 1974).

2. The Guild of Benthic Carnivores

Little work has been done on behavioral relationships between benthic carnivorous fish species, and indeed, there appear to be fewer overt interactions between them as compared to the herbivorous species. There are, however, anecdotal accounts that may be of interest to the fish behaviorist, and Hobson (1974) has provided a detailed treatment of predatory methods in fishes.

When a new source of food such as an exposed sea urchin or an abandoned fish nest becomes available, many species of predators are usually attracted. Benthic fish eggs appear to be one of the most universally acceptable food items on the reef, even for fishes such as *Centropyge* angelfish which normally feed on algae and detritus (Lobel, 1975). It is little wonder that many fishes show vigorous defense of their nesting site and/or possess cryptic eggs. Recent observations suggest that some benthic carnivores and omnivores such as labrids and chaetodontids form mixed species aggregations much like many herbivorous fish (Section III,A,1). These groups show *en masse* invasions of vigorously defended nests of fish such as *Abudefduf abdominalis* (G. Ludwig, University of Hawaii, personal communication). These groupings may remain intact as the individuals roam over the reef invading series of nests. Similar associations may well form wherever fish prey on the benthic egg masses of larger fish which defend their nest.

It is also common for predators to follow groups or individuals of different feeding specializations. Many predators such as labrids and fistularids are found near the forefront of mixed species schools of herbivores (Section III,A,1). They appear to take advantage of the cover and/or flushing effect of the school in order to attack their prey (Barlow, 1974a; W. Bengeyfield, unpublished report). Fistularids in particular are frequently observed to follow large herbivores such as scarids and acanthurids and prey upon small fishes and invertebrates that are exposed by the feeding movements of the herbivore. Such relationships are, however, transient events, and the predator may leave its host, adopt another, or swim alone. In contrast, other associations appear to be more permanent and may have significance outside of the context of feeding. Of particular fascination is the association of small goat fish (frequently *Parupeneus* spp.) with equally sized or larger labrids (Itzkowitz, 1974; G. W. Barlow, University of California Berkeley, personal communication; G. Losey, personal observation). On many tropical reefs, individual goatfish can be observed following and feeding beside an individual labrid. This at first appears to be a transient phenomena until prolonged observations are made. While there is no concrete evidence to support it, there appears to be some sort of at least temporary one-way bond between the goatfish and its labrid. On many occasions, a goatfish that had become separated from its labrid has been observed to cease feeding and swim rapidly about the area until again encountering the same labrid individual, and then resume following and feeding. Of course, nonsystematic observations of this sort are extremely prone to exaggeration and error, but agreement between observers suggests that such "following" associations warrant further attention.

B. Interaction between Feeding Guilds

1. Cleaning Symbiosis

Cleaning symbiosis in fishes was first introduced to the scientific community by Limbaugh (1961) as a mutualism in which cleaning organisms remove ectoparasites and other material from the body of cooperating host fish. Feder (1966) provided an extensive review of earlier studies. In the idealized situation, the host fish approaches the cleaning fish or shrimp and assumes an invitation posture or pose and may change coloration, rest on the bottom, etc. The cleaner then inspects the body of the host and may remove and ingest items from the host. Limbaugh (1961) claimed that the presence of cleaners was critical to the health of host fishes on a Caribbean reef. Subsequent reports have indicated that cleaning interactions occur in perhaps the majority of fishes in both fresh and marine waters (Abel, 1971; Cressey and Lachner, 1970; Youngbluth, 1968; Losey, 1971, 1972a, 1974a; Hobson, 1971; Potts, 1973a,b; Wyman and Ward, 1972; von Wahlert, 1961; Ayling and Grace, 1971; Arndt, 1973).

Detailed studies have now revealed that there is considerable variability both in the symbiotic status of the relationship and in the form of the behavior involved. Youngbluth (1968) and Losey (1972a) removed cleaner fish from Hawaiian reefs to test Limbaugh's (1961) hypothesis that cleaning is essential to the health of reef fishes. Neither study revealed any gross change in the condition of fish deprived of cleaning. Losey (1972a) suggested that cleaning might exist as a commensalism or even a parasitism when the production rate of ectoparasites was low and the cleaner fed largely on its host's tissues and mucus. Cleaning could of course operate as a mutualism when rates of ectoparasitic infections were high. In support of the hypothesis of mutualism, Hobson (1971) found seasonal changes in the standing crop of ectoparasites on a fish in California which will not tolerate cleaners during its breeding season. Atkins and Gorlick (ms.) have shown that the presence of cleaner fish on reefs at Enewetak Atoll had a significant effect on the structure of the population of an ectoparasitic copepod. Losey (1974a) indicated that production rates of ectoparasites on a Puerto Rican reef were orders of magnitude greater than that found in Hawaii and that cleaning on this reef probably was mutualistic. Wyman and Ward (1972) found that cleaning symbiosis occurred between *Etroplus maculatus* and *E. suratensis* in aquaria only during an outbreak of disease. Cleaning symbiosis appears to exist as a *potential* mutualism that is of advantage to the host individuals only when the rate of infection by ectoparasites exceeds critical levels that can be adequately tolerated or dealt with by their own defense mechanisms. At other times, cleaners may exist as commensals or parasites and feed on fish scales, mucus, and occasional ectoparasites without seriously affecting the host individuals.

The question then arises as to how the symbiosis continues to exist when the evident survival value for the hosts is reduced to a commensalism or even reversed to a parasitism. Wyman and Ward (1972) indicated that the symbiosis between *Etroplus* spp. appeared in aquaria only when one of the species was infected. This is obviously not the case for many, if not most, marine species. Presence of ectoparasites is not a necessary prerequisite for responding to a cleaner (Youngbluth, 1968; Losey, 1971; Losey and Margules, 1974). However, there is much variability in the form of the interaction between marine cleaners and their hosts (Fig. 3). Some highly preferred host species are frequently pursued for cleaning or even attacked by *Labroides* spp. of cleaners and rarely pose or solicit the services of a cleaner. Other species of hosts may pose for long periods and receive little attention from the cleaners (Losey, 1971). Depriving

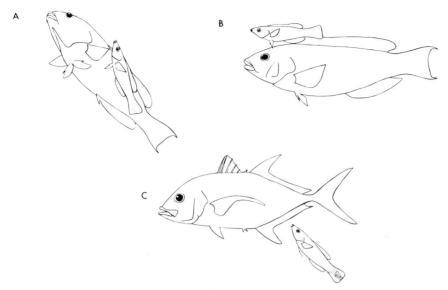

Fig. 3. "A" depicts a common "tail-down" pose orientation in a labrid host fish and typical inspection by a *Labroides* sp. of cleaner fish. Note the contact indicated between flank of the host and the pelvic, anal, and caudal fins of the cleaner. "B" illustrates pelvic-ride behavior seen in *Labroides* spp. in which they actively pursue a swimming host and contact it with their flickering pelvic fins. "C" depicts a parasitic attack on the anal fin of a passing host fish. Contact in this case is limited to biting of the host's fin.

hosts of cleaning can increase the amount of posing (Losey, 1971, 1975a), while exposing small groups of hosts to prolonged cleaning in an aquarium can greatly decrease the amount of posing for the cleaner (P. D. Atkins, unpublished report). In fact, after many hours, the hosts may begin to avoid the cleaner as would be expected in a parasitic relationship.

The answer appears to lie in a separation between the ultimate or evolutionary cause of the relationship and the proximate causes of response in the individual. Fricke (1966) found that host fishes would pose for a realistic model of a cleaner fish. Losey (1971) duplicated his results but also found that many host fishes would respond to a variety of unrealistic fish models and even learn to respond to bizarre "cleaners" such as paper clips and fishing lures as long as they could rub against the side of the fish. Stimulation of a host fish by a moving fish model can serve as a reinforcer for conditioning of complex tasks in at least some fish as long as it can rub against the fish's body (Losey and Margules, 1974). Tactile stimulation is the most probable source for this reinforcement (Losey, 1971). The motivation to respond to the stimulus of a cleaner model is a consummatory behavior in the host, *Chaetodon auriga,* in that it shows effects of satiation and deprivation while infection by ectoparasites has only peripheral effects on this response (Losey, 1975a, 1977).

Marine cleaning organisms have developed various means of delivering tactile stimulation to their hosts. Youngbluth (1968) described pelvic ride behavior in *Labroides phthirophagus* in which the cleaner positioned itself with its venter close to the head or trunk of its host (Fig. 3B). During pelvic ride the cleaner contacts the host with its twitching pelvic fins (Losey, 1972a; Losey and Margules, 1974). Wickler (1968) described mouth prodding in *L. dimidiatus*. Potts (1973b) described "stabilization" behavior in *L. dimidiatus* in which the cleaner contacted the host as in pelvic ride and appeared to stimulate the host to pose. *Gobiosoma* species of cleaners use flicks of their caudal fins against the host's body and produce a sensation much like the pelvic ride of *Labroides* on human skin (Losey, 1974a). Cleaner shrimp contact the host with waving antennae and delicate walking legs during cleaning. It appears that host fish learn to interact with the cleaner in order to receive tactile stimulation and not to purposely "have ectoparasites removed." As long as the hosts are not actually cleaned or painfully bitten too often, the gentle tactile stimulation received during inspection behavior maintains the pose response (Fig. 3). The evolution of the symbiosis between *Chaetodon auriga* and its cleaner, *Labroides phthirophagus,* appears to have involved a "behavioral parasitism" by the cleaner. The cleaner appears to have taken advantage of a tactile reward system in its host in order to feed on its body surfaces with apparent cooperation. The tactile reward system does not appear to have evolved for the purpose of cleaning symbiosis and appears to be present in many fishes if not most vertebrates (Losey, 1975a, 1977). Anecdotal study of naive "host" fish supports this opinion. A male *Istiblennius striatus* collected from a high tidal pool at Enewetak Atoll showed initial avoidance of cleaners in an aquarium and undoubtedly lacked experience as a host fish. Within one day, however, the blenny began to spend nearly all of its time soliciting the attentions of the cleaner. After removal of the cleaner, the blenny spent much time "soliciting" next to other fishes in the tank until it was eaten by a small moray eel while "soliciting" in front of this predator.

This hypothesis explains a variety of phenomena that have been observed regarding cleaning behavior. Host fish may continue to respond to cleaners even when these cleaners themselves are parasitic on their hosts that lack ectoparasites. The hosts continue to pose because of a preponderance of positive tactile stimulation. However, hosts may cease to pose for a hungry cleaner in an aquarium because it preys on them continually with obviously painful results. Fish learn to pose for new cleaners (Herald, 1964) and other bizarre objects that deliver gentle tactile stimulation.

In my admittedly biased opinion, many fish behaviorists can gain additional insight into the behavior of their subjects by remaining attentive to cleaning symbiosis. On many occasions I have compared notes with a colleague after watching captive fish only to find that I had noted a variety of symbiotic behaviors while my colleague had noted only social interactions. Behavior that appears to be related to cleaning symbiosis is perhaps more recognizable if one thinks of it as interspecific allogrooming. Fish may follow another individual and frequently stop in front of it or even crowd it into a corner and perform the "pose" solicitation display. Hermit crabs, parrotfish, or even small moray eels may be the object of these solicitations. Fish may also adopt the habit of hovering in the bubble stream from an aquarium airstone, probably as a source of tactile stimulation. Behavior of this sort is particularly common in captive marine reef fish and may grow to occupy a large portion of its time in the stimulus poor environment of the aquarium.

It will also be of interest to investigate the contribution of tactile stimulation to the form of other contact and close proximity behaviors such as courtship, parental behavior, etc. Does reinforcement by tactile stimulation help to shape the form of these behaviors? "Glancing" by young cichlids that feed on parental mucus (Ward and Barlow, 1967) is an obvious candidate for investigation. Is the response of the parent shaped by stimulation from the young in an obvious analogy to cleaning symbiosis?

2. *Parasitic Feeding Relationships*

Parasitism may refer to a relationship in which one symbiont is harmed while the other benefits, or where one species population shows a depressed growth rate while the other flourishes, or when there is a one-way metabolic dependency of the parasite on the host. Through the use of one or more of these definitions, many interspecific relationships such as Batesian mimicry may be classed as parasitic. Concepts and experimental paradigms of parasitology may frequently be applied to these relationships with considerable profit to the researcher (see Section IV,B). The breadth of this section, however, will be addressed toward cases of overt behavioral parasitism such as feeding on scales and mucus.

Teleost fish scales are frequently thought of as a hard armor coating that is of little or no food value. However, the large number of fish species that feed entirely on scales and/or mucus testifies to their importance as a food. The bony ridge scale of teleosts contains up to 50% organic material and, as a dermal structure, it is covered by epidermal and dermal tissues that are removed with the scale. Parasitic scale feeding has been reported for both marine and freshwater fishes (Marlier and Lelup, 1954; Hoese, 1966; Roberts, 1970; Major, 1973).

The tropical marine fish, laie (*Scomberoides lysan*), shows an interesting change from parasitic to predatory feeding habits in its ontogeny (Fig. 4) (Major, 1973). The young are equipped with outwardly curving teeth and are found schooling with atherinids and other "bait fish" such as *Pranesus insularum*, their host species. They approach the host from above and behind and scrape against their sides thus knocking off scales that are subsequently ingested. The

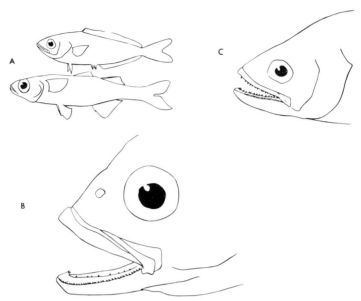

Fig. 4. "A" illustrates the typical predatory position of a young *Scomberoides lysan* above one of its hosts, *Pranesus insularum*. In "B," the head of the young *S. lysan* is greatly enlarged to demonstrate the preponderance of small, outward curving teeth on the outside of its jaw. These teeth are used to remove scales from their hosts. In "C," a small adult *S. lysan* is pictured in the same scale as "A." Note the change in dentition to primarily large teeth toward the center of the jaw.

host schools do not appear to avoid or show any loss in susceptibility to infection by this common parasite. Thus, the young gain the protection of a large school (e.g., see Hobson, 1968) and a plentiful food supply. As the laie age, however, they attain a much larger size than their hosts. They lose the outward curving teeth in favor of the grasping and cutting dentition of a predator. At the same time, they forsake the protection of the school for the life of a solitary predator and ingest the entire body of their former hosts. Major found a parallel development in two species of the genus *Oligoplites*.

The laie serves as an excellent example of changes in morphology that demand and are paralleled by changes in behavior. It also illustrates that one of the major distinctions between ectoparasitism and predation is the relative size of the symbionts: Many of the differences between ectoparasitism and predation such as physical intimacy, destruction of host, etc., all appear to stem from differences between the size of the host/prey and the parasite/predator. Major (1973) mentions the "stalking" behavior of the laie which is of speculative interest in the light of recent findings in cleaning symbiosis (Section III,B,1). The laie swam just forward and above the first dorsal fin of its host and often had at least one of its pelvic fins extended to within 2 to 3 mm of its host's dorsum. It also frequently extended its anal fin. The position and posture are identical to the "pelvic ride" behavior described for the cleaner fish, *Labroides phthirophagus* (Youngbluth, 1968). The single major difference appears to be that the cleaner delivers mild tactile stimulation to its host during pelvic ride behavior (Losey, 1972a; Losey and Margules, 1974), while the laie has not been reported to make actual contact with its host. This lack of tactile stimulation and associated response of the host appears to be the greatest behavioral difference between cleaner fish and the juvenile laie! While Major (1973) does not discuss their significance, he lists unidentified invertebrates as a portion of the gut contents of juvenile laie. Are these ectoparasitic invertebrates? Is the stalking position of the laie representative of an evolutionary stage in the development of cleaning by *Labroides* species? Are laie in fact delivering tactile stimulation to their hosts? If the last possibility is true it would explain why hosts such as *Pranesus insularum* do not appear to avoid the laie. In this case we would be forced to call the laie a possible if incompletely developed cleaner fish since ingestion of scales and biting of its hosts are also common attributes of the cleaning wrasse, *Labroides*.

Some other ectoparasitic fish appear to feed on the mucus of other fishes instead of scales. *Plagiotremus* (*Runula*) species dart out and feed on the sides of larger fishes and even swimmers. While they possess long sharp canines that are capable of cutting flesh and removing scales, these appear to be defensive weapons that are not brought to bear on their hosts (Hobson, 1968; Springer and Smith-Vaniz, 1972). Mucus feeding is probably common in cleaner fishes as well (Section III,B,1) and is well documented as a juvenile feeding mechanism in certain cichlid fishes (Ward and Barlow, 1967). Benson and Muscatine (1974) have indicated the potential importance of mucus as a food supply in the marine environment. Some species, however, such as *Plagiotremus laudandus* definitely do remove scales from certain hosts with small scales such as *Pterocaesio* spp. (G. Losey, personal observation) but may depend on mucus from other hosts such as holocentrids which have large scales.

IV. SYMBIOSES INVOLVING A SMALL NUMBER OF SPECIES

A. Goby/Shrimp Relationships

Many marine gobies (Gobiidae) inhabit sand or mud burrows from the intertidal zone to depths of 100 m or more. But many of these fish live in partnership with a burrow-digging shrimp and are incapable of digging and maintaining their own burrows. The observer usually finds one or two gobies resting or feeding at the mouth of the burrow while the shrimp continually digs and maintains the burrow (Fig. 5). The California blind goby, *Typhlogobius,* is an apparent excep-

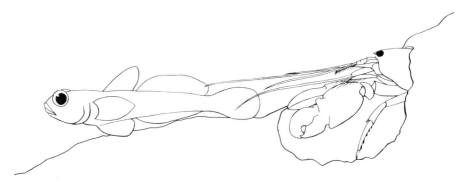

Fig. 5. A goby is pictured in the "guard" position at the entrance to its burrow. Its shrimp "partner" is typically in contact with the fish's caudal fin while outside of the burrow.

tion and probably remains deep in the burrow. But the many eyed species such as *Psilogobius* in Hawaii and *Amblyeleotris* in Japan appear to have similar behavior. The goby serves the function of a visual monitor of the environment and warns the shrimp of approaching objects through visual and tactile stimuli.

Communication between goby and shrimp was investigated by Moehring (1972) for the goby, *Psilogobius mainlandi,* and its two alternative hosts, *Alpheus rapax* and *Alpheus rapacida.* As might be expected in a mutualistic relationship (Losey, 1971), she found special signals and responses in both shrimp and goby that appeared to serve the function of symbiotic association. The presence of a goby at the entrance to the burrow favored the occurrence of burrowing behavior by the shrimp. Flicking and beating of the goby's tail served as a warning of danger to the shrimp and led to withdrawal of the shrimp within the hole. Communication from the shrimp to the goby was largely concerned with the location of the shrimp: When the shrimp was within its burrow, the goby fed and was active in its interaction with other gobies. When the shrimp was out near the mouth of the burrow, the goby assumed a guarding position and, when the shrimp responded to a warning signal of the fish, guarding behavior was again favored by the goby. Nearly all symbiotic signals were in the tactile sensory mode.

Moehring points out an interesting problem regarding communication between symbionts. Marler (1961) has suggested five types of messages that can be transmitted: species identifying, sexual, individual recognition, motivational, and environmental. Moehring points out that a single signal may serve different functions in social and symbiotic communication. A courtship action by a goby may serve as a motivational display of readiness to mate to another goby and simultaneously serve as an environmental message of an absence of predators to its symbiotic shrimp. Thus, the symbiologist may be faced with a particularly difficult problem in deciphering the relationship between causation (perhaps sexual motivation in this example) and symbiotic function. As indicated for cleaning symbiosis (Section III,B,1), there may well be disparity between the proximate and ultimate causes of behavior, particularly in a symbiosis.

Moehring also indicated an interesting relationship regarding the spacing of individuals. *Alpheus rapax* tend to group when isolated from symbiotic gobies, whereas *A. rapacida* females defend territories and are paired with males. However, since communication between shrimp is largely tactual, animals live in close proximity to one another when isolated from gobies. Gobies that are isolated from shrimp defend large territories and use largely visual communication. Symbiotic animals, however, show a compromise in territory size. This example clearly demonstrates the importance of studying a symbiotic animal under the natural conditions of its symbiosis and without its symbiont. While in this case the major effect appears to have been due to mechanical interaction between symbionts, the next section will indicate both behavioral and physiological differences between associated and nonassociated individuals.

B. Anemone/Fish Associations

Many fishes have been found in association with coelenterate hosts (Dales, 1966). The most extensive associations are within the pomacentrid fishes where species of genera such as *Pomacentrus, Chromis, Dascyllus, Amphiprion*, etc., range from facultative to apparently obligatory symbionts in stoney corals and sea anemones (Fig. 6). Many plankton-feeding species retreat into the cover of finger corals such as *Acropora* and *Pocillopora* upon the approach of a large object and during the evening. The apparently more specialized anemone fish spend much of their time within the tentacles of their host anemones and use it as

Fig. 6. An *Amphiprion* sp. of anemone fish is pictured in lateral contact with its host anemone.

shelter, similar to the coral dwelling species. These species are capable of acclimating to their anemone so that they are free to contact its nematocyst-laden tissues in a manner that could cause anything from a painful sting to paralysis and death in an unacclimated fish. These so-called anemone fish have been the subject of much research, frequently with conflicting results. Mariscal (1972) and Allen (1972) have provided ample review of the research on the behavior and ecology of the anemone fish as well as the nature of the acclimation process. However, recent results necessitate the inclusion of an update on this topic here.

Mariscal (1970) provided a milestone series of experiments that served to clarify a series of methodological errors of some previous workers and outline the methodology for proper investigation of the phenomenon of acclimation to sea anemones. He was able to narrow down the possibilities to some change in the mucous coating of an acclimated fish's skin. After acclimation, either the presence of some new compound inhibited nematocyst discharge or some compound that formerly elicited discharge was absent. Any additional compounds could have been manufactured by the acclimating fish or obtained from the anemone.

Foster (1975) investigated the acclimation process in *Amphiprion* spp. and *Dascyllus* spp. She found similarly complex but qualitatively different acclimation behavior in *Dascyllus* spp. of facultative anemone fish. Similar to *Amphiprion,* acclimation behavior progressed from minimal contact and nematocyst discharge in the initial stages of acclimation. This grades into total vigorous contact and complete lack of nematocyst discharge in the acclimated fish. Fish in the process of acclimation possessed discharged nematocysts in their mucus that were lacking in fully acclimated fish. However, acclimated fish had both discharged and undischarged nematocysts in their gut contents, which they apparently ingested while "nibbling" the tentacles of the anemone. Thus, acclimating and unacclimated fish had a continuous input of nematocyst toxin. Electrophoretic examination of the mucus of the fish showed that after acclimation, a unique protein was present that was not evident in unacclimated fish mucus or in the anemone or its toxin. The process of acclimation appears to result in the production of a unique protein that inhibits nematocyst discharge. Continuous contact with the anemone, and possibly receipt of nematocyst toxin, is necessary for maintenance of this inhibitory mucus. Current investigations are being conducted on the precise nature of this mechanism. Schlichter (1972) has also found a unique protein in the mucus of acclimated anemone fish, but he also found this protein in the mucus of the anemone. He suggested that this is a nematocyst inhibitor that is produced by the anemone for control of its stinging cells. The more sensitive disk-gel electrophoretic method used by Schlichter (1972) suggests that Foster (1975) may have failed to detect the protein in the mucus of her anemones due to differing stains and electrophoretic techniques.

Foster also made a variety of revealing behavioral observations that can best be reviewed in the context of the parasitologist's stages of interaction: attraction phase, infection phase, maintenance phase, and escape of the symbiont. Anemone fish show both visual and olfactory attraction to anemones, but the most strongly attractive stimulus is an anemone with a symbiotic fish already present. Infection is accomplished by eliciting limited nematocyst discharge that apparently triggers the production of a chemical inhibitor of nematocyst discharge. Not only were all anemones studied susceptible to infection by all anemone fish, but apparently many other fish as well. Foster observed both *Dendrochirus brachypterus* and *Acanthurus dussumieri* to inhabit potent anemones in captivity, and Smith (1973) and Abel (1960) have observed *Labrisomus kalisherae* and *Gobius bucchichii* in acclimated association with potent anemones in the field. It appears that while anemone fish have developed special behavior to take advantage of a biochemical process, many other fish may possess the necessary biochemical pathways but lack the behavior. The maintenance phase is accomplished by continued ingestion of nematocysts and their toxin in order to provide continued production of the nematocyst inhibitor. While the escape phase is of little importance in this type of mutualism, it results in a loss of the nematocyst inhibitor and necessitates reacclimation.

A variety of differences can be found between acclimated, "symbiotic" fish and "nonsymbiotic" fish without anemones. Eibl-Eibesfeldt (1960) and Mariscal (1972) noted that nonsymbiotic anemone fish lacked the strength of territorial defense found in fish with anemones. Foster (1975) alluded to the possibility of poor condition and a lack of vigor and coloration in chronically nonsymbiotic *Amphiprion chrysopterus* held in the laboratory. Symbiotic fish will dart quickly into an anemone, while nonsymbiotic fish rarely if ever dart directly into total contact with anemones. While this highly adaptive behavior is certainly not surprising, Foster found additional complications. When symbiotic fish were removed from their anemones to have their mucus sampled, 3 out of 30 individuals did not reenter their anemones immediately upon reintroduction to the aquarium. Control fish whose mucus coating had not been disturbed reentered their anemone without fail (three individuals with 12 replicates each). Thus, even during the maintenance phase, the fish have some means of predicting their immunity of nematocyst discharge without having to be stung each time. Finally, the presence of a unique mucous protein in symbiotic fish is an obvious difference from the nonsymbiotic condition. These examples further illustrate the importance of studying both symbiotic and nonsymbiotic individuals (see also Section IV,A).

C. Mimetic Relationships

Mimetic relationships are a unique type of symbiosis that involves a minimum of three parties, usually three species: the mimic, the model, and the third party or the animal that fails to distinguish between the model and the mimic (see

Wickler, 1968). Fish mimicry has been reviewed by Randall and Randall (1960) and Springer and Smith-Vaniz (1972) and so will receive only passing mention here. Many of the mimetic relationships in fishes involve parasitic feeding as discussed above. The mimic wears the guise of some harmless or even beneficial species in order to attack its prey. Other mimetic relationships involve escape from predation by resemblance to inedible or dangerous species or attraction of prey through the use of baits and lures.

One of the most interesting mimetic complexes that has been studied involves several species of three genera of blennies, *Meiacanthus, Plagiotremus (Runula)*, and *Ecsenius* (Springer and Smith-Vaniz, 1972; Losey, 1972b, 1975b). *Meiacanthus* spp. possess a pair of long canine teeth complete with venom-producing glands and a groove for the injection of venom into the wound. Their teeth are used as a protection against predation by biting the predator's mouth and throat after which they are released, frequently little harmed by the experience. Predators soon learn to avoid the colorful reef blenny. It appears that wherever a species of *Meiacanthus* occurs, it is mimicked by a species of *Plagiotremus* and *Ecsenius*. *Plagiotremus*, as discussed above, is a fish parasite and uses the guise of the inoffensive *Meiacanthus* to approach its prey. Since *Meiacanthus* uses its fangs only when it is attacked, most reef fish ignore its presence. Thus *Plagiotremus* is probably better able to approach its prey and may also enjoy a degree of predator protection due to its mimetic form. *Ecsenius* spp. are benthic herbivores and probably enjoy some degree of predator protection. This is suggested by their relatively open swimming and grazing behavior as compared with other reef blennies.

In the Red Sea, *Meiacanthus nigrolineatus* feeds on benthic invertebrates and is found close to the bottom near the microhabitat of its mimic *Ecsenius gravieri*. *Ecsenius gravieri* is a far more precise mimic of *M. nigrolineatus* than is the sympatric mimic, *Plagiotremus townsendi,* which is not found in such close association with the substratum. In the Marshall Islands, however, *Meiacanthus atrodorsalis* is a plankton feeder and is found hovering over the reef in the microhabitat of its mimic, *Plagiotremus laudandus,* which frequently schools with the model species. As might be expected, *P. laudandus* is a closer mimic of the model than the sympatric, *Ecsenius bicolor,* which is again closely associated with the substratum. It appears that the degree of behavioral and ecological association between the species has a profound effect on the strength of the selective pressure for the mimicry and thus the relative degree of resemblance by the two mimics.

While many examples of mimicry appear to be immediately obvious, it is necessary to employ caution in estimating the relative contributions of mimicry and independent convergence to the evolution of the mimic, as well as the importance of this mimicry to the survival of the species. Several species of

Plagiotremus display a dark horizontal stripe against a light background on their flank. Similar color patterns are found in many juvenile labrid fishes and in many elongate fishes in general (Barlow, 1972). It is tempting to hypothesize that the ectoparasitic *Plagiotremus* mimic the inoffensive labrids in order to more effectively approach their prey. However, the common occurrence of stripes in elongate fish dictates the use of caution in this interpretation. In addition, Losey (1968) found that striped as opposed to barred color patterns were more common among species of *Hypsoblennius* that inhabited visually homogeneous backgrounds. Several species showed a tendency to change from barred to striped patterns when they moved from visually disruptive to homogeneous backgrounds. He suggested that stripes afforded fewer visual cues of movement against a homogeneous background due to the lower number of moving, light/dark interfaces. These findings suggest caution in suggesting mimicry as a major factor in the evolution of *Plagiotremus*.

In other cases, mimicry has obviously played a major role in the evolution of the species, but its importance to the survival of the individual may be overestimated. The predaceous blenny, *Aspidontus taeniatus,* has been thoroughly documented as a mimic of the cleaning wrasse, *Labroides dimidiatus* (Randall, 1958; Wickler, 1960, 1961, 1963, 1968; reviewed by Springer and Smith-Vaniz, 1972). It is depicted as using its similarity to the benign cleaner in order to approach reef fishes and tear off fin membranes. However, adult fishes appear to have learned to distinguish between the model and the mimic such that only young fish are deceived (e.g., see Randall, 1958; Wickler, 1968), and the mimic appears to have little or no effect on the relationship between the cleaner and its hosts (Losey, 1974b). However, recent observations suggest that this may not always be the major function of the mimicry. While fin membranes have always demanded the majority of the attention in the diet of *A. taeniatus,* it may not be the most important type of food in their diet. Reexamination of gut content data from Randall (1958) shows that fin membranes were found in only 50% of the individuals, while 60% had eaten benthic fish eggs (eight individuals sampled). The four individuals that I sampled at Enewetak Atoll had all fed entirely on benthic fish eggs from pomacentrid, and gobiid fishes and the cleaner fish, *L. dimidiatus,* was also found to feed on these eggs. In addition, the only fish seen to chase the mimic were benthic pomacentrids, which frequently chase the cleaner as well, and various fish such as acanthurids solicited cleaning from the mimic and were not attacked (G. Losey, personal observation). It appears that many *A. taeniatus* may benefit from the mimicry by enjoying at least partial protection from predation, similar to cleaner fish, and perhaps rely on aggressive mimicry only when fish eggs are rare. This popular and frequently cited case of mimicry certainly deserves detailed examination under a variety of field conditions in order to properly assess its characteristics (Fig. 7).

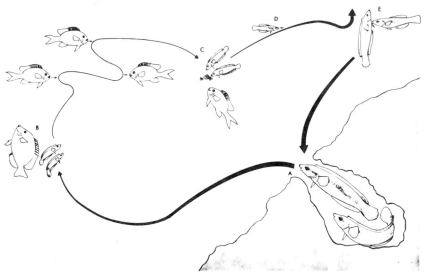

Fig. 7. Schematic of a typical hour in the life of a pair of adult cleaner mimics, *Aspidontus taeniatus,* observed at Enewetak Atoll (Eniwetok). In "A" the pair is inside of their rock burrow where one of the pair usually "stood guard" at the entrance. On close approach by a diver, this individual frequently emitted sharp grunting sounds. Eggs were found in the burrow with the male and female pair. At point "B" the pair has left the burrow to forage for food. They are both "ignoring" a fish that is posing as if it mistook the two *A. taeniatus* for *Labroides dimidiatus* cleaner fish. The mimics were never observed to attack posing hosts. Between "B" and "C," and far from their refuge, they are being attacked by nesting pomacentrid fishes and eating eggs from the pomacentrid nests. At "D" they are attacked by a *L. dimidiatus* far from their refuge just as this cleaner attacks members of its own species. At "E" it is cleaned by a *L. dimidiatus* that lives adjacent to its refuge.

V. CONCLUDING REMARKS

A. Research Guidelines in Symbiosis

Some general conclusions can be drawn concerning what appear to be profitable guidelines for research on symbiotic behavior. The first regards methods of categorization of symbioses as mutualism, commensalism, parasitism, etc. As outlined in the first section of this chapter, methods ranging from harm vs. benefit to the degree of metabolic dependency are available and may have variable utility for workers ranging from behaviorists to physiological parasitologists. The most important points to bear in mind are (1) all categorizations invoke an artificial compartmentalization upon a continuum of nature and should be used only as broad indicators; and (2) every researcher can probably profit by considering several methods of categorization. Each can result in additional insight into the dynamics of the relationship and lead to the formulation of testable hypotheses. Cleaning symbiosis serves as an example: Based upon a harm vs. benefit classification, cleaning relationships at least approach a state of mutualism. Thus, we might expect both symbionts to initiate interactions and have special signals and responses that function only in the symbiosis; and indeed they do. On the other hand, some cleaner fish appear to have an obligate metabolic dependency on their hosts while the hosts have no such dependency. According to Cheng (1967), this defines the category of parasitism. Thus, we might expect the parasite or cleaner to ultimately play the active role in initiating and maintaining the interaction and overcome the host's defensive mechanisms; and indeed, it appears that they do. Tactile stimulation by the cleaner appears to shape the behavior of its hosts and allows the cleaner to penetrate well into the "personal space" of its hosts.

The second conclusion is that much of the conceptual framework of the parasitologist may be applied to the study of behavioral symbioses. The phases of attraction, infection, establishment, maintenance, and escape of the parasite are common stages of research on endoparasites. Application of these terms to the anemone fish symbiosis draws attention to the possibility of a difference between infection and establishment of the anemone fish in an anemone and the maintenance of this relationship; and indeed one was found. The fish appears to demand a continual input of nematocyst toxin in order to maintain its immunity. Nibbling behavior has probably developed to provide ingestion of the toxin after acclimation has nearly or completely inhibited discharge of nematocysts into the epidermis.

A further usage of the parasitologists' approach is found in the concepts of susceptibility and immunity. Susceptibility infers that a host possesses the essential niche requirements of its symbionts. Immunity indicates that a susceptible host has gained effective defenses against infection, establishment, or maintenance of the parasite. For example, if a fish is not deceived by the guise of a mimic, we must determine whether it was susceptible to the mimic. Had it experienced the model? Or might it have been immune to the mimic? Had it experienced both the model and the mimic and learned to discriminate between them?

A third conclusion is that both symbiotic and nonsymbiotic preparations of all symbionts should be studied. Even though the nonsymbiotic condition might be unnatural or even pathological, considerable insight can be gained as to the nature of the relationship. Several examples in this chapter demonstrate the importance of this approach. From a behavioral standpoint, the territory size of the nonsymbiotic and symbiotic gobies and shrimps is particularly revealing.

B. Symbiotic Guidelines for Research on Social Behavior

I suggest that research on social behavior or intraspecific interactions might profit by attending to the methods and results of research on symbioses. In many cases, the methods and results of research on symbioses may have little or only in consequential applications, but in other examples, they may prove to be revealing.

The phases of interaction might again be borrowed from the parasitologist and applied to social interactions such as pair bonding. The processes of attracting, establishing, and maintaining a viable couple may well involve differing amounts of chemical, visual, acoustic, and tactile communication in the context of sexual or agonistic tendencies, in the various phases of interaction.

Symbiologists are obviously forced to consider the adaptive value and evolution of the behavior of each species separately and study their contribution to the symbiosis. The study of social behavior, however, frequently concentrates on the evolution of the system of signals and responses with less attention paid to the adaptive value of different roles within the system. However, relationships such as allogrooming can be profitably approached as a "symbiosis of roles" between groomer and groomee, even though each individual is capable of engaging in both roles. In many subordinate primates, grooming of a dominant serves to appease its aggression and maintain social relationships (Doyle, 1974). The behavior of groomer and groomee reflects this adaptive value: the groomer performs prolonged and intent movements that impart tactile stimulation to the groomee, while the latter remains more or less passive. The situation involves a striking parallel to cleaning symbiosis where the cleaner appears to enjoy the major benefit (Losey, ms.).

The study of symbioses also provides a clear demonstration of the relationship between the ultimate causes or adaptive significance of a behavior and the proximate causes of its occurrence in the individual. The proximate causes such as stimulus/response and motivational mechanisms are necessarily only an approximation to the ultimate factor. In many cases where there is strong pressure for precision, such as in the preservation of the individual or successful transmission of germ plasm, the proximate causes may be a close approximation of the ultimate. In other cases, such as behavioral symbioses or the phoretic relationships of some authors (Cheng, 1967), "mistakes" are not costly and the proximate may be a crude satisfaction of the ultimate goal. Cleaning symbiosis provides an exceptionally clear example: the host fish *Chaetodon auriga* responds largely on the basis of positive reinforcement by tactile stimulation from the cleaner fish. This "tactile hedonism" provides only the crudest approximation to the probable ultimate advantage of having ectoparasites removed. There is clear methodological danger in the tempting assumption that the ultimate adaptive factors play an important role in the proximate responses of the individual. In fact, many of the efforts of ethologists may be summarized as the study of how proximate causal factors satisfy the ultimate causes of behavior.

A final guideline is obvious for students of both interspecific and intraspecific interactions. The behavior of all animals is adapted to serve the ultimate goals of environmental, symbiotic, and social demands. While response to environmental variables is usually an obvious concern, it is all too easy for the symbiologist to ignore intraspecific interactions and for the social behaviorist to ignore symbioses. Thresher's discovery that the serial territoriality of *Eupomacentrus partitus* disappeared in the absence of conspecifics is a startling demonstration of the dangers for the symbiologist. Barlow's indication of extraspecific imposition of social grouping in the manini reveals a type of social organization that might not be noticed for this species if its symbiotic relationships were ignored. I have little doubt that the parallel study of symbiotic and social behavior will draw continually closer together in contributing to our understanding of ethology.

REFERENCES

Abel, E. F. (1960). Liaison facultative d'un poisson (*Gobius bucchichrii* Steindachner) et d'une anémone (*Anemonia sulcata* Penn.) en Méditerranée. *Vie Milieu* **11**, 517–531.
Abel, E. F. (1971). Zur ethologie von Putzsymbiosen einheimischer süsswasser Fische in naturalichen Biotop. *Oecologia* **6**, 133–151.
Albrecht, H. (1969). Behavior of four species of Atlantic damsel-fishes from Columbia, South America, (*Abudefduf saxatilis, A. taurus, Chromis multilineata, C. cyanea;* Pisces Pomacentridae). *Z. Tierpsychol.* **26**, 662–676.
Allee, W. C., Emerson, A. E., Park, O., Park, T., and Schmidt, K. P. (1949). "Principles of Animal Ecology." Saunders, Philadelphia, Pennsylvania.
Allen, G. R. (1972). "The Anemonefishes." T. F. H. Publications, New York.
Arndt, R. G. (1973). Cleaning symbiosis in some Florida brackish water cyprinodonts. *Mar. Aquarist* **4**, 5–13.
Atkins, P. D., and Gorlick, D. L. (ms.) Effects of cleaning by *Labroides dimidiatus* (Labridae) on reef fishes and fish ectoparasites at Enewetak Atoll.
Ayling, A. M., and Grace, R. V. (1971). Cleaning symbiosis among New Zealand fishes. *N. Z. J. Mar. Freshwater Res.* **5**, 205–218.
Barlow, G. W. (1972). The attitude of fish eye-lines in relation to body shape and to stripes and bars. *Copeia* pp. 4–12.
Barlow, G. W. (1974a). Extraspecific imposition of social grouping among surgeonfishes (Pisces: Acanthuridae). *J. Zool.* **174**, 333–340.
Barlow, G. W. (1974b). Contrasts in social behavior between Central American cichlid fishes and coral-reef surgeon fishes. *Am. Zool.* **14**, 9–34.
Benson, A. A., and Muscatine, L. (1974). Wax in coral mucus: Energy transfer from corals to reef fishes. *Limnol. Oceanogr.* **19**, 810–814.
Buskirk, H. W., Powell, G. V. L., Wittenberger, J. F., Buskirk, R. E., and Powell, T. V. (1972). Interspecific bird flocks in tropical highland Panama. *Auk* **89**, 612–624.

Cheng, T. C. (1967). Marine molluscs as hosts for symbioses. *Adv. Mar. Biol.* **5,** 1–424.

Cressey, R. F., and Lachner, E. A. (1970). The parasitic copepod diet and life history of diskfishes (Echeneidae). *Copeia* pp. 310–318.

Dales, R. P. (1966). Symbiosis in marine organisms. *In* "Symbiosis" (S. M. Henry, ed.), Vol. 1 pp. 299–326. Academic Press, New York.

deBary, A. (1879). "Die Erscheinungen der Symbiose." *Vers. Deut. Naturforscher und Aerzte zu Cassel,* 1878, Strassburg.

Doyle, G. A. (1974). Behavior of prosimians. *Behav. Nonhum. Primates* **5,** 155–338.

Eibl-Eibesfeldt, I. (1960). Beobachtungen und Versuche an Anemonenfischen (*Amphiprion*) der Maldiven und der Nicobaren. *Z. Tierpsychol.* **17,** 1–10.

Feder, H. M. (1966). Cleaning symbiosis in the marine environment. *In* "Symbiosis" (S. M. Henry, ed.), Vol. 1, pp. 327–380. Academic Press, New York.

Foster, M. A. (1975). The comparative acclimation behavior of several pomacentrid fishes to tropical sea anemones. Ph.D. Dissertation, University of Hawaii, Dept. of Zoology, Hawaii, Honolulu.

Fricke, H. (1966). Zum Verhalten des Putzerfisches, *Labroides dimidiatus. Z. Tierpsychol.* **23,** 1–3.

Heiligenberg, W. (1965). The suppression of behavioral activities by frightening stimuli. *Z. Vergl. Physiol.* **50,** 660–672.

Helfrich, P., Piyakarnchana, T., and Miles, P. S. (1968). Ciguatera fish poisoning. 1. The ecology of ciguateric reef fishes in the Line Islands. *Occas. Pap. Bishop Mus.* **23,** 305–369.

Herald, E. S. (1964). Cleanerfish for a cleaner aquarium. *Pac. Discovery* **17,** 28–29.

Hobson, E. S. (1965). Diurnal-nocturnal activity of some inshore fishes in the Gulf of California. *Copeia* pp. 291–302.

Hobson, E. S. (1968). Predatory behavior of some shore fishes in the Gulf of California. *U. S., Bur. Sport Fish. Wildl., Res. Rep.* **73,** 1–92.

Hobson, E. S. (1971). Cleaning symbiosis among California inshore fishes. *Fish. Bull.* **69,** 491–523.

Hobson, E. S. (1972). Activity of Hawaiian reef fishes during the evening and morning transitions between daylight and darkness. *Fish. Bull.* **70,** 715–740.

Hobson, E. S. (1973). Diel feeding migrations in tropical reef fishes. *Helgoläender Wiss. Meeresunters.* **24,** 361–370.

Hobson, E. S. (1974). Feeding relationships of teleostean fishes on coral reefs in Kona, Hawaii. *Fish. Bull.* **72,** 915–1031.

Hoese, H. D. (1966). Ectoparasitism by juvenile sea catfish, *Galeichthys felis. Copeia* pp. 880–881.

Itzkowitz, M. (1974). A behavioural reconnaissance of some Jamaican reef fishes. *Zool. J. Linn. Soc.* **55,** 87–118.

Jones, R. S. (1968). Ecological relationships in Hawaiian and Johnston Island Acanthuridae (Surgeonfishes). *Micronesica* **4,** 309–361.

Keys, A. B. (1928). Ectoparasites and vitality. *Am. Nat.* **62,** 279–282.

Limbaugh, C. (1961). Cleaning symbiosis. *Sci. Am.* **205,** 42–49.

Lincicome, D. R. (1971). The goodness of parasitism. *In* "Aspects of the Biology of Symbiosis" (T. C. Cheng, ed.), pp. 139–228. Univ. Park Press, Baltimore, Maryland.

Lobel, P. (1975). Comparative ecology and reproductive biology of the Hawaiian pygmy angelfishes (*Centropyge:* Pomacanthidae). Honors Thesis, University of Hawaii, Dept. of Zoology, Hawaii, Honolulu.

Lorenz, K. (1966). "On Aggression." Harcourt, Brace, and World, New York.

Losey, G. S. (1968). The comparative behavior of some Pacific fishes of the genus *Hypsoblennius* Gill (Blenniidae). Ph.D. Dissertation, Scripps Institution of Oceanography, La Jolla, California.

Losey, G. S. (1971). Communication between fishes in cleaning symbiosis. *In* "Aspects of the

Biology of Symbiosis" (T. C. Cheng, ed.), pp. 45–76. Univ. Park Press, Baltimore, Maryland.

Losey, G. S. (1972a). The ecological importance of cleaning symbiosis. *Copeia* pp. 820–833.

Losey, G. S. (1972b). Predation protection in the poison-fang blenny, *Meiacanthus atrodorsalis,* and its mimics, *Ecsenius bicolor* and *Runula laudandus* (Blenniidae). *Pac. Sci.* **26,** 129–139.

Losey, G. S. (1974a). Cleaning symbiosis in Puerto Rico with comparison to the tropical Pacific. *Copeia* pp. 960–970.

Losey, G. S. (1974b). *Aspidontus taeniatus:* Effects of increased abundance on cleaning symbiosis with notes on pelagic dispersion and *A. filamentosus* (Pisces, Blenniidae). *Z. Tierpsychol.* **34,** 430–435.

Losey, G. S. (1975a). Cleaning symbiosis and other allogrooming behavior. *Ani. Behav. Soc. Abstr.* p. 46.

Losey, G. S. (1975b). *Meiacanthus atrodorsalis:* Field evidence of predation protection. *Copeia,* pp. 574–576.

Losey, G. S. (1977). Host motivation incleaning symbiosis: *Chaetodon auriga.* (In preparation.)

Losey, G. S., and Margules, L. (1974). Cleaning symbiosis provides a positive reinforcer for fish. *Science* **184,** 179–180.

Low, R. M. (1971). Interspecific territoriality in a pomacentrid reef fish, *Pomacentrus flavicauda* Whitely. *Ecology* **52,** 648–654.

McClure, H. E. (1967). The composition of mixed species flocks in lowland and sub-montane forests of Malaya. *Wilson Bull.* **79,** 131–154.

MacDonald, C. (1973). Reproductive behavior and social dynamics of the yellowtail damselfish, *Microspathodon chrysurus* (Perciformes: Pomacentridae). M.S. Thesis, University of Puerto Rico, Dept. of Zoology.

Major, P. F. (1973). Scale feeding behavior of the leatherjacket, *Scomberoides layson* and two species of the genus *Oligoplites* (Pisces: Carangidae). *Copeia,* pp. 151–154.

Mariscal, R. N. (1970). An experimental analysis of the protection of *Amphiprion xanthurus* Cuv. and Val. and some other anemone fishes from sea anemones. *J. Exp. Mar. Biol. Ecol.* **4,** 134–149.

Mariscal, R. N. (1972). Behavior of symbiotic fishes and sea anemones. *In* "Behavior of Marine Animals" (H. E. Winn and B. L. Olla, eds.), Vol. 2, pp. 327–360. Plenum, New York.

Marler, P. (1961). The logical analysis of animal communication. *J. Theor. Biol.* **1,** 295–317.

Marlier, G., and Lelup, N. (1954). A curious ecological "niche" among the fishes of Lake Tanganyika. *Nature (London)* **174,** 935–936.

Moehring, J. L. (1972). Communication systems of a goby-shrimp symbiosis. Ph.D. Thesis, University of Hawaii, Dept. of Zoology, Hawaii, Honolulu.

Morse, D. H. (1970). Ecological aspects of some mixed species foraging flocks of birds. *Ecol. Monogr.* **40,** 119–168.

Moynihan, M. (1960). Some adaptations which help to promote gregariousness. *Proc. Int. Ornithol. Congr., 12th, 1958* Vol. 2, pp. 523–541.

Moynihan, M. (1962). The organization and probable evolution of some mixed species flocks of neotropical birds. *Misc. Coll. Smithson. Inst.* **143,** 1–140.

Moynihan, M. (1968). Social mimicry: Character convergence versus character displacement. *Evolution* **22,** 315–331.

Myrberg, A. A., Jr. (1972). Ethology of the bicolor damselfish, *Eupomacentrus partitus* (Pisces: Pomacentridae): A comparative analysis of laboratory and field behaviour. *Anim. Behav. Monogr.* **5,** 197–283.

Myrberg, A. A., Jr. (1973). Underwater television—a tool for the marine biologist. *Bull. Mar. Sci.* **23,** 824–836.

Myrberg, A. A., Jr., and Thresher, R. E. (1974). Interspecific aggression and its relevance to the concept of territoriality in reef fishes. *Am. Zool.* **14**, 81–96.

Nursall, J. R. (1974a). Some territorial behavioral attributes of the surgeon fish *Acanthurus lineatus* (L.) at Heron Island, Queensland. *Copeia,* pp. 950–959.

Nursall, J. R. (1974b). Character displacement and fish behavior, especially in coral reef communities. *Am. Zool.* **14**, 1099–1118.

Odum, E. P. (1959). "Fundamentals of Ecology." Saunders, Philadelphia, Pennsylvania.

Potts, G. W. (1973a). Cleaning symbiosis among British fish with special reference to *Crenilabrus melops* (Labridae). *J. Mar. Biol. Assoc. U. K.* **53**, 1–10.

Potts, G. W. (1973b). The ethology of *Labroides dimidiatus* (Cuv. and Val.) (Labridae; Pisces) on Aldabra. *Anim. Behav.* **21**, 250–291.

Randall, J. E. (1958). A review of the labrid fish genus *Labroides,* with description of two new species and notes on ecology. *Pac. Sci.* **12**, 327–347.

Randall, J. E. (1961). A contribution to the biology of the convict surgeonfish of the Hawaiian Islands, *Acanthurus triostegus sandvicensis. Pac. Sci.* **15**, 215–272.

Randall, J. E., and Randall, H. A. (1960). Examples of mimicry and protective resemblance in tropical marine fishes. *Bull. Mar. Sci. Gulf Carrib.* **10**, 444–480.

Rasa, O. A. E. (1969). Territoriality and the establishment of dominance by means of visual cues in *Pomacentrus jenkinsi* (Pisces: Pomacentridae). *Z. Tierpsychol.* **26**, 825–845.

Roberts, T. R. (1970). Scale-eating American characoid fishes, with special references to *Probolodus heterostomus. Proc. Calif. Acad. Sci.* [4] **38**, 383–390.

Sale, P. F. (1974). Mechanisms of co-existence in a guild of territorial fishes at Heron Island. *Proc. Int. Coral Reef Symp., 2nd, 1974* Vol. 1, pp. 193–206.

Sale, P. F. (1975). Reef fishes and other vertebrates: A comparison of social structures. *Anim. Behav. Soc. Abstr.* p. 62.

Schlichter, D. (1972). Chemische Tarnung. Die stoffliche Grundlage der Anpassung von Anemonenfischen an Riffanemonen. *Mar. Biol.* **12**, 137–150.

Smith, W. L. (1973). Record of a fish associated with a Caribbean sea anemone. *Copeia* pp. 597–598.

Springer, V. G., and Smith-Vaniz, W. F. (1972). Mimetic relationships involving fishes of the family Blenniidae. *Smithson. Contrib. Zool.* **112**, 1–36.

Syrop, S. B. (1974). Three selected aspects of the territorial behavior of a pomacentrid fish, *Pomacentrus jenkinsi.* M.S. Research Report, University of Hawaii, Dept. of Zoology, Hawaii, Honolulu.

Thresher, R. E. (1974). Territorial defense by a reef fish, *Eupomacentrus planifrons* (Cuvier): A field and laboratory analysis. M.S. Thesis, University of Miami, School of Marine and Atmospheric Science, Coral Gables, Florida.

Trivers, R. L. (1971). The evolution of reciprocal altruism. *Q. Rev. Biol.* **46**, 35–57.

Vuilleumier, F. (1967). Mixed species flocks in patagonian forests, with remarks on interspecies flock formation. *Condor* **69**, 400–404.

von Wahlert, G. (1961). Le comportement de nettoyage de *Crenilabrus melanocercus* (Labridae, Pisces) en Méditerranée. *Vie Milieu* **12**, 1–10.

Ward, J. A., and Barlow, G. W. (1967). The maturation and regulation of glancing off the parents by young orange chromides (*Etroplus maculatus:* Pisces-Cichlidae). *Behaviour* **29**, 1–56.

Wickler, W. (1960). Aquarienbeobachtungen an *Aspidontus,* einem ektoparasitischen Fisch. *Z. Tierpsychol.* **17**, 277–292.

Wickler, W. (1961). Über das Verhalten der Blenniiden *Runula* und *Aspidontus* (Pisces: Blenniidae). *Z. Tierpsychol.* **18**, 421–440.

Wickler, W. (1963). Zum problem der Signalbildung, am Beispiel der Verhaltensmimikry zwischen *Aspidontus* und *Labroides* (Pisces: Acanthopterygii). *Z. Tierpsychol.* **20**, 657–679.

Wickler, W. (1968). "Mimicry in Plants and Animals." Weidenfeld & Nicolson, London.

Wyman, R. L., and Ward, J. A. (1972). A cleaning symbiosis between the cichlid fishes *Etroplus maculatus* and *Etroplus suratensis*. I. Description and possible evolution. *Copeia* pp. 834–838.

Youngbluth, M. J. (1968). Aspects of the ecology and ethology of the cleaning fish, *Labroides phthirophagus* Randall. *Z. Tierpsychol.* **25,** 915–932.

2

Behavioral Toxicology and Teleost Fish

H. MARCUCELLA and C. I. ABRAMSON

I. Introduction 33
II. Conditioning and Learning 35
    A. Respondent Conditioning 35
    B. Operant Conditioning 40
III. Behavioral Toxicity 57
    A. Response Acquisition 58
    B. Response Retention 63
    C. Steady State Responding 68
IV. Summary 70
    References 71

I. INTRODUCTION

Recent evidence indicates that fish, an extremely valuable resource, are quickly becoming scarce. One consequence of this scarcity is the increasing concern for fish survival and a growing interest in identifying the levels of various chemical pollutants which are "safe" for fish and other aquatic life. Although the lethal concentrations and effects of many chemical pollutants, e.g., cyanide (Dondoroff *et al.*, 1966) and pesticides (McCann and Jasper, 1972), have been well documented, the long term indirect effects of sublethal concentrations upon the fish's ability to adapt to naturally occurring changes in its environment are unclear. However, evidence is accumulating that indicates that chemical agents may be behaviorally toxic even though symptoms of structural or biochemical toxicity are not detectable (Thompson and Lilja, 1964). Behavioral toxicity is said to have occurred when the introduction of a chemical agent into the fish's environment produces a change in its behavior without a corresponding anatomical or physiological change. To be behaviorally toxic the chemical must induce a behavior change that exceeds the normal range of variability, i.e., inappropriate given the existing environmental conditions. Although any change in behavior would indicate behavioral toxicity, toxicologists and ecologists are particularly interested in those chemically induced changes that decrease the animal's ability to adapt to its environment. For example, the introduction of a chemical substance may (1) increase the time required to learn to escape or avoid noxious stimuli, (2) decrease the animal's sensitivity to subtle changes in its environment, or (3) interfere with the animal's ability to retain previously learned behavior.

As Thompson and Schuster (1968) note, the study of toxic effects on the behavioral level offers ecologists and environmentalists two major advantages. First, those chemical agents that produce only behavioral changes that have serious and possibly irreversible deleterious effects on the animal's ability to adapt may be identified and controlled. Second, the identification of the behaviorally toxic effects of chemical agents may provide an early warning system which may allow the detection of toxicity before irreversible structural and biochemical damage has occurred.

However, behavioral toxicology requires reliable measures and a precise control over animal behavior under specified experimental conditions. Experimental psychology has offered much to meet this need. The fine grained analysis and control over the behavior of rats, pigeons, and primates developed by researchers in respondent and operant conditioning laboratories has contributed greatly to the recent progress in both behavioral toxicology and pharmacology. However, conditioning processes in other species, e.g., teleost fish, have not been as intensively studied. As a result, much less precise control over the behavior of individual fish is currently available to behavioral toxicologists.

The purpose of the present chapter is to demonstrate the feasibility of using teleost fish as subjects in behavioral toxicology experiments. To accomplish this, we will first review the existing literature on both operant and respondent conditioning in fish. Then, after familiarizing the reader with the techniques and procedures currently available for controlling fish behavior, a review of the literature examining the effect of various chemical substances on conditioned fish behavior will be presented. Finally, the implications of the findings of these studies for future work in behavioral toxicology with fish will be discussed.

No attempt was made to limit the review of behaviorally toxic substances to only those chemicals commonly classified as environmental pollutants. Instead, any chemical agent that has been shown to influence conditioned behavior has been included. Although these chemicals are not environmental pollutants, their effects upon behavior clearly fall within the broad definition of behavioral toxicity of Thompson and Schuster (1968). In addition, the procedures developed in these studies may prove useful in determining whether environmental pollutants will produce similar effects under similar conditions.

II. CONDITIONING AND LEARNING

In the late nineteenth and early twentieth centuries, the study of fish behavior was considered the domain of comparative psychologists and ethologists who were primarily concerned with instinctive and social behavior. Although a few learning experiments were performed (e.g., Thorndike, 1911), the study of learning and conditioning in fish had to await the arrival of experimental psychologists who wished to test the generality of their recently identified learning principles. For the most part fish were chosen as subjects simply because they were easily available and inexpensive to maintain. However, it quickly became obvious that fish behave quite differently from rats or pigeons on a variety of standardized learning tasks. Bolstered by the possibility of being able to develop a phylogenetic scale of learning, an intensive effort to discover as many behavioral differences as possible led to the creation of a vast literature, cataloging learning differences among fish, rats, and pigeons. Many of these early findings generated considerable controversy among experimental psychologists. For example, one major concern was whether the observed differences in performance reflected differences in procedures or learning capacity. Many of these controversies have yet to be resolved, and the reader is advised to consult Bitterman (1968) and Mackintosh (1969) for excellent reviews of these important comparative issues. The present chapter will not focus on comparative issues but rather will provide a general overview of respondent and operant conditioning phenomena in teleost fish.

A. Respondent Conditioning

Respondent conditioning is a procedure for creating new or conditioned reflexes. In respondent conditioning paradigms, learned reflexes can be established by repeatedly pairing a neutral stimulus in close temporal contiguity with a second stimulus (unconditioned stimulus) which reliably and without training elicits an unconditioned response (UCR). Following training, the previously neutral stimulus, now referred to as a conditioned stimulus (CS), is also able to elicit the response (conditioned response). Early laboratory demonstrations of classical conditioning phenomena in fish were reported by McDonald (1922) and Westerfield (1922). McDonald conditioned blunt-nosed minnows (*Pimephales notatus*) to inhibit a flight response elicited by the onset of a vibrating string.

Pairing food with the vibrating string inhibited the fear reaction. Westerfield (1922) used a similar procedure to condition mud minnows (*Umbra* spp.) to differentially respond to two tones of different frequencies.

Since that time numerous studies have been conducted with a variety of unconditioned stimuli (UCS) and responses (UCR). For example, Froloff (1925, 1928) conditioned flight produced by electric shock to visual and mechanical stimuli. Bull (1928–1939) conditioned responses to a wide range of conditioned stimuli (CS) including changes in temperature, salinity, and direction of water flow as well as to visual, olfactory, gustatory, and tactual cues.

More recently, Otis *et al.* (1957) conditioned respiratory and cardiac inhibition by pairing electric shock (UCS) with illumination changes (CS). Aggressive behavior has also been classically conditioned. Adler and Hogan (1963) conditioned Siamese fighting fish (*Betta splendens*) to extend their gill membrane, a common component of aggressive behavior in this species, to mild electric shock by pairing shock with exposure to a mirror image of the subject (UCS).

In a related experiment, Thompson and Sturm (1965b), using mirror image as the UCS, conditioned four components of the aggressive display of *Betta splendens* by pairing mirror presentations with the onset of a red light (CS). Frontal approach to mirror image, fin erection, gill cover erection, and undulatory movements all came to be elicited by the red light. They also reported that the rate of acquisition of the four responses differed greatly. Fin erection was most rapidly acquired, while frontal approach to the mirror required the most CS–UCS pairing in order to reach the specified criterion.

Thompson and Sturm (1965b) also ruled out the possibility of a sensitizing effect to CS onset by demonstrating that stimulus control over the conditioned aggressive display could be acquired. For example, in a second experiment, green light presentations, always followed by mirror presentations, were randomly alternated with red light presentations which were never followed by the mirror presentations. Only the green stimulus elicited aggressive behavior. No responses were elicited by red light.

Instrumental responses of fish have also been respondently conditioned by autoshaping procedures. Brown and Jenkins (1968) demonstrated that pigeons will begin pecking a response key if the key is occasionally illuminated for 8 sec. and, independently of the pigeon's behavior, immediately followed by food delivery. Squier (1969) reported that repeated pairings of a lighted key and reinforcement will also elicit key pressing in fish (*Tilapia*).

1. Variables Influencing Respondent Conditioning

Many procedural variables have been shown to influence the strength of classical conditioning. These variables include CS intensity, CS–UCS interval, and partial vs. continuous reinforcement.

a. CS–UCS Intensity. Woodward (1971) demonstrated that high CS intensity produced greater suppression of respiratory activity than low CS intensity. Greater respiratory suppression of Japanese carp (*Cyprinius carpio*) elicited by a 5 msec 7 mA DC shock was conditioned to a high intensity difference in illumination CS than a low intensity difference. For the first five of ten CS–UCS trials half the subjects were trained with high CS intensity and the remainder with low intensity CS. Half of the subjects in the low intensity condition were shifted to the high intensity condition, and half of the subjects in the high intensity condition were shifted to the low intensity condition. The results showed that respiratory activity was suppressed by both high and low intensity CS; however, the greater the intensity of the CS the greater the amount of response suppression. A similar effect for UCS intensity with goldfish (*Carassius auratus*) was reported by Scobie (1973).

b. CS–UCS Interval. Numerous studies have attempted to determine the optimal CS–UCS interval. For example, Noble *et al.* (1959) examined the effect of CS–UCS interval on the frequency of CR's elicited by the CS. One hundred five live-bearing tooth carps (*Molliensia* sp.) were assigned to one of six groups and trained with one of the following CS–UCS intervals: 0.5, 1.0, 1.5, 2.0, 3.0, or 4.0 sec. The intertrial interval for all groups averaged 1 min. The UCS (50 mA shock) duration was 1 sec, and the CS (increase in illumination from 35 to 400 foot candles) overlapped and terminated with the UCS. Three types of responses were recorded on each trial: (a) vigorous forward movement, (b) backing away, and (c) cessation of movement.

The frequency of conditioned responses (combined) increased to a maximum as the CS–UCS interval was increased to 2.0 sec, and then declined as the CS–UCS interval further increased to 4.0 sec; i.e., the optimal CS–UCS interval for fish was larger than that reported for humans (Deese, 1952; Woodworth and Schlosberg, 1954).

However, Klinman and Bitterman (1963) argued that the results of the Noble *et al.* (1959) study did not reflect a species difference but were due to differences in test period durations. In the Noble *et al* experiment, every tenth trial was a test trial, identical to all other trials, except that the UCS was omitted and any response of the fish during the period between CS onset to 1 sec following its termination was recorded. Unfortunately, this procedure was confounded because the time interval in which a response could be recorded during testing increased as the CS–UCS duration used in training was increased. When test trials were controlled for the duration, the optimal CS–UCS interval for both frequency and magnitude of responding decreased to 0.5 sec.

Three groups of subjects were trained with CS–UCS intervals of either 0.5, 2.0, or 4.0 sec. The CS, light onset, overlapped and terminated with the UCS, a

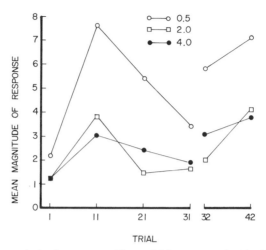

Fig. 1. Mean magnitude of response to CS per trial for groups trained in either a 0.5, 2.0, or 4.0-sec CS–UCS interval. [Taken from Klinman and Bitterman (1963).]

15 volt AC shock of 0.1-sec duration. On trials 1, 11, 21, 31, 32, and 42 the UCS was omitted and all activity (CR) during a 5.0-sec presentation of the CS was recorded. Between test trials 31 and 32, all subjects were returned to their home tanks for 2 hr.

The average magnitude of responding per test trial for each group is presented in Fig. 1. Clearly, the response magnitude of the 0.5-sec group was greater than that of either the 2.0- or 4.0-sec group.

However, additional studies by Klinman and Bitterman (exp. II and III, 1963) cast doubt on the generality of their earlier findings. For example, significant differences among groups trained at different CS–UCS intervals were not obtained (1) when the same species (*Mollensia* sp.) was trained with a longer intertrial interval (4.0 vs. 1.0 min), or (2) when a different species (*Carassius auratus*) was trained under conditions identical to those in their original experiment.

In further studies of the effect of the CS–UCS interval, Bitterman (1964) demonstrated that (1) strictly simultaneous pairing of the CS and UCS did not produce conditioning, (2) response magnitude was lower with trace than delay conditioning at comparable CS–UCS intervals, (3) response magnitude increased as CS–UCS intervals increased from 0 to 1.0 sec, and (4) the primary effect of increasing the CS–UCS interval beyond 1.0 sec was to increase the latency of the conditioned response. However, response magnitude eventually reached the same level as it did when shorter CS–UCS intervals were used.

c. Partial vs. Continuous Reinforcement. In a series of experiments on human eyeblink conditioning, Humphreys (1939) demonstrated that the presence of the UCS (air puff) on 50% of the conditioning trials did not affect response acquisition but increased its resistance to extinction. Opposite effects on intermittent CS–UCS pairing were found in goldfish. Gonzalez *et al.* (1961a) placed subjects on either a 50 or 100% reinforcement schedule in which the UCS was 0.5-sec shock and the CS was light onset. The intertrial interval equaled 3.0 min and the CS–UCS interval equaled 4.5 sec. Seven sessions of conditioning preceded 11 days of extinction. The 100% reinforced animals responded at a higher frequency than the 50% reinforced animals, yet resistance to extinction did not differ between groups.

In a second experiment, Gonzalez *et al.* (1961a) extended these findings by demonstrating that there was no significant difference between partially and consistently reinforced groups either after 10 or 20 sessions of training or after a sequence of conditioning and extinction sessions.

In a follow-up study, Gonzalez *et al.* (1962b) examined the effects (a) of spaced trials (a 24-hr intertrial interval), (b) of alternating extinction and conditioning trials, and (c) of alternating pairs of extinction and conditioning days.

In the previous studies, inconsistently reinforced animals were presented with the same number of trials as those consistently reinforced, but the UCS was omitted on one-half of the trials. Inconsistent reinforcement can also be programmed by presenting inconsistently reinforced animals with twice the number of trials as the consistent group. In this latter procedure the number of US presentations rather than the number of trials each group received is equated. While this difference in scheduling reinforcers does not appear to affect the behavior of the rat, Gonzalez *et al.* (1962a, 1963) reported some evidence that the partial reinforcement effect in fish can be obtained when the number of reinforcers received by each group is equated. Gonzalez *et al.* (1963) exposed three groups of African mouthbreeders (*Tilapia macrocephala*) to a respondent conditioning procedure in which a CS (light onset) was repeatedly followed by a 0.5-sec shock of moderate intensity. Conditioned stimulus onset preceded shock onset by 4.5-sec and terminated with it. Trials were presented on the average of once every 3 min, and general activity during CS presentations was recorded. One group of subjects (consistent) received five light–shock pairings per session for 20 sessions. A second group (partial I) received ten CS presentations per session for 20 sessions, but only five CS presentations per session were followed by shock onset. The third group (partial II) were consistently reinforced for eight sessions (five pairings per session) and then partially reinforced for 12 sessions.

The average number of responses elicited by the CS for each group during training and extinction has been presented in Fig. 2. More responses per session were elicited by the CS during training for the consistently reinforced group.

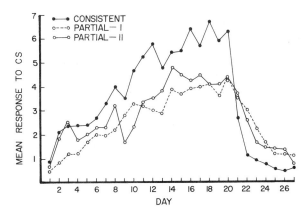

Fig. 2. Mean response to CS per session for consistently reinforced and both partially reinforced groups. Responses were extinguished during sessions 21–27. [Taken from Gonzalez *et al.* (1963).]

However, both partially reinforced groups were more resistant to extinction. That is, with an equated reinforcement procedure, the partial reinforcement effect was obtained.

However, the partial reinforcement effect observed when the equated reinforcement procedure was used appeared to be limited to African mouthbreeders. When Berger *et al.* (1965) studied the effects of equated reinforcement, equated trials, constant and variable CS–UCS intervals, long and short runs of nonreinforcement, biased and balanced patterns of partial reinforcement, and two different extinction procedures in goldfish, no partial reinforcement effect was observed.

In a further attempt to demonstrate the partial effect in goldfish, Behrend and Bitterman (1968) trained goldfish and African mouthbreeders in the same situation as Gonzalez *et al.* (1963). The results confirmed that African mouthbreeders show the partial reinforcement effect, but that goldfish do not, even under training conditions which produced the effect in mouthbreeders.

B. Operant Conditioning

The study of how the consequences of fish behavior come to control behavior has had a long and varied history. A variety of procedures and apparatus have been employed to demonstrate that fish can be taught a variety of responses. One of the earliest demonstrations of operant or instrumental conditioning in fish was provided by Triplett in 1901, who reported that perch (*Morone americanus*) will stop attacking minnows if previously separated from them by a glass wall. Since that time, numerous other studies have demonstrated that fish will learn a variety of tasks in a variety of situations both to obtain positive reinforcers and to avoid or escape from negative reinforcers.

i. Positive Reinforcement

A positive reinforcer is defined as any stimulus whose presentation increases the future probability of a response. Food is perhaps the most commonly used positive reinforcer with fish to establish new behaviors. However, the mere fact that an organism has learned a specific response, e.g., pressing, does not tell us whether or when the organism will emit the response. That is, once learned, operant behavior must be maintained by a schedule of positive reinforcement. In this section we will briefly describe (1) the role of several reinforcement parameters in maintaining operant behavior, and (2) the relationship between environmental stimuli and these response–reinforcer relationships.

a. **Reinforcement Parameters.** The contribution of reinforcement parameters to the maintenance of operant behavior can be measured while reinforcement is in effect or following its removal. When reinforcement conditions are still in effect, the contribution of a parameter can be measured by noting what changes in behavior, e.g., response frequency, occur when the value of the parameter is changed. The effect of a reinforcement parameter can also be measured by noting the parameter's effect on the resistance of the behavior to change when reinforcement is eliminated. The type of reinforcer employed, the frequency or schedule of reinforcement, the size or magnitude of the reinforcer, and the delay between the response and the subsequent delivery of the reinforcer are parameters of reinforcement that have been shown to be important determiners of maintained behavior.

i. Types of reinforcers. In addition to hundreds of studies demonstrating that food is an effective reinforcer for fish, there is also considerable evidence that visual and conditioned reinforcers will maintain fish behavior.

(a) Visual reinforcement. Thompson (1963) demonstrated that Siamese fighting fish (*Betta splendens*) would emit a swimming response if responses were followed by the presentation of an image of a *Betta*. The most effective stimulus was a mirror image of the subject. Models of *B. splendens* were somewhat effective as a reinforcer but only if the model was in motion.

Goldstein (1967) replicated these original findings and demonstrated that the contingency between responding and stimulus presentations is important in maintaining responding, i.e., responding was maintained at a much lower rate by noncontingent stimulus presentations. Results of later experiments indicated that response rate was related to several other parameters. For example, response rate was directly correlated with the degree of color difference between the model and *B. splendens* (Thompson and Sturm, 1965a). Responding maintained by visual reinforcement, unlike food maintained responding, extinguishes quickly (Hogan, 1967) and does not increase in frequency when reinforced on fixed ratio schedules (Hogan *et al.*, 1970; Turnbough and Lloyd, 1972).

Responding is unaffected by (a) the duration of stimulus presentation (5–40 sec) (Hogan *et al.*, 1970), (b) changes in the brightness of the model (Grabowski and Thompson, 1968), or (c) by the presence of a continuously available mirror. Response rate has also been shown to be greater for dominant vs. subordinate *Betta* and to decrease with habituation (Baennizer, 1970), as well as with contingent vs. noncontingent punishment (Fantino *et al.*, 1972).

Fantino *et al.* (1972) also reported that *Betta's* preference for visual versus food reinforcement was related to the food deprivation level. At moderate deprivation levels (48–120 hr), all subjects responded to produce visual reinforcement even when a food producing response was concurrently available. At high deprivation levels (240 hr), subjects responded to produce food.

(b) Conditioned reinforcement. A conditioned reinforcer has been defined as a stimulus that acquires its reinforcing properties during the life span of the organism (Kelleher and Gollub, 1962). Procedurally, these stimuli acquire reinforcing properties, for many species, by frequent pairing with an unconditioned reinforcer, e.g., food or water. In like fashion, the pairing procedure is also effective with fish. Sanders (1940) reported that neutral stimuli repeatedly paired with an unconditioned reinforcer will acquire the ability to reinforce fish behavior. Fish were first placed in the second compartment of a three compartment tank and reinforced with food for swimming into the first compartment whenever a lamp in the second compartment was illuminated. Fish were then placed into the third compartment and reinforced with light onset for swimming into the second compartment whenever an amyl acetate solution was presented in the third compartment. In the first phase of Sander's study, food delivery followed the completion of both responses. Sanders demonstrated that the response of swimming into the second compartment could be reinforced by light presentation, a conditioned reinforcer. An alternative possibility is that the first response in the sequence was maintained by unconditioned negative reinforcement, e.g., escape from amyl acetate. Such an interpretation is unlikely, however, because when food was omitted the latency of both responses increased considerably.

In a second experiment, Sanders (1940) demonstrated that fish could be taught a new response with conditioned reinforcers in the absence of unconditioned reinforcement. Five naive fish were first placed in the second compartment and reinforced with food for swimming into the first compartment whenever a lamp in the second compartment was illuminated. Fish were then placed into the third compartment and reinforced for swimming into the second compartment by the onset of the light. In contrast to the first experiment, food was no longer presented, i.e., fish were removed from the tank immediately after swimming into the second compartment.

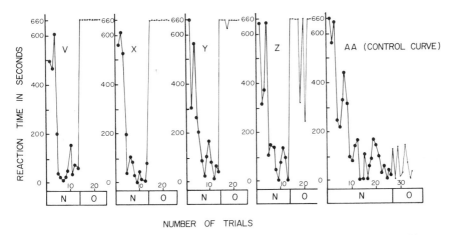

Fig. 3. Reaction time (response latency in sec) per trial for both normal (N) and lesioned (O) conditions. [Taken from Sanders (1940).]

Figure 3 shows response latencies per trial (time to swim into the second compartment) for all subjects. Only the large filled circles in the left half of each individual graph are of interest here (normal, N). The small filled circles represent response latencies following tectal lesions and will not be discussed. Figure 3 shows that the time between the presentation of the olfactory stimulus and the response (in seconds) decreased over trials, and that the shape of the curves resembles that of standard learning curves.

More recently, Salzinger *et al.* (1968) demonstrated that the presentation, during extinction, of auditory stimuli previously paired with reinforcement increased resistance to extinction. Following training on a fixed ratio ten schedule of reinforcement, the responses of goldfish were extinguished. In one condition, the feeder solenoid continued to operate and the water continued to be disturbed as it had been when the reinforcer was delivered. In the second, only the feeder solenoid was operated, and in the third condition, no feedback was provided. Resistance to extinction was greatest for animals in condition one and lowest for those in condition three.

ii. Schedules of reinforcement. The vast majority of the conditioning literature indicates that when responses are intermittently reinforced, both response rate and resistance to extinction increase. In a discrete trial procedure, half of the subjects are reinforced on every trial (continuous reinforcement) while the other half of the subjects are reinforced on only some percentage of trials (usually 50%). The responses of both groups are then extinguished. Intermittently reinforced rats emit more responses to some criterion of extinction (partial reinforcement effect). There is considerable evidence that this effect is not found with fish, i.e., continuously reinforced fish emit more responses in extinction than do partially reinforced fish. For example, Wodinsky and Bitterman (1959) reported that the group of African mouthbreeders (*Tilapia macrocephala*) which were partially reinforced emitted fewer responses in extinction than the group which had been consistently reinforced. However, repeated alternation of conditioning (three sessions) and extinction conditions did eventually produce the partial reinforcement effect. The lack of a partial reinforcement effect during initial extinction was found to be unrelated to intertrial interval and deprivation level (Longo and Bitterman, 1960), the pattern of reinforced trials, i.e., random or alternating (Gonzalez *et al.*, 1961b).

However, the appearance of a partial reinforcement effect in fish does appear to be related to reinforcement frequency during training. Typically, as mentioned previously, trial frequency for intermittent and consistently reinforced groups is equated in partial reinforcement effect experiments. When the number of reinforcements each group receives is equated, the partial reinforcement effect is obtained, i.e., intermittently reinforced responses of fish are more resistant to extinction than continuously reinforced responses in both free operant and discrete trial situations (Gonzalez *et al.*, 1962a). When goldfish response requirement was minimal and reinforcement was large, similar effects were obtained with equated trial procedures.

iii. Delay of reinforcement. In a series of related studies, Bitterman and his colleagues examined the effect of several variables on resistance to extinction in fish. Delayed reinforcement, unlike with the rat (Crum *et al.*, 1951) did not produce greater resistance to extinction in fish (Gonzalez *et al.*, 1963). However, greater resistance to extinction was obtained when reinforcement was delayed and trials were massed (Gonzalez *et al.*, 1965).

iv. Magnitude of reinforcement. In a free operant situation resistance to extinction was positively related to frequency and amount of reinforcement (Gonzalez *et al.*, 1967). In discrete trial situations, the amount of reinforcement increased resistance to extinction only at low response requirements (Gonzalez and Bitterman, 1967).

Lowes and Bitterman (1967) examined the effect of reinforcement magnitude shifts on performance. Goldfish were trained to nose a lighted target. Responses to the target turned out the light and were immediately followed by reinforcement. In the acquisition phase, half of the goldfish received a small reinforcement, half received a large reinforcement. Following acquisition, the magnitude of reinforcement was switched for both groups. The results showed no contrast effect and no performance decrement when the downward shift in reinforcement magnitude was introduced.

Mackintosh (1971), in a series of experiments with goldfish, confirmed the previous finding that goldfish show no decline in performance when shifted from a large to a small magnitude of reinforcement. Furthermore, he confirmed the

notion that goldfish did extinguish more slowly after training with large reinforcement than with small reinforcement (Gonzalez and Bitterman, 1967; Gonzalez et al., 1967).

Gonzalez (1972) studied the effect of patterning as a function of reinforcer
magnitude. Goldfish were trained on a single alternating schedule of reinforcement (reinforced–nonreinforced trials). The results showed that this schedule
produced longer response latencies following reinforcement delivery than after
nonreinforcement only when the reinforcement was large. The effect was not
obtained when either the reward was small or when the schedule of reinforcement
was a quasirandom 50% schedule with large reward.

Gonzalez et al. (1972) also studied the effect of reinforcement shifts on runway performance in goldfish. In experiment I they examined different reinforcement magnitudes on resistance to extinction in the runway. Goldfish were divided into three groups and reinforced with 1, 4, or 40 worms with spaced trials
(one per day). Animals failed to show the inverse relation between magnitude of
reinforcement and resistance to extinction which is found in the rat. In experiment II they attempted to find the depression effect which is also found in rats
when reinforcer magnitude is decreased. In one phase, one group of goldfish was
reinforced with one worm, while the other received 40 worms. On the basis of
their performance in the runway, the 40-worm group was divided into three
matched groups: 40–40 (each response reinforced), 40–1, and 40–40 (no reinforcement). The results showed no difference in performance when reinforcement magnitude was shifted.

In contrast, a shift in performance produced by a shift in reinforcer magnitude
has been reported by Raymond et al. (1972). They trained groups of goldfish to
swim a runway for either a large or small reinforcer. After 20 days of training
half of the fish in each group were shifted to the other reinforcer magnitude. The
subjects rapidly shifted swimming speeds when magnitudes were reversed.
Groups shifted from large to small reinforcements rapidly decreased their swimming speeds, and the small to large groups increased their speed. This study was
criticized by Gonzalez et al. (1972) because the reinforcer was visible to the fish
before the trial began. In order to confirm their findings, Wolach et al. (1973)
replicated their experiment but this time food was not visible to the subjects.
Goldfish were trained for 25 days with either large or small magnitudes of
reinforcement. Then half of the subjects in each group were shifted to the other
reinforcement magnitude.

Figure 4 shows the reciprocal of the mean starting speed per blocks of three
trials. The mean starting speed equaled the time from the opening of the start
door until the fish was 9.0 cm into the swimway. The L-L and S-S groups were
trained with the large or small reinforcer throughout training, while the reinforcer
magnitude for the S-L and L-S groups was shifted at the point represented by the
dashed vertical line.

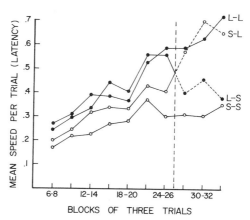

Fig. 4. Mean starting speed per trial (seconds) for blocks of three trials for groups with larger (L) and smaller (S) rewards. The dashed vertical line indicates that point at which reinforcer magnitude was shifted for the L-S and S-L groups. [Taken from Wolach *et al.* (1973).]

The shifted subjects changed starting speeds immediately following the shifts in reinforcer magnitude. The starting speeds of subjects shifted to a larger reward increased, while those of the subjects shifted to the smaller reward decreased.

In using a simultaneous contrast procedure, Gonzalez and Powers (1973) trained goldfish to press a lighted target for food. Different reinforcer magnitudes were signaled by the color of the target. A trial began by the lowering of the target and a series of five responses were reinforced with either one worm or ten worms. The control group was reinforced with only one worm per response. Although the experimental group showed evidence of reward magnitude discrimination, their overall performance did not differ from controls. The experimental group, however, did show a negative successive contrast effect which was not reported by Gonzalez *et al.* (1972), Lowes and Bitterman (1967), or Mackintosh (1971).

b. Discrimination Learning. The responses of fish maintained by reinforcing stimuli like those of other species can be brought under stimulus control; i.e., fish will learn to respond in the presence of stimuli that signal reinforcement and learn not to respond in the presence of stimuli which signal nonreinforcement. Evidence exists from these discrimination learning studies that fish can make a variety of discriminations including brightness (Deterline, 1957), shapes (see Chapter 3), and wavelength of light (see Chapter 3).

While interest in sensory capacities of fish has been increasing recently, much of the early literature in discrimination learning focused on a comparison of such learning in fish and other animals. This interest was generated by several early findings that behavior of fish on certain discrimination learning tasks differed significantly from that of other species, e.g., rats or pigeons. The important theoretical implications of these early findings for then current learning theory and for generalization of learning principles to species other than the rat generated many experiments that attempted to isolate the critical features of these experiments that were responsible for the differences in performance. The phenomena of probability learning and habit reversal in fish received most of this attention.

i. Habit reversal. Habit reversal studies have occupied a central position in the fish learning literature because early evidence suggested that the performance of fish in habit reversal experiments was qualitatively different from that of the rat. In the standard habit reversal procedure, subjects are presented with two stimuli, one correlated with reinforcement (S+) and the other with extinction (S-) until a predetermined discrimination criterion is reached. Then, the reinforcement contingencies associated with each stimulus are reversed and training continues until the discrimination criterion is again reached. This reversal procedure is usually repeated for either a specified number of reversals or until the number of errors per reversal (responses to S-) reaches asymptotic levels.

A correction procedure may or may not be used. When a correction procedure is used, the subjects are allowed to respond during the trial until a correct response is emitted; i.e., only the first correct response can terminate the trial. In a noncorrection procedure, the first response on a trial, whether correct or incorrect, terminates the trial and initiates the intertrial interval.

Although the discriminative performance of rats improves over successive reversals (Mackintosh, 1965; Sperling, 1965), Wodinsky and Bitterman (1957) reported that discrimination performance of African mouthbreeders (*Tilapia macrocephala*) on a line tilt discrimination shows little improvement over successive discrimination reversals.

A second group, trained to discriminate horizontal from vertical lines with a correction procedure, also showed little improvement. Wodinsky and Bitterman's results were later confirmed by Deterline (1957) with brightness and by Bitterman *et al.* (1958) with position. In the Bitterman *et al.* (1958) study some improvement over successive reversals did appear, but it was much less than that observed in rats.

Warren (1960) extended these findings to red paradise fish (*Macropodus opercularis*) for a black–white discrimination. In addition, Warren reported that overtraining (continued discrimination training after the discrimination criterion had been met), in contrast to rat studies (Paul, 1965), further impeded reversal learning. Mackintosh *et al.* (1966) argued that Warren's (1960) failure to observe the overtraining effect was primarily due to the lack of irrelevant inconspicuous stimuli in the experimental situation, a requirement found necessary with octopus in an earlier study (Mackintosh and Mackintosh, 1963). Yet even when Mackintosh *et al.* (1966) introduced irrelevant cues, no overtraining reversal effect was found. They did demonstrate, however, that the introduction of irrelevant cues eliminated the deleterious effect of overtraining reported by Warren (1960).

In an extensive study of habit reversal in goldfish and African mouthbreeders using spatial, visual, visual spatial, and Riopelle problems, Behrend *et al.* (1965) found no improvement over reversals as a function of amount of reinforcement or training. More recent evidence has suggested that progressive improvement over successive reversals can be obtained with fish. For example, Setterington and Bishop (1967), using small widely separated plastic beads as stimuli and an unlimited correction procedure where the targets were withdrawn after each incorrect response, reported substantial improvement over a series of 80 left–right discrimination reversals.

Progressive improvement in habit reversal performance has also been obtained in successive rather than simultaneous discrimination procedures (Woodard *et al.*, 1971; Mackintosh and Cauty, 1971). Mackintosh and Cauty (1971) reported that rats, pigeons, and fish show significant improvement over a series of right–left discriminations, but rats improve significantly more than pigeons which in turn improve more than goldfish. Mackintosh and Cauty (1971) also replicated the finding of Woodard *et al.* (1971) that in a successive discrimination procedure, fish improve over a series of red–green discrimination reversals. Thus, in general it appears that the performance of fish during a sequence of discrimination reversals differs from that of rats and pigeons. However, it appears that the difference is one of quantity; i.e., fish do improve but the degree of improvement is less than that observed for the rat or pigeon.

ii. Probability learning. In the typical probability learning experiment, unlike those on habit reversal, the subject is reinforced in the presence of both discriminative stimuli. However, the probability of reinforcement of responding to both stimuli is usually less than 1.0. For example, responding in the presence of one stimulus may be reinforced 75% of the time while the other only 25% (75:25 problem). Much attention has been focused on the apparent differences between rats and fish in probability learning experiments. For example, Bitterman *et al.* (1958) reported that rats tend to maximize on a 70:30 problem while African mouthbreeders tend to match. That is, rats responded to the higher probability stimulus more than 70% of the time, while fish distributed their responses such that a proportion of their responses to each stimulus matched the probability of reinforcement associated with it. Similar findings were reported for goldfish (Behrend and Bitterman, 1966). These findings contradicted that of an earlier study (Bush and Wilson, 1956) which reported that paradise fish maximize on a 75:25% problem.

The appearance of probability matching rather than maximizing appears to depend on several features of the discrimination situation. First, matching precision increases as the reinforcement ratio approaches 50:50 (Behrend and Bitterman, 1961). Second, probability matching in fish appears to depend on the presence of a guidance procedure (Bitterman *et al.,* 1958; Behrend and Bitterman, 1961). In the guidance procedure both targets are withdrawn following an unreinforced response, and only the target that was scheduled to be reinforced on that trial is reintroduced. The guidance procedure, in effect, forces responding to both stimuli. When the procedure was not used fish tended to maximize, i.e., respond exclusively to the stimulus associated with the higher probability of reinforcement. However, conflicting data have been reported by Marrone and Evans (1966), who demonstrated that African mouthbreeders will match three (20:60:20%) choice and two (30:70% and 80:20%) choice spatial problems without a guidance procedure if a swimming response was required.

Weitzman (1967) suggested that the difference in performance between rats and fish can be attributed to differences in apparatus and procedures which were designed to accommodate the physical differences between the species. When rats were trained under conditions resembling those of fish, both species tended to match. When rats were trained in situations similar to Bitterman *et al.* (1958), they tended to maximize.

2. Negative Reinforcement and Punishment

In the previous section we have seen that a variety of conditioned and unconditioned stimuli can acquire control over operant behavior of fish, and that changes in various parameters of these stimuli, e.g., the schedule and magnitude of reinforcement, affect both the frequency of this behavior and its resistance to extinction. We have also seen that a variety of environmental stimuli can acquire differential control over these response–reinforcer relationships.

In the following section we will see that aversive events also acquire control over fish behavior. For example, fish will also respond to escape or avoid aversive events or will stop responding when responses are followed by the presentation of an aversive event. Environmental stimuli which reliably predict the occurrence of an aversive event also acquire control over responding. For example, fish will learn to respond in the presence of stimuli that signal avoidable shocks and will supress responding in the presence of stimuli that signal unavoidable shock.

a. Escape and Avoidance Conditioning. In escape conditioning, the subject responds to terminate the aversive event, while avoidance procedures allow the subject to avoid the aversive event entirely by emitting a specific response prior to the onset of the event. Most avoidance conditioning studies employing fish as subjects use discrete trial procedures in which a stimulus signals impending shock, but a few recent studies have attempted to demonstrate avoidance conditioning in a free operant avoidance procedure as well.

  i. Discrete trial procedure.   In a discrete trial procedure the subject is presented with a series of avoidance trials, separated by intertrial intervals in which no contingency is in effect. The onset of each trial is signaled by the onset of an environmental stimulus (CS) which is followed by the onset of the aversive event (UCS) after some time interval (CS–UCS interval). If the subject responds during the CS–UCS interval, the CS is terminated, the shock avoided, and the animal returns to the intertrial interval. If the subject fails to respond during the CS–UCS interval, both the CS and UCS are presented until a response occurs (escape procedure).

  The acquisition of discrete trial avoidance behavior is influenced by a great many factors including the duration of the CS–UCS interval, the effect of prior respondent fear conditioning, the duration of the intertrial interval, stimulus modality, shock intensity and power, inescapable shock, species differences, and respondent stimulus–reinforcer contingencies.

Factors influencing discrete trial avoidance

  (a) *CS–UCS interval.*   Behrend and Bitterman (1962) examined the acquisition of an avoidance response (jumping a hurdle in a fish shuttle box) as a function of the duration of the CS–UCS interval: 2.5, 5.0, 10.0, 20.0, 40.0, or 60.0 sec. Subjects were given ten trials per day for 20 days with a mean intertrial interval of 3 min. Each trial began with the onset of the CS (light) followed at the appropriate interval by the onset of the UCS (0.25-sec intermittent shock). Each trial was terminated by the avoidance response or by the experimenter if no response occurred for 15 sec. A response in the presence of the CS alone terminated the CS and prevented the onset of shock, while a response in the presence of both light and shock terminated both stimuli and returned the subjects to the intertrial interval.

  Figure 5 shows the mean number of trials to reach three different criteria of avoidance conditioning as a function of the duration of the CS–UCS interval. Criteria were the first avoidance response (open circles), nine avoidance responses in the ten trials of any one session (open circles, dashed line), and ten avoidance responses in the ten trials of any one session (closed circles). The data of Fig. 5 show that the mean number of trials to reach the two more stringent criteria decreased as the duration of the CS–UCS interval increased. Asymptotic performance levels appeared somewhere between 20 and 40 sec. The datum point at the 2.5-sec CS–UCS interval for the most stringent criterion was not plotted because very few of these animals reached this criterion.

  (b) *Prior fear conditioning.*   Discrete trial avoidance conditioning can be facilitated by prior fear conditioning. Typically, the subjects are exposed to a

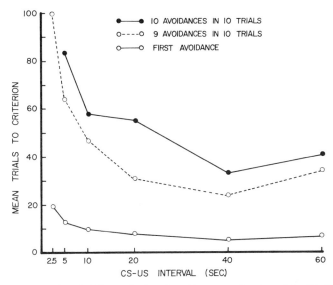

Fig. 5. Mean number of trials to criterion of avoidance as a function of the CS–UCS interval used in training for three criteria of avoidance. [Taken from Behrend and Bitterman (1962).]

number of CS–UCS pairings with no avoidance response possible. During testing all animals are exposed to the standard avoidance procedure at a fixed CS–UCS interval. For example, Behrend and Bitterman (1964) examined the effect of prior fear conditioning at a number of CS–UCS intervals between 0 and 1 sec on the subsequent acquisition of the avoidance response. Subjects were assigned to one of 11 groups which differed with respect to the duration of the CS–UCS interval. Following four sessions of conditioning, each animal was given one session of avoidance training (ten trials) at a CS–UCS interval of 20 sec.

The results are presented in Fig. 6. The mean number of avoidance responses increased and the mean avoidance latency decreased as the CS–UCS interval used during fear conditioning increased. Results consistent with Behrend and Bitterman (1962) have also been reported by Brookshire and Frumkin (1969). However, they noted that facilitation did not occur if, during testing, they used a CS–UCS interval of 10 sec instead of a 30-sec CS–UCS interval; a result that suggests that Behrend and Bitterman's (1962) findings were somewhat determined by their choice of a 20-sec test interval. Although some fear conditioning facilitates avoidance, extended fear conditioning training has also been shown to interfere with avoidance aquisition (Pinckney, 1967; Frumkin and Brookshire, 1969).

(c) *Intertrial interval.* Pinckney (1966) examined the effects of intertrial interval duration on the acquisition of a shuttle box avoidance response. Different

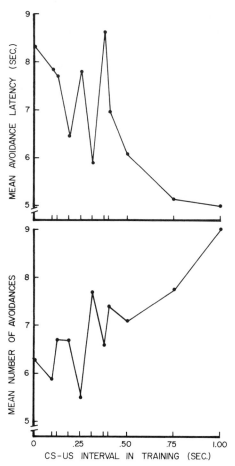

Fig. 6.　Mean avoidance latency in seconds (top panel) and mean number of avoidance responses (bottom panel) as a function of the CS–UCS interval used during prior fear conditioning. [Taken from Behrend and Bitterman (1964).]

groups of Mexican swordtails (*Xiphophorus helleri*) were given five sessions (20 trials per session) of avoidance training at different intertrial intervals: 0.5, 1, 2, 5, 10, and 20 min. The CS (light)–UCS (5-sec shock) interval was 15 sec. Animals trained with longer intertrial intervals acquired the avoidance response more quickly than those animals trained at shorter intervals.

　(d) *Stimulus modality.*　To examine the effect of stimulus modality on avoidance learning, Jacobs and Popper (1968) trained two groups of pinfish (*Lagodon rhumboides*) to avoid with either a visual CS or an auditory CS.

Subjects trained with visual stimuli needed much less time to meet the avoidance criterion than those trained with auditory stimuli.

Stimulus location also appears to influence acquisition of avoidance responding (Gallon, 1974). The onset of a light CS was presented in either the same, the opposite, or both compartments with respect to the location of the fish. Avoidance acquisition was much faster and reached a higher asymptote for the same side CS group. When light offset was used as the CS, no differential effect of signal location was observed.

(e) *Shock intensity.* Bintz (1971) assigned goldfish to one of five groups which differed in the intensity of shock used as UCS. Avoidance performance was shown to be an inverted U function of shock intensity. However, when the same subjects were tested at different shock intensities, the higher intensity shock produced better avoidance performance. A similar U-shaped function relating avoidance responding to shock intensity was reported by Gallon (1972).

Zerbolio and Wickstra (1973) studied the effect of various shock intensities (7.5, 10, 15, or 20 volts AC) and durations (100, 200, or 400 msec) on shuttle box avoidance in goldfish. Avoidance performance is also an inverted U function of power (intensity × duration). As power increased, acquisition rates increased, then decreased.

(f) *Inescapable shock.* Padilla *et al.* (1970) studied the effect of inescapable shock on shuttle box avoidance conditioning in goldfish. They first demonstrated reduced responsiveness 24 hr after exposure to inescapable shock. Similar findings have been reported for other organisms (Overmier and Seligman, 1967). However, Padilla *et al.* (1970) also demonstrated, in a second experiment, that the interference effect of inescapable shock disappears in 72 hr. Padilla (1973) also demonstrated that inescapable shock interferes with avoidance performance by goldfish whether presented prior to escape–avoidance training or interpolated between blocks of escape–avoidance training.

(g) *Species differences.* Wodinsky *et al.* (1962) reported the avoidance learning, measured by trials to criterion and mean avoidance latency on criterion session, of goldfish to be superior to that of beau gregories. Similar findings have been reported by Behrend and Bitterman (1962). They reported that acquisition of avoidance for mollies (*Mollensia sp.*) to be slower than that of goldfish.

(h) *Respondent stimulus reinforcer contingencies.* Several investigators have recently suggested that shuttle box avoidance responding in fish may be a species specific response of fish similar to that of pecking in pigeons (Brown and Jenkins, 1968; Gamzu and Schwartz, 1973). For example, Woodard and Bitterman (1971) reported that a CS which has been previously paired with an aversive stimulus will elicit the hurdle jumping response in a shuttle box whether or not the response avoids the aversive stimulus. This information, along with that of Horner, Longo, and Bitterman (1960), who demonstrated that light elicited activity from goldfish confined in a small chamber following pairing with shock, led

Woodard and Bitterman (1973b) to postulate that the shuttle box avoidance response emitted by fish in the presence of the CS was not maintained because of its consequences but was elicited by the CS. They provided evidence for this hypothesis by demonstrating that the frequency of initial responding (at least one hurdle crossing on any trial) was as high when a response in the presence of CS did not terminate the trial and avoid the shock as when the response did terminate the trial and avoid shock. Woodard and Bitterman (1971) suggest that all data on avoidance conditioning in goldfish can be accounted for, at least in part, in classical conditioning terms and question whether avoidance learning in goldfish has been demonstrated.

Scobie and Fallon (1974), independently of Woodard and Bitterman (1973b), also provided considerable evidence that respondent stimulus–reinforcer contingencies are involved in discrete trial avoidance conditioning. However, in contrast to the findings of Woodard and Bitterman (1973b), they also reported a reliable operant response–reinforcer component.

Goldfish (*Carassius auratus*) were assigned to one of four experimental conditions across which the opportunity to avoid shock and terminate the CS was varied. The CS (a change in either hue or brightness) was 10 sec in duration; UCS was a 0.10-sec presentation of 0.88 volt, 60 Hz AC/cm shock, and trials were presented at an average interval of 70 sec. The CS remained on until the UCS was presented or, in the two CS termination groups, a shuttle response was emitted. The probability of a response during the CS, per session, for each condition is presented in Fig. 7.

For all groups, the probability of a response during the CS increased over sessions regardless of whether a response avoided shock (A) or not ($\bar{\text{A}}$) or terminated the CS (T) or not ($\bar{\text{T}}$). However, asymptotic levels of responding (0.85) were significantly higher for the group that could avoid shock and terminate the CS (TA). When, in a second experiment, the CS–UCS interval was increased to 20 sec, the difference among the various groups failed to reach statistical significance.

Scobie and Fallon (1974) also demonstrated that the high frequency of responding in the groups that could not avoid shock and terminate the CS was due to the stimulus–reinforcer contingency; i.e., groups of fish trained with CS only, UCS only, or with unpaired CS–UCS presentations responded much less frequently than the paired CS–UCS group.

The CS–shock contingency also influences the extinction of discrete trial avoidance behavior. Wallace and Scobie (1977) examined the effect on avoidance responding of several extinction procedures in which either the contingency between the CS and shock and/or between the response and shock was altered. As would be predicted from the acquisition data presented in Fig. 7, removing the response–shock contingency without altering the stimulus–shock

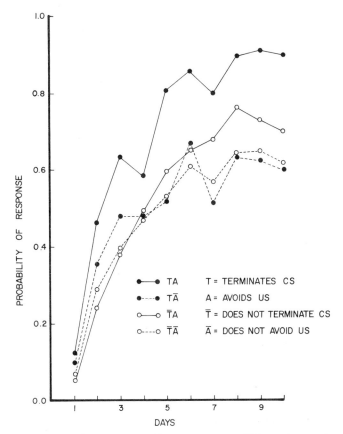

Fig. 7. The probability of at least one avoidance response per CS interval per session for fish trained under conditions in which a response did (T) or did not (T̄) terminate the CS and did (A) or did not (Ā) avoid the UCS. [Taken from Scobie and Fallon (1974).]

contingency had little effect on previously established levels of avoidance responding.

ii. Sidman avoidance. In the Sidman or free operant avoidance procedure, there is no exteroceptive warning stimulus to signal impending shock onset. The only cues to signal shock onset are temporal; i.e., (1) the shock–shock (S–S) interval, the intershock interval in the absence of responding, and (2) the response–shock interval (R–S), the duration of the shock-free interval produced by a response.

Behrend and Bitterman (1963) were the first to demonstrate free operant avoidance in fish. Goldfish were exposed to a Sidman avoidance procedure for twenty 20-min sessions. The R–S and S–S intervals were both 20 sec. Shock intensity was 6 volt AC, for a duration of 0.25 sec. Control subjects were yoked to experimental animals such that they received shock whenever the experimental animals failed to avoid. Experimental animals increased their response rate (breaking photocell in shuttle box) while yoked controls showed no increase over base line response rates.

Pinckney (1968) extended the results of Behrend and Bitterman (1963) by examining the effect of varying the R–S intervals: 2, 5, 10, 15, 20, or 40 sec, and exposing the subjects to 6 hr of avoidance training. The S–S interval was held constant for all subjects at 5.0 sec. The highest terminal response rate was obtained for the 15- and 20-sec R–S groups, and the fewest shocks were received by the 40-sec R–S animals. Little change in responding was observed for the 2-, 5-, and 10-sec groups.

b. Conditioned Suppression and Punishment. Conditioned suppression of responding in goldfish has been demonstrated by Geller (1963). Lever pressing was first established and then maintained on a variable interval (VI) 2-min schedule of food reinforcement. A conditioned suppression procedure in which a flashing light followed by shock onset was superimposed on the schedule of food reinforcement. The results showed that lever pressing gradually decreased in the presence of the flashing light.

In a later study, Geller (1964) examined the effect of intermittent shock presentations on conditioned suppression. For one group of goldfish, shock was delivered after every CS presentation, while for a second group, shock followed only one-half of the CS presentations. As in the previous experiment, responding was suppressed in the presence of the CS regardless of whether the CS reliably or inconsistently predicted shock. However, during extinction the inconsistently shocked animals recovered more quickly than those for which the signal was always followed by shock. Thus, Geller's failure to find a partial reinforcement effect with conditioned suppression is consistent with the earlier results of Longo and Bitterman (1960) and Bitterman *et al.* (1958) with conditioned fear responding.

Response suppression has also been obtained when the aversive event is response contingent. Punishing responses suppresses responses regardless of whether behavior is maintained by some schedule of reinforcement or unconditioned species-specific behavior. An example of punishment's effect on this latter behavior has been provided by Melvin and Ervey (1973), who examined the effect of moderate and intense punishment on the aggressive display of *Betta splendens*. Forty *Betta* were assigned to one of five groups; one group served as a habituation control and was never punished while fish in the other four groups were punished with either a moderate 7-volt or intense 13-volt shock on either trials 15–30 or 46–60. Trials were initiated after 20 min of adaptation to the chamber. In each trial a mirror was presented for 120 sec, and the occurrence and duration of aggressive displays (gill cover extension) were recorded. When a fish extended its gill covers on a punishment trial a 0.5-sec shock was administered.

Punishment administered early in the sequence of trials (16–30) had differential effects depending on intensity. Only intense punishment led to response suppression. This marked suppression was also exhibited by animals receiving intense punishment during trials 45–60. In contrast, the late administration of the 7-volt punishment had a facilitative effect on display duration, i.e., duration increased.

Punishment has also been shown to suppress food maintained responding in goldfish (Geller, 1963; Woodard and Bitterman, 1971). In the Woodard and Bitterman (1971) study, each response to a nipple from which goldfish had been trained to take liquid food was punished with a brief AC shock administered through a pair of stainless steel electrodes placed on (1) either side of the animal, (2) over and under it, or (3) in front and in back of it. All electrode orientations suppressed responding, but the most suppression was obtained with the front–back electrode arrangement.

In the Geller (1963) study, a discriminated punishment procedure was employed. Fish were first trained to press for worms on a 2-min variable interval schedule. At 45-min intervals, a 3-min flashing light which signaled a change to a continuous reinforcement schedule was activated. After several such presentations, a punishment contingency was added such that each response during the light stimulus was shocked (7 volts for 0.3 sec). Complete suppression of responding during the flashing light occurred within 11 sessions, yet responding during the light-off periods was unaffected.

III. BEHAVIORAL TOXICITY

Conditioning studies can be conveniently divided into those that are concerned with the acquisition of a response and those concerned with examining the influence of variations in some parameter, e.g., reinforcement magnitude on stable behavior maintained by schedules of reinforcement. Studies examining the effects of drugs on fish behavior can also be divided along these lines. In addition, because many studies using fish have attempted to understand the biochemical basis of learning, much attention has also been focused on the effect of certain chemicals on the retention of learned responses.

The intent of this section is to examine whether conditioned behavior of fish can be systematically altered by the introduction of chemical substances. We did not limit our discussion to only those substances labeled as environmental pollutants that are likely to be present in the organism's natural environment. Nor did we limit our discussion to only those studies that exposed subjects to various chemical substances in a way likely to occur under natural circumstances (immersion vs. injection). Our major interest is to ascertain whether existing experimental procedures allow the degree of control necessary to detect systematic changes in behavior. An analysis of the behavioral effects of toxic environmental pollutants awaits future researchers.

A. Response Acquisition

A variety of drugs have been found to either facilitate or inhibit the acquisition of responding in a variety of learning situations. The standard procedure is to expose fish to a given drug some time prior to initial acquisition and compare the behavior of the drug group with that of a nondrug group on the acquisition of a particular learning task. The effects of a variety of drugs, including actinomycin D, piracetam, scotophobin, and ethanol, have been examined.

1. Actinomycin D

Batkin *et al.* (1966) injected Japanese carp (*Cyprinus carpio*) with actinomycin D 1 hr prior to training on the first two sessions of training of a visual discrimination task. Fish, reinforced for swimming a T maze by access to open water, were given 40 training trials per session. Sessions one and two were conducted on successive days, but session three was conducted 11 or 15 days following session two. Experimental animals were injected intracranially with actinomycin D 1 hr prior to both sessions one and two, while control animals were injected with saline. Pretraining injections of actinomycin D had little effect on response acquisition. However, drug-injected animals did emit significantly more correct responses on session three than saline-injected controls.

2. Piracetam

Piracetam has been reported to enhance learning in rats (Wolthius, 1971). Bryant *et al.* (1973a) extended these findings to the goldfish. Eighteen hours prior to shuttle box avoidance training, experimental animals were exposed to a solution of 400 mg piracetam in 4 liters of home tank water. The fish remained in the solution for the duration of training. However, training occurred in the absence of the drug. During training each fish received ten sessions of dark avoidance conditioning. At the start of each trial, the stimulus light in the unoccupied compartment of the shuttle box was illuminated, and if the subject did not respond (hurdle jump) within 15 sec, shock (7 volts for 0.1 sec) was turned on in the unilluminated compartment for 45 sec. Drug-treated animals acquired avoidance behavior more quickly than controls, so that by the fourth day of training the piracetam animals were emitting significantly more correct avoidance responses than controls.

3. Scotophobin

Scotophobin, a molecule formed in the brains of rats that have learned to avoid a darkened compartment, has also been thought to play a biochemical role in learning. Bryant *et al.* (1972) injected goldfish (*Carassius auratus*) with synthetic scotophobin prior to light or dark avoidance conditioning. Scotophobin appeared to interact with learning in a specific way; that is, it facilitated acquisition of dark avoidance. Fish were trained (in groups of five to ten) to avoid the dark compartment of a large aquatic shuttle box. Fish were exposed to ten training trials per day for 4 days. Trials were initiated by the onset of a stimulus light in one end of the tank, and 15 sec later shock was presented in either the same compartment (light avoidance) or the unilluminated compartment (dark avoidance). Fish were injected intracranially with various doses of synthetic scotophobin (12.5 mg to 120 mg) 48 hr prior to training. Scotophobin appeared to have specific effects; i.e., it facilitated acquisition of dark avoidance but interfered with the acquisition of light avoidance. The mechanism mediating this effect is not clear.

4. Ethanol

A number of studies have shown that ethanol influences response acquisition in a number of experimental situations. Ryback (1969a) found that ethanol inhibited maze learning in goldfish when compared to water controls. Fish trained in ethanol were first placed in a 495 mg% ethanol solution for 6 hr, then placed in the maze which was filled with 630 mg% ethanol solution; i.e., fish were trained while blood alcohol levels were rising. All subjects spontaneously swimming through the maze were trained to avoid bumping into a glass barrier by always "going right." Exposure to the ethanol solutions prior to and during training significantly impaired acquisition. Ethanol animals needed an average of 75 trials to reach criterion (18 of 20 trials correct), while water controls reached criterion in 17.4 trials.

Different concentrations of ethanol and congener content also appear to influence maze learning (Ryback, 1969b). In experiment I, different subjects were exposed to ethanol solutions of different concentrations, either 400 mg% or 650 mg%, both prior to and during training. Exposure to the 400 mg% solution appeared to facilitate acquisition compared to water controls, but exposure to the 650 mg% appeared to inhibit acquisition.

Facilitation of acquisition has also been reported by other investigators. Petty *et al.* (1973) examined the effects of various concentrations of ethanol on the acquisition of shuttle box avoidance behavior. Three hr prior to training and during training, ethanol animals were placed in either a 428, a 628, or a 856 mg% ethanol solution (856 mg% equals 48 liters of 95% ethanol in 4.25 liters of water). All subjects received 20 trials of dark avoidance training (see above). The

CS interval was equal to 10 sec, and the UCS was a 0.7-volt shock for 0.1 sec pulsed each second for 50 sec. The mean number of correct dark avoidance responses for fish treated at each ethanol concentration and for water controls is presented in Fig. 8.

A dose-related facilitation of avoidance acquisition is apparent. The lowest concentration used did not facilitate acquisition, but both higher concentrations did so. The greatest effect was obtained with the intermediate concentration (628 mg%). Facilitation of acquisition was not correlated with increased frequency of escape or irrelevant responses (bottom panel). However, it is not clear from the data of these studies whether the facilitative effect was indicative of a change in

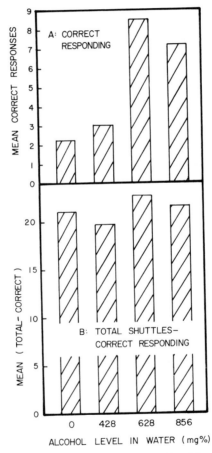

Fig. 8. Mean number of correct shuttle responses (top panel) and the mean number of total minus correct shuttles (bottom panel) for four groups of goldfish pretreated and trained in water containing various concentrations of ethyl alcohol (mg%). [Taken from Petty *et al.* (1973).]

the rate of learning or a change in the organism's sensitivity to shock, a point later addressed by Scobie and Bliss (1974).

A later study by Bryant *et al.* (1973b) found that duration of exposure to ethanol, 3 or 6 hr had no differential effect on dark avoidance acquisition. Bryant *et al.* (1973b) also provided evidence that the facilitative effect of ethanol on the acquisition of dark avoidance was not due to an ethanol-induced decrease in the animal's sensitivity to light.

A failure to find a differential effect of exposure time was also reported by Scobie and Bliss (1974). Both 0.5-hr and 6-hr exposure to a 745 mg% solution of ethanol facilitated the acquisition of a shuttle box avoidance response.

However, in a second experiment Scobie and Bliss (1974) did provide evidence that the facilitative effect of ethanol on the acquisition of shock avoidance was due to ethanol's ability to increase the effectiveness of shock as a reinforcer. Fish were trained to escape a shock intensity (0.55 volt/cm) that supported a low but nonzero rate of responding in untreated fish. Different groups of animals were exposed to either a 0, 350, or 745 mg% ethanol solution 1.5 hr prior to and during training. Figure 9 shows the probability of escape per blocks of five training trials for ethanol and control animals.

Fish exposed to and trained in the ethanol solutions emitted many more escape responses than water controls. The difference between the ethanol groups was

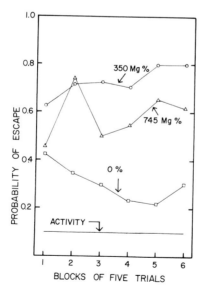

Fig. 9.   Mean probability of escape in blocks of five trials as a function of ethanol concentration. The horizontal solid line indicates general activity level averaged over all groups. [Taken from Scobie and Bliss (1974).]

not significant. In support of these data, Scobie and Bliss also demonstrated that exposure to ethanol also lowered shock thresholds. 0.1-sec 60-Hz shock was administered to loosely restrained goldfish every 10 sec. Intensity was increased until a motor reaction was observed and then decreased until no reaction was observed. Shock threshold was taken as the intensity half-way between these values.

The effect of ethanol on shock thresholds was determined by two methods. In the first method, base line thresholds were recorded and then fish were exposed to various concentrations of ethanol. Thresholds were again determined immediately following exposure and after every 5 min for 30 min. In the second method, animals were first exposed to ethanol for either 0.5 hr or 6 hr, and then thresholds were determined while the animal remained in the ethanol solution.

Figure 10 shows shock thresholds (expressed in terms of the base line thresholds) as a function of time since ethanol administration or (right panel) following either 30-min or 6-hr exposure to ethanol. Higher concentrations of ethanol produced lower thresholds. The effects seem to reach asymptotic levels

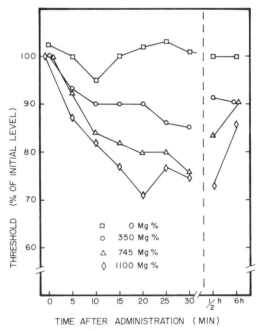

Fig. 10. Changes in shock thresholds (expressed in terms of the base line threshold) as a function of time since administration of several concentrations of ethanol (left panel). Data to the right of the dashed vertical line represent thresholds following either 30-min or 6-hr exposure to the selected concentrations of ethanol. [Taken from Scobie and Bliss (1974).]

30 min following exposure. The effect of ethanol on thresholds also seems to attenuate following a 6-hr exposure.

B. Response Retention

A drug can influence retention in two ways. First, the presentation of a drug following acquisition of a response may have a direct effect upon the retention of that response. Essentially, this effect is examined by a posttraining drug administration procedure where the drug is not present during acquisition and retention testing but is present during the period between training and testing. Retention may also be influenced by manipulating a drug state so that the drug state in which retention is tested differs from that in which the response is acquired. The former procedure has been used extensively to investigate the biochemical bases of learning, while the latter has been used to investigate the phenomena of state-dependent learning (Girden and Culler, 1937; Overton, 1966), i.e., conditions in which responses acquired in a drug state are not emitted in the nondrugged state but reappear when the animal is subsequently drugged.

1. Posttraining Drug Effects

a. Puromycin. Puromycin is an antimetabolite which has been shown to cause specific and reversible inhibition of protein synthesis in living systems. An early study by Agranoff and Klinger (1964) demonstrated that intracranial injections of puromycin immediately following response acquisition interfered with the retention of that response. Goldfish were first trained to avoid shock by swimming over a barrier to the dark side of a shuttle box. The onset of a lamp on one side of the box initiated a trial, and 20 sec later a 3-volt AC 0.2-sec shock was presented for 20 sec in the illuminated side of the chamber unless the goldfish crossed from the light to the dark side of the box prior to the onset of the shock.

Seventy-two goldfish were first given 20 shock avoidance trials with a 5-min rest period after every five trials and then divided into two groups. One-half of one group was injected intracranially with 10 μl of saline while the other group was immediately injected with 90 μg of puromycin. Seventy-two hr later all animals were returned to the avoidance apparatus for ten additional trials, again with 5-min rest periods every five trials (retention test).

The fish injected with puromycin emitted fewer correct responses than the control groups during the retention test, even though the performance of both groups was indistinguishable at the end of training. Agranoff and Klinger (1964) also reported that puromycin injected 72 hr prior to acquisition had no effect on acquisition, and that the disruptive effect was eliminated when goldfish were injected after several training sessions.

Davis *et al.* (1965) demonstrated that the inhibitory effect of puromycin on the emission of the shuttle box avoidance response was a function of the interval between the last training trial and injection. Similar findings were reported by Agranoff *et al.* (1965). Intercranial injections of 170 μg of puromycin in 10 μl of 0.5 *M* NaCl were given to different groups of subjects at different times following trial 20 of the first session of initial acquisition of avoidance responding. Injections were given at intervals of 0, 30, 60, and 90 min following training. All subjects then received ten additional training trials on day 4 of the experiment.

The results are plotted in Fig. 11 in terms of retention scores which were calculated by subtracting the predicted score from the score achieved. The predicted normal day 4 score (if the animal was not drugged) was predicted from the day 1 score of individual subjects. A regression of day 1 scores on day 4 scores was derived from the performance of 29 control fish in previous work.

Figure 11(A) shows that performance on the retraining or retention trials improves as the interval between training and treatment was increased. The effect of 170 μg of puromycin injected at various times following acquisition produced a retention deficit gradient similar in form but greater in magnitude to that

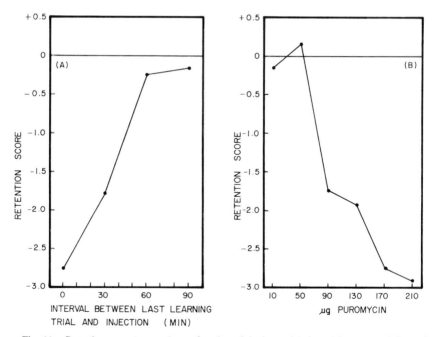

Fig. 11. Retention score (see text) as a function of the interval (minutes) between training and injection (left panel) and dosage (in micrograms) of puromycin (right panel). [Taken from Agranoff *et al.* (1966).]

produced by a 90-μg injection (Davis et al., 1965). Similar effects were also reported by Davis (1968).

Retention scores were also shown to vary as a function of amount of puromycin injected (Agranoff et al., 1965). These data are presented in Fig. 11(B). Injections of 50 μg of puromycin or less had no significant effect, while injections of 90 μg or more produced retention deficits.

Potts and Bitterman (1967) suggested that the effect of puromycin may be restricted to conditioned fear situations. Two groups of animals were trained to swim a simple maze for food reinforcement. On the twenty-eighth training trial (one or two per day), the fish were not fed but shocked intermittently for 30 sec. Experimental fish were immediately injected with 170 μg of puromycin while controls were injected with saline. One week following injections all animals were given three additional reinforcement trials. The mean swimming times on the three retraining trials were shorter for puromycin fish than for saline controls.

Potts and Bitterman (1967) demonstrated that the effect of puromycin is not limited to situations in which injections depress behavior, but puromycin will also increase activity if injected immediately following exposure to a conditioned fear procedure that suppressed behavior. Kristt et al. (1970) provided additional evidence in support of Potts and Bitterman's (1967) suggestion that the effect of puromycin is specific to the retention of conditioned fear by demonstrating that puromycin injected immediately following the acquisition of a response maintained by positive reinforcement did not disrupt the retention of the response. That is, puromycin animals performed as well as saline-injected controls.

Further evidence in support of the fear conditioning hypothesis was provided by Huber and Longo (1970), who demonstrated that puromycin also interfered with the retention of a classically conditioned fear response (Longo and Bitterman, 1960). During training, fish were given 60 light–shock pairings. For the first 50 pairings, a 10-sec light was followed by a 0.1-sec mild electric shock. During trials 51–60, the CS–UCS interval was increased to 20 sec. Fish were intracranially injected with 200 μg of puromycin in 10 μl of saline either 0, 24, or 48 hr following training. Three days following injections, all animals were given ten test trials in which a 20-sec CS was presented without shock. When performance between the last ten training trials and the ten test trials was compared, all puromycin groups showed marked retention deficits compared to saline-injected controls, regardless of injection delay. Huber and Longo also reported deficits following extended training, an effect not observed in avoidance situations where continued training prevents the deficit. In contrast, Schoel and Agranoff (1972) reported that the injection of 195 μg of puromycin either immediately or 4 hr following training had very little effect upon classically conditioned heart rate deceleration in goldfish.

Puromycin has also been shown to inhibit the extinction of a shuttle box avoidance response (Braud and Broussard, 1973). Three groups of ten fish were given 100 trials (over five sessions) of avoidance training in a procedure identical to that of Agranoff and Klinger (1964). Immediately following each of two (20 trial) extinction sessions (no shock), animals were injected with puromycin or saline. The third group was injected with puromycin following a 16-hr delay. Seventy-two hr after the second extinction session, each animal was given 20 additional extinction trials.

With multiple extinction sessions, with injections following each extinction, the number of responses per extinction did not decline for those fish injected with puromycin immediately after each extinction session. Response decreases were obtained for both saline and delayed puromycin groups.

In a similar experimental situation, Springer *et al.* (1975) demonstrated that puromycin injected prior to training did not affect acquisition but did produce severe retention deficits 72 hr later in groups of fish injected with puromycin 24, 16, 8, 4, or 0 hr prior to or 0 or 0.25 hr following avoidance training.

b. Actinomycin D.   Effects on retention of avoidance responding similar to those of puromycin have also been observed for actinomycin D. Agranoff *et al.* (1967) injected 2 μg of actinomycin D intracranially immediately after training on shuttle box avoidance and observed that performance on test trials was imparied.

c. Flurothyl.   Unlike puromycin and actinomycin D, exposure to flurothyl appears to facilitate avoidance responding. Riege and Cherkin (1973) trained goldfish to suppress a spontaneous swimming response by presenting a 2 volt/cm shock for swimming on one trial. When shocked fish were treated 3 min following training with a 16-min exposure to convulsion-producing solutions of flurothyl, the retention of the avoidance response, when compared to that of untreated controls, was facilitated; i.e., response suppression was greater 16, 64, or 256 hr following shock for treated animals than for untreated controls. Suppression scores of treated fish exposed to one trial of noncontingent shock did not differ from controls.

d. Diethyldithiocarbamate (DEDTC).   DEDTC, a chelating compound considered to be the active metabolite of the antialcoholic drug Antabuse, is quite toxic to fish and exposure to concentrations greater than 100 mg/liter is invariably fatal (Danschler and Fjerdingstad, 1975). However, at lower concentrations it has the paradoxical effect of facilitating the retention of avoidance responding in goldfish. Danschler and Fjerdingstad (1975) first trained several groups of animals to avoid shock in a discrete trial light avoidance procedure. A 20-sec shock followed a 10-sec CS unless a shuttle response was emitted in the presence of the CS. Trials were presented on the average of once every 30 sec. Immediately following the first training session, different groups of experimental animals were exposed for 1 hr to different concentrations of DEDTC: 1.25, 2.25, 3.125, 7.5, 10, 15, 25, or 100 mg/liter. Control animals were also trained to avoid but were not exposed to DEDTC. On session two all surviving animals were again trained on the high avoidance procedure.

The effect of exposure to DEDTC was clearly related to concentration. At low concentrations, 1.25, 2.25, or 3.125 mg/liter, no difference between control and experimental animals was noted. Increasing the concentration to 7.5 mg/liter increased the mortality rate from 0 to 10% but at the same time, for surviving animals, significantly increased the proportion of correct avoidance responses emitted by the DEDTC animals. Exposure to concentrations greater than 7.5 mg/liter greatly increased the mortality rate and impaired the avoidance behavior of the surviving animals.

The facilitative effect of 7.5 mg/liter was observed only when animals were exposed to the DEDTC solution immediately after the first session. No effect was observed when the same concentration of DEDTC was applied 24 hr after the first training session.

The results of Danschler and Fjerdingstad are important in two respects. First, they show that toxins can produce marked behavioral effects in fish in the absence of permanent structural or biochemical changes. Second, they emphasize the importance of defining behavioral toxicity in terms of a change in behavior without regard to direction. In the Danschler and Fjerdingstad study, avoidance behavior first improved with increases in the concentration of DEDTC but then deteriorated as the concentration of DEDTC was further increased.

2. State-Dependent Learning

In the previous section we have seen that presentation of drugs during the interval between training and retention test sessions may act to inhibit or facilitate performance. Drugs also influence retention by virtue of their differential presence during testing and training. For example, Ryback (1969a) reported that retention of a "go right" discrimination, learned in a Y maze, was a function of the drug state of the animal during training and testing. Goldfish were divided into four groups of eight and trained in the maze daily (50 trials per day) until a criterion of 18 correct out of 20 turns was obtained. Half of the fish were trained in alcohol while the other half were trained in water. All fish trained in alcohol were placed into a 495 mg% alcohol solution for 6 hr and then trained in a maze filled with a 630 mg% alcohol solution. During testing half of the alcohol fish were placed in a water-filled maze and half of the water-trained animals were tested in an alcohol-filled maze.

Fish trained and retrained under the same drug conditions showed no performance decrement, while fish trained and tested under different conditions made many more errors during testing than both the water–water and alcohol–alcohol groups. Similar findings were reported by Ryback (1969b) and Richardson (1972).

Scobie and Bliss (1974) reported the state-dependent effect with goldfish in an avoidance situation. They also reported that decrements in performance during testing were dose related, with poor performance associated with greater changes in the drug state. Although Ryback (1969a) reported that at moderate dosages 400 mg% extended exposure to the drug state eliminated the state-dependent effect, Scobie and Bliss (1974) reported that at higher dosages (745 mg%) extended exposure to ethanol did not eliminate the decrement increase.

In contrast, Braud and Weibel (1969) reported that discriminative stimuli associated with specific drug states acquired control over drug-induced behavior even after the drugs were discontinued. During the base line phase of the experiment, *Betta splendens* were exposed to twenty 120-sec mirror presentations in a modified Thompson and Sturm (1965a) apparatus in the presence of red or green illumination. Two measures of aggressive behavior were recorded, latency of response and total time aggressing per trial.

During the treatment phase on different sessions, *Betta splendens* were placed in either a morphine–sulfate–water solution (40 mg/liter) or a phenergan–water solution (20 mg/liter) prior to being placed into the apparatus. Following pretreatment fish were given 50 trials of mirror presentations in the presence of either red or green illumination. The pairing of colors and drugs was consistent for each subject. For example, for half of the subjects, red was paired with morphine and green with phenergan. Four days following training all subjects were tested in undrugged water. After training, all subjects evidenced enhanced aggressive behavior in the presence of the stimulus previously associated with the aggressive potentiating drug (morphine) and decreased aggressive behavior in the presence of the stimulus previously associated with the aggression depressing drug (phenergan).

C. Steady State Responding

The experiments reviewed thus far examined the effects of several chemical agents on either the acquisition or the retention of a newly acquired response. Behavioral toxicity may also be demonstrated by examining chemically induced changes in either the rate or pattern of schedule-maintained behavior. The standard procedure is to first reinforce responding on a particular reinforcement schedule until stable responding is obtained. The subject is then exposed to the chemical agent, and resulting changes in this stable pattern of responding are recorded.

Such a procedure allows one to measure the time required for recovery from different dosages and concentrations of the chemical substance as well as drug–

environment interactions. Frequently, the behavioral effects of a drug depend on the schedule of reinforcement maintaining the behavior to the extent that identical dosages of the same drug may have opposite effects on behavior maintained by different reinforcement schedules (Dews, 1955).

Unfortunately, very few studies using fish as subjects have attempted to measure the effects of a chemical substance upon well-established schedule-maintained patterns of responding. One of the few studies to do so is that of Wilson *et al.* (1970). The responses of African mouthbreeders (*Tilapia macrocephala*) were first reinforced on a variable ratio (VR) 2 schedule of reinforcement for ten sessions. On session 11, a 30-sec CS (light) followed by a 120volt AC shock was presented. Suppression was produced by the CS in all

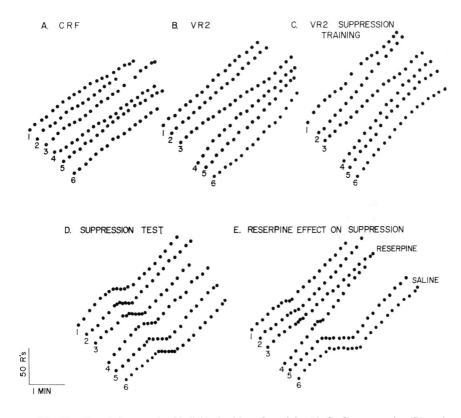

Fig. 12. Cumulative records of individual subjects for training (A, B, C), suppression (D), and drug conditions (E). Responses emitted during the interval from 20 to 10 sec after the first post-CS response is emitted are plotted in 10-sec intervals. All other responses are plotted in 15-sec intervals. [Taken from Wilson *et al.* (1970).]

subjects. One hr prior to a subsequent suppression session, half of the subjects were injected with a saline solution. Suppression was reduced in reserpined subjects but not in saline controls. Cumulative records for continuous reinforcement (CRF), VR2, suppression, and reserpine sessions for each session are presented in Fig. 12. Responses are plotted in 10-sec intervals from 20 sec before each CS onset to 10 sec after the first post-CS response was emitted. Responses emitted at all other times are plotted in 15-sec intervals.

Golub *et al.* (1972) examined the effects of a 170 μg injection of puromycin on behavior maintained by a VI 3-min schedule of reinforcement for 3 to 6 weeks. The injections of puromycin were given to four goldfish immediately following the final base line session and to four other fish 19.5 hr following the session. Controls received saline injections. Intracranial injections of puromycin had no significant effects upon food-maintained responding, a finding that is consistent with Kristt *et al.* (1970).

IV. SUMMARY

An examination of the fish learning literature has shown that a variety of responses can be either respondently or operantly conditioned and that a variety of chemicals affect the acquisition, retention, and maintenance of these responses. However, several limitations of the existing data are readily apparent. Although there are literally hundreds of studies examining learning phenomena in fish, most of these studies have provided only group data. Thus, much information is available about learning in the average fish of various species, but very little information is available as to whether individual fish behave in a similar manner. Substantial between-subject variability reported in many of these experiments further clouds the issue.

Furthermore, the majority of the studies reviewed have limited their focus to the first few trials of response acquisition and have not examined the conditions under which learned behavior is maintained over long periods of time. For example, very few studies have examined the effects of various reinforcement parameters, e.g., frequency or delay of reinforcement, on steady state behavior. As a result, a fine-grained experimental analysis of fish behavior similar to that available for other species is lacking.

In addition, with few exceptions, most investigations have depended on statistical vs. experimental control over variability. As a result, we do not at present possess the degree of experimental control over fish behavior that is needed to assess the effect of subtle environmental changes. This substantial amount of within and between-subject variability also creates difficulties for behavioral toxicologists, for it is very likely that the more subtle behavioral effects induced by chemical agents will be obscured.

Additional problems exist for behavioral toxicologists. For example, although there is abundant evidence that many chemicals have a behaviorally toxic effect, we need to know more about how variations in the concentration of and duration of exposure to these chemicals affect the behavior of individual organisms over longer time spans. The range of chemical substances studied needs to be expanded to include those chemicals that have been classified as environmental pollutants. At present, the existing literature contains little information useful to ecologists and toxicologists. This lack of information is not the fault of individual investigators, for their purpose in conducting many of the studies reviewed in this chapter was to identify the biochemical basis of learning, and not to establish the science of behavioral toxicology. Their contribution, nonetheless, has been significant in that they clearly demonstrated the feasibility of extending the study of behavioral toxicity to the behavior of fish. However, the problems facing behavioral toxicology are much different and require different research strategies.

The major pressing concern, then, for behavioral toxicologists is to obtain reliable and precise measures and control over the behavior of individual fish for extended periods of time. Such control would provide behavioral toxicologists with a very sensitive yardstick against which to measure both the transient and long-term effects of most chemical pollutants. Once such information is obtained, ecologists and environmentalists will be able to objectively determine acceptable pollution levels, i.e., levels that will minimize the possibility of economic hardship and maximize that of fish survival.

ACKNOWLEDGMENT

The second author would like to acknowledge the support of Patricia Rauso during the preparation of this chapter.

REFERENCES

Adler, N., and Hogan, J. (1963). Classical conditioning and punishment of an instinctive response in Betta splendens. *Anim. Behav.* **11,** 351–354.

Agranoff, B. W., and Klinger, P. D. (1964). Puromycin effect on memory fixation in the goldfish. *Science* **146,** 952–953.

Agranoff, B. W., Davis, R. E., and Brink, J. J. (1965). Memory fixation in the goldfish. *Proc. Natl. Acad. Sci. U.S.A.* **54,** 788–793.

Agranoff, B. W., Davis, R. E., and Brink, J. J. (1966). Chemical studies on memory fixation in goldfish. *Brain Res.* **1,** 303–309.

Agranoff, B. W., Davis, R. E., Casola, L., and Lim, R. (1967). Actinomycin D blocks formation of memory of shock-avoidance in goldfish. *Science* **158,** 1600–1601.

Baennizer, R. (1970). Visual reinforcement, habituation, and prior social experience of siamese fighting fish. *J. Comp. Physiol. Psychol.* **71,** 1–5.

Batkin, S., Woodard, W. T., Cole, R. E., and Hall, J. B. (1966). RNA and actenomycin-D enhancement of learning in the carp. *Psychon. Sci.* **5**, 345–346.

Behrend, E. R., and Bitterman, M. E. (1961). Probability-matching in the fish. *Am. J. Psychol.* **74**, 542–551.

Behrend, E. R., and Bitterman, M. E. (1962). Avoidance-conditioning in the goldfish: Exploratory studies of the CS–US interval. *Am. J. Psychol.* **75**, 18–34.

Behrend, E. R., and Bitterman, M. E. (1963). Avoidance in the fish. *J. Exp. Anal. Behav.* **6**, 47–52.

Behrend, E. R., and Bitterman, M. E. (1964). Avoidance conditioning in the fish: Further studies of the CS–UCS interval. *Am. J. Psychol.* **77**, 15–28.

Behrend, E. R., and Bitterman, M. E. (1966). Probability matching in the goldfish. *Psychon. Sci.* **6**, 327–328.

Behrend, E. R., and Bitterman, M. E. (1968). Partial reinforcement and classical conditioning in two species of fish. *Psychon. Sci.* **11**, 167–168.

Behrend, E. R., Domesick, V. B., and Bitterman, M. E. (1965). Habit reversal in the fish. *J. Comp. Physiol. Psychol.* **60**, 407–411.

Berger, B. D., Yarczower, M., and Bitterman, M. E. (1965). Effect of partial reinforcement on the extinction of a classically conditioned response in the goldfish. *J. Comp. Physiol. Psychol.* **59**, 399–405.

Bintz, J. (1971). Between and within-subject effect of shock intensity on avoidance in goldfish (Carassius auratus). *J. Comp. Physiol. Psychol.* **75**, 92–97.

Bitterman, M. E. (1964). Classical conditioning in the goldfish as a function of the CS-US interval. *J. Comp. Physiol. Psychol.* **58**, 359–366.

Bitterman, M. E. (1968). Comparative studies on learning in the fish. *In* "The Central Nervous System and Behavior" (D. Ingle, ed.), pp. 257–270. Univ. of Chicago Press, Chicago, Illinois.

Bitterman, M. E., Wodinsky, J., and Candland, D. K. (1958). Some comparative psychology. *Am. J. Psychol.* **71**, 94–110.

Braud, W. G. and Broussard, W. J. (1973). Effect of puromycin on memory for shuttle extinction in goldfish and barpress extinction in rat. *Pharmacol., Biochem., Behav.,* **1**, 651–656.

Braud, W. G., and Weibel, J. K. (1969). Acquired stimulus control of drug-induced changes in aggressive display in Betta splendens. *J. Exp. Anal. Behav.* **12**, 773–777.

Brookshire, K., and Frumkin, K. (1969). CS–US interval and conditioned fear facilitation of shuttle box avoidance learning in the goldfish. *Psychon. Sci.* **16**, 115–116.

Brown, P. L., and Jenkins, H. M. (1968). Autoshaping of the pigeons key peck. *J. Exp. Anal. Behav.* **11**, 1–8.

Bryant, R. C., Santos, N. N., and Byrne, W. L. (1972). Synthetic scotophobin in goldfish: Specificity and effect on learning. *Science* **177**, 635–636.

Bryant, R. C., Petty, F., and Byrne, W. L. (1973a). Effects of piracetam (SKF 38462) on acquisition, retention, and activity in the goldfish. *Psychopharmacologia* **29**, 121–130.

Bryant, R. C., Petty, F., Warren, J., and Byrne, W. L. (1973b). Facilitation by alcohol of active avoidance performance in the goldfish. *Pharmacol., Biochem. Behav.* **1**, 523–529.

Bull, H. O. (1928–1939). Studies on conditioned responses in fish. Parts I-IX. *J. Mar. Biol. Assoc. U. K. Dove Mar. Lab. Rep.*

Bush, R. R., and Wilson, T. R. (1956). Two choice behavior of paradise fish. *J. Exp. Psychol.* **51**, 315–322.

Crum, J., Brown, W. L., and Bitterman, M. E. (1951). The effect of partial and delayed reinforcement on resistance to extinction. *Am. J. Psychol.* **64**, 228–237.

Danscher, G., and Fjerdingstad, E. J. (1975). Diethyldithiocarbamate (Antabuse): Decrease of brain heavy metal staining pattern and improved consolidation of shuttle box avoidance in goldfish. *Brain Res.* **83**, 143–155.

Davis, R. E. (1968). Environmental control of memory fixation in goldfish. *J. Comp. Physiol. Psych.* **65**, 72–78.

Davis, R. E., Bright, P. J., and Agranoff, B. W. (1965). Effect of ECS and puromycin on memory in fish. *J. Comp. Physiol. Psychol.* **60**, 162–166.

Deese, J. (1952). "The Psychology of Learning." McGraw-Hill, New York.

Deterline, W. A. (1957). The effect of successive acquisitions and extinctions on operant discrimination learning in fish. Doctoral Dissertation, University of Pittsburgh, Pittsburgh, Pennsylvania (unpublished).

Dews, P. B. (1955). Studies on behavior. I. Differential sensitivity to pentobarbitol of pecking performance in pigeons depending on the schedule of reward. *J. Pharmacol. Exp. Ther.* **113**, 393.

Dondoroff, P., Teduc, G., and Schneider, C. R. (1966). Acute toxicity to fish of solutions containing complex metal cyanides in relation to concentrations of molecular hydrocyanic acid. *Trans. Am. Fish. Soc.* **95**, 6–22.

Fantino, E., Weigele, S., and Lancy, D. (1972). Aggressive display in the siamese fighting fish (Betta splendens). *Learn. Motiv.* **3**, 457–468.

Froloff, J. P. (1925). Bedingte reflexe bei fischen. I. *Pfluegers Arch. Gesamte Physiol. Menschen Tiere* **208**, 261–271.

Froloff, J. P. (1928). Bedingte reflexe bei fischen. II. *Pfluegers Arch. Gesamte Physiol. Menschen Tiere* **220**, 339–349.

Frumkin, K., and Brookshire, K. (1969). Conditioned fear training and latter avoidance learning in the goldfish. *Psychon. Sci.* **16**, 159–160.

Gallon, R. (1972). Effects of shock intensity on shuttle box avoidance conditioning in goldfish. *Psychol. Rep.* **31**, 855–858.

Galton, R. (1974). Spatial location of a visual signal and shuttle box avoidance acquisition by goldfish (Carassius auratus). *J. Comp. Physiol. Psychol.* **86**, 316–321.

Gamzu, E., and Schwartz, B. (1973). The maintenance of key pecking by stimulus-contingent and response-independent food presentation. *J. Exp. Anal. Behav.* **19**, 65–72.

Geller, I. (1963). Conditioned "anxiety" and punishment effects on operant behavior of goldfish (Carassius auratus). *Science* **141**, 351–353.

Geller, I. (1964). Conditioned suppression in goldfish as a function of a shock-reinforcement schedule. *J. Exp. Anal. Behav.* **7**, 345–349.

Girden, E., and Culler, E. (1937). Conditioned responses in curarized striate muscle in dogs. *J. Comp. Psychol.* **23**, 261–274.

Goldstein, S. R. (1967). Mirror image as a reinforcer in siamese fighting fish: A repetition with additional controls. *Psychon. Sci.* **7**, 331–332.

Golub, M., Cheal, M. C., and Davis, R. C. (1972). Effect of electroconvulsive shock and puromycin on operant responding in goldfish. *Physiol. Behav.* **8**, 573–578.

Gonzalez, R. C. (1972). Patterning in the goldfish as a function of magnitude of reinforcement. *Psychon. Sci.* **28**, 53–55.

Gonzalez, R. C., and Bitterman, M. E. (1967). Partial reinforcement effect in the goldfish as a function of amount of reward. *J. Comp. Physiol. Psychol.* **64**, 163–167.

Gonzalez, R. C., and Powers, A. S. (1973). Simultaneous contrast in goldfish. *Anim. Learn. Behav.* **1**, 96–98.

Gonzalez, R. C., Longo, N., and Bitterman, M. E. (1961a). Classical conditioning in the fish: Exploratory studies of partial reinforcement. *J. Comp. Psychol.* **54**, 452–456.

Gonzalez, R. C., Eskin, R. M., and Bitterman, M. E. (1961b). Alternating and random partial reinforcement in the fish with some observations on asymptotic resistance to extinction. *Am. J. Psychol.* **74**, 561–568.

Gonzalez, R. C., Eskin, R. M., and Bitterman, M. E. (1962a). Extinction in the fish after partial and consistent reinforcement with number of reinforcements equated. *J. Comp. Physiol. Psychol.* **55**, 381–386.

Gonzalez, R. C., Milstern, S., and Bitterman, M. E. (1962b). Classical conditioning in the fish: Further studies of partial reinforcement. *Am. J. Psychol.* **75**, 421–428.

Gonzalez, R. C., Eskin, R. M., and Bitterman, M. E. (1963). Further experiments on partial reinforcement in the fish. *Am. J. Psychol.* **76**, 366–375.

Gonzalez, R. C., Behrend, E. R., and Bitterman, M. E. (1965). Partial reinforcement in the fish: Experiment with spaced trials and partial delay. *Am. J. Psychol.* **78**, 198–207.

Gonzalez, R. C., Holmes, H. K., and Bitterman, M. E. (1967). Resistance to extinction in the goldfish as a function of frequency and amount of reward. *Am. J. Psychol.* **80**, 269–275.

Gonzalez, R. C., Potts, A., Pitcoff, K., and Bitterman, M. E. (1972). Runway performance of goldfish as a function of complete and incomplete reduction of reward. *Psychon. Sci.* **27**, 305–307.

Grabowski, J. G., and Thompson, T. (1968). Effects of visual reinforcer brightness and color on operant behavior of siamese fighting fish. *Psychon. Sci.* **11**, 111–112.

Hogan, J. A. (1967). Fighting and reinforcement in the siamese fighting fish (Betta splendens). *J. Comp. Physiol. Psychol.* **64**, 356–389.

Hogan, J. A., Kleist, S., and Hutchings, C. S. L. (1970). Display and food as reinforcers in the siamese fighting fish (Betta splendens). *J. Comp. Physiol. Psychol.* **70**, 351–357.

Horner, J. L., Longo, N., and Bitterman, M. E. (1960). A classical conditioning technique for small aquatic animals. *Am. J. Psychol.* **73**, 623–626.

Huber, H., and Longo, N. (1970). The effect of puromycin on classical conditioning in the goldfish. *Psychon. Sci.* **18**, 279–280.

Humphreys, L. G. (1939). The effect of random alternation of reinforcement of the acquisition and extinction of conditioned eyelid reactions. *J. Exp. Psychol.* **25**, 141–158.

Jacobs, D. W., and Popper, A. N. (1968). Stimulus effectiveness in avoidance behavior in fish. *Psychon. Sci.* **12**, 109–110.

Kelleher, R. T., and Gollub, L. R. (1962). A review of positive conditioned reinforcement. *J. Exp. Anal. Behav.* **5**, 543–597.

Klinman, C. S., and Bitterman, M. E. (1963). Classical conditioning in the fish: The CS–US interval. *J. Comp. Physiol. Psychol.* **56**, 578–583.

Kristt, S. A., Freimark, S. J., and Salzinger, K. (1970). The effect of puromycin on retention of a positively reinforced response in goldfish. *Psychon. Sci.* **20**, 181–183.

Longo, N., and Bitterman, M. E. (1960). The effect of partial reinforcement with spaced practice on resistance to extinction in the fish. *J. Comp. Physiol. Psychol.* **53**, 169–172.

Lowes, G., and Bitterman, M. E. (1967). Reward and learning in the goldfish. *Science* **157**, 455–457.

McCann, J. A., and Jasper, R. L. (1972). Vertebral damage to Bluegills exposed to acutely toxic pesticides. *Trans. Am. Fish. Soc.* **2**, 317–327.

McDonald, H. E. (1922). Ability of Pimephales notatus to form associations with sound vibrations. *J. Comp. Psychol.* **2**, 191–193.

Mackintosh, N. J. (1965). Selective attention in animal discrimination learning. *Psychol. Bull.* **64**, 124–150.

Mackintosh, N. J. (1969). Comparative studies of reversal and probability learning: Rats, birds, and fish. *In* "Animal Discrimination Learning" (R. M. Gilbert and N. S. Sutherland, eds.), pp. 137–162. Academic Press, New York.

Mackintosh, N. J. (1971). Reward and aftereffects of reward in learning of goldfish. *J. Comp. Physiol. Psychol.* **76**, 225–232.

Mackintosh, N. J., and Cauty, A. (1971). Spatial reversal learning in rats, pigeons, and goldfish. *Psychon. Sci.* **22**, 281–282.

Mackintosh, N. J., and Mackintosh, J. (1963). Reversal learning in Octopus vulgaris lamarck with and without irrelevant cues. *Q. J. Exp. Psychol.* **15**, 235–242.

Mackintosh, N. J., Mackintosh, J., Safriel-Jorne, O., and Sutherland, N. S. (1966). Overtraining, reversal, and extinction in the goldfish. *Anim. Behav.* **14**, 314–318.

Marrone, R., and Evans, S. (1966). Two choice and three choice probability learning in the fish. *Psychon. Sci.* **5**, 327–328.

Melvin, K. B., and Ervey, D. H. (1973). Facilitative and suppressive effects of punishment on species-typical aggressive display in Betta splendens. *J. Comp. Physiol. Psychol.* **83**, 451–457.

Noble, M., Gruender, A., and Meyer, D. R. (1959). Conditioning in fish (Molliensia sp.) as a function of the intertrial interval between CS and US. *J. Comp. Physiol. Psychol.* **52**, 236–239.

Otis, L. S., Cerf, J. A., and Thomas, G. J. (1957). Conditioned inhibition of respiration and heart rate in the goldfish. *Science* **126**, 263–264.

Overmier, J. B., and Seligman, M. E. P. (1967). Effects of inescapable shock upon subsequent escape and avoidance responding. *J. Comp. Physiol. Psychol.* **63**, 28–33.

Overton, D. A. (1966). State dependent learning produced by depressant and atropine-like drugs. *Psychopharmacologia* **10**, 6–31.

Padilla, A. M. (1973). Effects of prior and interpolated shock exposures on subsequent avoidance learning by goldfish. *Psychol. Rep.* **32**, 451–456.

Padilla, A. M., Padilla, C., Ketterer, T., and Giacalone, D. (1970). Inescapable shocks and subsequent escape/avoidance conditioning in goldfish (Carassius auratus). *Psychon. Sci.* **20**, 295–296.

Paul, C. (1965). Effects of overlearning upon single habit reversal in rats. *Psychol. Bull.* **63**, 65–72.

Petty, F., Bryant, R. C., and Byrne, W. L. (1973). Dose related facilitation by alcohol of avoidance acquisition in the goldfish. *Pharmacol., Biochem., Behav.* **1**, 173–176.

Pinckney, G. A. (1966). The effect of intertrial interval on avoidance learning in fish. *Psychon. Sci.* **6**, 497–498.

Pinckney, G. A. (1967). Avoidance learning in fish as a function of prior fear conditioning. *Psychol. Rep.* **20**, 71–74.

Pinckney, G. A. (1968). Response consequences and Sidman Avoidance behavior in the goldfish. *Psychon. Sci.* **12**, 13–14.

Potts, A., and Bitterman, M. E. (1967). Puromycin and retention in the goldfish. *Science* **158**, 1594–1596.

Raymond, B., Aderman, M., and Wolach, A. H. (1972). Incentive shifts in the goldfish. *J. Comp. Physiol. Psychol.* **78**, 10–13.

Richardson, E. J. (1972). Alcohol-state dependent learning: Acquisition of a spatial discrimination in the goldfish (Carassius auratus). *Psychol. Rec.* **22**, 545–553.

Riege, W. H., and Cherkin, A. (1973). Retroactive facilitation of memory in goldfish by flurothyl. *Psychopharmacologia* **30**, 195–204.

Ryback, R. S. (1969a). State-dependent or dissociated learning with alcohol in the goldfish. *Q. J. Stud. Alcohol, Part A* **30**, 598–608.

Ryback, R. S. (1969b). Effects of ethanol, bourbon and various ethanol levels on Y maze learning in the goldfish. *Psychopharmacologia* **14**, 305–314.

Salzinger, K., Friemark, S. J., Fairhurst, S. P., and Wolkoff, F. D. (1968). Conditioned reinforcement in the fish. *Science* **160**, 1471–1472.

Sanders, F. K. (1940). Second order olfactory and visual learning in optic tectum of goldfish. *J. Exp. Biol.* **17**, 416–434.

Schoel, W., and Agranoff, B. W. (1972). The effect of puromycin on retention of conditioned cardiac deceleration in the goldfish. *Behav. Biol.* **7**, 553–565.

Scobie, S. R. (1973). Unconditioned stimulus intensity and cardiac conditioning in the goldfish. (Carassius auratus). *Physiol. Behav.* **11,** 31–34.

Scobie, S. R., and Bliss, D. (1974). Ethol alcohol: Relation to memory for aversive learning in goldfish (Carassius auratus). *J. Comp. Physiol. Psychol.* **86,** 867–874.

Scobie, S. R., and Fallon, D. (1974). Operant and Pavlovian control of a defensive shuttle response in goldfish (Carassius auratus). *J. Comp. Physiol. Psychol.* **86,** 858–866.

Setterington, R. G., and Bishop, H. E. (1967). Habit reversal improvement in the fish. *Psychon. Sci.* **7,** 41–42.

Sperling, S. E. (1965). Reversal learning and resistance to extinction: A review of the rat literature. *Psychol. Bull.* **63,** 281–297.

Springer, A. D., Schoel, W. M., Klinger, P. D., and Agranoff, B. W. (1975). Anterograde and retrograde effects of electroconvulsive shock and of puromycin on memory formation in the goldfish. *Behav. Biol.* **13,** 467–481.

Squier, L. H. (1969). Autoshaping by responses with fish. *Psychon. Sci.* **17,** 177–178.

Thompson, T. (1963). Visual reinforcement in siamese fighting fish. *Science* **141,** 55–57.

Thompson, T., and Lilja, P. (1964). "Behavioral Toxicity of DDT," Psychol. Tech. No. PR 64-3. Department of Psychiatry, University of Minnesota, Minneapolis.

Thompson, T., and Schuster, E. R. (1968). "Behavioral Pharmacology." Prentice-Hall, Englewood Cliffs, New Jersey.

Thompson, T., and Sturm, T. (1965a). Visual-reinforcer color and operant behavior in siamese fighting fish. *J. Exp. Anal. Behav.* **8,** 341–346.

Thompson, T., and Sturm, T. (1965b). Classical conditioning of aggressive display in siamese fighting fish. *J. Exp. Anal. Behav.* **8,** 397–403.

Thorndike, E. L. (1911). "Animal Intelligence." Macmillan, New York.

Triplett, N. (1901). The educability of the perch. *Am. J. Psychol.* **12,** 354–360.

Turnbough, P. D., and Lloyd, K. E. (1972). Two visual reinforcers for operant responding in siamese fighting fish (Betta splendens). *Proc. 80th Annu. Conv. Am. Psychol. Assoc.* pp. 749–750.

Wallace, J., and Scobie, S. R. (1977). Avoidance extinction in goldfish. *Learn. Motiv.* **8,** 18–38.

Warren, J. M. (1960). Reversal learning by paradise fish (Macropodus opercularis). *J. Comp. Physiol. Psychol.* **53,** 376–378.

Weitzman, R. A. (1967). Positional matching in rats and fish. *J. Comp. Physiol. Psychol.* **63,** 54–59.

Westerfield, F. (1922). The ability of mud-minnows to form associations with sounds. *J. Comp. Psychol.* **2,** 187–190.

Wilson, W. L., Darcy, J. M., and Haralson, J. V. (1970). Reserpine and conditioned suppression in the fish Tilapia h. macrocephala. *Psychon. Sci.* **20,** 47–49.

Wodinsky, J., and Bitterman, M. E. (1957). Discrimination-reversal in the fish. *Am. J. Psychol.* **70,** 569–576.

Wodinsky, J., and Bitterman, M. E. (1959). Partial reinforcement in the fish. *Am. J. Psychol.* **72,** 184–199.

Wodinsky, J., Behrend, E. R., and Bitterman, M. E. (1962). Avoidance conditioning in two species of fish. *Anim. Behav.* **10,** 76–78.

Wolach, A. H., Raymond, B., and Hurst, J. W. (1973). Reward magnitude shifts with goldfish. *Psychol. Rec.* **23,** 371–376.

Wolthius, O. L. (1971). Experiments with UCB 6215, a drug which enhances acquisition in rats: Its effects compared with those of metamphetamine. *Eur. J. Pharmacol.* **16,** 283–297.

Woodard, W. T. (1971). Classical respiratory conditioning in the fish: CS intensity. *Am. J. Psychol.* **84,** 549–554.

Woodard, W. T., and Bitterman, M. E. (1971). Classical conditioning of goldfish in the shuttle box. *Behav. Res. Methods & Instrum.* **3,** 193–194.

Woodard, W. T., and Bitterman, M. E. (1973a). Further experiments on probability learning in goldfish. *Anim. Learn. Behav.* **1,** 25–28.

Woodard, W. T., and Bitterman, M. E. (1973b). Pavlovian analysis of avoidance conditioning in the goldfish (Carassius auratus). *J. Comp. Physiol. Psychol.* **82,** 123–129.

Woodard, W. T., Schoel, W. M., and Bitterman, M. E. (1971). Reversal learning with singly presented stimuli in pigeons and goldfish. *J. Comp. Physiol. Psychol.* **76,** 460–467.

Woodworth, R. S., and Schlosberg, H. (1954). "Experimental Psychology" (rev. ed.). Holt, New York.

Zerbolio, D. J., and Wickstra, L. L. (1975). The effect of power (US intensity × US duration) on shuttle box avoidance acquisition in goldfish. *Bull. Psychon. Soc.* **5,** 345–347.

3

Vision in Fishes: Color and Pattern

DAVID NORTHMORE, FRANCES C. VOLKMANN, and DEAN YAGER

I.	Introduction	79
	A. General Introduction	79
	B. Psychophysical Methods	80
II.	Spatial Vision	82
	A. Discrimination Thresholds	82
	B. Discrimination and Classification of Shapes	97
III.	Chromatic Vision	114
	A. Spectral Sensitivity	114
	B. Color Discrimination	124
	References	129

I. INTRODUCTION

A. General Introduction*

The design for an aquatic visual system must meet a stiff set of specifications, stiffer than for most aerial visual systems because of the photic conditions peculiar to the underwater scene. Light is colored by the selective filtering action of water and dissolved substances, it is scattered and refracted by suspended particles making distant objects appear faint and blurred, and more often than not, it is scarce. During evolution, these factors must have shaped the color vision, pattern vision, and visual sensitivity of fishes, and presumably shaped them as multifariously as the light environments they inhabit.

*We wish to express.our appreciation to John Volkmann for help with German translations and for contributions to and criticisms of the manuscript.

In this chapter we cannot hope to do justice to the variety of visual adaptations in fishes, the largest class of vertebrates, still less to the range of visual behavior that fishes are capable of. Instead, our standpoint will be in the laboratory, where the number of usable species is limited and their behavior can be controlled. The studies that we shall present attempt to show what a fish *can* respond to visually, rather than what it *does* respond to as it behaves in its natural habitat. By way of justification for this approach, we shall indicate how such results may be useful in uncovering the mechanisms of vision generally.

In animal and human psychophysical experiments, in which one seeks the connection between visual stimuli and perception or behavior, much reliance is put upon the determination of thresholds because these are held to be the most appropriate data to relate to physiological mechanisms. The experiments on contrast and spectral sensitivity fall into this class because the characteristics of single unit responses and visual pigments are readily correlated. Lest one should think of threshold data as too artificial to have anything to do with behavior, it should be appreciated that a major problem for underwater vision is the *detection* of objects. The boundary of a fish's visual world can only extend as far as its contrast or color discrimination thresholds will allow under prevailing conditions of illumination and water quality.

Many spatial factors in vision, the effect of target size on visibility for example, can be studied by threshold determinations, but the investigation of pattern discrimination proceeds in the laboratory by discovering how fish classify stimuli of various shapes. Since very little information is available on the physiological mechanisms of pattern processing in fish, one has to be content with isolating the features in a stimulus that the animal uses to perform its discrimination in the hope that physiological feature detectors will be found for future correlation. The experiments on shape discrimination to be reviewed have less appeal to relevance than even the psychophysical experiments since the stimuli employed are highly artificial, having been chosen usually on the basis of a hypothesis to be tested.

B. Psychophysical Methods

Psychophysical studies with fish are concerned with the same sort of measures used in human psychophysical studies: both reduce to the study of relations between stimulus variables and simple responses. The essential problem in fish psychophysical studies is to devise methods of establishing stimulus–response relations that might be established with humans simply by giving instructions. We will not present an extended discussion of animal psychophysical methods here, since three comprehensive reviews have recently been published (Stebbins, 1970; Blough and Yager, 1972; Northmore and Yager, 1975); rather, we will outline several broad categories of psychophysical methods used to investigate visual functions in fish, and refer to published papers which describe the methods fully.

1. Reflex Methods

It is often convenient to use a fish's innate stereotyped responses to visual stimuli as a means of measuring its powers of detection and discrimination. Of the many responses that might be employed, the most useful are those that do not wane with repeated elicitation.

One such visual response is the dorsal light reflex which is shown by the tilting of a fish about its longitudinal axis in the direction of a lateral source of light, the angle of tilt varying in a monotonic fashion with the difference in stimulation of the two eyes (Thibault, 1949). Making use of this fact, Silver (1974) used her subjects, neon tetras, as null detectors to perform photometric matching between a constant white light and different monochromatic lights.

Optomotor responses are usually studied in the laboratory by rotating an array of stripes around a fish contained in a stationary glass cylinder. If the stripes rotate at more than some threshold speed, a fish subject will either swim along with the stripes or orient to them like a compass needle orients to a magnet (Harden Jones, 1963). Using monochromatic light to illuminate or project the stripes, spectral sensitivity curves have been derived for a variety of species (Grundfest, 1932a; Cronly-Dillon and Muntz, 1965; Cronly-Dillon and Sharma, 1968).

Other untrained behaviors dependent upon light have suggested themselves: Blaxter (1964) measured the least amount of light required by herring for feeding, avoiding a barrier, and phototaxis, and obtained different spectral and absolute sensitivities for each of the three activities.

2. Training Methods

a. Respondent. These methods, which are also called Pavlovian or classical conditioning methods, depend upon establishing a conditioned response (CR) by correlating the occurrence of a visual stimulus (CS) with another stimulus (UCS) that reliably elicits some conveniently measurable response (UCR). The CR is then used to indicate whether the animal can discriminate the CS from other stimuli, be they stimuli which have not been correlated with the UCS, or simply the absence of the CS.

The responses most commonly conditioned for the purpose of fish psychophysics are shock-induced increases in swimming activity, and the inhibition of respiration and heart rate. The conditioning of gross activity is most simply achieved by confining the fish in a small tank equiped with carbon or stainless steel electrodes placed at either end for delivering brief AC shocks for the UCS, and a detector of water currents such as a paddle or self-heating thermistor for registering the CR (Bull, 1928; Horner et al., 1960; Northmore and Muntz, 1974). Methods of conditioning heart rate and respiration have been described by Hester (1968), Schwassmann and Krag (1970), and Northmore and Yager (1975).

b. Operant. In operant conditioning, the animal's behavior is maintained by administering reinforcement immediately following the desired response. A version of the operant method, the two-choice procedure, has been applied to the study of fishes' powers of discriminating colors and shapes (e.g., Muntz and Cronly-Dillon, 1966; Herter, 1953; Sutherland, 1968b), and for measuring acuity (Weiler, 1966; Wilkinson, 1972) and spectral sensitivity (Yager, 1967).

Although discrimination is best studied in the two-choice situation where the positive and negative stimuli are presented simultaneously, there are applications for methods in which the stimuli are presented successively on a single panel, particularly in the study of stimulus generalization and similarity (Yarczower and Bitterman, 1965; Yager et al., 1971). Conditioned suppression, a relatively new technique combining operant and respondent conditioning, has proved valuable for obtaining psychophysical thresholds in various animals (Smith, 1970), and has been shown to be applicable to goldfish (Geller, 1964).

c. Avoidance Methods. Goldfish can be trained to avoid electric shock by swimming out of a compartment in which a warning stimulus is presented. An automated two-compartment apparatus was described by Horner et al. (1961) which has been used to obtain a scotopic spectral sensitivity curve for a cichlid fish (Tavolga and Jacobs, 1971), and to demonstrate color mixture in the carp (Oyama and Jitsumori, 1973).

II. SPATIAL VISION

A. Discrimination Thresholds

1. Contrast Sensitivity

For an object to be visible under water, the light reflected from it must present a contrast with its surroundings by reflecting either a greater or lesser amount of light than its background, the water space light. The contrast of an object can be quantified by the expression $(B_t - B_o)/B_o$, where B_t and B_o are the luminances of the target object and space light measured from the position of the observer's eye. As a target object moves away from the observer, the amount of light entering the eye from the direction of the object undergoes changes from two causes: first, absorption and scattering attenuate light from the object; and second, the amount of light scattered into the eye increases as the underwater path between observer and object lengthens. This second factor accounts for a fog or veiling light which appears to envelop receding objects. The net result of absorption and scattering is that the contrast of a target declines with distance in an exponential fashion (Duntley, 1963).

An ability to detect low contrasts would obviously be an advantage to a fish because its sensitivity to contrast determines the range at which avoiding action can be taken from a predator, or the maximum distance that individuals may stray from a school without losing contact, to cite just two examples. Not surprisingly, some students of fish vision have entertained the possibility that fishes might possess mechanisms to enhance their contrast sensitivity (Baylor and Shaw, 1962; Hester, 1968). Just how sensitive fishes are to contrast, and how this sensitivity is affected by variables such as the state of adaptation and the size of the target, will be seen from some of the experiments to be reviewed.

a. Adapting Luminance. For animals and humans alike, the presence of a steady background light desensitizes the eye to increments of light by an amount that depends upon the background luminance. Over a certain range of background luminances, where Weber's law holds, the just detectable luminance increment, ΔI, increases in proportion to the background luminance, I. The ratio $\Delta I/I$, also known as the Weber fraction, equals the contrast threshold when contrast is defined as above. Human psychophysical experiments typically show that as background luminance increases from very low values, contrast threshold falls in two phases, threshold being determined by the rods in the first phase, and by the cones in the second. Weber's law holds accurately only for background luminances in the moderate photopic range (3–4 log units above the cone threshold) when the contrast threshold reaches an asymptote of about 0.01 for large targets (Blackwell, 1946).

The first systematic study of fish contrast sensitivity was performed by Hester (1968) using a classical conditioning technique on goldfish (*Carassius auratus*). The restrained fish was set up facing a screen onto which were projected stimulus spots of various diameters and luminances, superimposed upon a steady background of light. Both stimulus spots and background were projected in green light of the same spectral composition. Electrodes applied to the body surface picked up periodic potentials which, from the records presented, appear to have been caused by breathing movements rather than the electrocardiogram that Hester claimed he was recording. Whatever the record represented, it was possible to condition a pause in it by pairing the light stimulus (0.5 sec) with an electric shock.

Hester's data showed that, as background luminance was raised by 4 log units, the contrast threshold of the goldfish fell, demonstrating that over the range of backgrounds used, Weber's law was not obeyed. Moreover, contrast threshold fell in an apparently discontinuous manner, reminiscent of the rod–cone discontinuity seen in human data. The lowest contrast threshold attained in Hester's experiments was about 0.05.

That Weber's law can be obeyed in fish, at least over a limited range of background luminances, was shown with a two-choice training method in another cyprinid, the rudd (*Scardinius erythrophthalmus*), with contrast thresholds between 0.03 and 0.07 being obtained (Muntz and Northmore, 1970, 1971). More recently, a respiratory conditioning technique on restrained fish (Northmore and Yager, 1975) has been used to measure the thresholds of goldfish to various diameters of circular targets projected upon a tungsten light background whose luminance was varied over a much wider range than hitherto used (Northmore, 1977). The graphs of increment threshold versus background luminance for two goldfish shown in Fig. 1 demonstrate the extent to which Weber's law holds. A discontinuity in the increment threshold function, similar to the rod–cone break in human data, appears at backgrounds of about 1 mL, close to where Hester (1968) found one.

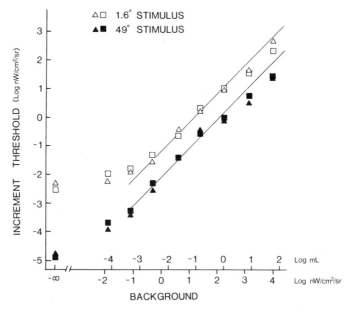

Fig. 1. Log increment thresholds of two goldfish (shown by triangles and squares) for circular test patches of 533 nm light as a function of log radiance and luminance of a white tungsten-light background. Data were obtained by respiratory conditioning using two diameters of stimulus spot. (open symbols, 1.6° stimuli; filled symbols, 49° stimuli) Lines of slope = 1 represent Weber's law (Northmore, 1977).

b. Spatial Summation. The detectability of a target depends upon the angle it subtends at the eye. A mass of human psychophysical data (e.g., Blackwell, 1946) shows that as a luminous circular test disk is increased in area, the threshold luminance for its detection falls inversely with area until a certain size is reached, and then falls little, if at all, thereafter. Over the linear portion of the threshold vs. area function, when the observer's eye is said to obey Ricco's law, the product of stimulus area and its threshold luminance is a constant. The implication of Ricco's law is that the visual system sums the light flux from a target, provided that the target is smaller than a critical area, sometimes called the Ricco area. Electrophysiological recordings from the visual systems of animals, including fish (Spekreijse et al., 1972; Easter, 1968), demonstrate that single units at various levels of the visual system sum light flux in a manner predicted by Ricco's law. In most cases, the area of complete summation can be related to the size of a unit's receptive field center. Indeed, a method often used to determine the receptive field dimensions is to plot the threshold as a function of stimulus diameter on the retina.

Hester found that the threshold contrast declined with target area as predicted by Ricco's law, but the limit of summation depended upon the luminance of the background field onto which the target was projected; at low background luminances, Ricco's law was obeyed up to the largest targets used (3.23° diameter), while at higher luminances only up to about 100′ of arc. Unfortunately, the stimulus diameters were not made sufficiently large to assess the limit of complete summation at low background luminances, or the maximum contrast sensitivity attainable.

Thresholds as a function of stimulus size have also been measured in the rudd using a conditioned activity response (Northmore and Muntz, 1974). The stimulus in this experiment was a slowly moving bar of monochromatic light to which the threshold decreased as bar width increased, approximately according to Ricco's law. Threshold reached a minimum at about 4° of visual angle and then increased, an unusual result for psychophysics but one that is typically obtained for retinal ganglion cells in fish owing to the presence of extensive antagonistic surrounds in the receptive field organization (MacNichol et al., 1961; Daw, 1968; Spekreijse et al., 1972).

In order to be able to relate spatial summation to the size of receptive fields plotted in electrophysiological experiments, Northmore (1977) has extended Hester's work by measuring thresholds to a wide range of stimulus diameters and adapting background luminances in goldfish, using the respiration conditioning technique. Full summation was found for circular stimuli subtending up to a diameter of 25°–30° of visual angle in the dark adapted state, but only up to about 3° under light adaptation (see Fig. 2). It may be significant that the range of summation areas corresponds well to the size range of the receptive field centers of goldfish retinal ganglion cells (Jacobson and Gaze, 1964; Daw, 1968; Easter,

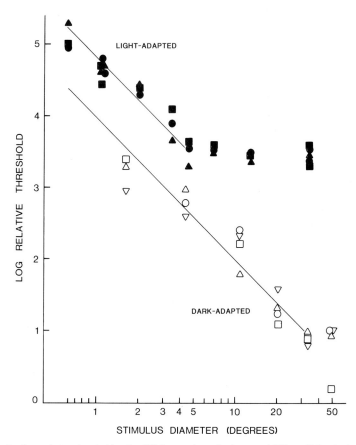

Fig. 2. Log relative thresholds of goldfish to various sized spots of 533 nm light obtained under full dark adaptation, and against a white tungsten-light background of 0.1 mL. Vertical separation of dark- (open symbols) and light-adapted data (filled symbols) is arbitrary. Straight lines are drawn to represent the range of stimulus diameters over which Ricco's law was found to hold. Data obtained by respiratory conditioning (Northmore, 1977).

1968; Spekreijse *et al.,* 1972; Beauchamp and Lovasik, 1973; Wartzok and Marks, 1973). Thus, both psychophysical and electrophysiological measures of areal summation in cyprinids bespeak a concern for sensitivity, presumably at the expense of acuity.

That the goldfish does indeed possess a high absolute, or dark-adapted, sensitivity has been shown by Powers (1977) using classical conditioning of heart rate and respiration. A large test disk (136° diameter) could be detected at about one-tenth of the human absolute threshold or at a radiance that effectively stimulated only one in 15,000 goldfish rods. Unlike the absolute threshold, contrast thresholds of goldfish and rudd compare less well to human thresholds and certainly offer no support for any special contrast-enhancing mechanism (Baylor and Shaw, 1972). Nevertheless, a physiological mechanism that contributes substantially to both kinds of sensitivity is the ability of these cyprinid visual systems to sum the effects of light over large retinal areas (Northmore, 1977).

   c. **Spatial Frequency Analysis.** It can fairly be said that the study of human spatial vision has undergone a revolution since the introduction of spatial frequency analysis (Sekuler, 1974). Much of the success of the approach stems from the theoretical results of looking at the visual system as a device that is susceptible to analysis by linear systems theory, but for our present purposes, spatial frequency analysis has the merit of providing a rather complete description of a visual system's performance. So far, the revolution has barely penetrated into animal psychophysics, and fish have been ignored, although there is good justification for employing them in this type of investigation. A problem for the application of spatial frequency analysis in humans is that the visual system is conspicuously nonhomogeneous in its spatial distribution of receptors and visual neurons. However, many fishes, the goldfish for example, have remarkably uniform retinas with a uniform mapping of the visual field onto the surface of the tectum. Thus, for these animals any statement made about the characteristics of one part of the visual field will probably be true of any other part, and may be applied with some confidence to global descriptions of function such as the modulation sensitivity function (contrast sensitivity vs. spatial frequency).

   The standard procedure for determining the modulation sensitivity function involves generating upon the screen of an oscilloscope a grating pattern whose luminance profile is sinusoidal perpendicular to the bars of the grating. For different settings of spatial frequency, measured in terms of the number of cycles per degree of visual angle, the contrast threshold is determined by finding the minimum depth of modulation that the subject can just distinguish from an unmodulated display of the same average luminance. For this purpose, contrast is defined as $(B_{max} - B_{min})/(B_{max} + B_{min})$, where B_{max} and B_{min} are the peak and trough luminances of the grating display.

   In this manner, D. P. M. Northmore and C. A. Dvorak (in preparation), using the respiratory conditioning technique on a 9-cm goldfish, obtained the modulation sensitivity function shown in Fig. 3. The points show contrast sensitivity, the inverse of contrast threshold, plotted against spatial frequency. The goldfish modulation sensitivity function is similar in shape to the human and cat functions (Bisti and Maffei, 1974) in that sensitivity falls off above and below a spatial frequency of maximum sensitivity. The high frequency loss is attributable jointly to a decline in image contrast due to the optics of the eye, and to the limit of resolution of the visual pathways. The image contrast of high spatial frequency gratings is reduced by optical aberrations, diffraction, and scattering, which all

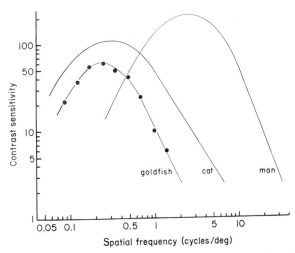

Fig. 3. The points show contrast sensitivity [1/(threshold contrast)] to sinusoidal gratings for a 9-cm goldfish. Stationary gratings with a mean luminance of 23 cd/m² were presented on an oscilloscope at an effective underwater distance of 30 cm. Thresholds were determined by respiratory conditioning (D. P. M. Northmore and C. A. Dvorak, in preparation). The curves for cat and man were obtained at 2 cd/m² by Bisti and Maffei (1974).

tend to smooth out the peaks and troughs of a grating pattern. If the modulation sensitivity function is followed down to the abscissa, which it typically meets at a steep angle (Westheimer, 1972), the intercept gives the spatial frequency of a grating of unity contrast that can just be resolved. Half the period of this grating is the "minimum separable" measured in conventional grating acuity determinations (see next section). A plausible extrapolation of the goldfish data predicts that the finest unity contrast grating discriminable would have a spatial frequency of 2 cycles per degree, corresponding to a grating acuity of 15 min of arc. The low frequency decline in contrast sensitivity is generally explained by lateral inhibitory mechanisms, such as antagonistic surrounds in receptive fields tending to reduce the response of visual neurons to uniform illumination (Cornsweet, 1970).

The lowest contrast threshold achieved by the goldfish used in this study (0.017) was smaller than the lowest value (0.05) obtained by Hester for circular targets, but is still greater than values obtained for cat and man with gratings. It should be noted, however, that the contrast threshold obtained in an experiment depends to a great extent upon the psychophysical methods used. Of special interest is the displacement of the modulation sensitivity function to lower frequencies as compared to man's and the consequent superiority of the fish at this end of the spectrum.

The disposition of the modulation sensitivity function makes good ecological sense when one considers the often murky waters that goldfish inhabit. Water with suspended particles will not only reduce the contrast of all objects, as discussed above, but because the particles generally differ from water in their refractive indexes, they will also diffuse the edges of images, making them look fuzzy. Obviously, the high spatial frequencies comprising an image will suffer more attenuation from this cause than will low frequencies—in systems theory parlance, murky water is a low-pass filter—so that there is no point in having contrast sensitivity at high frequencies where no contrast exists. Small objects or fine details must, therefore,be examined at close range where, in terms of visual angle, they are neither small nor fine. At the other extreme, large objects, such as features of the underwater terrain or predators, present looming blurs of relative darkness or lightness which, to our eyes, shade imperceptibly into the water space light. It is for this blurry world without sharp outlines that the goldfish's low spatial frequency response seems to be designed.

2. Acuity

A measurement of a subject's acuity is a measurement of the finest detail of a test pattern that the subject can correctly detect, identify, or locate in space (Riggs, 1965). A variety of test patterns have been used including letters of the alphabet, fine lines, and Landolt C's, but the principal pattern employed in the experiments to be reviewed here is the black and white grating pattern. When the bars of such a grating are fine enough to be only just resolvable, the bar spacing, measured in terms of the visual angle subtended at the eye, is called the minimum separable angle.

Much can be learned about the acuity of an animal from a study of the structure of its eye, particularly the retina and the optical components, of which the lens is the only element of importance in fishes. The dominant idea about the role of the retina in grating resolution derives from von Helmholtz (1924), who proposed that adjacent bars of a grating can be resolved by the eye when one row of relatively unstimulated retinal cones separates two rows of stimulated cones. From measurements of the intercone spacing in the retina and the focal length of the lens, several workers have calculated the "morphological acuity" for a variety of fish species. One of the tasks of this section is to examine the assumptions upon which these morphological predictions of acuity are made, the assumptions being that (1) acuity is limited by the retina, not by the optics, and (2) there is a demonstrable basis for the Helmholtzian principle, or at least that it holds for fishes.

a. Structural Considerations. An important determinant of an animal's acuity is the size of its eye. Large eyes are superior in this respect for two reasons: their pupillary apertures are larger, and they form larger retinal images.

The resolution of optical instruments is ultimately limited by the effects of diffraction which are more severe in a lens system of small aperture. The acuity of the human eye improves with pupil diameter up to about 1.5 mm, as predicted from the diffraction pattern, but increases in pupil diameter beyond this size lead to no further improvement in acuity because the decreased effects of diffraction are offset by worsening optical aberrations (Riggs, 1965). Direct inspection of grating images formed by fish lenses shows that resolution increases with lens diameter, but not as much as if diffraction were the only limiting factor (Tamura, 1957). Spherical aberration, one of the factors that adversely affects acuity, can be reduced by stopping down a lens with an iris. Fish lenses, however, would benefit little from being stopped down, since they are remarkably free of spherical aberration, apparently because of their concentric structure of layers whose refractive index increases toward the center (Pumphrey, 1961). In fact, the typical teleost pupil is about the same diameter as the lens and cannot be constricted (unlike the elasmobranch pupil) because the lens protrudes through the iris (Walls, 1963). It has been claimed that fish lenses also produce very little chromatic aberration (Pumphrey, 1961; Sadler, 1973), though subsequent work has shown that the focal length of teleost lenses lengthens considerably with increasing wavelength (Sivak, 1974; Scholes, 1975). Nevertheless, there is general agreement that acuity in the few fishes studied is not limited by their optics because the measured resolution of their lenses is better than the behavioral and morphological acuities (Tamura, 1957; Charman and Tucker, 1973).

Improved acuity should result from enlargement of the eye and retinal image, but only if the resolving power of the retina does not decrease proportionately to eye size, as it might if the number of retinal cells remained constant during growth. Cell counts in fish retinae at different stages of growth show that cone density does decline, but not as quickly as expansion of the retinal image (Lyall, 1957; O'Connell, 1963). Johns and Easter (1975) found that a ninefold growth in the retinal area of goldfish was accompanied by a decline in ganglion cell density by a factor of only three. Thus, given the enlarged image and addition of cells at the retinal margin, the resolving power of a fish eye should improve as it grows. Such a phenomenon has been observed of the behaviorally determined grating acuity in a cichlid fish, *Aequidens portalagrensis* (Baerends *et al.,* 1960). During its growth, sufficient cones are added to the retina to maintain the receptor packing constant, while enlargement of the optics leads to an improved resolution in the image.

The high acuity of the primate fovea is achieved by a combination of several design features: foveal cones are more slender and tightly packed than elsewhere, rods are excluded, far fewer receptors converge upon the higher order cells of the retina, and the cell layers overlying the receptors are displaced away from the foveal center. Various fish species exhibit a spectrum of retinal specialization ranging from a true fovea, resembling in many ways the primate fovea, to a virtually homogeneous distribution of cell types over the retina.

The three species of serranid basses studied by Schwassmann (1968) each possess a well-defined foveal depression in the temporal retina containing a high concentration of narrow cones, no rods, and a greatly increased density of ganglion cells indicating reduced summation of receptor signals. That the foveae in these basses do possess an enhanced acuity was suggested by electrophysiological recording from the optic tectum, where the foveal representation is magnified about five times in comparison to other parts of the retina. Schwassmann also found many single unit receptive fields that were small enough to be described as punctiform.

Active pelagic species typically have areas of higher cone density in the temporal half of the retina (Tamura, 1957; O'Connell, 1963; Tamura and Wisby, 1963; Anctil, 1969). The precise position of the area, whether above, on, or below the horizontal meridian of the eye, seems to correlate with a species' feeding habits. An area in the ventrotemporal retina, for example, should make for higher acuity in an upward-fore direction, and fish with such a placement of the area do tend to approach their food in this direction (Tamura, 1957). Sluggish, demersal species such as goldfish, if they have an area at all, tend to have a slight preponderance of cones in the dorsotemporal retina for examining objects on the bottom (Hester, 1968; Schellart, 1973).

In some species, the retinal area of specialization takes the form of a thickened horizontal band containing greater numbers of receptors and other cells (Munk, 1970). These bands presumably have higher acuity and movement sensitivity than the rest of the retina and may be used for scanning the water surface for prey. Mud skippers, which spend most of their time out of water, probably use their band-shaped areas for detecting prey and predators moving over the intertidal mud and sand flats.

A striking feature of many teleost retinas, and one whose function is obscure, is the regular mosaic arrangement of receptors seen microscopically in flat-mounted sections (Lyall, 1957; Engström, 1963). A gridlike regularity is also evident in the layout of retinal bipolar and ganglion cells (Podugol'nikova and Maksimov, 1975). Comparative surveys show that fishes needing to detect fast moving prey tend to have particularly well-formed, regular mosaics (Anctil, 1969).

For an animal to make the greatest use of its retinal resolution, it must be able to focus objects at different distances. The necessary mechanisms of accommodation in fish appear to have developed in close association with areas of retinal specialization. Accommodation in fishes is achieved not by deformation of the lens, which is usually spherical, but by its displacement relative to the retina (for recent reviews, see Sivak, 1975; Schwassmann, 1975). The typical teleost accommodative mechanism involves an intraocular muscle, the *retractor lentis,* which pulls the lens toward the retina. Thus, in the relaxed state the eye is focused for near objects, whereas accommodation for distant objects requires the contraction of the *retractor lentis.* There appears to be some variation among species with regard to the direction of lens movement, the direction depending upon the retinal position of the area of highest cone density. In the pelagic fishes studied by Tamura and Wisby (1963), the principal component of lens movement is in the plane of the pupil, apparently providing fine focusing for the temporal area of high acuity. Many predatory fish which aim themselves in the direction of their prey possess a pupil elongated anteriorly to allow rostrocaudal lens movements for focusing images on their temporal areas. Goldfish, on the other hand, accommodate by moving the lens mostly perpendicular to the pupil plane, while movement of the rainbow trout lens takes place with components in both directions equally (Sivak, 1973). The axis of accommodative lens movements is related to the direction of most acute vision, which in turn is related to the feeding habits of the fish (Tamura and Wisby, 1963; Sivak, 1973).

b. Psychophysical Results. The limited behavioral data that exist on fish acuity are, to all appearances, concordant with the Helmholtzian principle that for two lines to be resolved at least one row of relatively unstimulated cones must intervene between two stimulated rows.

Brunner (1935) showed behaviorally that at the highest illumination level used, the minnow (*Phoxinus laevis*) could resolve gratings that subtended a visual angle of 10.8', which was estimated to be close to the subtense of one cone diameter. The convict fish (*Microcanthus strigatus*), a coral dweller, was trained by Yamanouchi (1956) to discriminate vertical and horizontal gratings. The minimum separable of 5' are agreed well with the figure derived from the separation of cones in the area of high cone density in the temporal retina. Weiler (1966) trained oscars (*Astronotus ocellatus*) to discriminate targets of dots from a uniform gray target with a resulting minimum separable of 5.3' that was said to approximate the diameter of single retinal cones. The acuities of the skipjack tuna and little tunny were measured by Nakamura (1968) by training the fish to swim down an alleyway at the end of which was a vertical or horizontal grating pattern projected onto a screen (see Muntz, 1974, for critique). The lowest behavioral value for the minimum separable, 5.6', was slightly greater than the cone spacing of 4.3' calculated for the temporal retina by Tamura and Wisby (1963). A two-choice training method was employed by Wilkinson (1972) to measure the grating acuity of goldfish. Horizontal and vertical gratings could be discriminated above chance level when the bar spacing was greater than 22', which agrees well with Hester's (1968) figure of 24' for the morphological acuity derived from his estimates of cone density.

A problem afflicting all these experiments to some extent is that the distance from eye to test pattern could not be accurately controlled, and in some, estimates of acuity depended upon the experimenter judging the position relative to the stimuli at which the animals appeared to make their choice (Yamanouchi, 1956; Nakamura, 1968). Another source of uncertainty is the wide variation in cone density occurring over the retina in some species, particularly those with well-developed temporal areas. In experiments on free-swimming fish, one may have to assume that the part of the retina with the highest acuity is being used to discriminate a fine test pattern. The use of conditioning techniques with restrained fish solves the first problem, and to some extent the second also (Hester, 1968; Northmore and Yager, 1975). A further complication to interpretation is the choice of behavioral criterion taken to indicate that a target is just resolvable. Because of erratic discrimination in Wilkinson's experiments, her goldfish did not approach 100% correct responding even with the coarsest gratings used. Consequently, a somewhat flat psychometric function relating detection probability to grating size resulted. If the more conventional threshold criterion of 50% detection probability had been adopted, the data would have yielded a minimum separable of 1° 5′ rather than the 22′ claimed. Also, since acuity depends upon the luminance of the test pattern, the effects of stimulus luminance need to be investigated before any firm conclusions can be drawn about the relationship between receptor spacing and acuity. In man, acuity improves over about 2.5 log units of test luminance above the cone threshold and then levels out (Shlaer, 1937), and qualitatively similar acuity–luminance functions have been determined in several fish species (Nakamura, 1968; Brunner, 1935; Yamanouchi, 1956).

Methodological problems notwithstanding, these fish acuity experiments, together with other behavioral determinations of animal acuity (Muntz, 1974), all suggest a strong correlation between receptor spacing and acuity, as required by the Helmholtzian principle. However, much of what has been learned recently of the anatomy and physiology of the retina, including the fish retina, leads one to wonder why the Helmholtz principle should work at all.

The implication of the principle is that the visual system is capable of discriminating differences in the amount of light absorbed by adjacent receptors. A plausible anatomic basis for such a mechanism exists in the human fovea where one-to-one connections linking cones, bipolars, and ganglion cells are possible (Polyak, 1941), and appropriately enough, it is in this region of the retina that intercone spacing is a good predictor of acuity (Green, 1970). In fishes, on the other hand, there is nothing approaching a one-to-one ratio of cones to ganglion cells, even in foveate species such as the basses (Schwassmann, 1968). Moreover, the goldfish, whose retina is the least specialized of the species studied behaviorally, has an overall convergence ratio of cones to ganglion cells of 3.3

(Schellart, 1973) and yet appears to be capable of resolving the bars of gratings subtending an angle close to the intercone spacing.

A physiologic basis for the Helmholtz principle is not forthcoming from single unit studies either. Ganglion cells in the goldfish retina have receptive field centers often found to subtend as much as 30°, although the smallest types recorded were 3 × 3° and 1° × 4° (Beauchamp and Lovasik, 1973; Wartzok and Marks, 1973). On the face of it, ganglion cells look too gross to constitute the functional unit corresponding to single cones in the human fovea. However, it could be argued that the diameter of a ganglion cell field is largely irrelevant to the resolving power of the visual system in the same sense that the size of foveal cones appears to be irrelevant to human vernier acuity (Westheimer, 1972). In both instances, higher levels of visual processing may extract information by averaging over many ganglion cells. This hypothesis implies that information about the presence or absence of a grating cannot be extracted from a single ganglion cell, but only by looking at the signals from a number of them with overlapping fields.

Nevertheless, there is evidence suggesting that information about gratings at the behavioral limit of resolution *can* be extracted at the single cell level in the retina. Schwassmann (1975) reported that some goldfish retinal ganglion cells are capable of responding to the movement of gratings with a bar spacing as fine as 17' of arc, a figure falling within the range of behavioral acuities for goldfish determined by Wilkinson, and Northmore and Dvorak. There still remains the problem of how receptive fields, vastly greater than a cone diameter, can have such a fine acuity. One possibility is that small subunits within the receptive field are responsible for intercone comparisons and that these signal to the ganglion cell the presence of nonuniformities anywhere within the field. The subunits hypothesized as the mechanism of directionally selective cells constitute a model for such a system (Barlow *et al.*, 1964; Wartzok and Marks, 1973). An alternative hypothesis merely requires the ganglion cell to respond as a function of the total light flux falling upon its center. As a grating pattern moves across the field, the cell's impulse discharge is modulated, the degree of modulation varying inversely with the grating's spatial frequency. Grating acuity will then depend upon how small a modulation the cell can signal and upon the sensitivity of subsequent neural elements to detect very small modulations. According to this hypothesis, the grain of the receptor mosaic must be fine enough to signal flux changes without excessive variability, but is otherwise irrelevant.

3. Orientation Thresholds

The orientation in space of visual stimuli has provided the basis for a number of questions regarding fish visual behavior. Investigators have tested a variety of species on a simple horizontal–vertical discrimination (for examples, see Herter, 1929; Meesters, 1940; Schulte, 1957; Mackintosh and Sutherland, 1963; Clark,

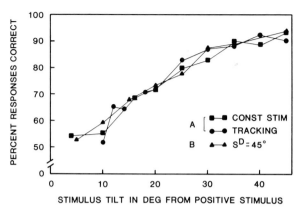

Fig. 4. Orientation thresholds in the goldfish. Percentage correct responses as a function of stimulus orientation in degrees from the orientation of the positive stimulus. A, positive stimulus = vertical; B, positive stimulus = 45° oblique. (Redrawn from Volkmann *et al.*, 1974, p. 878.)

1961, 1963; Tester and Kato, 1966; Saxena, 1966; Volkmann, 1972). Typically, the experiments have used redundant striped patterns or rectangular forms in simultaneous discrimination tasks, and have compared the speed of learning of this discrimination with that of learning other discriminations related to shape, brightness, or color (see Section II,B below). Research has also been aimed at determining the effects of stimulus orientation on transfer behavior to shape stimuli; this work will be summarized in Section II,B,3 below.

The question of how small a difference in visual orientation a fish can discriminate has received little attention. The results of a two-choice discrimination study are shown in Fig. 4 (Volkmann *et al.*, 1974; Volkmann, 1975).

One group of goldfish was trained to respond to vertical stripes, and another to 45° oblique stripes, the negative stimuli for both groups being stripes of various orientations between vertical and 45°. The position of the positive stimulus was varied randomly from trial to trial, and correct responding was reinforced with food pellets.

Results showed that the best fish were able to achieve thresholds of about 14°–16° of tilt from the positive orientation, although most of the thresholds were higher. It is impossible to say, of course, that these values represent the discriminatory capacity of the animals, but it is clear that the fish can discriminate visual orientation at least this well. The results showed, moreover, that performance was as good when the positive stimulus was oblique as it was when the positive stimulus was vertical. This contrasts with results commonly found in humans and some other species, which show better discrimination around the vertical or horizontal than around oblique orientations (Appelle, 1972).

4. Detection of Motion

There are at least three classes of moving stimuli that may be important to a fish and that may involve different physiological mechanisms for their detection: prey objects, predators, and moving surfaces. Measures of motion detection have been made with three different methods: orientation and pseudorheotropism, optokinetic nystagmus, and conditioned responses. There have been very few systematic studies of motion thresholds, but we will briefly summarize the available results.

a. Orientation to Moving Backgrounds. Lyon (1904) first showed, in a convincing series of experiments, that visual stimuli are very important for a fish to maintain a given position in a moving stream of water. Fish swim with a moving background so as to eliminate relative motion. A comprehensive review of rheotropism in fishes has been presented by Arnold (1974).

The threshold rate of motion may be very low for some species. Harden Jones (1963) reported that some small pike (*Esox lucius* L.) showed an orientation toward a particular point on a moving cylinder, to background speeds as slow as 0.2°/sec. Thresholds depend on a variety of factors that have not been investigated very systematically, including direction of movement, whether nasal or temporal, species, size of field, and temperature (Arnold, 1974).

b. Eye Movements. Restrained goldfish show optokinetic nystagmus for stimulus angular velocities greater than 1.6°/sec (Easter, 1972). Boulet found that free-swimming perch showed nystagmus in response to a 4° sphere moving at 3°/sec. Easter (1972) further reported that pursuit velocity varied linearly with stimulus speed up to 40°/sec, but that eye velocity was only about 70% as fast as target velocity. Eye velocity was also a function of target contrast, state of adaptation of the eyes, and angular subtense of the target, and may also be related to the relative numbers of retinal ganglion cells responding selectively to movement in a nasal or temporal direction (Cronly-Dillon, 1964).

c. Conditioned Responses. Ingle (1968b) used a conditioned heart rate procedure to study movement detection in goldfish. The relative sensitivity of the fish to nasal and temporal directions of movement was determined by presenting moving stimuli for 10 sec, followed by an electric shock; after training, the heart rate was slowed during stimulus presentation and before the shock. When a single black spot was moved at 12°/sec, all fish responded more strongly when the stimulus moved nasally, and when the spot moved at 3°/sec, all fish responded more strongly when it moved temporally. However, when multiple spots were moved at 12°/sec, the larger response was elicited by temporal movement. These puzzling results suggest that there are at least two motion-detecting systems in goldfish: one for object motion detection, and one for surface motion detection.

B. Discrimination and Classification of Shapes

1. Definitions and Approach

Sutherland (1961), drawing on Bingham (1914), has emphasized a distinction in usage between the terms *form* and *shape*. Form refers to the geometrical, structural properties of the figure itself, and is unaffected by changes in the orientation, size, color, or brightness of the figure. Shape, on the other hand, is taken to be determined partly by the form of a figure and partly by variables related to the presentation of the form to an observer, notably the orientation of the figure in space. All stimuli which differ in form also differ in shape, but not all stimuli which differ in shape also differ in form. Thus, a normally oriented square (one in which the contours are horizontal and vertical) and a square oriented 45° from the normal (a diamond) have the same form but different shapes. A square and a circle differ in both form and shape. A large and a small figure, or figures which have been reversed from black-on-white to white-on-black, differ, of course, in neither form nor shape.

Although the distinction between form and shape is useful in specifying a stimulus, it is most probably not made phenomenally. The psychological dimension is shape alone: we do not see a square vs. a square-rotated 45°; we see a square vs. a diamond. Apparently, the species of fishes that have been tested also classify the square and the diamond differently, as we shall see below.

The approach here will be to separate form from shape in our discussion of stimulus variables. The distinction will not be made, however, in our discussion of possible bases of discrimination or generalization made by the fish in responding to spatial stimuli.

In preparing this review, we have drawn on a variety of experiments conducted over approximately the last 50 years.* These experiments vary widely in number of fish tested, number of trials, and other important aspects of design. Sometimes much of the relevant information has simply not been reported by the investigators. Moreover, the relatively recent requirement that only positive results lead to publication could mean that different experiments may seem to agree

---

*The present summary omits (a) most material based on physiological manipulations such as lesions, ablations, and rearrangements; (b) material specifically related to ontological development; (c) material on intraretinal and interocular transfer, in which the emphasis is primarily on neural pathways and processing rather than on the discrimination of pattern per se; and (d) material in which animals are taught visual discriminations, but in which the major focus of interest is in memory and learning processes.

more than they should, and that data on indiscriminable forms or shapes are not reported.

Though many early experiments used few animal subjects, the research as a whole is remarkable for its care, patience, and sensitivity. Herter (1953) provides an excellent review for those interested in this material at the experimental level. Much of the early research has also been summarized in English in Sutherland's (1961) monograph. The more recent work by Sutherland (e.g., 1968b, 1969) is also especially useful.

2. Experiments on Form Discrimination

Form discrimination in fishes has been approached in the laboratory in a variety of ways. In an early study, Maes (1930) placed partitions containing holes of different shapes and sizes across aquaria, and counted the number of times the fish swam through each hole to get from one part of the tank to another. He also used rectangular holes varying in size, and concluded that both form and size controlled the frequency of passage.

Meesters (1940) conducted an unusual experiment which showed training on visual forms in a natural setting. He placed an opaque partition in a large aquarium containing sticklebacks. Then for some time he fed all the animals on one side food that was very "compact" and rounded in shape (small pieces of earthworm), and all the animals on the other side a very "loose-membered" food (Enchyträen). Finally, he presented pairs of visual stimuli to the fish, to see whether they would approach compact or loose figures in spontaneous choices. Their choices were determined almost entirely by the forms on which they had been fed. It would be useful to have more laboratory studies on the recognition of forms which are natural and relevant for the various species of fish. The ethological literature, which is not included here, provides a guide for this research.

Figure 5 presents selections representative of form discriminations that have been studied experimentally in the laboratory with fishes. The stimulus forms used may appear at first glance to be wholly arbitrary; they are certainly not "natural" stimuli for aquatic species. However, in some instances the choice was determined by theoretical considerations such as Gestalt laws of organization, or by various models of neurophysiological coding and feature extraction (e.g., Barlow, 1972; Corcoran, 1971; Deutsch, 1962; Dodwell, 1970; Sutherland, 1963, 1968a, 1974; Zusne, 1970). These apparently unnatural forms may thus reveal features which an animal uses for discrimination or classification.

It has been known for many years that fish can discriminate between a variety of forms that are common to human experience (Herter, 1953). As examples, Fig. 5 shows that the species indicated are able to discriminate the pairs of stimuli shown, i.e., between a circle and a square (Fig. 5 A), a diamond and a cross (Fig. 5 E), and the forms LEER and WURM (Fig. 5 N). The figure is incom-

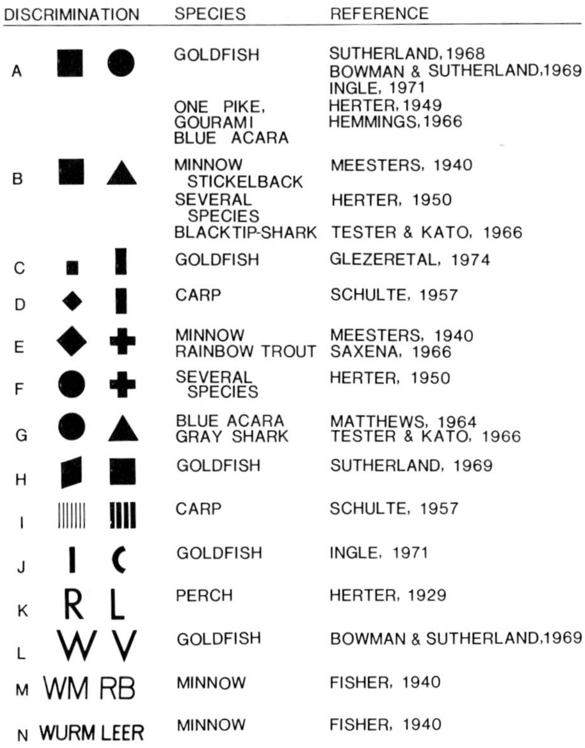

DISCRIMINATION	SPECIES	REFERENCE
A ■ ●	GOLDFISH	SUTHERLAND, 1968
		BOWMAN & SUTHERLAND, 1969
		INGLE, 1971
	ONE PIKE,	HERTER, 1949
	GOURAMI	HEMMINGS, 1966
	BLUE ACARA	
B ■ ▲	MINNOW	MEESTERS, 1940
	STICKELBACK	
	SEVERAL	HERTER, 1950
	SPECIES	
	BLACK TIP-SHARK	TESTER & KATO, 1966
C ▪ ▐	GOLDFISH	GLEZER ET AL, 1974
D ◆ ▐	CARP	SCHULTE, 1957
E ◆ ✚	MINNOW	MEESTERS, 1940
	RAINBOW TROUT	SAXENA, 1966
F ● ✚	SEVERAL	HERTER, 1950
	SPECIES	
G ● ▲	BLUE ACARA	MATTHEWS, 1964
	GRAY SHARK	TESTER & KATO, 1966
H ▰ ■	GOLDFISH	SUTHERLAND, 1969
I ▦ ▥	CARP	SCHULTE, 1957
J I ⦅	GOLDFISH	INGLE, 1971
K R L	PERCH	HERTER, 1929
L W V	GOLDFISH	BOWMAN & SUTHERLAND, 1969
M WM RB	MINNOW	FISHER, 1940
N WURM LEER	MINNOW	FISHER, 1940

Fig. 5. Illustrative shape discriminations used with various species of fish. For explanation see text.

plete, however, in that it does not specify the exact sizes of the stimuli, the precise length–width ratios of rectangles and parallelograms, and in some experiments, whether the stimuli were black-on-white or white-on-black. These can be important considerations, as we shall see below.

The experiments shown in Fig. 5 were typically conducted using a simultaneous discrimination task in an operant procedure; the fish were required to swim to the correct target and perform a "nosebang" response for food reinforcement. Discrimination is said to have occurred when a criterion such as 18 correct responses in 20 consecutive trials is reached.

The total number of trials to reach criterion has sometimes been used to assess the discriminability of the form stimuli for the fish. It is difficult to generalize from results obtained with this approach, however. Speed of learning may depend on a large number of variables in addition to the discriminative stimuli themselves, variables such as previous training, level of food deprivation, water temperature, time of year, and so on, as well as on species and the details of methodology. Stimulus similarity is more adequately approached through techniques designed to determine either psychophysical discriminatory thresholds, as discussed above (Section II,A), or generalization, as determined by transfer of the conditioned response to other stimuli, as will be discussed in Section II,B,3.

Thus, the experiments summarized in Fig. 5 cannot be directly compared in such a way as to assess relative difficulty of discriminations. A few pairs stand out, however, on the basis of comments of the investigators. A particularly difficult discrimination for the lemon sharks used by Clark (1961, 1963) and for the tropical fishes used by Hemmings (1966) was the square–circle discrimination. The tropical fishes required pretraining on a rectangle–circle discrimination before they could perform it at all (see also Hemmings and Matthews, 1963). The circle–square discrimination was learned by Bowman and Sutherland's goldfish in approximately 85 trials, however. The discriminations shown in Fig. 5 H and L are relatively more difficult for the goldfish. The striped-figures discrimination (Fig. 5 I) required over 700 trials before Schulte's carp reached criterion. The fish apparently see the stimuli paired in these discriminations as highly similar to each other. In terms of the relative ease of discrimination, on the other hand, Schulte noted that the diamond–rectangle discrimination (Fig. 5 D) was easier for carp than the circle–cross discrimination (Fig. 5 F). A shape discrimination which will be discussed below, that between a horizontal and a vertical rectangle (see Fig. 6 J), was accomplished by goldfish in fewer than 50 trials (Mackintosh and Sutherland, 1963).

Several investigators have pointed out that in general fish perform color and brightness discriminations more readily than they perform form discriminations, especially if the hues or luminances used differ markedly (Schaller, 1926, minnows; Horio, 1938, carp; Ingle, 1965, 1968a, goldfish; Saxena, 1966, trout). We have made the same observations in our own laboratories. Nevertheless, some investigators have found that responses to form may predominate over responses to color or brightness when the hues or brightnesses are very similar and when the forms used are highly dissimilar (Horio, 1938).

Discrimination between the geometric figures shown in Fig. 5 A–J suggests that the fishes tested must make use of properties of the stimulus such as curvature, abrupt corners, horizontal vs. vertical extent, and "in-pointing" vs. "out-pointing" angles in performing form discriminations. Discrimination between the line figures shown in Fig. 5 K–N suggests additional properties such as the relative number of upward or downward pointing angles (Fig. 5 L) and the relative number of vertical or horizontal line sigments (Fig. 5 N). A detailed analysis of the degree to which the animals might be using certain of these specific properties, however, requires first a review of their responses to form and shape stimuli on transfer tests.

3. Transfer Experiments on the Classification of Spatial Stimuli: Effects of Specific Stimulus Properties

Figure 6 summarizes a variety of transfer effects in fishes, chosen to exemplify some possible properties used by the animals in classifying spatial stimuli. Whenever possible, the figure shows examples not only of stimuli to which the fish do transfer, but also of related stimuli to which they do not transfer. Thus in Fig. 6 D, goldfish trained to respond to a square when it is presented with a circle will transfer that response to an inverted triangle of the same area when it is presented with a circle. However, the response does not transfer from the square to an upright (base down) triangle presented with a circle (Sutherland, 1968b). It is important to keep in mind when reading the figure that it shows degree of

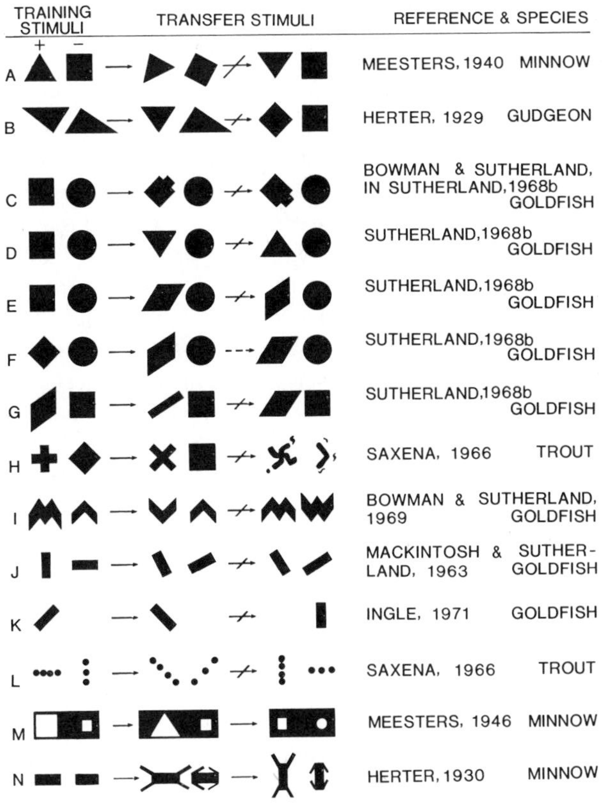

Fig. 6. Illustrative shape stimuli showing positive and negative transfer effects in various species of fish. For explanation see text.

transfer (→, transfer; →, weak transfer; ↛, no transfer) from the positive *train-ing* shape to each of the left-hand members of the transfer pairs. It does not mean that the animals transferred or did not transfer from one pair of *transfer* stimuli to the other, or that the middle pair was necessarily presented before the right-hand pair.

Figure 6 supplements and extends Fig. 5 in suggesting some of the major properties of shapes which fish might use in classifying these stimuli. Prominent among them are properties related to (a) discontinuities in figural contour, (b) parts of figures vs. whole figures, (c) orientation of principal contours, and (d) size. We shall discuss each of these, along with (e) other Gestalt properties such as outline vs. filled-in shapes, black–white reversals, and figure-ground relations.

a. Discontinuities in Figural Contour.   Figure 6 B shows the stimuli which Herter used in one of many experiments on shape classification (1929, 1950, 1953). Two gudgeon were trained as shown in the figure; a third gudgeon was trained with the triangle pointing up as the positive stimulus. On transfer tests, the two fish always preferred a triangle with the apex pointing down, and the third fish always preferred a triangle with the apex pointing up. All three chose a diamond, with apexes pointed both up and down, over a square (Herter, 1929). As a general conclusion from many experiments, Herter held that the learning of forms by fish "is directed toward the apexes (or corners)" (1953, p. 249). According to this interpretation, Meesters' fish in the experiment shown in Fig. 6 A did not transfer from an upright to an inverted triangle because the apex was no longer pointed up. Moreover, it has been a common finding that goldfish trained to respond to the square in a square–circle discrimination typically do not transfer to a 45° rotation of the square (a diamond) when it is presented with the circle. Herter's interpretation would presumably be that the corners are now in the wrong orientations. Sutherland has more recently maintained that "There appears to be a completely different rule written into the store for a right angle made by a junction of horizontal and vertical lines than for all other right angles" (1968b, p. 44). Thus, corners and angles are important to Sutherland's model as they are to Herter, but with some important restrictions, as indicated below.

An extensive study by Bowman and Sutherland investigated transfer based on the number and orientation of apexes, or "points" located on form stimuli (Sutherland, 1968b; Bowman and Sutherland, 1969). An example of their stimuli is shown in Fig. 6 I. Different groups of goldfish were trained on stimuli oriented upward, downward, or sideward. All groups transferred the response to other stimuli which contained points, based on (a) the relative number of points in the new stimuli (e.g., fished trained as in Fig. 6 I transferred to whichever stimulus of a new pair contained *more* points) and (b) the orientation of the points. Transfer was good to points oriented upward or sideward, regardless of which of these orientations was present in the training shape. Transfer did not occur to the appropriate number of points if they were oriented downward (Fig. 6 I, right-hand figure).

In an earlier experiment that bears on this point, Hager (1938) trained minnows to discriminate stripe number, and found that they learned more readily when the stripes were vertical than when they were horizontal. The fish discriminated five from six vertical stripes after 155–345 training trials. Smaller numbers of stripes were easier; larger ones were not reported.

In another study related to discontinuities in stimulus contour (Fig. 6 C), Bowman and Sutherland (Sutherland, 1968b) investigated the effect of adding a knob to the square or diamond stimulus in order to mediate transfer that would not occur to the stimulus without the knob. The knob breaks the contour by making the stimulus more complex, by adding a protuberance which might be treated like a point or apex, and by adding two 90° "in-pointing" angles. Goldfish transferred from a square-with-knob to a diamond-with-knob, but only if the knob was located in the top half of the figure.

Experiments such as these indicate that corners, apexes, number of points, and protuberances are properties of shapes that are salient stimuli for fish. They raise questions, however, about possible differences in importance to the fish of different parts of a shape, and about the specific effects of the orientation in space of these discontinuities on transfer behavior.

b. Parts of Figures Versus Whole Figures. Bowman and Sutherland's (1969) experiments on transfer mediated by knobs and points, along with other transfer experiments, led Sutherland to hypothesize that goldfish discriminate between shapes in terms of differences in their top halves only (Sutherland, 1968b). Figure 6 shows considerable support for this notion: in Fig. 6 A, it is not entirely clear why Meesters' minnows transferred to the shapes tilted by 20° (middle figures), but it is clear that if they were discriminating the tops of the figures only, both figures in the right-hand pair would look similar to the original negative training square and transfer would not be expected to occur. In an experiment with one minnow, Meesters himself varied the tops and the bottoms of the training figures independently, and found that the fish responded primarily to the tops (see Fig. 9 A and B below).

The transfer behavior shown in Fig. 6 C and I is also explained neatly by Sutherland's hypothesis. The right-hand figures in Fig. 6 I are particularly interesting: transfer to the left-hand figure of this pair would be expected if the animals were discriminating in terms of (a) absolute number of points at the top, (b) number of points at the bottom, or (c) the positive training figure as a whole. Instead, the stimuli appear to be classified according to the relative number of points at the top, and the animals did *not* choose the left-hand figure, even though it was identical to the original positive training shape.

Figure 6 D, E, and F summarizes additional experiments by Sutherland (1968b): in each case the transfer results can be explained by the hypothesis that the animals were attending to the tops of the shapes only.

Results which might call into question Sutherland's interpretation are sparse: in Fig. 6 B, the transfer on the part of Herter's minnows from the training shape on the left to the diamond in the right-hand pair cannot be accounted for in this way. In addition, Schulte (1957) found that carp learned to discriminate portions of circular stimuli on the basis of *either* their tops or bottoms. Finally, Matthews (1964) found that blue acaras which had been trained to discriminate between a circle and an upright equilateral triangle (Fig. 5 G) failed to transfer to a cricle vs. a pear shape with a rounded base, straight sides, and a pointed apex. This latter shape looks like a triangle on top and a circle on the bottom. Matthews suggests that the fish were attending to the *bases* of these figures, rather than to their tops.

Additional experiments led Matthews (1964) to the conclusion that fish do not attend to specific parts of shapes only, but rather form a "concept" of a triangle or a circle as a whole. Additional information is needed to determine the relative importance of the tops or bottoms of figures which differ in size. It would also be especially interesting to correlate such additional results with the feeding habits of surface or bottom-feeding species of fish.

c. Orientation of Principal Contours.   Figure 6 J, K, and L summarizes some effects of stimulus rotation in transfer experiments. Figure 6 A, G, H, and N is also relevant.

As an initial specific question, one might ask: over what changes in stimulus orientation is the response invariant, i.e., over what range of tilts will transfer occur to a given form? In an early study, Meesters (1940) investigated this question using a triangle vs. square discrimination (see Fig. 5 B). He found that sticklebacks and minnows transferred about 75% of the time to the stimuli when they were tilted 20°, 67% of the time to the stimuli tilted 30°, and hardly at all to the stimuli tilted by more than 30°. Mackintosh and Sutherland (1963) performed a systematic study of transfer effects in goldfish to 1- × 5-cm rectangles presented at right angles to each other in various orientations (Fig. 6 J). Animals trained with horizontal vs. vertical rectangles transferred 88% of the time to rectangles rotated by up to 30° from their original positions, but transfer broke down when the stimuli were rotated 40°. A second group of animals, trained on two oblique stimuli (oriented at 45° in opposite directions), took significantly longer to learn the original discrimination; two of the eight goldfish did not reach criterion in 160 trials. The animals in group II were not tested with rotations in the same way as those in group I, but were required to choose their original training shape and avoid their original negative shape when each was presented with a blank field. Results were interpreted as showing (a) that the animals had an initial tendency to choose either shape over the blank field, and (b) that "the fish had not learned to discriminate between the two oblique rectangles in terms of their total configuration but had learned separately the different orientations of the positive and the negative" (Mackintosh and Sutherland, 1963, p. 139).

There is ample evidence that fish, like many other animals, tend to treat mirror-image stimuli as similar. An example is shown in Fig. 6 K, in which Ingle (1971) found that goldfish transferred from an oblique rectangle to its mirror image, but not from an oblique rectangle to a vertical one. On the basis of the results of Volkmann *et al.* (1974), it is clear that goldfish can discriminate orientation differences smaller than any of those discussed here (see Section II,A,3 above). The question here is one of classification rather than discrimination, although mirror-image stimuli may provide a special case of both.

A different but related question concerns the role of the orientation of principal contours in mediating the classification of different shapes. This question is also related to the orientation of figural discontinuities (Section II,B,3,a above). Fisher (1940), a student of Herter's, performed a series of experiments on the discrimination of letters of the alphabet by minnows (see Fig. 5 M and N for examples). The letters were altered in various ways, and were presented singly and in combinations of up to three or four. Fisher concluded that it was important whether the vertical or the horizontal members of the stimulus pattern predominated. Although features such as gaps and curvature were also important, Fisher attributed the performance of the animals to how well the horizontal or vertical orientation was preserved when the stimuli were transformed.

Figure 6 G illustrates some work by Sutherland which bears on this question. He found that, for goldfish trained on these stimuli, the most important difference between the parallelogram and the square was the point or apex at the top of the parallelogram, contrasted with the lack of points at the top of the square. Although the presence of oblique contour was not itself sufficient to mediate transfer (see Fig. 6 G, right-hand figures), transfer was better to an oblique rectangle with principal contours in the same orientation as the training shape (Fig. 6 G, middle figures) than to a mirror-image rectangle (Sutherland, 1968b).

Ingle (1971) has argued that fish can perhaps use properties such as "parallelness" of left and right sides to distinguish among some shapes, and that these animals might be less sensitive to parallelness when it is oriented obliquely (a diamond) than when it is oriented normally (a square). He thus accounts for the fact that training on a circle transfers more readily to a diamond than to a square. Presumably, this unequal sensitivity in the two orientations makes the diamond resemble the circle more than the square to a goldfish.

Two experiments by Saxena also provide evidence on the relative importance of contour orientation in mediating transfer across shapes. Figure 6 H shows that, with trout, a cross vs. diamond discrimination transferred to the same forms rotated by 45° (an X vs. square discrimination). It did not transfer, however, to the somewhat irregular figures presented in Fig. 6 H, far right. This was true even though the incomplete contours of the negative figure matched the right-hand side of the original training figure, and the so-called positive transfer figure appears to a human to match the original training cross better than the X does. Thus, the trout must have been using properties other than contour orientation, perhaps solidity vs. "looseness" as determinants of transfer.

Finally, Fig. 6 L provides information on the relative importance of number and orientation in mediating transfer (Saxena, 1966). The trout, trained to discriminate four horizontal disks from three vertical ones, responded to *number* when the stimuli were both tilted by 45°, but to *orientation* when the stimuli were tilted by 90°.

In general, the data reviewed here would seem to indicate that the species studied are sensitive to the orientations of principal contours in visual stimuli, but that orientation is not among the most salient variables in determining the shapes to which the animals will or will not transfer. Stimuli must be tilted by large amounts before transfer breaks down. As we have argued previously, life in an aquatic environment surely is not tuned to the discrimination of small differences in *visual* orientation (Volkmann *et al.*, 1974).

d. Stimulus Size. It is a common finding that animals which have been trained to discriminate between two shapes transfer the discrimination when the shapes are made larger or smaller (Sutherland, 1961, 1968a; Glezer *et al.*, 1974). There are a number of reasons for expecting that this type of behavior would occur: The animal, typically, is trained with a variety of angular stimulus sizes, since it views the stimuli from different distances during training (Ingle, 1971). Although the fish shows size constancy (Meesters, 1940) and is thus presumably able to discriminate both size and distance, the reinforcement contingencies of training produce discriminations based on *shape,* and may also favor generalization across similarly shaped stimuli of different absolute or angular sizes. This generalization, moreover, is not symmetrical; a number of experiments have shown that transfer is better to larger shapes than to smaller ones (Schulte, 1957, carp; Mackintosh and Sutherland, 1963, goldfish; Saxena, 1966, trout). Mackintosh and Sutherland (1963), for example, trained goldfish to discriminate between a horizontal and a vertical rectangle, each 5 × 1 cm. When tested on larger (10 × 2 cm) rectangles, the animals performed even better than they had with the training stimuli. Transfer also occurred to smaller (2.5- × 0.5-cm) rectangles, though these stimuli were not discriminated as well as were the training stimuli. Volkmann (1972) found that goldfish which did not learn a horizontal–vertical discrimination with single 2.5- × 0.5-cm rectangles learned it readily with 5- × 1-cm rectangles or with a redundant pattern of stripes each 0.5 cm wide and 1 cm apart. When tested later with the single small rectangles, they performed at 90% correct or better over 100 trials. It is of some theoretical interest (Sutherland, 1968b) that redundancy can substitute for size in establishing a discrimination,

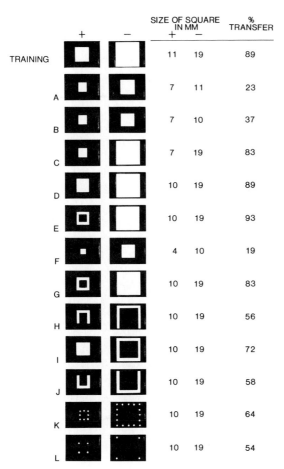

Fig. 7. Transfer effects to a variety of rectangular stimuli in the trout. (Redrawn from Saxena, 1966, p. 85.)

and that the discrimination can subsequently be transferred readily to a stimulus the size of a single element in the redundant pattern.

Another question related to size discrimination concerns the conditions under which the fish responds to the absolute size of a positive stimulus and those under which it responds relatively, to the smaller or larger of two stimuli. In an early experiment, Herter (1929) trained minnows to choose between squares 3 and 1 cm on a side, or between circles of those diameters. When tested with the training forms along with identical forms varying in size, the animals chose relatively rather than absolutely. Meesters (1940) found in a similar study that when the differences in stimulus size were large, the fish chose absolutely; when the differences were small, they chose relatively. In addition, the tendency toward a relative choice increased with an increase in the time interval between training and testing.

Saxena (1966) studied the responses of two trout to a variety of stimulus squares which differed in size, black–white relations, and completeness of contour. Her experiment is summarized in Fig. 7. Saxena interpreted the results as showing that (a) whenever the original positive stimulus, or one very close to it in size, was available, the fish chose it on an absolute basis. (b) Whenever the original negative stimulus was present, the fish tended to avoid it. (c) These response tendencies were maintained with either filled-in or outline shapes. (d) Incomplete contours produced behavior at chance levels. Conclusions (c) and (d) will be discussed in more detail below. The conditions of this experiment thus appear to favor choice on an absolute basis.

A final question concerns the relative importance of size and form in determining how fish classify visual stimuli. Figure 6 M shows an experiment of Meesters (1940) in which a single minnow was seen to use size rather than form in transferring from a large square vs. a small square to a large triangle vs. a small square. When both transfer stimuli were small, however, the fish responded according to form and chose the square. In a different (conditioned avoidance) situation, Ingle (1971) trained goldfish to discriminate a large circle from a large square presented at a fixed distance from the restrained fish. He then required the animals to learn the opposite discrimination using small stimuli. For example, fish trained to avoid the large square subsequently learned to avoid the small circle. Finally, the animals were again presented with the large stimuli, with no shock. In this test, the fish responded to the large square on which they were originally trained rather than to the small circle on which they were most recently trained. Thus size is a potent property of visual stimuli for the fish, and may in fact predominate over form when the two properties lead to different behaviors.

e. Other Stimulus Properties.   Figures 7 and 8 show examples of some additional properties of stimuli that may affect transfer. A number of investigators have studied *filled-in vs. outline shapes.* Meesters (1940) found that minnows and sticklebacks trained on a triangle vs. square discrimination with either outline or filled-in stimuli transferred the discrimination readily to the other type. Schulte (1957) trained carp on a diamond vs. rectangle discrimination with solid black stimuli (Fig. 5 D) and showed that they transferred to heavy outlines of the stimuli, but not to thin outlines. Saxena (1966) found that trout transferred a size discrimination learned with white squares (Fig. 7) to white outlines of the stimuli (Fig. 7 E). The discrimination transferred reasonably well even when a small outline shape was presented with a large white one (Fig. 7 G), but was marginal to a small white square vs. a large outline square (Fig. 7 I). It is possible that the order of presentation of the various stimulus transformations in

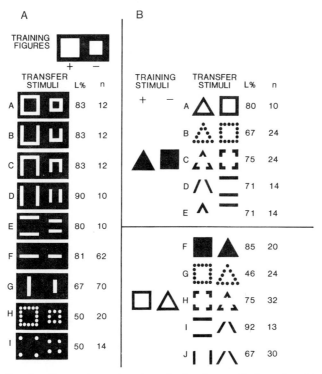

Fig. 8. Transfer effects to incomplete shapes in the minnow. (Redrawn from Meesters, 1940, pp. 103 and 115.)

these tests influenced the results, which seem to indicate that the fish chose an outline over a white square even after training on white squares. Alternatively, the fish may see the outline figures as *black* squares and respond to them on that basis (see below). Sutherland (1969) found that goldfish showed significant transfer to an outline parallelogram when it was presented with a circle, but not to an outline square presented with a circle. These animals also performed better, however, on the original parallelogram vs. circle discrimination than they did on the original square vs. circle discrimination.

The degree of transfer to *incomplete outlines* is also exemplified in Fig. 7 and especially in Fig. 8; transfer behavior to stimuli of this type is most probably also related to the discrimination of specific parts of stimuli, as discussed above. Figure 8 shows a variety of transfer tests to figures of incomplete outlines, performed by Meesters (1940). The responses to these stimuli are very interesting, although they come from only one or two minnows. The animals transferred reasonably well to lines representing the training squares on the right-hand side of Fig. 8, regardless of the orientation of the lines or which parts of the squares they represented (Fig. 8 L–O). Some of Meesters' data, however, suggest that transfer was better to two lines representing the horizontal sides of the squares than to two lines representing the vertical sides. The animals showed some transfer to lines representing the figures on the left-hand side of Fig. 8 (Fig. 8 D,E,I,J), and to lines representing the corners or apexes of the figures (Fig. 8 C,H). When shapes were represented with dotted lines, however, no transfer occurred (Fig. 8 B,G,R,S). These findings are supported by Saxena's data on the trout (Fig. 7 K,L). Meesters summarized his own work by saying that figures with interrupted lines do not seem to be equivalent to the training figures for fish, although dashed lines produce better transfer than do dotted lines. Even so, transfer occurs when only the corners are retained.

Figures 7 and 8 also illustrate some examples of transfer to *black–white reversals* of the training stimuli. Meesters (1940) found good transfer of a triangle vs. square discrimination from either black to white or white to black in minnows (Fig. 8 A–F). Meesters also noted, however, that if only one of the figures was reversed, the fish discriminated on the basis of brightness and chose the black figure. Mackintosh and Sutherland (1963) found that goldfish trained to discriminate black horizontal from black vertical rectangles when these stimuli appeared on a white background learned significantly faster than another group of animals trained with white rectangles on a black background. On subsequent transfer tests, both groups transferred to reversals of the stimuli, but transfer was incomplete. The fish originally trained with white figures transferred better than those trained with black. Sutherland (1968b) suggested that this apparent preference for black over white shapes in his studies might be due to the fact that in training, the bait showed up more conspicuously against black stimuli than against white ones. However, we have found that goldfish respond better to black on white stimuli than to white on black, even when reinforcement is delivered through a tube centered between the two-choice stimuli after the appropriate response has been made. Thus the preference for black over white figures may reflect a more basic characteristic of these fish than the conditions of their training in the laboratory.

The behavior of fish to black–white reversals may supply information on *figure-ground relations* for these animals. Little serious work has been done in this area, but one small study by Meesters is summarized in Fig. 9. It shows that one animal, trained to discriminate a black diamond from a black cross, transferred to forms which maintained the tops (but not the bottoms) of the figures (Fig. 9 A,B), and to a series of stimuli in which, from a human point of view, the shapes were increasingly embedded in a white background which took on figural characteristics. The fish continued to respond to the original black shapes throughout the series, indicating a highly *stable* figure-ground response.

It has been noted more recently by Sutherland (1961) that goldfish respond best to shapes which stand out from the background on which they are mounted

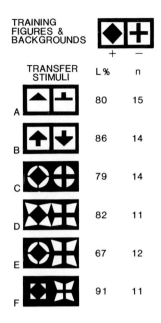

Fig. 9. Transfer effects to embedded figures and possibly ambiguous figure-ground stimuli in the minnow. (Redrawn from Meesters, 1940, p. 116.)

(stereometric shapes). In general this appears to be the case, although we have found that optically projected shapes serve as salient stimuli for the fish as long as the white lighted background is not too bright (Volkmann, 1972).

The older literature contains many references to other Gestalt properties of shapes and the "organized" manner in which fish respond to them. Among these are the illusions (see Fig. 5 N) and the constancies (Meesters, 1940). Many of the individual examples of discriminations which come from this literature are unconvincing; as a whole, however, the data suggest that the way in which the fish responds to visual shape is not as different from the way we humans respond to it as we might have thought.

As a summary illustration of the transfer approach to shape recognition, Fig. 10 presents the results of a study by Sutherland (1969) showing "similarity rankings" of 20 shapes by goldfish. The top and the bottom shapes were the original training figures; the intermediate shapes are arranged in decreasing order of transfer from the square. Such an illustration provides clues as to how, in one experiment, goldfish use such properties as parts of shapes, corners, points, contour orientation, and size, in arriving at their classification. It would be interesting to know how humans classify the same set of shapes.

Fig. 10.   Rank order of transfer shapes in the goldfish. The shapes are arranged in decreasing order of transfer from the square. The first and last shapes in each column are the training shapes. H, horizontal parallelogram; V, vertical parallelogram. A horizontal bar is drawn at the crossover point—i.e., shapes above the bar were treated as increasingly equivalent to the square, shapes below the bar were treated as increasingly equivalent to the parallelogram. (Redrawn from Sutherland, 1969, p. 167.)

4.Some Possible Basic Discriminations Related to Spatial Vision

A list of basic discriminations, constructed on the basis of experimental evidence, can aid the pattern recognition theorist by emphasizing a finite number of specific features which a species might abstract from the visual environment. Although the present list is bound to be incomplete, the reader will immediately recognize in it discriminations which suggest that fishes abstract many of the same stimulus features that appear to be used by higher animals (Corcoran, 1971; Deutsch, 1962; Dodwell, 1970; Levine, 1969; Sutherland, 1963, 1968a, 1974). Unfortunately, we are still lacking for the fish an analysis of single unit responses to specific features of form and shape stimuli comparable to that which has provided a rich source of information and ideas about the central processing of visual stimuli in mammals (Barlow, 1972; Hubel and Wiesel, 1962, 1965, 1968; Kuffler, 1973). Information about basic discriminations in these fishes, drawn from various experimental situations, may aid in the search for neural mechanisms of coding in these animals.

a. Figure-Ground Discriminations. Any organism obviously has to separate figure from ground in order to survive in a visual environment. The data reviewed here suggest that fish not only make these basic discriminations, but that contours seen as figures are highly stable (Meesters, 1940), and that the species studied tend to treat dark stimuli rather than light stimuli as figures in ambiguous situations (Mackintosh and Sutherland, 1963).

b. Discriminations Related to Visual Orientation. Orientation is coded early in the visual system of mammals, and is a primary feature of cells which make up ocular dominance columns in Brodmann's Area 17 (Hubel, 1975). The coding of orientation may provide the basis for discriminations of horizontal and vertical proportion, or relative width in the horizontal and vertical dimension. Sutherland's model is explicitly designed for such computations (1963, 1968a,b, 1969). It is a surveyor's model, which computes successive distances around a contour as a function of the directions north, south, east, and west. Basically, this discrimination requires codings of the horizontal and vertical dimensions, and their comparison. It deals with single, unified figures. A second discrimination is that of the statistical predominance of specific orientations in a shape, for example, horizontals and verticals. This discrimination requires the identification of some subshapes as mainly horizontal, others as mainly vertical, without discrimination of exact proportions, but with a discrimination of relative proportions (recall the WURM–LEER experiment by Fisher, 1940). A fast-acting mechanism for accurately estimating small numbers of events (horizontals and verticals, here) is needed, such as the "subitizer" in humans (Kaufman et al., 1949). For many species, the mechanism appears indeed to be tuned to the horizontal and vertical orientations more precisely than to oblique orientation (Appelle, 1972), though this does not appear to be the case, at least behaviorally, for the goldfish (Volkmann et al., 1974, see above). A third discrimination is that of the orientation of the principal contours of a figure. This, of course, requires that orientation be coded in such a way that specified sets of tilts, namely, those above threshold for the animal, can be discriminated and compared.

Whatever the coding system for orientation may be, it permits mirror images to be treated similarly, since generalization to mirror image stimuli is a common finding in the species of fish studied. With extensive training, however, mirror images are discriminated (Mackintosh and Sutherland, 1963; Campbell, 1971; Ingle, 1971), indicating that the code for two-mirror image stimuli must be very similar but not identical.

c. Curvature. For this discrimination the system must evaluate orientation over length: if orientation changes over length, the edge or contour is curved. It is possible, of course, that curvature is discriminated more directly, by "curvature detectors," for example. These would most likely exist at a higher level of processing than analyzers for orientation and length (Barlow, 1972).

d. Discriminations Related to Contour Discontinuities. These include angles, corners, points, knobs, subforms, and other discontinuities discussed above. One basic discrimination in this class might be angular sharpness: if the apex of an angle were coded as two different tilt codes, such a discrimination could be accounted for. A second discrimination would encode the number of these discontinuities (Bowman and Sutherland, 1969). These discriminations may also be involved in specifying a figure as "compact" or "loose" (Meesters, 1940).

e. Texture and Texture Density. Little research has been conducted in this area with fishes. Meesters (1940) found that minnows can discriminate differing densities of vertical stripe patterns. Ingle (1967, 1968b) showed that a moving textured stimulus affects visually guided behavior differently than does a moving small spot. One might speculate that a large textured field provides a particularly good stimulus for the so-called "second" visual system (Held, 1968; Ingle, 1967; Schneider, 1967; Trevarthen, 1968a,b), and might be coded as *ground* in a figure-ground discrimination.

f. The Constancies: Size, Orientation, Brightness. It would be difficult to imagine the fish performing the discriminations described here without the operation of perceptual constancies similar to those of humans. For example, size constancy, which refers to the relatively unchanging appearance of the size of an object at different distances, requires information about the size of the object's retinal image and its distance. We have seen that fish can be trained to discriminate the size of objects, and to discount size in classifying objects of the same shape but different size (Mackintosh and Sutherland, 1963). Little information is available on the appreciation of cues to distance in fishes, except that Meesters (1940) found evidence of size constancy in minnows. In an aquatic world in which size may signal the primary difference between prey and predator, its constancy in highly developed form would appear to be essential for survival.

III. CHROMATIC VISION

A. Spectral Sensitivity

The sensitivity of an animal to a light of a given wavelength ultimately depends upon the ability of its visual pigments in the retina to absorb light and set in train the chemical and electrical reactions in the receptors leading to a visual sensation. The appropriate measure of this ability is the pigment's absorption spectrum (the proportion of incident light absorbed as a function of wavelength) as it exists within the receptor (Dartnall, 1962). Until the advent of microspectrophotometry, which enables pigments to be studied *in situ* within receptors (Liebman and Entine, 1964; Marks, 1965), visual pigments had been characterized by extracting them from the retina using a detergent and measuring their absorption spectra *in vitro*. The absorption spectra so obtained are of similar shape with a maximum absorption at a characteristic wavelength, the λ_{max}. These methods of extraction and analysis applied to the retinae of fishes have revealed a variety of pigments unequaled by any other class of vertebrates (Lythgoe, 1972). The result of these findings has been to stimulate enquiry into the adaptiveness of pigments of different λ_{max} for the visual needs of fishes living in waters as different in color as pea soup and weak tea (Lythgoe, 1968; Munz and McFarland, 1973; Muntz, 1975). However, any discussion of the suitability of an animal's visual pigments for vision in a given environment necessarily makes assumptions about how the pigments determine spectral sensitivity. It may be valid to assume that the absorption spectrum of a single visual pigment predicts the spectral sensitivity when only receptors containing that pigment are operative, as may be the case for scotopic (dark-adapted) vision. However, when several receptor types each containing a different pigment act in concert to determine the visual response, as in photopic (light-adapted) vision, the complexity of processes intervening between light absorption and behavior makes any such simple assumptions suspect. In this section we shall examine some of the attempts to explain fish spectral sensitivity in terms of visual pigments as well as present a few of the major results.

One method of measuring an animal's spectral sensitivity is to present monochromatic lights of different wavelengths but equal quantal content and record the magnitude of some convenient behavioral response that is evoked. The function arrived at by plotting response magnitude against wavelength might be termed a "response spectrum." Thibault (1949) used this method when he measured the angle that carp tilted when their two eyes were unequally illuminated (dorsal light reflex) and plotted the angle as a function of wavelength. A serious drawback to the response spectrum is that its shape will be influenced by the relation between stimulus intensity and response magnitude. Therefore, a more satisfactory characterization of spectral sensitivity, the "action spectrum," is generally used.

An action spectrum is obtained by finding the quantal flux required to produce some criterion response for each of a variety of monochromatic stimuli. The inverse of the criterion flux, the sensitivity, is then plotted against wavelength to yield the action spectrum. The responses employed may be continuous in nature, such as the angle of tilt toward a light source, or probabilistic, such as the proportion of correct responses that the animal makes in a two-choice discrimination.

1. Spectral Sensitivity Curves and Their Interpretations

a. Scotopic. Since Crescitelli and Dartnall (1953) showed that the absorption spectrum of the rhodopsin extracted from the human retina was a good fit to the human scotopic action spectrum, similar satisfactory matches have also been made for other terrestrial vertebrates (Muntz, 1974), supporting the generalization that the pigments obtained by detergent extraction of the retina are rod pigments (Dartnall, 1960).

Since pigments from a large number of fishes have been studied by extraction methods—518 in a recent list for teleosts alone (Ali and Wagner, 1975)—it would be useful to be able to predict their scotopic spectral sensitivity from these data. Unfortunately, the necessary behavioral experiments have been done on all too few species, and those that have are not especially convincing. In order to make the correlation between a behavioral action spectrum and a pigment absorption spectrum, account must be taken of certain factors, some of which appear to be particularly important to the interpretation of fish spectral sensitivity (Dartnall, 1953).

The first factor to be considered is absorption of light, especially at short wavelengths, by the optical media of the eye. The corneas and lenses of deep sea and nocturnal fishes tend to absorb very little down to wavelengths as short as 400 nm. At the other extreme are fishes with strongly pigmented corneas, lenses, and retinas. The cichlid, *Astronotus ocellatus,* for example, possesses yellow corneas absorbing light strongly up to about 550 nm (Muntz, 1973). In species with yellow corneas, the pigment is usually concentrated in the dorsal parts, and may also be present in the lens, retina, and reflective tapetum behind the receptors (Moreland and Lythgoe, 1968; Muntz, 1972). Too few species have been studied to be able to make any definitive statement about the influence of short-wavelength absorbing pigment on the dark-adapted spectral sensitivity, but two behavioral results are mentioned because their interpretation involves possible effects of photostable screening pigments. The effects of yellow corneas are more apparent in the light-adapted data on *Perca* and *Blennius* (Fig. 11, and see later).

An early attempt to compare the scotopic spectral sensitivity of a fish with its extractable pigment was made by Grundfest (1932a) using the optometer response of a sunfish (*Lepomis* sp.) to an array of wires rotating around it. The dark-adapted action spectrum for this response peaked in the same general region of the spectrum as the pigment absorption spectrum (540 nm), but was much narrower, a finding that Grundfest attributed to light filtering by photostable colored pigments in the eye. This suggestion has yet to be substantiated.

Tavolga and Jacobs (1971) used a shuttle-box avoidance method to measure the dark-adapted spectral sensitivity of a cichlid (*Tilapia heudelotii macrocephala*). The resulting action spectrum was bell-shaped and maximal at about 525 nm, a reasonable figure for a porphyropsin λ_{max}, but any detailed comparison with a pigment absorption spectrum cannot be made because many species of *Tilapia* have yellow corneas (Muntz, 1973).

A second factor that particularly affects the prediction of fish spectral sensitivity is the high density of visual pigment that their retinas often contain (Denton *et al.*, 1971; Muntz, 1973). The higher the density of pigment in a receptor, the broader will be its absorption spectrum, making it inappropriate to fit the spectral sensitivity with a curve taken straight from a nomogram such as Dartnall's (1953) or Munz and Schwanzara's (1967) without correction.

Dark-adapted spectral sensitivity curves of the goldfish and rudd, as determined by two-choice operant methods, were distinctly broader than the absorption spectrum of the pigments extracted from these fishes (Yager, 1968; Muntz and Northmore, 1973). In the case of the rudd, a better fit to the data was obtained by applying a correction to the absorption spectrum for the high optical density of pigment found in this retina (Muntz and Northmore, 1971; Denton *et al.*, 1971). Density corrections, however, are not the complete answer to fitting scotopic spectral sensitivity curves. This can be seen from Powers' (1977) dark-adapted spectrum for goldfish obtained with the respiratory conditioning method, shown in Fig. 11, together with the goldfish pigment absorption spectrum (λ_{max} 522 nm), with and without correction for a maximum optical density of 0.4.

Gruber (1969) used a conditioned response of the nictitating membrane of the lemon shark (*Negaprion brevirostris*) to obtain a dark-adapted action spectrum whose peak agreed fairly well with the rhodopsin of λ_{max} 502 nm extracted from this animal. However, as was the case with goldfish, the action spectrum was broader than the pigment absorption spectrum.

A number of fishes are known to possess paired pigment systems consisting of mixtures of rhodopsin and porphyropsin (Lythgoe, 1972; Ali and Wagner, 1975) and in some species the relative proportions of the two pigment types change with environmental factors such as light intensity, photoperiod, temperature, and season (Bridges, 1972). In the rudd, for example, lengthening days in the spring cause the proportion of rhodopsin in its retina to increase, a change which affects both the rods and cones (Dartnall *et al.*, 1961; Loew and Dartnall, 1976). The scotopic sensitivity of this fish has been measured behaviorally, and in keeping with the pigment changes, was found to become relatively more blue sensitive under 20 hr of artificial light per day as compared to 4 hr (Muntz and Northmore, 1973).

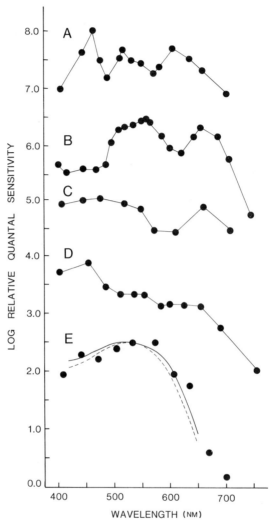

Fig. 11. Behavioral spectral sensitivity curves. A, shanny (*Blennius pholis*); light-adapted sensitivity at cornea; two-choice training method (Wainwright, 1973). B, perch (*Perca fluviatilis*); light-adapted sensitivity at cornea; two-choice training method (Cameron, 1974). C, rudd (*Scardinius erythrophthalmus*); light-adapted sensitivity at cornea; classical conditioning of activity (Northmore and Muntz, 1974). D, goldfish (*Carassius auratus*); light-adapted sensitivity at cornea; two-choice training method (Yager, 1967). E, points: dark-adapted sensitivity at retina of goldfish; classical conditioning of respiration (Powers, 1977). Dashed curve: porphyropsin absorption spectrum $_{max}$ 523 nm from nomogram; continuous curve: absorption spectrum corrected for maximum pigment density of 0.4.

Last in the list of factors tending to complicate the interpretation of scotopic spectral sensitivity data, and one so far little explored, is the possible variation in spectral sensitivity along different lines of sight. This could be the result of uneven distribution of photostable pigments in the cornea, lens, retina or tapetum, or of the visual pigments over the retina. The dorsal and ventral halves of a fish's retina may have different densities of visual pigment and, in a paired pigment system, different proportions of rhodopsin and porphyropsin (Denton *et al.*, 1971).

In conclusion, no behavioral spectral sensitivity experiment on fish has shown a match between the scotopic action spectrum and the pigment absorption spectrum quite as convincing as that shown for mammals. Even when all the factors discussed here have been taken into account, the extractable pigment seems to provide only a guide to the shape of the spectral sensitivity curve. The residual failures of correspondence (see Fig. 11) are most likely attributable to the operation of cone mechanism even in the dark-adapted state, raising the possibility that some fishes are capable of true wavelength discrimination close to their absolute threshold.

b. Photopic. Any interpretation of photopic or light-adapted spectral sensitivity must not only contend with the same factors affecting scotopic spectral sensitivity, but also the simultaneous operation of several receptor types each with different spectral sensitivities. The shape of an animal's photopic action spectrum will therefore be determined both by what the pigments are in the photopic receptors, and by the way in which their signals are combined. Let us consider for a moment an animal whose light-adapted vision is mediated by three cone types, each maximally sensitive to short, medium, or long wavelengths. Signals from each type may be thought of as converging upon a set of channels concerned with transmitting different aspects of the retinal image. For example, there may be "brightness" channels which convey a weighted sum of the three cone outputs, and others in which the cone signals are differenced in order to accentuate chromatic or spatial features of a stimulus. It is conceivable, therefore, that two different behavioral measures of spectral sensitivity could tap different subsets of channels, yielding quite distinct action spectra.

The most extensive behavioral studies of photopic spectral sensitivity in fishes have been done on two members of the carp family, the goldfish and rudd. The spectral sensitivities of individual cones are known from intracellular recording in carp (Tomita *et al.*, 1967) and microspectrophotometry (MSP) in goldfish (Liebman and Entine, 1964; Marks, 1965; Harosi and MacNichol, 1974), the results of both techniques revealing three classes of cone with peak sensitivities at 455, 530, and 625 nm. MSP examination of the cone pigments of the rudd has similarly shown three types (Loew and Dartnall, 1976). However, the rudd retina is more complicated than that of the goldfish because its visual pigments undergo seasonal shifts in the proportion of rhodopsin- and porphyropsin-type pigments present in the receptors. Loew and Dartnall's data show that both rods and cones participate in this shift, and that the λ_{max} of the pigment in a given cone lies within one of the following ranges: 450–460, 507–523, and 570–625 nm. Under conditions of short daylength, the cone pigments shift to their longest wavelength value.

In keeping with the MSP results, the behavioral spectral sensitivity curves of carp and goldfish show peaks, or at least humps of sensitivity, at about the same spectral locations as the λ_{max} of the cone pigments (Thibault, 1949; Cronly-Dillon and Muntz, 1965; Yager, 1967, 1969; Thorpe, 1971). The rudd, on the other hand, due to its changeable pigments, would be expected to show peaks of sensitivity that move with changing conditions of daylength. However, no such effect was found by Muntz and Northmore (1970), and the rudd's spectral sensitivity curves continued to display maxima at about 620 nm, 510 nm, and at short wavelengths near 400 nm, in spite of the expected changes in the *extractable* pigments with altered daylength. A possible reason for the lack of daylength effect is that the pigment changes are not complete and do not occur uniformly over the retina (Denton *et al.*, 1971). Therefore, the animals could have detected the test stimuli with the same pigments at all daylengths.

An important feature shared by the behavioral spectral sensitivity curves of the freshwater fishes (Fig. 11 B–D) is their broad spectral sensitivity extending well into long wavelengths, where experimenters report that they cannot see lights that their subjects can. This is readily explained by the spectral position of their long-wavelength-sensitive pigment as compared to primates (Marks *et al.*, 1964; Brown and Wald, 1964). The adaptive significance of this far-red sensitivity seems to be that the ponds and lakes that these fishes inhabit are usually colored by substances that shift the spectral distribution of available light under water to longer wavelengths (Lythgoe, 1975; Muntz, 1975).

A more surprising feature of the cyprinid results (Fig. 11 C,D) is the high short-wavelength sensitivity obtained in many behavioral experiments (Thibault, 1949; Yager, 1967; Muntz and Northmore, 1970, 1971; Beauchamp and Rowe, 1977). In some cases, maximum sensitivity was found at wavelengths as short as 400 nm with appreciable sensitivity in the near ultraviolet. This, and other reported instances of fishes responding to ultraviolet radiation (Breder, 1959), suggest that information useful to a fish can be gleaned in this spectral region, even under water. Indeed, near ultraviolet is transmitted sufficiently well by clear ocean water for there to be more quanta at 350 nm than at 700 nm at a depth of 10 m (Jerlov, 1968), although ultraviolet is heavily absorbed by the yellow substances dissolved in most fresh waters.

High sensitivity at short wavelengths is not invariably the rule in cyprinids, however. The use of the optomotor response yielded action spectra with low short-wavelength sensitivity in goldfish as it did in a species of sunfish (Cronly-Dillon and Muntz, 1965; Grundfest, 1932b). A possible reason for this effect is that a fish's ability to detect moving stripes projected in blue light is poorer because of low acuity and movement sensitivity in the short-wavelength mechanism. Most classical conditioning methods have also demonstrated a reduced sensitivity at short wavelengths compared to the two-choice training methods (Northmore and Muntz, 1974; Shefner and Levine, 1976). One possible explanation is that fish in classical conditioning situations, being passively stimulated, cannot use the parts of their retinas most sensitive to blue light for the detection of the stimuli. In support of this idea is the finding that spectral sensitivity depends upon the region of retina stimulated, at least for the performance of the dorsal light reflex (Thibault, 1949; Lang, 1967). Whatever the precise mechanisms involved, we seem to have here an instance of different behaviors being actuated by different sets of receptors, detectors, or channels.

Recently, the light-adapted spectral sensitivity of two perciform fishes has been studied behaviorally: the freshwater perch (*Perca fluviatilis*) (Cameron, 1974), and the marine shanny (*Blennius pholis*), a rocky shore fish (Wainwright, 1973). Their action spectra, shown in Fig. 11(A,B), were obtained with two-choice training methods, similar in principle to that used by Muntz and Northmore (1970), and both represent spectral sensitivity at the cornea. The cone pigments have been analyzed in both species by MSP (Loew and Lythgoe, in preparation). The two cone pigments found in the perch, both porphyropsins with their λ_{max} in the spectral regions 535–540 and 615–620 nm, corresponded well with the prominent peaks in the action spectrum. The pigment situation in the shanny is more complicated because, like the rudd, this species appears to have a rhodopsin–porphyropsin pigment system. However, the three pigments found with λ_{max} at about 500, 535, and 570 nm could account for the peaks in the middle- and long-wavelength regions of the spectrum, although there are indications of a short-wavelength-sensitive mechanism for which no pigment was found. The sensitivity of both species fell off at the shortest wavelengths tested, and this can probably be explained by the presence of yellow pigment in their corneas (Moreland and Lythgoe, 1968). It is also noteworthy that compared to the shanny, the spectral sensitivity of the freshwater perch is biased toward longer wavelengths, a difference that accords with the redder light environment of fresh waters.

It has been stated that elasmobranchs have mainly, if not entirely, rod retinas and therefore have no color vision (Walls, 1963). Although MSP data are lacking, histology shows that some sharks do have cones, and Gruber (1969) has examined the spectral sensitivity of the lemon shark to find out whether its visual system is duplex. Gruber's classical conditioning technique yielded light-adapted curves that were unimodal in shape, like his dark adapted curves, but broader, and shifted to longer wavelengths suggesting the operation of two or more photopic receptors.

A single-peaked light-adapted action spectrum has also been reported by Silver (1974) working with a teleost, the brilliantly colored neon tetra. Using the dorsal light reflex, Silver obtained a curve that seemed to be fitted by a porphyropsin-type pigment of λ_{max} 535 nm, a result that might have been expected of a dark-adapted freshwater fish had her lights not been nine log units above the human absolute threshold. This action spectrum may well have been a composite of at least two receptor mechanisms because a slight shoulder of sensitivity could be discerned at 600–620 nm in the data of each animal. Chromatic adaptation, as was done by Yager (1969), is necessary to resolve the underlying components in such cases.

c. Models of Photopic Spectral Sensitivity. Brightness in the photopic visual system is usually thought to be conveyed by a summation of signals from the several cone types. Since animals appear to be performing a brightness discrimination when required to detect a monochromatic light, a plausible model of the photopic action spectrum is that the brightness channels carry some function of the weighted sum of the light quanta caught by the three receptor types. This, the "additive" model, predicts that the spectral sensitivity S_λ will be given by

$$S_\lambda = k_1 \cdot A_\lambda + k_2 \cdot B_\lambda + k_3 \cdot C_\lambda$$

where A_λ, B_λ, and C_λ are the spectral sensitivities of the three receptor types given by the absorption spectrum of the pigment each receptor contains. This model, which generates a smooth action spectrum without pronounced peaks or troughs, has been applied by Yager (1967,1969) to fit his goldfish spectral sensitivity curves obtained with tungsten and colored adapting lights.

However, the photopic action spectrum obtained for the rudd by Muntz and Northmore (1970) exhibited distinct maxima and minima that were poorly fitted by the additive model. Muntz and Northmore proposed that for a fish to detect a monochromatic stimulus at threshold, it was necessary for only one receptor type, the most sensitive at that wavelength, to signal the presence of the stimulus. If the rudd has three photopic receptors, then its action spectrum should appear in three segments, each segment being fitted by the spectral sensitivity of a single cone type. This was called the "envelope" model.

Some spectral sensitivity curves, such as those of perch and shanny (see Fig. 11), display peaks and troughs that cannot be fitted by an envelope of conventional pigment absorption spectra, and are still less adequately fitted by the smooth function predicted by the additive model. Another striking example shown in Fig. 11(C) is the action spectrum for the rudd obtained using a classically conditioned increase in swimming activity in unrestrained fish (Northmore and Muntz, 1974). The stimulus, which was paired with electric shock, consisted of a large, diffuse patch of monochromatic light flashed on a screen that was continuously illuminated with a broad-band tungsten light. The spectral sensitivity curve displays a profound trough of sensitivity, strongly suggesting a subtractive interaction between the long- and middle-wavelength-sensitive receptor mechanisms, similar to the interactions invoked by Sperling and Harwerth (1971) to account for the increment-threshold spectral sensitivity of primates. The existence of inhibitory interrelations between receptor mechanisms in perch was clearly demonstrated by Cameron (1974) in a two-color mixing experiment. The wavelength of a red monochromatic light was chosen so that it stimulated the long-wavelength-sensitive receptors considerably more than the middle-wavelength-sensitive receptors, and its luminance was fixed so that it could be detected by the fish about 30% of the time. If a weak light of similar wavelength were added, the probability of detecting the pair increased as one would expect if the two lights were being summed within the same receptor type. If the added light was of dissimilar wavelength, a green for example, the added light actually reduced the detectability of the mixture as compared to the red light alone. The effect can be explained by the existence of mutually inhibitory connections between receptor types, an arrangement consistent with the electrophysiological findings in fish retinas (MacNichol *et al.,* 1961), and the mechanisms of color discrimination to be considered in the next section (see also Guth *et al.,* 1969).

It still remains for a satisfactory explanation to be given for the strikingly different forms of photopic action spectra that have been obtained in related species; in particular, the smooth, additive-type function of Yager's (1967) goldfish result (Fig. 11 D) as compared to the action spectra showing pronounced troughs and peaks. Again, we feel that the cause of the differences is likely to be procedural, rather than species differences, although the appropriate within-species comparisons of experimental method have yet to be done. In the two-choice apparatus employed by Yager and Thorpe, the goldfish were adapted with a white or colored light prior to each trial, and then tested in darkness soon after the extinction of the adapting light. In the experiments generating the more peaked action spectra, the two-choice and classical conditioning experiments on rudd, for example, the monochromatic test stimuli were superimposed on broad-band, tungsten-light backgrounds, Under the latter set of conditions, the fish may have been detecting the stimuli not just by brightness differences but also by color differences between stimulus and background. This notion is supported by the fact that the most profound dip in sensitivity occurs near the spectral point that humans call yellow, and where goldfish experience monochromatic lights as being least saturated (Yager, 1967; Shefner and Levine, 1976).

B. Color Discrimination

For more than 20 years, various species of fish have been subjects for an extensive series of experiments on physiological, anatomical, and photochemical mechanisms of color vision. We will not attempt a comprehensive review of that literature in this chapter; reference will be made to pertinent studies in discussions of psychophysical results, and references to review articles and recent experiments are included in the bibliography.*

To assert that an animal has color vision is to say that it can discriminate between two stimuli composed of different sets of wavelengths of light when all other cues, such as luminance, size, shape and location, have been eliminated. If this ability can be demonstrated, then there are a number of psychophysical functions that can be determined from which inferences can be made about the characteristics of the physiological mechanisms that are necessary to mediate the discriminations. When precise psychophysical and physiological data are obtained from the same species, theoretical color discrimination models may be tested by developing explicit linking hypotheses between the two kinds of data.

There are many types of discriminations which depend on spectral composition, and which have been used in investigations of human color vision (Graham, 1965: Chaps. 12, 13, 15–17; Jameson and Hurvich, 1972: Chaps. 14, 16, 19–22). We will review here some of the studies on color vision in fish that have used the same types of procedures.

1. Discrimination between Different Spectral Distributions

No species of fish has been shown *not* to be able to discriminate different spectral distributions, when all other cues are eliminated. The best early experiments were a series by von Frisch (1912, 1913, 1924, 1925), who demonstrated that a minnow, *Phoxinus*, was able to choose a test tube with colored paper in it from a series of 50 tubes graded from white to black; when colored tubes were compared directly, blue, green, and red were distinguished, while red and yellow were regularly confused. However, in these experiments, as in most early work on fish color vision, possible brightness cues were not adequately controlled: the series of grays may not have included a brightness which was equal to the subjective brightness of the original colored tube, as perceived by the fish.

In two later studies, brightness cues were controlled much more carefully. Hurst (1953), working with the bluegill sunfish, demonstrated red–green discrimination, using a forced-choice technique; stimulus luminances were varied by a factor of 45 to 1. McLeary and Bernstein (1959) demonstrated that goldfish could discriminate between colored papers in combination with density filters.

*For example, Crescitelli and Dartnall (1954), Jacobson (1964), Kaneko (1970), Kaneko and Hashimoto (1969), Liebman and Entine (1964), MacNichol and Svaetichin (1958), Marks (1965), Norton et al. (1968), Schwanzara (1967), Spekreijse et al. (1972), Stell (1967, 1975), Svaetichin (1953), and Tomita et al. (1967).

Their subjects were trained to discriminate between a red and a green stimulus that had been selected to be of equal brightness to humans. These animals were then tested for generalization with bright and dim red and bright and dim green stimuli; a preliminary brightness discrimination study had shown that the different sets of colored stimuli overlapped in brightness. Under these circumstances, the goldfish generalized perfectly according to hue; that is, they maintained responding to the appropriate color despite a wide variation in brightness.

A number of other experiments have led to the conclusion that many fishes can discriminate colors (e.g., Reeves, 1919; Arora and Sperry, 1963; Muntz and Cronly-Dillon, 1966). This result is not surprising, given the known physiological mechanisms which are differentially responsive to wavelengths. (see footnote on page 124). The inferences that can be made about color vision mechanisms are limited, however; many of these discriminations could be made by *either* dichromatic or trichromatic visual systems (Yager and Jameson, 1968; Muntz, 1968).

2. Wavelength Discrimination Function

This function, an extension of the crude color discriminations described above, describes the minimal change in wavelength of a monochromatic light that allows detection of color differences. Monochromats cannot discriminate

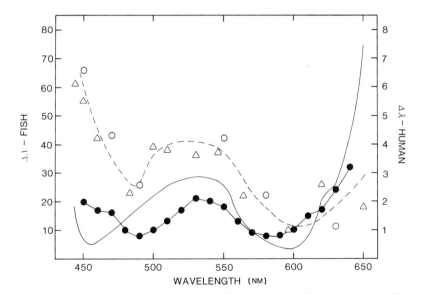

Fig. 12. Wavelength discrimination functions. Open circles, goldfish (Yarczower and Bitterman, 1965); triangles, minnow (Wolff, 1925); smooth curve, theoretical function for goldfish (Yager, 1967); closed circles, median measurements from eight different experiments on humans (Graham, 1965, Fig. 12.1).

between any two wavelengths. The human dichromat's wavelength discrimination function (just discriminable wavelength difference as a function of wavelength) shows excellent discrimination at the neutral point (about 500 nm for red–green defects) and increases rapidly at longer and shorter wavelengths. The human trichromatic wavelength discrimination function has two minima near 500 and 590 nm, with poor discrimination only at the spectral extremes. There is some experimental evidence that the minnow (Wolff, 1925) and the goldfish (Yarczower and Bitterman, 1965) have wavelength discrimination functions with characteristics similar to those of the trichromatic human observer (Fig. 12). In both studies, however, brightness cues were not controlled, and thus no strong statement about trichromacy can be made from these data; however, a trichromatic theoretical model does adequately account for the goldfish results (Yager, 1967).

3. Color Mixture

The most direct test of mono-, di-, or trichromacy would involve determination of the number of primary stimuli required in a mixture to match any other light in color. However, the experimental difficulties that would have to be overcome in obtaining complete color-mixture functions in a nonverbal subject are virtually intractable. Hamburger (1926) has shown that there are complementary color pairs for the minnow, just as for humans. Fish trained to a "white" light reacted to certain mixtures of yellow and blue, red and green, and orange and blue (mixtures which appeared white to a human observer) just as they did to white light. One other experiment on color mixture has been published, and it is very limited, although the data are excellent as far as they go. Oyama and Jitsumori (1973) trained carp to discriminate a yellowish-red (645 nm) and a yellowish-green (530 nm) from a yellow stimulus (576 nm); the hue names are, of course, as a normal human observer sees them. Brightness cues were adequately controlled. Discrimination training was then given between the 576 nm stimulus and a series of different mixtures of 645 nm + 530 nm. Some of the mixtures were indistinguishable from the 576-nm light, for the carp. This is analogous to the performance of a human observer on an anomaloscope, in which the subject sets a mixture of yellowish-red and yellowish-green to match a slightly reddish yellow, as a measure of the characteristics of the color discrimination system.

4. Saturation Discrimination

Another function that can be used to assess the type of color vision in an organism is the spectral saturation function. Spectral lights of equal brightness usually differ not only in hue but also in saturation. Estimations of degree of saturation are very difficult to make, even for a human observer. However, a monotonically related psychophysical measure of saturation is "least-colorimetric-purity," the least amount of a spectral light that must be added to white light to make it just detectably different in color from the white alone; the higher the saturation, the less the required monochromatic light.

The form of this function is strongly dependent on the specific characteristics of the color vision mechanism: if saturation is at zero at all wavelengths, then the organism is a monochromat; if most wavelengths can be discriminated from a white stimulus, except for one or two points in the spectrum, then it is probably a dichromat; and if the organism can discriminate all wavelengths from white and there are no points in the spectrum where saturation approaches zero, as with a normal human, then the organism probably has trichromatic vision.

Yager (1967,1974) used a two-choice operant conditioning technique to measure the least-colorimetric-purity function in the goldfish at 12 wavelengths. The goldfish could discriminate all the wavelengths from white, and the form of the function was accounted for by a trichromatic model of the visual system that postulates a summation of response from different types of cones to yield a brightness response, and interactions between activities initiated in the different types of cones to yield opponent chromatic responses at the neural level. An investigation of a white-monochromatic discrimination at much more closely spaced spectral points confirmed that no neutral point existed (Shefner and Levine, 1976).

5. Chromatic Contrast and Adaptation

In human color vision, color perception can be altered by preadaptation to a chromatic stimulus (successive contrast) or by surrounding a stimulus with a chromatic annulus (simultaneous contrast). Both of these effects have been demonstrated in fish. Herter (1950) showed that the visual system of several species of fish exhibited simultaneous color contrast. For example, a fish trained positively to a green stimulus on a neutral background would also respond positively to an objectively gray stimulus when it was presented against a red background. Yager (1974) showed that, in the goldfish, chromatic preadaptation produced alterations in color discrimination which suggested that they were exhibiting successive contrast: red adaptation resulted in an increase in the amount of green light which had to be added to a "white" light for the mixture to be discriminable from the "white" light alone. The same result obtained for a human observer in the same situation, the reason being that the red preadaption caused the "white" stimulus also to appear green. Similarly, green adaptation resulted in higher least-colorimetric-purity in the red region of the spectrum. A theoretical model, which allowed the computation of perceived hues of the "white" light following chromatic adaptation, gave a satisfactory account of the results.

6.Color Vision by the Rod System

Powers and Easter (1975) have reported some evidence which suggests that the hue percept of the goldfish in the *scotopic* state is similar to the hue produced by long-wavelength ("red") light in the *photopic* state. This result is consistent with the physiologic findings of Raynauld (1972) and Beauchamp and Daw (1972), and anatomical evidence by Scholes (1975), that rods and long-wavelength absorbing cones are connected by similar neural pathways to the ganglion cells.

7. Psychological Color Space

In humans, the "color circle is closed," which means that the colors of the long-wave end of the spectrum (red) and the short-wave end (violet or reddish-blue) are more similar perceptually to each other than they are to the middle-wave part of the spectrum (yellowish-green). That this is also true for minnows was shown by Wolff (1925) in his experiment on stimulus generalization and wavelength discrimination with spectral lights. Yager's (1974, Fig. 5) model of goldfish color vision also predicts that this should be true for that species.

8. Color Constancy

With a human observer, it is well known that objects in the visual field tend to retain their original perceived hues when the overall illumination is changed from "white" light to a strongly chromatic illuminant. This phenomenon is called color constancy, and has been attributed to change in the "adaptation level" of the visual system (e.g., Helson, 1943,1964) and to lateral opponent induction effects (Jameson and Hurvich, 1964). Color constancy, at the physiological level, depends in part on the existence of chromatically and spatially opponent receptive fields in the visual system, and these mechanisms are known to exist in fish (e.g., MacNichol *et al.,* 1961).

Burkamp (1923) has shown that several species of fish demonstrate color constancy. With white illumination, he trained subjects to feed from dishes that were painted with a particular color, and to ignore other colors, and white, gray, or black dishes. His fish still chose the same dish when the whole tank was subsequently illuminated with either the same color light as the dish with food, or its complement; adequate controls for nonvisual cues were introduced. The result was obtained even though, when the complementary illuminant was used, almost no light was reflected from the training dish. This finding is consistent with the human results and theoretical models.

ACKNOWLEDGMENTS

We would like to express our appreciation to Ros Becker and Martha Romeskie for their beautiful drawings, and to Jeanne Downs for her patience and skill in typing most of this long manuscript.

REFERENCES

Ali, M. A., and Wagner, H. J. (1975). Visual pigments: Phylogeny and ecology. *In* "Vision in Fishes: New Approaches in Research" (M. A. Ali, ed.), pp. 481–516. Plenum, New York.

Anctil, M. (1969). Structure de la rétine chez quelques téléostéens marins du plateau continental. *J. Fish. Res. Board Can.* **26,** 597–628.

Appelle, S. (1972). Perception and discrimination as a function of stimulus orientation: The "oblique effect" in man and animals. *Psychol. Bull.* **78,** 266–278.

Arnold, G. P. (1974). Rheotropism in fishes. *Biol. Rev. Cambridge Philos. Soc.* **49,** 515–576.

Arora, H. L., and Sperry, R. W. (1963). Color discrimination after optic nerve regeneration in the fish *Astronotus ocellatus. Dev. Biol.* **7,** 234–243.

Baerends, G. P., Bennema, B. E., and Vogelzang, A. A. (1960). Über die Änderung der Sehschärfe mit dem Wachstum bei Aequidens portalegransis (Hensel) (Pisces, Cichlidae). *Zool. Jahrb., Abt. Allg. Zool. Physiol. Tiere* **88,** 67–78.

Barlow, H. B. (1972). Single units and sensation: A neuron doctrine for perceptual psychology? *Perception* **1,** 371–394.

Barlow, H. B., Hill, R. M., and Levick, W. R. (1964). Retinal ganglion cells responding selectively to direction and speed of image motion in the rabbit. *J. Physiol. (London)* **173,** 377–407.

Baylor, E. R., and Shaw, E. (1962). Refractive error and vision in fishes. *Science* **136,** 157–158.

Beauchamp, R. D., and Daw, N. W. (1972). Rod and cone input to single goldfish optic nerve fibers. *Vision Res.* **12,** 1201–1212.

Beauchamp, R. D., and Lovasik, J. V. (1973). Blue mechanism response of single goldfish optic fibers. *J. Neurophysiol.* **36,** 925–939.

Beauchamp, R. D., and Rowe, J. S. (1977). Goldfish spectral sensitivity: A conditioned heart rate measure in restrained or curarized fish. *Vision Res.* **17,** 617–624.

Bingham, H. C. (1914). A definition of form. *J. Anim. Behav.* **4,** 136–141.

Bisti, S., and Maffei, L. (1974). Behavioural contrast sensitivity of the cat in various visual meridians. *J. Physiol. (London)* **241,** 201–210.

Blackwell, H. R. (1946). Contrast thresholds of the human eye. *J. Opt. Soc. Am.* **36,** 624–643.

Blaxter, J. H. S. (1964). Spectral sensitivity of the herring, *Clupea harengus* L. *J. Exp. Biol.* **41,** 155–162.

Blough, D. S., and Yager, D. (1972). Visual psychophysics in animals. *Handb. Sens. Physiol.* 8, Part 4, 732–763.

Bowman, R., and Sutherland, N. S. (1969). Discrimination of "W" and "V" shapes by goldfish. *Q. J. Exp. Psychol.* **21,** 69–76.

Breder, C. M. (1959). Studies on social groupings in fishes. *Bull. Am. Mus. Nat. Hist.* **117,** 393–482.

Bridges, C. D. B. (1972). The rhodopsin-porphyropsin visual system. *Handb. Sens. Physiol.* **7,** Part 1, 417–480.

Brown, P. K., and Wald, G. (1964). Visual pigments in single rods and cones of the human retina. *Science* **144,** 45–52.

Brunner, G. (1935). Über die Sehschärfe der Elritze (*Phoxinus laevis*) bei vershiedenen Helligkeiten. *Z. Vergl. Physiol.* **21,** 296–316.

Bull, H. O. (1928). Studies on conditioned responses in fishes. Part I. *J. Mar. Biol. Assoc. U.K.* **15,** 485–533.

Burkamp, W. (1923). Versuche über Farbenwiedererkennen der Fische. *Z. Sinnesphysiol.* **55,** 133–170.

Cameron, N. E. (1974). Chromatic vision in a teleost fish: *Perca fluviatilis* L. Ph.D. Thesis, University of Sussex, England.

Campbell, A. (1971). Interocular transfer of mirror images by goldfish. *Brain Res.* **33,** 486–490.

Charman, W. N., and Tucker, J. (1973). The optical system of the goldfish eye. *Vision Res.* **13**, 1–8.

Clark, E. (1961). Visual discrimination in lemon sharks. *Abstr. Symp. Pap., Pac. Sci. Congr., 10th*, pp. 175–176.

Clark, E. (1963). The maintenance of sharks in captivity. Part II. Experimental work on shark behavior. Congr. Int. Aquariol., *1st, 1960* Vol. D, pp. 1–10.

Corcoran, D. W. J. (1971). "Pattern Recognition." Penguin Books, Baltimore, Maryland.

Cornsweet, T. N. (1970). "Visual Perception." Academic Press, New York.

Crescitelli, F., and Dartnall, H. J. A. (1953). Human visual purple. *Nature (London)* **172**, 195–196.

Crescitelli, F., and Dartnall, H. J. A. (1954). A photosensitive pigment of the carp retina. *J. Physiol. (London)* **125**, 607–627.

Cronly-Dillon, J. R. (1964). Units sensitive to direction of movement in goldfish optic tectum. *Nature (London)* **203**, 214–215.

Cronly-Dillon, J. R., and Muntz, W. R. A. (1965). The spectral sensitivity of the goldfish and clawed tadpole under photopic conditions. *J. Exp. Biol.* **42**, 481–493.

Cronly-Dillon, J. R., and Sharma, S. C. (1968). Effect of season and sex on the photopic spectral sensitivity of the three-spined stickleback. *J. Exp. Biol.* **49**, 679–687.

Dartnall, H. J. A. (1953). The interpretation of spectral sensitivity curves. *Br. Med. Bull.* **9**, 24–30.

Dartnall, H. J. A. (1960). Visual pigments of colour vision. *In* "Mechanisms of Colour Discrimination" (Y. Gallifret, ed.), pp. 147–161. Pergamon, Oxford.

Dartnall, H. J. A. (1962). The photobiology of visual processes. *In* "The Eye" (H. Davson, ed.), 1st ed., Vol. 2, pp. 523–533. Academic Press, New York.

Dartnall, H. J. A., Lander, M. R., and Munz, F. W. (1961). Periodic changes in the visual pigment of a fish. *Prog. Photobiol. Prve. Int. Congr., 3rd, 1960* pp. 203–213.

Daw, N. W. (1968). Colour-coded ganglion cells in the goldfish retina: Extension of their receptive fields by means of new stimuli. *J. Physiol. (London)* **197**, 567–592.

Denton, E. J., Muntz, W. R. A., and Northmore, D. P. M. (1971). The distribution of visual pigments within the retina in two teleosts. *J. Mar. Biol. Assoc. U.K.* **51**, 905–915.

Deutsch, J. A. (1962). A system for shape recognition. *Psychol. Rev.* **69**, 492–500.

Dodwell, P. C. (1970). "Visual Pattern Recognition." Holt, New York.

Duntley, S. Q. (1963). Light in the sea. *J. Opt. Soc. Am.* **53**, 214–233.

Easter, S. S. (1968). Excitation in the goldfish retina: Evidence for a non-linear intensity code. *J. Physiol. (London)* **195**, 253–271.

Easter, S. S. (1972). Pursuit eye movements in goldfish (*Carassius auratus*). *Vision Res.* **12**, 673–688.

Engström, K. (1963). Cone types and cone arrangements in teleost retinae. *Acta Zool. (Stockholm)* **44**, 179–243.

Fisher, P. (1940). Untersuchungen über das Formsehen der Elritze. *Z. Tierpsychol.* **4**, 797–867.

Geller, I. (1964). Conditioned suppression in goldfish as a function of shock-reinforcement schedule. *J. Exp. Anal. Behav.* **7**, 345–349.

Glezer, V. D., Leushina, L. I., Nevskaya, A. A., and Prazdnikova, N. V. (1974). Studies on visual pattern recognition in man and animals. *Vision Res.* **14**, 555–584.

Graham, C., ed. (1965). "Vision and Visual Perception." Wiley, New York.

Green, D. G. (1970). Regional variations in the visual acuity for interference fringes on the retina. *J. Physiol. (London)* **207**, 351–356.

Gruber, S. H. (1969). The physiology of vision in the lemon shark, *Negaprion brevirostris (Poey):* A behavioral analysis. Ph.D. Dissertation, University of Miami, Coral Gables, Florida.

Grundfest, H. (1932a). The sensibility of the sunfish, *Lepomis,* to monochromatic radiation of low intensities. *J. Gen. Physiol.* **15**, 307–328.

Grundfest, H. (1932b). The spectral sensibility of the sunfish as evidence for a double visual system. *J. Gen. Physiol.* **15**, 507–524.

Guth, L., Donley, N., and Marrocco, R. (1969). On luminance additivity and related topics. *Vision Res.* **9**, 537–575.

Hager, H. J. (1938). Untersuchungen über das optische differenzierungsvermögen der Fische. *Z. Vergl. Physiol.* **26**, 282–302.

Hamburger, V. (1926). Versuche über Komplementär-Farben bei Ellritzen. *Z. Vergl. Physiol.* **4**, 286–304.

Harden Jones, F. R. (1963). The reaction of fish to moving backgrounds. *J. Exp. Biol.* **40**, 437–446.

Harosi, F. I., and MacNichol, E. F. (1974). Visual pigments of goldfish cones. Spectral properties and dichroism. *J. Gen. Physiol.* **63**, 279–304.

Held, R. (1968). Dissociation of visual functions by deprivation and rearrangement. *Psychol. Forsch.* **31**, 338–348.

Helson, H. (1943). Some factors and implications of color constancy. *J. Opt. Soc. Am.* **33**, 555–567.

Helson, H. (1964). "Adaptation Level Theory. An Experimental and Systematic Approach to Behavior." Harper, New York.

Hemmings, G. (1966). The effect of pretraining in the circle/square discrimination situation. *Anim. Behav.* **14**, 212–216.

Hemmings, G., and Matthews, W. A. (1963). Shape discrimination in tropical fish. *Q. J. Exp. Psychol.* **15**, 273–278.

Herter, K. (1929). Dressurversuche an Fischen. *Z. Vergl. Physiol.* **10**, 688–711.

Herter, K. (1950). "Vom Lernvermögen der Fische. Moderne Biologie: Festschrift für H. Nachtsheim," pp. 163–179. Berlin.

Herter, K. (1953). "Die Fischdressuren und ihre sinnesphysiologischen Grundlagen." Akademie-Verlag, Berlin.

Hester, F. J. (1968). Visual contrast thresholds of the goldfish (*Carassius auratus*). *Vision Res.* **8**, 1315–1336.

Horio, G. (1938). Die Farb- und Formdressur an Karpfen. *Japn. J. Med. Sci. 3* **4**, 395–402.

Horner, J. L., Longo, N., and Bitterman, M. E. (1960). A classical conditioning technique for small aquatic animals. *Am. J. Psychol.* **73**, 623–626.

Horner, J. L., Longo, N., and Bitterman, M. E. (1961). A shuttle box for fish and a control circuit of general applicability. *Am. J. Psychol.* **74**, 114–120.

Hubel, D. H. (1975). Monkey visual cortex: Normal structure and function. Friedenwald Award Lecture, Association for Research in Vision and Ophthalmology, Sarasota, Florida.

Hubel, D. H., and Wiesel, T. N. (1962). Receptive fields, binocular interaction and functional architecture in the cat's visual cortex. *J. Physiol. (London)* **160**, 106–154.

Hubel, D. H., and Wiesel, T. N. (1965). Receptive fields and functional architecture in two non-striate visual areas (18 and 19) of the cat. *J. Neurophysiol.* **28**, 229–289.

Hubel, D. H., and Wiesel, T. N. (1968). Receptive fields and functional architecture of monkey striate cortex. *J. Physiol. (London)* **195**, 215–243.

Hurst, P. M. (1953). Color discrimination in the bluegill sunfish. *J. Comp. Physiol. Psychol.* **46**, 442–445.

Ingle, D. (1965). Interocular transfer in goldfish: Color easier than pattern. *Science* **149**, 1000–1002.

Ingle, D. (1967). Two visual mechanisms underlying the behavior of fish. *Psychol. Forsch.* **31**, 44–51.

Ingle, D. (1968a). Interocular integration of visual learning by goldfish. *Brain, Behav. Evol.* **1**, 58–85.

Ingle, D. (1968b). Spatial dimensions of vision in fish. *In* "The Central Nervous System and Fish Behavior" (D. Ingle, ed.), pp. 51–59. Univ. of Chicago Press, Chicago, Illinois.

Ingle, D. (1971). Vision: The experimental analysis of visual behavior. *Fish Physiol.* **5**, 59–77.

Jacobson, M. (1964). Spectral sensitivity of single units in the optic tectum of the goldfish. *Q. J. Exp. Physiol. Cogn. Med. Sci.* **49**, 384–393.

Jacobson, M., and Gaze, R. M. (1964). Types of visual response from single units in the optic tectum and optic nerve of the goldfish. *Q. J. Exp. Physiol. Cogn. Med. Sci.* **49,** 199–209.

Jameson, D., and Hurvich, L. (1964). Theory of brightness and color contrast in human vision. *Vision Res.* **4,** 135–154.

Jameson, D., and Hurvich, L., eds. (1972). *Handb. Sens. Physiol.* **7,** Part 4.

Jerlov, N. G. (1968). "Optical Oceanography." Am. Elsevier, New York.

Johns, P. R., and Easter, S. S. (1975). Retinal growth in adult goldfish. *In* "Vision in Fishes: New Approaches in Research" (M. A. Ali, ed.), pp. 451–457. Plenum, New York.

Kaneko, A. (1970). Physiological and morphological identification of horizontal, bipolar, and amacrine cells in goldfish retina. *J. Physiol. (London)* **207,** 623–633.

Kaneko, A., and Hashimoto, H. (1969). Electrophysiological study of single neurons in the inner nuclear layer of the carp retina. *Vision Res.* **9,** 37–55.

Kaufman, E. L., Lord, M. W., Reese, T. W., and Volkmann, J. (1949). The discrimination of visual number. *Am. J. Psychol.* **42,** 498–525.

Kuffler, S. W. (1973). The single-cell approach in the visual system and the study of receptive fields. *Invest. Ophthalmol.* **12,** 794–813.

Lang, H. J. (1967). Über das Lichtrückenverhalten des Guppy (*Lebistes reticulatus*) in farbigen und farblosen Lichtern. *Z. Vergl. Physiol.* **56,** 296–340.

Levine, M. D. (1969). Feature extraction: A survey. *Proc. IEEE* **57,** 1391–1407.

Liebman, P. A., and Entine, G. (1964). Sensitive low light level microspectrophotometer: Detection of photosensitive pigments of retinal cones. *J. Opt. Soc. Am.* **54,** 1451–1459.

Loew, E. R., and Dartnall, H. J. A. (1976). Vitamin A_1/A_2-based visual pigment mixtures in cones of the rudd. *Vision Res.* **16,** 891–896.

Lyall, A. H. (1957). The growth of the trout retina. *Q. J. Microsc. Sci.* [N. S.] **98,** 101–110.

Lyon, E. P. (1904). On rheotropism. I. Rheotropism in fishes. *Am. J. Physiol.* **12,** 149–161.

Lythgoe, J. N. (1968). Visual pigments and visual range underwater. *Vision Res.* **8,** 997–1012.

Lythgoe, J. N. (1972). List of vertebrate visual pigments. *Handb. Sens. Physiol.* **7,** Part 1, 604–624.

Lythgoe, J. N. (1975). Problems of seeing colours under water. *In* "Vision in Fishes: New Approaches in Research" (M. A. Ali, ed.), pp. 619–634. Plenum, New York.

Mackintosh, N. J., and Sutherland, N. S. (1963). Visual discrimination by the goldfish: The orientation of rectangles. *Anim. Behav.* **11,** 135–141.

McLeary, R. A., and Bernstein, J. J. (1959). A unique method for control of brightness cues in the study of colour vision in fish. *Physiol. Zool.* **32,** 284–292.

MacNichol, E. F., and Svaetichin, G. (1958). Electric responses from the isolated retinas of fishes. *Am. J. Ophthalmol.* **46,** 26–40.

MacNichol, E. F., Wolbarsht, M. L., and Wagner, H. G. (1961). Electrophysiological evidence for a mechanism of color vision in the goldfish. *In* "Light and Life" (W. D. McElroy and B. Glass, eds.), pp. 795–816. Johns Hopkins Press, Baltimore, Maryland.

Maes, R. (1930). La vision des formes chez les poissons. *Ann. Soc. R. Zool. Belg.* **60,** 103–130.

Marks, W. B. (1965). Visual pigments of single goldfish cones. *J. Physiol. (London)* **178,** 14–32.

Marks, W. B., Dobelle, W. H., and MacNichol, E. F. (1964). Visual pigments of single primate cones. *Science* **143,** 1181–1183.

Matthews, W. A. (1964). Shape discrimination in tropical fish. *Anim. Behav.* **12,** 111–115.

Meesters, W. A. (1940). Über die Organization des Gesichtsfeldes der Fische. *Z. Tierpsychol.* **4,** 84–149.

Moreland, J. D., and Lythgoe, J. N. (1968). Yellow corneas in fishes. *Vision Res.* **8,** 1377–1380.

Munk, O. (1970). On the occurrence and significance of horizontal band-shaped retinal areae in teleosts. *Vidensk. Medd. Dansk Naturh. Foren.* **133,** 85–120.

Muntz, W. R. A. (1968). On criteria for trichromatic vision: A reply to Yager and Jameson. *Anim. Behav.* **16,** 32.

Muntz, W. R. A. (1972). Inert reflecting and absorbing pigments. *Handb. Sens. Physiol.* **7,** Part 1, 529–565.

Muntz, W. R. A. (1973). Yellow filters and the absorption of light by the visual pigments of some Amazonian fishes. *Vision Res.* **13,** 2235–2254.

Muntz, W. R. A. (1974). Comparative aspects in behavioural studies of vertebrate vision. *In* "The Eye" (H. Davson and L. T. Graham, Jr., eds.), Vol. 6, pp. 155–226). Academic Press, New York.

Muntz, W. R. A. (1975). Behavioural studies of vision in a fish and possible relationships to the environment. *In* "Vision in Fishes: New Approaches in Research" (M. A. Ali, ed.), pp. 705–717. Plenum, New York.

Muntz, W. R. A., and Cronly-Dillon, J. (1966). Colour discrimination in goldfish. *Anim. Behav.* **14,** 351–355.

Muntz, W. R. A., and Northmore, D. P. M. (1970). Vision and visual pigments in a fish, *Scardinius erythrophthalmus* (the rudd). *Vision Res.* **10,** 281–298.

Muntz, W. R. A., and Northmore, D. P. M. (1971). The independence of the photopic receptor systems underlying visual thresholds in a teleost. *Vision Res.* **11,** 861–876.

Muntz, W. R. A., and Northmore, D. P. M. (1973). Scotopic spectral sensitivity in a teleost fish (*Scardinius erythrophthalmus*) adapted to different daylengths. *Vision Res.* **13,** 245–252.

Munz, F. W., and McFarland, W. N. (1973). The significance of spectral position in the rhodopsins of tropical marine fishes. *Vision Res.* **13,** 1829–1874.

Munz, F. W., and Schwanzara, S. A. (1967). A nomogram for retinene$_2$-based visual pigments. *Vision Res.* **7,** 121–148.

Nakamura, E. L. (1968). Visual acuity of two tunas, *Katsuwonus pelamis* and *Euthynnus affinis*. *Copeia* No. 1, pp. 41–49.

Northmore, D. P. M. (1977). Spatial summation and light adaptation in the goldfish visual system. *Nature (London),* **268,** 450–451.

Northmore, D. P. M., and Muntz, W. R. A. (1974). Effects of stimulus size on spectral sensitivity in a fish (*Scardinius erythrophthalmus*), measured with a classical conditioning paradigm. *Vision Res.* **14,** 503–514.

Northmore, D. P. M., and Yager, D. (1975). Psychophysical methods for investigations of vision in fishes. *In* "Vision in Fishes. New Approaches in Research" (M. A. Ali, ed.), pp. 689–704. Plenum, New York.

Norton, A., Spekreijse, H., Wolbarsht, M., and Wagner, H. (1968). Receptive field organization of the S-potential. *Science* **160,** 1021–1022.

O'Connell, C. P. (1963). The structure of the eye of *Sardinops caerulea, Engraulis mordax,* and four other pelagic marine teleosts. *J. Morphol.* **113,** 287–329.

Oyama, T., and Jitsumori, M. (1973). A behavioral study of color mixture in the carp. *Vision Res.* **13,** 2299–2308.

Podugol'nikova, T. A., and Maksimov, V. V. (1975). Morphological types of bipolar cells identified by regular grids of their axonal expansions in the inner plexiform layer of the herring retina. *Neurophysiology* **7,** 47–51.

Polyak, S. L. (1941). "The Retina." Univ. of Chicago Press, Chicago, Illinois.

Powers, M. K. (1977). Visual sensitivity of the goldfish. Ph.D. Dissertation, University of Michigan, Ann Arbor.

Powers, M. K., and Easter, S. S. (1975). A behavioural test of rod-red cone convergence in the goldfish retina. *In* "Vision in Fishes: New Approaches in Research" (M. A. Ali, ed.), pp. 743–748. Plenum, New York.

Pumphrey, R. J. (1961). Concerning vision. *In* "The Cell and the Organism" (J. A. Ramsay, ed.), pp. 193–208. Cambridge Univ. Press, London and New York.

Raynauld, J. P. (1972). Goldfish retina: Sign of the rod input in opponent color ganglion cells. *Science* **177**, 84–85.

Reeves, C. D. (1919). Discrimination of light of different wavelengths by fish. *Behav. Monogr.* **4**, No. 3, 1–106.

Riggs, L. A. (1965). Visual acuity. *In* "Vision and Visual Perception" (C. H. Graham, ed.), pp. 321–349. Wiley, New York.

Sadler, J. D. (1973). The focal length of the fish eye lens and visual acuity. *Vision Res.* **13**, 417–423.

Saxena, A. (1966). Lernkapacität, Gedächtnis und Transpositions-vermögen bei Forellen. *Zool. Jahresber., Abt. Allg. Zool. Physiol. Tiere* **69**, 63–94.

Schaller, A. (1926). Sinnesphysiologische und psychologische Untersuchungen an Wasserkäfern und Fischen. *Z. Vergl. Physiol.* **4**, 1–38.

Schellart, N. A. M. (1973). Dynamics and statistics of photopic ganglion cell responses in isolated goldfish retina. Doctoral Thesis, University of Amsterdam, Amsterdam, The Netherlands.

Schneider, G. E. (1967). Contrasting visuomotor functions of tectum and cortex in the golden hamster. *Psychol. Forsch.* **31**, 52–62.

Scholes, J. H. (1975). Colour receptors, and their synaptic connexions, in the retina of a cyprinid fish. *Philos. Trans. R. Soc. London, Ser. B* **270**, 61–118.

Schulte, A. (1957). Transfer- und Transposition-versuche mit monokular dressierten Fischen. *Z. Vergl. Physiol.* **39**, 432–476.

Schwanzara, S. (1967). The visual pigments of freshwater fishes. *Vision Res.* **7**, 121–148.

Schwassmann, H. O. (1968). Visual projection upon the optic tectum in foveate marine teleosts. *Vision Res.* **8**, 1337–1348.

Schwassmann, H. O. (1975). Refractive state, accommodation, and resolving power of the fish eye. *In* "Vision in Fishes: New Approaches in Research" (M. A. Ali, ed.), pp. 279–288. Plenum, New York.

Schwassmann, H. O., and Krag, M. H. (1970). Relation of visual field defects to retinotectal topography in teleost fish. *Vision Res.* **10**, 29–42.

Sekuler, R. (1974). Spatial vision. *Annu. Rev. Psychol.* **25**, 195–232.

Shefner, J. M., and Levine, M. W. (1976). A psychophysical demonstration of goldfish trichromacy. *Vision Res.* **16**, 671–673.

Shlaer, S. (1937). The relation between visual acuity and illumination. *J. Gen. Physiol.* **21**, 165–188.

Silver, P. H. (1974). Photopic spectral sensitivity of the neon tetra (*Paracheirodon innesi* (Myers)) found by the use of a dorsal light reaction. *Vision Res.* **14**, 329–334.

Sivak, J. G. (1973). Interrelation of feeding behavior and accommodative lens movements in some species of North American freshwater fishes. *J. Fish. Res. Board Can.* **30**, 1141–1146.

Sivak, J. G. (1974). The refractive error of the fish eye. *Vision Res.* **14**, 209–213.

Sivak, J. G. (1975). Accommodative mechanisms in aquatic vertebrates. *In* "Vision in Fishes: New Approaches in Research" (M. A. Ali, ed.), pp. 289–297. Plenum, New York.

Smith, J. C. (1970). Conditioned suppression as an animal psychophysical technique. *In* "Animal Psychophysics" (W. C. Stebbins, ed.), pp. 125–159. Appleton, New York.

Spekreijse, H., Wagner, H. G., and Wolbarsht, M. L. (1972). Spectral and spatial coding of ganglion cell responses in goldfish retina. *J. Neurophysiol.* **34**, 73–86.

Sperling, H. G., and Harwerth, R. S. (1971). Red-green cone interactions in the increment-threshold spectral sensitivity of primates. *Science* **172**, 180–184.

Stebbins, W. C., ed. (1970). "Animal Psychophysics." Appleton, New York.

Stell, W. (1967). The structure and relationships of horizontal cells and photoreceptor-bipolar synaptic complexes in the goldfish retina. *Am. J. Anat.* **121**, 401–424.

Stell, W. (1975). Structural studies of functional pathways in goldfish retina. *In* "Vision in Fishes: New Approaches in Research" (M. A. Ali, ed.), pp. 81–90. New York.

Sutherland, N. S. (1961). The methods and findings of experiments on the visual discrimination of shape by animals. *Exp. Psychol. Soc., Monogr.* **1**, 1–68.

Sutherland, N. S. (1963). Shape discrimination and receptive fields. *Nature (London)* **197**, 118–122.

Sutherland, N. S. (1968a). Outlines of a theory of visual pattern recognition in animals and man. *Proc. R. Soc. London, Ser. B* **171**, 297–317.

Sutherland, N. S. (1968b). Shape discrimination in the goldfish. *In* "The Central Nervous System and Fish Behavior" (D. Ingle, ed.), pp. 35–50. Chicago: Univ. of Chicago Press, Chicago, Illinois.

Sutherland, N. S. (1969). Shape discrimination in rat, octopus, and goldfish: A comparative study. *J. Comp. Physiol. Psychol.* **67**, 160–176.

Sutherland, N. S. (1974). Object recognition. *In* "Handbook of Perception" (E. C. Carterette and M. P. Friedman, eds.), Vol. 3, pp. 157–185. Academic Press, New York.

Svaetichin, G. (1953). The cone action potential. *Acta Physiol. Scand.* **29**, Suppl. 106, 565–600.

Tamura, T. (1957). A study of visual perception in fish, especially on resolving power and accommodation. *Bull. Jpn. Soc. Sci. Fish.* **22**, 536–557.

Tamura, T., and Wisby, W. J. (1963). The visual sense of pelagic fishes, especially the visual axis and accommodation. *Bull. Mar. Sci. Gulf Caribb.* **3**, 433–448.

Tavolga, W. N., and Jacobs, D. W. (1971). Scotopic thresholds for monochromatic light in the cichlid fish, *Tilapia heudelotii macrocephala*. *Vision Res.* **11**, 713–718.

Tester, A. L., and Kato, S. (1966). Visual target discrimination in blacktip sharks (*Carcharhinus melanopterus*) and grey sharks (*C. menisorrah*). *Pac. Sci.* **20**, 461–471.

Thibault, C. (1949). Action de la lumière blanche et monochromatique sur la posture des poissons téléostéens. *Arch. Sci. Physiol.* **3**, 101–124.

Thorpe, S. A. (1971). Behavioral measures of spectral sensitivity of the goldfish at different temperatures. *Vision Res.* **11**, 419–433.

Tomita, T., Kaneko, A., Murakami, M., and Pautler, E. L. (1967). Spectral response curves of single cones in carp. *Vision Res.* **7**, 519–531.

Trevarthen, C. B. (1968a). Two mechanisms of vision in primates. *Psychol. Forsch.* **31**, 299–337.

Trevarthen, C. B. (1968b). Vision in fish: The origins of the visual frame for action in vertebrates. *In* "The Central Nervous System and Fish Behavior" (D. Ingle, ed.), pp. 61–94. Univ. of Chicago Press, Chicago, Illinois.

Volkmann, F. C. (1972). An improved experimental situation for studying visual psychophysics in the goldfish, with data on the discrimination of the vertical. *Percept. Mot. Skills* **35**, 271–280.

Volkmann, F. C. (1975). Behavioural studies of the discrimination of visual orientation and motion by the goldfish. *In* "Vision in Fishes: New Approaches in Research" (M. A. Ali, ed.), pp. 731–741. Plenum, New York.

Volkmann, F. C., Zametkin, A. J., and Stoykovich, C. A. (1974). Visual discrimination of orientation by the goldfish, *Carassius Auratus*. *J. Comp. Physiol. Psychol.* **86**, 875–882.

von Frisch, K. (1912). Sind die Fische farbenblind? *Zool. Jahrb., Abt. Allg. Zool. Physiol. Tiere* **33**, 107–126.

von Frisch, K. (1913). Weitere Untersuchungen über den Farbensinn der Fische, *Zool. Jahrb., Abt. Allg. Zool. Physiol. Tiere* **34**, 43–68.

von Frisch, K. (1924). Sinnesphysiologie des Wassertiere. *Verh. Dtsch. Zool. Ges.* **29**, 21–42.

von Frisch, K. (1925). Farbensinn der Fische und Duplizitätstheorie. *Z. Vergl. Physiol.* **2**, 393–452.

von Helmholtz, H. (1924). "Physiological Optics" (transl. by J. P. C. Southall). Opt. Soc. Am., New York.

Wainwright, A. W. (1973). Vision in a teleost fish: *Blennius pholis L.* Ph.D. Thesis, University of Sussex, England.

Walls, G. L. (1963). "The Vertebrate Eye and its Adaptive Radiation." Hafner, New York.

Wartzok, D., and Marks, W. B. (1973). Directionally selective visual units recorded in optic tectum of the goldfish. *J. Neurophysiol.* **36,** 588–604.

Weiler, I. J. (1966). Restoration of visual acuity after optic nerve section and regeneration in *Astronotus ocellatus. Exp. Neurol.* **15,** 377–386.

Westheimer, G. (1972). Visual acuity and spatial modulation thresholds. *Handb. Sens. Physiol.* **7,** Part 4, 170–187.

Wilkinson, F. (1972). A behavioural measure of grating acuity in the goldfish. M.A. Thesis, Dalhousie University, Halifax, N.S., Canada.

Wolff, H. (1925). Das Farbenuntercheidungsvermögen der Ellritze. *Z. Vergl. Physiol.* **3,** 279–329.

Yager, D. (1967). Behavioral measures and theoretical analysis of spectral sensitivity and spectral saturation in the goldfish. *Vision Res.* **7,** 707–727.

Yager, D. (1968). Behavioral measures of the spectral sensitivity of the dark-adapted goldfish. *Nature (London)* **220,** 1052–1053.

Yager, D. (1969). Behavioral measures of spectral sensitivity in the goldfish following chromatic adaptation. *Vision Res.* **9,** 179–186.

Yager, D. (1974). Effects of chromatic adaptation on saturation discrimination in goldfish. *Vision Res.* **14,** 1089–1094.

Yager, D., and Jameson, D. (1968). On criteria for assessing type of colour vision in animals. *Anim. Behav.* **16,** 29–31.

Yager, D., Buck, S., and Duncan, I. (1971). Effects of temperature on the visually evoked tectal potential and brightness perception in goldfish. *Vision Res.* **11,** 849–860.

Yamanouchi, T. (1956). The visual acuity of the coral fish *Microcanthus strigatus* (Cuvier and Valenciennes). *Publ. Seto Mar. Biol. Lab.* **5,** 133–156.

Yarczower, M., and Bitterman, M. E. (1965). Stimulus generalization in the goldfish. *In* "Stimulus Generalization" (D. J. Mostofsky, ed.), pp. 179–192. Stanford Univ. Press, Stanford, California.

Zusne, L. (1970). "Visual Perception of Form." Academic Press, New York.

4

The Function of the Teleost Telencephalon in Behavior: A Reinforcement Mediator

KAREN LEE HOLLIS and J. BRUCE OVERMIER

I.	Introduction	137
	A. From Smell to Synthesis: The Evolutionary Puzzle of the Forebrain	137
	B. Anatomical and Ontogenetic Aspects of the Teleost Telencephalon	141
	C. Telencephalon as Rhinencephalon	145
	D. Rhinencephalon vs. Limbic System: The Leftovers Don't Smell	146
II.	Analysis of the Role of the Telencephalon	148
	A. Critical Examination of Hypotheses	148
	B. "Secondary" Reinforcement and Species-Specific Behaviors ...	154
III.	Telencephalon Ablation, Behavior, and Reinforcement	157
	A. Scheme for Organizing Data	157
	B. Review of the Data	158
IV.	Comparative Psychological Research: A Comment	176
	References	188

I. INTRODUCTION

A. From Smell to Synthesis: The Evolutionary Puzzle of the Forebrain

The cerebral hemispheres, a multisensory integrative system and hypothesized site of most "higher" mental processes, have evolved from the anterior one-third of the primitive vertebrate embryo's neural tube. While the hindbrain and mid-

brain divisions of the neural anlage have also undergone major evolutionary development, the dramatic anatomical and functional changes within the forebrain
have probably contributed most to man's unique adaptations. Before we can even
ask the most puzzling of questions, namely, how the primarily olfactory
functions of the nascent forebrain are related to man's cognitive processes and
how this relationship developed during evolution (Darwin, 1871; Thorndike,
1911), we must determine just what role the forebrain plays in the behavior of
those vertebrates where its olfactory functions are still substantial, for example in
Teleostei (bony fish).

The neurobehavioral study of the teleost telencephalon is one approach to the
analysis of the evolutionary development of the brain. Although Teleostei is
representative of a divergent lineage from primitive Osteichthyes (Hodos, 1970;
Nelson, 1969) (Fig. 1), the ancestral stock from which terrestrial vertebrates
evolved, the basic features of the teleost brain are quite similar to those of their
more primitive ancestors (Jerison, 1973). In addition, the great numbers of living
species which comprise this group with their divergent, but well-studied, behavioral repertoires make them excellent subjects for neurobehavioral analysis
(Fryer and Iles, 1972).

Traditionally, answers to neurobehavioral questions have been sought through
surgical manipulation of nervous structures. The brain is invaded by stimulation,
ablation, or lesion, and the resultant behavioral alterations are measured, the
description of these alterations forming the basis from which inferences of neural
function are then made. Following this historical precedent, the role of the
telencephalon in the behavior of teleosts has been studied largely by means of the
ablative technique.

The first scientific report by Desmoulins, 150 years ago, of a teleostean
telencephalon ablation concluded that little change, if any, occurred as a result of
the "decortication." Although this may not be surprising, investigators over the
next 100 years failed to observe any significant changes other than a decreased
amount of activity; furthermore, these researches were carried out on a variety of
teleost species. Indeed, as late as 1939, Meader asserted that "when normal and
operated individuals occupied the same aquarium, the [ablates'] only distinguishing characteristic was the head wound" (p. 13). This bit of history in itself
demonstrates just how elusive the answers to our questions regarding teleost
telencephalic function can be. Yet, as is typical of an emergent area of research,
more sophisticated observational techniques applied to behaviors more complex
than postural maintenance, locomotion, and feeding—which are all normal in
ablated fish (Segaar, 1965; Savage, 1969b)—have revealed that very significant
behavioral changes *do* result from telencephalon ablation.

The more sophisticated observations on telencephalon-ablated fish have revealed that behaviors important to both the species and the individual's survival
are disturbed. In brief, agonistic, reproductive, and parental behaviors clearly
suffer, and within the domain of "learned behaviors," although some kinds of

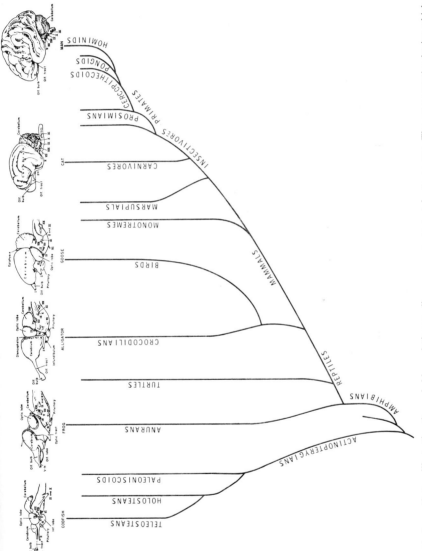

Fig. 1. A phylogenetic tree illustrating the probable evolutionary divergences among vertebrate groups. The representative brains which appear at the ends of the branches show the gross relationships of brain structures across vertebrates. (After Hodos, 1970.)

learning such as classical conditioning seem unimpaired, others, such as anticipatory flight and avoidance of dangerous, noxious events, are severely disrupted.* Moreover, temporal delays—even brief ones of a few seconds—introduced between the occurrence of a response and the delivery of the reward dramatically interfere with the acquisition and the maintenance of a learned response.

One goal of our own research is to provide a basis for a coherent account of the full range of known behavioral disturbances that result from removal of the telencephalon in the teleost fish. The thesis to be presented here is that the teleost telencephalon mediates complex reinforcement processes. The hypothesis is that the telencephalon of the fish is "involved in the utilization of changes in conditioned motivational reactions as reinforcers ('secondary' or 'conditioned' reinforcers) for the acquisition and maintenance of behaviors" (Flood *et al.*, 1976).

The notion of a telencephalic reinforcement mechanism as this hypothesis postulates for the teleost is one which has generated theoretical interest in quite a different circle; this hypothesis is related to a recent theoretical explanation of mammalian limbic system function. Although the divergent evolution of teleosts and mammals may make this at first seem inappropriate, nonetheless, we believe that a careful survey of the neuroanatomical and behavioral data reviewed below suggest that the teleost telencephalon is clearly the cognate of the mammalian limbic system which also functions, *sui generis,* in a wide range of species-specific and learned behavior patterns. Although both the research and theory of the teleost telencephalon have dichotomized the domains of species-specific and learned behaviors, we will suggest a scheme utilizing the reinforcement notion

---

*In the typical classical, or Pavlovian, conditioning paradigm, a neutral stimulus is paired in time with another stimulus, an unconditioned stimulus (UCS), which is capable of eliciting an unconditioned response (UCR) prior to any training. The stimuli are presented independently of the animal's behavior. As a result of such pairings, the neutral stimulus acquires the ability to elicit a response, a conditioned response (CR), which is, typically, closely related to the UCR; this neutral stimulus has, thus, become a conditioned stimulus (CS). In the instrumental conditioning paradigm, on the other hand, reinforcement is presented contingent on some behavior designated by the experimenter; reinforcement, here, refers to the presentation of a positive reinforcer (e.g., food) or the termination of a negative reinforcer (e.g., electric shock). As a result of this manipulation, the probability of the designated behavior increases. Negative reinforcement can be classified further as either escape or avoidance training. Escape training involves the termination of an *unconditioned* negative reinforcer (e.g., electric shock) contingent on some response. There exists no opportunity to avoid the shock. Avoidance behavior, nonetheless, may be characterized as a kind of escape behavior in which the animal escapes a *conditioned* negative reinforcer. That is, in the typical avoidance paradigm, some stimulus reliably precedes shock; in time, as a result of these pairings, this stimulus acquires aversive properties and it thus becomes a conditioned negative reinforcer. If the animal makes the appropriate response during this stimulus, the conditioned negative reinforcer is terminated; the unconditioned negative reinforcer (shock) is avoided. Thus, both paradigms involve the termination of a negative reinforcer—in escape training it is unconditioned, in avoidance training it is conditioned.

which integrates the data obtained from typical learning experiments with those of species-specific behavior. Organization of these dichotomous domains of research under such a scheme suggests a heretofore unrecognized common basis of both process and neurological substrate for the development, maintenance, and integration of *all* behavior sequences. Tests of this hypothesis will be discussed.

A brief review of the gross anatomy and ontogeny of the vertebrate brain and of the telencephalon itself is included here to illustrate the neuroanatomical and neurophysiological basis of homology between the teleost telencephalon and the mammalian limbic system. We shall also discuss the arguments and interpretive difficulties presupposed by questions of homology.

B. Anatomical and Ontogenetic Aspects of the Teleost Telencephalon

The vertebrate brain has three divisions: the hindbrain, the midbrain, and the forebrain. These divisions, which appear as three distinct bulges on the anterior end of the neural tube, lose their segmental character during ontogenetic and phylogenetic development. The hindbrain, or rhombencephalon, becomes differentiated into the medulla (mylencephalon), an enlargement of the spinal cord, and the metencephalon, consisting of the cerebellum and pons. The metencephalon is an outgrowth of the medulla itself. The midbrain, or mesencephalon, has developed no major subdivisions; it consists of a core of nervous structures collectively termed the tegmentum. In nonmammalian vertebrates, however, there exists a dorsal enlargement of mesencephalic tissue, the tectum. The forebrain, or prosencephalon, is differentiated into the diencephalon and the telencephalon. The diencephalon consists of the thalamus, hypothalamus, and posterior pituitary, and remains little changed throughout the vertebrates (Gordon, 1972). The remainder of the forebrain, the telencephalon,* is located just anterior to the thalamic and hypothalamic structures and contains six major differentiable nuclear regions in the dorsal, dorsomedial, dorsolateral, ventral, ventromedial, and central or deep areas (Fig. 2).

Although the telencephalon may take on a somewhat different appearance in the many vertebrate species, based upon neuroanatomical and neurophysiological similarities, these telencephalic nuclear regions may be further characterized

---

*Dorsally, the teleostean telencephalon (Fig. 2) appears as two laterally situated lobes, distinct from the larger and more caudal mesencephalic lobes (optic tectum). While most of the diencephalon is located posterior and inferior to the telencephalon, the preoptic nucleus is situated at the juncture of the telencephalic lobes and the remainder of the diencephalic structures. Though incorrect, it is perhaps because of the *apparent* separability of these diencephalic and telencephalic divisions that the term "forebrain" is commonly used to refer specifically to the telencephalon. This convention will not be employed in this paper.

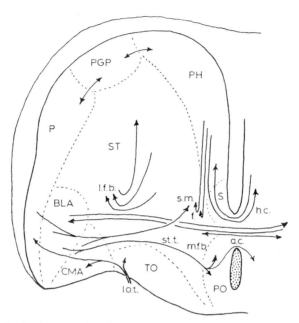

Fig. 2. A sketch of a coronal section through the telencephalon of a representative teleost illustrating both the major telencephalic regions and fiber tracts. BLA, basolateral amygdala; CMA, corticomedial amygdala; P, piriform area; PGP, primordial general pallium; PH, primordial hippocampal formation; PO, preoptic area; S, septal nuclei; ST, striatum; TO, olfactory tubercle; a.c., anterior commissure; f., fornix; h.c., hippocampal commissure; l.f.b., lateral forebrain bundle; l.o.t., lateral olfactory tract; m.f.b., medial forebrain bundle; s.m., stria medullaris; st.t., stria terminalis. The arrows indicate the course of fiber bundles. (After Schnitzlein, 1968.)

as hippocampal, amygdaloid, piriform, pallial, striatal, and septal. Thus, unmistakable "landmarks" allow the neuroanatomist to characterize a core of nervous tissue in the telencephalons of both frogs and monkeys as "hippocampal" despite the fact that in the latter this plus related structures become much more highly differentiated and are commonly referred to as the "limbic system."

Although the teleost also possesses differentiable telencephalic nuclear regions, the use of homologous anatomical terminology to describe these nuclei is not universally accepted (cf. Scalia and Ebbesson, 1971). The controversy exists primarily because the teleost telencephalon is singularly characterized among vertebrates by its unique ontogenetic development. Some have argued that this divergent ontogenetic process of teleosts results in a highly specialized structure, both morphologically and functionally (e.g., Nieuwenhuys, 1967).

In all vertebrates, the forebrain arises from the anterior portion of the embryonic neural tube; the side walls of this tube consist of two thickened plates, connected dorsally, rostrally, and ventrally by a thin epithelial membrane. Together, these membraneous and thickened parts enclose a single median ventricle. For most vertebrates, increases in the size of the neural structure are accomplished by an evagination, or outpouching, of the lateral side walls. This, together with the inversion of the dorsal portion of the side walls, results in lateral paired ventricles (Fig. 3c). The forebrain of teleosts, on the other hand, consists of two *solid* lobes separated by but one median ventricle. Expansion in the teleosts is accomplished by a bending outward, or eversion (Fig. 3B). While the ventral parts of the thickened side walls essentially maintain their embryonic position during development, the dorsal parts begin to bulge, proliferating laterally and ventrally. In so doing, they invade the ventricular space, which becomes T shaped. The epithelial membrane, which connects the two side walls dorsally, gradually broadens by a flattening of its cubical (or cylindrical) cells, eventually covering the whole medial, dorsal, and also the greater portion of the lateral surface of the hemispheres. Consequently, the points of attachment, the taenae, of this roof plate, or tela, are shifted laterally, proceeding, in most teleost species, to such a great extent that they are finally found at the ventrolateral side of the forebrain. All this is accompanied by an increase in the intraventricular space (Nieuwenhuys, 1959, 1967; Aronson, 1963; Segaar and Nieuwenhuys, 1963; Segaar, 1965; Aronson and Kaplan, 1968).

As a consequence of eversion, the ependymal matrix layer, which borders the ventricle, far exceeds the meningeal surface; although the whole dorsal and

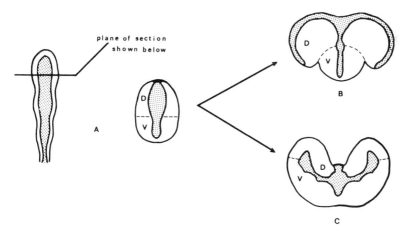

Fig. 3. Diagrammatic representation of the teleost and mammalian forebrain during ontogenesis: development from tube-shaped early embryonic state (A), through lateral eversion to form the adult stage as found in most teleosts (B), and through inversion and evagination of the anterior end of the neural tube to the adult stage as found in most mammals (C). Dotted line indicates boundary between the dorsal and ventral areas found in the neural tube anlage. Stippled area represents ventricular space.

medial surface and also a large part of the lateral surface are covered by the ependymal matrix, the meningeal surface is found only at the base of the telencephalon. This, of course, has vascular implications; blood vessels pass to and from the telencephalon only through this ventral meningeal surface (Nieuwenhuys, 1967; Segaar, 1965; Segaar and Nieuwenhuys, 1963). Anatomically, as Nieuwenhuys (1967) points out, the process of eversion is just the opposite of the familiar inversion and evagination seen in mammals. The eversion process, however, may not be a simple one in which the topographical position in the adult brain clearly reflects embryonic origin.

If we assume the process of eversion does, in fact, result in a highly specialized structure with unique functions, then, of course, the study of the teleost telencephalon would not likely provide us with much information regarding the functional evolution of the vertebrate cerebrum (see Bernstein, 1970; Hodos, 1970). Ontogenetic differences across species do not always imply functional diversity, however. Aronson (1967) has suggested that the process of eversion is not necessarily one which results in specialized function; on the contrary, it may be "an adaptation to fit the forebrain into the smallest possible space" (p. 190). If this is the case, avoidance of identifying nuclear regions of the teleost telencephalon by using only regional descriptions (e.g., dorsal, ventral) may be counterproductive to good science because it eliminates one source of hypotheses about the participation of these telencephalic structures in behavior.

Similarities of structural relations between the teleost telencephalon and that of other, higher vertebrates have convinced many investigators that eversion is not a crucial issue. Schnitzlein (1968), among others (e.g., Droogleever-Fortuyn, 1961), has pointed out that the anatomical relationships, cell types, and fiber connections among major nuclear regions of the teleost telencephalon are similar to those found in other vertebrates. On this basis, he has characterized these nuclear regions of the teleost telencephalon; these are illustrated in Fig. 2. The primordial hippocampal formation is situated dorsomedially, "characterized by its position between the primordial general pallium and the precommissural septal area" (Schnitzlein, 1968). Ventrally situated is the olfactory tubercle which extends somewhat ventromedially. The amygdaloid complex, which consists of the corticomedial and basolateral amygdala, and the piriform area are located laterally. Dorsally, between the hippocampal formation and the piriform region, is the primordial general pallium. These structures form what is termed the pallial tissue layer. The subpallial tissue layer consists of the precommissural septum, located ventromedially, and the striatum, situated centrally, deep within the hemisphere. In mammals, these structures constitute a part of what is known as the "limbic system." Although the characterization of pallial structures is disputed (Scalia and Ebbesson, 1971), the identification of the subpallial structures is generally agreed upon by most investigators (Aronson and Kaplan, 1968). Notwithstanding the similar anatomical relationships between the nuclear regions of fish and higher vertebrates, across teleost species there appear dramatic enlargements and diminutions—and even additions—of certain pallial areas; moreover, most of the experimental studies have been done on species, such as members of the family Cyprinidae, which have less highly differentiated telencephalons. Care must be taken, therefore, when possible generalizations and extrapolations suggest themselves.

Despite what appear to be overwhelming obstacles in an evolutionary approach to the understanding of the relationship between the teleost telencephalon and mammalian limbic system, many workers believe such an approach to be promising (Isaacson, 1974; Ebbesson *et al.,* 1972; Ingle, 1965b; Aronson, 1970). In addition, because the teleost telencephalon possesses no neocortex, the teleost fish provides a unique biological preparation for the study of the limbic system with certain advantages over mammalian subjects. For example, surgical invasion of limbic structures in mammals is accompanied by collateral damage to neocortical structures, which could, in turn, be directly or indirectly responsible for any behavioral deficits observed. Neurobehavioral analysis of the teleost can provide information on the role the paleolimbic structures play before the introduction of the neocortex and perhaps provide some insights into the behavioral contribution of the "added" neocortex in other vertebrates.

C. Telencephalon as Rhinencephalon

The olfactory nerves, which arise from the nasal mucosa, terminate in the olfactory bulbs, the latter being located in most teleost species just anterior to the telencephalon. The olfactory bulbs, in turn, send fibers via the olfactory tracts to the telencephalon and possibly in some species to the contralateral bulb. Apparently, there are also *efferent* fibers from the hemispheres to the bulbs (Döving and Gemne, 1966; Hara and Gorbman, 1967). That is, the telencephalon receives afferents from the olfactory bulbs which, in turn, are modulated by the telencephalon itself. Behavioral and other physiological evidence have corroborated the telencephalon's obvious role in olfaction.

Wrede (1932), extending the earlier work of Strieck (1925), conducted a series of experiments also involving olfactory and gustatory discriminations. By comparing blinded, but otherwise intact, minnows (*Phoxinus* sp., family Cyprinidae) plus blinded, telencephalon-ablated minnows on their responses to various stimuli, she demonstrated that although the intact subjects both "smelled" and "tasted," telencephalon-ablated subjects could only make discriminations via their sense of taste. When required to discriminate stimuli which activate both receptor systems (e.g., skin slime) from those that activate only one (e.g., salt), the ablated group made many mistakes. Thus, although ablated fish can still detect the slime, skin slime is easily confused with some other substances because integration of the two systems is no longer possible. This evidence, then, supports the conclusions of Herrick (1924) that the telencephalon of teleosts functions to integrate taste and smell.

Olfactory function has also been demonstrated by degenerative anatomical techniques. For example, Scalia and Ebbesson (1971) have used axonal degeneration to determine the terminus of olfactory fibers; they found three major synaptic fields, and these are all in the ventral telencephalon. In addition, they found that the bulk of the telencephalon does *not* receive primary olfactory fibers.

D. Rhinencephalon vs. Limbic System: The Leftovers Don't Smell

Form and function, the bases of homology, are inseparable partners in the evolutionary development of the brain. If, indeed, one's goal is the understanding of this evolutionary process through the study of the function of the teleost telencephalon, then one must necessarily encourage pursuit of the question of homology.

The basis for determining the existence of homologous relationships between neural structures is not absolute; various criteria have been used, either by themselves or in combination with others. Similarities of topography/topology, fiber connections, and cell origin and structure are those most often employed; others include histochemical composition, electrophysical activity, *and the behavior* of the organism following lesions and/or stimulation of the area in question (Campbell and Hodos, 1970). The use of homologous terminology in the naming of the nuclear areas of the teleost telencephalon, for example, is at present based upon similarities of topological relationships, fiber connections, and cytoarchitecture between teleost telencephalon and mammalian limbic system. Unfortunately, the question of homology is typically left to stand on these anatomical bases alone. This is unfortunate because the behavioral data base provides dramatic parallels as well. Indeed, Campbell and Hodos (1970) argue vigorously that a multilevel convergence of evidence—anatomical, physiological, *and behavioral*—is necessary to answer questions of homology, any one criterion alone being insufficient.

In pursuit of the question of homology, then, we will briefly explore the physiological and behavioral similarity between the teleost telencephalon and the mammalian limbic system. Mammalian limbic structures were at one time commonly referred to as rhinencephalic—smell brain. Herrick (1933) and Papez (1937) asserted early that limbic structures participate in memorial and associative processes and provide the neural bases for emotional experience. Yet, experimental studies which followed did not always confirm these assertions. Part of the difficulty was the ambiguity of what constituted "emotion," and the different constellations of structures which authors subsumed under the rubric, "rhinencephalon." Pribram and Kruger's (1954) comprehensive treatise on the subject attempted to alleviate the prevailing disquiet. Based upon the type of connections between each telencephalic structure and the olfactory bulb, they characterized three systems of the rhinencephalon. This tripartition consisted of (a) the primary olfactory system, structures which have direct connections with the olfactory bulb; (b) the second system which receives fibers from the primary olfactory system but has no direct connections with the olfactory bulb; and (c) the third system which receives fibers from the second system but not from the first system or olfactory bulb. The second and third systems are both connected by efferents to the hypothalamus.

The systematic delineation of these telencephalic structures which are *not directly* olfactory in nature demanded further research into their functions. Why, for example, is the reduction of the primary olfactory system in microsmatic animals (e.g., cat, monkey) not accompanied by a similar reduction of the second and third systems. The presumption is that this is because these two systems subserve other than olfaction. Research on the structures belonging to Pribram and Kruger's second and third systems—presently grouped under the term "limbic system"—has revealed many and varied functions of limbic structures. Neuropsychological (behavioral–physiological) research has shown that selective limbic ablations and lesions in mammals have little impact upon general sensorimotor functions. Such lesions, however, have dramatic effects upon species-specific behavior. Lesions of the amygdala, hippocampus, and cingulate disrupt threat behavior, aggression, and social dominance (e.g., Rosvold *et al.*, 1954; Dicks *et al.*, 1969; Bard, 1950) and impair and disorder reproductive and parental behaviors—though all components seem available (e.g., Kimble *et al.*, 1967; Michal, 1965; Slotnick, 1967). In addition, Fuller *et al.* (1957) describe a loss of initiative. In learning contexts, limbic ablations do not impair classical conditioning—at least of autonomic responses (Shumilina, 1966; Thompson, 1964). In contrast, hippocampal lesions impair delayed response learning (Rosvold and Sczwarcbart, 1964) and reversal learning (Mahut, 1971; Kimble, 1969) and produce perseveration and reduced response flexibility (Butter, 1969). Septal lesions increase resistance to extinction of simple appetitive tasks (Butters and Rosvold, 1968), and increase the persistance of some responses—a loss of inhibition (Zucker, 1965; Ellen *et al.*, 1964). The most dramatic effects of various limbic lesions are on avoidance behaviors; such lesions impair both passive and active (McCleary, 1961; Brady *et al.*, 1954) avoidance learning as well as resulting in loss of previously acquired active avoidance responses (Tracy and Harrison, 1956; Olton and Isaacson, 1968).*

There is a striking identity between fish and mammals of the behavioral competences that are unimpaired (e.g., classical conditioning) or impaired (e.g.,

---

*Isaacson (1974) provides an excellent overview of current research of the limbic system [although in a discussion of the evolution of this structure, he erroneously asserts (p. 223) that telencephalon ablation in fish does not drastically interfere with learning tasks].

reversal learning, tasks involving delays, and avoidance learning) by invasion of telencephalic structures. The convergence of behavioral and neuroanatomical evidence just sketched strongly supports a homologous relationship between the telencephalon of teleosts and higher vertebrates. It should not be surprising, then, that there exist similarities of theory as well.

The behavioral deficits in limbic-lesioned mammals have led to assertion that mammalian limbic structures participate in (a) short-term memorial (Scoville and Milner, 1957), (b) general arousal (Kaada, 1960), (c) selective inhibitory (Douglas and Pribram, 1966), and (d) motivational and/or reinforcer (Gloor, 1960; Vanderwolf, 1971) functions or processes. The hypotheses offered to account for the effects of teleost telencephalic ablations are similar to those for mammalian limbic functions.

As we next review the theory regarding the functions of the teleost telencephalon, we will see how behavioral and physiological parallels between the mammalian limbic system and teleost telencephalon have led to parallel theorizing. We will also discover, in our discussion of the methodology how these theoretical parallels have, in turn, suggested similar methodological treatment. Certainly, whatever the final answer to the question of homology—and the data do not warrant finality at this point—the issue has been, and continues to be, a heuristic device of considerable merit.

II. ANALYSIS OF THE ROLE OF THE TELENCEPHALON

A. Critical Examination of Hypotheses

Despite the fact that inferences regarding the function of the teleost telencephalon parallel the carefully formulated theoretical explanations of the mammalian limbic system, attempts to account theoretically for the considerable selective, specific effects of telencephalic ablation in teleosts are generally more informal and imprecise. The most serious flaw of the hypotheses we shall consider is their failure to integrate the deficits observed in *both* species-specific and learned behaviors. These attempts might be viewed as exemplary of what Weiskrantz (1968) would call the "tinkering" phase of theory building; that is, in its early stages, "the only validation [of an inference] depends on the utility of the inference itself and on the consequences that can be derived from it" (p. 413). Having served research well in this regard, we propose that a present evaluation of hypotheses be made in terms of their potential ability to (a) account for the existing learning data, (b) integrate, parsimoniously, the disruptive effects of telencephalon ablation on learned behaviors with those of species-specific behaviors, and (c) make substantive predictions. In a paper dealing with theoretical issues such as these, the review of the data and the discussion of current theory raise a question of sequence. Our decision has been to discuss the theory first, indicating as we go along the basic observations which led to formulation of these hypotheses. Although their relative merits will be more obvious later in our review of the data, acquaintance with the hypotheses will aid the reader in the conceptualization of the effects of telencephalon ablation in teleosts. Nonetheless, we will not attempt an exhaustive review of the bases and criticisms of these hypotheses. A more thorough treatment of current hypotheses can be found in Flood *et al.* (1976); we will here try to merely build upon and extend their review.

We should first like to make the reader aware that the term ''hypothesis'' will be used loosely here; the attention given the function of the teleost telencephalon consists mostly of sketchily defined inferences with few of the formal properties characteristic of hypotheses. Nonetheless, these inferences about telencephalon function align themselves with one of four explanatory notions: short-term memory, nonspecific arousal, inhibition of dominant responses, and utilization of secondary reinforcement. Because of the informality of these hypotheses, then, we will here attempt merely to evaluate their potential viability, pointing out where revision is necessary if they are to merit serious consideration.

Before we begin consideration of hypotheses of telencephalic function, note should be made that except for olfaction, sensory functions of the telencephalon-ablated teleost are unimpaired. With respect to vision, Nolte (1932) reported that the telencephalon was not essential for color vision in sticklebacks (*Gasterosteus aculeatus,* family Gasterosteidae), minnows (*Phoxinus* sp., family Cyprinidae), and carp (*Carassius carassius,* family Cyprinidae). More recent data (Bernstein, 1961a, 1962) from goldfish (*Carassius auratus,* family Cyprinidae) have confirmed that, at most, only a temporary suppression of color vision ensued following telencephalic extirpation. Also, sensitivity to brightness was unimpaired in ablated goldfish (Bernstein, 1961b). Finally, Hosch (1936) reported that shape perception was not disrupted by ablation in minnows. In modalities other than vision, temperature sensing by European minnows (*Phoxinus* sp.) (Berwein, 1941) and sensitivity to pain in goldfish (Savage, 1969b) are unaffected by ablation of the telencephalon.

1. Short-Term Memory

The short-term memory hypothesis (Beritoff, 1971; Savage, 1968a,b, 1969a,b; Peeke *et al.* 1972) suggests that the telencephalon is integral to the functioning of a temporary ''holding'' system for event representations as well as the transfer of this event information from short- to long-term memory. This hypothesis was based upon the observation that ablated fish were impaired in certain tasks whose commonality appeared to be that the signal-to-respond, the response, and the reinforcer were not temporally contiguous (e.g., tasks in which delivery of the reinforcer was delayed a few seconds and tasks involving avoidance learning). Telencephalon-ablated goldfish were impaired in a simple operant task when a delay was introduced between the response and the reinforcer, but were not impaired when reinforcement was immediate (Savage, 1969b). In avoidance tasks, these animals do not evidence maintained activation following onset of the avoidance signal, as if they have ''forgotten'' the cue (Savage, 1969a).

The short-term memory process itself is thought to be a temporary and rapidly fading bioelectrical coding of information which normally is transferred to long-term memory, an altogether different process based upon protein synthesis (Agranoff and Davis, 1968). Removal of the telencephalon which was hypothesized to be a potentiator of the short-term memory process would disrupt the normal transfer to long-term memory and hence impair task acquisition. However, it was argued that manipulations which might intensify neural traces of events could compensate, at least in part, for the loss of the short-term memory potentiating function of the telencephalon. Consistent with this view, Savage (1968b) observed that massing of trials ameliorated the deficits of telencephalon-ablated goldfish in avoidance learning. Indeed, when normal and ablated fish were trained in an avoidance task under spaced and massed conditions, the massed-trial ablated group performed nearly as well as the massed-trial normal group. Ablates in the spaced-trial condition performed the poorest of all groups, as would be expected. Similarly, Flood and Overmier (1971) reported that massing of trials of a food-getting task facilitated acquisition.

Data obtained in Savage's own laboratory, however, have provided a difficult hurdle for the short-term memory hypothesis. In a more direct test of this hypothesis, Overmier and Savage (1974) compared normal and ablated goldfish in a classical trace conditioning paradigm, in which the conditioned stimulus is terminated a few seconds prior to the onset of the unconditioned stimulus. Unfortunately for the hypothesis, there were *no* differences between the performances of normals and ablates, suggesting that telencephalon-ablated fish are capable of forming an association between the shock stimulus and the ''memory trace'' of the signal presented earlier. Of course, one might argue that the telencephalic short-term ''memory'' is of stimulus–response or response–reinforcement events, and *not* the stimulus–stimulus events of classical conditioning.

Although the short-term memory hypothesis still remains a viable explanatory device in the domain of learned behaviors, it has not generally been applied to the explanation of the species-specific behaviors of telencephalon-ablated fish, though Peeke *et al.* (1972) have used it to account for the failure of telencephalon-ablated goldfish to show long-term habituation of futile predatory responses. This lack of integration of ethological and learned behaviors is, perhaps, its most serious flaw as it is difficult to understand how the loss of a memory subsystem would produce the many and varied species-specific deficits that are observed in telencephalon-ablated fish.

2. Nonspecific Arousal

The nonspecific arousal hypothesis, which accounts for behavioral impairments in terms of the loss of a telencephalic arousal function (Herrick, 1933; Aronson, 1948, 1970; Aronson and Kaplan, 1963, 1965, 1968; Kaplan and Aronson, 1967, 1969), is an especially compelling inference in the light of both the activity data and much of the ethological literature on telencephalon-ablated teleosts. Polimanti (1913), Janzen (1933), and Hosch (1936) early observed in several species that the spontaneous activity level of ablates decreases substantially, although they are quite capable of normal locomotion. Janzen, for example, describes ablated goldfish as suffering from a lack of "initiative."

Extirpation of the telencephalon also affects species-specific behaviors, resulting in increased thresholds for elicitation, but generally not in their timing nor in their organization (e.g., Hale, 1956b; Aronson and Kaplan, 1968; but see Segaar, 1965). From these data, the telencephalon would appear to subserve a simple energizer or arousal function for behaviors organized and integrated in other, lower centers in the brain.

The nonspecific arousal hypothesis could potentially be applicable to the full range of behavioral phenomena, species-specific as well as learned behaviors; but, as presently formulated, it has difficulty in explaining the selectivity with which the learned behaviors are affected. For example, (a) classically conditioned and escape, but *not* avoidance, responses are readily learned, and (b) a discrimination problem, but *not* a simple operant response whose reinforcer is delayed a few seconds, is learned following telencephalon ablation (see Flood *et al.*, 1976). While a corollary to this hypothesis suggests that "simple" learning tasks should be least affected by extirpation of the telencephalon, the empirically constructed "continuum of difficulty" that would result—with, for example, classical conditioning, escape, and discrimination training at one end and avoidance and simple operant-with-delay of reinforcement training at the other—is, logically, untenable.

Another serious flaw of the arousal hypothesis is that it has little predictive power. "Facilitation" by the telencephalon can be achieved either through inhibitory *or* excitatory processes (Aronson and Kaplan, 1968); thus, some behaviors normally excited by the telencephalon would suffer deficits following telencephalon ablation, while other behaviors normally inhibited or attenuated by the telencephalon would be expected to increase following the ablation. Because this hypothesis itself offers no independent means by which to judge whether a particular behavior is modulated through excitatory or inhibitory mechanisms, the nonspecific arousal hypothesis can do little more than offer *ad hoc* explanations for the behavioral alterations we observe. For example, although one observes that telencephalon-ablated goldfish extinguish sooner in avoidance tasks (Hainsworth *et al.*, 1967) and are generally less active, they take *longer* to extinguish responding in appetitive tasks (Flood and Overmier, 1971); in the ethological domain, although they do not exhibit as much aggressive behavior, nest digging behavior is occassionally increased markedly (in sticklebacks, Segaar, 1965). If the nonspecific arousal hypothesis is to serve any useful function in our understanding of the telencephalon, the mechanism(s) of this "facilitation," as well as the means by which to determine how behaviors will be affected, must be more precisely formulated.

3. Inhibition of Dominant Responses

Outside the context of the nonspecific arousal hypothesis, the importance of the role of inhibition has received much attention. When the scattered and loosely formulated references to a telencephalic inhibitory mechanism are pooled, a third process—and what might be considered a corollary to nonspecific arousal— emerges. It is that *some* of the behavioral deficits which result from telencephalon ablation are attributable to the loss of the ability to inhibit dominant responses, either innate or learned. We should like to point out that this "hypothesis" has been advanced only as an explanation of certain specified behavioral alterations. Segaar (1965) postulated a failure of telencephalic inhibition to account for the increase of nest fanning and sand digging in sticklebacks following ablation. Ingle (1965a) reasoned that inhibition might account for the deficits of telencephalon-ablated fish in complex appetitive tasks: ablates could no longer inhibit competing exploratory responses.

The attention given this hypothesis by Flood *et al.* (1976), however, has demonstrated that a great deal more of the behavior of telencephalon-ablated fish can be explained by reference to loss of inhibition of dominant responses. In the domain of learned behaviors, the failure to inhibit incompatible, species-specific defense reactions (e.g., freezing) can explain the avoidance deficits of ablates. Also, the impairments of operated fish in (a) position habit reversal in T mazes in which, for example, left swimming must come to replace right swimming (Warren, 1961; paradise fish, *Macropodus opercularis,* family Anabantidae; Frank *et al.,* 1972: goldfish), and (b) passive avoidance learning in which, for example, subjects must cease to enter a place they previously frequented (Overmier and Flood, 1969: goldfish), are explicable as failures to inhibit a previously learned response when the correct response is changed. Bridging the gap between the domains of learned and species-specific behaviors, Peeke *et al.* (1972) observed that telencephalon-ablated goldfish emitted many more (i.e., failed to inhibit) predatory bites at brine shrimp enclosed in a glass tube than did normals, and again, unlike normals, they did not evidence any transfer of learning when this unattainable food was offered on successive days.

Indeed, this hypothesis has little difficulty handling most of learned behavioral impairments with the exception of the temporal delay data. This exception may prove to be a difficult hurdle, however, for it is not easily understood how dominant responses could so suddenly—and severely—interfere with an already acquired response when the reinforcer is then delayed a few seconds. Readily amenable to testing in the sphere of learned behaviors, a problem occurs when one wants to test the hypothesis' viability in the ethological domain. The lack of some independent means to judge "dominant" and "nondominant" behaviors *within* the species-specific hierarchy reduces the present definition to circular reasoning; that is, the behavior persists because it is dominant and is dominant because it persists. In addition to persistence, per se, one would want some independent and corroborating measure of a behavior's dominance; otherwise, with respect to naturalistic behaviors, at least, the inhibition of dominant response hypothesis, like the nonspecific arousal hypothesis, has little predictive power.

4. Utilization of Secondary Reinforcement

The last hypothesis to be considered is, interestingly enough, the progeny of the two-process mediational theory of learning (Rescorla and Solomon, 1967), originally developed by Mowrer (1947) to account for avoidance behavior and extended to appetitive behaviors as well (Spence, 1956). This theory purports that avoidance behavior involves two separate and sequential processes: (a) the classical conditioning of motivational reactions to a signal, and (b) the instrumental learning of a response, in part, attributable to this conditioned motivation. Avoidance behavior, for example, is thought to be the result of elicitation of a classically conditioned motivational state ("fear") evoking a response, the reinforcement for which is the termination of the signal and its associated conditioned aversive motivation. This type of reinforcer is termed "conditioned" or "secondary" since, to be effective, it must have a history of being paired with an unconditioned or primary reinforcer, one which is capable of reinforcing the responses without previous training.

Learned avoidance behavior of teleost fish is the most severely affected by telencephalon ablation; an explanation of this disruption might be found in two-process theory. Because classical conditioning proceeds normally in telencephalon-ablated fish, the impairment in avoidance learning would necessarily have to lie in the instrumental process. The instrumental process involves both the evocation of the response by the classically conditioned motivational state *and* the reinforcement of the response by the termination of this state; thus, either or both aspects of the instrumental process might be impaired by ablation. Testing of the "response evocation" component revealed, however, that after telencephalon-ablated goldfish were trained to avoid shock in the presence of a *tone* by shuttle crossing and were subsequently classically conditioned with *light*–shock pairings, they were capable of "transferring" the shuttle response to instances of light presentation in the shuttlebox (Overmier and Starkman, 1974). Thus, this transfer-of-control experiment demonstrated that the classically conditioned mediational (''fear'') state is, indeed, capable of evoking the response in telencephalon-ablated fish.

Two-process theory leaves but one alternative to account for the avoidance deficit of ablates: the telencephalon ''is involved in the utilization of changes in conditioned motivational reactions as reinforcers ('secondary' or 'conditioned' reinforcers) for the acquisition and maintenance of behaviors'' (Flood *et al.,* 1976). That is, the avoidance behavior of ablated fish is impaired because, although the shock signal elicits the conditioned motivational state and this is capable of evoking a response, the termination of this signal does not function as a secondary reinforcer for the telencephalon-ablated fish as it does for the normal animal.

In the context of other learned behaviors, the secondary reinforcement hypothesis would predict that *any* behaviors which involve the utilization of secondary reinforcement for their acquisition or maintenance would be impaired. The avoidance case is one of secondary *negative* reinforcement, since the *termination* of a noxious warning stimulus reinforces the response; *positive* (appetitive) secondary reinforcement should be equally ineffective for the telencephalon-ablated teleost.

Indeed, disruption of positive secondary reinforcement is implicated in the explanation of ablates' inability to acquire or maintain a response under delayed reinforcement conditions. It has been demonstrated in mammals (Grice, 1948) that, under conditions of short delays of primary reinforcement, secondary reinforcers are necessary to bridge the delay; elimination of these conditioned secondary reinforcers greatly impairs both response acquisition and maintenance in normal monkeys and rats. Because telencephalon-ablated goldfish are impaired by short delays of primary reinforcement which do not disrupt normal fish (Savage, 1969b), the hypothesis that the telencephalon mediates secondary reinforcement is made plausible. Of course, further testing of the viability of the secondary reinforcement hypothesis is essential but, fortunately, operant psychology offers well-developed experimental methodologies dealing with the subject of secondary reinforcement.

B. "Secondary" Reinforcement and Species-Specific Behaviors

A ''major shortcoming'' of this secondary reinforcement hypothesis, admit its authors, is its *apparent* lack of relevance to naturalistic behaviors. It has been demonstrated, however, that, in fish as well as other animals, some species-specific events—sight of a rival male (Thompson, 1963; Siamese fighting fish, *Betta splendens,* family Anabantidae) or a courting female (Sevenster, 1968: stickleback), for example—may serve as reinforcers for a variety of responses arbitrarily selected by the experimenter. This, of course, cannot be construed as proof that species-specific behaviors are reinforced, or are reinforcing, in the context of their *naturally* occurring sequence. Yet, such results are strongly suggestive and do demonstrate their *potential* in this regard and provide a basis for closer examination of the secondary reinforcement hypothesis in naturalistic settings. Indeed, Glickman and Schiff (1967) have reviewed a body of electrical brain stimulation data in mammals which suggested to them that activation by appropriate stimuli of species-typical consummatory response patterns constitutes "reinforcement." In this regard, it is worth noting that secondary reinforcers are known to be elicitors of anticipatory consummatory (e.g., Miller and DeBold, 1965) and species-typical responses (e.g., Hogan, 1961; Bolles, 1971).

Having stepped, if but tentatively, onto the foreign soil of naturalistic behaviors, the secondary reinforcement hypothesis finds itself with somewhat of a "language" problem. The term "secondary" reinforcer, as used by learning theorists to mean a stimulus that must be paired with a "primary" reinforcer to be effective, is, at best, difficult to understand in a naturalistic setting. While Flood *et al.* (1976) explicitly state that the focus of the deficit is *secondary* reinforcement, and not reinforcement per se, this may merely reflect the context in which they developed their hypothesis; the "language problem" may not exist except in the vocabulary of operant psychology. That is to say, although the operant definition of conditioned reinforcement—efficacy through pairing—is clearly different from that of primary reinforcement and does not readily embrace species-specific reinforcement, the underlying mechanism (or mechanisms) may be such that telencephalon ablation selectively affects traditional secondary and species-specific reinforcement processes while not affecting those of primary reinforcement. The basis, then, for differentiating between reinforcers may not be pairings per se but, for example, the "strength" of the reinforcers, traditional secondary and species-specific reinforcement being weaker (defined behaviorally in terms of resistance to extinction, rate of responding, etc.) than traditional primary reinforcers (e.g., Hogan, 1974). This very approach to apparent "differences" between species-specific and traditional primary reinforcers has recently been suggested by Roper (1975), who observed that he could mimic—with the primary reinforcer food—the highly variable responding of mice for nest materials by changing the food reinforcement parameters, that is, increasing the distance between the operandum and the reinforcement dispenser, using a low level of deprivation, etc.

Successful integration by the reinforcement hypothesis (as we will henceforth refer to it) of learned and species-specific behavior requires certain assumptions: (a) reinforcement is important to the normal integrity of species-specific behavior sequences; and (b) the reinforcing properties of the terminal species-specific events are reduced in effectiveness following telencephalic ablation just as are secondary reinforcers. Given these assumptions, it follows that telencephalic ablation should disrupt species-specific behavior sequences. Additionally, these assumptions would predict that when *arbitrarily selected responses* are maintained by species-specific events as reinforcers (e.g., Thompson, 1963), telencephalic ablation should lead to a disruption of performance. If this prediction were confirmed, the data would provide evidence that secondary reinforcers and naturalistic reinforcers share some common element, whatever its basis.

The conceptualization of species-specific behaviors which the above requires is not an unreasonable one. A growing body of literature provides evidence that the opportunity to engage in species-specific behaviors is, indeed, reinforcing and that, minimally, the potential for reinforcement to serve an important function within the context of naturally occurring behavioral sequences does exist (Craig, 1918; Hinde and Steel, 1972; Rasa, 1971; Thomas, 1974). That the utilization of species-specific reinforcers will be impaired following telencephalon ablation, as is the case with secondary reinforcers, remains to be tested; however, we are optimistic, based upon observations that the opportunity to engage in aggressive behavior is reinforcing to Siamese fighting fish (Thompson, 1963) and that the aggressive behavior of this same species is disrupted following telencephalon ablation (Noble, 1939; Noble and Borne, 1941; Shapiro *et al.*, 1974).

The commonality of function with respect to learned and species-specific behaviors that we are postulating for the teleost telencephalon is an idea which gains credibility in the light of recent research in higher vertebrates. A quite similar idea is suggested by Thompson and Ledoux (1974) for the "ensemble of nervous sites" in the rat which appears to function in both the retention of learned visual discrimination tasks (that is, brightness and pattern discrimination) and this species' innate preference for the dark. When control groups and groups of rats which sustained lesions in one of ten brain regions of the "visual memory system" were tested for their dark preference, the results indicated a significantly lower preference for the dark in those rats with lesions in five of the particular sites. These regions, then, apparently subserve both learned and instinctive behaviors. The authors interpret their data to suggest that "the lesion-induced deficits seen in both classes of adaptive behavior have a *common* basis; namely, the interference with the expression (or the disruption) of associations between visual stimuli and an *emotion* (see Mowrer, 1960)" (Thompson and Ledoux, 1974, p. 79; italics ours). We view these data and the authors' interpretation as an indication that nervous structures which are implicated in the regulation of both learned and species-specific behavior may, indeed, possess commonality of function in their regulation of those behaviors, and that this commonality may be expressed via a reinforcement-like process.

If, after testing the reinforcement hypothesis in the domain of species-specific behavior, we find evidence to suggest that the utilization of species-specific reinforcement by fish is impaired following telencephalon ablation, our next endeavor will be to find this "common element" shared by species-specific and secondary reinforcement—but not, as our ethologist friends and colleagues advise, before we drop the term "secondary"!

III. TELENCEPHALON ABLATION, BEHAVIOR, AND REINFORCEMENT

A. Scheme for Organizing Data

Behaviors which are known to be affected by telencephalon ablation have traditionally been dichotomized as "learned" or "species specific." But our preceding analysis has provided a sound basis for believing that reinforcement-like processes play an important role in the control and maintenance of *all* behaviors. Our desire to account for the deficits in species-specific behaviors of telencephalon-ablated teleosts by reference to a reinforcement process impels us to organize existing data in such manner as to facilitate identification of the reinforcing event. One such scheme for organizing existing data and suggesting new research bearing on the validity of the organizing scheme appears in Table I. According to the scheme, responses and reinforcers each are conceived of as belonging to one of two generic types: (a) traditional and pan-species, or (b) naturalistic and species specific. A response/reinforcement matrix is thus created, the cells of which characterize "classes" of behavioral sequences based upon the generic type both of the response and of the stimulus which reinforces or maintains it.

Existing studies and the resulting data on the behavior of telencephalon-ablated teleosts can be classified easily in this manner. We will now review the data subsumed under each of these behavioral classes and, based upon the reinforcement hypothesis, delineate possible explanations and discuss promising lines of research which are suggested.

TABLE I

Scheme for Organizing Researches Based on the Generic Nature of Responses and Reinforcers

| | Reinforcers | |
Responses	Traditional, pan-species	Naturalistic, species-specific
Traditional, pan-species	Class 1	Class 3
Naturalistic, species-specific	Class 4	Class 2

B. Review of the Data

1. Pan-Species Reinforcers Contingent on Pan-Species Behaviors (Class 1)

Class 1 in Table I represents, not surprisingly, the largest body of literature. The familiar paradigms of learning theorists, classical and instrumental conditioning, are readily adapted to the study of the behavior of telencephalon-ablated fish. In this cell, then, nosing underwater disks and swimming over barriers, etc.—traditional, arbitrary, experimenter-selected "pan-species" behaviors— are studied, maintained by reinforcers equally arbitrarily selected and "pan-species," such as food, electric shock, etc. Here, too, we find predominant subject species: the psychologists' ubiquitous white rat is replaced, in these classical and instrumental conditioning paradigms, with the equally ubiquitous goldfish (*Carassius auratus*) and African mouthbreeder (*Tilapia* sp.). In our review of the experimental studies subsumed under this behavioral class, we will consider separately the paradigms of classical and instrumental conditioning.*

a. Classical Conditioning. A comprehensive review of the literature on the role of the telencephalon in learning by Flood *et al.* (1976) suggests that acquisition of a classically conditioned response is not at all affected by telencephalon ablation. This statement requires qualification, however, because all such classical conditioning research to date has relied on an aversive stimulus as the unconditioned stimulus (US), namely, electric shock. Flood *et al.* suggest that this experimental imbalance is probably due to the difficulties that arise with respect to the response-independent delivery of nonaversive US's like food or brain stimulation. While the latter would involve surgical techniques complicated by our lack of information on the potential reinforcement sites within the teleost brain, the former presents a difficult mechanical problem. It would be necessary, in alimentary conditioning procedures, to present the US directly into the fish's mouth to avoid confounding of classical conditioning and instrumental approach behaviors. In addition, both suggest measurement problems: one must identify a reliable, unconditioned response (UR) and conditioned response (CR) if one is to index the learning. Progress on these problems is being made, and we can anticipate being in a position to conduct alimentary classical conditioning studies in the near future (Grimm, 1960; Demski, 1973; Boyd and Gardner, 1962).

Nonetheless, the defensive classical conditioning literature based on several species, predominantly cyprinids, indicates that, when the conditioned response is measured via gross motor movements (deflection of a paddle), conditioning

---

*For basic descriptions of these paradigms, see the footnote on p. 140. For more complex clarification, comparison, and examples with fish, see Bitterman (1966).

proceeds as rapidly in ablates as in normal fish (Baru, 1951, 1955; Karamyan, 1956) regardless of stimulus modality other than olfaction, of course (Kholodov, 1960). Furthermore, the response magnitudes of normals and ablates do not differ from one another (Overmier and Curnow, 1969). A similar pattern is found when an autonomic index of conditioning, heart rate, is employed (Bernstein, 1961a,b). Moreover, equality of the conditioned bradycardia response between normal and telencephalon-ablated goldfish obtains (a) in a situation dependent upon interocular transfer (Bernstein, 1962) and (b) in both delayed conditioning and trace conditioning paradigms (Overmier and Savage, 1974). In the delay paradigm, the US is contiguous with the CS, while in the trace paradigm there is a temporal gap between them and, thus, only a "neural trace" of the CS is present during the US.

While the data indicate that defensive classical conditioning in teleosts is not affected by extirpation of the telencephalon and, by inference, suggest that the telencephalon does not participate in the classical conditioning "process," this is not true of instrumental conditioning—where decrements are considerable, albeit selective.

b. Instrumental Conditioning—Positive Reinforcement. When the response is a simple one, such as swimming from point A to point B whereupon reinforcement is obtained, no significant differences between the response times of normal and telencephalon-ablated goldfish are found (Savage, 1969b). The acquisition of this simple response is, however, profoundly slower in ablates than in normals whenever a temporal and/or spatial separation is introduced. For example, breaking a photocell beam in one area of the tank 19.2 cm from where reinforcement is subsequently obtained results in slower acquisition of this free-operant task (Savage and Swingland, 1969). Yet, telencephalon-ablated goldfish, after extended training, eventually do perform this response at the same rate as do normals (Savage 1969b). Several parameters of the acquisition of a simple response to obtain food by ablated goldfish were investigated by Flood and Overmier (1971) in a discrete trial procedure. They reported that, although at asymptote ablates do not differ from normals in any of three typical learning indices—latency to leave the start chamber, total time to swim to the goal box, and number of trials to reach asymptote—the performance of telencephalon-ablated fish early in training is significantly inferior, an effect which is ameliorated by the massing of trials. The response acquisition of ablates is best characterized as slow, initially, followed by rapid improvement—the reverse of normals. Interestingly, and we will elaborate on this finding later, Flood and Overmier also observed that, while telencephalon-ablated fish are "slow to start," once having reached asymptotic performance, they are more persistent after the withdrawal of food than normals; that is, they manifest greater resistance to extinction than normals. Hale (1956a) has reported that telencephalon-ablated sunfish (*Lepomis cyanellus,* family Centrarchidae) are slower than normals in entering the goal box of a Welty-type divided aquarium—in which subjects must swim from one compartment, through a hole in the divider, to the other, smaller compartment—and that this inferiority persists throughout training. Hale, however, terminated training after only 15 trials, probably before his subjects reached asymptote. Moreover, Hale, interested primarily in group facilitation of learning, also reports that homogeneous groups of three fish, normals or ablates, perform the task more quickly than isolates, although, again, the ablated groups are inferior to the normal groups. These data corroborate the earlier, unpublished studies of Hillowitz (1945) and Berman (1945).

The T maze is a more complicated task than the straight runway. Although Warren (1961) reported that telencephalon-ablated paradise fish made more errors in learning a positional habit in a T maze (that is, the reinforcer is always obtained in the same arm of the T), Frank *et al.* (1972) observed equivalent acquisition in goldfish. Both studies agree, however, that successive reversals of this position habit proved more difficult for ablated than for normal fish. However, as we have seen in other tasks, although they persisted in the previously learned response longer, the telencephalon-ablated fish did eventually learn the reversals to the same criterion as did the normals (Warren, 1961; Frank *et al.,* 1972). Warren (1961) also investigated the performance of telencephalon-ablated paradise fish on a series of 12 "umweg" problems of increasing difficulty. More complicated mazes than the simple T, the series was presented three times to groups of normal and telencephalon-ablated fish. When neither group showed progressive improvement, performance on individual problems was analyzed. Interestingly, the telencephalon-operated group was superior on one of the problems, the least difficult, equal to the normal group on five, and inferior on the remaining six.

A pattern is evident in the data. From the simple runway task to the umweg problem, these data would suggest a rather straightforward relationship between increasing the number of task-incompatible response alternatives available to the fish and the impairment suffered as a result of telencephalon ablation. However, data obtained from discrimination and from discriminated choice problems, other methods of increasing task "complexity" and incompatible response alternatives, preclude such simply analysis. In these, responses are reinforced when they occur in the presence of a particular stimulus (S^D) but not reinforced when they occur in the absence of that stimulus, or in the presence of a different stimulus (S^Δ). Most vertebrate organisms can learn to perform the required response in the presence of the S^D and inhibit this response in the presence of the S^Δ, even when there is no explicit "penalty" for responding during S^Δ. The discrimination problem provides, perhaps, a more unbiased assessment of performance than we have seen in that whenever the performance index is derived from *both* S^D and S^Δ conditions (e.g., percentage correct response), the spontaneously lower activity levels of the telencephalon-ablated fish cannot confound the results as it can in, say, a straight runway task where speed is the usual measure. Indeed, when the percentage of correct responses is employed, ablated goldfish do not differ from normals when they must respond in the presence, but not in the absence, of one stimulus (Kholodov, 1960) or must choose to respond to one of two stimuli (Savage, 1969b). Further, Flood (1975) reports no differences in the long-term retention of such discriminated choice behavior in this same species.

Despite the ease with which the telencephalon-ablated goldfish learned the discrimination problem of Savage (1969b), when he exposed his subjects to a 5-sec delay of reinforcement, the performance of the operated group deteriorated rapidly. Similar results are reported by Beritoff (1971) using visual, as well as auditory, stimuli.

A summary of the impact of telencephalon ablation on instrumental tasks employing positive reinforcement certainly needs to stress the selectivity with which tasks are affected. Simple instrumental tasks, either discriminative or nondiscriminative, are minimally affected. With increasing numbers of alternative task-incompatible responses available, increasing deficits appear—but only in the acquisition of these tasks. Finally, delays of reinforcement produce substantial impairment of both simple and complex behaviors. We view this latter impairment as quite independent of discrimination behavior per se because as we have previously noted, telencephalon-ablated fish are extremely sensitive to delays of but a few seconds in the simplest of locomotor response tasks.

We have noted earlier that delays of reinforcement are thought to be bridged by secondary reinforcers; therefore, these data are clearly consonant with the reinforcement hypothesis. With respect to the remaining observations, the ablates' absence of impairment in discrimination problems, usually regarded as "complex" tasks, may seem anomolous juxtaposed with findings which suggest a relationship between increasing task difficulty, in terms of task-incompatible responses, and the impairment shown by these animals. Both findings, however, may be consistent with the reinforcement hypothesis. Early in the acquisition of tasks with many incompatible responses, the primary reinforcer is much delayed; under such conditions of delay, initial learning must depend more heavily on the utilization of secondary reinforcers in the maze. With extended training, increments in mastery of the task would lead to shorter and shorter delays of reinforcement, and the dependence on conditioned reinforcers would be diminished relative to that on the primary reinforcer. Hence, any impairment suffered by telencephalon-ablated fish should be primarily in the *acquisition* of these tasks, as has been reported.

Discrimination tasks, on the other hand, do not necessarily require utilization of secondary reinforcers—at least in mammals (Bauer and Lawrence, 1953). This latter observation suggests a straightforward test of the reinforcement hypothesis. We know that S^D's acquire the ability to reinforce behavior through association with the primary reinforcer, although they do not necessarily act in that capacity in the simple discrimination task. The classical test of this notion (Skinner, 1936) involved presenting the S^D, following discrimination training, contingent upon some response and observing whether the rate of that response increased. Similarly, one might compare normal and telencephalon-ablated fish with respect to the reinforcing property of S^D's. The reinforcement hypothesis would predict that, while these stimuli may function quite well as S^D's for both groups, they are capable of functioning as conditioned reinforcers to strengthen new responses only in the normal group.

c. Instrumental Conditioning—Negative Reinforcement.

Even more striking than the selectivity with which positively reinforced tasks are affected by telencephalon ablation is that which is observed in instrumental training with aversive stimuli. Despite evidence which suggests that ablates do not differ from normals in their responsiveness to shock is measured by activity levels of goldfish (Savage, 1969b), it is within the paradigms of escape and avoidance that we find the most marked contrast in the degree of impairment resulting from ablation.

Escape behavior per se has not been studied in telencephalon-ablated fish. Nonetheless, information can be obtained from the trials of avoidance training during which the animals failed to avoid (i.e., failed to respond during the signal, prior to shock), because trials in which an avoidance response is not made is then similar to an escape training trial. When the median latencies of a response on such ''escape'' trials were compared, Hainsworth *et al.* (1967) found no difference between normal and telencephalon-ablated goldfish. These findings were confirmed by Savage (1969a). However, deficits in escape behavior do appear in ablated animals when the task permits great variability of responding. Kaplan and Aronson (1967) reported that, in an avoidance task in which the opportunities for variability of responding were so great as to initially require guiding of the response, the escape behavior of ablated African mouthbreeders was poorer than that of controls. Earlier in our review of the positive reinforcement literature, we noted that the opportunity for variability of responding was an important variable in the degree of impairment suffered by telencephalon-ablated fish. Nonetheless, we need to follow-up these observations in a pure escape training task, unconfounded by the methodological problems that the opportunity for avoidance creates.

Study of avoidance tasks dominated limbic lesion research for many years (McCleary, 1966) and continues to be a valuable tool in the understanding of the mammalian limbic system. Probably as a result, the avoidance task has found its way into the behavioral study of the teleost telencephalon as well. The available literature suggests that extirpation of the teleost telencephalon significantly impairs learning all types of avoidance tasks. Hainsworth *et al.* (1967) compared the avoidance behavior of normal, sham-operated, and telencephalon-ablated goldfish in a simple, one-way shuttlebox. When the telencephalon was removed prior to avoidance training, acquisition of the correct response in these animals was severely impaired or prevented; when the ablation was performed after training, the previously learned response was all but lost. Additional experiments (Kaplan and Aronson, 1967; Savage, 1968a, 1969a; Fujita and Oi, 1969; Overmier and Gross, 1974) have confirmed these findings in a two-way shuttlebox; furthermore, the deficits obtained appear to be independent of species of fish (cf. African mouthbreeder, goldfish), signal modality, and length of the signal shock interval (Savage, 1969a).

Dewsbury and Bernstein (1969) reported that, in a "shuttlebox" with a negligible barrier, telencephalon-ablated and control goldfish do not differ; but in the same shuttlebox with a larger barrier, differences are substantial. These observations led them to believe that the reported avoidance deficits were merely an artifact of "behavioral alterations" present in telencephalon-ablated fish, not at all related to these animals' ability to learn an avoidance task. More recent evidence, however, suggests that, in intact goldfish, aversive classical conditioning results in a CR which simulates "avoidance behavior" (Woodard and Bitterman, 1973; Scobie and Fallon, 1974). To the extent that the experimentally designated "avoidance response," crossing the barrier, resembles the elicited unconditioned response of gross motor movement and "flight" behavior, the "avoidance task" may, in fact, reduce to classical conditioning of a motor response to the signal, and be only artifactually related to avoidance contingencies per se. The more difficult and/or complex the response—e.g., the larger the barrier—the less likely it is for the barrier crossing response to be elicited by the unconditioned aversive stimulus. This possible confounding, juxtaposed with the knowledge that ablates do classically condition as well as normals, suggests that the Dewsbury and Bernstein experiment needs to be replicated with the appropriate classical conditioning control group.

Much earlier in our discussion of learned behaviors, we noted that, because the ablated fish are less active than normals, an analysis based upon latencies of active responses would be biased in favor of normal fish and could artifactually account for some observed deficits. A similar problem arises in the active avoidance task, too, because the fish is called upon to perform the requisite response during the short signal period if it is to avoid. Thus, failure to avoid could be attributed to lowered activity levels rather than to an interference with learning ability. Data derived from *passive* avoidance and discriminated go/no-go avoidance tasks, however, refute this argument; the learning indices of both of these tasks are based not on vigor of responding but on withholding of responding. Overmier and Flood (1969) first trained goldfish in an instrumental appetitive discrimination in which swimming into a goal box during the presentation of S^D was reinforced with food. Following criterion performance, fish were tested in a *passive* avoidance task in which, by remaining in the start box during the S^D, shock could be avoided; swimming into the goal box resulted in shock. As before, telencephalon-ablated fish were severely hampered in the acquisition of the passive avoidance response. Also, Savage reported that not only were ablated goldfish impaired in a simple discriminative go/no-go avoidance task, when there was no contingency present for responding in S^Δ (1969a), but when incorrect responses (responses in the presence of S^Δ) were punished, ablates avoided shock more poorly in *both* the go and no-go task components than did controls (1968a)! This clearly rules out activity decrements as a potential basis for explanation of the inferiority of ablated fish.

Despite the large difference between normal and telencephalon-ablated fish in avoidance tasks, we should like to note that ablates *do* eventually learn to avoid if training is continued for a sufficiently great number of trials (Hainsworth *et al.,* 1967; Kaplan and Aronson, 1967; Overmier and Gross, 1974; Overmier and Starkman, 1974). The performance of these animals, however, is quite variable and unstable during the course of acquisition (e.g., Kaplan and Aronson, 1967), the instability being further demonstrated by faster extinction of the avoidance response in ablated animals than in normals (e.g., Hainsworth *et al.,* 1967).

A proper summary of the effects of telencephalon ablation on avoidance behavior is equivocal pending systematic replication of the Dewsbury and Bernstein (1969) experiment. The available data strongly suggest, however, that ablation consistently and reliably interferes with *all* types of avoidance learning, regardless of the species, signal modality, shock parameters, or task demands. Of all the deficits in learned behaviors suffered by telencephalon-ablated teleost fish, the impairment in the acquisition of avoidance is clearly the most dramatic.

The reinforcement hypothesis, because it is the progeny of two-factor avoidance theory, accounts easily for these data. If we assume, with contemporary avoidance theory, that the instrumental avoidance response—either active or passive—is reinforced primarily by the termination of "fear" motivation elicited by the warning signal for shock, a secondary reinforcer, it follows that disruption and impairment of the utilization of secondary reinforcement would greatly hamper the learning of such avoidance responses.

More interesting, however, is the ability of the reinforcement hypothesis to account for the decreased resistance to extinction of telencephalon-ablated fish in instrumental avoidance tasks, especially as it contrasts with the increased resistance to extinction of ablates in food-reinforced tasks. Extinction, as it is typically defined and employed in experiments cited above, is removal of the primary reinforcer, positive or negative, from the situation. It should be obvious, however, that extinction procedures so conceived are not symmetrical with respect to appetitive and avoidance instrumental tasks. In appetitive tasks, the removal of the primary reinforcer (food) results in a situation not previously encountered, while in negatively reinforced tasks, removal of the primary reinforcer (shock) duplicates exactly the state of affairs representative of successful avoidance! Reference to this asymmetry of extinction procedures coupled with current theories of extinction can help us to understand why telencephalon-ablated fish extinguish most rapidly in avoidance tasks while normal fish extinguish most rapidly in appetitive tasks.

When extinction is instituted in avoidance tasks, shock is no longer presented when the subject fails to respond; ''avoidance'' responses continue to terminate the shock signal and its conditioned aversive state which, according to currently supported theory (Solomon and Wynne, 1953; Solomon and Brush, 1956), is *exactly* what reinforces avoidance behavior in the first place. Thus, the avoidance behavior of normal fish should continue. In contrast, it should be expected that telencephalon-ablated fish, for which such secondary reinforcement is disrupted or ineffective, would discontinue responding sooner than normals.

Compare this with the situation commonly thought to exist in the extinction of positively reinforced behavior. According to the currently accepted theory (Amsel, 1958), nonreinforcement of previously reinforced responses, as in extinction, produces a state of ''frustration'' in the animal; this frustration reaction is an aversive motivational state—a notion, incidently, supported by ethological data (Tinbergen, 1952; McFarland, 1965). Other behaviors, which do not have a past history of reinforcement in this context, do not produce this state of frustration. Because the termination of frustration, like the termination of all conditioned aversive states, can function as a reinforcer for behavior, behaviors *incompatible* with the previously learned response are reinforced by frustration reduction and gradually come to replace the now unreinforced frustration-inducing response.

The reinforcement hypothesis maintains that telencephalon-ablated fish cannot utilize reinforcement which results when such conditioned aversive states are terminated. For these animals, then, incompatible behaviors will not be reinforced by frustration reduction, and the learned behavior should persist longer. Additionally, to the extent that reversal learning is a ''compound'' task of learning a new response *plus* extinguishing the old response, this analysis of the increased resistance to extinction of ablated fish provides some purchase on the explanation of the poorer reversal learning by ablated fish.

The reinforcement hypothesis seems to fare quite well as an explanatory device of learned behavior. Because we know that extirpation of the telencephalon impairs naturalistic behaviors as well, it remains for us to demonstrate that a disrupted reinforcement mechanism can account for the impairment. To do this one must first show (a) that the terminal species-specific events of selected natural behavior chains (e.g., courtship) can function as reinforcers for arbitrarily selected operant responses, and then (b) that telencephalic ablation which disrupts the natural species-specific behavior sequence also eradicates the power of the terminal species-specific event to reinforce an arbitrary operant. Of course, as a control, one must also demonstrate that the selected arbitrary operant continues to be capable of being controlled by previously effective pan-species reinforcers. Second, if we can additionally show that the species-specific behavior sequence can be controlled by primary pan-species reinforcers and that such control survives ablation of the telencephalon, then we will have taken two important steps toward implicating a reinforcement mechanism in the operation of naturally occurring behaviors and its disruption as the source of the behavioral deficits in telencephalon-ablated fish. The first category of experiments corresponds to class 3 in the matrix of Table I while the second corresponds to class 4. We shall see that all the desired data are not yet available, although many pieces of it are.

Before discussing these areas of research, we need to first review the effects of telencephalon ablation on species-specific behavior sequences as they occur in the natural context; this is, of course, the data of class 2, where species-specific behaviors, the reinforcement hypothesis would maintain, are reinforced by naturally occurring species-specific events.

2. Species-Specific Reinforcers Contingent on Species-Specific Behaviors (Class 2)

The effects of telencephalon ablation on species-specific behaviors are many and varied, and, therefore, are here organized under their separate headings.

a. **Schooling Behavior.** As Segaar (1965) notes, it was probably Kumakura who, in 1928, first discovered that the telencephalon influenced behaviors other than olfaction. He found that goldfish, *Carassius auratus,* which normally show a tendency to school, did not do so following extirpation of the telencephalon. The effect was transitory; the tendency to school returned within 2 weeks. The same transitory effect was found in *Phoxinus laevis* as well (Hosch, 1936; Berwein, 1941). Hosch (1936) noted, however, that when his minnows eventually schooled, they remained together longer than did the unoperated animals. In addition, Berwein (1941) found that a school of telencephalon-ablated *Phoxinus* would accept a strange fish into the school faster than would an intact comparison group. More drastic effects than those noted above in Cyprinidae have been observed, however. A permanent reduction in schooling was obtained in the percoid, *Box salpa* (Wiebalck, 1937), in the gobiid, *Gobio fluviatilis* (Hosch, 1936), and in several species of cichlids (Noble, 1936). Aronson and Kaplan (1968) have suggested that this permanent deficit is possibly due to the "more complexly organized forebrains in these [Perciform] species" (p. 111).

Koshtoiants *et al.* (1960) have shown that the "group effect," the consumption of less oxygen by a school of fish than by the total of its isolated members, disappears following telencephalon ablation in several species of *Smaris* and *Mullus* (both family Percoidae), and in *Phoxinus* and *Carassius carassius.* This evidence correlates well with their observation that ablates show less activity in isolation but more activity when in the school.

If one were to generalize, then, across the species studied so far, it appears that, although removal of the telencephalon impairs schooling behavior to a greater or lesser extent, it is not permanently eliminated. Whether these deficits are due to a disruption of schooling tendencies per se or to disruption of olfaction remains to be investigated, however, because none of these experiments employed an olfactory control (e.g., an olfactory tract sectioned group). A more recent study by Hemmings (1966) makes clear the fact that olfaction does, indeed, play an important role in fish schooling (see also Todd, 1971).

b. Aggressive Behavior. The study of the effects of telencephalon ablation on the aggressive behavior of Teleostei reveals a similar pattern: there exist quantitative deficiencies in the aggressive behavior following decerebration; however, once fighting is elicited, it reportedly does *not* differ in any way from that shown by intact fish (Hale, 1956b; Fiedler, 1967, 1968; Karamyan *et al.,* 1967; Shapiro *et al.,* 1974). Extensive decrements in aggressive behavior were observed in stickleback *Gasterosteus aculeatus* (Schönherr, 1955; Segaar, 1961, 1965; Segaar and Nieuwenhuys, 1963), as well as in the jewel fish, *Hemichromis bimaculatus* (Cichlidae), the fighting fish, *Betta splendens,* and the live-bearing swordtail, *Xiphophorus maculatus* (Cyprinodontidae) (Noble, 1939; Noble and Borne, 1941). Hale (1956b) observed the agressive behavior of the sunfish, *Lepomis cyanellus,* following the removal of small to large parts of the telencephalon. Extensive lesions resulted in marked quantitative deficiencies in aggressive behavior. Generally, the greater the lesion, the more marked was the deficiency; after a certain, very large, quantity was extirpated, the fish were never observed to *initiate* fighting. As in previous studies, however, fighting could always be elicited, albeit with higher intensity stimuli.

c. Reproductive Behavior. Research indicates that an intact telencephalon also is integral to nest building, sexual activity, and parental behaviors (Segaar, 1965). Aronson (1948, 1949), studying the function of the telencephalon in the West African mouthbreeder, *Tilapia macrocephala* (Cichlidae), found that telencephalic ablation produced a marked decline in the frequency of reproductive behaviors; however, *none* of these were completely eliminated. Overmier and Gross (1974) reported on the nest building behavior of a related species, the East African mouthbreeder, *T. mossambica,* and also found that although nest building in telencephalon-ablated fish was greatly impaired, all but one of seven ablated fish did dig a partial nest.

A similar pattern of ablation-produced deficits has been observed in other species as well. In *Tilapia macrocephala, Gasterosteus aculeatus, Hemichromis bimaculatus,* and *Betta splendens,* and several viviparous species of the family Cyprinodontidae (e.g., *Xiphophorus*), nearly complete ablation produced substantial deficits but not usually total elimination of all reproductive behaviors

(Noble, 1936, 1937, 1939; Noble and Borne, 1941). Kamrin and Aronson (1954) corroborated these observations in *Xiphophorus maculatus*. This same pattern of ablation-produced deficits has more recently been observed in *Hemihaplo-chromis philander* (Ribbink, 1972) and the paradise fish, *Macropodus opercularis* as well (Davis *et al.*, 1976; Kassel *et al.*, 1976; Schwagmeyer *et al.*, 1977). Davis and his collaborators report, for example, that although the building of a foam bubble nest and spawning were frequently (but not always) eliminated in telencephalon-ablated subjects, other reproductive behaviors like lateral and frontal displays were only decreased in frequency, while approach behavior and coloration changes were not at all affected.

Noble (1936, 1937), and later Noble and Borne (1941), had attempted to localize the organization of reproductive behavior patterns within specific areas of the telencephalon. On the basis of data obtained from animals with small localized lesions, they concluded that the organization of the various components of reproductive patterns is specifically localized in different telencephalic areas. This interpretation, however, suffers from their discovery that some of the *same* deficits were produced by lesions in different parts of the telencephalon. Unfortunately, these data are available in short abstracts only, and histological results are not provided.

This same localized approach has been undertaken by Segaar and Nieuwenhuys (1963; Segaar, 1961, 1965), who have done certainly the most extensive work in this area. First, quantitative measurements of the parental, aggressive, and sexual behaviors of *Gasterosteus aculeatus* were taken each day of control males' 2-week breeding cycle. Aggression was measured as a number of bites against a rival male, sexual drive as number of zig-zags in the presence of a female, and parental behavior as the duration of fanning the nest. These behaviors were found to vary, with respect to one another, in a specific and predictable pattern. After removal, in experimental subjects, of the dorsorostral or lateral parts of both telencephalic hemispheres, or after coagulation of these areas, aggression remained abnormally low between spawning and hatching while sexual behavior occurred briefly, then abruptly dropped to zero. Following bilateral mediocaudal lesions, aggression was higher than usual, sexual behavior abnormally continuous, and parental behavior depressed. After total extirpation of the telencephalon, intensive, frequent, and persistent nest fanning and digging of sand were observed during the reproductive stage. What is, perhaps, most interesting is that these three behavior patterns (aggressive, sexual, and parental) maintained this altered equilibrium not only in the first, experimental, breeding cycle but in subsequent cycles as well.

We must pause to consider the conclusions reached by Macey *et al.* (1974) in their study of telencephalon localization of a reproductive behavior and the implications their results have for all ablative studies. Macey *et al.* placed electrolytic lesions in six areas of the forebrain of killifish, *Fundulus heteroclitus*

(Cyprinodontidae). Both lesioned and sham-operated control fish were then tested for the spawning reflex response elicited by injection of neurohypophysial hormones. Only lesions of the nucleus preopticus, a hypothalamic area typically left intact in teleost ablative studies (see footnote p. 00), severely impaired or abolished the spawning reflex response; *localized* telencephalic lesions *did not*. These data are supported by the finding that electrical stimulation in the nucleus preopticus of an unrelated species, *Lepomis macrochirus* (Centrarchidae), elicits certain elements of spawning behavior in that species (Demski and Knigge, 1971). However, Macey *et al.* note that this is not consistent with the findings that telencephalic ablations produce severe impairment of all reproductive behaviors, including the spawning reflex, for example, as reported by Kamrin and Aronson (1954) in another cyprinodont, *Xiphophorus maculatus*. Macey *et al.* suggest, however, that ablation of the telencephalon would, of course, interrupt afferent pathways to the preoptic nucleus. Even if the preoptic nucleus were to remain intact, these pathways—which would, presumably, transmit the relevant information to the preoptic nucleus—would be destroyed.

Perhaps a slight epistemological digression is in order. Although the results of Macey *et al.* suggest that the deficits produced by the ablation are merely artifacts of interruptions elsewhere in the system, more detailed investigations are needed before we can draw such a conclusion. Nonetheless, these data are included as a reminder of the "risks" of the ablative technique and the theoretical limitations these risks impose. We will return to this issue later.

From the perspective of our scheme (Table I), the researches of two behavioral classes, 3 and 4, remain to be discussed. These classes are, respectively, pan-species responses followed by species-specific reinforcers (pan-species responses→species-specific reinforcers) and species-specific responses followed by pan-species reinforcers (species-specific responses→pan-species reinforcers).* These data are generally important to any effort to bridge the "psychology–ethology gap" as well as provide critical tests of the reinforcement hypothesis for species-specific behavior.

We have earlier described how the reinforcement hypothesis accounts for the behavior of telencephalon-ablated teleosts in learned tasks (class 1, pan-species responses→pan-species reinforcers) and how this hypothesis might *logically* be extended to include disruptions of naturalistic behaviors (class 2, species-specific responses→specific reinforcers). As we shall show in the following sections, (a) species-specific events can function as reinforcers for pan-species responses (see

---

*For the remainder of the discussion, the behavioral classes corresponding to cells 3 and 4 of the matrix will be referred to in the following manner: "pan-species responses→species-specific reinforcers" and "species-specific responses→pan-species reinforcers," respectively. Our use of the arrow is intended to connote both a contingent and dependent relationship between the response and reinforcer.

discussion of class 3), and (b) species-specific behaviors are amenable themselves to modulation by the presentation of known pan-species reinforcers (see discussion of class 4). These are *insufficient* but *necessary* to our hypothesis, although they do form part of an *unnecessary* but *sufficient* complex for the condition that species-specific behavior sequences are maintained by species-specific "terminal" events. This meets what Mackie (1965) has referred to as the INUS condition for determining "causality."

3. Species-Specific Reinforcers Contingent on Pan-Species Behaviors (Class 3)

The reinforcement hypothesis' account of the disruption of species-specific behavior sequences in the natural environment is predicated upon the assertion that, following telencephalic ablation, certain ethological events lose their reinforcing function in the natural context and thus produce the deficits in behavior. It follows, then, that these ethological events also would cease to be effective when used as species-specific reinforcers in the laboratory, hence the importance of the study of the behavioral class, pan-species responses→species-specific reinforcers (class 3). Unfortunately, until 1976 *no* experiments had tested the efficacy of species-specific reinforcement following telencephalon ablation. Although researchers are now beginning to use telencephalon ablations to study species-specific reinforcement (e.g. Davis, et al., 1976), the body of literature dealing with this topic in *normal* animals, itself an area of relatively recent and expanding interest, is considerable (Hinde, 1958; Hinde and Steel, 1972; Hinde and Stevenson, 1969; Shettleworth, 1972). We will review those studies of reinforcement by species-specific events in Teleostei.

After reading Forselius' "Study of Anabantid Fishes" (1957), in which the elaborate agonistic behavior of the male *Betta splendens* is finely detailed, one is not surprised that the marked and prepotent territorial behavior of the male in the presence of other male conspecifics might have suggested to some that the sight of a rival and/or the opportunity to engage in agonistic behavior would be reinforcing. In an early attempt to test this hypothesis (Hogan, 1961), the sight of another male *B. splendens* was made contingent upon both locomotor (swimming in a straight alley) and lever pressing responses. Although the operant data suggested that "learning" of these responses was not taking place, the subjects' behavior suggested that associations had been formed but had interfered with the to-be-learned response. For example, they displayed at both the lever and the door to the goal box. Subsequently, with the use of more sensitive techniques, Thompson (1963, 1966) and Thompson and Sturm (1965a) demonstrated that male *B. splendens* will perform an operant response (swimming through one or more rings) when this response is followed by presentations of mirror images or models. Later, Goldstein (1967), using a yoked control procedure, refuted the suggestion that these findings were an artifact of general activity increases. More recently, Goldstein (1975) has made observations which suggest that the aggressive motivation-reducing (reinforcing) properties of such displays, especially against omega males, play an important role in the establishment of stable communities of *B. splendens.*

Hogan (1967) too was able to replicate the species-specific reinforcer properties of display in *B. splendens,* although he noted that the use of these reinforcers resulted in less rapid improvement in acquisition, lower asymptotic performance, and more rapid extinction when compared to performance maintained by food reward. In addition, Hogan *et al.* (1970) reported that the "partial reinforcement effect," the paradoxically greater resistance to extinction following conditions in which only some responses are reinforced, was obtained in this species when food was used as a reward but not when exposure to the sight of a mirror image was employed.

We have not explored the question of whether species-specific reinforcement is qualitatively or merely quantitatively different from traditional "primary" reinforcement, as these experiments might imply. Fortunately, the viability of the reinforcement hypothesis is not dependent upon the resolution of the qualitative/quantitative issue. We would suggest that the data to date demonstrate that weak reinforcers do not reliably produce the partial reinforcement effect; hence, species-specific reinforcers are likely to be members of the class of "weak reinforcers." Such a suggestion finds support in a number of recent studies comparing a primary food reinforcer with other reinforcers, including nest-building, aggression, etc. (Roper, 1975; Hogan, 1974; Macdonald and de Toledo, 1974).

Whether the distinction between species-specific and pan-species reinforcers is qualitative or quantitative, the viability of the reinforcement hypothesis in the domain of species-specific behavior would be increased by experiments which demonstrate that *certain* species-specific reinforcers are incapable of maintaining pan-species responses following telencephalon ablation. The species-specific reinforcers in question would, we hypothesize, be those which maintain the behavior in the natural context and which are disrupted by ablation of the telencephalon. Identification of these reinforcers may be a difficult task. The research we have just reviewed provides us with one possibility, however, and we are presently preparing in our laboratory to replicate this research in telencephalon-ablated *Betta splendens.* The display behavior of *B. splendens* has been successfully classically conditioned by Thompson and Sturm (1965b). Further, we know that telencephalon-ablated fish classically condition equally as well as normals. Part of our testing will involve the classical conditioning of this display behavior in telencephalon-ablated fish. Should we find that ablated fish classically condition as well as normals, a crucial test of the hypothesis would be to determine whether the opportunity to display at a rival will now fail to serve as an adequate reinforcer for an operant response. Some recent work by Davis and his collaborators (Davis *et al.*, 1976; Kassel *et al.*, 1976) do indeed suggest that the opportunity to display at a rival is "less reinforcing" of locomotor responses (swimming through a ring) in telencephalon-ablated paradise fish.

A related strategy is suggested by two other studies. French (1942) demonstrated that *Carassius auratus* would learn to swim through a maze to reach a goal box where conspecifics were present, and Angermeier *et al.* (1963) suggested that changes in motor behavior can serve as reinforcement for the same species. It is certainly worth investigating whether the reduced "social behavior" and activity levels of telencephalon-ablated fish are, to any degree, related to an impaired effectiveness of these reinforcers.

Of the remaining studies of species-specific reinforcement in teleosts which may have potential relevance to explanation of the behavior of telencephalon-ablated fish, one is especially interesting in its implications. The data of Sevenster (1968, 1973) deserve special attention here because they may be viewed as a bridge between the species-specific reinforcement (cell 3) and "pure" ethological (cell 2) approaches. As in the experiments we have just reviewed, Sevenster employed species-specific reinforcers to maintain responding; however, the operant responses which he selected to be reinforced were unique in their apparent similarity to the natural behaviors which would normally be found in that reinforcer context. Thus, in male *Gasterosteus aculeatus,* the sight of a gravid female or rival male served as reinforcers for (a) biting the small green knob of a glass rod, a behavior topographically similar to the aggressive leaf-biting of territorial males, and (b) swimming through a narrow ring, a behavior topographically similar to males' "creeping through the nest." Although both responses were performed when reinforced with presentation of a female, the rod-biting yielded rather lower rates of responding. These lower rates were attributable to reinforcement-to-response latencies that were very long. Sevenster interpreted these data to suggest motivational incompatibility of response and reinforcer: the male normally inhibits his aggressive behavior in the latter stages of courtship. Biting a rod, an "aggressive" behavior, was motivationally incompatible with the courtship behavior that the female elicited. That is, in this case, the reward had an after effect which suppressed further responding. This interpretation was supported by evidence that (a) response rate increased substantially in extinction sessions during which the male no longer saw the gravid female, (b) "exposures," noncontingent presentations of the female, had the same suppressing effect on subsequent responses as did reinforcers, and (c) responses which followed unreinforced bites on a variable ratio schedule had very short latencies, while the response which immediately followed the reinforcer was much delayed. This motivational incompatibility should not, then, be present for the ring-swimming response→female reinforcer combination nor for rod-biting when it is subsequently reinforced with a rival *male;* indeed, the data bear this out as well. Although the former response may not be homologous with "creeping through the nest'' in the behavior of this species, rod biting for a rival male represents an experimental situation whose inferences about reinforcement in ethological behavior may well be valid. Leaf biting in territorial males occurs in the presence of rivals; if a behavior which is judged similar to leaf biting—and which is shown to be incompatible with courtship behavior—can be increased by the presentation of a rival male, the possibility that these behaviors are reinforced by contingent events in their natural context has clearly gained support.

In our review of species-specific reinforcement, we have focused on those studies which have dealt with behaviors which are known to be affected by telencephalon ablation (reproduction, aggression, etc.) and also with species (*Gasterosteus, Betta, Carassius*) whose behavior in the natural context has already been studied following removal of the telencephalon. While this approach does, indeed, provide a logical foundation upon which the reinforcement hypothesis might be built, different tools are available to us as well. The experimental architecture could be varied by choosing to investigate behavioral events which have *not* been previously studied in telencephalon-ablated subjects but are *known* to be effective species-specific reinforcers. The work of Losey and Margules (1974; see also Chapter 1) is an excellent example. The presentation of a moving model of a cleaner fish, *Labroides phthirophagus* (Labridae), was employed as a positive reinforcer for a photocell-crossing response in *Chaetodon auriga* (Chaetodontidae), a host species. The data suggest that the cleaning symbiosis is reinforcing for the host fish. Given this as a starting point, one might endeavor to study in telencephalon-ablated host fish both whether the cleaning symbiosis in the natural context is disrupted and whether exposure to the cleaner fish now will fail to reinforce some pan-species, experimenter-selected response in ablates, as the reinforcement hypothesis suggests.

Regardless of the approach, and of course, what we may eventually find here, the study of this behavioral class (pan-species responses→species-specific reinforcers) is certain to answer some of our questions regarding telencephalon function in the teleost. Further, underlying the reinforcement hypothesis are certain assumptions about the properties and mechanisms of reinforcers in general. Therefore, tests of this hypothesis are bound to facilitate our understanding of the reinforcement process—one of the most basic issues in psychology.

4. Pan-Species Reinforcers Contingent on Species-Specific Behaviors (Class 4)

Equally important to the reinforcement hypothesis, however, is the research of the remaining behavioral class in which species-specific responses are reinforced with pan-species reinforcers (class 4, Table I). This response–reinforcer class both contrasts with and parallels, on several levels, the research on reinforcement with species-specific events (class 3) which we have already delineated. These areas represent parallel lines of research in that they raise issues about laboratory investigations of species-specific behavioral "events" and reinforcement operations. While class 3 explores the extent to which the occurrence of species-specific events can reinforce, class 4 explores the extent to which species-specific behaviors themselves are modifiable by other reinforcers. They also suggest answers to questions of the necessity and sufficiency of such reinforcement operations for the control of behavior. In this regard, both lines of research may well be taken as evidence that a reinforcement mechanism could *potentially* be operating in the ethological context from which the species-specific behavior was derived, as we have suggested earlier (Section III,B,3).

These behavioral classes contrast with one another to the extent that to date their researches have relied upon quite different experimental paradigms, the "reward" or response incrementing paradigm in research on behavioral class 3, and punishment or response decrementing paradigm in research on the behavioral class 4. As Table II illustrates, these are but two of four basic experimental paradigms which test the effectiveness of a stimulus event in the control of behavior. Reflection on our review of species-specific research in class 3 reveals that only positive reinforcement paradigms were employed with fish (e.g., the species-specific reinforcer was presented contingent upon a pan-species response and the occurrence of that response increased); one might also ask whether an operant response could be maintained if negative reinforcement were employed; that is, will withdrawal of an "aversive" species-specific event (e.g., sight of predator model) contingent upon the occurrence of an arbitrary operant reinforce that operant? Also, one might ask whether an operant response could be suppressed by means of either punishment paradigm, presenting an aversive species-specific event contingent on some response or withdrawing a positive species-specific event contingent on some response. These latter paradigms, negative

TABLE II

Basic Instrumental Paradigms

Hedonic quality of stimulus event	Response-contingent operations	
	Present stimulus event	Withdraw stimulus event
Positive	Reward operation (positive reinforcement)[a]	Peanlty operation (punishment)
Negative	Punishment operation (punishment)	Escape/avoidance operation (negative reinforcement)

[a] The names for the operations which appear in parentheses are the technical terms psychologists commonly use.

reinforcement and punishment, have yet to be investigated in the research belonging to behavioral class 3.

Study of the "reverse" relationship of species-specific responses→pan-species reinforcers in Teleostei to date has relied solely upon an aversive paradigm, punishment. For example, Adler and Hogan (1963) demonstrated that the gill cover extension response of *Betta splendens* elicited by a mirror image could be suppressed by the presentation of a brief shock, and the suppressive effect obtained by punishment was of greater magnitude than that produced by noncontingent presentations of shock. Very recently, Murray (1973) has obtained data which suggest that the penalty operation may selectively depress components of aggressive display behavior in *B. splendens*. Bridging the gap between this behavioral class and the ethological literature, Thomas (1974) has shown that the intensity of species-specific foraging behavior in *Gasterosteus aculeatus* is increased when acceptable food objects are found but decreased when unacceptable food objects are encountered.

The research potential of this behavioral class remains to be fully exploited. In addition to punishment, other experimental paradigms, which we delineated earlier, could be used. For example, the reward paradigm has been successful in strengthening species-specific behaviors in dogs (Konorski, 1967), hamsters (Shettleworth, 1975), pigeons (Azrin and Hutchinson, 1967), and rats (Ulrich *et al.*, 1963); similarly, the escape paradigm has been successfully used to strengthen species-specific behaviors in cats and chicks (Thorndike, 1911). We can only wonder as to the insights these other paradigms would yield in ablated teleosts.

The importance of both this latter behavioral class and species-specific reinforcement, as well as the methodological logic of our approach, can be properly summarized as follows: the reinforcement hypothesis is that the teleost telencephalon is involved in the utilization of "secondary" reinforcement. While this hypothesis has fared well in the domain of traditional learned behaviors, its application to the explanation of the disruption of species-specific behaviors following telencephalon ablation is not intuitively obvious. We have tried to clarify this application. Rather than to assume that there must be *different* telencephalic mechanisms for species-specific and pan-species behaviors, we are attempting to extend the reinforcement hypothesis derived from learning experiments to include ethological behaviors by proposing two corollaries. These are that (a) the species-specific behaviors which are disrupted by telencephalon ablation are reinforced in their natural context, and (b) the cause of this disruption is the inability of these animals to utilize the reinforcement which would, in the natural context, maintain these behaviors. These corollaries may be tested by means of the four reinforcement techniques delineated in Table II within the confines of the response–reinforcement relationships, species-specific reinforcement of pan-species behaviors (class 3), and pan-species reinforcement of species-specific behaviors (class 4). Finally, while these researches do not "prove" the necessity of reinforcement in the natural context, they do establish the potential for it to function in this manner; this approach is consistent with that of many ethologists (e.g., Hinde and Steel, 1972; Rasa, 1971). Clearly, only a convergence of evidence obtained from the behavioral classes 3 and 4 can lend credence to the notion that reinforcement is necessary for behaviors in the natural context and can provide support for the reinforcement hypothesis as an explanation of telencephalic function in Teleostei.

IV. COMPARATIVE PSYCHOLOGICAL RESEARCH: A COMMENT

Since the ancient Egyptians 5000 years ago made detailed observations of *Tilapia nilotica* (Cichlidae), the sacred symbol of rebirth after death (Chimits, 1957), simple basic curiosity is perhaps a commonality which has led many of us to ask questions of teleost behavior. Questions about the mechanisms and processes of, say, defending territories from intruders or learning to avoid aversive events in our shuttleboxes, etc., establish some common ground among those of us who study the behavior of Teleostei. Yet, the methods we employ are diverse, indeed, and the methodology is that which identifies us as ethologists, neurophysiologists, comparative psychologists, etc. We would like to pursue the methodological diversity here briefly, as it is certainly the case that the answers we obtain to our behavioral questions are determined—and sometimes motivated—by the methodologies we employ. Generally, comparative neurobehavioral researches fall into two "camps," indirect comparative behavioral study and direct surgical manipulation.

The indirect method employs behavioral similarities and differences as indices both of evolutionary commonalities and divergences and of relative primitiveness of selected behavioral competencies. Ethologists have used the indirect method to determine homologies of species-specific behaviors within taxonomic groups which are known to be somewhat related (Lorenz, 1941). Comparative psychologists, focusing on *differences* rather than on similarities, have used the indirect method to determine divergencies of learning mechanisms and problem-solving capacities (see Bitterman, 1975).

The indirect method is best explained by its most influential proponent, M. E. Bitterman (1960, 1965, 1975). According to Bitterman (1965), whose primary interest is the neurobehavioral processes underlying learning phenomena, "one way to study the role of the brain in learning is to compare the learning of animals with different brains. Differences in brain structure may be produced by surgical means or they may be found in nature. . ." (p. 396). Thus, the learning of some specific problem by fish is compared with that of earthworms, turtles, pigeons, rats, and monkeys in an attempt to discover *qualitative* differences in these animals' learning competences.

The methodology necessitates that the logically inescapable sensory, motor, and/or motivational differences between the species selected be controlled by "systematic variation," that is, a comparison of these animals' performance over a *wide* range of task variables (sensory, motor, and motivational; Masterton *et al.*, 1974). Systematic variation would enable one to map the functional relationships between parameters and patterns of behavior; basically different functional relationships would then imply *qualitatively different* learning, or other behavioral processes. The data do, in fact, suggest that some animals respond differently than others when faced with particular learning problems. Bitterman and his associates have found, for example, that when a reward is shifted after a period of training from a large to a small amount, goldfish and turtles continue to respond at the same rate while the performance of rats suffers a "depression effect" (Bitterman, 1975).

This approach to the comparative study of behavior has been severely criticized by Hodos and Campbell (1969), among others, for several reasons. According to Hodos and Campbell, one cannot draw "inferences about the phylogenetic development of behavior patterns" based upon "data from animals which represent divergent lineages" (p. 337). In his earlier papers (Bitterman, 1965), Bitterman typically classified his subjects for analysis "in accordance with the conventional scale of complexity—monkey at the top and earthworm at the bottom" (p. 408). Notwithstanding the fact that fish (as well as pigeons, rats, and monkeys) do represent a distinct evolutionary line from primitive amphibia (see Fig. 1), the criticism of what appears to be a "Scala Naturae" may be a straw man argument. Bitterman has never claimed that one neurobehavioral process *evolved* from the other; that is, his inferences are not about the phylogenetic *development* of behavior. Particular species are selected because they are more likely to evidence differences in their behavior. These differences "provide a much broader picture of the evolution of behavior" (Bitterman, 1975, p. 704) *only* to the extent that they suggest that functional divergences of learning processes have taken place. The inferences are restricted to the processes themselves, and not their development!

More valid a criticism and the subject of Hodos and Campbell's paper entitled, "Why there is no theory in comparative psychology" (1969), is that this approach provides little more than a catalog of species differences, when one of the goals of comparative psychology *should* be the investigation of "systematic trends in behavior which hopefully would vary reliably with other taxonomic indexes. . ." (p. 349). Although we would agree that the evolution of behavior is a legitimate goal of *comparative* psychology, it is difficult to assert, *a priori,* which of all approaches will and will not provide us with this information—and, consequently, of which approaches we shall permit the title "Comparative."*

Curiously, what we believe the most formidable problem of the indirect approach has, for the most part, escaped indictment. This problem emerges from the logic which underlies systematic variation. Systematic variation cannot guarantee that artifactual performance differences have been eliminated. One can never be sure that any observed performance differences are not attributable to the failure to manipulate "just one more" of the countless variables—perhaps one assumed too trivial to control—and, thus, the crucial question becomes "How many systematic replications are sufficient?" For example, the failure of fish to show the phenomenon of progressive improvement in a successive habit reversal task stood for 16 years (since Wodinsky and Bitterman, 1957) as a solid piece of evidence of phyletic differences until Engelhardt et al. (1973) demonstrated that sufficient modification of the apparatus and training conditions would yield such a pattern of improvement in fish. At best an inefficient way of solving the problem, Bitterman has admitted (1975) that "systematic variation is a rather expensive control procedure" (p. 703).

Lest the reader think that the weapons with which to combat the methodological enemy lie with the other camp of comparative research, we will quickly discover that although one adversary retreats, others, equally formidable, take the stand. The techniques of ablation, lesioning, and stimulation—the direct surgical manipulation of neural processes—must suffer criticism as well.

One such criticism is that these treatments are disruptive to the normal functioning of the organism, making deductions about the mechanisms of normal function insecure. Another criticism is that all organisms are "integrated mechanisms" which function as a whole, and it would thus be impossible to ascertain the role of one neural mechanism through surgical intervention without interference with others. The undeniable logic of this statement has been humorously parodied by the suggestion that one might someday propose that "the personality" is controlled by the nose since its removal would produce substantial changes in the personality of the individual. While this remark was certainly facetious, its intent was to illustrate the potential for faulty logic underlying interpretation of surgical manipulation in an integrated organism. Indeed, we earlier discussed the finding of Macey et al. (1974) which suggested that telencephalic ablation might affect behavior by depriving the preoptic nucleus of critical input, the specific function under investigation being localized in the preoptic nucleus rather than in the telencephalon per se.

As a result of the problems raised by the concept of "the integrated organism," some safeguards may have become apparent but are worth noting here.

*Simple classification of behavior patterns and competences, e.g., the botanization of behavior, may well be another legitimate goal—and no less an intriguing one, though perhaps less grandiose.

Because the telencephalon may function, for example, primarily in the reinforcement of behavior, it may effect behavior—or itself be affected—indirectly via its connections with other neural mechanisms. Therefore, we must design our experiments in such manner as to ameliorate the inevitable confounding. The possible confounding effects of arousal differences were tested in one experiment by measuring the response of normal and ablated fish to shock independently of the avoidance paradigm (Savage, 1969b). Appropriate control procedures require more than just good experimental design; they require a concentrated effort to keep all hypothesized functions of the telencephalon *and* related structures in mind so as to construct experiments which will minimize the disruption of one function while testing another. For example, recent evidence (Wenzel, 1974; Cain, 1974) suggests that the *olfactory bulb* of higher vertebrates subserves behavioral functions seemingly unrelated to olfaction per se. This is likely true of fish as well. Inclusion of an olfactory tract sectioned or bulbectomized group would provide a basis for obtaining the "double dissociation" needed to assess differences produced by the loss of telencephalic structures and distinguish these differences from those produced by removal of olfaction and/or other functions subserved by the olfactory bulb.

Prophesies of doom are commonly exaggerated; the success of others who have employed these techniques make the risks look less foreboding. Weiskrantz' (1968) comments may be worth repeating here: "...there are no logical grounds for determining in advance whether some specific treatments are going to affect the inner workings of the organism differently from others.... Whether we affect the brain indirectly through its receptor system or directly through surgical techniques is irrelevant to the question, and, if we wish to maintain that we cannot deduce anything about brain manipulations without prior knowledge as to how the brain works, then, similarly, we must say this of any treatment, and thus logically commit ourselves to a nihilism to which few could subscribe in practice" (pp. 401–402). We do not claim that our techniques provide us with the refined analysis that we would, at some point, require. Yet, they do tell us what questions we must next ask and what form our analyses should take. Moreover, these treatments allow researchers to identify gross parallels of function across species, as we have done in this paper.

These methodological criticisms make it clear that a chauvinistic devotion to our methods and rabid refutation of their criticisms are foolhardy; clearly, neither "camp" can win the battle for the "mind." It is only the combination of neuroanatomical, neurobehavioral, physiological, ethological, and psychological data that can answer final questions of brain processes. Although one piece of information may be meager, another, especially if obtained via a different method of analysis, may reinforce and corroborate one's hypothesis. What is required, then, is a multilevel approach producing *cumulative converging lines of evidence,* each piece reinforcing and corroborating existing evidence while providing further refinement of the data. It is this approach that characterizes the analysis of the teleost telencephalon promoted in this paper.

The research on the function of the teleost telencephalon is a good example of Weiskrantz' "tinkering phase." The fish brain is still a mysterious organ—witness the fact that the first stereotaxic atlas of the goldfish brain has just recently been published (Peter and Gill, 1975)! Ingle (1965b) cites a statement of Herrick (1924, p. 44) that is still most appropriate to this research: "...and there is a long, long road to travel before we shall be able to understand in any but the most shadowy outlines what a fish's mind is really like."

How ironic is the fact that our references to "the telencephalon," a structure which in man is thought responsible for the subtleties of logic and abstractive capacity, are themselves products of this same abstraction! That is, there is no such structure as "the teleost telencephalon," except as it exists in our own "forebrain." We alluded to the exaggerations and diminutions of structures across species earlier in this paper and yet proceeded to review the data of telencephalic function in teleost species which are as distantly related and structurally different as goldfish and gobies! Our "comparative" study of Teleostei leaves much to be desired. As Table III illustrates, only a few species have been selected for study, and rather unsystematically at that. In fact, of the 27 orders of Teleostei, we have sampled from but four. Even more discouraging is the fact that, of the 200 families which comprise these four orders, we have selected from but a dozen, and even within these families, only a few species have been studied. We would certainly urge a greater representation if we wish to generalize to as large a group as Teleostei; yet, perhaps even more is required of us. More detailed neuroantomical and neurophysiological study, especially as this approaches a comparative analysis of the teleostean telencephalon, would be illuminating.

In our attempt to understand the function of the teleost telencephalon, several hypotheses have been offered, but the large gaps in the experimental literature make any evaluation of hypotheses somewhat premature. We have tried to outline the variety of contingencies—positive reinforcement, negative reinforcement, etc.—which have not been applied to certain behavioral classes of our scheme (see Fig. 1). These researches will, we are certain, provide new insights into the neuropsychology of the teleost telencephalon and the nature of reinforcement itself. Indeed, we hope that this chapter has provided some stimulus for the filling-in of those "gaps."

TABLE III

Taxonomic Classification of 27 Orders of Teleostei

Order	Suborder	Superfamily	Family
Osteoglossiformes			Diplomystidae
			Ictaluridae
Clupeiformes			Bagridae
			Cranoglanididae
Salmoniformes			Siluridae
			Schilbeidae
			Pangasiidae
			Amblycipitidae
			Amphiliidae
			Akysidae
			Sisoridae
			Clariidae
			Heteropneustidae
			Chacidae
			Olyridae
	Siluroidei		Malopteruridae
			Mochochidae
			Ariidae
			Doradidae
			Auchenipteridae
			Aspredinidae
			Plotosidae
			Pimelodidae
Cypriniformes			Ageneiosidae
			Hypophthalmidae
			Helogeneidae
			Cetopsidae
			Trichomycteridae
			Callichthyidae
			Loricariidae
			Astroblepidae
		Characoidae	Characidae
			Gymnotidae
			Electrophoridae
		Gymnotoidae	Apteronotidae
Anguilliformes	Cyprinoidei		Rhamphichthyidae

TABLE III (*Continued*)

Order	Suborder	Superfamily	Family

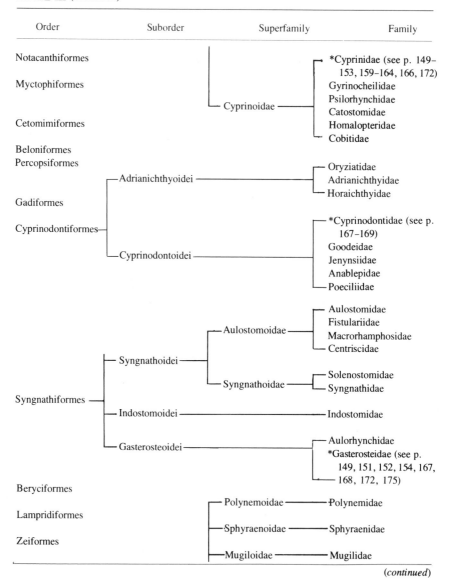

Notacanthiformes
Myctophiformes
Cetomimiformes
Beloniformes
Percopsiformes
Gadiformes
Cyprinodontiformes—
Syngnathiformes —
Beryciformes
Lampridiformes
Zeiformes

Cyprinoidae — *Cyprinidae (see p. 149–153, 159–164, 166, 172), Gyrinocheilidae, Psilorhynchidae, Catostomidae, Homalopteridae, Cobitidae

Adrianichthyoidei — Oryziatidae, Adrianichthyidae, Horaichthyidae

Cyprinodontoidei — *Cyprinodontidae (see p. 167–169), Goodeidae, Jenynsiidae, Anablepidae, Poeciliidae

Syngnathoidei — Aulostomoidae — Aulostomidae, Fistulariidae, Macrorhamphosidae, Centriscidae

Syngnathoidae — Solenostomidae, Syngnathidae

Indostomoidei — Indostomidae

Gasterosteoidei — Aulorhynchidae, *Gasterosteidae (see p. 149, 151, 152, 154, 167, 168, 172, 175)

Polynemoidae — Polynemidae

Sphyraenoidae — Sphyraenidae

Mugiloidae — Mugilidae

(continued)

TABLE III (*Continued*)

Order	Suborder	Superfamily	Family

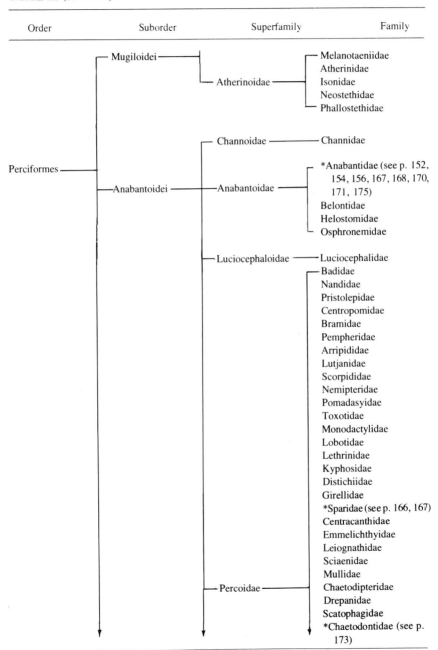

Mugiloidei

Atherinoidae — Melanotaeniidae
Atherinidae
Isonidae
Neostethidae
Phallostethidae

Channoidae ——— Channidae

Perciformes

Anabantoidei — Anabantoidae — *Anabantidae (see p. 152, 154, 156, 167, 168, 170, 171, 175)
Belontidae
Helostomidae
Osphronemidae

Luciocephaloidae — Luciocephalidae
Badidae
Nandidae
Pristolepidae
Centropomidae
Bramidae
Pempheridae
Arripididae
Lutjanidae
Scorpididae
Nemipteridae
Pomadasyidae
Toxotidae
Monodactylidae
Lobotidae
Lethrinidae
Kyphosidae
Distichiidae
Girellidae
*Sparidae (see p. 166, 167)
Centracanthidae
Emmelichthyidae
Leiognathidae
Sciaenidae
Mullidae
Percoidae — Chaetodipteridae
Drepanidae
Scatophagidae
*Chaetodontidae (see p. 173)

TABLE III (*Continued*)

Order	Suborder	Superfamily	Family
Perciformes (*Continued*)	Percoidei	Percoidae (*Continued*)	Enoplosidae
			Histiopteridae
			Oplegnathidae
			Percichthyidae
			Serranidae
			Grammistidae
			Plesiopidae
			Acanthoclinidae
			Opistognathidae
			Kuhliidae
			*Centrarchidae (see p. 160, 167, 171)
			Priacanthidae
			Cepolidae
			Rainfordiidae
			Apogonidae
			*Percidae (see p. 166, 167)
			Lactariidae
			Labracoglossidae
			Bathyclupeidae
			Pomatomidae
			Rachycentridae
			Carangidae
			Menidae
			Coryphaenidae
			*Cichlidae (see p. 162–164, 167, 168)
			Sillaginidae
			Branchiostegidae
		Chirrhitoidae	Cirrhitidae
			Aplodactylidae
			Chironemidae
			Cheilodactylidae
			Latridae
		Trichodontoidae	Trichodontidae
		Champsodontoidae	Champsodontidae
		Chiasmodontoidae	Chiasmodontidae
		Ammodytoidae	Ammodytidae
			Hypoptychidae
		Embiotocoidae	Embiotocidae

(*continued*)

TABLE III (*Continued*)

Order	Suborder	Superfamily	Family

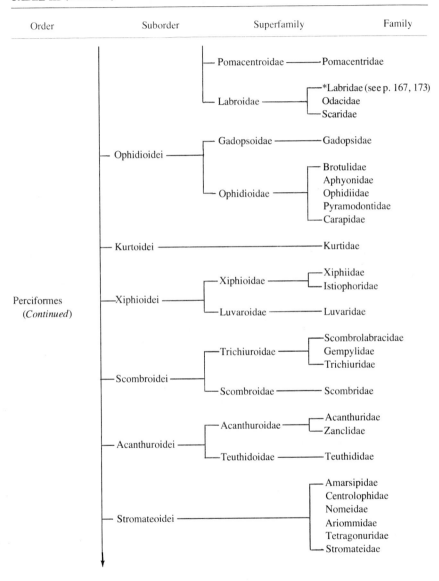

Pomacentroidae ——— Pomacentridae

Labroidae —
- *Labridae (see p. 167, 173)
- Odacidae
- Scaridae

Ophidioidei —

Gadopsoidae ——— Gadopsidae

Ophidioidae —
- Brotulidae
- Aphyonidae
- Ophidiidae
- Pyramodontidae
- Carapidae

Kurtoidei ——————————— Kurtidae

Xiphioidei —

Xiphioidae —
- Xiphiidae
- Istiophoridae

Luvaroidae ——— Luvaridae

Scombroidei —

Trichiuroidae —
- Scombrolabracidae
- Gempylidae
- Trichiuridae

Scombroidae ——— Scombridae

Acanthuroidei —

Acanthuroidae —
- Acanthuridae
- Zanclidae

Teuthidoidae ——— Teuthididae

Stromateoidei ———
- Amarsipidae
- Centrolophidae
- Nomeidae
- Ariommidae
- Tetragonuridae
- Stromateidae

Perciformes
(*Continued*)

TABLE III (*Continued*)

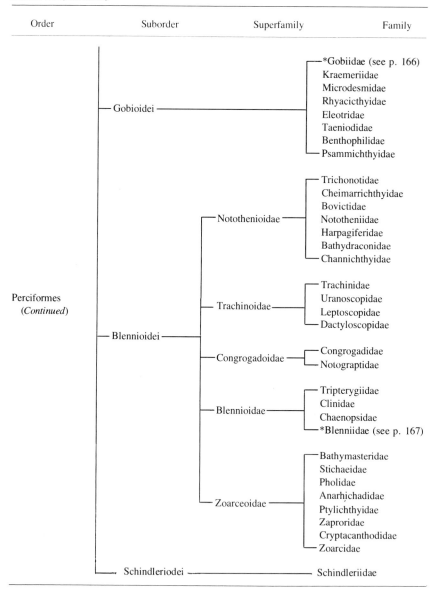

Order	Suborder	Superfamily	Family
Perciformes (*Continued*)	Gobioidei		*Gobiidae (see p. 166) Kraemeriidae Microdesmidae Rhyacicthyidae Eleotridae Taeniodidae Benthophilidae Psammichthyidae
	Blennioidei	Notothenioidae	Trichonotidae Cheimarrichthyidae Bovictidae Nototheniidae Harpagiferidae Bathydraconidae Channichthyidae
		Trachinoidae	Trachinidae Uranoscopidae Leptoscopidae Dactyloscopidae
		Congrogadoidae	Congrogadidae Notograptidae
		Blennioidae	Tripterygiidae Clinidae Chaenopsidae *Blenniidae (see p. 167)
		Zoarceoidae	Bathymasteridae Stichaeidae Pholidae Anarhichadidae Ptylichthyidae Zaproridae Cryptacanthodidae Zoarcidae
	Schindleriodei		Schindleriidae

TABLE III (*Continued*)

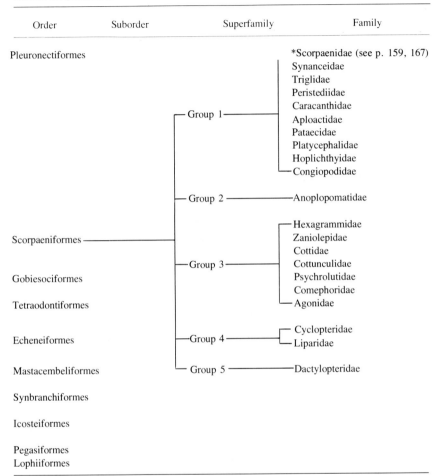

Order	Suborder	Superfamily	Family
Pleuronectiformes			*Scorpaenidae (see p. 159, 167)
			Synanceidae
			Triglidae
			Peristediidae
		Group 1	Caracanthidae
			Aploactidae
			Pataecidae
			Platycephalidae
			Hoplichthyidae
			Congiopodidae
		Group 2	Anoplopomatidae
			Hexagrammidae
			Zaniolepidae
Scorpaeniformes			Cottidae
		Group 3	Cottunculidae
Gobiesociformes			Psychrolutidae
			Comephoridae
Tetraodontiformes			Agonidae
Echeneiformes		Group 4	Cyclopteridae
			Liparidae
Mastacembeliformes		Group 5	Dactylopteridae
Synbranchiformes			
Icosteiformes			
Pegasiformes			
Lophiiformes			

*Scorpaenidae (see p. 159, 167)

^{a} Orders arranged after Gosline (1971). An asterisk indicates families which have been studied in behavioral experiments exploring telencephalic function using the ablative technique. The numbers in parentheses indicate text pages for reference studies.

ACKNOWLEDGMENTS

Preparation of this manuscript was supported by a grant from NIMH (MH-13,558) to J.B.O. and by grants to the Center for Research in Human Learning from NICHHD (HD-01136) and NSF

(GB-35703X). Requests for reprints should be sent to J. B. Overmier, Department of Psychology, University of Minnesota, Minneapolis, Minnesota 55455.

REFERENCES

Adler, N., and Hogan, J. A. (1963). Classical conditioning and punishment of an instinctive response in *Betta splendens*. *Anim. Behav.* **11,** 351–354.

Agranoff, B. W., and Davis, R. E. (1968). The use of fishes in studies on memory formation. *In* "The Central Nervous System and Fish Behavior" (D. Ingle, ed.), pp. 193–201. Univ. of Chicago Press, Chicago, Illinois.

Amsel, A. (1958). The role of frustrative nonreward in noncontinuous reward situations. *Psychol. Bull.* **55,** 102–119.

Angermeier, W. F., Hitt, J., and Wilbourn, J. (1963). Change in motor activity as reinforcement in rats, chickens, and fish. *J. Genet. Psychol.* **103,** 161–165.

Aronson, L. R. (1948). Problems in the behavior and physiology of a species of African mouthbreeding fish (*Tilapia macrocephala*). *Trans. N. Y. Acad. Sci.,* **11,** 33–42.

Aronson, L. R. (1949). An analysis of reproductive behavior in the mouthbreeding cichlid fish, *Tilapia macrocephala* (Bleeker). *Zoologica (N.Y.)* **34,** 133–158.

Aronson, L. R. (1963). The central nervous system of sharks and bony fishes with special reference to sensory and integrative mechanisms. *In* "Sharks and Survival" (P. W. Gilbert, ed.), pp. 165–241. Heath, Boston, Massachusetts.

Aronson, L. R. (1967). Forebrain function in teleost fishes. *Trans. N. Y. Acad. Sci.,* Ser. 2, **29,** 390–396.

Aronson, L. R. (1970). Functional evolution of the forebrain in lower vertebrates. *In* "Development and Evolution of Behavior: Essays in Memory of T. C. Schneirla." (L. R. Aronson *et al.,* eds.), pp. 75–107. Freeman, San Francisco, California.

Aronson, L. R., and Kaplan, H. (1963). Forebrain function in avoidance conditioning. *Am. Zool.* **3,** 483–484.

Aronson, L. R., and Kaplan, H. (1965). Effect of forebrain ablation on the acquisition of a conditioned avoidance response in the teleost fish, *Tilapia h. macrocephala. Am. Zool.* **5,** 654.

Aronson, L. R., and Kaplan, H. (1968). Function of the teleostean forebrain. *In* "The Central Nervous System and Fish Behavior" (D. Ingle, ed.), pp. 107–125. Univ. of Chicago Press, Chicago, Illinois.

Azrin, N. H., and Hutchinson, R. R. (1967). Conditioning of the aggressive behavior of pigeons by a fixed-interval schedule of reinforcement. *J. Exp. Anal. Behav.* **10,** 395–402.

Bard, P. A. (1950). Central nervous mechanisms for the expression of anger in animals. *In* "Feelings and Emotions: The Moosehart Symposium" (M. L. Reymert, ed.), pp. 211–237. McGraw-Hill, New York.

Baru, A. V. (1951). "K Sravnitel'noi Fiziologii Uslovnykh Refleksov." Avtoreferat, Leningrad.

Baru, A. V. (1955). "Voprosy Sravnitel'noi Fiziologii i Patologii Vysshei Nervoi Deyatel'nosti." Medgiz, Leningrad.

Bauer, F. J., and Lawrence, D. H. (1953). Influence of similarity of choice point and goal cues on discrimination learning. *J. Comp. Physiol. Psychol.* **46,** 241–248.

Beritoff, J. S. (1971). "Vertebrate Memory: Characteristics and Origin." Plenum, New York.

Berman, H. M. (1945). The effect of various groupings of normal and forebrainless goldfish on their learning ability. Master's Thesis, University of Chicago, Chicago, Illinois.

Bernstein, J. J. (1961a). Loss of hue discrimination in forebrain-ablated fish. *Exp. Neurol.* **3,** 1–17.

Bernstein, J. J. (1961b). Brightness discrimination following forebrain ablation in fish. *Exp. Neurol.* **3,** 297–306.

Bernstein, J. J. (1962). Role of the telencephalon in color vision of fish. *Exp. Neurol.* **6,** 173–185.

Bernstein, J. J. (1970). Anatomy and physiology of the central nervous system. *Fish Physiol.* **4,** 1–90.

Berwein, M. (1941). Beobachtungen und Verusche über das gesellige Leben von Elritzen. *Z. Vergl. Physiol.* **28,** 402–420.

Bitterman, M. E. (1960). Toward a comparative psychology of learning. *Am. Psychol.* **15,** 704–712.

Bitterman, M. E. (1965). Phyletic differences in learning. *Am. Psychol.* **20,** 396–410.

Bitterman, M. E. (1966). Animal learning. *In* "Experimental Methods and Instrumentation in Psychology" (J. B. Sidowski, ed.), pp. 451–484. McGraw-Hill, New York.

Bitterman, M. E. (1975). The comparative analysis of learning. *Science* **188,** 699–709.

Bolles, R. C. (1971). Species specific defense reactions. *In* "Aversive Conditioning and Learning" (F. R. Brush, ed.), pp. 183–234. Academic Press, New York.

Boyd, E. S., and Gardner, L. C. (1962). Positive and negative reinforcement from intracranial stimulation of a teleost. *Science* **136,** 648–649.

Brady, J. V., Schreiner, L., Geller, I., and Kling, A. (1954). Subcortical mechanisms in emotional behavior: The effect of rhinencephalic injury upon the acquisition and retention of a conditioned avoidance response in cats. *J. Comp. Physiol. Psychol.* **47,** 179–186.

Butter, C. M. (1969). Perseveration in extinction and in discrimination reversal tasks following selective frontal ablations in *Macaca mulatta. Physiol. Behav.* **4,** 163–171.

Butters, N., and Rosvold, H. E. (1968). Effect of septal lesions on resistance to extinction and delayed alternation in monkeys. *J. Comp. Physiol. Psychol.* **66,** 389–395.

Cain, D. P. (1974). The role of the olfactory bulb in limbic mechanisms. *Psychol. Bull.* **81,** 654–671.

Campbell, C. B., and Hodos, W. (1970). The concept of homology and the evolution of the nervous system. *Brain, Behav. Evol.* **3,** 353–367.

Chimits, P. (1957). *Tilapia* in ancient Egypt. *FAO Fish. Bull.* **10,** 1–5.

Craig, W. (1918). Appetites and aversions as constituents of instincts. *Biol. Bull. (Woods Hole, Mass.)* **34,** 91–107.

Darwin, C. (1871). "The Descent of Man, and Selection in Relation to Sex." Vol. 1. vi + 409 pp.; Vol. 2. viii + 436 pp. Appleton, New York.

Davis, R. E., Kassel, J., and Schwagmeyer, P. (1976). Telencephalic lesions and behavior in the teleost, *Macropodus opercularis:* Reproduction, startle reaction, and operant behavior in the male. *Behav. Biol.* **18,** 165–178.

Demski, L. S. (1973). Feeding and aggressive behavior evoked by hypothalamic stimulation in a cichlid fish. *Comp. Biochem. Physiol. A* **44,** 685–692.

Demski, L. S., and Knigge, K. M. (1971). The telencephalon and hypothalamus of the bluegill (*Lepomis macrochirus*): Evoked feeding, aggressive and reproductive behavior with representative frontal sections. *J. Comp. Neurol.* **143,** 1–16.

Dewsbury, D. A., and Bernstein, J. J. (1969). Role of the telencephalon in performance of conditioned avoidance responses by goldfish. *Exp. Neurol.* **23,** 445–456.

Dicks, D., Myers, R. E., and Kling, A. (1969). Uncus and amygdala lesions: Effects on social behavior in the free-ranging rhesus monkey. *Science* **165,** 69–71.

Douglas, R. J., and Pribram, K. H. (1966). Learning and limbic lesions. *Neuropsychologia* **4,** 197–220.

Döving, K. B., and Gemne G. (1966). An electrophysiological study of the efferent olfactory system in the burbot. *J. Neurophysiol.* **29,** 665–674.

Droogleever Fortuyn, J. (1961). Topographical relations in the telencephalon of the sunfish, *Eupomotis gibbosus. J. Comp. Neurol.* **116,** 249–263.

Ebbesson, S. O., Jane, J. A., and Schroeder, D. M. (1972). A general overview of major interspecific variations in thalamic organization. *Brain, Behav. Evol.* **6**, 92–130.

Ellen, P., Wilson, A. S., and Powell, E. W. (1964). Septal inhibition and timing behavior in the rat. *Exp. Neurol.* **10**, 120–132.

Engelhardt, F., Woodard, W. T., and Bitterman, M. E. (1973). Discriminative reversal in the goldfish as a function of training conditions. *J. Comp. Physiol. Psychol.* **85**, 144–150.

Fiedler, K. (1967). Ethologische und neuroanatomische Auswirkungen von Vorderhirnexstirpationen bei Meer brassen (Diplodus) und Lippfischen (Crenilabrus, Perciformes, Teleostei). *J. Hirnforsch.* **9**, 481–563.

Fiedler, K. (1968). Verhaltenswirksame Strukturen im Fischgehirn. *Zool. Anz.* **31**, 602–616.

Flood, N. B. (1975). Effect of forebrain ablation on long-term retention of a food-reinforced shape discrimination. *Psychol. Rep.* **86**, 783–786.

Flood, N. B., and Overmier, J. B. (1971). Effects of telencephalic and olfactory lesions on appetitive learning in goldfish. *Physiol. Behav.* **6**, 35–40.

Flood, N. B., Overmier, J. B., and Savage, G. E. (1976). The teleost telencephalon and learning: An interpretive review of data and hypotheses. *Physiol. Behav.* **16**, 783–798.

Forselius, S. (1957). Studies of Anabantid fishes. *Zool. Bidr. Uppsala* **32**, 93–597.

Frank, A. H., Flood, N. B., and Overmier, J. B. (1972). Reversal learning in forebrain ablated and olfactory tract sectioned teleost, *Carassius auratus*. *Psychon. Sci.* **26**, 149–151.

French, J. W. (1942). The effect of temperature on the retention of a maze habit in fish. *J. Exp. Psychol.* **31**, 79–87.

Fryer, G., and Iles, T. D. (1972). "The Cichlid Fishes of the Great Lakes of Africa." T. F. H. Publications, Inc., Ltd., British Crown Colony of Hong Kong.

Fujita, O., and Oi, S. (1969). [Effect of forebrain ablation and inter-trial intervals upon conditioned avoidance responses in the goldfish.] *Annu. Anim. Psychol. (Tokyo)* **19**, 39–47.

Fuller, J. L., Rosvold, H. E., and Pribram, K. H. (1957). The effect on affective and cognitive behavior in the dog of lesions of the pyriform-amygdala-hippocampal complex. *J. Comp. Physiol. Psychol.* **50**, 89–96.

Glickman, S. E., and Shiff, B. B. (1967). A biological theory of reinforcement. *Psychol. Rev.* **74**, 81–109.

Gloor, P. (1960). Amygdala. *Handb. Physiol., Sect. 1: Neurophysiol.* **2**, 1395–1420.

Goldstein, S. R. (1967). Mirror image as a reinforcer in Siamese fighting fish: A repetition with additional controls. *Psychon. Sci.* **7**, 331–332.

Goldstein, S. R. (1975). Observations on the establishment of a stable community of adult male and female Siamese fighting fish (*Betta splendens*). *Anim. Behav.* **23**, 179–185.

Gordon, M. S. (1972). "Animal Physiology: Principles and Adaptations," 2nd ed. MacMillan, New York.

Gosline, W. A. (1971). "Functional Morphology and Classification of Teleostean Fishes." Univ. Press of Hawaii, Honolulu.

Grice, G. R. (1948). The relation of secondary reinforcement to delayed reward in visual discrimination learning. *J. Exp. Psychol.* **38**, 1–16.

Grimm, R. J. (1960). Feeding behavior and electrical stimulation of the brain of *Carassius auratus*. *Science* **131**, 162–163.

Hainsworth, F. R., Overmier, J. B., and Snowdon, C. T. (1967). Specific and permanent deficits in instrumental avoidance responding following forebrain ablation in the goldfish. *J. Comp. Physiol. Psychol.* **63**, 111–116.

Hale, E. B. (1956a). Social facilitation and forebrain function in maze performance of green sunfish, *Lepomis cyanellus*. *Physiol. Zool.* **29**, 93–107.

Hale, E. B. (1956b). Effects of forebrain lesions on the aggressive behavior of green sunfish, *Lepomis cyanellus*. *Physiol. Zool.* **29**, 107–127.

Hara, T., and Gorbman, A. (1967). Electrophysiological studies of the olfactory system of the goldfish, *Carassius auratus* L. I. Modification of the electrical activity of the olfactory bulbs by other central nervous structures. *Comp. Biochem. Physiol.* **21**, 185–200.

Hemmings, C. C. (1966). Olfaction and vision in fish schooling. *J. Exp. Biol.* **45**, 449–464.

Herrick, C. J. (1924). "Neurological Foundations of Animal Behavior." Holt, New York.

Herrick, C. J. (1933). The functions of the olfactory parts of the cerebral cortex. *Proc. Natl. Acad. Sci. U.S.A.* **19**, 7–14.

Hillowitz, S. (1945). The effects of forebrain removal on learning in goldfish. Master's Thesis, University of Chicago, Chicago, Illinois.

Hinde, R. A. (1958). The nest-building behaviour of domesticated canaries. *Proc. Zool. Soc. London* **131**, 1–48.

Hinde, R. A., and Steel, E. (1972). Reinforcing events in the integration of canary nest-building. *Anim. Behav.* **20**, 514–525.

Hinde, R. A., and Stevenson, J. G. (1969). Sequences of behavior. *Adv. Study Behav.* **2**, 267–296.

Hodos, W. (1970). Evolutionary interpretation of neural and behavioral studies of living vertebrates. *In* "The Neurosciences: Second Study Program" (F. O. Schmitt, ed.), pp. 26–39. Rockefeller Univ. Press, New York.

Hodos, W., and Campbell, C. B. G. (1969). *Scala Naturae:* Why there is no theory in comparative psychology. *Psychol. Rev.* **76**, 337–350.

Hogan, J. A. (1961). Motivational aspects of instinctive behavior in *Betta splendens*. Doctoral Dissertation, Harvard University, Cambridge, Massachusetts.

Hogan, J. A. (1967). Fighting and reinforcement in the Siamese fighting fish (*Betta splendens*). *J. Comp. Physiol. Psychol.* **64**, 356–359.

Hogan, J. A. (1974). On the choice between eating and aggressive display in the Siamese fighting fish (*Betta splendens*). *Learn. Motiv.* **5**, 273–287.

Hogan, J. A., Kleist, S., and Hutchings, C. S. L. (1970). Display and food as reinforcers in the Siamese fighting fish (*Betta splendens*). *J. Comp. Physiol. Psychol.* **70**, 351–357.

Hosch, L. (1936). Untersuchungen über Grosshirnfunktionen der Elritze (*Phoxinus laevis*) und des Gründlings (*Gobio fluviatilis*). *Zool. Jahrb., Abt. Allg. Zool. Physiol. Tiere* **57**, 57–98.

Ingle, D. J. (1965a). Behavioral effects of forebrain lesions in goldfish. *Proc. 73rd Annu. Conv. Am. Psychol. Assoc.* pp. 143–144.

Ingle, D. J. (1965b). The use of the fish in neuropsychology. *Perspect. Biol. Med.* **8**, 241–260.

Issacson, R. L. (1974). "The Limbic System." Plenum, New York.

Janzen, W. (1933). Untersuchungen über Grosshirnfunktionen des Goldfisches (*Carassius auratus*). *Zool. Jahrb., Abt. Allg. Zool. Physiol. Tiere* **52**, 591–628.

Jerison, H. J. (1973). "Evolution of the Brain and Intelligence." Academic Press, New York.

Kaada, B. R. (1960). Cingulate, posterior orbital, anterior insular and temporal pole cortex. *Handb. Physiol., Sect. 1: Neurophysiol.* **2**, 1345–1372.

Kamrin, R. P., and Aronson, L. R. (1954). The effects of forebrain lesions on mating behavior in the male platyfish, *Xiphophorus maculatus*. *Zoologica (N. Y.)* **39**, 133–140.

Kaplan, H., and Aronson, L. R. (1967). Effect of forebrain ablation on the performance of conditioned avoidance response in the teleost fish, *Tilapia h. macrocephala*. *Anim. Behav.* **15**, 438–448.

Kaplan, H., and Aronson, L. R. (1969). Function of forebrain and cerebellum in learning in the teleost *Tilapia heudelotii macrocephala*. *Bull. Am. Mus. Nat. Hist.* **142**, 141–208.

Karamyan, A. I. (1956). "Evolution of the function of the cerebellum and cerebral hemispheres." Medgiz, Leningrad (transl. by Israel Program for Scientific Translations, 1962, OTS no. TT 61-31014).

Karamyan, A. I., Malukova, I. V., and Sergeev, B. F. (1967). Participation of the telencephalon of bony fish in the accomplishment of complex conditioned-reflex and general behavior reactions.

In "Behavior and Reception in Fish," pp. 109–144. Academy of Science, USSR, Moscow. (Transl. by Bureau of Sport Fisheries and Wildlife, OTS no. PB 184929T).

Kassel, J., Davis, R. E., and Schwagmeyer, P. (1976). Telencephalic lesions and behavior in the teleost, *Macropodus opercularis:* Further analysis of reproductive and operant behavior in the male. *Behav. Biol.* **18,** 179–188.

Kholodov, Y. A. (1960). Simple and complex food obtaining conditioned reflexes in normal fish and in fish after removal of the forebrain. *Works Inst. Higher Nerv. Act., Physiol. Ser.* **5,** 194–201 (transl. by Natl. Sci. Found., Washington, D.C., 1962).

Kimble, D. P. (1969). Possible inhibitory functions of the hippocampus. *Neuropsychologia* **7,** 235–244.

Kimble, D. P., Rogers, L., and Hendrickson, C. W. (1967). Hippocampal lesions disrupt maternal, not sexual, behavior in the Albino rat. *J. Comp. Physiol. Psychol.* **63,** 401–407.

Konorski, J. (1967). "Integrative Activity of the Brain." Univ. of Chicago Press, Chicago, Illinois.

Koshtoiants, K. S., Maliukina, G. A., and Aleksandriuk, S. P. (1960). The role of the forebrain in the "group effect" in fish. *Sechenov Physiol. J. USSR* **46,** 1209–1216 (transl. by Natl. Sci. Found., Washington, D.C.).

Kumakura, S. (1928). Versuche an Goldfischen, denen beide Hemisphären des Grosshirns exstirpiert worden waren. *Nagoya J. Med. Sci.* **3,** 19–24.

Lorenz, K. (1941). Vergleichende Bewegungsstudien an Anatinen. *J. Ornithol.* **89,** Suppl., 194–294.

Losey, G. S., and Margules, L. (1974). Cleaning symbiosis provides a positive reinforcer for fish. *Science* **184,** 179–180.

McCleary, R. A. (1961). Response specificity in the behavioral effects of limbic system lesions in the cat. *J. Comp. Physiol. Psychol.* **54,** 605–613.

McCleary, R. A. (1966). Response-modulating functions of the limbic system: Initiation and suppression. *Prog. Physiol. Psychol.* **1,** 209–272.

Macdonald, G. E., and de Toledo, L. (1974). Partial reinforcement effects and type of reward. *Learn. Motiv.* **5,** 288–298.

Macey, M. J., Pickford, G. E., and Peter, R. E. (1974). Forebrain localization of the spawning reflex response to exogenous neurohypophysial hormones in the killifish, *Fundulus heteroclitus. J. Exp. Zool.* **190,** 269–280.

McFarland, D. J. (1965). Hunger, thirst, and displacement pecking in the Barbary dove. *Anim. Behav.* **13,** 293–300.

Mackie, J. L. (1965). Causes and conditions. *Am. Philos. Q.* **2,** 245–264.

Mahut, H. (1971). Spatial and object reversal learning in monkeys with partial temporal lobe ablations. *Neuropsychologia* **9,** 409–424.

Masterton, R. S., Skeen, L. C., and RoBards, M. J. (1974). Origins of anthropoid intelligence. *Brain, Behav. Evol.* **10,** 322–353.

Meader, R. G. (1939). Notes on the functions of the forebrain in teleosts. *Zoologica (N. Y.)* **24,** 11–14.

Michal, E. K. (1965). The effects of lesions in the limbic system on courtship and mating behavior of male rats. Doctoral Dissertation, University of Illinois, Urbana.

Miller, N. E., and DeBold, R. C. (1965). Classically conditioned tongue-licking and operant bar pressing recorded simultaneously in the rat. *J. Comp. Physiol. Psychol.* **59,** 109–111.

Mowrer, O. H. (1947). On the dual nature of learning—a re-interpretation of "conditioning" and "problem-solving." *Harv. Educ. Rev.* **17,** 102–148.

Murray, C. A. S. (1973). Conditioning in *Betta splendens* (Doctoral Dissertation, University of Pennsylvania, 1973). *Diss. Abstr. Int. B* **34,** 1778.

Nelson, G. J. (1969). Origin and diversification of teleostean fishes. *Ann. N. Y. Acad. Sci.* **167,** 18–30.

Nieuwenhuys, R. (1959). The structure of the telencephalon of the teleost *Gasterosteus aculeatus*. *Proc. kon. ned. Akad. Wet. Ser. C* **62,** 341–362.

Nieuwenhuys, R. (1967). The interpretation of the cell masses in the teleostean forebrain. *In* "Evolution of the Forebrain" (R. Hassler and H. Stephan, eds.), pp. 32–39. Georg Thieme Verlag, Stuttgart.

Noble, G. K. (1936). The function of the corpus striatum in the social behavior of fishes. *Anat. Rec., Suppl.* **64,** abstr. no. 76, p. 34.

Noble, G. K. (1937). Effect of lesions of the corpus striatum on the brooding behavior of cichlid fishes. *Anat. Rec., Suppl.* **70,** abstr. no. 53, p. 58.

Noble, G. K. (1939). Neural basis of social behavior in vertebrates. *Collect. Net* **14,** 121–124.

Noble, G. K., and Borne, R. (1941). The effect of forebrain lesions on the sexual and fighting behavior of *Betta splendens* and other fishes. *Anat. Rec., Suppl.* **79,** abstr. no. 138, p. 49.

Nolte, W. (1932). Experimentelle Untersuchungen zum Problem der Lokalisation des Assoziationsvermögens im Fischgehirn. *Z. vergl. Physiol.* **18,** 255–279.

Olton, D. S., and Isaacson, R. L. (1968). Hippocampal lesions and active avoidance. *Physiol. Behav.* **3,** 719–724.

Overmier, J. B., and Curnow, P. F. (1969). Classical conditioning, pseudoconditioning, and sensitization in "normal" and forebrainless goldfish. *J. Comp. Physiol. Psychol.* **68,** 193–198.

Overmier, J. B., and Flood, N. B. (1969). Passive avoidance in forebrain ablated teleost fish, *Carassius auratus*. *Physiol. Behav.* **4,** 791–794.

Overmier, J. B., and Gross, D. (1974). Effects of telencephalic ablation upon nest-building and avoidance behaviors in East African mouthbreeding fish, *Tilapia mossambica*. *Behav. Biol.* **12,** 211–222.

Overmier, J. B., and Savage, G. E. (1974). Effects of telencephalic ablation on trace classical conditioning of heart rate in goldfish. *Exp. Neurol.* **42,** 339–346.

Overmier, J. B., and Starkman, N. (1974). Transfer of control of avoidance behavior in normal and telencephalon ablated goldfish (*Carassius auratus*). *Physiol. Behav.* **12,** 605–608.

Papez, J. W. (1937). A proposed mechanism of emotion. *AMA Arch. Neurol. Psychiatry* **38,** 725–743.

Peeke, H. V., Peeke, S. C., and Williston, J. S. (1972). Long-term memory deficits for habituation of predatory behavior in the forebrain ablated goldfish (*Carassius auratus*). *Exp. Neurol.* **36,** 288–294.

Peter, R. E., and Gill, V. E. (1975). A stereotaxic atlas and technique for forebrain nuclei of the goldfish, *Carassius auratus*. *J. Comp. Neurol.* **159,** 69–102.

Polimanti, O. (1913). Contributions à la physiologie du système nerveux central et du mouvement des poissons. *Arch. ital. Biol. (Pisa)* **59,** 383–401.

Pribram, K. H., and Kruger, L. (1954). Functions of the "olfactory brain." *Ann. N. Y. Acad. Sci.* **58,** 109–138.

Rasa, O. A. E. (1971). Appetence for aggression in juvenile damsel fish. *Z. Tierpsychol., Suppl.* **7.**

Rescorla, R. A., and Solomon, R. S. (1967). Two-process learning theory: Relationships between Pavlovian conditioning and instrumental learning. *Psychol. Rev.* **74,** 151–182.

Ribbink, A. J. (1972). The behavior and brain function of the cichlid fish, *Hemihaplochromis philander*. *Zool. Afr.* **7,** 21–41.

Roper, T. J. (1975). Nest material and food as reinforcers for ratio responding in mice. *Learn. Motiv.* **6,** 327–343.

Rosvold, H. E., and Sczwarcbart, M. K. (1964). Neural structures involved in delayed response performance. *In* "The Frontal Granular Cortex and Behavior" (J. M. Warren and K. Akert, eds.), pp. 1–15. McGraw-Hill, New York.

Rosvold, H. E., Mirsky, A. F., and Pribram, K. H. (1954). Influence of amygdalectomy on social behavior in monkeys. *J. Comp. Physiol. Psychol.* **47,** 173–178.

Savage, G. E. (1968a). Function of the forebrain in the memory system of the fish. *In* ''The Central Nervous System and Fish Behavior'' (D. Ingle, ed.), pp. 127–138. Univ. of Chicago Press, Chicago, Illinois.

Savage, G. E. (1968b). Temporal factors in avoidance learning in normal and forebrainless goldfish (*Carassius auratus*). *Nature (London)* **218**, 1168–1169.

Savage, G. E. (1969a). Telencephalic lesions and avoidance behaviour in the goldfish (*Carassius auratus*). *Anim. Behav.* **17**, 362–373.

Savage, G. E. (1969b). Some preliminary observations on the role of the telencephalon in food-reinforced behaviour in the goldfish, *Carassius auratus*. *Anim. Behav.* **17**, 760–772.

Savage, G. E., and Swingland, I. R. (1969). Positively reinforced behaviour and the forebrain in goldfish. *Nature (London)* **221**, 878–879.

Scalia, F., and Ebbesson, S. O. E. (1971). The central projections of the olfactory bulb in a teleost (*Gymnothorax funebris*). *Brain, Behav. Evol.* **4**, 376–399.

Schnitzlein, H. N. (1968). Introductory remarks on the telencephalon of fish. *In* ''The Central Nervous System and Fish Behavior'' (D. Ingle, ed.), pp. 97–100. Univ. of Chicago Press, Chicago, Illinois.

Schönherr, J. (1955). Über die Abhangigkeit der Instinkthandlungen vom Vorderhirn und Zwischenhirn (Epiphyse) bei *Gasterosteus aculeatus* L. *Zool. Jahrb. (Physiologie)* **65**, 357–386.

Schwagmeyer, P., Davis, R. E., and Kassel, J. (1977). Telencephalic lesions and behaviour in the teleost *Macropodus opercularis:* Effects of telencephalon and olfactory bulb ablation on spawning and foam nest building. *Anim. Behav.,* in press.

Scobie, S. R., and Fallon, D. (1974). Operant and Pavlovian control of a defensive shuttle response in goldfish (*Carassius auratus*). *J. Comp. Physiol. Psychol.* **86**, 858–866.

Scoville, W. B., and Milner, B. (1957). Loss of recent memory after bilateral hippocampal lesions. *J. Neurol., Neurosurg. Psychiatry* **20**, 11–21.

Segaar, J. (1961). Telencephalon and behavior in *Gasterosteus aculeatus*. *Behaviour* **18**, 256–287.

Segaar, J. (1965). Behavioural aspects of degeneration and regeneration in fish brain: A comparison with higher vertebrates. *Prog. Brain Res.* **14**, 143–231.

Segaar, J., and Nieuwenhuys, R. (1963). New etho-physiological experiments with male *Gasterosteus aculeatus,* with anatomical comment. *Anim. Behav.* **11**, 331–344.

Sevenster, P. (1968). Motivation and learning in sticklebacks. *In* ''The Central Nervous System and Fish Behavior'' (D. Ingle, ed.), pp. 233–245. Univ. of Chicago Press, Chicago, Illinois.

Sevenster, P. (1973). Incompatibility of response and reward. *In* ''Constraints on Learning: Limitations and Predispositions'' (R. A. Hinde and J. Stevenson-Hinde, eds.), pp. 265–283. Academic Press, London.

Shapiro, S., Schuckman, H., Sussman, D., and Tucker, A. M. (1974). Effects of telencephalic lesions on the gill cover response in Siamese fighting fish. *Physiol. Behav.* **13**, 749–755.

Shettleworth, S. (1972). Constraints on learning. *Adv. Study Behav.* **4**, 1–68.

Shettleworth, S. (1975). Reinforcement and the organization of behavior in golden hamsters: Hunger, environment, and food reinforcement. *J. Exp. Psychol.: Anim. Behav. Proces.* **104**, 56–87.

Shumilina, A. E. (1966). The significance of the frontal lobes in conditioned reflex activity in the dog. *In* ''Frontal Lobes and Regulation of Behavior: Symposium 10.'' Proceedings of XVIII International Congress of Psychology, Moscow, pp. 103–109.

Skinner, B. F. (1936). The reinforcing effect of a differentiating stimulus. *J. Gen. Psychol.* **14**, 263–278.

Slotnick, B. M. (1967). Disturbances of maternal behavior in the rat following lesions of the cingulate cortex. *Behaviour* **29**, 204–236.

Solomon, R. L., and Brush, E. S. (1956). Experimentally derived conceptions of anxiety and aversion. *In* "Nebraska Symposium on Motivation" (M. R. Jones, ed.), pp. 212–305. Univ. of Nebraska Press, Lincoln.

Solomon, R. L., and Wynne, L. C. (1953). Traumatic avoidance learning: Acquisition in normal dogs. *Psychol. Monogr.* **67,** No. 4 (Whole No. 354).

Spence, K. W. (1956). "Behavior Theory and Conditioning." Yale Univ. Press, New Haven, Connecticut.

Strieck, F. (1925). Untersuchungen über den Geruchs- und Geschmackssin der Elritze (*Phoxinus laevis A.*). *Z. vergl. Physiol.* **2,** 122–154.

Thomas, G. (1974). The influences of encountering a food object on subsequent searching behavior in *Gasterosteus aculeatus L. Anim. Behav.* **22,** 941–952.

Thompson, R. (1964). A note on cortical and subcortical injuries and avoidance learning in rats. *In* "The Frontal Granular Cortex and Behavior" (J. M. Warren and K. Akert, eds.), pp. 16–25. McGraw-Hill, New York.

Thompson, R., and Ledoux, J. E. (1974). Common brain regions essential for the expression of learned and instinctive visual habits in the albino rat. *Bull. Psychon. Soc.* **4,** 78–80.

Thompson, T. (1963). Visual reinforcement in Siamese fighting fish. *Science* **141,** 55–57.

Thompson, T. (1966). Operant and classically conditioned aggressive behavior in Siamese fighting fish. *Am. Zool.* **6,** 629–641.

Thompson, T., and Sturm, T. (1965a). Visual-reinforcer color, and operant behavior in Siamese fighting fish. *J. Exp. Anal. Behav.* **8,** 341–344.

Thompson, T., and Sturm, T. (1965b). Classical conditioning of aggressive display in Siamese fighting fish. *J. Exp. Anal. Behav.* **8,** 397–403.

Thorndike, E. L. (1911). "Animal Intelligence." Macmillan, New York.

Tinbergen, N. (1952). "Derived" activities; their causation, biological significance, origin, and emancipation during evolution. *Q. Rev. Biol.* **27,** 1–32.

Todd, J. H. (1971). The chemical language of fishes. *Sci. Am.* **224,** 98–108.

Tracy, W. H., and Harrison, J. M. (1956). Aversive behavior following lesions of the septal region of the forebrain in the rat. *Am. J. Psychol.* **69,** 443–447.

Ulrich, R., Johnston, M., Richardson, J., and Wolff, P. (1963). The operant conditioning of fighting behavior in rats. *Psychol. Rec.* **13,** 465–470.

Vanderwolf, C. H. (1971). Limbic-diencephalic mechanisms of voluntary movement. *Psychol. Rev.* **78,** 83–113.

Warren, J. M. (1961). The effect of telencephalic injuries on learning by Paradise fish, *Macropodus opercularis. J. Comp. Physiol. Psychol.* **54,** 130–132.

Weiskrantz, L. (1968). Treatments, inferences, and brain function. *In* "Analysis of Behavioral Change" (L. Weiskrantz, ed.), pp. 400–414. Harper, New York.

Wenzel, B. M. (1974). The olfactory system and behavior. *In* "Limbic and Autonomic Nervous Systems Research" (L. V. DiCara, ed.), pp. 1–40, Plenum, New York.

Wiebalck, U. (1937). Untersuchungen zur Function des Vorderhirns bei Knochenfischen. *Zool. Anz.* **117,** 325–329.

Wodinsky, J., and Bitterman, M. E. (1957). Discrimination reversal in fish. *Am. J. Psychol.* **70,** 569–576.

Woodard, W. T., and Bitterman, M. E. (1973). Pavlovian analysis of avoidance conditioning in the goldfish (*Carassius auratus*). *J. Comp. Physiol. Psychol.* **82,** 123–129.

Wrede, W. L. (1932). Versuche über den Artduft der Elritzen. *Z. vergl. Physiol.* **17,** 510–519.

Zucker, I. (1965). Effect of lesions of the septal-limbic area on the behavior of cats. *J. Comp. Physiol. Psychol.* **60,** 344–352.

Sound Detection and Sensory Coding by the Auditory Systems of Fishes

RICHARD R. FAY

I. Introduction 197
II. Sound Detection 198
    A. Underwater Sound 198
    B. Structure and Function of Peripheral Auditory Systems 201
    C. Auditory Sensitivity 206
III. The Analysis of Auditory Information 211
    A. Frequency Discrimination Experiments 211
    B. Masking Experiments 213
    C. Mechanisms of Frequency Analysis 216
IV. Auditory Localization 219
    A. Lateral-Line System and Localization 220
    B. Inner Ears and Localization 220
V. Auditory Electrophysiology 224
    A. Responses of the Inner Ear 224
    B. Responses of the Eighth Nerve and Brain 227
VI. Conclusion 229
    References 231

I. INTRODUCTION

The structures and functions of the auditory systems of fishes have been investigated by scientists of rather diverse backgrounds since the beginning of this century. The particular emphasis and methods associated with the disciplines of zoology, physiology, anatomy, psychology, biophysics, and the various fields of engineering have all been applied here, as they have been in most modern studies of sensory systems. In some cases, the fish auditory system is chosen as a convenient preparation for the study of certain phenomena of general biological interest. For example, the experiments of Furukawa and his associates on the electrophysiology of the goldfish auditory system did not stem from an interest in goldfish, or even from a particular interest in fish sensory systems, but rather were designed to study hair cell physiology and synaptic processes in a uniquely suitable vertebrate nervous system. Similarly, my own psychophysical investigations of frequency analysis in the goldfish (Fay, 1969, 1970a,b, 1972, 1974a) were designed as investigations of sensory coding and information processing by nervous systems, and not simply as contributions to the physiology of fishes. In other cases, however, the experimental subject was indeed the subject of the experiment, as in the studies of auditory sensitivity of the tuna (Iverson, 1967) and of the cod (Buerkle, 1967), for example.

Such diverse approaches and experimental orientations have led to numerous attempts to bring together a large and heterogenius literature from various points of view (see the reviews by Parker, 1918; von Frisch, 1936; Kleerekoper and Chagnon, 1954; Griffin, 1955; Moulton, 1963; Tavolga, 1965, 1971; van Bergeijk, 1967a; Enger, 1968; Lowenstein, 1971; Popper and Fay, 1973). Such a list of past and present reviews tends to argue against the value of my introducing yet another one here. However, most of the previous attempts at a synthesis of information have dealt primarily with the fishes and how they hear, from evolutionary (Pumphrey, 1950; van Bergeijk, 1967a), physiological (Lowenstein, 1971), and anatomical–behavioral (Moulton, 1963) points of view. This chapter, on the other hand, deals primarily with auditory systems, and how they function as receptors and analyzers of acoustic information among the fishes. The functions of these systems are always compared to those of other vertebrate classes in attempts to illuminate general principles of vertebrate auditory mechanisms.

Fishes may respond to a variety of underwater mechanical disturbances through several mechanoreceptive sensory systems, and we may attribute these responses to stimulation of the auditory, vestibular, lateral-line, or cutaneous systems depending upon the nature of the disturbance and the known receptive properties of the sensory organs possibly involved. An understanding of auditory function in fishes, then, must begin with analysis of the adequate stimuli and of the sensitivities of the receptor organs.

II. SOUND DETECTION

A. Underwater Sound

The treatment of underwater sound here will be qualitative simply because a visualization of physical events is more valuable than quantitative relationships in the present context. Quantitative treatments of most phenomena can be found in any text on acoustics, and a good intuitive discussion can be found in van Bergeijk (1964).

As an object vibrates under water, sound propagates away from the source as a mechanical disturbance consisting of particle movements with a particular displacement amplitude (d) and fluctuations of hydrospheric pressure (p) above and below ambient values. Both sound pressure and particle displacement can be important in the stimulation of auditory receptor organs of fishes. In ideal, boundaryless conditions, the characteristic impedance of the medium (defined as the product of the medium's density and the velocity of sound in cm/sec) determines the ratio between sound pressure (in dynes/cm²) and the particle displacement (in centimeters) for a particular sound frequency.* Thus, a value for particle displacement amplitude may be calculated from a measured sound pressure value once the impedance of the medium and the frequency of the signal are known. However, in the vicinity of underwater sound sources and of large impedance discontinuities such as an air–water interface, the impedance [the ratio between sound pressure and particle displacement (p/d)] may vary unpredictably, making the specification of d from measurements of p impossible. In most cases, p/d drops from its ideal value, and this is equivalent to a decrease in the impedance of the medium (toward the value for air), or an increase in the displacement amplitude for a given sound pressure level. These changes in p/d normally occur in association with two distinct acoustic phenomena; near-field effects and standing wave patterns.

1. Near and Far Fields

The important near-field vs. far-field distinction was made clear by Harris and van Bergeijk in 1962. Since that time, the concept has been reviewed and restated many times, primarily in quantitative terms (e.g., Harris, 1964; van Bergeijk, 1967a; Siler, 1969). The near field can be viewed as a region surrounding an underwater sound source in which relatively large hydrodynamic motions occur in addition to that particle motion associated with the elastic propagating sound wave. It may be helpful here to think of the hydrodynamic motions as due to the streaming of the highly incompressable water around the vibrating sound source. As van Bergeijk (1967a) has pointed out, if water were completely incompressable, these near-field motions would be the only type of phenomenon produced.

The amplitude of this hydrodynamic motion is inversely proportional to the square of the distance from a monopole sound source. Since the particle motion

---

*Strictly, the characteristic impedance of the medium equals the ratio between sound pressure and particle velocity under ideal conditions. In this chapter, the ratio between pressure and particle displacement will be used to indicate relative impedance values. Displacement is more easily visualized than velocity, and one can be calculated from the other once the frequency is known.

associated with the elastic propagating wave declines simply in direct proportion with distance, a certain distance exists at which the amplitude of both displacement effects are equal, and beyond which the hydrodynamic displacement amplitude falls below the other. This point is defined as the boundary between the near and far fields, and it occurs at a distance of about 1 wavelength/2π from a monopole source. In the present context, the importance of the near field is that it is a region within which the major particle displacement component will vary in amplitude relative to sound pressure depending upon the distance of measurement from the source, among other factors. In the far field, the major displacement component remains proportional to sound pressure regardless of distance.

2. Standing Waves

Another common cause of changes in p/d is standing wave patterns. A standing wave may be generated by a propagating wave striking a large impedance discontinuity, such as an air–water interface, and reflecting back onto itself. If reflection is perfect, a static spatial pattern will be generated consisting of areas of relatively high sound pressure fluctuations alternating at ¼ wavelength intervals with areas of relatively high particle displacement amplitude. At a pressure minimum (node), p/d will approach zero since particles are vigorously moving to and from with little compression occurring. At a pressure maximum (antinode), however, p/d will approach infinity since compression occurs at the same time from both directions and little particle motion takes place. If the sound reflection is not perfect, the resulting pattern will have both stationary and progressing components. Here again, the importance of the standing wave pattern is that a measure of either pressure or displacement alone is not adequate to completely specify the amplitude of the stimulus impinging upon the fish.

Near fields and standing wave patterns are inevitable in almost all laboratory investigations of underwater hearing (Parvelescu, 1964), and clearly create problems for experimental attempts to measure the auditory sensitivity of fishes which are sufficiently sensitive to both the pressure and the motional components of the stimulus. In order to measure sound pressure sensitivity absolutely, it is necessary to demonstrate that the sound pressure level is indeed controlling the animal's response independently of displacement amplitude. Measurements with a calibrated hydrophone will then provide the appropriate values for the stimulus levels.

For absolute measurements of displacement sensitivity, the displacement amplitude must be shown to control the animal's response. However, additional problems arise here since meaningful measurements of displacement amplitude are difficult to obtain. The accelerometers normally used must be specially calibrated and prepared for their use under water (Cahn *et al.*, 1969), and those sufficiently sensitive for most applications are rather large and may alter the properties of the acoustic field in which they are placed. Note, too, that displacement is a vector quantity with direction, and measurements in various directions require at least two accelerometers, one for use horizontally, and one for use vertically. Finally, for any particular system under study, the direction of greatest sensitivity would have to be determined before a single value for absolute sensitivity would be meaningful.

B. The Structure and Function of Peripheral Auditory Systems

1. Morphology

The inner ears and lateral-line organs of fishes have a common embryological origin and comprise the acoustico-lateralis system (see review by Lowenstein, 1971). Specialized mechanoreceptive ciliated receptor cells (hair cells) are found in each organ of the system. Lateral-line hair cells have been found to be displacement sensitive since a deformation of the cilia modulates activity in innervating sensory nerve fibers (Flock, 1965). Each cell has a bundle of stereocilia with one asymmetrically placed kinocilium. Movement of the stereocilia toward the kinocilium causes depolarization and excitation of sensory nerves, while movements away from the kinocilium cause hyperpolarization and inhibition.

In the lateral-line systems of fishes and amphibia, the hair cell cilia are imbedded in a gelatenous cupula which may lie in pits or canals, or stand free on the body surface. These cells respond to water particle movements at frequencies up to 200–300 Hz, at a minimum amplitude in the low angstrom range (Dijkgraaf, 1963). While it appears that both the organs of the ear and lateral-line system respond to water particle displacements at frequencies below 200–300 Hz, the otolithic organs are likely to be the more sensitive (Weiss, 1966, 1969) due to the more massive ciliary restraint provided by the otolith as compared to the cupula (see Section II,B,2).

The inner ears of fishes are composed of the pars superior (semicircular canals and utriculus) with a vestibular function, and the pars inferior (normally the sacculus and lagena) for which an auditory function is simply presumed in most cases. The utriculus, sacculus, and lagena are otolithic organs in which a hair cell macula is overlain by an otolithic membrane and a solid calcium carbonate otolith. The maculae of the sacculus and lagena are oriented almost vertically with the otolith suspended laterally. The saccular macula is generally more elongated than the lagena, and is suggested by the available data to be the most important auditory organ in most species (e.g., von Frisch, 1938; Dijkgraaf, 1950, 1952; Moulton and Dixon, 1967; Furukawa and Ishii, 1967a; Fay, 1974b).

The general morphology of the pars inferior varies considerably among species [see Moulton (1963) and Baird (1974) for a discussion of this variability, and Retzius (1881) for some beautiful drawings of the ears of over 30 species]. One of the best known examples of this variability occurs between members of the superorder Ostariophysi (goldfish, carp, catfish, minnow, and others) and all other species. The Ostariophysi are characterized by a chain of movable bones, the Weberian ossicles (Weber, 1820), which connect the anterior membranes of the swimbladder to the perilymphatic and endolymphatic fluid systems of the inner ear [see van Bergeijk (1967a) and Popper (1971a) for a more complete introduction to the morphological literature on the Weberian ossicle systems.] Figure 1 shows the principal structures and the manner of their connection very clearly. Notice that the most anterior ossicle (scaphium) ends in contact with the unpaired perilymphatic sinus which communicates equally with both sacculi via the endolymphatic transverse canal.

Figure 2 illustrates that the saccular otolith of the Ostariophysi (*Cyprinus idus* in this case) is relatively small and elongated while it is quite massive and more disk shaped in the non-Ostariophysi (e.g., *Lucioperca sandra*). Note that the

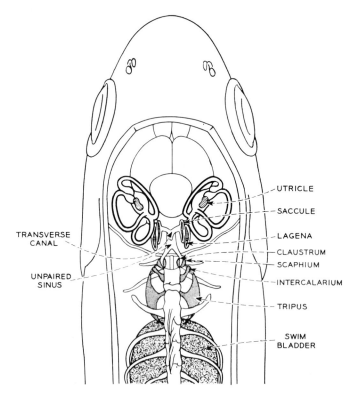

Fig. 1. Dorsal view of the peripheral auditory system of an ostariophysine fish showing the swim bladder, the Weberian ossicles, and the inner ears. The shaded portions of the saccule, lagena, and utricule represent otoliths. Taken from van Bergeijk (1967a), after von Frisch (1938).

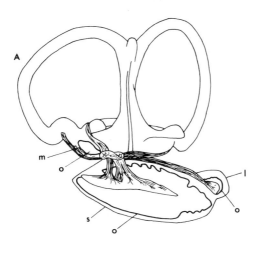

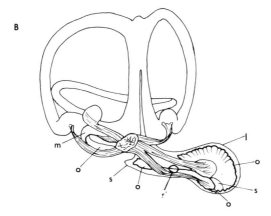

Fig. 2. Medial views of the inner ears of two typical fish species. The nonostariophysine *Lucioperca sandra* is shown in A, and the ostariophysine *Cyprinus idus* is in B. The striated structures are the various branches of the eighth nerve and the maculae which they innervate. l, lagena; m, utriculus; o, otoloth; s, sacculus; si, transverse canal. Taken from Popper and Fay (1973), after Retzius (1881).

transverse canal does not appear in the non-Ostariophysi and that the endolymphatic systems of the two ears do not communicate as in the Ostariophysi. The ultrastructure of the otolithic maculae has been well described for the sacculus (Hama, 1969) and the lagena (Saito, 1973) of the goldfish. Of particular significance is the observation that the dorsal portion of the macula is composed of cells in which the kinocilium is oriented dorsally, while in the ventral macula, the kinocilium of each hair cell is oriented ventrally. Efferent-type synapses at the base of the hair cells are common in the goldfish, and there is evidence for both convergent and divergent innervation patterns. Nerve fibers from the sacculus and lagena enter the medulla as part of a dorsal root of the eighth nerve, and ascend to the dorsal acousticolateral nucleus (Aronson, 1963). Some large diameter fibers from the anterior portion of the sacculus are known to run caudally to terminate bilaterally on the paired Mauthner cells of the medial reticular nuclei.

2. Modes of Stimulation

In order for stimulation of the otolithic organs to occur, it appears that a relative shearing motion must take place between the otolith, to which the cilia are attached through "tectorial tissue" (Wever, 1973) and the apical membrane of the hair cell. The mechanical disturbances causing this motion may reach the ear through several possible routes. The most general route involves simple tissue conduction in which the particle motion associated with all acoustic phenomena is taken up by body tissue, including the receptor cells of the ear. Of course, little attenuation of the acoustic signal occurs as it passes through the fish's body since most tissue offers no significant impedance discontinuity in a water medium. A relative motion across the hair cell cilia can occur in this case since the very dense otolith would tend to move at an amplitude and phase different from that of surrounding tissue. Since this principle of stimulation is similar to that of an accelerometer and operates in all vestibular organs, the distinction between an auditory and vestibular organ in some species may be made only on the basis of the type of neural information processing to which the afferent signals are subjected by the brain. This inertial system would clearly be displacement sensitive, and its sound pressure sensitivity would clearly vary with distance within the near field.

Another mode of auditory stimulation involves the swim bladder and its mechanical coupling to the fluid systems of the ear (von Frisch, 1938; van Bergeijk, 1967a). The swim bladder, like any gas bubble under water, expands and contracts in response to sound pressure fluctuations by an amount which is, within limits, independent of frequency. These relatively large movements of the swim bladder wall may be transmitted to the inner ears where a relative motion is set up across the hair cell cilia.

In the Ostariophysi, these movements are transmitted by the Weberian ossicles to the unpaired sinus, to the transverse canal, and then to the sacculi where the otoliths are engaged in movement by frictional forces. In certain nonostariophysine families such as the clupeids (Wohlfart, 1936), the mormyrids (Stipetic, 1939), and the anabantids (Schneider, 1942), alternatives to the Weberian ossicles appear which tend to bring the swim bladder (or other gas bubble) into closer relation to the ear. In some of these cases, the amplified displacment impinges upon the macula, and not upon the otolith as in the Ostariophysi. Any system making use of a bubble of gas in this way would be pressure sensitive since the displacement amplitude reaching the ear would be proportional to the sound pressure level reaching the swimbladder, and not to the displacement amplitude of the acoustic stimulus. This system would cease to operate in a pressure node of a standing wave, and would exhibit a sound pressure threshold which would not vary with distance within the near field.

As van Bergeijk (1967a) has pointed out, the presence of a bladder is not proof that it is used for hearing in any particular species since a transmission pathway to the ear and a sensory macula with appropriately oriented hair cells are also necessary. While the Ostariophysi clearly make some use of the swim bladder in hearing, the extent of its involvement in the hearing of the non-Ostariophysi may be quite variable, and nonexistent in some cases. As the transmission pathway between the ear and the bladder becomes less efficient, a point is reached where the ear's response to direct particle movement will exceed its response to that particle movement produced by the bladder's response to sound pressures, even under far-field conditions. Such variation in the efficiency of coupling may well contribute to wide species differences in absolute sensitivity evident, for example, in Tavolga and Wodinsky's (1963) survey of hearing in nine marine non-Ostariophysi.

It is important to note here, finally, that both modes of stimulation require that the fluids of the inner ear are free to move, and are not totally encapsulated by rigid bone. Wever (1969) refers to this as the mobilization principle of Lempert, and shows how the operation of all vertebrate ears requires a pressure release system, such as the air-bounded round window membrane of the cochlea. Wever (1969, 1971) further argues that the swim bladder contributes to the hearing sensitivity of fishes as a fluid-mobilizing mechanism. Alternatively, von Frisch (1938) and van Bergeijk (1967a) refer to a region of very thin bone forming part of the ventromedial saccular wall which may provide a pathway for the release of pressure and for the mobilization of endolymphatic fluid (Baird, 1974).

The operation of both the pressure and the displacement mode of stimulation has been analyzed only recently in the electrophysiological experiments of Fay and Popper (1974, 1975). In one experiment, saccular receptor potentials were correlated with the goldfish's position within a standing wave. As the fish was moved from a region of high p/d (pressure maximum) to an area of low p/d, the response declined as if the system were pressure sensitive. With the swim bladder filled with water, however, the system responded as if it were displacement sensitive, but with an overall loss in sensitivity of about 35 db. These data were then compared to the displacement sensitivity determined by direct vibration of the head in order to calculate the point within the near field (or the p/d value) at which the direct response of the ear to displacement would exceed that produced by the effect of sound pressure on the swim bladder. For the goldfish and catfish, displacement was found to predominate only at extremely close range (2 and 0.02 cm at 50 and 1250 Hz, respectively). In similar experiments with the nonostariophysine *Tilapia macrocephala* (mouthbreeder), the response of the sacculus to displacement was about equal to that of the Ostariophysi, while the sound pressure sensitivity was so poor that it could not be measured at all. The mouthbreeder's auditory response, therefore, would remain under the control of particle displacement at source distances greatly exceeding those for catfish and goldfish, and perhaps extending into the far field.

C. Auditory Sensitivity

1. Behavioral Audiograms

Questions of auditory sensitivity normally require a behavioral answer, and the one most often accepted is the pure tone audiogram determined in quiet. Popper and Fay (1973) have presented the audiograms for 21 teleost species which have appeared in the recent literature. Since that review, audiograms for several other species have appeared (Chapman, 1973; Chapman and Sand, 1973; Chapman and Hawkins, 1973; Offutt, 1974; Tavolga, 1974). Although audiograms comprise the bulk of the psychophysical literature, the experiments and data will not be re-reviewed here. The electrophysiological experiments of Fay and Popper (1974, 1975) are clear in showing that meaningful statements about auditory sensitivity in fishes must include both pressure and displacement threshold measurements. Unfortunately, the majority of published audiograms are simply sound pressure values, and even in the majority of these, no attempt was made to demonstrate that sound pressure, and not particle displacement, determined the response. There are, however, several exemplary studies which are valuable in illustrating some of the experimental approaches to the problems of obtaining valid pressure and displacement sensitivity measures.

2. Near-Field Manipulation

In a study of hearing in the catfish, Poggendorf (1952) was the first to use variations of the p/d of the stimulus to test for the operation of pressure- or displacement-sensitive systems. By making pressure gradient measurements throughout his experimental tank, Poggendorf found that displacement increased relative to pressure near the surface of the water. Behavioral pressure thresholds were then determined for the catfish as a function of the distance of the fish from the surface. In general, pressure thresholds were found to be independent of distance, indicating that the catfish was pressure sensitive under these conditions. Unfortunately, however, in this and other studies of fish hearing using the near-field manipulation (e.g., Enger, 1967a; Fay, 1969), the acoustic conditions under which sensitivity to pressure or displacement normally occurs were not determined, and we are left with a rather lifeless number expressing the animal's sensitivity occurring under conditions which bear no known relation to those existing in its usual environment.

The recent psychophysical experiments of Chapman and Hawkins (1973) on the hearing of cod were carried out in a very large acoustic range so that true far-field conditions could be achieved. The cod's pressure sensitivity was shown to be independent of distance well within the near field at frequencies above 50 Hz, indicating that the animal was responding to pressure under all conditions tested. While the point at which the response to sound pressure would be overtaken by the response to direct displacement was not measured directly, a full set of predictions were made based upon the estimated displacement sensitivity of the sacculus and calculations of near-field amplitude. In similar experiments by Chapman and Sand (1973) on two species of flatfish (both lack a swim bladder), the animals were simply found to be displacement sensitive even into the far field, with best threshold levels falling between 10^{-8} and 10^{-9} cm at about 150 Hz. It is noteworthy that in both of these field experiments, the day-to-day variation in ambient pressure noise was measured and compared with sensitivity values in order to determine whether or not particular thresholds were masked.

One final point about the design of the near-field type of experiment must be made. Chapman and Hawkins (1973) have quite correctly pointed out that a threshold which is proportional to sound pressure regardless of distance from the source is not necessarily an indication that the system studied is pressure sensitive, since a displacement-sensitive system would also respond in this way in the far field. In other words, it is necessary to prove that the distance manipulations occur within the near field before such an experiment has any value at all. Only in a free field and only using well-understood sound-source types is it possible to calculate the location of the near-field boundary with any confidence.

3. Standing Wave Manipulations

In experiments of a different type, Cahn et al. (1969) generated standing waves in a long, water-filled tube, and were able to measure particle movement as well as sound pressure. Behavioral thresholds for two species of grunt were measured at two points within the standing wave, and were expressed in terms of both sound pressure and particle velocity. It was found that as the p/d decreased from the equivalent of a far-field situation, thresholds for a 400 Hz tone remained constant in sound pressure units, but varied widely in velocity units. Under the same conditions at 100 Hz, however, particle movement thresholds remained constant as pressure thresholds varied. It was thus shown that these species simply shift from displacement sensitivity to pressure sensitivity as frequency increases from 100 to 400 Hz in the far field. These data do not indicate, however, at what point within the near field (or at what p/d) the response to the 400-Hz tone would come under the control of displacement amplitude.

4. Criticisms of the Behavioral Audiogram

The behavioral audiogram is generally accepted as the answer to questions of auditory sensitivity, even though very few have been determined using an entirely appropriate set of methods. The question arises now whether or not the information provided by even the valid audiogram is of sufficient value to warrant the effort necessary for its determination. The audiogram is primarily a measure of the bandwidth of hearing (high and low hearing range) and absolute sensitivity. These data are often used to characterize the auditory capabilities of a particular species for comparison with others, such as in the study by Masterton *et al.* (1969) on the mammals. Bandwidth may be estimated from electrophysiological measures of the frequency response of more peripheral auditory mechanisms, and it can be shown that the only unique feature of the behavioral measure is that it could reveal a significantly narrower bandwidth than that determined by more peripheral processes. However, considering the difficulties associated with the measurement and interpretation of the behavioral audiogram, electrophysiological approaches to the question may be more reasonable alternatives, particularly since the organ under study can be clearly identified, and the stimulus can be directly applied and therefore adequately specified.

While the behavioral threshold provides the best answer to questions of absolute sensitivity, the typical audiogram is not particularly valuable in providing predictions about which acoustic signals may or may not be detected under most conditions of stimulation. Audiograms are either determined in quiet, in which case the ambient noise levels are shown not to determine the threshold, or under well-controlled noise levels where precise measurements of the masking effects can be made. Clearly, the definition of a "quiet" condition (those noise levels not causing masking) must be derived from the results of a masking experiment. While most of the existing audiograms for fishes are intended to represent the sensitivity of the species in quiet, few studies included the manipulation of noise level necessary to confirm that masking had not occurred. Thus, most of the published threshold values for fishes may be masked to an unknown extent, and thus may be measures of ambient noise spectra in laboratories all over the world as much as they are of some property of the auditory systems of fishes.

The final point here is that ambient noise levels probably determine the detectability of most signals to which a fish may respond in its usual environment. This is certainly true of man and the mammals. This means that it is the masked threshold, and not the "absolute" quiet threshold, which allows predictions about the detectability of signals under the usual environmental conditions. Clearly, a species with a particularly low quiet threshold would have no necessary advantage over a less "sensitive" species if signal detectability were determined for both by ambient noise levels. These considerations suggest that, in general, species differences in the quiet threshold would correlate with the ambient noise levels under which a particular species evolved. It is reasonable to assume, for example, that selective pressures operated to lower absolute sensitivity only to the point where the ambient noise levels became the major factor determining signal detectability. Further increases in absolute sensitivity without a corresponding improvement in filtering capability would be biologically meaningless.

As a conclusion to this section on the auditory sensitivity of fishes, a call is made, not for more audiograms, but for more thorough studies of pressure and displacement sensitivity in a limited number of carefully selected species. For questions specifically made about auditory bandwidth, an electrophysiological answer would probably be more easily obtained and interpreted than a behavioral one. If the question is one of sensitivity, on the other hand, the well-conditioned masking experiment provides a more useful answer than the determination of thresholds under uncontrolled ambient noise.

5. The Determinants of Auditory Sensitivity and Bandwidth

While the literature abounds with attempts to describe the auditory sensitivity of fishes using the audiogram, few studies have been designed to analyze the determinants of sensitivity and bandwidth. It has long been thought that the Ostariophysi tend to have a wider bandwidth and greater sound pressure sensitivity than the unspecialized nonostariophysines, and the presence of the Weberian ossicles in the former provided a ready explanation. Poggendorf (1952) provided the first real evidence, however, when he showed that pressure sensitivity of the catfish declined by 35 db or so across a wide frequency range when the ossicular chain was interrupted. The flat loss demonstrated that the highly damped ossicular system may well provide greater overall sensitivity, but is not responsible for the greater hearing bandwidth of the Ostariophysi. It must be noted here that van Bergeijk (1967a) interpreted Poggendorf's data as showing that the bandwidth contracted by 2000 Hz due to the interference with the ossicles. A close look at the original data reveals no indication of such a change.

Species differences in hearing bandwidth have also been attributed to the dimensions of the swim bladder. The hypothesis here is that the size of the bladder, and therefore the resonant frequency, would determine the range of best hearing. Popper (1971b) tested this idea by comparing the sensitivity of 5- and 11-cm on goldfish. Since no significant differences were found in the audiograms, evidence was provided that the intact swim bladder is rather broadly tuned and would not contribute significantly to species differences in bandwidth. These tentative conclusions have been recently reinforced through biophysical studies of the response of intact swim bladders to sound. Popper (1974) has found, for example, that the internal sound pressure and phase response of the goldfish swim bladder is an approximately flat function of frequency between 50 and 1600 Hz. In studies with the cod, Sand and Hawkins (1973) also found the swim bladder to be heavily damped with a resonance occurring far above the frequency of best hearing. The authors pointed out that such a system would insure a relative constancy of auditory sensitivity for individuals of different sizes, and a stability of sensitivity during rapid depth changes.

Evidence is accumulating, then, that neither the morphology of the Weberian ossicles nor the dimensions of the swim bladder can account for the differences in hearing bandwidth occurring between species. The recent electrophysiological experiments of Fay and Popper (1974, 1975) lend support to this and go further in suggesting the important role of the dimensions of the otoliths and of the fluid systems of the inner ear in determining the bandwidths of hearing. Fig. 3 shows three independent auditory bandwidth measures for goldfish, catfish, and

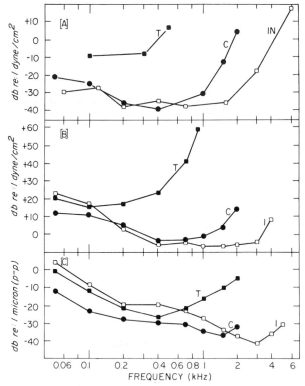

Fig. 3. The frequency response and hearing sensitivity of *Tilapia macrocephala* (T), *Carassius auratus* (C), *Ictalurus punctatus* (I), and *Ictalurus nebulosus* (IN). The curves in A are behavioral thresholds for *Tilapia* (Tavolga, 1974), for *Carassius* [values derived from the audiograms for goldfish plotted together in Popper and Fay (1973)], and for *Ictalurus nebulosus* (Poggendorf, 1952). The curves in B show the sound pressures in decibels (db) relative to (re:) 1 dyne per sq cm necessary to evoke a 1 μV (rms) microphonic response from the sacculi of the three species shown (Fay and Popper, 1974, 1975). The curves in C show the peak displacement of the head necessary to evoke a 1 μV microphonic from the same species (Fay and Popper, 1974, 1975).

mouthbreeder. The upper panel (A) shows the behavioral sound pressure audio-grams taken from various sources. Note that only the curve for the catfish was shown to be determined by sound pressure level, and not by displacement amplitude (Poggendorf, 1952). The middle and lower panels show the 1-μV isopotential functions of frequency determined through the recording of saccular potentials evoked by underwater sound (B), and by direct vertical vibration of the head (C). The sound pressure functions (B) for the goldfish and catfish were shown to be determined by the sound pressure level since deflation of the swim bladder caused a marked reduction of the response, at least for frequencies above 160 Hz. Deflation of the swim bladder in the mouthbreeder, on the other hand, had no effect. The implication here is that the particle motion associated with the generation of underwater sound was the effective stimulus component. Swim bladder deflation caused no change in the response to vibration in any species.

A comparison of A and B shows that behavioral and electrophysiological measures of auditory bandwidth give quite similar values. This correspondence is a strong suggestion that the sacculus is the receptor organ responsible for the behavioral performance. This same conclusion was reached in another elec-trophysiological study of the goldfish sacculus (Colnaghi, 1975), and in a recent study of the carp (Fay, 1974b). Of course, less of a correspondence would be expected for the mouthbreeder data since the plotted values are determined by the levels of particle movement in the acoustic field, and these bear no necessary relation to the sound pressure levels generated. A comparison of curves B and C shows that the species differences in bandwidth appear to be about the same, whether the Weberian ossicles or the swim bladder are involved in the response or not. This is a good indication that such bandwidth differences among species are determined by the mechanical properties of the inner ears and have little to do with the dimensions of more peripheral structures.

III. THE ANALYSIS OF AUDITORY INFORMATION

This section is primarily concerned with frequency analysis since the majority of experiments on information processing have focused on this topic. In be-havioral terms, the processes of frequency analysis are most often defined by experiments on the analysis of complex signals into their components (e.g., masking studies) and by experiments on pitch perception (e.g., frequency dis-crimination).

A. Frequency Discrimination Experiments

The most common psychophysical measure of frequency analysis is successive pure tone frequency discrimination limens (DL's). Popper and Fay (1973) have reviewed the existing fish data in some detail, and to my knowledge, no new studies have appeared since that time. However, it is valuable to have another look at the data as they are plotted together in Fig. 4 for comparison with the same psychophysical measures made for the mammals, and for the performance of the human skin. Clearly, the fish data fell into two groups, with most values for the goldfish and minnow (Ostariophysi) falling below those for the three non-Ostariophysi studied by Dijkgraaf (1952). The exceptions here are the data for the minnow collected by Stetter (1929) using methods very similar to those used in studies of stimulus generalization along the frequency dimension for the goldfish (Fay, 1970b). While the differences between the two groups of values may suggest a real sensitivity difference (Travolga, 1971; Enger, 1968), more data are necessary before this suggestion can be considered more seriously. At any rate, it is clear that for the goldfish and the minnow, at least, discriminative

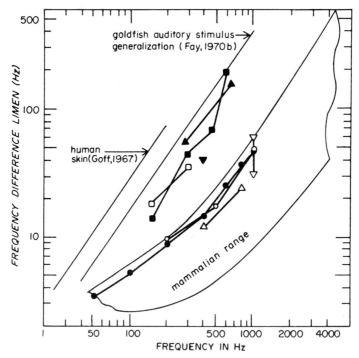

Fig. 4. Auditory frequency discrimination thresholds for fishes compared with those for the human skin, and with those for certain mammals, excluding man (Fay, 1974c). Filled circles, *Carassius auratus* (Fay, 1970a); open circles, *Carassius auratus* (Jacobs and Tavolga, 1968); inverted open triangles, *Phoxinus laevis* (Wohlfahrt, 1939); filled triangles, *Phoxinus laevis* (Stetter, 1929); open triangles, *Phoxinus laevis* (Dijkgraaf and Verheijen, 1950); filled squares, *Sargus annularis*; open squares, *Gobius niger*, inverted filled triangles, *Corvina nigra* (Dijkgraaf, 1952).

behavior is quite unlike that of the human skin, and falls within the limits of the performance of mammalian auditory systems below 1000 Hz. Based upon the presently available data, then, it is an error to regard the fishes as inferior to the mammals in this aspect of frequency analysis.

B. Masking Experiments

Other important data on frequency analysis come from experiments on masking in which the ability to analyze complex signals into individual components is measured. In general, the design and interpretation of masking experiments have evolved from the notion of the mammalian cochlea as a set of mechanical filters which distributes activity along the basilar membrane according to frequency. Thus, signals of widely different frequency would not interfere with (mask) each other since information about them is carried to the brain in spatially separate channels. Obviously, a measure of the masking of one signal frequency by another would provide valuable data on the degree to which frequency components are resolved by the ear. While it is rather unlikely that fishes use this type of peripheral–mechanical mechanism for frequency analysis, the masking paradigm remains quite valuable in analyzing the general filtering properties of any auditory system. In fact, the application of these experiments to the fishes may reveal which frequency analytic capabilities do not require the initial frequency-to-place transformation characteristic of the mammalian cochlea.

1. Wide Band Masking: Critical Masking Ratios

One of the more valuable experiments here involves the masking of tones by broad band noise (Fletcher, 1940; Hawkins and Stevens, 1950). The measure of interest is the critical ratio (CR) or the difference, in decibels, between the level of uniform spectrum noise in a 1-Hz wide band and the level of the masked tone at threshold. If this CR is very large, the masking effect of the noise is great, and the frequency analytic capabilities of the system under study are poor. Another way to view a large CR value is to assume that a wide portion (bandwidth) of the noise contributes to the masking of the tone. By making the assumption that the power of a restricted band of noise surrounding the tone in frequency equals the power of the tone at masked threshold (Fletcher, 1940), one can then estimate the width of the band of noise which is actually effective in masking the tone.

While only one experiment of this kind has been reported in the fish hearing literature (Fay, 1974a), tentative values can be derived from other studies in which at least some of the criteria for the determination of a valid CR were met. These data are plotted together in Fig. 5 along with an indication of the mammalian range of values. The important point here is that the CR values for the goldfish, and many of the estimates for the other species as well, fall generally in line with the mammalian values. That is to say, the fishes do not appear to be

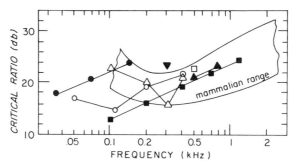

Fig. 5. Critical masking ratio values for the goldfish, *Carassius auratus* (filled squares) (Fay, 1974a), compared with those for certain mammals, including man (Fay, 1974a), and with preliminary values determined for certain other teleost species. Filled circles, *Gadus morhua* (Buerkle, 1968); open circles, *Gadus morhua* (Chapman and Hawkins, 1973); open squares, *Carassius auratus;* filled triangles, *Holocentrus rufus;* inverted filled triangles, *Tilapia macrocephala;* open triangles, *Lagodon rhomboides* (Tavolga, 1974).

qualitatively different from the mammals in their ability to analyze a complex signal into its tonal and noise components. It is interesting to note here that the frequency DL (in hertz) and the critical ratio bandwidth (in hertz) approximately double in size with a doubling of the frequency at which they are measured.* This is an indication that a single physiological mechanism may underlie both processes. Finally, note that under usual conditions in the more natural environment, the range of CR's illustrated here predicts that most species will detect only those signals which fall at least 15 to 25 db above ambient noise spectrum levels.

2. The Critical Masking Bandwidth

The critical ratio masking experiment allows one to estimate the bandwidth within which signals interfere with each other only after making several critical assumptions about the way in which signals are detected by the auditory system. Other types of masking paradigms have been designed, however, which allow the width of this band, the critical band, to be measured directly (see Scharf, 1970, for a review). In the classical experiment of this type, the masked threshold for a tone is measured as a function of the width of a masking band centered at the frequency of the tone. As the width of the noise band increases from a very narrow value, the masking effect also increases, indicating that masking is determined by noise power. As the noise band is widened further, however, a point is reached where masking no longer increases, and the threshold becomes independent of total noise power (bandwidth). In other words,

---

*The slope of the goldfish CR function is 3 db/octave. Since a 3-db difference corresponds to a 2:1 power ratio, and thus to a 2:1 bandwidth ratio, we can say that the critical ratio bandwidth doubles with a doubling of the frequency at which it is measured.

the additional noise power of the wider band falls outside the limits of a filterlike mechanism, and does not contribute to the masking of the signal at the center of the band. The noise bandwidth at which this transition occurs is known as the critical bandwidth, and has come to be accepted as a fundamental unit in the quantitative description of auditory analysis in man and the other mammals.

In a recent study, Tavolga (1974) has performed this kind of experiment with the goldfish by measuring the masked threshold for a 500-Hz tone as a function of the width of a surrounding noise band. Just as in the experiments with man (e.g., Greenwood, 1961) and on the monkey (Gourevitch, 1970), the threshold for the tone increased with noise bandwidth, but only up to a certain point. For the goldfish, this critical bandwidth value occurred at about 200 Hz, a value almost twice as large as that found for man, but about equal to that found for the monkey. Again, the goldfish has been found not to differ qualitatively, or even quantitatively, from the mammals in its frequency analyzing capabilities.

3. Narrow Band Masking

Further support for the existence of filterlike processes in the auditory systems of fishes comes from studies of tonal masking in the goldfish (Tavolga, 1974) and noise masking in the cod (Buerkle, 1969). Some of the data from both experiments are plotted together in Fig. 6 as the relative thresholds for tones masked by tones (goldfish), and for narrow bands of noise masked by the same noise bands (cod). It is quite clear here that masking is most effective when the frequencies of the masker and the signal are similar, and that the masking effect declines with the frequency separation between the masker and the signal. At a

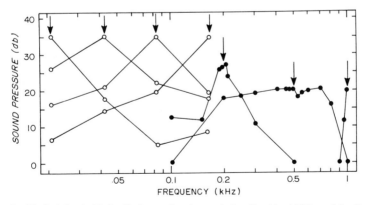

Fig. 6. Masked thresholds for *Gadus morhua* (open circles, Buerkle, 1969), and for *Carassius auratus* (filled circles, Tavolga, 1974). The ordinate is sound pressure in decibels with an arbitrary reference. The arrows indicate the frequency of the tone to be detected in each case. The curves for the goldfish are thresholds for tones masked by tones, while the curves for the cod are thresholds for narrow bands of noise masked by the same narrow noise bands.

qualitative level, at least, these data resemble those for man (Wegel and Lane, 1924).

C. Mechanisms of Frequency Analysis

In general, the data from both the discrimination and the masking experiments show that the fishes, and the goldfish in particular, are able to analyze the frequency components of auditory signals with a precision not clearly different from that of those mammals which have been tested. These functional similarities have prompted the view that the mechanisms responsible for this analysis are the same in the fishes and in the mammals. For example, van Bergeijk (1967b) suggested that the saccular macula could respond differentially to different sound frequencies, although rather crudely, so that a "place" princi-ple at the periphery could be assumed to account for any similarities between the fishes and the mammals in frequency analysis.

Although there is no biophysical evidence for this type of spatial analysis, evidence from neurophysiological experiments suggest that some sort of frequency-to-place transformation does occur. The kinds of data most relevant here are the frequency tuning curves of single saccular nerve fibers. Such curves exist only for the goldfish (Furukawa and Ishii, 1967a) and for the sculpin (Enger, 1963), and even in these cases, the data must be considered only pre-liminary. Nevertheless, some of the curves published for the goldfish are plotted in Fig. 7 along with some low-frequency units from the cat auditory nerve (Kiang *et al.,* 1965). The fish curves (A) clearly show that there are at least two types of saccular units, one responsive throughout the frequency range of hearing by the goldfish, and one responsive primarily to the low frequencies.* Furukawa and Ishii (1967a) did not find the frequency point of best response (characteristic frequency) to be continuously distributed across individual fibers as in the mam-mals, but rather found many examples of the two basic types shown in Fig. 7. Enger (1963) appears to have encountered the same two types of frequency response characteristics in his studies on the sculpin eighth nerve. At any rate, it appears that while the degree of tuning in the goldfish fibers is clearly inferior to that of the cat, some sort of frequency analysis based upon the relative activity in at least two populations of nerve fibers is theoretically possible.

---

*Note that the neural response thresholds here are expressed in units of sound pressure impinging upon the fish. It is reasonable to assume that the "tuning" evident in the threshold curve for the high-frequency unit of the goldfish is caused by mechanical properties of the auditory system peripheral to the receptor cell macula. The same can be said for the low-frequency leg of the low-frequency unit curves. Since spatially coded information about sound frequency can only exist where the slopes of the unit tuning curves differ to some extent, it is clear that the goldfish can use such a code only in a restricted frequency region above about 250 Hz.

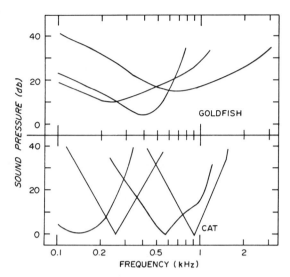

Fig. 7. A comparison between the unit tuning curves of fibers from the eighth nerve of the goldfish (Furukawa and Ishii, 1967a) and of the cat (Kiang *et al.*, 1965), for frequencies below 1000 Hz. The thresholds for the cat are plotted relative to the threshold at the best frequency for each unit. The thresholds for the goldfish are plotted relative to an arbitrary sound pressure level.

Further evidence for a peripheral analysis comes from the electrophysiological masking experiments of Sand (1971) in which evoked potentials from the saccular nerve of the goldfish were attenuated by noise to the degree that the frequency components of the signal and the masker were similar. This same pattern was found in behavioral studies of temporary threshold shift (Popper, 1973), in which overstimulation of the goldfish with a pure tone of a particular frequency caused an elevation of thresholds only for tones in the same frequency range. Finally, Sand (1974) has presented evidence from studies on the saccular potentials of the perch which show that the relative degree of saccular stimulation due to horizontal and vertical vibration depends to some extent upon the frequency of stimulation. This is an indication that the direction of movement of the otolith may be frequency dependent.

1. Spatial and Temporal Coding

It is clear, then, that some degree of frequency analysis may occur at the receptor level in some fish species. The critical question now, however, is whether or not this initial analysis is necessary and sufficient to account for the kinds of analytic capabilities which have been revealed behaviorally. In Fig. 7, for example, it is quite obvious that the relative activity present in the two types of goldfish eighth nerve fibers would change little if at all with changes in the stimulating frequency below 300 Hz or so. The superior ability of the goldfish to detect tones against a background of noise (to filter) thus bears no relation to the extremely broad tuning characteristics of the two fiber groups. The auditory nerve fibers of the cat transmit far more spatially coded information about stimulus frequency than do the goldfish fibers, yet the abilities of the goldfish and the cat in signal detection and in frequency discrimination are about equal below 400 Hz or so. This is a suggestion that the underlying physiological mechanism is the same in both species, and that it is not dependent upon the frequency-to-place transformation occurring at the periphery.

What, then, is the meaning of data from experiments on masking, the critical band, and temporary threshold shift which suggest some sort of spatial distribution of frequency within which signals interact to the extent that their frequency contents are similar? It is interesting to consider here that the best alternative to the peripheral analysis theory is the notion of a central analysis of temporal patterns in which there may occur a time-to-place transformation. Licklider (1959) has shown how a simple neuronal network can act as an autocorrelator which compares a train of nerve spikes with delayed replicas of itself. In this way, temporal patterns such as periodicities existing within one fiber are recorded to produce differential activity across a spatial array of fibers. It is important to understand here that the end result of such a process is a spatial transformation which may have many elements in common with the frequency-to-place spatial transformation performed by the mammalian cochlea. Thus, experimental evidence suggesting a spatial or "place" analysis of frequency does not necessarily bear on the question of a peripheral, as opposed to a central, "place principle" of frequency analysis.

2. Experimental Approaches

In order for such a temporal analysis of frequency to occur, it is necessary that temporal properties of the stimulating waveform be preserved in the firing patterns of auditory neurons. The experiments of Furukawa and Ishii (1967a) have demonstrated, at least at a qualitative level, that this phase locking indeed occurs in individual saccular nerve fibers of the goldfish. However, in order to provide direct evidence that this temporally coded information is used by the nervous system in analyzing frequency, an appropriate neural analyzing network must be demonstrated to exist in the brain. This demonstration has not yet been made, and there remains a significant challenge to the neurophysiologist to attempt it.

One approach to this demonstration is illustrated in the experiments of Mountcastle et al. (1969) in which a temporal code for "flutter" frequency discrimination on the skin was indicated as the result of quantitative comparisons between the error made in psychophysical judgments of frequency and the time "jitter" observed in the phase locking of central neurons. Another approach could involve a comparison between input and output neurons in their frequency-

and time-selective properties. We know that in the goldfish, for example, saccular nerve fibers are rather broadly tuned at two frequency regions, and a demonstration of more sharply tuned central neurons with a continuous distribution of characteristic frequencies would suggest the operation of a time-to-place transforming mechanism. More convincing evidence for the hypothetical autocorrelator might come from a demonstration that certain central neurons are "tuned" to particular pulse repetition rates, or respond with a greater probability to a train of acoustic transients characterized by a particular interpulse interval. Neurons with these properties have been reported in the cat cortex (Goldstein *et al.*, 1971) and in the rat cochlear nucleus (Møller, 1969), but they have not yet received quantitative and systematic study. Note here that these monaural interval-sensitive neurons which may represent the output of an autocorrelator are similar to the binaural interval-sensitive neurons (e.g., Goldberg and Brown, 1969) which are thought to possibly reflect the output of a cross-correlator (Jeffress, 1948).

The only behavioral evidence specifically indicating the operation of a temporal analyzer in fishes comes from the experiment of Fay (1972), in which stimulus generalization methods were used to determine how the goldfish analyzes information contained in amplitude-modulated signals. The goldfish was shown to be capable of acquiring information about both the carrier and the modulation frequencies, and responded to a 1000-Hz tone modulated at 40 Hz as if it had elements in common with a 40-Hz pure tone. This latter result is equivalent to a demonstration of periodicity pitch (Small, 1970), a phenomenon which has been considered evidence for the existence of a temporal analysis of waveform in the human psychoacoustical literature [see von Békésy (1972) and Wightman (1973) for some possible alternative explanations for the periodicity pitch phenomena].

IV. AUDITORY LOCALIZATION

The ability to acquire information about the spatial location of sound sources is considered to be extremely important for the survival of mammalian species (Masterton *et al.*, 1969), and one would expect the same to be true for the fishes. As van Bergeijk (1964) has pointed out, however, a fish receiving pressure stimuli via the swimbladder would be unable to localize the source of sound because both ears would be stimulated equally, and always from the same direction. In other words, interaural differences in time of arrival, phase, or intensity would appear to be impossible in this situation. Even small movements of the fish would be of little value here since the orientation of the swimbladder within the sound field would have no effect on the magnitude of its response to sound pressure. Only movements large enough to place the fish in areas of discriminably different sound pressure levels would provide the necessary cues. Note here that the fish's ability to discriminate differences in intensity is in general quite poor (Jacobs and Tavolga, 1967).

A. Lateral-Line System and Localization

Van Bergeijk (1964) has argued that the lateral-line system is uniquely suited for localization and may well have been involved in the many demonstrations of the fish's ability to orient to, or seek out, nearby underwater sound sources (see Erulkar, 1972, for a review of the literature here). Individual receptor cells of the lateral-line system are directionally sensitive to the motional (vector) component of the underwater sound stimulus (Flock, 1965), and these receptors are arranged in a three-dimensional array over the body surface. By comparing the input from several spatially separate receptors, differences in time, phase, and intensity may be used by the nervous system to locate the direction of origin of a mechanical disturbance. Unfortunately, however, there is very little real data to support this view. For example, while Schwartz (1967) has shown that some fishes can localize the source of small surface waves using the lateral-line organs of the head, there is no behavioral evidence that the same system is used to localize the source of acoustic phenomena. In fact, those studies of localization in which the responsible receptor system was identified (Moulton and Dixon, 1967; Schuijf, 1975) indicated that the lateral-line system was not involved.

B. Inner Ears and Localization

1. Time Difference Cues

The experiment of Moulton and Dixon (1967) is important because it showed that the goldfish could make conditioned and unconditioned responses to sound (tail flip) based upon input to the central nervous system from the sacculi. The tail flip response to one side was eliminated when the saccular branch of the eighth nerve was cut on one side, and the response was eliminated completely by cutting the nerve bilaterally. Since the fish was restrained when tested for localization, it appears inescapable that the directional response is processed on the basis of some types of interaural differences. This is a somewhat startling conclusion even granting that the sacculi were not stimulated via the swim bladder in this case, since the cues of interaural time, phase, and intensity would be severely attenuated in the underwater environment. The velocity of sound under water is approximately 1500 m/sec, or a bit over 4 times its velocity in air. Assuming that the ears of the goldfish are no more than 1 cm apart, then the maximum interaural difference in time (max Δt) is about 7 μsec. This value is about 10 to 100 times smaller than the max Δt available to most mammals.

Interaural differences in intensity would also seem to be exceedingly small since most fishes are very small in relation to the wavelengths of sounds detected, and would offer no significant impediment to sound traveling through the body.

Moulton and Dixon have hypothesized that interaural time is the relevant cue, and that the central analyzing mechanism includes the paired Mauthner cells (M cells) of the teleost brainstem. Each M cell has a giant axon which decussates at the level of the cell body and runs down the spinal cord to innervate contralateral body musculature. While excitatory input to each cell arrives via ipsilateral saccular nerve fibers, rapid electrically transmitted inhibition occurs at the axon hillock via fibers from the contralateral sacculus (Furukawa, 1966). Given this pattern of rapid contralateral inhibition, it is clear that a certain range of in-teraural differences in arrival time would result in the excitation of the M cell ipsilateral to the leading ear, and in inhibition of the contralateral M cell. In this way, information about which ear was stimulated first could be coded in the nervous system. While the exceedingly small interaural time differences possibly involved here are considered to be a problem for the more "primitive" nervous systems of the fishes (van Bergeijk, 1964), it should be pointed out that the human auditory system is capable of resolving interaural time differences in the low microsecond range (Tobias and Zerlin, 1959). Note here that the variability of thresholds and of relative rise times of excitatory and inhibitory events are the critical factors involved in the neuronal processing of such small time dif-ferences, and not the absolute conduction velocities of neurons, nor the absolute latencies of synaptic events. Finally, it must be emphasized that the M cell body may be capable of processing the interaural time information (which may be transmitted to other areas of the brain) in spite of the fact that nearly simultaneous activity in the M-cell axons causes mutual inhibition to occur (Diamond, 1971).

2. Intensity Difference Cues

The Mauthner cell system appears to be well adapted for the processing of interaural time information which could be used in directional orientation to sound. There are, however, alternatives for localization which could be based upon an effective $\Delta t_{\Delta I}$ cue existing between at least two otolithic organs. Consider, for example, that the hair cell receptors of the ear are directionally sensitive, and that the paired otolithic maculae are oriented at an angle with respect to the rostrocaudal, the dorsoventral, and the transverse body axis. In studies on the perch, Sand (1974) has confirmed that the direction of the greatest sensitivity to vibration for each saccular macula is different for stimulation in the horizontal plane, and that the sacculi and the lagenae show different axes of best sensitivity in the vertical planes. Thus, a comparison of the neural activity from the two sacculi would give some information about the location of a monopole source (van Bergeijk, 1964) in the horizontal plane, and a comparison between the sacculi and lagenae could provide some directional information in the vertical plane. While it must not be forgotten that the sacculi would tend to be equally stimulated via the swim bladder, particularly in the Ostariophysi, the additional directional stimulation caused by the direct effect of particle movement on the saccular otoliths may become detectable, especially at the lower frequencies where the swim bladder mode of stimulation is relatively less efficient. In any case, the lagenae of the Ostariophysi would be affected far less than the sacculi by the response of the swim bladder, and could be used to process directional information.

While this type of system could provide some of the cues for localization, it appears by itself not to be sufficient. For example, a condensation transient arriving from the fish's right could not be distinguished from a rarefaction arriving from the left since both would have identical effects on the otoliths of the ear (assuming no usable time differences exist). In general, the system making use of the directional characteristics of two or more receptor organs suffers from the inability to tell right from left, or front from back, even though it is able to distinguish between other sources which are not located 180° apart. This ambiguity can be resolved if the detection system is also capable of noting the phase angle between pressure and particle movement. For example, the otoliths of the lagena may indicate that water particle movements are occurring along the transverse axis (that the signal source is located either directly to the right or left). For a source to the right, a particle movement from right to left would be accompanied by an initial pressure increase (compression), while a particle movement in the opposite direction would be accompanied by a pressure decrease. For a source located to the left, these relationships between pressure polarity and displacement direction would simply be reversed.

Furukawa and Ishii (1967b) have shown that a compression pulse compresses the goldfish swim bladder, causing the fluid in the sinus impar to move away from the sacculi, thus drawing the saccular otoliths upward toward the transverse canal opening. A rarefaction pulse causes the otoliths to be pushed downward. Simply by noting whether the dorsal or ventral hair cell group is stimulated first, the goldfish is theoretically able to determine stimulus polarity. Piddington (1972) has shown in behavioral studies that the goldfish is indeed able to discriminate the polarity of acoustic transients such as those produced accidently during swimming (Moulton, 1960). In summary, then, an ostariophysine may be able to determine the direction of a sound source with a 180° ambiguity by noting the direction of particle movement using the lagenar otoliths. By simultaneously noting the direction of movement of the saccular otoliths, the polarity of the pressure wave is determined, and the direction of the sound source is determined exactly. While this theory of localization is incomplete and overspeculative at this point, it is perhaps worth noting that the swim bladder is considered to be necessary for localization, and that the Ostariophysi may be superior in their ability to localize compared with those species which lack a special connection between the swim bladder and the ear. This view contrasts sharply with other conceptions which consider the swim bladder and the Weberian ossicles to render the otolithic ear useless for localization (van Bergeijk, 1964). Of course, the fact remains that localization cannot occur unless the motional component of the stimulus is detected either by the lateral-line system or by the organs of the ear. This would mean that those fishes using the swim bladder for pressure detection would be able to detect the presence of a signal at amplitudes lower than those necessary for localization (van Bergeijk, 1964).

3. Experimental Approaches

While it is now clear that underwater sound localization by fishes does occur, the kind of behavioral data necessary to confirm the operation of one or the other of several hypothetical mechanisms is lacking, and very difficult to obtain. The long history of conflicting studies [reviewed by van Bergeijk (1964), Erulkar (1972), and Kleerekoper and Chagnon (1954)] is most probably due to the use of exceedingly complex stimulus fields in which the fish may have been in the position of a human observer attempting to localize in an unfamiliar reverberation chamber. The weight of evidence from field experiments in which the stimulus field is probably more simple (e.g., Popper et al., 1973; Schuijf et al., 1972; Nelson and Gruber, 1963) indicates that fishes and sharks do indeed localize sound sources. The challenge that now exists is to combine rational psychophysical methods with a simplification of the acoustic field in order to identify the acoustic conditions and the auditory structures necessary for localization to occur. The technique developed by Fay (1969) in which the restrained fish is classically conditioned to respond to a signal emanating from a particular direction would most likely be of value here (see also Fay and MacKinnon, 1969). A similar approach was used by Chapman (1973) in psychophysical experiments on the differential masking effects of signals emanating from different directions in a free field. In a later study, Chapman and Johnstone (1974) determined that cod and haddock could be conditioned to discriminate differences in sound source location as small as 20°. This experiment also provided data strongly suggesting that the nervous system keeps separate the input from different receptor organs, or from populations of hair cells with different orientations, which are stimulated to different degrees depending upon the sound source direction. It is thus shown that the capacity for directional hearing allows an improvement in the signal-to-noise ratio for signal detection in fishes as in man [see Jeffress (1972) for a review of the human psychoacoustical literature on these and related points of binaural signal detection].

Quite recent papers by Schuijf (1975) and by Schuijf and Buwalda (1975) report studies on the directional hearing of cod which were carried out using instrumental appetitive conditioning under the nearly ideal conditions of a natural acoustic range (fjord). The ability of the cod to discriminate between sound sources located 22° apart was shown to depend upon the operation of the two intact labyrinths, and not upon the operation of the lateral-line system (Schuijf, 1975). Schuijf and Buwalda (1975) went on to demonstrate that the phase or temporal relationships between the sound pressure and the particle displacement components of the acoustic stimulus were responsible for at least some aspects of directional hearing in the cod. Valuable evidence is thus provided for a theory of directional hearing which is similar in most respects to that described earlier in this section. The reader is referred to Schuijf (1976) for a more complete and analytical treatment of the theory.

V. AUDITORY ELECTROPHYSIOLOGY

A. Responses of the Inner Ear

By far, the bulk of our knowledge of inner ear electrophysiology in fishes comes from a series of studies on the goldfish by Furukawa, Ishii, Matsurra, and their colleagues at Osaka University. This section is primarily a review of their work.

1. The Origin of the Saccular Microphonic

Matsuura *et al.* (1971a,b) studied the generation of hair cell microphonic potentials (MP) in the goldfish sacculus, and the effects produced by the local application of ionic solutions, metabolic inhibitors, and ototoxic drugs. The basal ends of the hair cells were found to communicate directly with the perilymph which, in turn, communicates with intracranial fluids. Substances applied in small drops onto the floor of the skull acted directly on the basal membranes of the hair cell receptors. Applied in this way, KCl solutions severely depressed MP, presumably by depolarizing the receptor cell membrane. This finding is consistent with the view that the saccular MP is generated exclusively by the polarization of the receptor membrane, particularly since there is no analog in the goldfish sacculus of the endocochlear DC potential of the mammalian cochlea. Matsuura *et al.* also found that perfusing the endolymphatic space with NaCl had very little effect on MP in the goldfish while such a procedure severely depresses MP in mammals. The suggestion here is that while the flow of K^+ ions between the endolymph and the hair cells is responsible for the MP in mammals, Na^+ appears to carry the current in the fishes.

The finding that ouabain suppressed MP only when it was applied to the basal membranes of the hair cells suggested that Na^+ is continuously being extruded from the receptor cell into the perilymph. The finding that the ototoxic antibiotics streptomycin and kanamycin reduced MP only when applied to the apical, endolymphatic side of the hair cell was interpreted as new evidence for the site of action of these drugs.

2. *The Frequency Doubling Effect*

In general, the otolithic microphonic potentials of the fishes show some intriguing features which set them apart from those generated in the mammalian cochlea. The most striking feature of the grossly recorded microphonic is that it contains a large component at twice the frequency of the stimulus (e.g., Zotterman, 1943; Cohen and Winn, 1967; Furukawa *et al.*, 1972a; Fay, 1974b). This frequency doubling is similar to that observed in the lateral-line microphonic (Kuiper, 1956) and in responses from the amphibian (Capranica *et al.*, 1966) and the reptilian (Hepp-Reymond and Palin, 1968) ear. Furukawa *et al.* (1972a) studied this aspect of the response in detail by recording from restricted regions of the saccular macula with microelectrodes. The response appeared as a half-wave rectified version of the stimulus waveform with the negative peaks clipped off. The remaining positive peaks of the MP occurred during the compression

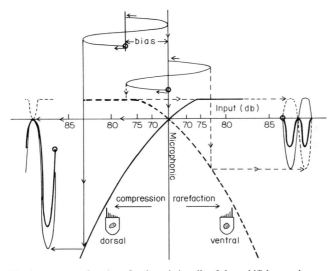

Fig. 8. The input–output functions for those hair cells of the goldfish saccular macula oriented dorsally (solid line), and for those oriented ventrally (dashed line). The input (displacement) waveforms are shown at the top, and the output (microphonic) waveforms are projected to the right for the unbiased input, and to the left for the biased input. The thin solid line in the output waveforms represents the output of the dorsally oriented cells, and the thin dashed lines represent the output of the ventrally oriented cells. The heavy solid line in the output waveforms shows the sum of the thin solid and dashed lines (the sum of the outputs from hair cells of both orientations). The open circles on both the input and output waveforms indicate the starting point of the functions. Modified from Furukawa and Ishii (1967b).

phase of the stimulus in the dorsal macula, and during the rarefaction phase in the ventral portion of the macula. When these two potentials are added algebraically, as they are when recordings are made from the endolymphatic fluid, the sum is a somewhat distorted waveform at twice the frequency of the stimulus. Fig. 8 shows graphically how this would occur by the addition of the outputs of the two generators shown to operate 180° out of phase with each other.

Note what this model predicts about the gross microphonic if the otolith were biased toward one direction or the other. If, for example, the otolith were displaced upward (to the left in Fig. 8), the dorsal hair cells would be operating almost entirely in their linear range while the ventral hair cells would be operating primarily in the range of maximal clipping. The resultant output waveform would thus tend to be a replica of the input waveform with an added DC shift. Notice that within a certain range of bias, the amplitude of the fundamental frequency component of the response is a function of the amplitude of the bias. Such behavior was confirmed in a study of the saccular potentials of the carp (Fay, 1974b). A slow periodic bias was impressed on the otolith by adding a very low frequency tone to the higher frequency stimulating waveform. Fig. 9 shows the types of responses produced by such a bitonal stimulus as a function of the amplitude of the low-frequency biasing component. As the amplitude of the low-frequency component (H) is raised, the response to the higher component (G) is modulated in amplitude at twice the frequency of the low component. The 180° phase reversal which occurs between each adjacent burst is due to the alternate predominance in the response of the dorsal and ventral hair cell groups. Notice that the particular electrode location used here tends to emphasize the

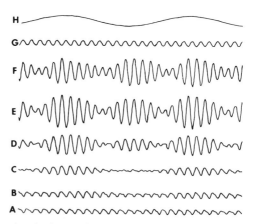

Fig. 9. Saccular microphonic waveforms from the carp in response to an 800-Hz (G) and a 50-Hz (H) tonal mixture. The response was band-pass filtered at 800 Hz in A–F to show amplitude and phase changes in the fundamental frequency component. A, response to 800 Hz at 10 db re: 1 dyne/cm². B, response to the 800-Hz component in the presence of the 50-Hz component at −10 db.

response from one hair cell group. This pattern of response corresponds quite well to the predictions of the model shown in Fig. 8.

3. Postsynaptic Potentials in Auditory Nerve Fibers

In a series of three papers (Ishii *et al.*, 1971a,b; Furukawa *et al.*, 1972b), the relationships between the microphonic potential, synaptic events, and spike initiation in afferent fibers were studied in the goldfish. Intracellular postsynaptic potentials (PSP's) were recorded from large saccular nerve units quite close to their peripheral origin, and were compared to the intramacularly recorded MP's. The synaptic transmission between the hair cells and the innervating fibers was found to be chemically mediated since a manipulation of the postsynaptic membrane polarization altered the size of the EPSP's, and a strong DC polarization reversed the EPSP's electrical sign. A consistent delay of about 0.5 msec occurred between peaks in the microphonic response and the peaks of the EPSP's indicating, again, that ephaptic transmission is unlikely here. The EPSP is quite brief (a rise time of about 0.34 msec) and is observed to occur spontaneously as all-or-nothing quantal events. Finally, it was observed that EPSP's are easily fatigued during high-frequency stimulation so that, for example, the onset of a 1500-Hz tone burst causes a single EPSP of relatively long duration. Since the microphonic always precedes the EPSP and does not fatigue in this way, the view that the microphonic in an epiphenomenon accompanying the release of transmitter substance is rejected in favor of the view that the microphonic is the cause of, or at least the trigger for transmitter release. It should be emphasized here that these experiments with the goldfish remain the only studies of vertebrate auditory neurophysiology in which graded postsynaptic potentials in single eighth nerve fibers have been analyzed.

B. Responses of the Eighth Nerve and Brain

There have been relatively few studies of neural response in the central auditory systems of fishes. Only Enger (1963) and Furukawa and Ishii (1967a) have systematically analyzed unit responses from the eighth nerve, and only Enger (1973), Grözinger (1967), Page (1970), Page and Sutterlin (1970), and Piddington (1971b) have analyzed the responses of central structures in any detail.

In Enger's (1963) study of the sculpin auditory nerve, four types of units were identified on the basis of the pattern of spontaneous discharge, which ranged from no activity at all through "regular," "irregular," and "burst" activity. These four types also differed somewhat in adaptation rates, threshold, frequency response, and phase locking. While the basis for these kinds of differences remains unknown, Enger (1963) has offered the suggestion that the two basic types of frequency response functions observed could provide the basis for a spatial analysis of frequency.

The same kinds of differences between the response properties of neuron populations have been observed in the saccular fibers of the goldfish (Furukawa and Ishii, 1967a). Large fibers from the anterior portion of the macula were most responsive at 800 Hz (see Fig. 7), showed clear adaptation, and were silent in the absence of stimulation. These S1 fibers were observed to discharge during the rarefaction, the compression, or during both phases of the stimulating waveform. The implication here is that some fibers innervate the dorsal macula, others innervate the oppositely oriented hair cells of the ventral macula, and the third group innervates hair cells of both orientations. Smaller diameter fibers from the posterior portion of the macula (S2 fibers) were spontaneously active, were most sensitive at about 300 Hz (see Fig. 7), showed little adaptation, and responded to only one or the other phase of the stimulus. A third group of fibers studied originated from the lagena and responded only to rather intense vibrations of the head. Here again, differences among the two populations of saccular fibers in adaptation rate, spontaneous discharge, and best frequency remain unexplained. Phase locking to stimulus frequencies in excess of 1000 Hz was observed, although not quantitatively analyzed.

Most recently, both the tuning and the phase-locking of goldfish saccular neurons have been more quantitatively studied (Fay, 1978). Two broad and overlapping classes of neurons were described to be similar in some respects to the S1 and S2 fibers of Furukawa and Ishii (1967). Measures of sensitivity and frequency response suggested that the low frequency type was responsive to particle displacement while the high frequency type probably responded to sound pressure via the swim bladder. Thus, the independent information about displacement and pressure required by Schuijf's (1976) theory of sound localization may be provided by a single organ (the sacculus) for frequencies at which both neuron types respond (100–300 Hz). The responsiveness of saccular neurons was expressed as the degree of phase-locking as a function of stimulus frequency. While there is great variation among neurons in these frequency response functions, there is, for any stimulus frequency between 70 and 1000 Hz, a group of neurons which phase-lock with great accuracy.

There are several studies of unit responses in more central structures. In general, latencies increase and phase locking deteriorates at higher neural centers (Grözinger, 1967). Although Page (1970) states that the bandwidth of single fibers contracts at higher levels of the system, quantitative analysis has yet to be made. Perhaps the most surprising observations come from the study of Page and Sutterlin (1970) in which responses from midbrain tegmental units were found to be responsive to both visual and auditory stimulation, and appeared to be quite sharply tuned at 200 Hz. Piddington (1971a) has demonstrated the existence of a descending inhibitory system in the auditory pathway of the goldfish, and has shown some of the presumed consequences of the system's operation in free-swimming animals (Piddington, 1971b). Enger (1973) demonstrated the same degree of frequency-dependent masking in units of the goldfish medulla that Sand (1971) showed in the saccular nerve. Enger (1967a,b) has also recorded the activity of units from the medulla in several species in attempts to determine whether the input system involved was pressure or displacement sensitive. Clearly, most studies of central auditory neurophysiology have been designed primarily as demonstrations, and not as systematic or quantiative investigations of the neural coding of auditory information.

VI. CONCLUSION

The auditory capacities of the fishes appear to differ from those of the mammals in one basic respect. That is, hearing for the fishes is confined to the frequency range below 3 kHz or so where the temporal analysis of the stimulus waveform by the nervous system is most likely to occur. Most mammals hear best in the frequency range between 3 and 10 kHz where the spatial analysis of frequency performed mechanically by the cochlea provides the CNS with most of the information it gets about a particular sound's frequency content. Man may be an exception among the mammals in this respect in that he has particularly poor high-frequency hearing (Masterton *et al.,* 1969), and may use a temporal analysis of waveform to a greater degree than most other mammals. The birds, reptiles, and amphibians certainly tend to fall between the fishes and the mammals in the frequency range of best hearing, but there are not yet any clear indications of the degree to which spectral or temporal analysis are used in information processing for those species.

Aside from the observation that fishes simply do not receive or process information at the higher, mammalian range of frequencies, there are no data to suggest that the hearing of fishes is at all less well developed than for the mammals. The data suggest, on the other hand, that the capacities for auditory information processing, the detection of signals in noise, and the simultaneous and successive analysis of frequency of the fish auditory system do not differ significantly from those of the mammalian systems. An interesting and important question which arises now is whether the mechanisms for auditory analysis used by the fishes are similar to those used by the mammals in dealing with signals in the same low-frequency range. There are no real answers to this question at present because the types of mechanisms involved are simply not known for any species. This lack of understanding is due, in part, to the view of the mammalian auditory system as a set of filters operating entirely in the frequency domain. Responses of the systems to low-frequency stimuli have been neglected, primarily because our conceptual and electronic tools, still under the influence of Helmholz, are more geared to a spectral analysis of frequency than to a temporal analysis of waveform. Since the spectral component of vertebrate auditory analysis may be of relatively less importance for the nonmammals, and may not exist at all for the fishes, these species may provide superior preparations for psychophysiological studies of the mechanisms for auditory analysis in the time domain.

The ears of fishes, and of at least some amphibians and reptiles, are quite unlike those of the mammals and the birds in that the kinocilium of the hair cell receptor is present throughout life, and in that the axes of greatest hair cell sensitivity are often mixed (opposed) on the macula or the auditory papilla. Since activity in afferent fibers is initiated only when the stereocilia are displaced toward the kinocilium, and since hair cells of the cochlea are all oriented in the same direction, it is not surprising that the neurally coded output of the mammalian cochlea is, essentially, a half-wave rectified version of the input waveform (Rose *et al.*, 1967). In other words, only those details of the stimulating waveform which occur in one direction (polarity) are preserved in the temporal pattern of spike activity. Due to the double orientation of the hair cells in the ears of fishes, reptiles, and amphibians, however, details of the complete stimulus waveform are preserved. For symmetrical waveforms such as tones, then, the fish would acquire temporally coded information at twice the rate of the mammal. For asymmetrical waveforms such as transients and noise, on the other hand, the fish would acquire information in greater detail.

The apparent inferiority of the mammals in this aspect of temporal coding has recently been challenged by evidence that the inner and outer hair cells of the cochlea may actually operate in approximate phase opposition (Zwislocki and Sokolich, 1974). For a given direction of movement of the basilar membrane, the direction of the shear forces acting on the hair cell stereocilia is thought to be different for the inner and the outer hair cells due to a difference in the mode of coupling between the stereocilia and the overlying tectorial membrane. In any case, the demonstration that some units of the mammalian eighth nerve tend to fire during an upward movement of the basilar membrane, while others tend to fire for a movement in the opposite direction, is quite significant here because it suggests that hair cell receptors operating in phase opposition is a common feature of vertebrate acoustico-lateralis systems. While the function of this type of arrangement in the mammals is currently thought to be related to the "sharpening" of eighth nerve unit tuning curves (additional filtering), some of the possible functions identified for the fishes are quite different. For example, the determination of the polarity of transients is made possible by this arrangement, and this, in turn, would aid in the ability to localize for a system making use of the directional characteristics of the otolithic maculae (see Section IV,B,2). The double orientation also increases the absolute speed with which information is relayed to the brain since excitation will occur at the same latency whether the stimulating waveform begins with a condensation or a rarefaction. Finally, the density of temporally coded information is doubled as a result of the opposed cells, and this would appear to be an advantage for any central nervous system analysis of temporal structure. In any case, the common occurrence of this kind of organization among the vertebrates is a relatively new observation, and its implications for the neural coding of auditory information remain an exciting topic for future investigation.

ACKNOWLEDGMENTS

The preparation of this chapter was supported by NSF Grant BNS 76-02031 and an Intramural Research Support grant (No. 781-466-75) from The Bowman Gray School of Medicine to the author. I am grateful to Dr. James A. Harrill, chairman of the Section of Otolaryngology, for his generous support to this and other work.

Sincere appreciation is expressed to E. Glen Wever and to the late Georg von Békésy for their past support of my work on the comparative psychophysiology of hearing. I would like to take this opportunity to thank Bob Cole, Art Popper, Ian Cooke, and especially Jeff Bitterman for their assistance to me when it was most needed. Finally, I thank Bill Uttal for his thoughtful criticisms of this manuscript, and for a stimulating friendship.

REFERENCES

Aronson, L. R. (1963). The central nervous system of sharks and bony fishes with special reference to sensory and integrative mechanisms. *In* "Sharks and Survival" (P. Gilbert, ed.), pp. 165-242. Heath, Boston, Massachusetts.

Baird, I. L. (1974). Some aspects of the comparative anatomy and evolution of the inner ear in submammalian vertebrates. *Brain, Behav. Evol.* **10**, 11-36.

Buerkle, U. (1967). An audiogram for the Atlantic Cod, *Gadus morhua* L. *J. Fish. Res. Board Can.* **24**, 2309-2319.

Buerkle, U. (1968). Relation of pure tone thresholds to background noise level in the Atlantic Cod (*Gadus morhua*). *J. Fish. Res. Board Can.* **25**, 1155-1160.

Buerkle, U. (1969). Auditory masking and the critical band in Atlantic Cod (*Gadus marhua*). *J. Fish. Res. Board Can.* **26**, 1113-1119.

Cahn, P., Siler, W., and Wodinsky, J. (1969). Acoustico-lateralis system of fishes: Tests of pressure and particle velocity sensitivity in grunts, *Haemulon sciurus* and *Haemulon parrai*. *J. Acoust. Soc. Am.* **46**, 1572-1578.

Capranica, R., Flock, A., and Frischkopf, L. (1966). Microphonic response from the inner ear of the bullfrog. *J. Acoust. Soc. Am.* **40**, 1262.

Chapman, C. J. (1973). Field studies of hearing in teleost fish. *Helgol. Wiss. Meeresunters.* **24**, 371-390.

Chapman, C. J., and Hawkins, A. D. (1973). A field study of hearing in cod, *Gadus morhua* L. *J. Comp. Physiol.* **85**, 147-167.

Chapman, C. J., and Johnstone, A. D. F. (1974). Some auditory discrimination experiments on marine fish. *J. Exp. Biol.* **61**, 521-528.

Chapman, C. J., and Sand, O. (1973). A field study of hearing in two species of flatfish, *Pleuronectes platessa* (L) and *Limauda limauda* (L), family *Pleuronectidae*). *Comp. Biochem. Physiol.* **47**, 371-385.

Cohen, M. J., and Winn, H. E. (1967). Electrophysiological observations on hearing and sound production in the fish *Porichthys notatus*. *J. Exp. Zool.* **165**, 355-370.

Colnaghi, G. L. (1975). Saccular potentials and their relationship to hearing in the goldfish. *Comp. Biochem. Physiol.* **50A,** 605-613.

Diamond, J. (1971). The mauthner cell. *Fish Physiol.* **5,** 135-216.

Dijkgraaf, S. (1950). Untersuchungen uber die funktionen des Ohrlabrinths bei Meeresfischen. *Physiol. Comp. Oecol.* **2,** 81-106.

Dijkgraaf, S. (1952). Uber die schallwahrnehrnung bei meeresfischen. *Z. Vergl. Physiol.* **34,** 104-122.

Dijkgraaf, S. (1963). The function and significance of the lateral line organs. *Biol. Rev. Cambridge Philos. Soc.* **38,** 51-105.

Dijkgraaf, S., and Verheijen, F. (1950). Neue versuche über das tonunterscheidungsvernögen der elritze. *Z. Vergl. Physiol.* **32,** 248-256.

Enger, P. S. (1963). Single unit activity in the peripheral auditory system of a teleost fish. *Acta Physiol. Scand.* **59,** Suppl. 3, 9-48.

Enger, P. S. (1967a). Effect of the acoustic near field on the sound threshold in fishes. *In* "Lateral Line Detectors" (P. Cahn, ed.), pp. 239-248. Indiana Univ. Press, Bloomington.

Enger, P. S. (1967b). Hearing in herring. *Comp. Biochem. Physiol.* **22,** 527-538.

Enger, P. S. (1968). Hearing in fish. *In* "Hearing Mechanisms in Vertebrates" (A. V. S. de Rueck and J. Knight, eds.), pp. 4-17. Little, Brown, Boston, Massachusetts.

Enger, P. S. (1973). Masking of auditory responses in the medulla oblongata of goldfish. *J. Exp. Biol.* **59,** 415-424.

Erulkar, S. D. (1972). Comparative aspects of spatial localization of sound. *Physiol. Rev.* **52,** 237-360.

Fay, R. R. (1969). "Auditory Sensitivity of the Goldfish Within the Acoustic Near Field," Rep. No. 605, pp. 1-11. U.S. Nav. Submar. Med. Cent., Groton, Connecticut.

Fay, R. R. (1970a). Auditory frequency discrimination in the goldfish (*larassius auratus*). *J. Comp. Physiol. Psychol.* **73,** 175-180.

Fay, R. R. (1970b). Auditory frequency generalization in the goldfish (*larassius auratus*). *J. Exp. Anal. Behav.* **14,** 353-360.

Fay, R. R. (1972). Perception of amplitude modulated auditory signals by the goldfish. *J. Acoust. Soc. Am.* **52,** 660-666.

Fay, R. R. (1974a). Masking of tones by noise for the goldfish (*larassius auratus*). *J. Comp. Physiol. Psychol.* **84,** 708-716.

Fay, R. R. (1974b). Sound reception and processing in the carp: Saccular potentials. *Comp. Biochem. Physiol.* **49,** 29-42.

Fay, R. R. (1974c). Auditory frequency discrimination in vertebrates. *J. Acoust. Soc. Am.* **56,** 206-209.

Fay, R. (1978). The coding of information in single auditory nerve fibers of the goldfish. *J. Acoust. Soc. Am.* (in press).

Fay, R. R., and MacKinnon, J. R. (1969). A simplified technique for conditioning respiratory mouth movements in fish. *Behav. Res. Methods & Instrum.* **1,** 123-124.

Fay, R. R., and Popper, A. N. (1974). Acoustic stimulation of the ear of the goldfish (*larassius auratus*). *J. Exp. Biol.* **61,** 243-260.

Fay, R. R., and Popper, A. N. (1975). Modes of stimulation of the teleost ear. *J. Exp. Biol.* **62,** 379-387.

Fletcher, H. (1940). Auditory patterns. *Rev. Mod. Phys.* **12,** 47-65.

Flock, Å. (1965). Electron microscope and electrophysiological studies of the lateral line canal organ. *Acta Oto-Laryngol., Suppl.* **199,** 1-88.

Furukawa, T. (1966). Synaptic interaction at the mauthner cell of goldfish. *Prog. Brain Res.* **21A,** 44-70.

Furukawa, T., and Ishii, Y. (1967a). Neurophysiological studies on hearing in goldfish. *J. Neurophysiol.* **30,** 1377-1403.

Furukawa, T., and Ishii, Y. (1967b). Effects of static bending of sensory hairs on sound reception in the goldfish. *Jpn. J. Physiol.* **17,** 572–578.

Furukawa, T., Ishii, Y., and Matsuura, S. (1972a). An analysis of the microphonic potentials of the sacculus of goldfish. *Jpn. J. Physiol.* **22,** 603–616.

Furukawa, T., Ishii, Y., and Matsuura, S. (1972b). Synaptic delay and time course of post synaptic potentials of at the junction between hair cells and 8th nerve fibers of the goldfish. *Jpn. J. Physiol.* **22,** 617–635.

Goff, G. (1967). Differential discrimination of frequency of cutaneous mechanical viberation. *J. Exp. Psychol.* **74,** 294–299.

Goldberg, J. M., and Brown, P. B. (1969). Response of binaural neurons of dog superior olivary complex to dicliotic tonal stimuli some physiological mechanisms of sound localization. *J. Neurophysiol.* **32,** 613–636.

Goldstein, M. H., deRebaupierre, F., and Yeni-Komshian, G. H. (1971). Cortical coding of periodicity pitch. *In* "Physiology of the Auditory System" (M. B. Sach, ed.), pp. 299–306. Natl. Educ. Consultants, 1971, Baltimore, Maryland.

Gourevitch, G. (1970). Detectability of tones in quiet and in noise by rats and monkeys. *In* "Animal Psychophysics" (W. C. Stebbins, ed.), pp. 67–98. Appleton, New York.

Greenwood, D. D. (1961). Auditory masking and the critical band. *J. Acoust. Soc. Am.* **33,** 484–502.

Griffin, D. R. (1955). Hearing and acoustic orientation in marine animals. Papers on marine biology and oceanography. *Deep-Sea Res.* **3,** Suppl., 406–417.

Grozinger, B. (1967). Elektro-physiologische Untersuchungen an der Horbahn der Schleie (*Tinca tinca* (L.)). *Z. Vergl. Physiol.* **57,** 44–76.

Hama, K. (1969). A study of the fine structure of the saccular marula of the goldfish. *Z. Zellforsch. Mikrosk. Anat.* **94,** 155–171.

Harris, G. G. (1964). Considerations on the physics of sound production by fishes. *In* "Marine Bio-acoustics" (W. N. Tavolga, ed.), Vol. I, pp. 233–249. Pergamon, Oxford.

Harris, G. G., and van Bergeijk, W. A. (1962). Evidence that the lateral line organ responds to near field displacements of sound sources in water. *J. Acoust. Soc. Am.* **34,** 1831–1841.

Hawkins, J. E., and Stevens, S. S. (1950). The masking of pure tones and of speech by white noise. *J. Acoust. Soc. Am.* **22,** 6–13.

Hepp-Reymond, M. C., and Palin, J. (1968). Patterns in the cochlear potential of the Tokay gecko (*Gekko gecko*). *Acta Oto-Laryngol.* **65,** 270–292.

Ishii, Y., Matsuura, S., and Furukawa, T. (1971a). Quantal nature of transmission at the synapse between hair cells and 8th nerve fibers in the goldfish. *Jpn. J. Physiol.* **21,** 79–89.

Ishii, Y., Matsuura, S., and Furukawa, T. (1971b). An input-output relation at the synapse between hair cells and 8th nerve fibers in goldfish. *Jpn. J. Physiol.* **21,** 91–98.

Iverson, R. T. B. (1967). Response of the yellowfin tuna (*Thumus albacares*) to underwater sound. *In* "Marine Bio-acoustics" (W. N. Tavolga, ed.), Vol. II, pp. 105–121. Pergamon, Oxford.

Jacobs, D. W., and Tavolga, W. N. (1967). Acoustic intensity lineus for the goldfish. *Anim. Behav.* **15,** 324–335.

Jacobs, D. W., and Tavolga, W. N. (1968). Acoustic frequency discrimination in the goldfish. *Anim. Behav.* **16,** 67–71.

Jeffress, L. A. (1948). A place theory of sound localization. *J. Comp. Physiol. Psychol.* **41,** 35–39.

Jeffress, L. A. (1972). Binaural signal detection: Vector theory. *In* "Foundations of Modern Auditory Theory" (J. V. Tobias, ed.), Vol. II, pp. 349–367. Academic Press, New York.

Kiang, N. Y. S., Watanabe, T., Thomas, E., and Clark, L. (1965). "Discharge Patterns in Single Fibers of the Cat's Auditory Nerve," M.I.T. Res. Monogr. No. 35. MIT Press, Massachusetts.

Kleerekoper, H., and Chagnon, E. (1954). Hearing in fish with special reference to *Semotilus atromaculatus*. *J. Fish. Res. Board Can.* **11,** 130–152.

Kuiper, J. (1956). "Microphonic Effects of the Lateral Line Organ." Publication of the Biophysics Group, Natuurkundig Laboratorium, Gröningen.

Licklider, J. C. R. (1959). Three auditory theories. *In* "Psychology: A Study of a Science" (S. Koch, ed.), Vol. I, pp. 41–144. McGraw-Hill, New York.

Lowenstein, O. (1971). The labyrinth. *Fish. Physiol.* **5**, 207–240.

Masterton, B., Heffner, H., and Ravizza, R. (1969). The evolution of human hearing. *J. Acoust. Soc. Am.* **45**, 966–985.

Matsuura, S., Ikeda, K., and Furukawa, T. (1971a). Effects of K^+, Na^+, and ouabain on microphonic potentials of the goldfish inner ear. *Jpn. J. Physiol.* **21**, 563–578.

Matsuura, S., Ikeda, K., and Furukawa, T. (1971b). Effects of streptomyacin, kamamyacin, quinine and other drugs on the microphonic potentials of the goldfish saccule. *Jpn. J. Physiol.* **21**, 579–590.

Møller, A. R. (1969). Unit responses in the cat coclilear nucleus to repetitive, transient sounds. *Acta Physiol. Scand.* **75**, 542–551.

Moulton, J. M. (1960). Swimming sounds and the schooling of fishes. *Biol. Bull.* **119**, 210–223.

Moulton, J. M. (1963). Acoustic behavior of fishes. *In* "Acoustic Behavior of Animals" (R. G. Busnel, ed.), pp. 655–687. Elsevier, Amsterdam.

Moulton, J. M., and Dixon, R. H. (1967). Directional hearing in fishes. *In* "Marine Bio-acoustics" (W. N. Tavolga, ed.), Vol. II, pp. 187–232. Pergamon, Oxford.

Mountcastle, V. B., Talbot, W., Sakata, H., and Hyvarinen, J. (1969). Cortical neuronal mechanisms in flutter vibration studied in unanesthetized monkeys. *J. Neurophysiol.* **32**, 452–484.

Nelson, D. R., and Gruber, S. H. (1963). Sharks: Attraction by low frequency sounds. *Science* **142**, 975–977.

Offutt, G. C. (1974). Structures for the detection of acoustic stimuli in the Atlantic codfish Gadus morhua. *J. Acoust. Soc. Am.* **56**, 665–671.

Page, C. H. (1970). Electrophysiological study of auditory responses in the goldfish brain. *J. Neurophysiol.* **23**, 116–128.

Page, C. H., and Sutterlin, A. M. (1970). Visual-auditory unit responses in the goldfish tegmentium. *J. Neurophysiol.* **23**, 129–136.

Parker, G. H. (1918). A critical survey of the sense of hearing in fishes. *Proc. Am. Philos. Soc.* **57**, 69–98.

Parvelescu, A. (1964). Problems of propagation and processing. *In* "Marine Bio-acoustics" (W. N. Tavolga, ed.), Vol. I, pp. 87–100. Pergamon, Oxford.

Piddington, R. W. (1971a). Central control of auditory input in the goldfish. I. Effect of shocks to midbrain. *J. Exp. Biol.* **55**, 569–584.

Piddington, R. W. (1971b). Central control of auditory input in the goldfish. II. Evidence of action in the free swimming animal. *J. Exp. Biol.* **55**, 585–610.

Piddington, R. W. (1972). Auditory discrimination between compressions and rarefactions by goldfish. *J. Exp. Biol.* **56**, 403–419.

Poggendorf, D. (1952). Die absoluten Horschwellen des Zwergwelses und Beitrage zur Physik des Webesschen Apparates der Ostariophysen. *Z. Vergl. Physiol.* **34**, 222–257.

Popper, A. N. (1971a). The morphology of the Weberian ossicles of two species of the genus *Astyanas* (Ostariophysi: Characidae). *J. Morphol.* **133**, 179–188.

Popper, A. N. (1971b). The effect of size on auditory capacities of the goldfish. *J. Audit. Res.* **11**, 239–247.

Popper, A. N. (1973). Pure tone auditory thresholds for the carp, *Cyprinus Carpio*. *J. Acoust. Soc. Am.* **54**, 327A.

Popper, A. N. (1974). The response of the swimbladder of the goldfish (*Carassius auratus*) to acoustic stimuli. *J. Exp. Biol.* **60**, 295–304.

Popper, A. N., and Fay, R. R. (1973). Sound detection and processing by teleost fishes: A critical review. *J. Acoust. Soc. Am.* **53**, 1515–1529.

Popper, A. N., Salmon, M., and Parvelescu, A. (1973). Sound localization by the Hawaiian squirrel fishes *Myripristus Gerndti* and *M. Argyromus. Anim. Behav.* **21**, 86–97.

Pumphrey, R. J. (1950). Hearing. *Symp. Soc. Exp. Biol.* **4**, 3–18.

Retzius, G. (1881). "Das Gehororgan der Wirbeltiere," Vols. I and II. Samson & Wallin, Stockholm.

Rose, J. E., Brugge, J. F., Anderson, D. J., and Hind, J. E. (1967). Phase locked response to low frequency tones in single auditory nerve fibers of the squirrel monkey. *J. Neurophysiol.* **30**, 769–793.

Saito, K. (1973). Fine structure of macula lagena in the teleost inner ear. *Kaibogaku Zasshi* **48**, 1–18 (In Japanese).

Sand, O. (1971). An electrophysiological study of auditory masking of clicks in goldfish. *Comp. Biochem. Physiol.* **40**, 1043–1053.

Sand, O. (1974). Directional sensitivity of microphonic potentials from the perch ear. *J. Exp. Biol.* **60**, 881–899.

Sand, O., and Hawkins, A. D. (1973). Acoustic properties of the cod swimbladder. *J. Exp. Biol.* **58**, 797–820.

Scharf, B. (1970). Critical bands. *In* "Foundations of Modern Auditory Theory" (J. V. Tobias, ed.), Vol. I, pp. 157–198. Academic Press, New York.

Schneider, H. (1942). Die Bedeutung der Atemhöle der Labrynthfische fur ihs Horvermogen. *Z. Vergl. Physiol.* **29**, 172–194.

Schuijf, A. (1976). The phase model of directional hearing in fish. In "Sound Reception in Fish" (A. Schuijf and A. Hawkins, Eds.), pp. 63–86. Elsevier, Amsterdam.

Schuijf, A. (1975). Directional hearing of cod (*Gadus morhua*) under approximate free field conditions. *J. Comp. Physiol.* **98**, 307–332.

Schuijf, A., and Buwalda, R. (1975). On the mechanism of directional hearing in cod (*Gadus morhua*). *J. Comp. Physiol.* **98**, 333–343.

Schuijf, A., Baretta, J. W., and Wildschut, J. (1972). A field investigation on the discrimination of sound direction in *Labrus berggylta. Neth. J. Zool.* **22**, 81–104.

Schwartz, E. (1967). Analysis of surface wave perception in some teleosts. *In* "Lateral Line Detectors" (P. Cahn, ed.), pp. 123–134. Indiana Univ. Press, Bloomington.

Siler, W. (1969). Near- and far-fields in a massive environment. *J. Acoust. Soc. Am.* **46**, 483–485.

Small, A. (1970). Periodicity pitch. *In* "Foundations of Modern Auditory Theory" (J. V. Tobias, ed.), Vol. 1, pp. 1–50. Academic Press, New York.

Stetter, H. (1929). Untersuchungen iber den Gehorsinn der Fische: Gesanders van *Phoxinus laevis* L. und *Ameiurus nebulosus* Raf. *Z. Vergl. Physiol.* **9**, 339–447.

Stipetic, E. (1939). Uber Gehororgan des Mormyriden. *Z. Vergl. Physiol.* **26**, 740–752.

Tavolga, W. N. (1965). Review of marine bio-acoustics. *Tech. Rep., NAVTRADEVCEN* 1212-1.

Tavolga, W. N. (1971). Sound production and detection. *Fish Physiol.* **5**, 135–205.

Tavolga, W. N. (1974). The critical band in fishes. *J. Acoust. Soc. Am.* **55**, 1323–1333.

Tavolga, W. N., and Wodinsky, J. (1963). Auditory capacities in fishes. *Bull. Am. Mus. Nat. Hist.* **126**, 177–240.

Tobias, J., and Zerlin, S. (1959). Lateralization-threshold as a function of stimulus duration. *J. Acoust. Soc. Am.* **31**, 1591–1594.

van Bergeikj, W. A. (1964). Directional and nondirectional hearing in fish. *In* "Marine Bioacoustics" (W. N. Tavolga, ed.), Vol. 1, pp. 281–300. Pergamon, Oxford.

van Bergeijk, W. A. (1967a). The evolution of vertebrate hearing. *In* "Contributions to Sensory Physiology" (W. D. Neff, ed.), Vol. 2, pp. 1–46. Academic Press, New York.

van Bergeijk, W. A. (1967b). Discussion. *In* "Marine Bio-acoustics" (W. N. Tavolga, ed.), Vol. II, pp. 244-245. Pergamon, Oxford.

von Békésy, G. (1972). The missing fundamental and periodicity detection in hearing. *J. Acoust. Soc. Am.* **51,** 631-637.

von Frisch, K. (1936). Uber den gehorsinn der fische. *Biol. Rev. Cambridge Philos. Soc.* **11,** 210-246.

von Frisch, K. (1938). The sense of hearing in fish. *Nature (London)* **141,** 8-11.

Weber, E. H. (1820). "De Aure et Auditu Hominis et Animalum. Pars I., De Aure Animalum Aquatilium," Lipsiae.

Wegel, R., and Lane, C. (1924). The auditory masking of one sound by another and its probable relation to the dynamics of the inner ear. *Phys. Rev.* **23,** 266-285.

Weiss, B. (1966). Auditory sensitivity in goldfish. *J. Audit. Res.* **6,** 321-335.

Weiss, B. (1969). Lateral line sensitivity in the goldfish. *J. Audit. Res.* **9,** 71-75.

Wever, E. G. (1969). Cochlear stimulation and Lempert's mobilization theory. *Arch. Oto-Laryngol.* **90,** 720-725.

Wever, E. G. (1971). The mechanics of hair cell stimulation. *Ann. Otol. Rhinol. Laryngol.* **80,** 786-805.

Wever, E. G. (1973). Tectorial reticulum of the labyrinthine endings of vertebrates. *Ann. Otol., Rhinol., & Laryngol.* **82,** 277-290.

Wightman, F. (1973). The pattern transformation model of pitch. *J. Acoust. Soc. Am.* **54,** 407-416.

Wohlfahrt, T. (1936). Das Ohrlabyrinth der Sardine (*Clupea pilchardus*) und seine Bezeihungen zur Schwimmblase und Seitenlinie. *Z. Morphol. Oekol. Tiere* **33,** 381-412.

Wohlfahrt, T. (1939). Untersuchungen uber das Tonunterscheidungsvemögen der Elritze. *Z. Vergl. Physiol.* **26,** 570-604.

Zotterman, Y. (1943). The microphonic effect of teleost labyrinths and its biological significance. *J. Physiol. (London)* **102,** 313-318.

Zwislocki, J., and Sokolich, W. (1974). Model of neuromechanical sound filtering in the cochlea. *J. Acoust. Soc. Am.* **56,** 521 (abstr.).

6

The Behavior of Turtles in the Sea, in Freshwater, and on Land

A. M. GRANDA and J. H. MAXWELL

I. Introduction 237
   A. Anatomy 238
   B. Temperature Control 240
   C. Respiration and Circulation 241
II. Systematics 242
III. Sensory Systems 244
   A. Vision 246
   B. Audition 249
   C. Chemoreception 251
IV. Major Behavior Patterns 251
   A. Learning 251
   B. Sleep 266
   C. Diving 268
   D. Hibernation 270
   E. Migration 272
   F. Reproduction 275
V. Conclusion 276
   References 276

I. INTRODUCTION

Turtles are distributed over land, sea and fresh waters. A particularly ancient form, they have changed little since the late Triassic era, about 220 million years ago. Even by the late Upper Jurassic (170 million years ago), fossilized remains show a present day morphology, and little can be gleaned of the direction or progression of their evolution. "There is no feature revealed by them (skulls) that cannot be rather closely matched in some group of turtles still living" (Parsons and Williams, 1961, p. 89). One must reach far into the past to the Permian age, about 300 million years ago, to find evidence of a small fossil reptile, *Eunotosaurus africanus,* whose ribs have just begun to form a distinct shell.

Turtles belong to the order Chelonia, alternatively known as Testudinata. They are contained in the class Reptilia and are vertebrates that share the common distinguishing characteristic of a vertebral column. Reptiles were the first vertebrates to free themselves completely from the water by developing an encased marine environment that could be deposited on land. Accordingly, reptiles differ from Amphibia which remain tied to the water for reproductive purposes and for the maintenance of body fluids; reptiles do not.

For whatever purpose, perhaps ancestral memory or simple affection, some reptilian species preferred to return to the water. Despite a consequent modification of limbs and body morphology, these atavists nevertheless retained the basic survival anatomy and capability so suitable for a water-free environment: lungs for oxygen exchange and the ability to enclose the fetal environment in a protective shell for safe deposit on land. The compulsion to lay shell-covered eggs on land is a strange *Persephone*-like arrangement, perhaps the price demanded by evolution for back-sliding into a water environment. All turtles, marine and otherwise, lay their eggs on land, often undergoing severe hardship to accomplish their task.

In general, turtles share the common construction of a stiff, sometimes bony, boxlike shell that encloses the hip and shoulder girdles and all of the internal organs. The head, neck, limbs and tail project through openings in the front and rear. On land, this tanklike structure permits little agility or maneuverability. The ponderous advance of the land turtle already has passed into mythology: land turtles are slow of gait—very slow and very steady. In water, however, movement is not seriously compromised. Certain pelagic forms, *Chelonia mydas* for example, have an elegance of movement that is delightful to observe. There are arabesques, swoops, sudden turns and dives that speak of a marvelous control of movement both subtle and swift.

A. Anatomy

The shell in all turtles is composed of an inner bony layer of regularly arranged elements and an outer layer of horny scaleplates called scutes that overlap the bony plates (cf. however, Trionychidae, the soft-shelled turtles). The scutes are labeled in Fig. 1(A); the several parts of the bony layer are labeled in Fig. 1(B). While there are some changes among the various species, the basic plan holds for all (Zangerl, 1969).

The skull is solid, without temporal openings, a feature that places turtles in the subclass Anapsida. All the more recent turtles lack teeth; instead, there is a

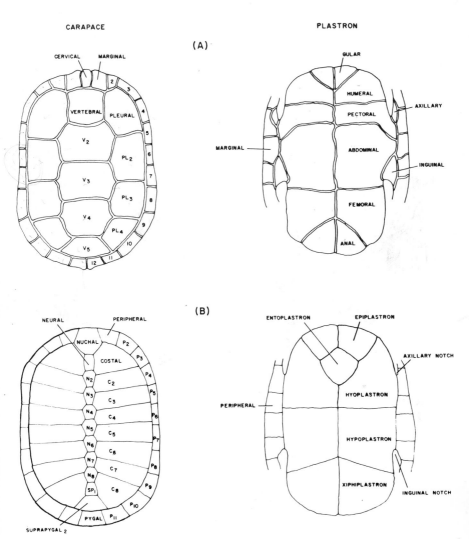

Fig. 1. (A) Scutes of the carapace and plastron; (B) bones of the carapace and plastron.

horny beak with a fairly sharp edge to it in some species, or a modified flattened grinding surface over part of it in others. There is some evidence of teeth in fossil remains, and it is more than likely that the course of evolutionary development fused these palatal teeth into a beak. Birds, too, one could guess, probably followed the same course in their own development. Figure 2 shows the skull bones and their more commonly associated names in three representative turtle species.

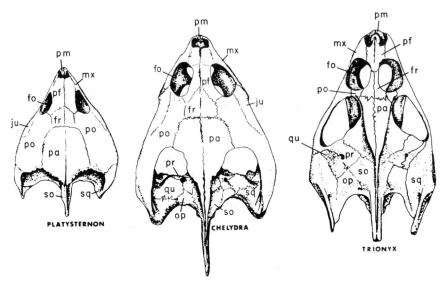

Fig. 2.   Skulls from three representative turtles showing the solidly roofed anterior portions and the erosion from behind of large sections of the posterior roofs. More advanced forms have larger portions eroded away. (Adapted from Holman, 1969.) fo, fossa orbitalis; fr, frontal; ju, jugal; mx, maxilla; op, opisthotic; pa, parietal; pf, prefrontal; pm, premaxilla; po, postorbital; pr, prootic; qu, quadrate; so, supraoccipital; sq, squamosal.

Of all visible body parts, the limbs poking through the shell openings display the most blatant diversity in adapting to various environmental media (cf. Fig. 3). Sea turtles, for example, have flippers that propel them efficiently through water, all four limbs orchestrated for efficient movement. Terrestrial breeds differ in having clawed appendages that are almost shovel-like in order to help in digging and clasping during reproduction and mating. The freshwater species all developed some form of webbing between their claws for paddling through water, the amount of webbing being intimately tied to the strength of attachment to aquatic life (Ernst and Barbour, 1972, p. 4).

B. Temperature Control

There are a number of additional characteristics of turtles that need to be considered in order to come to an appreciation of their behavior and its control. In freeing themselves from the water, reptiles developed a scaly skin with few surface glands for the retention of body water. They have no easy way to cool or warm their bodies. Turtles, as reptiles, are ectothermic animals and seek to avoid extremes of temperature. They hide in cool retreats when it is hot and seek warm surrounds or hibernate when cold. The seeking of proper climes is a preoccupation for most turtles and determines large segments of their behavior. Most sea turtles, however, are not so concerned. They live in fairly constant marine environments, although leatherbacks have been sighted along the North American coast off Canada and New England, far from their nesting sites to the south. The water temperature is colder here, a good 15°C below the temperature of water near the nesting beaches, and the possibility of some form of temperature regulation in these animals has been raised.

Mrosovsky and Pritchard (1971), for example, showed that egg temperatures of leatherbacks, as well as their body temperatures measured in off-shore waters, were significantly warmer by 3°C or more than their immediate environments. More dramatically, a leatherback turtle taken out of cold water at 7°C off the coast of Nova Scotia showed a deep-body temperature 18° above the water temperature (Frair et al., 1972). Both green and ridley turtles also are warmer than their immediate environments, but the temperature difference is not as great. While one could speculate on endothermic mechanisms operative in these animals (for which there is no evidence presently, but cf. Desmond, 1976), the results can be related plausibly to large body size and the simple conservation of heat produced by muscular activity (Frair et al., 1972).

C. Respiration and Circulation

Because of the shell and the special features of the shoulder and pelvic girdles, respiration is accomplished by contraction of the oblique abdominal muscles at the hind leg openings for inspiration, and by the ventral abdominal muscles which push the viscera against the lungs deflating them for expiration. In some aquatic species, additional oxygen may be drawn through vascular mucous membranes of the gullet and cloaca, possibly extending the length of time between breaths. The circulatory system that is dependent on this oxygen exchange is somewhat unique in turtles when compared to mammals or even to other reptiles such as the Crocodilia. Turtles have a three-chambered heart with two auricles and a single ventricle. The ventricle is incompletely divided, which means that venous blood returning to the right side of the heart through the sinus venosus mixes with oxygenated blood returning to the left auricle through the pulmonary veins. Contraction of the heart pumps out blood not fully oxygenated through the dorsal aorta to its various destinations. During prolonged diving, the blood from the tissues bypasses the pulmonary system and goes directly out the dorsal aorta. The invention is apparently unique and quite useful, for it draws almost exclusively from anaerobic glycolysis as an energy source during extensive periods under water (Millen et al., 1964). Because of this arrangement, perhaps a completed septal division of the ventricle similar to the crocodilian heart would have been more helpful, turtles appear incapable of protracted muscular activity requiring great energy expenditures (Bustard, 1973, p. 14). To pull a turtle's head out in any tug-of-war, one need only sustain the pull for a short time for the animal suddenly to give up. Their necks, of course, are powerfully muscled, but sustained activity requiring great effort is simply not possible.

II. SYSTEMATICS

All living land, marine and freshwater turtles fall into three, perhaps four, major lines of evolution. One line is represented by the very large leatherback turtle, the only member of the family Dermochelydae, a pelagic form adapted to life at sea. The leatherback is the largest of living turtles, with specimens known to range in weight from 318 to 726 kg and in carapace lengths from 118 to 244 cm (Ernst and Barbour, 1972, p. 249). The limbs are modified into flippers completely devoid of claws. The carapace is without scutes; instead, it is covered with a leathery skin having distinct axial ridges.

All other marine turtles are collected into the family Cheloniidae, often classified with the Cryptodiroidea (see below). These animals do have claws as well as a bony carapace covered with scutes. The family is made up of four genera of living turtles: the green turtle (*Chelonia mydas*), the hawksbill turtle (*Eretomochelys imbricata*), the loggerhead turtle (*Caretta caretta*), and the ridley turtle (*Lepidochelys kempii* and *L. olibacea*). The Cheloniidae are all large,

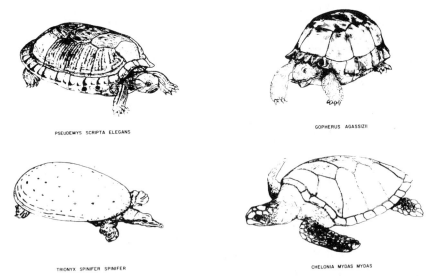

PSEUDEMYS SCRIPTA ELEGANS

GOPHERUS AGASSIZII

TRIONYX SPINIFER SPINIFER

CHELONIA MYDAS MYDAS

Fig. 3. Limb and shell adaptations among four species of freshwater, land, and sea turtles. See text.

though not as large as the Dermochelydae. The green turtle (cf. Fig. 3), the most famous family member, is especially valuable, being renown for its tasty flesh, its eggs, and its unique oil, useful it is said in the restoration of youthful appearance to those that desire it (Parsons, 1962).

The side-necked turtles, the Pleurodiroidea, make up a second line. These animals withdraw their heads by bending their necks laterally under the front of the carapace. The neck vertebrae have lateral processes for attachment of muscles that bend the neck in a horizontal plane. The living representatives of this family are restricted to the Southern Hemisphere (Australia, Africa, Madagascar, and South America). The side-necks are made up of two families, the Pelomedusidae, where the neck is completely retractile, and the Chelidae, the snake-necked turtles, where the neck cannot be completely retracted. None of these animals are represented in northern climes, although there are fossil remains to indicate they were once distributed there.

All the remaining turtles, both land and freshwater forms, are placed in the third line—the Cryptodiroidea or hidden-necked turtles. These animals all withdraw their heads by a vertical sigmoid-shaped bending of the neck. The bend is not seen, hence the name. The families in this group comprise many that are more commonly met. The Chelydridae are snapping turtles. Snappers have large heads with frontally placed eyes and very powerful jaws. They eat almost anything they can get into their mouths. In turn they are much valued for their delicious flesh. Mud and musk turtles are contained within the family Kinosternidae. These animals are usually small to medium in size, 8 to 20 cm in length. Their distinguishing feature is a set of musk glands on either side of the body bordering the carapace. The glands exude a foul-smelling secretion when the animals are disturbed. The largest family of living turtles, the Emydidae, are semiaquatic pond turtles widely distributed in the New World, Europe, Asia, and parts of Africa. The feet are elongated and the toes are webbed to varying degrees among species. The shell and skin of several forms are brightly colored with rich reds and yellows as well as the prevailing browns and greens. The grouping includes *Pseudemys* (cf. Fig. 3), the common slider and *Chrysemys,* the painted turtle, both popular experimental animals. Also included is the box turtle, *Terrapene,* which has a distinctive plastral hinge that allows almost complete closure of the shell.

Also included with Cryptodiroidea are the terrestrial turtles, called by some tortoises (Testudinidae). This family includes the largest living land turtles. The feet are webless, heavy clawed, and covered with hard scales. The openings in the shell can be neatly closed by almost all species when the limbs are retracted. In this position the limb scales complete the body armor. A typical representative is the gopher turtle, *Gopherus agassizii* (cf. Fig. 3), native to the United States and Mexico, with forelimbs and feet more specialized for digging. The most spectacular animals of this group, however, are the giant land turtles, *Testudo elephantopus* and *Testudo gigantea,* many over 120 cm long with weights of a few hundred kilograms (Van Denburgh, 1914; Schmidt and Inger, 1957, p. 29). They inhabit only islands: Madagascar and the Galapagos.

Three more families complete the Cryptodiroidea. There are the Platysternidae, a large-headed, long-tailed group found in southern Asia, and the Dermatamyidae, a small, short-tailed group inhabiting the fresh waters of Central America. We know little about them, although they are plentiful in number. Finally, there are the Carettochelyidae, a somewhat anomalous form. These animals have flat, paddle-shaped limbs and retract their heads in standard cryptodine form, but the body carapace is covered by a layer of soft skin instead of horny scutes. The bony layer is complete, and the marginal bones meet the rib plates as they do in most turtles. This latter characteristic prevents their classification with soft-shelled turtles, the last or fourth line of evolution (cf. below). The Carettochelyidae form a link between the Cryptodiroidea and the true soft-shelled turtles.

The Trionychidae, the soft-shelled turtles (cf. Fig. 3), are a distinct group often classified with the Cryptodiroidea: they withdraw their heads in standard "hidden-necked" fashion. Arguments, however, can easily be advanced to place them in a separate group. The soft-shells are adapted especially to an aquatic life. Their limbs are paddlelike with three claws on each, hence their name. The inner bony layer of the shell is much reduced and the horny scutes have been lost altogether. Both plastron and carapace bones are embedded in a thick, tough tissue that is rather smooth and leathery. The distal ends of the ribs are not fused to the shell, but project freely. The lips are not horny but rather fleshy as is the drawn out snout, a snorkel device for breathing. Serologic tests indicate that these animals are distinct from both the Cryptodiroidea and the Pleurodiroidea. The soft-shelled turtles are carnivorous and nasty in disposition, apparently willing to bluff and bite rather than remain passively secure inside an armored shell as turtle orthodoxy demands.

A scheme of classification is displayed in Table I to indicate the major relationships. The hierarchy is by no means settled.

√ **III. SENSORY SYSTEMS**

Sensory systems mediate between environment and organism, and turtles present the classical array of sensory receptors to cope with their surrounds. The senses of sight, hearing, somesthesis, smell and taste are obviously present, but aside from the concession that those senses are organized to the unique chelonian approach, we know very little about them in turtles or even in reptiles as a class. It is a pity, for nature in a fury of experimentation tried several variations in these animals for success in sensory information processing—unique structures, clever

TABLE I

Classification of Turtles

ass	Subclass	Order	Suborder	Superfamily	Family

ptilla-Anapsida-Testudines

Athecae (Without-shell turtles) ── **Dermochelidae** (Leatherback sea turtle. 1 genus; 1 species)

Thecophora (Fused-shell turtles)

— **Pleurodiroidea** (Side-necked turtles) —
- **Pelomedusidae** (Neck completely retractile. 3 genera; 15 species)
- **Chelidae** (Snake-necked turtles; not completely retractile. 10 genera; 20 species)

— **Cryptodiroidea** (Hidden-necked turtles) —
- **Cheloniidae** (Sea turtles. 4 genera; 5 species)
- **Dermatemyidae** (Central American freshwater turtles. 1 genus; 1 species)
- **Platysternidae** (Asian big-head turtles. 1 genus; 1 species)
- **Testudinidae** (Land turtles. 10 genera; 60 species)
- **Kinosternidae** (Musk and mud turtles. 4 genera; 25 species)
- **Emydidae** (Freshwater turtles. 25 genera; 70 species)
- **Chelydridae** (Snapping turtles. 2 genera; 3 species)

— **Trionychoidea** (Soft-shelled turtles) —
- **Carettochelidae** (Paddle-shaped limbs; soft-shell. 1 genus; 1 species)
- **Trionychidae** (7 genera; 27 species)

adaptations. In this section we outline the several sensory systems and describe the limits within which they operate to the extent we know anything at all about them. The behaviors and their technical control that we discuss in Section IV must very obviously depend on the range of information made available to the animals by their unique sensory structures. Our concern here is to describe the field on which that behavior and its information control is played.

✓ A. Vision

The eye of turtle is organized on sound vertebrate principles with some reptilian styling added as well as genuine chelonian touches. The eyeball has the usual tough outer sclera continuous with an unusually transparent cornea, the latter much more so than primate corneas. In common with some reptiles and many birds, but not with mammals, the sclera is reinforced with cartilage and small bones, the scleral ossicles. The reason for the reinforced sclera is to aid in a rather unusual method of accommodation. Unlike mammals which distort their crystalline lenses by relaxing the tension of the elastic envelope surrounding them, turtles squeeze the lens by action of the ciliary muscles. The result is to force the ciliary body to press against the lens all the way round and cause the lens to elongate from front to back. The front surface becomes more curved and thereby brings objects close by into focus. The scleral ossicles [cf. Fig. 4(A)] are important in this regard for they help to direct the force of the ciliary body and keep it against the lens periphery (cf. Bellairs, 1970, p. 345; Walls, 1942, p. 275). The lens is easily malleable, being soft and pliable, somewhat more so than in other vertebrates (Walls, 1942, p. 610).

The receptors of the retina are made up of cones and rods, and structures known as double cones [cf. Fig. 4(B)]. The ratio of cones and rods differs in different species, but the numbers are not known. Cones largely mediate photopic vision and provide the basis for an appreciation of color. In *Pseudemys scripta* and *Chelonia mydas,* the cones contain three different photopigments (Liebman and Granda, 1971), and that fact argues for the presence of color vision. These two species have rods as well, though they are not as plentiful as the cones; rods function mainly in dim-light vision. The photopigments of both species have absorption maxima (λ_{max}) congruent with their environments. *Pseudemys* have cone pigments absorbing maximally at 450, 522, and 620 nm, with a rod photopigment also at 522 nm. The arrangement is based on vitamin A_2, entailing a displacement to longer wavelengths characteristic of species located in fresh waters (Wald, 1939). *Chelonia,* on the other hand, have cone pigments at 445, 502, and 562 nm. The absorption peak of their rod photopigment is 502 nm. But here the base is vitamin A_1, a system characteristic of sea and land vertebrates (Wald, 1939), thereby providing a better match to prevailing light conditions.

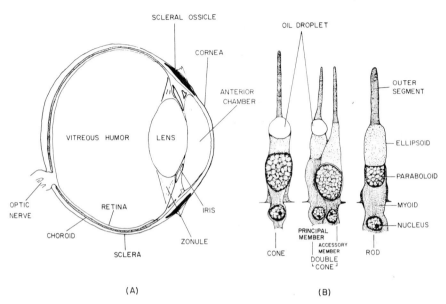

Fig. 4. (A) Hemisection of *Pseudemys* eye (courtesy of D.P.M. Northmore); (B) visual receptors in the retina of *Chelydra serpentina* showing single and double cones, also rods. (Adapted from Walls, 1942.)

The most unusual structures in the turtle's retina are colored oil globules (Liebman and Granda, 1975). The globules contain photostable, carotenoid pigments and appear as deeply saturated reds, oranges and yellows. Pale yellow and a colorless variety are also present, although not all colors are present in all species. Located at the border of the inner and outer segments, all light destined for the outer segment that contains the photopigment must first pass through the oil globule. Where deeply saturated in color, those globules act as rather sharp cut-off filters restricting the short-wavelength absorbing capability of the visual pigment. In essence, they act to shift the maximum absorption to longer wavelengths at a cost of overall reduced sensitivity. In studies deducing spectral sensitivity from electrical measurements, for example, the peak sensitivities derived from the recordings are shifted to longer wavelengths than would be expected from the absorption characteristics of the visual pigments. The explanation lies in the filtering effects of the brightly colored oil globules. Relative spectral sensitivities of the dark-adapted eyes of *Pseudemys* and *Chelonia* determined from electrical measurements are shown in Fig. 5 (Granda, 1962; Granda and O'Shea, 1972).

Pseudemys are most sensitive to red light at 645 nm, a characteristic sensitivity where the visual pigments are based on vitamin A_2. *Chelonia* are most sensitive to 520 nm, a blue–green light; that system is based on vitamin A_1. The vitamin

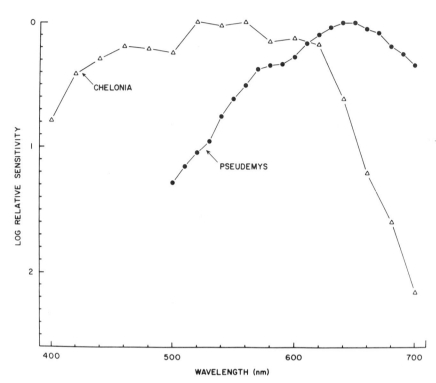

Fig. 5. Relative spectral sensitivity curves of *Chelonia* (Granda and O'Shea, 1972) and *Pseudemys* (Granda, 1962) arbitrarily equated at peak sensitivity.

systems with their characteristic absorptions are appropriate to the light distribution in their respective environments (Bridges, 1965).

The oil globules and their attendant cones are gathered into specialized areas of the retina. Turtles in general do not have well-defined foveas for high acuity and resolution as do the higher vertebrates. Yet in *Amyda,* the soft-shell turtle, Gillett (1923) described a fovea, and more recently Brown (1969) as well as Granda and Haden (1970) showed a distinct specialization of the receptor mosaic in *Pseudemys. Pseudemys* have a linear area centralis extending horizontally across the retina. The receptors are very concentrated and small here with a corresponding increase in density and number of colored oil globules. Below and above this area, receptor size gradually increases. The linear characteristic is apparently stabilized to the horizon, for as the animal is rotated, the linear area centralis remains effectively horizontal in all head positions. Brown suggested this facility could serve for the detection of relevant visual stimuli near or at the horizon, important for an animal living close to the ground. The concentration of receptors and oil globules seen in the central area is carried to the inferior temporal retina as well. To Granda and Haden this specialization suggested the ability of *Pseudemys* to devote that area to binocular vision with its advantage of depth perception. The temporal retina is the only area that has overlap in the visual field to allow for corresponding images in each eye.

B. Audition

The sounds that turtles produce are grunts or moans, a restricted expression that some have taken to argue that turtles as a class could not have bothered to develop an elaborate auditory system since they have so little occasion to use it. However, in some species, *Clemmys insculpta, Chrysemys picta, Pseudemys scripta,* and *Terrapene carolina,* Wever and Vernon (1956a,b) showed that there is considerable sensitivity to sounds below 1000 Hz. They did their measurements by recording the cochlear microphonic potentials from electrodes placed in the middle ear. Between 200 and 700 Hz, sensitivity was of the same order of magnitude as that measured in the cat. Sensitivity declined below 200 Hz and rapidly fell off above 700 Hz, so much so that at 3000 Hz no tests could be made without using dangerously high intensities. Similar work on the green turtle, *Chelonia mydas,* showed essentially the same features (Ridgeway *et al.,* 1969).

Work on single auditory unit responses in the cochlear nucleus of *Terrapene carolina* essentially corroborates the results derived from microphonic potentials. The majority of units reported by Manley (1970) were found to be rather sharply tuned, with characteristic frequencies at 140 or 400 Hz.

The relation of the electrical responses to the parameters of hearing is neither direct nor clear. The functional attributes of hearing need to be established by behavioral tests. Patterson and Gulick (1966), to establish this relationship, applied the head withdrawal technique of Granda *et al.* (1965) to the measurement of auditory thresholds, and were able to show a close correlation to the cochlear microphonic data through the range of 200–600 Hz (cf. Fig. 6).

The anatomy of the turtle auditory system is rather simple and straightforward. In *Pseudemys* the tympanic membrane is at the body surface and is connected to the extracolumella and the columella, bony structures that traverse the tympanic cavity as in Fig. 7(A). At the medial wall of the tympanic cavity, the columella expands to form the stapes which lies in the oval window of the otic capsule. The ear of *Chelonia mydas* makes no pretense of an external tympanic membrane [cf. Fig. 7(B)]. The area external to the extracolumella is undifferentiated from the rest of the surface tissue and is difficult to locate, buried as it is under cutaneous and subcutaneous layers.

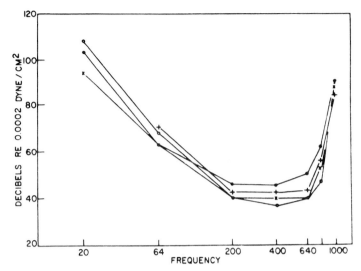

Fig. 6. Auditory thresholds for *Pseudemys* determined by behavioral tests. (Taken from Patterson, 1966.)

The inner ear is generally on the vertebrate plan. The auditory papilla, made up largely of hair cells, is located in the cochlear duct. The papilla in turn sits on the basilar membrane, a thin partition in the fluid path along which pressure discharges occur when sound is transmitted. Aerial sound first moves the tympanic membrane which in turn exerts alternating pressure through the columella to a footplate in the oval window. Here the pressures are transmitted to the

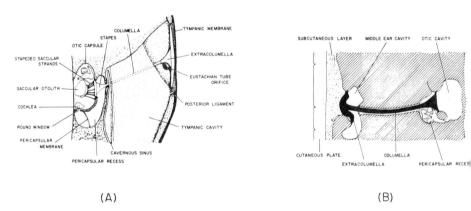

(A)   (B)

Fig. 7. (A) Peripheral auditory system of *Pseudemys*, dorsal view (Taken from Wever and Vernon, 1956a.) (B) Peripheral auditory system of *Chelonia*, dorsal view. (Taken from Ridgway *et al.*, 1969.)

cochlear fluid that sets in motion the basilar membrane. There has to be a return path to allow for movement of the fluid. In higher vertebrates this is accomplished by the free movement of a thin membrane known as the round window. In the turtle there is no round window to allow for fluid displacements. Instead there is a return pathway to the lateral surface of the columella footplate. When the footplate moves in, the displaced fluid is led to the outer face of the footplate. The footplate in this fashion operates within a closed fluid-filled system, a disadvantage since the mass loading on the plate that must be moved is increased substantially. The upper frequency range of hearing is thereby limited, for the sound pressure required for a particular displacement increases as the square of the frequency. At low frequencies there is little concern (Wever, 1974).

C. Chemoreception

Olfaction and taste are important sensory processes, but we know next to nothing about their operation. Some turtles go to elaborate lengths to produce foul-smelling odors; the musk turtle *Stenotherus odoratus* is a good example of this questionable talent. To produce an odorous substance implies the sensitivity to appreciate it, but there is little systematic work to argue an important role for these sensory processes in turtles of any species (cf., however, Scott, In press). All turtles with the apparent exception of the Testudinidae have glands that produce odorous substances.

The green turtle, *Chelonia mydas,* is capable of underwater chemoreception, and Manton *et al.* (1972a,b) devised a procedure that tested this ability rather well (see Section IV,A). The question concerned the role of chemoreception in orientation, possibly a dominant enough role to explain the extraordinary migration that sea turtles make. But one would be sorely put to accept a chemical gradient over large distances as a valid cue for orientation, although the idea is intriguing.

IV. MAJOR BEHAVIOR PATTERNS

A. Learning

Turtles have been taught to traverse runways, press keys, and solve mazes in order to earn the rewards of food, water, and air. Other solutions have involved avoidance responses to electric shock. In this section we discuss several types of learning situations that have been pursued successfully with turtles. The major portion of the discussion will be taken up with the detail of basic experiments, their techniques and results, experiments which by their design best take advantage of the turtle's physical structure and abilities.

1. Maze Learning

Some of the earliest behavioral studies on turtles involved maze learning with a variety of rewards including food (Yerkes, 1901; Tinklepaugh, 1932; Kirk and Bitterman, 1963; Ellis and Barcik, 1972), water (Seidman, 1949; Gonzales and Bitterman, 1962) and air (Morlock et al., 1968). There are several reasons why this technique is now in less favor than other operant conditioning techniques. Maze techniques are not very efficient: they do not lend themselves well to automation and the gathering of large quantities of data, and they usually require much handling of subjects. Virtually all turtles in the laboratory are captive wild animals that possess a high degree of natural wariness. The handling of even well-trained turtles often disrupts their behavior. But above all, turtles are poorly adapted for maze running; they lack, by reasons of anatomical structure and physiology, the maneuverability and quickness required to perform that task efficiently.

The early maze learning studies were simple demonstrations attesting to the fact that turtles could be taught a behavioral task. Certain performance characteristics were consistently noted. Turtles typically displayed a degree of hesitation at choice points which hinted at a degree of "thoughtfulness" (Yerkes, 1901; Tinklepaugh, 1932), a compliment that belied the fact that their performance was rather variable (Spigel, 1966; Hart et al., 1969). Turtles, too, often were found to develop strong position preferences (Casteel, 1911).

Other problems that arise in T-maze discrimination tasks are sometimes due to brightness or color preferences of the subjects, Mrosovsky and Boycott (1966) demonstrated a positive phototaxic response in Pseudemys that often was not obvious for many trials. For example, their turtles originally displayed a black perference that only slowly yielded to the experimental white variable. They suggested that the initial black preference may have been due to fear which was eliminated progressively to allow the underlying white preference to emerge. The lability of brightness preferences is supported by the findings of Anderson (1958), who showed that hatchling turtles often burrowed into the sand or moved into the shade when released in bright sunlight, but moved toward brighter areas when released at night. Clearly, the prevailing lighting conditions play a role in brightness preferences, and stimuli that are avoided in bright light (Spigel and Ellis, 1966) may be approached in darkness (Graf, 1972).

Changes in color preferences are often associated with the intensity of illumination. Most turtles prefer long-wavelength light when the choice is between two bright lights, but prefer short wavelengths when illumination is low (Graf, 1972; Sokol and Muntz, 1966). As Morlock (In press) points out, color preferences are probably the result of a basic positive phototaxis coupled with a shift in maximum spectral sensitivity from long to short wavelengths due to dark adaptation (Granda et al., 1972).

2. Operant Conditioning Techniques

Within recent years the majority of investigations involving instrumental techniques with turtles used some form of operant task that required the subject to operate a lever or key. Operant techniques are typically well suited for automation and the rapid accumulation of data. The animals usually do not have to be handled between trials, and the operant task can be designed to suit the subjects' behavioral repertoire.

3. Key Pressing Techniques

An instrumental technique designed by Bitterman (1964) has been used rather successfully for several purposes. The device was a two-choice, key pressing apparatus that allowed access to food reinforcement following correct performance. The floor plan of one configuration of an apparatus similar to Bitterman's appears in Fig. 8. The required response was to push one of two response keys

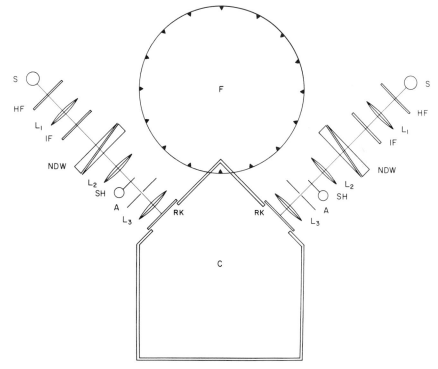

Fig. 8. Ground plan of basic key pressing apparatus. (Adapted from Bitterman, 1964, and Graf, 1967.) F, feeder magazine; RK, response key; S, light source; HF, heat filter; IF, interference filter; $L_{1...3}$, lenses; NDW, neutral density wedge; SH, shutter; A, aperture; C, chamber to hold animal.

(RK) mounted above the floor on both sides of the front of the chamber (C). The response keys were made of thin plexiglass that served as stimulus targets when light was projected onto them externally. Either target could be blocked off so that the apparatus could be used in single key procedures. The optical system shown in Fig. 8 permitted the presentation of stimuli whose color (IF), intensity (NDW), and duration (SH) could be controlled precisely. The feeder magazine consisted of a disk that was rotated in discreet steps. Bits of ground meat were attached to the disk and rotated into the chamber through an opening in the apex upon completion of the appropriate response. The meat reinforcement remained in the chamber for a preselected time during which a dim magazine lamp was lighted. The turtle normally seized the meat and submerged its head into the water at the bottom of the chamber in order to eat it. The primary advantages of the feeder magazine were (1) the food was presented in a well-controlled manner at a fixed location, and (2) the food was presented during a limited-access time interval whereby the food was removed if not taken. This procedure strongly tended to make the turtles take food promptly.

Bitterman found that well-tamed turtles could be magazine-trained rapidly, and the reinforcement time could be gradually reduced to 10 sec. The operant response was conditioned through a combination of baiting and shaping techniques. Turtles could be maintained for many months, their only supply of food being that obtained in the experimental chamber. Some animals were trained on a 20:1 reinforcement schedule, with the turtles receiving 10 reinforcements totaling 1 gm of hamburger each day, 6 days a week. Other turtles were run at 20 reinforcements per day, thereby receiving 2 gm of hamburger each day. There was no noticeable change in motivated behavior.

Bitterman and his colleagues used this technique to study certain types of learning in *Chrysemys picta*. For example, Kirk and Bitterman (1965) observed basic differences among the behaviors of mammals, fish, and turtles when presented with stimuli that were differentially associated with reinforcement. Mammals usually display "maximizing" behavior, where the most often rewarded stimulus is chosen nearly 100% of the time. Fish, on the other hand, display a "matching" form of behavior and choose stimuli with the same percentage rate at which they are reinforced. Turtles turned out to be an intermediate form. They used a "matching" strategy when required to choose between stimuli of different colors, a "visual task," but when the two targets were the same color, and reward was contingent upon position, a "spatial task," turtles either used a "maximizing" strategy or a nonrandom matching strategy such as reward following. Kirk and Bitterman concluded "...that random probability matching is a precortical phenomenon which tends to be suppressed by cortical development, more effectively in the spatial modality than in the visual."

In 1966, Holmes and Bitterman studied in *Chrysemys* another form of learning that earlier showed clear performance differences between fish and mammals.

They noted that fish failed to show progressive improvement in habit reversal while the same behavior was easy to demonstrate in mammals. In the "visual" task, turtles were taught to choose either a red or green stimulus, only one of which was rewarded. In the "spatial" task, stimuli were the same color and reward contingencies were determined by position. Reward contingencies were reversed for both spatial and visual tasks after a variety of interreversal periods. Progressive improvement was observed in all situations except when the inter-reversal period for the visual task was 4 days. Groups receiving more and less training between reversals showed improvement while the 4-day group did not. The curvilinear relationship was confirmed when another 4-day group was tested with no improvement. No reason for this unusual finding was given, and the authors noted that the results were unlike any found for other animals.

Sokol and Muntz (1966) used a single key version of Bitterman's apparatus to determine the scotopic spectral sensitivity of *Chrysemys picta*. Six turtles were trained using alternate stimulus-on, stimulus-off periods. Reinforcements were confined to stimulus-on periods at a 10:1 fixed ratio. During testing, the intensity of the stimulus was gradually reduced by five logarithmic units from the maximum light possible. A reversed or ascending series was also run. Ten test wavelengths from 389 to 700 nm were tested and response vs. intensity curves were obtained for each wavelength. Two scotopic spectral sensitivity curves were derived using response rate criteria. At each wavelength, one response criterion equaled the mean rate of the stimulus-off periods plus one standard deviation, while the other criterion was 1.67 standard deviations above the mean stimulus-off rate of response. The two averaged scotopic spectral sensitivity curves each showed a peak in the short wavelengths between 460 and 500 nm, and a secondary peak in the long wavelengths between 635 and 670 nm.

The data collected by Sokol and Muntz using this modified Bitterman apparatus were in agreement with electrophysiological findings (Deane *et al.*, 1958; Granda, 1962); the data showed a strong secondary peak in the long wavelengths. The finding of a major peak sensitivity in the short wavelengths prompted the authors to conclude that at least two types of receptors exist in the turtle retina, one dominant at high intensities and maximally sensitive to long wavelengths and the other dominant at low intensities and maximally sensitive to short wavelengths. These conclusions were partially verified by a later experiment also based on Bitterman's technique (Graf, 1967).

In Graf's (1967) study on the photopic spectral sensitivity of *Chrysemys picta*, flickering lights were used to provide illumination to the two keys of a Bitterman-type apparatus, and turtles were trained to respond to the more rapidly alternating light. On one key, variable chromatic illumination was sinusoidally alternated with a standard white light at a moderate rate of 13 cycles/sec. On the other key, the rate was high, 45 cycles/sec. By varying the luminance of the chromatic beam, it was possible to make a good luminance match with the

standard white beam, and the apparent flicker of the 13 cycles/sec key was
eliminated or greatly reduced. The 45 cycles/sec key appeared steady to Graf
himself, regardless of the luminance levels of the variable or standard beams. In
effect, then, the turtle was required to choose the steady key over the flickering
key. During the experiment, the luminance levels of the variable beams were
systematically varied and, at some luminance level, the subject's percent of
correct responses to the steady key fell to near chance, indicating that the 13
cycles/sec key also appeared steady. Graf produced a set of functions of percent
correct responses vs. optical density values of the variable beam for wavelengths
between 575 and 715 nm. The U-shaped functions that resulted allowed the
calculation of a threshold luminance value for each tested wavelength. From the
threshold luminance values, a relative spectral sensitivity curve was drawn. Peak
sensitivity was in the region 625–640 nm, a finding that agreed closely with the
conclusion of Sokol and Muntz (1966) that high luminance levels favor long
wavelengths.

4. Variations of the Key Pressing Technique

In 1969, Pert and Bitterman described still another operant task that turtles
could be trained to perform. Their technique involved training turtles to grasp a
nipple extended through the stimulus key. Meat paste was extruded in precise
amounts from the nipple tip by a syringe pump device. Each grasping response
displaced the nipple slightly, and that movement was detected by a phonograph
cartridge connected to automatic recording equipment.

The main advantage of Pert and Bitterman's technique over Bitterman's original method was that the instrumental and consummatory responses were now
more intimately related in time resulting in more rapid learning. Other advantages included the nearly complete elimination of pretraining (the nipple is self-
baiting and the turtles learned to grasp it for food immediately), and the increased
variety of rewards that can be delivered in controlled quantities.

These workers found that turtles would take food at a steady rate until they
were satisfied, although the rate of response might vary with the level of reward.
The response rate for a 0.02 ml reward, for example, was higher than for a 0.05
ml reward, although the total amount of food consumed per session was equal for
the two cases. Generally, for adult *Chrysemys*, satiation levels ranged from 5 to
12 ml of paste per session.

With intermittent reinforcement, responding was stable over long periods.
Increasingly long, variable-interval schedules produced lower rates of responding, although the rate of responding after each change stabilized rapidly. Many
hundreds of responses could be elicited in the course of one session, making it a
much more efficient system than the original apparatus and method.

Pert and Gonzales (1974) more recently used a two-key modification of the
nipple grasping technique in experiments on reward and learning, also in

Chrysemys. The authors noted that in experiments on the magnitude of reward, fish tend to obey the Law of Effect, i.e., reward directly strengthens the connections between stimulus and response, whereas rats do not strictly obey that rule: reward acts as a stimulus which is learned about and anticipated as a consequence of responding. Turtles were of interest in this regard because they broaden the range of phyletic comparison; they constitute a useful "intermediate" life form to speculate on.

The experimental apparatus consisted of a dimly illuminated experimental chamber and two manipulanda. The response key consisted of a translucent plexiglass disk fitted into a hole cut in the front of the experimental chamber. Pushing the disk activated a relay in an automated response circuit. The magazine key was similar to the response key except that it had two short lengths of surgical tubing extending through holes in the disk. The tubes were of unequal size and were used to deliver either a large, 0.35 ml, or a small, 0.02 ml, reward. The reward of meat paste was delivered by a syringe pump device as in the original design. Turtles were trained to press continuously the test key which was lighted with green or red light until the magazine key was lighted. A response to the magazine key would then result in a reinforcement. Responses to red or green light could be differentially reinforced with either large or small amounts of food.

In one experiment, large and small reinforcements were associated with differently colored lights. Plots of mean logarithm latency of the first response vs. days showed negative simultaneous contrast and a clear discrimination of reward magnitude. In a second experiment, clear differences in acquisition and extinction were found as a function of reward magnitude. In acquisition, latency of response declined under both large and small reward at about the same rate, but reached asymptotic levels of about 5 sec for the large reward group and about 12 sec for the small reward group. During extinction, resistance was significantly greater for the large reward group than for the small, and there was no crossover. The rate of approach to asymptote was about the same in the two groups. The large reward group also demonstrated a gradual increase in response latency when downshifted from large to small reinforcement conditions. The performance eventually came to equal that of a control group that had been kept continuously on small reinforcements. There was no evidence of negative successive contrast, i.e., overshooting of the control level of response latency. In a final experiment, using a single disk as both the response key and magazine key, the experimenters showed that turtles could demonstrate a positive behavioral contrast effect, that is, they not only were able to discriminate between a rewarded and nonrewarded stimulus color, but when the nonrewarded color was introduced, the response rate to the positive stimulus actually increased over the original training rate. The results of these experiments wre found to be quite similar to the effects seen in fish, but unlike those for rats. The authors suggested that perhaps the Law of Effect holds only for certain types of animals, or that indeed it might be a valid principle for all animals but is merely obscured by mammalian anticipatory or expectancy processes that are undeveloped in fish and turtles.

Another two-key operant paradigm was devised by Manton *et al.* (1972a,b) that was used to determine the detectability of certain water-borne chemicals by immature green turtles, *Chelonia mydas*.

Green turtles were trained and tested in an experimental chamber containing fresh water (marine green turtles easily tolerate the osmolarity demand for short periods). Water at 26°C flowed continuously at a rate of 8 liters/min from an inlet

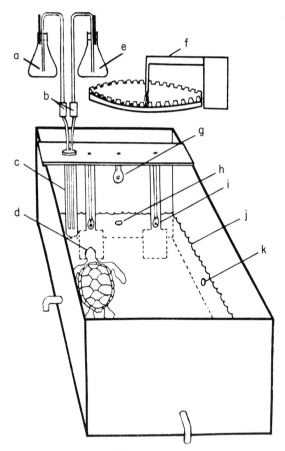

Fig. 9. Apparatus for chemoreception (Taken from Manton *et al.*, 1972a,b.) a, chemical or water reservoir; b, release valves; c, glass delivery tubes; d, turtle pressing left key; e, second reservoir; f, automatic feeder; g, overhead light; h, water inlet; i, key light; j, water level; k, one of three water outlets.

at the front of the tank, and then out through ports at the sides and rear. Two response keys equipped with small lamps were suspended in the water at the front of the tank, and an automatic feeder was positioned over the right key (see Fig. 9).

After the turtles were acclimated to feeding in the tank, they were taught to press the right key for food. They were then taught to press the left key until the onset of a small light, before shifting to the right key. The left lamp was lighted on an intermittent schedule to establish a steady rate of responding. Once the shift was made, a response on the right key within 20 sec of the left light's onset was followed by the illumination of the right key's lamp, and a small cube of meat was delivered. When the turtles learned the operant task well, the intensity of the light from the left lamp was gradually reduced and a chemical stimulus was released from an outlet near the left key substituting for the original light discriminant. The turtles gradually learned to press the left key continuously until a chemical stimulus was delivered, then to shift to the right key for reinforcement. The shift to the right key constituted a correct report of the chemical's presence. Plain water was used as a control stimulus.

When the percent of stimuli correctly reported was plotted against sessions for four chemicals (β-phenethylalcohol, isopentyl acetate, triethylamine, and cinnamaldehyde), it was clear that these chemicals could be easily distinguished from water. Mean correct detection for all four chemicals was 88.6%, while the mean false positive report for plain water in all sessions was 41.7%. Sea turtles could not distinguish the two amino acids, L-serine and glycine, from water controls. The percentages of correct reports and false positives in those cases were 80.2 and 79.1, respectively.

Apparently, olfaction rather than taste is responsible for the turtles' ability to detect chemicals in water. When zinc sulfate was applied to the olfactory mucosa for temporary anosmia, the turtles' ability to detect chemicals was completely disrupted for periods of up to 5 days, but control animals treated with either saline or magnesium sulfate were unaffected.

5. Lever Pressing Techniques

The first successful operant conditioning procedure for use with turtles was described by van Sommers in 1963. His technique involved training immature, air-deprived *Pseudemys* to press a lever for access to air.

Van Sommers' experimental chamber (cf. Fig. 10) consisted of a small, sealed, water-filled cylinder. In its roof was a smaller cylindrical recess into which a given amount of air (or other gas mixture) could be drawn by reducing the water volume of the main chamber a corresponding amount. The design of the chamber restrained the turtle in a way that placed its head directly beneath the air recess with its right front limb near a small lever mounted on the side wall of the chamber. The temperature of the water could be precisely controlled, and

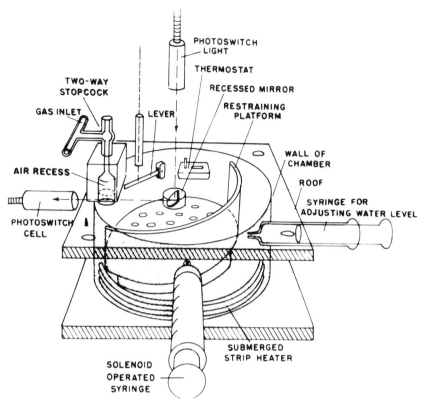

Fig. 10.   Lever pressing apparatus for air reinforcement. (Taken from van Sommers, 1963.)

there was a means of presenting lights to the animals through the transparent sides of the chamber and air recess.

Following acclimation and shaping of the lever pressing response for air, the time that reinforcement was available was reduced to a 5–10 sec period during which the turtle could breathe only with its head placed into the air recess. Responses were followed by a brief flash of yellow light to signal accessibility to air reinforcement. Water temperature was maintained at 25°C for most experiments.

The rate of responding under most conditions was rather slow as might be expected for a diving animal such as *Pseudemys*. The median number of reinforcements per minute was generally under two for all experimental conditions. Limiting of air access to either 5 or 10 sec resulted in a doubling of response rate for the shorter access time.

When 3-min extinction periods, signaled by a red light, were alternated with periods where all responses were reinforced, the rates of responding were markedly different for the two conditions, both in turn being different from a control "introductory" period where no alterations occurred and all responses were reinforced. Rates of responding during the extinction periods were lower than the introductory control period; rates of responding during the reinforced cycle of the alternating portion of the session were significantly higher than either of the other two conditions. The increased response rate during the reinforced period probably was an attempt to compensate for the additional air deprivation experienced during extinction, and not a demonstration of positive behavioral contrast.

In another alternating schedule, cycles of air alone were alternated with air contaminated with 10% CO_2, the latter signaled by a red light. Turtles could easily make the discrimination and markedly reduced their response rate in the presence of the contaminant.

In two final experiments, the effects of metabolic aspects of turtle respiration on response rates were investigated by altering the turtles' diet and the water temperature of the experimental chamber. A change from near starvation to a diet augmented with beef produced a clear increase in response and reinforcement rates. Improvement in the response rate was taken to be a reflection of the metabolic rate increase derived from greater energy supplies. When the water temperature of the chamber was increased from 22° to 32°C, response rates increased on the average by a factor of two. This finding agrees well with the Q_{10} approximation (the factor by which metabolic rate changes with a 10°C change in temperature) of 2.0–2.5 reported for physiological ranges by Prosser and Brown (1961, p. 166).

Crawford and Siebert (1964) found a Q_{10} of only 1.6, a factor somewhat smaller than that reported by van Sommers. Crawford and Siebert measured the lever pressing rate of *Pseudemys* for food reward as a function of temperature. The turtles were tested in a water-tight chamber filled to a depth of 1.9 cm with water from the turtles' home tank. The turtles each were given 10 min of continuous reinforcement in the shape of a small cube of cooked shrimp delivered by an automatic feeder. The range of water temperatures tested was 14° to 29°C, and the change in operant rate of the turtles was essentially linear over that range.

In later experiments, lever pressing responses for food were investigated by the manipulation of reinforcement schedules (Crawford *et al.*, 1966; Crawford and Adams, 1968). A fixed ratio schedule of 2 (FR 2) produced an increase in the response rate over a continuous schedule, but further increases failed to improve the rate. At FR 10, performance dropped off for all subjects with most showing severe declines at FR 5. Variable ratio reinforcements (VR) were very effective for turtles in this operant situation. Steady improvements in rate with little variance was seen up to a VR 13 schedule. Fixed interval reinforcement (FI) produced the highest response rates of any schedule tested, but the performance was also the most variable, and the rate-interval curves were rather flat, reflecting the fact that the subjects chosen for this part of the experiment originally had the highest continuous reinforcement rates of all the animals tested. Variable interval reinforcement (VI) produced more stable responding than FI, but the rate was rather low and fell off at intervals beyond 72 sec.

6. Avoidance and Escape Conditioning

Turtles in the laboratory are not always willing to take food when offered. Seasonal factors may be important. Turtles purchased or captured in the cool months often do not eat well for weeks when introduced into the laboratory, and even animals held over from the summer may experience disruptions in eating behavior. These problems may be minimized by the employment of carefully controlled lighting and heating that mimic warm weather conditions. Such measures, however, often fail to overcome ingrained cyclic patterns. Even when turtles are willing to eat, there are problems in obtaining reliable behavior because so little is known about controlling their motivation for food. Accordingly, many experimenters have turned to aversive stimuli to control behavior, with the majority of studies using electric shock.

Perhaps the first to use aversive stimuli with turtles was Olive Andrews, who in 1915 conditioned *Chrysemys* to selectively approach or avoid their feeding station by pairing electric shock with a whistle but not with a bell. She electrified a pair of forceps holding a bit of earthworm whenever the whistle was sounded, but disconnected the shock source whenever the bell sounded. In time, turtles apparently differentiated between the two stimuli to Andrews' satisfaction. Actually, it would only be necessary for the turtles to detect one of the auditory stimuli in order to successfully avoid shock. Nevertheless, Andrews' findings did indicate that turtles could hear something, and that in itself was a significant finding at the time.

Several years later, Poliakov (1930) employed a rather unique conditioned avoidance technique in order to confirm Andrews' findings. Poliakov fitted a small mechanical mallet device to the carapace and allowed the animal to move about while occasionally presenting auditory stimuli, either the tone of a pipe organ or a bell. Each auditory stimulus was followed by the activation of the mallet device which struck the turtle on the top of the head causing it to pull its head into its shell. After many pairings of the auditory stimuli and head tap, it was possible to elicit the head withdrawal response with the auditory stimuli alone.

In 1965, Granda *et al.* reported an avoidance behavior technique for turtles that has proven useful in the investigation of sensory functions. Their technique involved conditioned shock avoidance to light by head withdrawal (cf. Fig. 11). The turtle, *Pseudemys,* was first prepared by having two holes drilled through its lower jaw under anesthesia. Small stainless steel screws were then implanted.

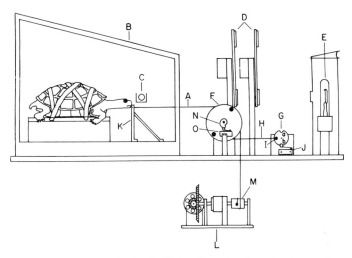

Fig. 11. Automated apparatus for head withdrawal conditioning. Experimenter is replaced by programmed head positioning device. See text. (Taken from Maxwell and Granda, 1975.) A, leader line; B, chamber; C, milk–glass target; D, wheels housing neutral density filters; E, light source; F through O, components of head positioning device.

During initial training, the turtle was placed in an experimental chamber and strapped to a platform facing a visual target that consisted of a circular light patch, 2 cm in diameter, projected onto a plexiglass plate. A nonstretchable nylon line was attached to the screws in the jaw and connected to a spring mounted in association with a wheel and microswitch arrangement, so that it was possible to detect head movements when the pulling force of the spring was overcome. A potentiometer was mounted onto the wheel's shaft to monitor the "strength" of the head movements. Small clips were attached to the jaw screws to allow the delivery of electric shock. The presentations of light stimuli and electric shock were under the control of automatic programming equipment.

At the beginning of each training session, the turtle was strapped to the platform in the chamber, and the shock clips and nylon line were attached to the jaw screws. Following 30–45 min. of dark adaptation, discreet training trials were presented. The turtle's head was pulled out by the experimenter to a pre-selected starting point from which measures of response amplitude were made. The light stimulus was then presented followed in 5 sec by electric shock. During acquisition, turtles escaped the electric shock by pulling their heads in. A response terminated both light stimulus and electric shock. With more training, the animals learned to avoid shock by responding within the grace period. A response in this period terminated the light stimulus and prevented shock delivery. The turtles were trained in this fashion to a criterion of 85% avoidance responses per 20-trial session for two consecutive sessions. Thereafter, the luminance of the stimulus was reduced in unit steps with the subjects trained to criterion at each step. Training continued until the luminance was reduced by two logarithmic units.

Testing consisted of a descending series of stimulus luminances, noting the latencies and amplitudes of the responses made. Ascending series were also employed but they were not as successful. Testing proceeded under extinction conditions, and the light was turned off after 5 sec if no response was made. Two nearly monotonic functions were obtained relating response latency and response amplitude to stimulus luminance. Response latency was inversely related to stimulus luminance: a maximum latency of about 2.4 sec was obtained for a very dim luminance value, while an asymptotic latency of 0.3–0.4 sec was obtained for the luminances three logarithmic units more intense. Response amplitude was directly related to stimulus luminance: the magnitude of the responses recorded increased by a factor of six over the ranges employed. Finally, extinction trials were run for 10 consecutive sessions with a fixed luminance two logarithmic units below the maximum level. Extinction was described as difficult to obtain, with resistances extending beyond several hundred trials.

Patterson and Gulick (1966) adapted the conditioned avoidance technique to obtain auditory thresholds, again in *Pseudemys*. Auditory stimuli in the range 20–1000 Hz were presented either through a speaker mounted above the animal's head or through an earphone mounted on the carapace. The learning of the avoidance response to an 85% criterion for two consecutive sessions took longer for auditory than for visual stimuli. In four turtles, 300–500 tone–shock pairings were required to reach criterion. Latency of response was also greater for audition than for vision, with latencies of up to 10 sec being recorded near threshold. Response latency and amplitude held the same relationship to stimulus intensity as they did in vision, with the strongest stimuli producing the largest responses with the shortest latencies.

Patterson (1966) reported the results of auditory sensitivity studies on *Pseudemys* employing this same conditioned head withdrawal technique. He found a peak sensitivity at 400 Hz with a threshold at that frequency of 40 db (re 0.0002 dyne/cm^2).

Dark adaptation curves were determined by Zwick and Granda (1968) in a later study for *Pseudemys* using the original experimental paradigm (Granda *et al.*, 1965), but with some critical modifications. Turtles were light adapted between trials by illuminating the front of the chamber with "white" tungsten light. Either a 1- or 5-min intertrial adaptation was given. Following the offset of the intertrial light adaptation, a "white" stimulus was presented at a fixed time in the dark. Only one stimulus was presented during any given dark period. Fixed intervals of 2, 5, 30, 60, 90 and 180 sec were employed.

Thresholds were determined in the following manner. Alternate periods of light and dark adaptation were presented with a single stimulus delivered during each dark period. Twenty cycles of alternating light and dark periods constituted a session. Thresholds were determined not by the method of limits, as in all previous experiments (Granda *et al.*, 1965; Patterson and Gulick, 1966; Patterson, 1966), but by a modified tracking procedure whereby the turtle's responses themselves determined the intensity of subsequent stimuli. An avoidance response caused the next stimulus to be reduced in intensity by 0.2 logarithmic units, while the absence of a response caused the next stimulus to be increased in intensity by a like amount. As before, testing trials were run during extinction.

The results showed that dark adaptation is fairly complete in *Pseudemys* by 90 sec in the dark. On the other hand, thresholds determined after either 5 or 1 min of light adaptation were essentially equal, indicating that a level of complete light adaptation could be maintained with the shorter of the two periods. The "Up and Down" tracking method employed was superior to the method of limits because it concentrated the intensities of the stimuli around the threshold, resulting in less variance and more reliability.

Granda *et al.* (1972) used similar procedures to determine the spectral sensitivity of *Pseudemys* under both light- and dark-adapted conditions. Dark adaptation curves were determined for 10 wavelengths ranging from 433 to 720 nm. Dark adaptation curves for long-wavelength light followed a course similar to white light, i.e., the curves reached asymptote at 90 sec in the dark. Curves for shorter wavelengths, however, took much longer to reach asymptote and displayed discontinuities indicative of the influence of more than one receptor system. Spectral sensitivity curves obtained at times in the dark ranging from 10 sec to 45 min showed a shift in peak sensitivity from 633 nm, early in dark adaptation, to 466 nm, when the turtle was well dark adapted.

Granda *et al.* (1972), with this same technique, utilized chromatic adaptation to isolate the receptor mechanisms. Spectral sensitivity curves were determined against red, green, and blue backgrounds equated for energy. The resultant curves displayed significant decreases in sensitivity appropriate to the spectral regions to which they were adapted. These curves were then used to derive theoretical spectral sensitivities of three underlying receptor mechanisms. The peak sensitivities of the theoretical mechanisms compared reasonably well with the known absorption maxima of the three classes of photopigments found by microspectrophotometry (Liebman and Granda, 1971).

In summary, turtles learn easily and well, with a persistance of effort that betrays little variance and high reliability. Those virtues are obviously purchased at the cost of a very limited repertoire and the capricious mercy of the immediate ambient milieu. Turtles are stubborn and conservative. They do not change their behavior easily—they rarely have cause to do so—but it can be demonstrated that they discriminate stimuli if appropriate to their sensory abilities. They also learn to manipulate levers for reinforcements, and this operant behavior can be brought effectively under control of schedules and amounts.

The following sections will describe major blocks of behavior in turtles, behaviors other than learning. Little is known about aspects of their migration or diving, for example, but the patterns are so invariable, so dominant that we are necessarily compelled to wonder at their purpose and control. These descriptive portions are necessarily brief because so little work has been done here.

√ B. Sleep

Sleep in turtles, indeed in all poikilotherms, is a controversial issue which centers on what sleep really is. One side of the argument is that sleep is an adaptation that allows homeotherms to conserve energy during periods of behavioral inactivity. Muscular activity diminishes during sleep with associated reductions in heart rate, body temperature and oxygen consumption. Also associated with behavioral sleep in homeotherms is a characteristic EEG record consisting of slow wave sleep (SWS) punctuated with episodes of desynchronized or "paradoxical" sleep (PS). A logical extention of the argument would hold that turtles, already existing in a state of reduced energy requirements, have less need of an energy conserving behavioral state such as true sleep. Activity, or the lack of it, is due to thermal conditions, with the level of activity mainly serving the purpose of maintaining optimal body temperature. States in turtles similar to what is commonly thought of as behavioral sleep might simply be postures assumed by these animals in order to absorb the maximum heat from the environment. On the other hand, behavioral immobility may be due to lower temperatures and the consequent lack of muscular responsiveness. Turtles also do not exhibit the EEG patterns associated with homeothermic sleep. Their EEG records during quiescence show no SWS but rather aperiodic high voltage spiking on a background of low voltage fast activity (LVF) (Walker and Berger, 1973).

Counterarguments hold that the fact turtles are already efficient users of energy does not mean that it would not be adaptive to conserve still more whenever possible. Also, these arguments hold, the EEG patterns associated with homeothermic sleep are merely signs of sleep and not sleep itself. This fact can be shown when the normal correspondence between the EEG and behavior is dissociated pharmacologically (Bradley, 1968). The absence of SWS or PS might only indicate the absence of an appropriate generator and not indicate the absence of sleep. Since sleep is most commonly viewed as a form of behavior, its existence or nonexistence in turtles should be determined from a set of behavioral criteria that is applicable to both homeotherms and poikilotherms. Flanigan *et al.* (1974) described such a set of criteria that might be useful in defining a state of sleep. In order for any animal to be considered asleep, it must (1) assume a stereotypical posture, (2) remain immobile, (3) possess an elevated threshold to arousing stimuli which may be indicated either by the level of stimulation for threshold response or by the latency, frequency, or duration of the behavioral response, and (4) recover rapidly to an awake state upon stimulation.

In an attempt to resolve the question of sleep, Flanigan and co-workers (1974; Flanigan, 1974) observed two species, *Terrapene carolina* and *Geochelone carbonaria,* for several days under conditions of constant illumination and temperature. During the course of the observations, electrographic recordings were made from chronically implanted electrodes. They characterized a wakefulness–sleep continuum that was associated with four well-defined states. The first was an active waking state during which the limbs were extended supporting the body, with the head elevated, and both eyes open. Respiration averaged about 1.9 breaths/min. Heart rate was rapid, averaging 34.6 beats/min. State two was characterized as quiet waking. The shell rested on the floor, but the animal's neck was extended and the head elevated with both eyes usually open. Respiration and heart rate were slightly reduced. In state three, one or more limbs were typically extended backward, parallel to the body's long axis and relaxed. The neck generally rested on the floor or hung over the edge of the plastron. The eyes were closed but occasionally opened for brief periods. Respiration rates averaged about 1.0 breaths/min. Heart rates averaged 19.4 beats/min, but tachycardia accompanied respirations. State four was an extension of state three, accompanied by even more profound relaxation and virtually no eye openings. The frequency of responding to electrical stimuli was approximately halved when the turtles moved from behavioral waking to states three and four. Concurrently, the latency of responses approximately doubled. EEG records were generally of the LVF type during waking. Spikes and sharp waves were occasionally seen during waking, but reached their peak levels during states three and four. Periods of SWS characteristic of homeothermic sleep were not observed, nor was there any evidence of PS. The investigators concluded mainly from the behavioral observations that sleep does occur in turtles.

Clearly, the electrophysiological components of turtle sleep are not comparable in form to mammalian sleep responses. Hartse and Rechtschaffen (1974) pointed out that the difference may be due to the lack of neocortical development in turtles. It is possible that the spikes observed during behavioral sleep in turtles are analogous to the subcortical limbic spikes recorded during SWS in mammals (Jouvet *et al.,* 1959). Like the turtle spikes, mammalian limbic spikes disappear upon arousal and, significantly, the limbic spikes are enhanced by decortication. It may be that limbic spikes reflect a more primitive type of sleep-associated neural activity that is overshadowed by mammalian neocortical activity. That activity is therefore evident in turtles which possess only a rudimentary neocortex.

√C. Diving

Freshwater turtles spend the greater part of their lives completely submerged under water. Observations on undisturbed laboratory turtles (*Pseudemys*) show that most of their time is spent lying quietly on the bottom of the tank with their eyes closed, apparently asleep. Usually about once an hour these animals open their eyes, raise their heads and the foreparts of the body, breathe, and then submerge again. The breathing periods are brief in duration, ranging from 0.5 to 4 min, and the durations do not correlate with the time spent submerged except in cases of unusually prolonged dives. Even when breathing, turtles do not have to break the surface. The lining of the nares is hydrophobic, and a small dimple in the surface film is formed once the water is cleared from them. The turtle can bob with its head motionless below the surface and breathe without any part of its body exposed (Belkin, 1964).

The quiet periods during which turtles remain submerged are not of extreme duration and might easily be matched by other air breathing animals. When pressed, however, turtles have a capacity to remain submerged far longer than all other tetrapod vertebrates (Dessauer, 1970). With the exception of sea turtles, most species are able to survive without oxygen for at least 12 hr at 22°C. Sea turtles apparently do not have the submergence capabilities of other turtles, and may only survive about 2 hr under the same conditions (Belkin, 1963a). Recently, however, green turtles were found in the Gulf of California in a dormant state for one to three or more months at a time, partially buried in the sandy bottom under water, or in sea caves or ledges (Felger *et al.,* 1976). The report raises the interesting issue of what physiological mechanisms could be involved.

There are several possible explanations for this remarkable ability. One factor is their low metabolic level (Altland and Parker, 1955; Belkin, 1965). They do not expend oxygen rapidly, and therefore do not use up their stored supply quickly. This fact cannot be the total answer, however, since all reptiles are poikilothermic with low metabolic rates, and yet none are nearly so capable of survival without oxygen as are turtles (Belkin, 1963a). Another possible factor is the turtle's ability to extract usable amounts of dissolved oxygen from water (Belkin, 1963b). The mechanisms are not well understood. It may be that buccopharyngeal and cloacal absorption play a role in oxygen uptake, but the rhythmic intake of water into the mouth and out the nares often observed in submerged animals more likely serves chemoreception than absorption (McCutcheon, 1943; Root, 1949). The uptake of water into the cloaca is not regular at all (Musacchia and Chladek, 1961), and it is more probable that such intake is unrelated to respiration (Jackson, 1969). On the other hand, it is possible in some species that the skin or other exposed tissue plays the major role in oxygen uptake (Root, 1949). It has been noted, for example, that the skin of *Sternotherus odoratus* and *Trionyx,* two highly aquatic turtles, is much more permeable to water than is the skin of semiaquatic turtles such as *Pseudemys* or *Chrysemys* (Klicka and Mahmoud, 1971; Ernst, 1968; Bentley and Schmidt-Nielsen, 1970). *Sternotherus* can survive indefinitely submerged in highly oxygenated water as can *Trionyx* (Gillette, 1970), while the degree of oxygenation makes very little difference in the survival times of *Pseudemys* (Belkin, 1963b). In addition to its apparent permeability to oxygen, the skin of *Sternotherus* is modified in other ways. This species possesses highly vascularized barbels on its chin and throat, and vascularized patches of skin between the scutes of its plastron (Klicka and Mahmoud, 1971). The barbels may serve a chemoreception function similar to that of the barbels of catfish, since *Sternotherus* often inhabit deep and murky river water where vision is restricted (Carr, 1952), but their possible role in aquatic respiration cannot be ruled out. Further adaptations of *Sternotherus* include a level of oxidative activity which is lower than that of other turtles, as well as an elevated myoglobin count, the latter factor being an aid to oxygen storage and diffusion (Klicka and Mahmoud, 1971).

Despite the capacity of some turtles to extract oxygen from the water, the primary means of survival under water appears to be anaerobic metabolism (Belkin, 1962; Robin *et al.,* 1964; Jackson, 1969). The evidence indicates that anaerobic glycolysis is of extreme importance to diving turtles. Turtles poisoned with iodoacetate, an inhibitor of anaerobic glycolysis, survive normally in air but succumb rapidly when held under water (Belkin, 1962). In addition, the large stores of glycogen in the tissues of turtles, stores that are larger than in other reptiles, indicate their importance in this regard. Turtles also have an enhanced ability to buffer poisonous by-products of metabolism which would otherwise build up to intolerable levels during prolonged dives. There are great changes in turtle blood and tissue chemistry accompanying dives that might easily kill other animals, but which are tolerated with ease by turtles (Dessauer, 1970).

Other Physiological Reactions to Diving

During dives, a slowing of heart rate, or bradycardia, is observed in turtles, and the rate may fall from 20–40 beats/min to 2–4 beats/min. Bradycardia usually begins immediately during voluntary dives (Belkin, 1964), but may not begin for several minutes during forced dives (White and Voss, 1966). Exercise may increase the heart rate slightly, but bradycardia usually does not abate until the first breath of air is taken. Hypercarbia (abnormally high levels of CO_2 in the blood) rather than anoxia appears to play the major role in maintaining bradycar-

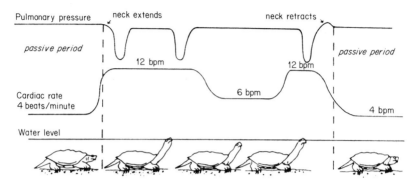

Fig. 12. Breathing pattern and corresponding cardiac rate of *Chelydra serpentina*. bpm, beats per minute. (Taken from Gaunt and Gans, 1969.)

dia, since turtles surfacing into a carbon dioxide atmosphere do not experience increased heart rate, while those surfacing into air or even pure nitrogen do (White and Ross, 1966).

Belkin (1964) suspects that the low heart rate associated with diving may be the ''normal'' rate and that tachycardia occurs during breathing to facilitate the rapid equilibration of the oxygen and carbon dioxide tensions of blood and tissue with that of the alveolar gas. Belkin also raises the possibility that turtles may have voluntary control over their heart rate. He observed that turtles (*Pseudemys*) very near the surface anticipated breathing by raising their heart rates, but if they dived again without breathing, bradycardia returned. *Chelydra serpentina* showed a similar increase in heart rate as breathing was anticipated, as well as bradycardia between widely separated breaths and when the turtle rested quietly below the surface (cf. Fig. 12, taken from Gaunt and Gans, 1969).

Another response to diving in turtles is the alteration of blood flow pattern. During breathing, about 60% of the heart's output is through the pulmonary artery to the lungs. During diving, blood flow through the pulmonary artery is greatly reduced due to the action of a functional ventricular shunt that allows most of the blood to bypass the lungs (Millen *et al.* 1964; White and Ross, 1966).

√ D. Hibernation

Turtles which reside in temperate climates are known to hibernate during the cold months of winter, although the depth of hibernation can vary significantly among individual specimens even in the same locale. Major differences in the onset and termination of hibernation are seen both within and between genera. The temperature of the water seems to be the primary determinant of when semiaquatic turtles hibernate, but there is apparently a large range of temperatures capable of triggering hibernation behavior. Some specimens enter and emerge from hibernation at lower temperatures than others, and thus may spend up to a month less time hibernating. Some turtles emerge to bask on favorable days in the winter and return to hibernation when cold weather returns. Low air temperatures are the primary stimuli for hibernating in terrestrial turtles. Because air temperatures fluctuate much more widely than do water temperatures, terrestrial turtles may spend short periods in semihibernation in the early fall only to become more active again during periods of warm weather. Finally, however, they are forced to burrow or find other substantial shelter when freezing weather occurs in late fall. In climates lacking severe winters, the shallow hibernation activity pattern may carry over the entire winter (Ernst and Barbour, 1972).

The location of the turtle's hibernaculum can vary. Semiaquatic turtles usually burrow into the mud at the bottom of a lake, pond, or waterway. Alternatively, they seek shelter under submerged logs or piles of vegetable debris. Still others enter muskrat burrows or lodges, and fewer still leave the water entirely to burrow some distance from the water or to retreat under logs or stumps. Terrestrial turtles generally burrow into loose soil or sand after the fall rains have improved the mechanical condition of the site. They generally form a shallow burrow of only a few inches at first, but go deeper and deeper as the soil temperature drops. In the coldest part of the winter, they may lie in a burrow 60 cm or more deep surrounded by a pocket of loose soil. In the spring, they reverse their position in the burrow and dig their way out as the soil warms. Terrestrial turtles may also burrow in the mud under water, under logs, stumps, or piles of debris, or even enter the burrows of mammals.

Turtles often congregate in favorable hibernating locations, with several animals sharing the same burrow or muskrat lodge, or settling into the mud together at the bottom of the pond. Thomas and Trautman (1937) reported finding an estimated 450 turtles in an area of about 2 × 15 m. The turtles all were buried in a foot of mud at the bottom of a partially drained canal, and all but a few were dead due to exposure to freezing temperatures. Woodbury and Hardy (1940) observed that desert tortoises often hibernate in communal dens which consist of excavations deep in gravel banks. The burrow is often shared with other animals in peaceful communism: red foxes, skunks, burrowing owls, rattlesnakes, gopher frogs, toads, and a variety of insects and spiders (Carr, 1952).

The phenomenon of hibernation plays a major role in determining the geographical range of some breeds of turtles, with the northern range often being limited by the depth to which the soil freezes in the winter. Turtles are killed by freezing, and those that burrow on land in the winter must dig below the frost line to survive. In climates where extreme winter cold causes the ground to freeze too deeply, turtles cannot survive. Even those turtles buried in the mud of lakes or ponds not solidly frozen may be killed if a heavy covering of ice and snow prevents fresh supplies of oxygen from dissolving into the water. It seems to be the general consensus among naturalists that cold weather is the major killer of turtles; large numbers are killed during severe winters, and even in mild winters, many turtles which emerge during specious warm weather are destroyed by a sudden fall in temperature (Schwartz and Schwartz, 1974).

E. Migration

A distinction should be made between the normal wanderings of turtles and actual migrations. All turtles wander to some degree, and even the most sedentary species move about. In contrast to the apparently random wanderings of individuals are the goal-directed movements of groups of turtles that occur on a fixed schedule. Included in the class of true migrants are the young of all freshwater or marine species which must find their way from the nesting site over long stretches of inhospitable terrain to reach their natural home in the water. The premier migrants of the turtle family are the marine turtles which traverse thousands of miles in the trip that takes them from their feeding grounds to the nesting beaches and back. The longest known migration was recorded for a single leatherback (*Dermochelys coriacea*) tagged in Surinam and recovered 11 months later in Ghana (Pritchard, 1973). Although the total distance traveled by this specimen was a prodigious 5900 km, perhaps the more remarkable feats of migration, considering distances traveled and pin point accuracies involved, are performed by turtles which nest on the beaches of small off-shore islands, the very beaches they previously emerged from as hatchlings.

Nine mature females (*Chelonia mydas*) tagged on the nesting beaches of Ascension, a tiny volcanic island in the mid-Atlantic, were recovered on the feeding grounds off the coast of Brazil at least 2252 km to the west. That the turtles recovered off Brazil were not just eccentric wanderers is attested to by the fact that there are no resident turtles at the nesting site. Ascension rises out of the depths of the ocean floor on a volcanic peak, and there are no flats of turtle grass to support even one turtle let alone the hundreds that come to nest. The nearest source of food for sea turtles based in the Western Hemisphere is Brazil. Similarly, *Chelonia* tagged at Tortuguero, Costa Rica, are never recovered in Costa Rican waters after the nesting season, indicating that the resident population is small and that the vast majority of turtles make regularly scheduled journeys over substantial distances in order to nest (cf. Fig. 13, taken from Carr and Ogren, 1960).

Very little is known about the migrating habits of sea turtles. The departure times from their feeding grounds and the routes taken to and from the nesting beaches are all unknown. It is possible to estimate how long the journeys must take by taking into account the swimming speeds of tagged individuals. Carr and Ogren (1960) reported estimates of up to 36.8 km per day for some individuals. This means that if Brazilian turtles take the most direct route to Ascension Island,

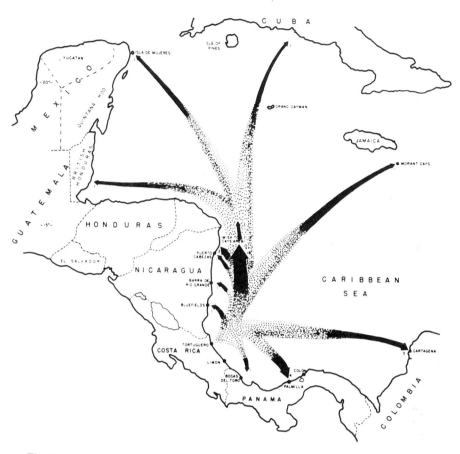

Fig. 13. Sites of recoveries of green turtles marked at Tortuguero, Costa Rica (1955–1959). (Taken from Carr and Ogren, 1960.)

it would take approximately 60 days to reach their destination. All of this time would be spent in the open sea where there would be little if any food available. Following this journey, mating and nesting take place over a 2-month period, all of this occurring at a foodless mid-ocean island. Finally, a return journey must be made, again over open seas, before the feeding grounds are reached. It is evident that most if not all nesting turtles undergo a long and perilous adventure of several months, all without food or much rest. It is no wonder then that nesting at Ascension Island occurs only on a 3-year cycle (Carr, 1965). On Tortuguero, turtles have been known to return after only 2 years, indicating perhaps that the journey to that site is not so arduous.

The most intriguing question concerning sea turtle migration is the manner of locating their nesting beaches. Tagging studies reveal that turtles return to the same locale, and occasionally even to the same precise spot, time after time. The mechanism by which such precise navigational feats are accomplished is largely unknown. Certain visual procedures can probably be ruled out. The accomodative mechanism in the eye is designed primarily for aquatic vision, and consequently sea turtles are myopic in air (Ehrenfeld and Koch, 1967). Celestial navigation is therefore impossible. Furthermore, the position of the turtle, low on the surface of the sea, makes it unlikely that it could sight an island goal from any great distance. It is possible that many of the nesting sites around the world could be found simply by following the coastline to the appropriate spot, but this possibility does not account for the fact that turtles also nest on islands.

One of the recent theories on turtle navigation involves the detection of chemical substances originating from the nesting site. Koch *et al.* (1969) discussed the various navigational procedures available to turtles migrating to Ascension Island and the weaknesses associated with each. They concluded that some sort of olfactory guidance system was indeed feasible considering the fact that calculations show that any substance released into the waters around Ascension would only be 100- to 1000-fold less concentrated in the Brazilian coastal region than in the waters immediately downstream. The problems associated with migrating up the chemical gradient are formidable, but there is at least indirect evidence that such behavior could take place. The olfactory lobes of sea turtles are quite large. Such development implies that the olfactory sense has a significant survival value. That the turtle can use its olfactory apparatus effectively is attested to by Manton *et al.* (1972a,b), who showed that sea turtles are capable of performing certain behavioral tasks the success of which depended on olfactory cues. Green turtles have been observed to perform a curious "smelling" behavior as they emerge from the surf (Koch *et al.,* 1969; Carr, 1965; Carr and Ogren, 1960). The animals press their snouts into the moist sand and hold it there as if to make a final verification of the correctness of their landfall.

How sea turtles navigate to and from their nesting beaches nevertheless remains a mystery. The tracking of turtles in the open sea is a difficult and costly task, and more efficient techniques are constantly sought. The use of miniature radio transmitters attached to the carapace or to a towed float has been attempted with only limited success, though the use of satellite-borne receivers may improve the value of this technique.

The second great group of turtle travelers includes the hatchlings from both marine and freshwater turtles. Groups of hatchlings emerge from their nests during the appropriate season and race overland to the body of water that is to be their permanent home. Although Daniel and Smith (1947) reported that in their experience *Caretta* sea turtles always placed their nests in sight of the sea, it is unlikely that this is a general rule. In most cases, the tiny hatchlings emerge from the nest out of direct sight of the water and at night. Often there are obstructions of varying sizes between them and their goal.

A general positive phototaxic response is one of the major factors responsible for the water approach behavior of hatchlings. At night, hatchlings emerging from the nest can be drawn off a direct course to the water by the light from a flashlight or lantern. There is some evidence that blue light is preferred by hatchlings, and they will approach it in favor of equally intense red light (Mrosovsky and Carr, 1967; Mrosovsky and Shettleworth, 1968). However, it also appears that the short-wavelength preference may simply reflect the spectral sensitivity of the turtle under the prevailing dark-adapted conditions (Granda and O'Shea, 1972; Granda *et al.*, 1972), and that the true preference may be only for brighter lights (Ehrenfeld, 1966; Mrosovsky, 1967; Anderson, 1958).

It is probably a consequence of phototaxis that sea turtles head toward the center of an open horizon. Mrosovsky and Shettleworth (1968) hypothesized that green turtles balance the brightness inputs to each eye and head toward the center of the brightest patch of horizon. Their hypothesis is supported by the fact that unilaterally blindfolded turtles circle toward the uncovered eye. It is possible that freshwater turtles may have to use a slightly different mechanism to find water because in their environment, the most open horizon is not always toward water. Perhaps in the case of freshwater turtles, orientation of hatchlings takes place through some negative response to dark masses of shadow formed by woodland vegetation (Anderson, 1958).

F. Reproduction

Reproduction activity is unique and strongly patterned. The male turtle has a distensible penis contained in the tail and he injects sperm into the female cloaca by mounting her and curving his longer tail under hers for insertion. Reproduction is thus sexual and there is internal fertilization. The sperm remains viable for a long time, in some species 3 to 4 years, and is stored by the female for future use in her genital tract. Whatever joys of copulation there are, for example the giant turtles of the Galapagos are known to bellow with lust (Van Denburgh, 1941, p. 225), reproduction apparently is not closely tied to copulation for efficiency. The female deposits many eggs—in some species they have parchment-like coverings, in others the shell is strongly calcified. The eggs are deposited in soil, sand, or rotted organic material. The female does this task in a nest skillfully and instinctively dug by alternate scoops of the hind legs. The hind leg ritual in nest building is apparently followed by all turtles, both land and water species. The resulting egg hole is flask shaped and rather narrow mouthed. Into it the female deposits from one to more than 100 eggs, the number depending on species, but also depending on maturity of the mother and on environmental conditions. Facts here are not particularly well documented. Egg laying can be and often is done several times a season. The nests are covered over soon afterward. The female roughs over the surface and leaves without a backward glance of maternal solicitude. The male is even less responsible, never having presumed the slightest degree of parental affection.

V. CONCLUSION

In summary, turtles are ancient life forms intimately tied to water or its near vicinity for a number of complex behaviors: reproduction, migration, diving— behaviors they are uniquely engineered to do. Turtles perform their activity with determination and little variability. Many of their stereotyped behaviors appear as programmed genetic instructions overriding ambient needs. That description is in keeping with the paucity of their neural architecture. The turtle brain is an ancient structure with little neocortical development. Yet it is the case that turtles behave in ways other than the programed behaviors ordained for survival. They show complicated learning functions capable of being brought under experimental control. They learn to detect and distinguish a variety of sophisticated sensory discriminanda and attach these cues to appropriate response repertoires: maze learning, lever pressing, and avoidance and escape conditioning.

Turtles have "simple" brains to direct their activities, and the puzzle we face is how such behaviors are possible. The answer is not that "simpler" brains allow simpler behaviors, but that "simpler" brains are more complicated than we believed, for relatively few neurons have the task of controlling a great deal of varied behavior with apparently little defined structure.

ACKNOWLEDGMENTS

The work presented here was supported by Public Health Service Grant EY01540 from the National Eye Institute, National Institutes of Health. We thank N. Mrosovsky and D. P. M. Northmore for their criticisms and suggestions.

REFERENCES

Altland, P. D., and Parker, M. (1955). Effects of hypoxia upon the box turtle. *Am. J. Physiol.* **180,** 421–427.
Anderson, P. K. (1958). The photic responses and water approach behavior of hatching turtles. *Copeia* pp. 211–215.
Andrews, O. (1915). The ability of turtles to discriminate between sounds. *Bull. Wis. Nat. Hist. Soc.* **13,** 189–195.

Belkin, D. A. (1962). Anerobiosis in diving turtles. *Physiologist* **5**, 105.

Belkin, D. A. (1963a). Anoxia: Tolerance in reptiles. *Science* **139**, 492–493.

Belkin, D. A. (1963b). Importance of aquatic respiration in the diving ability of turtles. *Fed. Proc., Fed. Am. Soc. Exp. Biol.* **22**, 635.

Belkin, D. A. (1964). Variations in heart rate during voluntary diving in the turtle, *Pseudemys concinna*. *Copeia* pp. 321–330.

Belkin, D. A. (1965). Critical oxygen tensions in turtles. *Physiologist* **8**, 109.

Bellairs, A. (1970). "The Life of Reptiles," Vol. II, pp. 283–590. Universe Books, New York.

Bentley, P. J., and Schmidt-Nielsen, K. (1970). Comparison of water exchange in two aquatic turtles, *Trionyx spinifer* and *Pseudemys scripta*. *Comp. Biochem. Physiol.* **32**, 363–365.

Bitterman, M. E. (1964). An instrumental technique for the turtle. *J. Exp. Anal. Behav.* **7**, 189–190.

Bradley, P. B. (1968). The effect of atropine and related drugs on the EEG and behavior. *In* "Anticholinergic Drugs and Brain Functions in Animals and Man" (P. B. Bradley and M. Fink, eds.), pp. 3–13. Elsevier, Amsterdam.

Bridges, C. D. G. (1965). Absorption properties, interconversions, and environmental adaptation of pigments from fish photoreceptors. *Cold Spring Harbor Symp. Quant. Biol.* **30**, 317–334.

Brown, K. (1969). A linear area centralis extending across the turtle retina and stabilized to the horizon by non-visual cues. *Vision Res.* **9**, 1053–1062.

Bustard, R. (1973). "Sea Turtles. Natural History and Conservation." Taplinger Publ., New York.

Carr, A. (1952). "Handbook of Turtles." Cornell Univ. Press, Ithaca, New York.

Carr, A. (1965). The navigation of the green turtle. *Sci. Am.* **212**, 79–86.

Carr, A., and Ogren, L. (1960). The ecology of migrations of sea turtles. 4. *Bull. Am. Mus. Nat. Hist.* **121**, 7–48.

Casteel, D. B. (1911). The discriminative ability of the painted turtle. *J. Anim. Behav.* **1**, 1–28.

Crawford, F. T., and Siebert, L. E. (1964). Operant rate in the turtle as a function of temperature. *Psychon. Sci.* **1**, 215–216.

Crawford, F. T., and Adams, P. M. (1968). The effect of schedules of reinforcement upon the response rate of turtles. *Psychon. Sci.* **11**, 153–154.

Crawford, F. T., Adams, P. M., and Whitt, J. M. (1966). Response rate of turtles to fixed ratio reinforcement. *Psychon. Sci.* **6**, 19–20.

Daniel, R. S., and Smith, K. U. (1947). The sea-approach behavior of the neonate loggerhead turtle. *J. Comp. Physiol. Psychol.* **40**, 413–420.

Deane, H. W., Enroth-Cugell, C., Gongaware, M. A., Neyland, M., and Forbes, A. (1958). Electroretinogram of freshwater turtle. *J. Neurophysiol.* **21**, 45–61.

Desmond, A. J. (1976). "The Hot-Blooded Dinosaurs." Dial Press, New York.

Dessauer, H. C. (1970). Blood chemistry of reptiles: Physiological and evolutionary aspects. *In* "Biology of the Reptilia" (C. Gans and T. S. Parsons, eds.), Vol. 3, pp. 1–72. Academic Press, New York.

Ehrenfeld, D. W. (1966). The sea-finding orientation of the green turtle (*Chelonia mydas*). Doctoral Dissertation, University of Florida, Gainesville (unpublished).

Ehrenfeld, D. W., and Koch, G. L. (1967). Visual accommodation in the green turtle. *Science* **155**, 827–828.

Ellis, K. R., and Barcik, J. D. (1972). Acquisition and suppression of an appetitive task in the fresh water turtle *Chrysemys picta marginata*. Paper presented at the convention of the *Am. Assoc. Adv. Sci.* pp. 115–116.

Ernst, C. H. (1968). Evaporative water-loss relationships of turtles. *J. Herpetol.* **2**, 159–161.

Ernst, C. H., and Barbour, R. W. (1972). "Turtles of the United States." Univ. of Kentucky Press, Lexington.

Felger, R. S., Cliffton, K., and Regal, P. J. (1976). Winter dormancy in sea turtles: Independent discovery and exploitation in the Gulf of California by two local cultures. *Science* **191**, 283–285.

Flanigan, W. F. (1974). Sleep and wakefulness in chelonian reptiles. II. The red-footed tortoise, *Geochelone carbonaria*. *Arch. Ital. Biol.* **112**, 253–277.

Flanigan, W. F., Knight, C. P., Hartse, K. M., and Rechtschaffen, A. (1974). Sleep and wakefulness in chelonian reptiles. I. The box turtle, *Terrapene carolina*. *Arch. Ital. Biol.* **112**, 227–252.

Frair, W., Ackman, R. G., and Mrosovsky, N. (1972). Body temperature of *Dermochelys coriacea*: Warm turtle from cold water. *Science* **177**, 791–793.

Gaunt, A. A., and Gans, C. (1969). Mechanics of respiration in the snapping turtle, *Chelydra serpentina*: (Linne). *J. Morphol.* **128**, 195–228.

Gillette, D. D. (1970). Breathing adaptations in *Trionyx*. *J. Int. Turtle Tortoise Soc.* **4**, 18–19.

Gillette, W. G. (1923). The histologic structure of the eye of the soft shelled turtle. *Am. J. Ophthalmol.* **6**, 955–973.

Gonzales, R. C., and Bitterman, M. E. (1962). A further study of partial reinforcement in the turtle. *Q. J. Exp. Psychol.* **14**, 109–112.

Graf, V. (1967). A spectral sensitivity curve and wavelength discrimination for the turtle *Chrysemys picta picta*. *Vision Res.* **7**, 915–928.

Graf, V. (1972). Behavioral Visual functions for *Chrysemys picta picta*. Preferences and frequency responses. *Brain, Behav. Evol.* **5**, 155–175.

Granda, A. M. (1962). Electrical responses of the light- and dark-adapted turtle eye. *Vision Res.* **2**, 343–356.

Granda, A. M., and Haden, K. W. (1970). Retinal oil globule counts and distributions in two species of turtles: *Pseudemys scripta elegans* (Wied) and *Chelonia mydas mydas* (Linnaeus). *Vision Res.* **10**, 79–84.

Granda, A. M., and O'Shea, P. J. (1972). Spectral sensitivity of the green turtle (*Chelonia mydas mydas*) determined by electrical responses to heterochromatic light. *Brain, Behav. Evol.* **5**, 143–154.

Granda, A. M., Matsumiya, Y., and Stirling, C. E. (1965). A method for producing avoidance behavior in the turtle. *Psychon. Sci.* **2**, 187–188.

Granda, A. M., Maxwell, J. H., and Zwick, H. (1972). The temporal course of dark-adaptation in the turtle, *Pseudemys*, using a behavioral avoidance paradigm. *Vision Res.* **12**, 653–672.

Hart, R. R., Cogan, D. C., and Williamson, L. L. (1969). Maze path selection in the turtle (*Chrysemys*): A quasi-comparative study. *Psychol. Rec.* **19**, 301–304.

Hartse, K. M., and Rechtschaffen, A. (1974). Effect of atropine sulfate on the sleep-related EEG spike activity of the tortoise, *Geochelone carbonaria*. *Brain, Behav. Evol.* **9**, 81–94.

Holman, J. G. (1969). The ancestral turtle. *J. Int. Turtle Tortoise Soc.* **3**, 16–19.

Holmes, P. A., and Bitterman, M. E. (1966). Spatial and visual habit reversal in the turtle. *J. Comp. Physiol. Psychol.* **62**, 328–331.

Jackson, D. C. (1969). Buoyancy control in the freshwater turtle, *Pseudemys scripta elegans*. *Science* **166**, 1649–1651.

Jouvet, M., Michel, F., and Courjon, J. (1959). L'activité électrique du rhinencéphale au cours de sommeil chez le chat. *C. R. Seances Soc. Biol. Ses. Fil.* **153**, 101–105.

Kirk, K. L., and Bitterman, M. E. (1963). Habit reversal in the turtle. *Q. J. Exp. Psychol.* **15**, 52–57.

Kirk, K. L., and Bitterman, M. E. (1965). Probability learning in the turtle. *Science* **148**, 1484–1485.

Klicka, J., and Mahmoud, I. Y. (1971). A comparative study of respiratory pigment concentrations in six species of turtles. *Comp. Biochem. Physiol. A* **38**, 53–58.

Koch, A. L., Carr, A., and Ehrenfeld, D. W. (1969). The problem of open-sea navigation. The migration of the green turtle to Ascension Island. *J. Theor. Biol.* **22**, 163–179.

Liebman, P. A., and Granda, A. M. (1971). Microspectrophotometric measurements of visual pigments in two species of turtle. *Pseudemys scripta* and *Chelonia mydas. Vision Res.* **11**, 105–114.

Liebman, P. A., and Granda, A. M. (1975). Super dense carotenoid spectra resolved in single cone oil droplets. *Nature (London)* **253**, 370–372.

McCutcheon, F. H. (1943). The respiratory mechanism in turtles. *Physiol. Zool.* **16**, 255–269.

Manley, G. A. (1970). Comparative studies of auditory physiology in reptiles. *Z. Vergl. Physiol.* **76**, 363–381.

Manton, M. L., Karr, A., and Ehrenfeld, D. W. (1972a). An operant method for the study of chemoreception in the green turtle, *Chelonia mydas. Brain, Behav. Evol.* **5**, 188–201.

Manton, M. L., Karr, A., and Ehrenfeld, D. W. (1972b). Chemoreception in the migratory sea turtle, *Chelonia mydas. Biol. Bull.* **143**, 184–195.

Maxwell, J. H., and Granda, A. M. (1975). An automated apparatus for the determination of visual thresholds in turtles. *Physiol. Behav.* **15**, 131–132.

Millen, J. E., Murdaugh, H. V., Jr., Bauer, C. B., and Robin, E. D. (1964). Circulatory adaptation to diving in the freshwater turtle. *Science* **145**, 591–593.

Morlock, H. C. (in press). Learning. *In* "Turtles: Research and Perspectives" (M. Harless and H. C. Morlock, eds.). Wiley, New York.

Morlock, H. C., Brothers, N., and Shaffer, L. (1968). Access to air as a reinforcer for turtles. *Psychol. Rep.* **23**, 1222.

Mrosovsky, N. (1967). How turtles find the sea. *Sci. J.* November, pp. 53–57.

Mrosovsky, N., and Boycott, B. B. (1966). Intra- and inter-specific phototactic behavior of freshwater turtles. *Behaviour* **26**, 215–227.

Mrosovsky, N., and Carr, A. (1967). Preference for light of short-wavelengths in hatchling green sea turtles, *Chelonia mydas,* tested on their natural nesting beaches. *Behaviour* **28**, 217–231.

Mrosovsky, N., and Pritchard, P. C. H. (1971). Body temperatures of *Dermochelys coriacea* and other sea turtles. *Copeia* No. 4, pp. 624–631.

Mrosovsky, N., and Shettleworth, S. J. (1968). Wavelength preferences and brightness cues in the water finding behavior of sea turtles. *Behaviour* **32**, 211–257.

Musacchia, S. J., and Chladek, M. I. (1961). Investigations of the cloacal bladders in turtles. *Am. Zool.* **1**, 376.

Parsons, J. J. (1962). "The Green Turtle and Man." Univ. of Florida Press, Gainesville.

Parsons, T. S., and Williams, E. E. (1961). Two Jurassic turtle skulls: A morphological study. *Bull. Mus. Comp. Zool.* **125**, 43–106.

Patterson, W. C. (1966). Hearing in the turtle. *J. Audit. Res.* **6**, 453–464.

Patterson, W. C., and Gulick, W. L. (1966). A method for measuring auditory thresholds in the turtle. *J. Audit. Res.* **6**, 219–227.

Pert, A., and Bitterman, M. E. (1969). A technique for the study of consummatory behavior and instrumental learning in the turtle. *Am. Psychol.* **24**, 258–261.

Pert, A., and Gonzales, R. C. (1974). The behavior of the turtle (*Chrysemys picta*) in simultaneous, successive, and behavioral contrast situations. *J. Comp. Physiol. Psychol.* **87**, 526–538.

Poliakov, K. L. (1930). Zur Physiologie des Riech und Höranalysators bei der Schildkröte, *Emys orbicularis. Russ. Physiol. J.* **13**, 161–178.

Pritchard, P. C. H. (1973). International migrations of South American sea turtles (*Cheloniidae* and *Dermochelidae*). *Anim. Behav.* **21**, 18–27.

Prosser, C. L., and Brown, F. H. (1961). "Comparative Animal Physiology." Saunders, Philadelphia, Pennsylvania.

Ridgway, S., Wever, E. G., McCormick, J., Palin, J., and Anderson, J. (1969). Hearing in the giant sea turtle, *Chelonia mydas. Proc. Natl. Acad. Sci. U.S.A.* **64,** 884–890.

Robin, E. D., Vester, J. W., Murdaugh, H. V., Jr., and Millen, J. E. (1964). Prolonged anaerobiosis in a vertebrate: anaerobic metabolism in the freshwater turtle. *J. Cell. Comp. Physiol.* **63,** 287–297.

Root, R. W. (1949). Aquatic respiration in the musk turtle. *Physiol. Zool.* **22,** 172–178.

Schmidt, K. P., and Inger, R. F. (1957). "Living Reptiles of the World." Hamish Hamilton Ltd., London.

Schwartz, C. W., and Schwartz, E. R. (1974). The three-toed box turtle in central Missouri: Its population, home range and movements. *Mo., Dep. Conserv.* Ser. No. 5, pp. 1–28.

Scott, T. R. (in press). The chemical senses. *In* "Turtles: Research and Perspectives" (M. Harless and H. C. Morlock, eds.). Academic Press, New York.

Seidman, E. (1949). Relative ability of the newt and the terrapin to reverse a direction habit. *J. Comp. Physiol. Psychol.* **42,** 320–327.

Sokol, S., and Muntz, W. R. A. (1966). The spectral sensitivity of the turtle, *Chrysemys picta picta. Vision Res.* **6,** 285–292.

Spigel, I. M. (1966). Variability in maze-path selection by turtle. *J. Genet. Psychol.* **75,** 21–27.

Spigel, I. M., and Ellis, K. R. (1966). Cerebral lesions and climbing suppression in the turtle. *Psychon. Sci.* **5,** 211.

Thomas, E. S., and Trautman, M. B. (1937). Segregated hibernation of *Sternotherus odoratus* (Latreille). *Copeia* p. 231.

Tinklepaugh, O. L. (1932). Maze learning of a turtle. *J. Comp. Psychol.* **13,** 201–206.

Van Denburgh, J. (1941). The gigantic land tortoises of the Galapagos Archipelago. *Proc. Calif. Acad. Sci.* **2,** Part I, 203–374.

van Sommers, P. (1963). Air-motivated behavior in the turtle. *J. Comp. Physiol. Psychol.* **56,** 590–596.

Wald, G. (1939). On the distribution of vitamin A_1 and A_2. *J. Gen. Physiol.* **22,** 391–415.

Walker, J. M., and Berger, R. J. (1973). A polygraphic study of the tortoise (*Testudo denticulata*). *Brain, Behav. Evol.* **8,** 453–467.

Walls, G. L. (1942). "The Vertebrate Eye and Its Adaptive Radiation." Cranbrook Inst. Sci., Bloomfield Hills, Michigan.

Wever, E. G. (1974). The evolution of vertebrate hearing. *Handb. Sens. Physiol.* **5,** Part I, 423–454.

Wever, E. G., and Vernon, J. A. (1956a). Sound transmission in the turtle's ear. *Proc. Natl. Acad. Sci. U.S.A.* **42,** 292–299.

Wever, E. G., and Vernon, J. A. (1956b). Auditory responses in the common box turtle. *Proc. Natl. Acad. Sci. U.S.A.* **42,** 962–965.

White, F., and Ross, G. (1966). Circulatory changes during experimental diving in the turtle. *Am. J. Physiol.* **211,** 15–18.

Woodbury, A. M., and Hardy, R. (1940). The dens and behavior of the desert tortoise. *Science* **92,** 529.

Yerkes, R. M. (1901). Formation of habits in the turtle. *Pop. Sci. Mon.* **58,** 519–525.

Zangerl, R. (1969). The turtle shell. *In* "Biology of the Reptilia" (C. Gans, A. d'A. Bellairs, and T. S. Parsons, eds.), Vol. 1, pp. 311–339. Academic Press, New York.

Zwick, H., and Granda, A. M. (1968). Behaviorally determined dark adaptation functions in the turtle, *Pseudemys. Psychon. Sci.* **11,** 239–240.

7

Visually Guided Behavior of Turtles

WILLIAM N. HAYES and LEONARD C. IRELAND

I. Introduction 281
II. The Testudinata 282
III. Depth Perception 285
IV. Visual Alarm Reactions 288
V. Optokinetic Responses 292
VI. Water-Finding Behavior 300
VII. Migration and Homing 305
VIII. Summary and Conclusions 313
    References 314

I. INTRODUCTION

One primary lesson of vertebrate comparative anatomy is that all vertebrates share a common body plan. In other words, all vertebrates have homologous structural characteristics derived from primitive morphological forms. Historically, unusual structural variations which initially appeared incompatible with this principle were eventually recognized as examples of adaptations reflecting basic vertebrate themes.

It is axiomatic that the structural characteristics of animals place precise and inflexible limits on their behavioral capabilities. Within these limits, however, does vertebrate behavior display the same conservation of basic design as does vertebrate anatomy? Are there systematic trends in behavior which vary reliably with other taxonomic indexes? Is it possible that there are general mechanisms of adaptation and survival? The answers to these questions must be considered primary goals of behavioral research (Hodos and Campbell, 1969). Clearly, our knowledge of the behavior of most vertebrates is insufficient for us to even begin to answer them. The principal task of today's behavioral scientist is the description of behavioral capacities at the species level, and the discovery and explanation of how each species' behavioral repertoire enables it to survive in its particular ecological niche.

If there are systematic trends in the behavior of vertebrates, then those species which appeared early in the course of evolution should display patterns of behavior which are to some degree fundamental. The behaviors of more recent vertebrates should be recognizable as variations on these early strategies. In the search for such basic patterns of behavior, it would be ideal if we could first observe the activities of the earliest vertebrates and then ascend the "phylogenetic tree" toward the present day, recording the behavioral variations of each new species. This, of course, is impossible. Many of the species we would wish to study disappeared millions of years ago. It is also not possible to reconstruct the phylogenetic tree using species of living vertebrates. The members of many classes of animals which have survived to the present day are structurally quite different from their ancestors, and we must assume that their behaviors may also be different. This is certainly true of the reptiles. There are no living representatives of the cotylosaurs, the earliest reptiles, nor of the therapsid reptiles which gave rise to the mammals. Most species of living reptiles appear highly specialized when compared to primitive forms. Nevertheless, comparative studies of the behavior of today's reptiles should allow us to gain some idea of general reptilian behavioral capabilities, and perhaps will allow us to make some reasonably accurate speculations concerning the behaviors of the ancient reptiles from which the mammals and birds are derived. In any case, it is the best we can do.

Many of the behavioral investigations performed with reptiles have been done with turtles, probably because of their ready availability rather than because of any particular taxonomic considerations. This is not entirely inappropriate. The Testudinata are a remarkably diverse and successful group. Further, the majority of behavioral studies performed with turtles have been concerned with visually guided behaviors. Again, this is not inappropriate. The vertebrates as a group have excelled in visual capabilities since very early in their history (Polyak, 1957; Walls, 1942). In this chapter, we review the literature concerning visually guided behavior in turtles, with particular emphasis on how such behaviors may contribute to their survival.

II. THE TESTUDINATA

Members of the order Testudinata, which number about 240 living species, are found over much of the surface of the earth, in most habitats which will support reptilian life in any form. The Testudinata are often roughly divided into three groups: the land tortoises, the freshwater terrapins, and the sea turtles. These classifications, however, are seldom used with any consistency. For example, tortoise shell is obtained from the hawksbill sea turtle (*Eretmochelys imbricata*), and the semiaquatic, freshwater dwelling *Macrochelys temmincki* is referred to as the alligator snapping turtle. All members of the order Testudinata may be properly called "turtles," and we will do so when referring to testudines in general. When speaking of a particular species, we will abide by American convention and refer to primarily aquatic and semiaquatic species as turtles, and to species which are primarily or entirely terrestrial as tortoises.

Scientists are, as yet, none too certain as to the early stages of turtle evolution (Colbert, 1969; Romer, 1968). The first animals recognized as true turtles made their appearance by the middle or late Triassic, approximately 200 million years

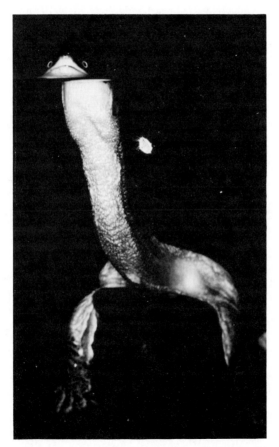

Fig. 1. A typical pleurodire, the common or eastern side-necked turtle of Australia (*Chelodina longicollis*). (Photograph courtesy of Professor Carl Gans).

ago. These animals already possessed many of the characteristics we associate with the turtles and tortoises of today: a body armored by a heavy shell, the lack of teeth along the margins of the jaws, and fewer bones in their skulls than in the skulls of the primitive cotylosaurs. By the late Mesozoic, roughly 80 million years ago, two suborders of turtles had appeared, the Pleurodira (see Fig. 1) and the Cryptodira (see Fig. 2). A pleurodire may usually be distinguished from the more numerous cryptodires by, among other things, the fact that it bends its neck laterally as it pulls its head into its shell. For this reason, pleurodires are usually referred to as side-necked turtles. These suborders have survived to the present day, and no additional suborders are currently recognized.

It has been suggested that the earliest turtles were marsh dwellers, and that the tortoises and sea turtles invaded their respective habitats via adaptive radiation (Goin and Goin, 1971). While this is not known with any certainty, it is clear that the living turtles occupy many different environments. Turtles may be found in habitats as diverse as oceans, swamps, hardwood forests, and deserts. In many cases, turtles display obvious structural adaptations to their habitats. For example, the limbs of the sea turtles are efficient, paddlelike flippers, and the shell of the East African pancake tortoise (*Malacochersus tornieri*) is so thin that is offers little or no defense against predators. The unusual shell of *M. tornieri* was apparently produced by selective pressures calling for improved locomotor energetics and the ability to wedge the body into narrow rock crevices (Ireland and Gans, 1972). It would be unusual indeed if significant changes in behavior did not accompany such radical structural modifications. A reasonably complete description of the living turtles may be found in Pritchard (1967).

Fig. 2.   The Indian soft-shelled turtle (*Lissemys punctata*), a cryptodire. (Photograph courtesy of Professor Carl Gans.)

III. DEPTH PERCEPTION

One of the first well-controlled studies of visually guided behavior in reptiles was performed by Yerkes (1904). He hypothesized that the responses of several different species of turtles to visual depth cues would vary as a function of their ecological niches. Specifically, Yerkes suggested that terrestrial turtles were more likely to display avoidance reactions when confronted with depth cues, since they are more likely to encounter dangerous irregularities in the terrain. Further, it is not difficult to conceive of how an approach response to depth cues could have survival value for semiaquatic turtles threatened by terrestrial or airborne predators. Yerkes tested the behavior of three species of turtles in his experiments: the common box turtle, *Terrapene carolina,* which is primarily a terrestrial animal; the spotted turtle, *Nanemys guttata* (now *Clemmys guttata*), which prefers marshy areas and spends part of its life in the water and part on land; and the painted turtle, *Chrysemys picta,* a relatively aquatic species.

Yerkes placed individuals of each species in the middle of a 30 × 60 cm platform which was elevated 30, 90, or 180 cm above a black cloth net. He observed the behavior of each species on the platform, and recorded the time it took for each turtle to descend or fall from it, if, in fact, the turtle eventually did so. He allowed a maximum time of 60 min for descent, an experimental procedure requiring great patience.

The results clearly supported Yerkes' hypothesis. As shown in Table I, the average time before descent was shortest for the relatively aquatic *C. picta* and longest for the terrestrial *T. carolina.* Also, failure to leave the platform within the 60-min test period was a common occurrence, and appeared at a lower platform height more frequently for *T. carolina* than for the other two species. Yerkes also tested a number of other turtle species, and reported that their

TABLE I

Descent Times and Failures to Descend for Three Turtle Species[a]

Height (cm)	C. picta		C. guttata		T. carolina	
	Mean time to descend (sec)	Failures	Mean time to descend (sec)	Failures	Mean time to descend (sec)	Failures
30	57	0	1626	11	2527	9
90	390	0	2941	30	3242	33
180	610	1	3600	40	3542	39

[a] After Yerkes, 1904.

performance was also consistent with his hypothesis. Yerkes observed, "This quantitative expression of the amount of hesitation clearly indicates a close relation between the demands of the natural environment of the species, so far as spatial relations are concerned, and the behavior of the animals."

In order to verify that the turtles' behavior depended upon visual information, and not some other aspect of the situation, Yerkes tested some animals with tin foil caps placed over their eyes. He found that *C. picta* now rushed off the platform without the slightest hesitation, irrespective of the platform height. *C. guttata* first tried to remove the blindfold, then moved about until an edge was encountered. It then retreated from the edge. For different reasons, *T. carolina* also failed to leave the platform. These turtles simply refused to move when their eyes were covered.

No further studies of depth perception in turtles are to be found in the literature for several decades, although depth perception was studied in many other animals (see Walk, 1965, for an excellent review). In 1961, Walk and Gibson reported on studies of depth perception in many animals, employing a new apparatus called the visual cliff (see Fig. 3). The visual cliff consists of a runway arranged so that the animal may descend a short distance to either side onto a piece of clear glass. Underneath the glass on one side of the runway, the visual array appears to be immediately underneath the glass. Beneath the glass on the other side the visual cues are arranged to appear at a relatively greater distance, say 3 or 4 ft. These two sides are respectively termed "shallow" and "deep." The glass, of course, prevents the animal from falling. When an animal is placed on the runway, it has three choices: it can remain on the runway, descend to the shallow side, or descend to the deep side.

One reason for the invention of the visual cliff appears to have been a desire to control certain nonvisual cues which might be associated with an actual cliff. For example, there might be differences in air currents or acoustic stimuli which could enable an animal to detect a dropoff. Also, an actual dropoff is dangerous for species with little ability to perceive or respond to depth. This, of course, is why Yerkes used a net in his experiments. One potential difficulty with using the visual cliff is that with repeated testing an animal could learn that it was not actually going to fall after stepping to either the deep or shallow sides. This means that the best indication of an animal's response to depth cues occurs on the first trial, before the animal has an opportunity to learn that the situation is not actually dangerous.

Walk and Gibson tested ten *C. scripta* on a visual cliff. The turtles were tested repeatedly for several days, in order to allow sufficient time for descent to occur. Walk and Gibson found that the turtles appeared to avoid the "deep" side, but that their performance was not nearly as impressive as that of the majority of other species tested (goats, pigs, sheep, rats, chickens, cats, dogs, monkeys, and human infants). Like Yerkes, Walk and Gibson suggested that the aquatic habitat

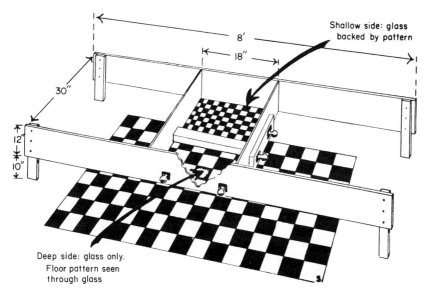

Fig. 3. Visual cliff. Reprinted with permission of Academic Press from Walk (1965).

of *C. scripta* might account for this species' relatively unimpressive response to depth. Their case would have been much stronger if they had tested any terrestrial turtles. Further, the initial descent of *C. scripta* was to the shallow side eight out of ten times, indicating that depth cues were apparently taken into consideration.

Routtenberg and Glickman (1964) compared the behavior of many different species on a visual cliff, including several species of terrestrial and aquatic turtles. Included in the terrestrial category were 18 *T. carolina* and one wood turtle (*Clemmys insculpta*). The aquatic turtles included 11 *C. scripta*, 12 *C. picta*, one false map turtle (*Graptemys pseudo-geographica*), and two mud turtles (*Kinosternon subrubrum*). Routtenberg and Glickman were not as patient as Yerkes or Walk and Gibson, allowing their subjects only 15 min to descend. This may be the reason for their report that 47% of the terrestrial group and 30% of the aquatic group failed to leave the runway on the first trial. Of the ten terrestrial turtles that descended, nine chose the shallow side. In the case of the aquatic turtles, nine of 18 chose the shallow side. It is not clear why the aquatic species in this study did so poorly relative to the *C. scripta* in Walk and Gibson's experiment. When a terrestrial vs. aquatic comparison was carried out for the data of the second trial, there was no significant difference. This difference between first and second trial results is another indication that the significant descent on the visual cliff is the first one, at least as far as investigations of depth perception are concerned. The two groups were also compared on the average

time they took to make the first descent. The aquatic group descended significantly earlier than the terrestrial group, a finding also consistent with Yerkes'
data.

Hertzler and Hayes (1967) performed experiments with *T. carolina* on a visual
cliff, intending to use the apparatus for evaluating the effects of lesions of the
visual system on responsiveness to distance cues. They introduced two variations
in the usual visual cliff procedure. First, no glass was used so as to insure that
there were no reflections, and a string was attached to the posterior of each turtle's
carapace. The experimenter held on to the string in order to prevent injury
the animals if they elected to descend to the deep side. This made the apparatus
not, strictly speaking, a visual cliff, but an actual cliff. Unlike the Yerkes task,
the turtles had the opportunity to choose between a shallow and a deep side. The
second variation in procedure was as follows: if the turtle did not begin moving
within 10 min on the first trial, and 2 min on the three succeeding trials, it was
lightly and repeatedly tapped on the rear of the carapace with a pencil. This
tapping resulted in locomotor behavior and, eventually, a choice. There is some
danger, of course, that this procedure could result in random activity on the part
of the animal. The preoperative performance on the cliff, however, of 16 *T.
carolina* (four trials each) was 60 of 64 descents to the shallow side. These
results are similar to those reported both by Yerkes and Routtenberg and
Glickman.

Comparisons between the pre- and postoperative performance of *T. carolina*
showed that sizable lesions of either the optic tectum or of the so-called general
cortex produced no significant change in behavior, whereas a combined ablation
of both of these areas resulted in chance level performance.

Recently, Ashe *et al.* (1975) extended the procedures of Routtenberg and
Glickman (1964) to a wide variety of additional species. Thirty-seven individuals
representing 29 different species were tested on the visual cliff for a 10 min
period, and their behavior scored as follows: (1) no response—no movement
during the 10 min; (2) no preference—movement occurred indiscriminately on
both sides of the cliff; or (3) preference for the centerboard and/or the shallow
side—movement was confined to the centerboard and/or the shallow side. It was
found that only those turtles classified as terrestrial exhibited a preference for the
centerboard and/or the shallow side, while the overwhelming majority of the
aquatic species exhibited no preference for one side or the other.

IV. VISUAL ALARM REACTIONS

When a vertebrate perceives a rapidly approaching object, it may behave in a
variety of ways. If the object has no particular positive significance, the animal
often displays some form of "alarm reaction" such as blinking, turning the head

or body away, or moving out of the object's path. In the case of many turtles, alarm reactions include the withdrawal of the head, tail, and legs into the shell. Many studies have been done on the alarm reactions of animals to visual stimuli (Walk, 1965). The testing procedures in most were quite informal, and did not allow the determination of the specific sensory cues involved. For example, the experimenter might simply move his hand toward the animal's face and record its response (Avery, 1928; Mowrer, 1936). In this situation the animal might be responding to air currents, odors, variations in temperature, or even acoustic stimuli in addition to or instead of visual cues. Such informal testing procedures also make it difficult to be sure that stimulus characteristics are identical from one trial to the next.

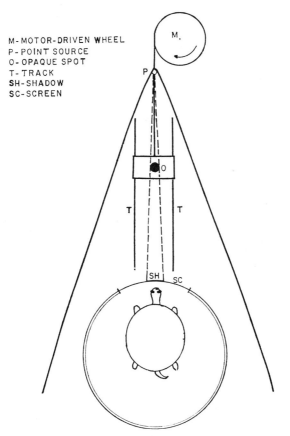

M- MOTOR-DRIVEN WHEEL
P- POINT SOURCE
O- OPAQUE SPOT
T- TRACK
SH- SHADOW
SC- SCREEN

Fig. 4. Diagram of apparatus used to elicit visual alarm reactions. Reprinted with permission of Bailliere Tindall from Hayes and Saiff (1967).

Schiff *et al.* (1962) introduced an optical technique which allows one to evaluate the contribution of nonvisual cues and allows precise control of stimulus characteristics. A round object was interposed between a point source of light and a translucent screen. This projected a clear, round shadow which could be seen from the opposite side of the screen (see Fig. 4). The size of the shadow could be varied by moving the round object toward or away from the light source. As the object moved toward the light, the shadow became smaller and vice versa. Schiff and his associates suggest that this technique can be used to isolate, under controlled conditions, the stimulus characteristics which signify "...an impending collision."

Schiff *et al.* tested rhesus monkeys (*Macaca mulatta*) with this procedure and observed that these animals "ducked" and exhibited other signs of alarm when the shadow was suddenly enlarged. When the shadow was suddenly made smaller, however, indications of interest rather than signs of alarm were observed. Schiff (1965) tested fiddler crabs (*Uca pugnax*), leopard frogs (*Rana pipiens*), and domestic chickens (*Gallus domesticus*) and found essentially the same results.

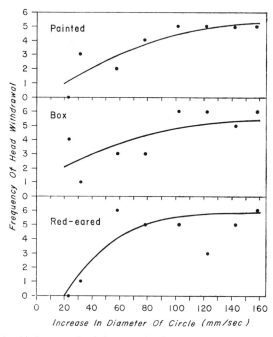

Fig. 5. Relationship between visual alarm reaction frequency and rate of increase in the diameter of the circular shadow. Taken from Hayes and Saiff (1967) with permission of Bailliere Tindall.

Hayes and Saiff (1967) extended this experimental approach to several species of turtles. In the first experiment, three turtles were used: one each of the species *Chrysemys scripta, Chrysemys picta,* and *Terrapene carolina.* Each turtle was exposed to circular shadows which enlarged at eight different velocities. Control trials were also given in which the shadow grew smaller, or in which the light was turned on and off. Also, an occasional trial was administered in which the animal was positioned so that the screen could be viewed with only one eye. Observers recorded whether the turtles exhibited withdrawal of the head into the shell. The findings were almost identical for the three individuals, and are presented in Fig. 5. As the velocity of shadow enlargement increased, so did the frequency of head withdrawal. The relationship appeared to be an exponential one. The trials with only one eye directed toward the screen also resulted in vigorous head withdrawal, indicating that binocular visual stimulation is not necessary for eliciting visual alarm reactions. No response was seen when the shadow was made smaller rather than larger, when the lights were off so that only auditory cues were present, or when the light were suddenly turned on or off. This indicates that, of all these potential cues, only a rapidly enlarging shadow is sufficient to elicit visual alarm reactions from these turtles.

Similar findings were reported by Ireland *et al.* (1969), who used equipment which allowed them to precisely measure the degree of head withdrawal in *C. scripta.* They arranged a photoelectric cell and a collimated light source so that the movements of a turtle's head brought about a proportional deflection of an oscilloscope beam (see Fig. 6). The amplitude of head withdrawal in *C. scripta* was found to vary as a function of the velocity of shadow enlargement. Also, Ireland *et al.* found that the alarm reaction decreased and eventually ceased to occur with repeated stimulus presentations.

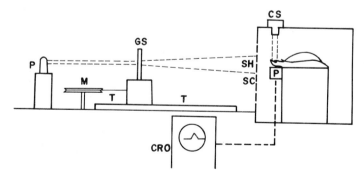

Fig. 6. Diagram of the apparatus used by Ireland *et al.* (1969) with permission of Bailliere Tindall. P, point source of light; M, motor driven wheel; GS, glass slide with opaque circle on it; T, tracks; SH, shadow; SC, screen; CS, collimated light source; P, photocell; CRO, cathode ray oscilloscope.

In brief, the visual cues produced by a rapidly approaching object appear sufficient to elicit head withdrawal in three species of turtles. This does not mean, of course, that other stimuli might not serve to alert the animal to approaching objects and elicit head withdrawal in real world situations.

V. OPTOKINETIC RESPONSES

Animals of many species exhibit behaviors which enable them to stabilize the image of the surrounding environment on the retina (Walls, 1942). Such behaviors are usually referred to as optokinetic responses. In the laboratory, optokinetic responses are usually elicited by moving a uniform stimulus pattern, consisting of alternating black and white vertical stripes, horizontally across an animal's visual field. Although it is not always necessary, it is usually the case that the pattern fills the entire visual field. Rotating striped cylinders, with the subject positioned either inside or outside, have been found convenient for the presentation of such stimulus patterns and are called optokinetic drums (see Fig. 7) (Smith and Bojar, 1938).

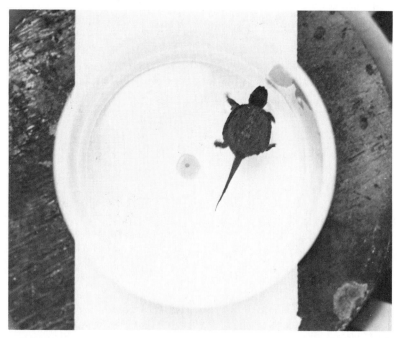

Fig. 7. Unrestrained *Chelydra serpentina* in an optokinetic drum. (Photograph by L. Ireland.)

There are three different kinds of optokinetic responses: (1) optomotor responses in which the animal follows the moving stripes by moving its entire body, (2) head nystagmus in which only the head is moved, and (3) eye nystagmus in which only the eyes move (Hayes and Ireland, 1972). An animal may track the stripes of an optokinetic drum by uninterrupted locomotion (optomotor response). However, when the animal moves only its head or eyes, the tracking angle is limited. Stripes will thereafter enter the opposite edge of the visual field and then cross it. Stabilization of these new images occurs by a rapid saccadic movement of the head or eyes in the direction opposite to that of stimulus motion, thus permitting focus on another stripe. The literature concerning optokinetic responses is large. Most of this work has been done with insects, fishes, and mammals, while little work has been done with reptiles.

There appear to have been no studies carried out on the optokinetic responses of testudines until quite recently. Hayes *et al.* (1968) reported on the eye and head nystagmus of *Chrysemys scripta,* the red-eared slider. In these experiments, the turtles were restrained on a plastic disk with rubber straps, and the disk was suspended within an optokinetic drum. As the cylinder revolved about the animal, observers counted both head and eye movements. This procedure was very reliable, giving interobserver correlation coefficients of +0.99.

Hayes *et al.* found that exposing the turtles to moving stripes for extended periods of time led to the habituation of optokinetic responses. During the first minute of testing, as shown in Fig. 8, the response rate was approximately 50 per minute. By minute 60 of testing, it had declined to between 10 and 20 per minute. During minute 61, the direction of motion of the stripes was reversed for

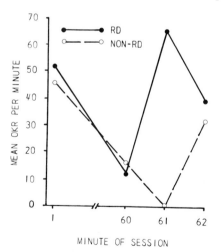

Fig. 8. OKR scores of RD and non-RD groups during the four test periods. (From Hayes *et al.,* 1968, with permission of the American Psychological Association.)

the RD (reversed direction) group in order to see how much of the response decrement was specific to the initial direction of movement. For the non-RD group, the drum was turned off for the same time period. It can be seen in Fig. 8 that reversing the drum restored the response rate to its initial level, or even higher, indicating that fatigue was not responsible for the response decrement. The non-RD group exhibited no head or eye nystagmus during the minute the drum was turned off. In minute 62, the drum was again set in motion in the original direction for both groups. The response rate was significantly lower than when the drum was first rotating in this direction, and the two groups did not differ significantly from each other. Additional experiments by Hayes *et al.* showed that habituation of head and eye nystagmus could be obtained after only a 5-min exposure to the moving drum, and that the effects of habituation could be detected up to 24 hr later. Further, an interesting day-to-day difference was found to occur when drums with different numbers of stripes were used. When the drum had 19 alternating black and white stripes set at equal intervals, the frequency of head and eye nystagmus increased from day to day over a 3-day period. If there were only four 1-in. wide black stripes, 90° apart, the frequency decreased over days. Thus, two different phenomena appeared to occur. When the drum had 19 stripes, sensitization occurred. When there were only 4 stripes, habituation took place. Currently, we have no explanation for this difference.

Hayes and Hertzler (1967) reported on the effects of cortical and tectal lesions on optokinetic responses in *C. scripta,* using 5 min tests in the same striped drums as those used by Hayes *et al.* They found that cortical lesions had no detectable effect on performance in either the 19 or 4 stripe condition. Lesions of the optic tectum, however, significantly reduced the frequency of head and eye nystagmus in the 19 stripe drum, but had no significant effect on performance in the 4 stripe drum. More extensive testing, using the two different drums, did reveal some effect of the tectal lesions in the 4 stripe drum (Hayes and Hertzler, 1967). On the basis of these experiments, it appears reasonable to conclude that the optic tectum plays some role in the production or regulation of optokinetic responses.

Hayes *et al.* demonstrated not only habituation of head and eye nystagmus, but also a phenomenon which bears some resemblance to the rebound effects reported by Sherrington (1947) for certain spinal reflexes. Sherrington reported that many reflexes not only recover to normal levels after a period of inhibition, but may even exhibit greater than normal amplitude and frequency. For example, the crossed extension reflex of the limb of a spinal dog may be inhibited by a flexion reflex, after which the extensor reflex will be intensified. Similar effects may be seen after inhibition of the so-called "mark-time" reflex, an alternating movement of the hind limbs which occurs on holding the animal up so that its limbs hang freely. This reflex is inhibited by pinching the skin of the tail. When the skin stimulation is stopped, "... the stepping movement sets in more vigorously and at quicker rate than before." Sherrington termed this phenomenon postinhibitory rebound or reflex rebound. Hayes *et al.* found that when the direction of rotation of the drum was reversed following several minutes of exposure, the frequency of eye and head nystagmus did not merely recover to original levels, but exceeded the original rate by a significant margin. According to Sherrington, this excess or overshoot may be due to the sudden removal of inhibition. Similar rebound effects have been reported for *Chrysemys picta* by Hogberg (1968).

Hertzler and Hayes (1969) demonstrated that optokinetic reflex rebound in *C. scripta* depended upon the integrity of the tectal commissure, which suggests that the buildup of inhibition, presumed to underlie the rebound effect, depends upon an interaction between the two tecta. Transection of the tectal commissure either prevents the buildup from occurring or prevents it from manifesting itself. At the same time, Hertzler and Hayes found no change in the rate of habituation of eye and head nystagmus. These results are shown in Fig. 9.

Hertzler and Hayes also conducted experiments which compared the performance of monocular and binocular turtles. This is another way of investigating the tectal interaction which presumably underlies the rebound effect, since it is widely agreed that there is nearly complete crossover of the optic nerve fibers at the optic chiasm in turtles (Polyak, 1957; Walls, 1942). They tested the turtles under three different conditions: (1) binocular, (2) monocular where the direction of stimulus motion past the open eye was from temporal-to-nasal, and (3) monocular where the direction of movement past the open eye was from nasal-to-temporal. The results are shown in Fig. 10. The frequency of optokinetic nystagmus in the two monocular conditions was quite different. When the movement of the stripes past the open eye was in the temporal-to-nasal direction, the frequency of nystagmus was nearly the same as for the binocular condition. However, when the movement past the open eye was in the opposite direction, nasal-to-temporal, the turtles displayed almost no responses. It is as if the turtle did not "see" the stripes when they were moving in this direction. During the period when the direction of motion of the drum was reversed (minute 31 in Fig. 10), only the binocular condition yielded a true rebound effect, i.e., a response rate which significantly exceeded that of the first minute of testing. With monocular turtles, reversing the drum from temporal-to-nasal past the open eye resulted in a marked decrease in the frequency of nystagmus, another indication that the monocular turtle does not "see" the movement when it is in the nasal-to-temporal direction. The other monocular condition, where reversal was from nasal-to-temporal, brought about a large increase in response rate. Since the response rate prior to the reversal was nearly at the zero level, and temporal-to-nasal stimulation is more effective, some increase is to be expected. The response rate was not higher than that seen during the first minute for the

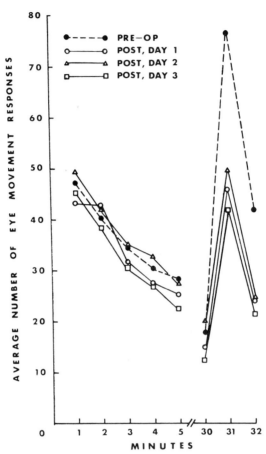

Fig. 9. Median preoperative and 3-day postoperative OKR scores of *Chrysemys scripta* with transections of the tectal commissure. (From Hertzler and Hayes, 1969, with permission of the American Psychological Association.)

temporal-to-nasal direction in the other monocular condition, an indication that this was not a true rebound effect.

Taken together, these findings indicate that reflex rebound of optokinetic eye and head nystagmus does not occur except in binocular turtles, where the inputs to the two eyes are simultaneously sent to both optic tecta. Manipulations which prevent tectal interaction from taking place appear to insure that no rebound effect occurs. Cutting the tectal commissure prevents rebound, as does covering one of the turtle's eyes. It is likely that unilateral lesions of the optic tectum would also prevent the inhibitory building-up from occurring.

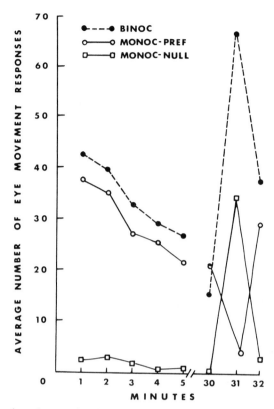

Fig. 10. Binocular and monocular OKR scores of *Chrysemys scripta*. Monocular performance is shown for both the preferred, or temporal-to-nasal direction of stimulus movement, and the null, or nasal-to-temporal direction. (From Hertzler and Hayes, 1969, with permission of the American Psychological Association.)

Hayes and Ireland (1972) investigated the optomotor behavior of *C. scripta*. Essentially the same procedures were used as in the experiments described above, except that unrestrained turtles were placed in a transparent, water-filled container. In the first experiment, seven different stimulus velocities were presented to the turtles for 4 successive days. An observer recorded the number of complete revolutions described by each subject during each two min exposure to each velocity. The results are shown in Fig. 11. The mean number of revolutions described by the turtles varied directly with the speed of the drum. The product moment correlation coefficient between the mean rpm of the turtles and the rpm of the drum was +0.92, indicating that about 85% of the variance among the means is accounted for by variation in drum velocity. It should be pointed out

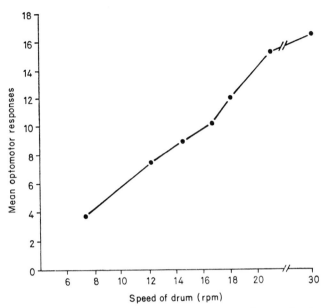

Fig. 11. Mean binocular optomotor response rate of *Chrysemys scripta* as a function of speed of drum rotation. (From Hayes and Ireland, 1972, with permission of S. Karger, Basel/New York.)

that the compensation brought about by the optomotor responses is far from perfect. The velocity of the turtles averages only about two-thirds that of the drum. In this experiment, the turtles also displayed head and eye nystagmus. With the turtle turning around rapidly, however, it was not possible to accurately record the frequency of these responses. It is almost certain that, by employing head and eye nystagmus in conjunction with optomotor responses, the turtles achieved a better stabilization of the moving stripes on the retina than is reflected by their optomotor scores.

In a second experiment performed by Hayes and Ireland, the same procedures were followed, except that the animals were rendered monocular by covering one eye with a mixture of black ink and waterproof epoxy. The turtles were presented with both temporal-to-nasal and nasal-to-temporal stimulation, at the same seven velocities as in the first experiment. There was a highly significant difference in responsiveness to nasal-to-temporal and temporal-to-nasal stimulation (see Fig. 12). When the direction of drum rotation was temporal-to-nasal, optomotor performance was directly related to drum velocity. When stimulus motion was in the opposite direction, the turtles essentially failed to respond. Even the temporal-to-nasal condition did not elicit very effective compensation. The fre-

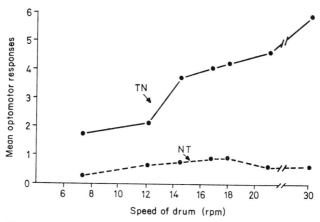

Fig. 12. Mean monocular optomotor response rate of *Chrysemys scripta* as a function of speed of drum rotation. TN, temporal-to-nasal; NT, nasal-to-temporal. (From Hayes and Ireland, 1972, with permission of S. Karger, Basel/New York.)

quency of optomotor responses was significantly less than under binocular conditions. Whereas the binocular condition produced an average ratio of turtle rpm to drum rpm of two-thirds, the temporal-to-nasal monocular performance ratio fell to one-quarter or one-fifth.

In another experiment of Hayes and Ireland, an attempt was made to habituate the optomotor response with 5 min of continuous exposure to stripes rotating at a constant 12.2 rpm. Also, the direction of motion was reversed during the sixth minute and re-reversed during the seventh, in order to determine whether any rebound effects might occur. No habituation was observed, nor was there any rebound effect. The only significant effect was an increase in the turtles' response rate over time. Thus, while both the head and eye nystagmus of the restrained turtle habituates and shows rebound effects, the optomotor response of the unrestrained turtle does not.

Preliminary investigations of the optokinetic responses of several other species of turtles have been performed. Snapping turtles (*Chelydra serpentina*) display optomotor responses, head nystagmus, and eye nystagmus when placed in an optokinetic drum (Ireland and Rose, 1976). Green sea turtles (*Chelonia mydas*) display all three types of optokinetic responses immediately after emerging from the nest (Ireland, 1976). Hatching loggerhead sea turtles (*Caretta caretta*) show head and eye nystagmus, but do not perform optomotor responses in an optokinetic drum (Ireland and Babcock, 1976). We have no explanation for their lack of optomotor behavior.

VI. WATER-FINDING BEHAVIOR

One of the primary adaptations which enabled the reptiles to invade dry land was the development of the amniotic egg, which made it unnecessary for them to lay their eggs in water. This adaptation almost seems superfluous in the case of many species of turtles. Many turtles lay their eggs close to the water and their young travel toward and enter the water immediately after emerging from the nest, spending much of their lives either in or near it.

For many years, behavioral scientists have been intrigued with the question of precisely how young turtles are able to find the water. The majority of studies concerned with the water-finding abilities of testudines have been done with sea turtles, although preliminary investigations have been performed with several semiaquatic, freshwater species (Anderson, 1958; Noble and Breslau, 1938; Ortleb and Sexton, 1964).

Immediately after hatching, young sea turtles usually head toward the ocean as rapidly as their flippers allow them to travel across the beach (see Fig. 13). Hatchling sea turtles almost always emerge from their nest at night. Nocturnal emergencies have numerous advantages. The tropical beaches where sea turtles

Fig. 13. Hatchling green sea turtles (*Chelonia mydas*) traveling through a tide pool and over rocks to reach the ocean. (From Carr, 1967. Reprinted by permission of Doubleday and Co., Inc.)

commonly nest often become extremely hot during the day. Exposure to such high temperatures serves to lower the activity level of hatchlings, and may prove fatal to them (Mrosovsky, 1968). Further, traveling toward the sea under the cover of darkness undoubtably provides some protection from both airborne and terrestrial predators.

Hatchling sea turtles are able to locate the water during the day as well as at night, under virtually all weather conditions, alone or in groups, and from locations from which they do not have a direct view of the ocean. Numerous studies have been performed to determine the sensory basis of this water-finding ability.

Carr and Ogren (1960) placed green sea turtle (*Chelonia mydas*) eggs in artificial nests on a beach facing in a different direction than the one from which the eggs were obtained. After emerging from the nests, the hatchlings had no difficulty making their way to the ocean, demonstrating that their ability to find the water did not depend upon an innate preference for traveling in a certain direction.

There is considerable circumstantial evidence which indicates that successful water-finding by sea turtles involves visual information. Green turtle and loggerhead (*Caretta caretta*) hatchlings traveling toward the water show a strong, positive reaction to light (Hooker, 1908, 1909; Parker, 1922; Hendrickson, 1958). The turtles will turn and move toward the beam of a flashlight shone across their path as if drawn by a magnet. If a sufficiently intense light is used, it is possible to induce green turtle hatchlings to return to the beach after they have entered the water (Carr and Ogren, 1960). Also, artificial lighting on roads near nesting beaches has been reported to disorient loggerhead hatchlings (McFarlane, 1963). Equally important, neither green turtle nor loggerhead hatchlings seem able to find the water if both eyes are blindfolded (Daniel and Smith, 1947; Carr and Ogren, 1960). Blindfolded hatchlings either wander randomly about the beach or simply remain stationary. Mrosovsky and Shettleworth (1968) performed the necessary control experiments to demonstrate that this disorientation is not due to the process of fitting blindfolds to the turtles' heads or to any irritation produced by the blindfolds.

It is not difficult to conceive of how light, particularly blue–green light reflected from the surface of the ocean, might serve as a valuable cue for locating the water. Hooker (1911) was the first to investigate the question of whether lights of particular wavelengths might play an important role in sea finding. He reported that loggerhead hatchlings avoided both red- and green-colored objects but tended to approach blue-colored ones. Hooker noted, however, that his stimuli were not spectrally pure and that the actual intensities of light reflected by his colored objects were not known.

Mrosovsky and Carr (1967) examined the responsiveness of green turtle hatchlings to lights of different wavelengths. In preparation for their experiments, they first dug a circular trench on the turtles' nesting beach. The trench measured about 0.3 m wide, 0.3 m deep, and 12 m in diameter. It was sufficiently deep to trap any hatchlings which fell in. Further, the trench was divided into 24 compartments of equal size so that the turtles could move only a short distance after entering. Large numbers of hatchlings could be placed in the center of this arena, and their directional tendencies scored by counting the number of turtles which were subsequently trapped in each compartment. Working at night, Mrosovsky and Carr first released a group of hatchlings in the arena without any artificial stimuli present, in order to determine the turtles' directional preferences under natural conditions. In this situation, virtually all the hatchlings entered compartments on the seaward side of the arena. Then, before weather conditions changed significantly, more groups of turtles were released and lights of different wavelengths and intensities were shone across their seaward travel path. When a red light of relatively low intensity was projected across their path, few of the turtles turned toward the light and the majority fell into seaward compartments. When a dim blue light was substituted, many more turtles oriented toward it, even though the blue light emitted somewhat less energy than the red one. Mrosovsky and Shettleworth (1968) later demonstrated that it was necessary for a red light to contain about 2.8 log units more energy than a blue one to be equally attractive to hatchlings. If a sufficiently intense red light was employed, however, the hatchlings preferred it to a blue one. These results suggest that hatchling green turtles have a preference for light of short wavelengths, in addition to a preference for intense light.

It is possible that this apparent preference for blue light simply indicates that the turtles' retinal receptors are differentially sensitive to lights of different wavelengths, and that the only variable determining their orientational tendencies is perceived intensity or brightness. In other words, it is possible that blue lights are simply perceived as being brighter than lights of other colors containing equivalent amounts of energy. Granda and O'Shea (1972) recorded the electroretinogram (ERG) of green turtles whose eyes were stimulated with a variety of monochromatic lights. The turtles proved to be most sensitive to light of about 520 nm, in the blue-green portion of the spectrum. However, as Mrosovsky (1972) pointed out, if Granda and O'Shea's data are examined closely, one finds that the eye of the green turtle can detect blue light containing approximately 2.0 log units less energy than a red one. Considering that a red light must be 2.8 log units more intense than a blue one to be equally attractive to hatchlings (Mrosovsky and Shettleworth, 1968), this leaves 0.8 log units of energy unaccounted for. This again suggests that the turtles' increased responsiveness to blue light may involve an actual preference for light of short wavelengths. Additional work will be necessary to clarify this point.

Adult female green turtles appear to employ similar visual cues to find the water after nesting. Ehrenfeld and Carr (1967) found that adult females were unable to find the water when fitted with binocular blindfolds. They also equipped the turtles with "spectacles" which could hold colored filters. The turtles successfully found the water when the spectacles were equipped with either red, green, or blue filters. A significant degree of disorientation was noted, however, when the red filters were used. This result was probably due to the turtles' minimal sensitivity to the red portion of the spectrum.

It should be noted that possessing a visual system maximally sensitive to the blue–green portion of the spectrum is not only potentially advantageous for finding the ocean but for living in it as well. In the aquatic habitat of the sea turtle, blue–green light penetrates the water with the least attenuation.

Considerations of color aside, light intensity appears to be an important cue for sea turtle water-finding behavior. Demonstrating that sea turtles are attracted by intense lights, however, does not prove that the intensity cues available under natural conditions actually serve to guide them toward the water.

The majority of beaches where sea turtles nest have an essentially simple topography consisting of an open stretch of sand slanting toward the ocean, backed by trees and other vegetation. Thus, there is usually a difference in light intensity between the open seaward horizon and the darker background tree line at all hours of the day and night, and under all weather conditions. Mrosovsky and Shettleworth (1968) performed experiments in which they manipulated these natural intensity cues. They erected barriers of dark cloth, about 1.5 m high and of various lengths, at different locations around the outside of a test arena of the same type and size employed by Mrosovsky and Carr (1967). The cloth served to produce a darkened background which, from turtle eye-level at the center of the arena, was sufficiently high to obscure any outside surface features. The location of the cloth was varied from test to test. In some experiments it was placed so as to extend the natural tree line. In others, it was located near the middle of the open seaward horizon. When green turtle hatchlings were tested at night in these situations, they almost always headed toward the center of the remaining open horizon, whether or not this travel path was the shortest route to the ocean. These results suggest that the turtles make use of intensity cues from a wide field of view, and that they use visual cues other than simply those available from the nearest body of water.

In further tests, Mrosovsky (1970) was able to show that both green and hawksbill (*Eretmochelys imbricata*) hatchlings deviated from the shortest route to the water in reaction to different positions of the sun. Mrosovsky (1970) also demonstrated that when a circular test arena was surrounded by an opaque wall, which was sufficiently high to prevent the hatchlings from seeing the ocean, shore, or treeline, hawksbill hatchlings became disoriented and wandered in all directions. When an even higher wall was erected around one portion of the arena, however, the majority of turtles chose paths in roughly the opposite direction. On the basis of these data, and other data cited above, Mrosovsky suggested that water-finding behavior might depend upon a simple tropotactic reaction to light: a simultaneous comparison of the light intensities arriving at the two eyes and reorientation of the body until the two are equal (Fraenkel and Gunn, 1961). Any stimulus in the field of view, therefore, might have some effect on orientation.

Experiments with unilaterally blindfolded hatchling greens and loggerheads (Daniel and Smith, 1947; Mrosovsky and Shettleworth, 1968) lend considerable support to this phototropotactic interpretation of water-finding behavior. Hatchlings with monocular blindfolds have a strong tendency to turn in circles, almost always moving in the direction of the open eye. Adult female green turtles with one eye covered also circle toward the open eye (Ehrenfeld and Carr, 1967). This is precisely the behavior one would expect from an animal attempting to equalize the intensities of the visual inputs to the two eyes. Yet, as Mrosovsky (1972) pointed out, a tropotactic reaction to light will not account for all aspects of hatchling orientation. Occasionally, a unilaterally blindfolded turtle circles toward its covered eye. If orientation depends strictly upon a tropotactic reaction to light intensity, this should never occur.

Mrosovsky and Shettleworth (1974) fitted hatchling green turtles with "goggles" which selectively occluded portions of their visual field (see Fig. 14). In

Fig. 14. Green sea turtle (*Chelonia mydas*) hatchling wearing rubber hood and goggles with the temporal field of the right eye occluded. (From Mrosovsky and Shettleworth, 1974, with permission of Brill, Leiden.)

general, their results indicate that visual inputs to the nasal field of view are associated with turning toward the midline of the body, while inputs to the temporal field of view are associated with turning away from the midline. The behavior of hatchlings with monocular blindfolds may be understood by assuming that visual inputs to the temporal field normally have a greater influence on orientation than nasal inputs. Thus, when all parts of the retina are stimulated equally, unilaterally blindfolded animals turn toward their open eye, away from the midline. The orientation of binocular animals, then, would depend upon the balance struck between the visual inputs in the left nasal and right temporal fields vs. those in the right nasal and left temporal fields. Since inputs to the temporal field appear to have a greater effect, the turtles would be expected to turn toward the eye receiving the greatest overall visual input. Occasionally, the majority of visual inputs to the open eye of a unilaterally blindfolded turtle might be to the nasal field and elicit circling toward the covered eye. Alternately, in a few turtles, inputs to the nasal field might be dominant over inputs to the temporal field. Also, a wide variety of congenital defects of the visual system might be expected to produce unusual circling behavior. A small number of green turtle hatchlings simply turn in circles on the beach after leaving the nest, never reaching the water (J. A. Frick, personal communication).

Further research will be necessary to specify the exact nature of these orientational mechanisms. In particular, studies should be performed to determine the precise areas of the retina which, when stimulated, produce contralateral and ipsilateral turning, and procedures should be devised to control for the possible effects of eye movements.

VII. MIGRATION AND HOMING

With the exception of studies of water-finding behavior, research concerning the sensory cues which guide turtles from place to place in their natural habitats has not kept pace with laboratory studies of their reactions to sensory stimuli, or with our knowledge of their sensory physiology. This is somewhat surprising, since determining the cues which turtles actually attend to in real world situations should serve to guide research in these other areas. Most studies of animal migration and homing ability have been performed with highly mobile vertebrates, especially birds, but a few investigators have concerned themselves with the relatively sedentary testudines.

The migratory champions among the Testudinata are the sea turtles (Carr, 1967). Of all the species of sea turtles, the migratory travels of *C. mydas* have been documented the most carefully. The travels of adult female *C. mydas* (see Fig. 15) have been partially charted by means of experiments in which tags of durable metal were attached to one of the forelimbs of nesting animals. It is

Fig. 15. A female green sea turtle (*Chelonia mydas*) returns to the sea after nesting on the beach at Tortuguero, Costa Rica. (Photograph by L. Ireland.)

virtually impossible to employ this technique with adult male *C. mydas* as they rarely, if ever, come ashore after leaving their natal beach as hatchlings. By means of tagging experiments carried out at Tortuguero, Costa Rica, Professor Archie Carr and his colleagues have found that: (1) the females appear to nest only every 2–4 years, rather than annually, (2) no adult female tagged at Tortuguero has ever been found nesting on any other beach, (3) the females show remarkable nest site tenacity, usually digging nests within a few kilometers of their last nesting site, (4) no adult female has been reported captured in the ocean off Tortuguero except during the nesting season, and (5) after leaving Tortuguero at the end of the breeding season, the females apparently travel to distant feeding grounds including those located off the coasts of Cuba, Florida, Nicaragua, the Yucatan Peninsula, and Venezuela (Carr, 1967; Carr and Carr, 1970, 1972; Carr and Ogren, 1960). These data thoroughly support the theory that *C. mydas* is migratory.

The best documented long distance migration of *C. mydas,* however, is an entirely open-ocean journey from feeding grounds along the eastern coast of Brazil to Ascension Island in the southern Atlantic, approximately 2250 km distant (Carr, 1975) (see Fig. 16). As there do not appear to be any ocean current systems which could passively carry the turtles from Brazil to Ascension, it is likely that the successful completion of this migration depends upon a sophisticated navigational capability.

Koch *et al.* (1969) suggested that both olfactory and visual stimuli might play roles in guiding *C. mydas* from Brazil to Ascension Island. They pointed out that the south equatorial current could provide an olfactory link between Ascension and the Brazilian mainland (see Fig. 16). Koch and his associates suggested that the turtles might backtrack the south equatorial in the general direction of Ascen-

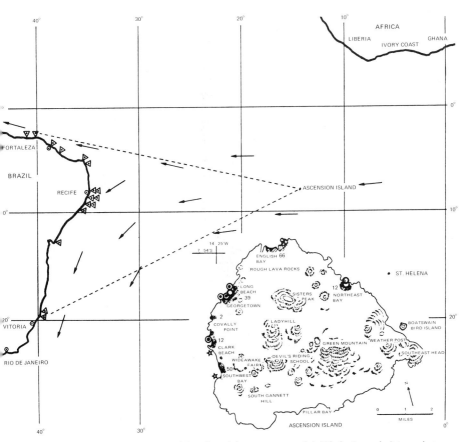

Fig. 16. Locations of recapture of female, adult green sea turtles (*Chelonia mydas*) tagged at Ascension Island. Triangles represent recoveries along the coast of Brazil. Hollow circles show recoveries of turtles that had been tagged and returned to nest after 2 years. Circles with dots show turtles that returned to nest after 3 years absence, presumably in Brazil. Stars represent turtles that returned to nest 4 years after they were tagged and presumably after having made two round trips to Brazil. Turtles recovered at Ascension had gone back to original nesting sites. Arrows suggest current trends. (From Carr, 1972, with permission of N.A.S.A.)

sion, by means of unspecified olfactory cues, and make course corrections by means of celestial cues.

Manton *et al.* (1972) reported that *C. mydas* is capable of underwater chemoreception, a rare adaptation for an air-breathing vertebrate, and it is possible that this ability evolved in response to selective pressures concerned with migratory abilities. Studies of the visual acuity of *C. mydas* in air indicate that the turtle is too near-sighted to make effective use of the stars for orientation, but might well obtain information from the position of the sun or moon (Ehrenfeld and Koch, 1967). The sensory basis of green turtle migration has not been investigated in the field, and the actual cues *C. mydas* uses during its long-distance journeys are unknown.

The travels of newborn green turtles are no less spectacular than those of adults. Hatchlings leaving their natal beach must eventually reach adult feeding areas which may be thousands of kilometers distant. There is a virtually complete lack of knowledge concerning the behavior or ecological niche of hatchling *C. mydas* from the time they leave the beach until they arrive at feeding grounds approximately 1 year later (Carr, 1972). This period in the life cycle of *C. mydas* has been referred to as the "lost year."

Until quite recently, our knowledge of the behavior of hatchling greens essentially ended at the waterline. Frick (1976), working off Bermuda with green turtles hatched from eggs brought from Tortuguero, Costa Rica, found that it was possible for a swimmer equipped with a face plate and flippers to keep a hatchling swimming in open ocean in view for up to 4 hr. Her research was designed to determine if the travel paths of hatchlings were random or nonrandom, whether the hatchlings showed evidence of accurate orientation when land was below the horizon, and if the hatchlings displayed a preferred direction of travel after leaving the beach. Frick was able to chart the travel paths of 26 turtles over distances up to 6.4 km. All tests were conducted during the day in calm, clear weather. Twelve hatchlings were released from beaches facing south, three from a beach facing west, and three from a beach facing north. Eight were released from a beach facing northeast and directly toward another shore approximately 0.6 km distant. The position of a hatchling over time was determined by observation of shore landmarks from a small boat accompanying the swimmer.

Frick found that the presence of neither the swimmer nor the boat appeared to influence the orientation of the hatchlings. When a swimmer or a boat blocked the path of a turtle, it simply dived under the obstacle, resurfaced, and continued on its original course. All the hatchlings spent most of their time swimming at or near the surface, occasionally diving to depths of up to 3 m. Nearly all the turtles swam steadily throughout the test periods. Swimming speeds averaged about 1.5 km/hr. The tracks of 24 hatchlings clearly showed nonrandom orientation. The tracks of turtles released from beaches facing the ocean usually approximated straight lines or took the form of gradual curves. Hatchlings released from the beach facing another shore initially swam straight out from land and then turned, adopting one of two possible headings which would take them into open ocean. Two hatchlings simply circled aimlessly. Whether these hatchlings showed any circling tendencies before entering the water was not reported. Hatchlings released on the same beach moved seaward on similar headings, regardless of whether they were released on different days or at different times of day. Turtles released on beaches facing different directions displayed different travel paths. In most cases, the departure courses of hatchlings appeared to be essentially extensions of the paths taken when crossing the beach to the sea. Hatchlings maintained these headings when the island was below the horizon from turtle eye level.

Ireland *et al.* (1976), also working off Bermuda with newborn turtles obtained from eggs brought from Tortuguero, equipped 11 *C. mydas* hatchlings with miniature acoustic transmitters and were able to follow them to sea at night in a small boat fitted with directional receiving equipment. Their findings are essentially identical to those of Frick (1976). The hatchlings swam steadily and directly away from the beach, and did not change their courses to any significant degree when land was below the horizon from turtle eye-level.

The observations of Frick (1976) and Ireland *et al.* (1976) constitute the first reports that sea turtle hatchlings are capable of accurate orientation in open ocean. Swimming rapidly away from the beach presumably has survival value in that it serves to take the hatchling rapidly beyond the reach of numerous inshore predators, and decreases the probability that it will be swept back to the beach by strong wave action. Whether the turtles eventually reorient to some common heading when well out from land is not known. Also, it is not known whether the hatchlings must actively swim toward adult feeding areas or whether they are simply carried there passively by ocean currents (Carr, 1972). The sensory basis of their straight-line travel has not been determined, but Ireland *et al.* (1976) noted that the turtles did not appear to simply orient toward the brightest portion of the sky or horizon, suggesting that the mechanisms involved in this straight-line travel are different from those involved in sea finding.

Homing behavior, the ability to return to a given location after wandering to or being displaced to another area, has also been reported or suggested for several terrestrial and semiaquatic turtles including *Chrysemys picta, Chrysemys scripta, Gopherus polyphemus,* and *Terrapene carolina* (Bogert, 1937; Breder, 1927; Cagle, 1944; Emlen, 1969; Gould, 1957, 1959; Gourley, 1974; Lemkau, 1970; Nichols, 1939; Williams, 1952; Woodbury and Hardy, 1948). The possible sensory basis of homing behavior was investigated in only a few of these studies. In each case, the authors were primarily concerned with the potential role of celestial cues.

Gould (1957) tested the possibility that *T. carolina* might use celestial cues for homing. He transported 43 box turtles in closed containers to open fields located from approximately 1 to 10 km from the areas where the turtles were captured. In order to accurately mark the turtles' travel paths after they were released in the presumably unfamiliar fields, Gould employed a technique devised by Breder (1927). Prior to release, a spool of thread was attached to the top of each animal's shell. One end of the thread was attached to a wooden stake and the thread unwound as the turtle walked away from the release site, marking the turtle's trail. All of the turtles were released and observed under clear skies at least once. Gould considered 22 of the animals suitable for his further experiments. Selection was based on whether a turtle traveled any appreciable distance during the first test period, which lasted for from 10 min to 2 hr, and whether or not it headed in approximately the homeward direction. Seventeen of these turtles were then released several more times, in most cases from two different fields with "home" lying in two different directions. Releases were carried out under clear, partly cloudy, or overcast skies. Gould reported that the turtles failed to orient in a homeward direction when the skies were either partly cloudy or overcast but continued to do so under clear skies, a result which appears to confirm his hypothesis that the turtles were choosing their travel paths with reference to some celestial cue or cues. Gould (1959), using similar procedures, obtained data which indicated that C. picta might also depend upon celestial cues for accurate homeward orientation.

Emlen (1969), however, was unable to confirm that C. picta could use celestial cues for homing. He captured 45 painted turtles in or on the shore of a small pond. Each turtle was marked for individual identification by filing notches along the margins of its shell. To aid in recognition from a distance, numbers were also painted on the dorsal surface of the shell. The turtles were released at six different locations. Three of the release sites were 100 m from the pond, to the north, south, and east. The three additional sites were located about 1.6 km from the pond, to the north, east, and west. The pond was not visible from turtle eye-level from any of the sites. Breder's (1927) thread technique was used to mark the travel path of each turtle. Emlen attempted to release each turtle at all of the six locations. This was not possible, as several of the animals escaped during testing. Tests were carried out only during the day. Each test had a duration of 2 hr.

Emlen found that the turtles displayed a marked tendency to orient in a homeward direction when released 100 m to the north, south, or east (see Fig. 17). This directional tendency disappeared entirely when they were released at any of the sites located 1.6 km from their home pond (see Fig. 18). Turtles released at 100-m sites under conditions of complete overcast continued to orient in a homeward direction (see Fig. 19), a finding which argues against the importance of celestial cues. Emlen also performed experiments in which turtles were released at the 100-m sites after their eyes were covered by blindfolds. With this procedure, he reported that there was a pronounced deterioration both in homeward orientation and in the straightness of the turtles' travel paths (see Fig. 20). He suggested that the visual recognition of local landmarks might play an important role in guiding the painted turtles back to their home ponds, and that such a simple, short range homing mechanism appeared appropriate to the needs of a relatively sedentary turtle such as C. picta. To date, the differences between the findings of Emlen (1969) and Gould (1959) concerning the role of celestial cues in the homing behavior of C. picta have not been resolved. Emlen's study,

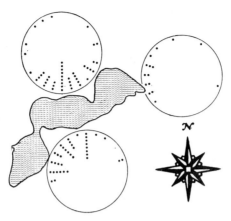

Fig. 17. Orientation of painted turtles (*Chrysemys scripta*) released 100 m from their home pond under clear skies. Each dot represents the direction taken by one turtle. (From Emlen, 1969, with permission of Brill, Leiden.)

however, appears to be the better designed of the two, and his findings appear more consistent with the demands of the ecological niche of *C. picta*.

Gourley (1974) performed experiments to determine if gopher tortoises (*Gopherus polyphemus*) employ solar cues for homing. He released 23 tortoises in an open field about 8 km from their home burrows, and tested the directional preferences of 37 tortoises in a circular arena, about 6 m in diameter, which

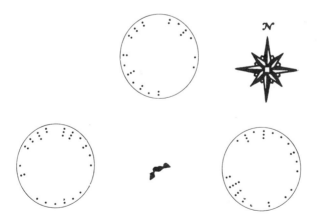

Fig. 18. Orientation of painted turtles (*Chrysemys scripta*) released about 1.6 km from their home pond. Each dot represents the heading of one turtle. (From Emlen, 1969, with permission of Brill, Leiden.)

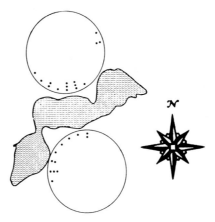

Fig. 19. Orientation of *Chrysemys scripta* released 100 m from their home pond under conditions of complete overcast. Dots indicate the travel paths of individual turtles. (From Emlen, 1969, with permission of Brill, Leiden.)

prevented the tortoises from seeing any topographical landmarks. Over half of the tortoises in each of these two groups displayed significant directional preferences in the course of repeated tests. These preferred directions, however, had no recognizable relationship to homeward directions and were widely divergent for tortoises captured in the same general area.

Gourley then subjected those tortoises which displayed a significant directional preference in the arena tests to a 6-hr shift in the light–dark cycle. To accomplish this, the tortoises were placed in a room in which the light was turned

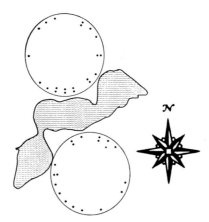

Fig. 20. Orientation of *Chrysemys scripta* released 100 m from their home pond when blindfolded. Each dot represents the direction taken by one turtle. (From Emlen, 1969, with permission of Brill, Leiden.)

on approximately 6 hr earlier than sunrise and off about 6 hr before dusk. The animals were maintained under these conditions for 7 days. When the tortoises were again tested in the arena, a significant change was noted in their directional preferences. The mean directional shift was about 90° counterclockwise. This result may be explained by assuming that: (1) the tortoises possess some form of "internal clock," (2) that the turtles must know the time of day in order to obtain accurate directional information from the position of the sun, and (3) that the tortoises' "clocks" were set back 6 hr by the shift in the light–dark cycle. The turtles appear to have misjudged the time and corrected their headings accordingly. Gourley's data, therefore, are somewhat paradoxical. Gopher tortoises appear capable of orienting on the basis of solar cues, but unable to use them to find their way home.

VIII. SUMMARY AND CONCLUSIONS

The general impression one gains is that among turtles, there is convincing evidence that the characteristics of a given individual's environment allow one to predict with reasonable accuracy how the animal will behave on a visual or actual cliff. A cautionary note is in order, however. None of the studies, so far, have been carried out with observers who were unaware of the hypothesis being tested. It is also possible that the presence of the human observer, particularly one who had some expectation as to what would happen, might influence the outcome of the study. In the future, it is to be hoped that less intrusive observational techniques will be utilized, such as time-lapse photography. This would greatly decrease the potential influence of the observer on the phenomenon he is observing.

Visual alarm reactions are obviously adaptive, allowing animals to avoid impending collisions. It is also important to note that the visual alarm reactions of turtles do not appear to be so rigid and inflexible that they cannot be modified by experience. This insures that the animal can eventually cease to respond to repetitive, irrelevant stimuli.

The adaptive significance of optokinetic and optomotor responses must be presumed to lie in the realm of compensation for the visual changes brought about during locomotion. Exactly how the compensatory systems have evolved and how they function in the field remain to be determined. In any case, it is clear that such behavior is widespread among the turtles thus far examined.

The water-finding ability displayed by both hatchling sea turtles after emerging from the nest and adult female sea turtles after laying their eggs is behavior with a clear goal and obvious survival value. Visual information appears to be absolutely critical for successful water finding. The essential cue appears to be light intensity, which is normally greater to seaward. The turtles appear to make use of intensity cues from a wide field of view (see also Verheijen and Brouwer, 1972). A possible preference for blue–green light has not been ruled out. Experiments with unilaterally blindfolded turtles suggest that they have a positive tropotactic response to light intensity. A simple tropotactic mechanism, however, could not produce the circling of hatchlings with monocular blindfolds toward the covered eye which is occasionally observed. The observations indicating that hatchlings react differently to visual inputs to the temporal and nasal fields of view may account for this phenomenon. As yet, there is no information which suggests that the mechanisms which control sea finding are different in hatchlings and adults.

It has been suggested that *C. mydas* depends upon both olfactory and visual cues for guidance during their long-distance migrations, but this hypothesis has not been tested in the field. Hatchling *C. mydas* are capable of straight-line orientation when out of sight of land. The sensory basis of this ability is unknown. The use of visual cues has been implicated in the ability of several species of turtles to display a consistent direction of travel or to perform accurate homing behavior. The studies reporting that testudines employ celestial cues, however, are not especially convincing, and much additional work needs to be performed in this area (see also Schmidt-Koenig, 1975).

The reader will quite probably have noted that we have omitted numerous studies on the abilities of turtles to learn visual discriminations. Burghardt (1977) has recently reviewed these studies in great detail, and we felt it unnecessary to include them here. In brief, testudines have been found capable of learning brightness, hue, size, form, and position discriminations. Little consideration, however, has been given to how these abilities aid the various species of turtles in coping with the demands of their particular ecological niches.

REFERENCES

Anderson, P. K. (1958). The photic responses and water-approach behavior of hatchling turtles. *Copeia* pp. 211–215.

Ashe, V. M., Chiszar, D., and Smith, H. M. (1975). Behavior of aquatic and terrestrial turtles on a visual cliff. *Chelonia* **2**, 3–8.

Avery, G. T. (1928). Responses of foetal guinea pigs prematurely delivered. *Genet. Psychol. Monogr.* **3**, 245–331.

Bogert, C. M. (1937). Note on the growth rate of the desert tortoise, *Gopherus aggassizi. Copeia* pp. 191–192.

Breder, R. (1927). Turtle trailing: A new technique for studying the life habits of certain testudinata. *Zoologica (N.Y.)* **9**, 231–243.

Burghart, G. M. (1977). Learning processes in reptiles. *In* "Biology of the Reptilia" (C. Gans and T. S. Parsons, eds.), vol. 7. Academic Press, New York (In press).

Cagle, F. R. (1944). Home range, homing behavior, and migration in turtles. *Misc. Publ., Mus. Zool., Univ. Mich.* **61**, 1–34.

Carr, A. (1967). "So Excellent a Fishe." Nat. Hist. Press, Garden City, New York.

Carr, A. (1972). The case for long range chemoreceptive piloting in *Chelonia. In* "Animal Orientation and Navigation" (S. Galler, K. Schmidt-Koenig, G. Jacobs, and R. Belleville, eds.), pp. 469–483. N.A.S.A., Washington, D.C.

Carr, A. (1975). The ascension island green turtle colony. *Copeia* pp. 547–555.

Carr, A., and Carr, M. H. (1970). Modulated reproductive periodicity in Chelonia. *Ecology* **51**, 335–337.

Carr, A., and Carr, M. H. (1972). Site fixity in the Caribbean green turtle. *Ecology* **53**, 425–429.

Carr, A., and Ogren, L. (1960). The ecology and migrations of sea turtles. IV. The green turtle in the Caribbean Sea. *Bull. Am. Mus. Nat. Hist.* **121**, 1–48.

Colbert, E. H. (1969). "Evolution of the Vertebrates." Wiley, New York.

Daniel, R. S., and Smith, K. U. (1947). The sea-approach behavior of the neonate loggerhead turtle (*Caretta caretta*). *J. Comp. Physiol. Psychol.* **40**, 413–420.

Ehrenfeld, D. W., and Carr, A. (1967). The role of vision in the sea finding orientation of the green turtle. (*Chelonia mydas*). *Anim. Behav.* **15**, 25–36.

Ehrenfeld, D. W., and Koch, A. L. (1967). Visual accommodation in the green turtle. *Science* **155**, 827–828.

Emlen, S. T. (1969). Homing ability and orientation in the painted turtle (*Chrysemys picta marginata*). *Behaviour* **33**, 58–76.

Fraenkel, G. S., and Gunn, D. L. (1961). "The Orientation of Animals." Dover, New York.

Frick, J. A. (1976). Orientation and behaviour of hatchling green turtles (*Chelonia mydas*) in the sea. *Anim. Behav.* **24**, 849–857.

Goin, C. J., and Goin, O. B. (1971). "Introduction to Herpetology." Freeman, San Francisco, California.

Gould, E. (1957). Orientation of box turtles *Terrapene c. carolina* (Linnaeus). *Biol. Bull.* **112**, 336–348.

Gould, E. (1959). Studies on the orientation of turtles. *Copeia* pp. 174–176.

Gourley, E. V. (1974). Orientation of the gopher tortoise, *Gopherus polyphemus. Anim. Behav.* **22**, 158–169.

Granda, A. M., and O'Shea, P. J. (1972). Spectral sensitivity of the green turtle (*Chelonia mydas mydas*) determined by electrical responses to heterochromatic light. *Brain, Behav. Evol.* **5**, 143–154.

Hayes, W. N., and Hertzler, D. R. (1967). Role of the optic tectum and general cortex in reptilian vision. *Psychon. Sci.* **9**, 521–522.

Hayes, W. N., and Ireland, L. C. (1972). A study of visual orientation mechanisms in turtles and guinea pigs. *Brain, Behav. Evol.* **5**, 226–239.

Hayes, W. N., and Saiff, E. I. (1967). Visual alarm reactions in turtles. *Anim. Behav.* **15**, 102–106.

Hayes, W. N., Hertzler, D. R., and Hogberg, D. K. (1968). Visual responsiveness and habituation in the turtle. *J. Comp. Physiol. Psychol.* **65**, 331–335.

Hendrickson, J. R. (1958). The green turtle Chelonia mydas (L.) in Malaya and Sarawak. *Proc. Zool. Soc. London* **130**, 455–535.

Hertzler, D. R., and Hayes, W. N. (1967). Cortical and tectal function in visually guided behavior of turtles. *J. Comp. Physiol. Psychol.* **63**, 444–447.

Hertzler, D. R., and Hayes, W. N. (1969). Effects of monocular vision and midbrain transection on movement detection in the turtle. *J. Comp. Physiol. Psychol.* **67**, 473–478.

Hodos, W., and Campbell, C. B. G. (1969). Scala naturae: Why there is no theory in comparative psychology. *Psychol. Rev.* **76**, 337–350.

Hogberg, D. K. (1968). The effects of cortical spreading depression, tectal and cortical lesions, and caffeine on optokinetic nystagmus habituation and reflex rebound in the painted turtle. Doctoral Dissertation, SUNY at Buffalo, Buffalo, New York (unpublished).

Hooker, D. (1908). Preliminary observations on the behavior of some newly-hatched loggerhead turtles (*Thalassochelys caretta*). *Carnegie Inst. Washington, Yearb.* No. 6, pp. 111–112.

Hooker, D. (1909). Report on the instincts and habits of newly-hatched loggerhead turtles. *Carnegie Inst. Washington, Yearb.* No. 7, p. 124.

Hooker, D. (1911). Certain reactions to color in the young loggerhead turtle. *Carnegie Inst. Washington Publ.* **132**, 71–76.

Ireland, L. C. (1976). Optokinetic behavior of the hatchling green sea turtle, *Chelonia mydas*. (In preparation).

Ireland, L. C., and Babcock, R. A. (1976). Optokinetic behavior of the hatchling loggerhead sea turtle, *Caretta caretta*. (In preparation).

Ireland, L. C., Frick, J. A., and Wingate, D. B. (1976). Nighttime orientation of hatchling green sea turtles (*Chelonia mydas*) in open ocean. (In preparation).

Ireland, L. C., and Gans, C. (1972). The adaptive significance of the flexible shell of the tortoise *Malacochersus tornieri*. *Amin. Behav.* **20**, 778–781.

Ireland, L. C., Hayes, W. N., and Laddin, L. H. (1969). Relation between frequency and amplitude of visual alarm reactions in *Pseudemys scripta*. *Anim. Behav.* **17**, 386–388.

Ireland, L. C., and Rose, E. L. (1976). Optokinetic behavior of the hatchling snapping turtle, *Chelydra serpentina*. (In preparation).

Koch, A. L., Carr, A., and Ehrenfeld, D. W. (1969). The problem of open-sea navigation: The migration of the green turtle to Ascension Island. *J. Theor. Biol.* **22**, 163–170.

Lemkau, P. (1970). Movements of the box turtle, *Terrapene c. carolina* (Linnaeus) in unfamiliar territory. *Copeia* pp. 781–783.

McFarlane, R. W. (1963). Disorientation of loggerhead hatchlings by artificial road lighting. *Copeia* p. 153.

Manton, M. L., Karr, A., and Ehrenfeld, D. W. (1972). A method for chemoreception study in the green turtle. *Brain, Behav. Evol.* **5**, 188–201.

Mowrer, O. H. (1936). "Maturation" vs. "learning" in the development of vestibular and optokinetic nystagmus. *J. Genet. Psychol.* **48**, 383–404.

Mrosovsky, N. (1968). Nocturnal emergence of hatchling sea turtles: Control by thermal inhibition of activity. *Nature (London)* **220**, 1338–1339.

Mrosovsky, N. (1970). The influence of the sun's position and elevated cues on the orientation of hatchling sea turtles. *Anim. Behav.* **18**, 648–651.

Mrosovsky, N. (1972). The water-finding ability of sea turtles. *Brain, Behav. Evol.* **5**, 202–225.

Mrosovsky, N., and Carr, A. (1967). Preference for light of short wavelengths in hatchling green sea turtles, *Chelonia mydas*, tested on their natural nesting beaches. *Behaviour* **28**, 217–231.

Mrosovsky, N., and Shettleworth, S. J. (1968). Wavelength preferences and brightness cues in the water finding behavior of sea turtles. *Behaviour* **32**, 211–257.

Mrosovsky, N., and Shettleworth, S. J. (1974). Further studies of the sea-finding mechanism in green turtle hatchlings. *Behaviour* **51**, 195–208.

Nichols, J. T. (1939). Range and homing of individual box turtles. *Copeia* pp. 125–127.

Noble, G. K., and Breslau, A. M. (1938). The senses involved in the migration of young fresh-water turtles after hatching. *J. Comp. Psychol.* **25**, 175–193.

Ortleb, E. P., and Sexton, O. J. (1964). Orientation of the painted turtle, *Chrysemys picta*. *Am. Midl. Nat.* **71**, 320–334.

Parker, G. H. (1922). The crawling of young loggerhead turtles toward the sea. *J. Exp. Zool.* **36**, 323–331.

Polyak, S. (1957). "The Vertebrate Visual System." Univ. Chicago Press, Chicago, Illinois.

Pritchard, P. (1967). "Living Turtles of the World." Crown T. F. H. Publications, New York.

Romer, A. S. (1968). "The Procession of Life." World Publ. Co., Cleveland, Ohio.

Routtenberg, A., and Glickman, S. E. (1964). Visual cliff behavior in undomesticated rodents, land and aquatic turtles, and cats (Panthera). *J. Comp. Physiol. Psychol.* **58,** 143–146.

Schiff, W. (1965). Perception of impending collision. *Psychol. Monogr.* **79,** No. 604.

Schiff, W., Caviness, J. A., and Gibson, J. J. (1962). Persistent fear responses in Rhesus Monkeys to the optical stimulus of "Looming". *Science* **136,** 982–983.

Schmidt-Koenig, K. (1975). "Migration and Homing in Animals." Springer-Verlag, Berlin and New York.

Sherrington, C. (1947). "The Integrative Action of the Nervous System," 2nd ed. Yale Univ. Press, New Haven, Connecticut (originally published, 1906).

Smith, K. U., and Bojar, S. (1938). The nature of optokenetic reactions in mammals and their significance in the experimental analysis of the neural mechanisms of visual functions. *Psychol. Bull.* **35,** 193–219.

Verheijen, F. J., and Brouwer, J. M. M. (1972). Orientation of *Podura aquatica* (L.) (Collembola, Insecta) in a natural angular radiance distribution. *Neth. J. Zool.* **22,** 72–80.

Walk, R. D. (1965). The study of visual depth and distance perception in animals. *In* "Advances in the Study of Behavior" (D. S. Lehrman, R. A. Hinde, and E. Shaw, eds.), vol. 1, pp. 99–154. Academic Press, New York.

Walk, R. D., and Gibson, E. J. (1961). The study of visual depth and distance perception in animals. *Psychol. Monogr.* **75** (No. 519).

Walls, G. L. (1942). "The Vertebrate Eye and its Adaptive Radiation." Cranbrook Inst. Sci., Bloomfield Hills, Michigan.

Williams, J. E. (1952). Homing behavior of the painted turtle and musk turtle in a lake. *Copeia* pp. 76–82.

Woodbury, A., and Hardy, R. (1948). Studies of the desert tortoise, *Gopherus agassizi. Ecol. Monogr.* **18,** 145–200.

Yerkes, R. M. (1904). Space perception of tortoises. *J. Comp. Neurol. Psychol.* **14,** 17–26.

8

The Gas Bubble Disease of Fish

G. C. McLEOD

I.	Introduction	319
II.	Adaptation to Supersaturation	320
III.	Supersaturation: An Environmental Problem	324
IV.	Experimental Induction of Gas Bubble Disease in Adult Atlantic Menhaden	324
V.	Testing Procedure for Gas Supersaturation	328
VI.	Symptomatology of Gas Bubble Disease in Menhaden	330
VII.	The Interaction of Changing Temperatures and Supersaturation of Gases in Adult Menhaden	332
VIII.	Conclusions	334
	References	338

I. INTRODUCTION

In the early nineteen hundreds, Gorham (1898, 1899), Marsh (1903, 1904), and Marsh and Gorham (1905), biologists at the Fisheries Aquarium at Woods Hole, noticed that apparently healthy fish in several aquaria suddenly began swimming erratically and lost equilibrium. Within several hours the fish were dead. There were gas vesicles beneath the cornea and in the loose connective tissue of the eye causing marked exopthalmia, and in the mucous membrane of the mouth and gills along the lateral lines of the fish and in the fins. All of the blood vessels were found to contain quantities of free gas, which varied from a few small bubbles to large bubbles which distended the bulbous of the heart. The main vessels of the gills were sometimes filled with gas bubbles extending into the capillaries. The gas-filled auricle was still beating without propelling any blood. Death was due to astasis caused by bubbles forming in the larger vessel of the systemic circulation in the heart, blocking the flow of blood.

Gorham and Marsh attributed the disease to an abnormal gas content of the aquaria water. An analysis of gas from tissues and blood vessels was 90–92% nitrogen, with the remainder oxygen. They suggested that hemoglobin can modify the effects of oxygen supersaturation by combining with the dissolved oxygen and removing it from its dissolved state. They concluded that "gas bubble disease" is caused by nitrogen gas.

Lobsters (*Homarus*) and the horseshoe crab (*Limulus*), mollusks, hydroids, and the sea spider were found to be susceptible to gas bubble disease. Some green algae were also reported to develop and emit gas bubbles which Marsh and Gorham presumed had originated during a period of water supersaturation.

Hughes (1968) reported the occurrence of gas bubble disease in lobsters (*Homarus americanus*) due to air leaks in a hatchery. Gas bubble disease was described in three species of bivalve mollusks by Malouf *et al.* (1972). After supersaturation had been produced by heating cold sea water in closed heat exchangers, water temperatures were raised from 1°–6°C to 20°C, giving oxygen saturations as high as 129%. Dissolved nitrogen levels were not reported. About 75% of oysters (*Crassostrea virginica* and *C. gigas*) held in the heated water developed symptoms, and about 10% of the affected oysters died. Hard clams (*Mercenaria mercenaria*) were less severely affected, and suffered few mortalities.

The first symptoms reported in the oysters were crescent-shaped conchiolin blisters in the shell bordering the mantle. Gas bubbles were observed in the gill filaments and in the outer layers of the mantle. In severe cases the shell cavity became filled with conchiolin blisters. Hard clams showed obvious lightening of the gill coloration due to the presence of bubbles preventing free blood circulation.

Marsh and Gorham (1905) described other instances of naturally supersaturated waters and suggested prevention of gas bubble disease by removal of excess dissolved gases by aeration. The supersaturation was corrected at Woods Hole Marine Fisheries Aquarium by replacing a leaky suction intake pipe.

II. ADAPTATION TO SUPERSATURATION

Water may be supersaturated in a number of ways (Lindroth, 1957; Weitkamp, 1972): (1) by a dissolved gas contained in a mixture containing a higher percentage of the gas than normally found in air; (2) by a gas dissolved under higher than atmospheric pressure; (3) by a gas dissolved at a lower temperature; and (4) by mixing two bodies of saturated water of different temperatures.

Gas bubble disease occurs only when the uncompensated total gas pressure is greater in the water than in the blood. At supersaturation the diffusion pressure between the dissolved gas phase and the atmospheric phase favors a net transfer of gases from the water to the air. If the transfer does not take place fast enough by diffusion, gas bubbles form. On the other hand, the gas bubble cannot form in the water unless gas nuclei are present, and unless the total dissolved gas pressure exceeds the sum of the compensating pressures, such as hydrostatic pressure. Therefore, hydrostatic pressure is a major preventative factor in gas bubble disease. The effect of hydrostatic pressure is to oppose gas bubble formation; for example, one cannot blow a bubble out of a tube immersed in water unless the gas bubble in the tube slightly exceeds the hydrostatic pressure at the end of the tube. In a similar manner, a bubble cannot form in water, blood, or in any tissue until the total gas pressure exceeds the sum of the atmospheric pressure. Normally, gas bubbles form in fresh water to a depth of about 1 m when total dissolved gas pressure is equal to 1.10 atm, but they do not form below that level.

Excessive total dissolved gas pressure relative to ambient atmospheric pressure is a threat to all organisms in the euphotic zone. If a fish or food organism were to remain within a meter of the surface in waters having a total dissolved gas pressure of 1.1 atm, they are capable of developing gas bubble disease, especially if their body pressures further decrease gas solubility by physical activity, metabolic heat, increased osmolarity, or decreased blood pressure. Hydrostatic pressure only opposes bubble formation—it does not decrease the kinetic energy of dissolved gas molecules except at extreme pressures. If this were not the case, aerobic animal life would be eliminated at or below a water depth equivalent to the pressure of oxygen because there would be no oxygen pressure to drive oxygen across the gill membranes and thence into the blood.

Another example will clarify the importance of total dissolved gas pressure. Eutrophic lakes often become supersaturated with photosynthetic dissolved oxygen, and such lakes commonly approach or exceed 120% of saturation values for oxygen, but this represents an additional dissolved oxygen gas pressure of only about 32 mm Hg (O_2 = 159.19 mm Hg × 0.02 = 31.03 mm Hg) which equals 1.011 atm of total dissolved gas pressures. The imbalance can be compensated for by metabolic oxygen consumption, blood pressure, or both. On the other hand, a thousandfold increase in the saturation level would only increase the total dissolved gas pressure by about 1.8 mm Hg, or 1.8 mm Hg × 760 mm Hg = 1.002 atm. This would not cause gas bubble disease.

In spring waters dissolved oxygen pressures may be low in dissolved nitrogen while other gas pressures are high. F. Schnieder (1971) showed that dissolved nitrogen was reported to be 121% of the air saturation value, whereas oxygen was 16% of the saturation value. The total gas pressure was 0.016 dry atmospheric pressure. Fish were living in this water and although they probably suffered from hypoxia, there were no symptoms of gas bubble disease (Water Quality Criteria, 1972).

A number of authors determined that bubble formation is promoted by boundary zones or surface interfaces which reduce surface tension and thereby decrease the dissolved gas pressure. Gas nuclei are apparently required for bubble formation. These nuclei are in a sense an equilibrium between an extremely high compressive energy of surface tension and the pressure of contained gases. Lack of gas nuclei may, in fact, account for those unusual circumstances where extremely high but uncompensated dissolved gas pressures in fact fail to cause bubble formation. Gas nuclei are produced by anything that increases gas solubility of surface tension, and they can be eliminated by extremely high pressure which drives them back into solution.

At a water depth of 30 m the air is at a pressure of 4 atm; since the solubility of gas in a liquid such as blood is proportional to the pressure of the gas, four times more nitrogen is dissolved in blood at 30 m than at the surface.

The gas volume control mechanism in near-surface dwelling fish works as follows (Hall, 1924): As the fish ascends, gas is released from the bladder through a gas-absorbing gland. As the bladder is filled, a countercurrent exchanger, a series of fine blood vessels, functions to allow the molecules to pass from the arterial vessels to other thin wall vessels. Blood at the end of the series of blood vessels next to the bladder is in equilibrium with high oxygen pressure in the bladder. As the blood starts back to the heart the venous capillaries carry off large quantities of oxygen. This oxygen is transferred to the incoming arterial system. Thus, venous blood at an oxygen pressure equal to that of the incoming arterial blood is established. The process prevents blood from carrying oxygen away from the swim bladder through the fine series of blood vessels called the rete mirabili, but does not account for the secretion of gas. The gas secretion is accomplished by a gland that secretes CO_2 and lactic acid in the blood; this in turn increases the oxygen pressure. As the oxygen is in equilibrium with gas in the swim bladder, an increase in pressure forces gas out of the blood and into the swim bladder (Jacobs, 1930; Scholander and van Dam, 1954). Scholander and van Dam (1954) cited the two principal steps, i.e., the chemical dissociation of the oxygen by the acid and/or CO_2 from the oxyhemoglobin and a countercurrent exchange (the retes), which retain gases inside of the swim bladder with minimal loss to the outside.

Further experiments raised a number of questions about the role of CO_2 and lactic acid. In reevaluating much of the evidence, it seemed clear that there is agreement that the retes act as an effective countercurrent diffusion exchange mechanism for oxygen, CO_2, and nitrogen. The question is how the oxygen is split off from the blood. Fishes that do not possess retes and which secrete only nitrogen into the swim bladder pose another problem (Scholander and van Dam, 1954; Scholander, 1957). Since in certain salmonoid fishes tested neither the nitrogen nor the oxygen capacity of blood is sufficiently large to account for the tension found in the swim bladder by a simple diffusion process, some sort of active transport must be taking place. There are two possibilities.

Perhaps nitrogen can diffuse into bubbles of oxygen, which then pass to the swim bladder, carrying both oxygen and nitrogen (Powers et al., 1932). Koch

(1934) proposed that gas solubilities are depressed locally through the action of a gas gland, allowing an inert gas such as nitrogen to diffuse across. Scholander and van Dam (1954) and Wittenberg (1958a) postulated an active secretion of oxygen in the form of minute bubbles (7 to 52 μm diameter) into which inert gases may diffuse and the bubbles then pass into the swim bladder with the inert gases. This assumes that oxygen is preferentially absorbed in fishes when nitrogen content of the fish swim bladder reaches such high values. Apparently the capillary network removes oxygen more rapidly than other gases.

Further work provided a concept of a watershell surrounding small bubbles which allows gas bubbles to become more enriched and the more soluble of the gases to dissolve in the surrounding water (Wyman *et al.*, 1952). The shell is essentially an air–water interface that supports a uniform diffusion gradient. Experimental findings agree quite well with the theoretical composition ratios of inert gases. The fact that the gas mixture normally present in the swim bladder contains argon and nitrogen in a proportion similar to air has been established for a number of species.

The main questions are (1) How is oxygen split off from the blood in the area of the gas gland? (2) How are gradients maintained in fishes that lack rete mirabile? (3) How are bubbles formed, since tremendous pressures would be required to form such a small bubble.

These questions may be answered by studying the dissociation curves of fish blood, and the role of carbon dioxide in this process. It would also be desirable to learn more about the gases initially diffused in the swim bladder—where they are diffused, what they are, and in what concentrations they exist. Perhaps a reverse process may indeed take place, with oxygen being secreted into a nitrogen bubble.

The physiological and behavioral data suggest a surface zone in the water mass which is a critical zone for the well-being of fish, and below which fish are quite safe.

Cage and live box studies in the Columbia and Snake Rivers conducted by Ebel (1969) have shown that fish probably need to remain below a depth of 2.5 m in water of 123–143% nitrogen saturation in order to remain free of gas bubble disease symptoms.

Leham (1973) suggested a critical zone concept based on a threshold of 110% gas concentration. When the river has a gas content of 110% gas saturation, fish can inhabit all depths of the river without harm. When the river is at 120% saturation on the surface, the critical zone is down to a depth of about 3 ½ ft, where the gas content is 110% saturation. Below this level fish should not be harmed. At 130% saturation, the critical zone is 6 ⅔ ft, and at 140% saturation the boundary of the critical zone is 10 ft.

It is known that the high gas contents of river waters occur during the high runoff periods. Salmon gill net fishermen recognize the fact that during periods

of high current such as the spring runoff or during changes in the tide below
Bonneville, salmon go into the deeper waters to avoid the higher water velocities. In doing so they are insuring that they remain well below the critical
zone. This rheotactic response minimizes their exposure to the supersaturated
water.

III. SUPERSATURATION: AN ENVIRONMENTAL PROBLEM

For a long while, supersaturation was thought to be a problem that was limited
to water supplies of fish facilities, although there were some reports that spill-
ways of hydroelectric dams in Sweden caused supersaturation. Ebel (1969, 1970,
1971) and Beiningen and Ebel (1971) reported that spillway dams caused gas
bubble disease and may be limiting factors for the existence of aquatic life on the
Columbia and Snake Rivers. Other investigators reported gas bubble disease
among fish living in the heated effluents of steam generating and nuclear power
plants (Marcello and Fairbanks, 1974; DeMont and Miller, 1972; Marcello and
Strawn, 1972).

The inverse relationship between temperature and gas solubility in water in-
duces dissolved gas supersaturation in the thermal effluent of a power plant.
When natural waters are at or near saturation levels with dissolved gases and the
water temperature is increased in passage through a plant condenser system
without any equilibration with the atmosphere, the water becomes gas supersaturated. The return to normal saturation levels is a slow process, and often does not
take place before the discharge water is cooled by mixing and heat loss to the
environment. Fishes attracted to heated effluents supersaturated with dissolved
gases may develop gas bubble disease and die.

Since the Pilgrim Nuclear Power Station menhaden mortality, concern over
the potential problem of gas bubble disease at coastal power plants has increased.
However, with only a few reported cases of gas bubble disease mortality of fish
in the thermal effluents of power generating stations, experimental work is
needed to determine what environmental conditions and power plant design
features and modes of operation lead to gas bubble mortality of fish.

IV. EXPERIMENTAL INDUCTION OF GAS BUBBLE DISEASE IN
   ADULT ATLANTIC MENHADEN

The recognition that fishes are attracted to power plant thermal discharges
which may be supersaturated with dissolved gas prompted an experimental program to determine the tolerance of important species to gas saturation. An initial
problem was that the Atlantic menhaden had never been successfully maintained

in the laboratory. Our program focused on the capture and maintenance of menhaden and then an induction of gas bubble disease.

Menhaden are usually collected by purse seining. The purse seine "set" consists of a carrier vessel and a purse boat. A spotter plane locates the school and directs the purse boat in setting the net. When the school is encircled, lead weights are released to close the net and trap the fish. The net is hauled aboard the purse boat with the aid of a hydraulic power block until the school is concentrated into the heavily constructed pocket of the seine, called the bunt. Then the carrier vessel comes alongside the bunt, the fish are further "dried up," and brailed into the fish hold of the carrier vessel.

The best time to transfer the menhaden was as soon as the carrier vessel was secured adjacent to the bunt (Fig. 1). The fish were then transferred from the bunt with a dip net into an aerated 2.4 m diameter tank aboard our collecting vessel (Fig. 2). Approximately 150 fish were transported to the holding facility at the New England Aquarium (Fig. 3).

The holding facility (Fig. 4) incorporated three biological filters to break down nitrogenous waste products and a mechanical filter to remove particulate matter. Water was gravity siphoned into the biological filters, and then air lifted back into the tank. The mechanical filter pumped water from the bottom center of the tank through a sand filter and back into the tank at about a 60 gal/min flow. This return line helps in aeration of the tank as well as creating a current which

Fig. 1.   Capture technique.

Fig. 2.   Transferal.

Fig. 3.   Holding facility.

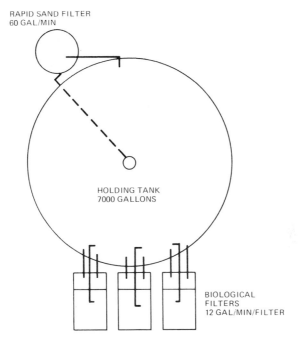

RAPID SAND FILTER
60 GAL/MIN

HOLDING TANK
7000 GALLONS

BIOLOGICAL
FILTERS
12 GAL/MIN/FILTER

Fig. 4.   Menhaden holding facility.

appears to aid in the schooling behavior of the fish. The walls of the holding facility were painted black to reduce the likelihood of fish colliding with the walls (J. H. Prescott, personal communication, 1974). The fish were fed finely grained food 4–5 times a day; total daily intake was approximately 5% of their body weight. Experimentation with various food sizes indicated that Purina tropical fish food gave the most efficient feeding since it remained in the water column long enough for maximum consumption.

No immediate losses were noted due to handling and transfer. However, during the first 2 weeks a total of 34 fish, or 22%, died, possibly from the effects of net damage. After the initial mortality, fish were maintained in outside pools for over a year. Standard water quality parameters were measured on a regular basis. During July and August the temperature remained about 20°C, but as cold weather set in the temperature steadily dropped to 13°C, and an abrupt color change occurred in some fish, from bright silver to black, possibly indicating thermal stress. Reduced feeding behavior and sluggishness were also noted. When the temperature was gradually increased to 18°–20°C, most of the darkened fish regained their original coloration, feeding behavior, and activity. It is presumed that those who did not recover were too weak to do so.

Salinity remained between 30 and 32 ppt, pH was maintained between 7.5 and 7.8, and dissolved oxygen between 6 and 7 ppm. Ammonia levels rose for 3 weeks to a maximum of 3.5 ppm until the bacterial population in the biological filter was established. Values then steadily declined to a stable level of 0.225 ppm, and the nitrate levels subsequently rose from 0.5 ppm to a maximum of 2.5 ppm. Nitrite also rose from 0.006 ppm to 1.5 ppm during the same period. Water changes were made as necessary to keep nitrate and nitrite levels below 3 ppm NO_3^- and 1.5 ppm NO_2^-.

V. TESTING PROCEDURE FOR GAS SUPERSATURATION

Twelve fish were used in each experiment: six in the test tank and six in the control tank. The test and control tanks were 145 gal capacity. A 50-gal pressure chamber was attached to the test tank as detailed in Fig. 5. The pressure chamber was constructed of 60 cm diameter PVC pipe. A 1 hp pump provided water circulation through the pressure chamber, and a ball valve on the return line to the test tank provided control of pressure and water flow. Original experiments used a venturi method of aeration in the pressure chamber; however, in later experiments an air compressor was added to allow for higher saturations.

The temperature, dissolved oxygen, and dissolved gas pressure were measured at regular intervals during the experiment in both the control and test tanks. Dissolved gas pressure was measured with a Weiss saturometer made by Eco

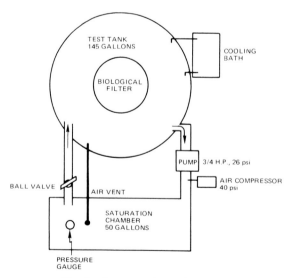

Fig. 5. Supersaturation testing system.

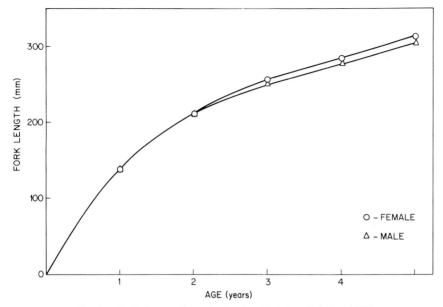

Fig. 6. Menhaden age determination (modified from Reintjes, 1969).

Enterprises, and the nitrogen saturation and total dissolved gas saturation calculated according to the equations:

$$\text{Total dissolved gas \% saturation} = (P_{atm} + \Delta P)/P_{atm}$$

where P_{atm} is the atmospheric pressure at time and altitude of saturometer reading and ΔP the saturometer reading.

% N_2 saturation

$$= \left[\frac{(P_{atm} + \Delta P) - [O_2/\beta O_2(22.41 \text{ ml/mmole}/32.00 \text{ mg/mmole}) \times 0.76] - P_{H_2O}}{(P_{atm} - P_{H_2O}) \times 0.7902} \ 100\right]$$

where O_2 is the oxygen concentration in mg/liter; βO_2 the Bunsen solubility coefficient for oxygen; P_{H_2O} the partial pressure of water vapor as a function of temperature; and T the observed temperature in °C.

As the test fish died, necropsies were performed as soon as possible. Weight, fork length, sex, and sexual maturation were determined and age estimated using a modification of a graph by C. E. Richards (Fig. 6). Of the 110 which died, fish length ranged from 225 to 330 mm, the average weight was 319 gm, 41% were males, and 59% were females. The majority of fish, 41.7%, were age two, 32.0% age three, 16.5% age four, and 9.7 age five.

VI. SYMPTOMATOLOGY OF GAS BUBBLE DISEASE IN MENHADEN

At 100% and 105% saturation of nitrogen, there are no gas bubbles externally or in any of the internal organs, although certain behavioral changes become apparent. At 100% saturation and up to 110% saturation of nitrogen, fish slough off mucus, swim erratically, and are more excitable than control fishes. The fishes are darker in color.

Although 110% saturation of nitrogen is not inferred as a definitive level of induction of gas bubble disease in fishes, behavioral changes similar to those observed at 105% were noted. Necropsies showed some evidence of emboli in the intestines, the pyloric ceca, and occasionally the operculum. Two fish died within 96 hr, one between 72 and 74 hr, and one between 80 and 96 hr. However, at 110% saturation symptoms of gas bubble disease did not appear in all fish.

At 115% saturation nitrogen, the same behavioral changes already cited are present, as are clearly defined external bubbles in some or all of the fins, and sometimes in the eye. Necropsy revealed 3–5 mm bubbles in the intestines and caeca.

At 120 and 130% nitrogen saturation, death occurred within 24 hr with classic symptoms of gas bubble disease. Temperatures of 15°–25°C made no significant

Fig. 7.   Exophthalmia in menhaden at high nitrogen saturations.

Fig. 8. Longitudinal line bubbles of the roof of the mouth.

Fig. 9. Bubbles in dorsal fin of menhaden.

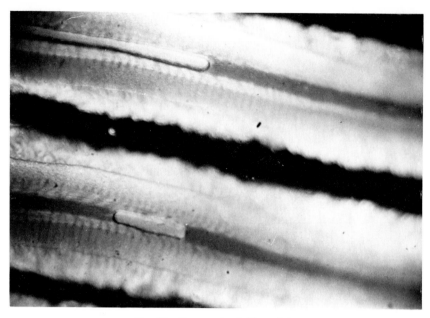

Fig. 10. Hemostasis of gill arterioles.

difference. Evidence of exopthalmia was apparent in the fish (see Fig. 7). Emboli were extensive in all high saturation test specimens in the pyloric ceca, intestines, eye, operculum, roof of mouth (see Fig. 8), epithelim of dorsal fin (see Fig. 9), mesentery, and gill arterioles (see Fig. 10). In two cases, the bulbous arteriosis was greatly distended by the presence of an embolus. The photomicrographs (Figs. 7–10) dramatically depict the classic symptoms of "gas bubble disease" in the specimens.

Figure 11 is a graphical summary of the percentage survival of adult menhaden to levels of supersaturation of nitrogen. Adult fish in our experiments succumb to gas saturations of 120–130% N_2 within 24 hr; at lower percentage saturations of N_2, fish may show symptoms of the gas bubble disease but may not die within the experimental period.

VII. THE INTERACTION OF CHANGING TEMPERATURES AND SUPERSATURATION OF GASES IN ADULT MENHADEN

As temperature plays an important role in the life of many fishes, it is important to determine its relationship to gas bubble disease. Temperature may be related to gas bubble disease in two ways: first, gas supersaturation at high temperatures may have a synergistic effect by lowering the thermal tolerance

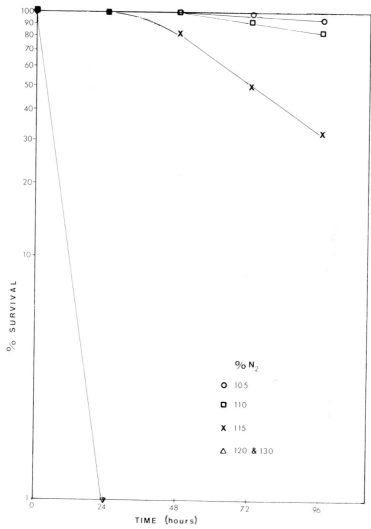

Fig. 11. Menhaden survival rate averaged over the temperature range of 15°–25°C.

level of fishes, and second, increased temperatures decrease the solubility of gases in the liquid and thereby increase the degree of gas saturation of the liquid. Technically, temperature and supersaturation are probably only significantly related by changes in solubility of dissolved gases with a temperature change. Increased supersaturation due to temperature rise defines the problem, rather than the lowering of thermal tolerance due to increased levels of dissolved gases. A

TABLE I
Development of Gas Bubble Disease Symptoms in Menhaden

% N₂ saturation	Observations
105	No external or internal bubbles
110	No external bubbles apparent, internal bubbles apparent only in intestines (1–3 mm)
115	External bubbles in some or all of the fins, sometimes in eye, bubbles usually ∼ 0.5–2.0 mm. Internal bubbles in intestines and ceca only. Bubbles in intestines 3–5 mm, ceca 1–3 mm
120	External bubbles in some or all of fins, always in the dorsal and caudal; operculum; roof of mouth; eyes. Internal bubbles in intestines, ceca, heart, bulbous arteriosis (with distention), swim bladder distention, hemostasis of gill arterioles with melanophores present, indicating stress. Bubbles maximum ∼ 10 mm at lower temperature and ∼ 5 mm at higher temperatures
130	External bubbles present in all fins, operculum, roof of mouth, eyes (exophthalmia with some bursting). Internal bubbles in all organs with severe distention of bulbous arteriosis and swim bladder, along entire length of gill arterioles in most cases, hemostasis obvious with melanophores present. Bubbles maximum ∼ 10 mm at lower temperatures and ∼ 5 mm at higher temperatures

review of the literature showed that most fish died due to symptoms of gas bubble disease, and that the lethal mechanism is not the same as that induced by high temperatures in saturated water (Ebel, 1971).

Tolerance of menhaden to temperatures between 15° and 30°C was determined in concert with gas saturation experiments. The most marked effect of temperature in gas saturation between 15° and 25°C is that the average bubble size at the lowest temperature condition was twice that at 25°C. At 30°C, all experimental fish died without gas saturation. The data are summarized in Tables I and II and in Fig. 12.

VIII. CONCLUSIONS

It is possible that physiological stress due to high activity levels can modify the tolerance of fishes to saturation. We have observed large schools of menhaden swimming for days in the discharge channel against an effluent water velocity of 8 knots. These fish have small bubbles in the fins. These bubbles are smaller than those induced by gas saturation in the laboratory. Presumably, swimming activity is a way of enhancing diffusion of the gas from the fish. The effect can be

TABLE II

Tolerance of Adult Menhaden to Gas Supersaturation at Varying Water Temperatures

Water temperature (°C)	Saturation (%)			Gas bubble disease: fish mortality in				Total number of fish tested	Survival (%)
	Nitrogen	Oxygen	Total	24 hr	48 hr	72 hr	96 hr		
30	No survival of fish								
25	130	130	125	12	—	—	—	12	0
	120	121	118	12	—	—	—	12	0
	110	112	107	0	0	0	1	12	92
	105	85	95	0	0	0	1	18	94
22	123	124	119	12	—	—	—	12	0
	115	91	108	0	2	2	2	12	50
	110	115	107	0	0	0	1	12	92
	105	92	100	0	0	0	0	18	100
15	130	134	126	12	—	—	—	12	0
	120	130	118	12	—	—	—	12	0
	110	110	105	0	0	1	1	12	83
	105	95	100	0	0	0	0	18	100

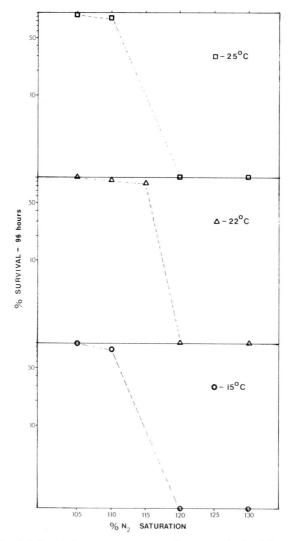

Fig. 12. Relationship between temperature and gas saturation in adult menhaden.

duplicated in the laboratory, and there is recovery from exposure to supersaturation. It is also possible that the small bubbles are of nitrogen only, whereas environmentally induced gas bubble disease creates bubbles of both O_2 and N_2.

Other considerations include the ability of fishes to detect and avoid water supersaturated with dissolved gases. Meldrim *et al.* (1974) found that the behavioral responses of some freshwater fish to supersaturated conditions varied with the species. Yellow perch have no definite response to supersaturated water, while silver minnows are very responsive. Stickney (1968) observed that Atlantic herring tend to avoid highly gas-saturated water.

The ability of fish to detect and avoid supersaturated environments may be altered by other factors. Meldrim *et al.* (1974) report that the behavioral response of the golden shiner to supersaturated conditions may change, depending on the water temperature associated with the exposure.

More information is needed in regard to the following questions: How much time do the fish spend at various locations? At what depths do migrants travel, and how much time do migrants spend at the various depths? How does their passage through and over dams influence their susceptibility to gas bubble disease? What are the actual mortalities to juveniles and adults? How can the high supersaturations be reduced or avoided? These are some of the questions that need to be answered in order to adequately define the problem and seek logical solutions. Past and current laboratory studies have and will continue to provide pertinent information on the supersaturation problem. However, it is unlikely these studies alone will ever really define the problem or provide final solutions.

It is obvious that there is a critical lack of factual information as to what is actually happening to migratory fish populations. The menhaden fishery is a good example. Although there have been menhaden along our eastern coastline for many years, it is only within the last 4 years that the fishery has become commercially important. From a few million tons 4 years ago, the annual landings are now estimated at 70 million tons. The reason for the migration of menhaden into the New England area is unknown. Presumably, the fish come from deeper water toward the coastline in April and May, and as the coastal waters warm up, migrate into harbors, rivers, and estuaries in July and August to spawn. Juveniles leave the area in late October and November. Not only is the reason for the presence of a large fishery in the area unknown, but its predictability is uncertain. One year, large numbers of the fish may be sighted in Massachusetts Bay; the following year schools of fish may be virtually absent from Massachusetts Bay, but may be present south of Cape Cod and in Buzzards Bay.

Presumably, the attraction of adult menhaden to certain regions of the coastline in April or May is due to the change in temperature resulting from effluent plumes from the power plant. The initial stimulus of a change in temperature is a reason for menhaden to enter an effluent canal. A second stimulus may be provided by the velocity of waters in the effluent canal. But why schools of fish would remain in a canal that has a high velocity of water, a temperature change some 15 degrees different from the ambient water temperatures and close to the thermal tolerance of the fish, and high gas supersaturation is unknown. The available laboratory and field evidence suggests that temperature is a strong initial stimulus for the migratory behavior. Once in the warmer plume of water being discharged from a coastal power plant, the velocities of the discharge waters become important stimuli that continually attract the fish to remain in the warm, supersaturated waters.

REFERENCES

Beiningen, K. T., and Ebel, W. J. (1971). Dissolved nitrogen, dissolved oxygen, and related water temperatures in the Columbia and Lower Snake Rivers, 1965–69. *Natl. Mar. Fish. Serv., Data Rep.* No. 56.

DeMont, J. D., and Miller, R. W. (1972). First reported incidence of gas bubble disease in the heated effluent of a steam electric generating station. *Proc. 25th Annu. Meet., Southeastern Assoc. Game & Fish Comm.* **25,** 392–398.

Ebel, W. J. (1969). Supersaturation of nitrogen in the Columbia River and its effect on salmon and steelhead trout. *Fish. Bull.* **68,** 1–11.

Ebel, W. J. (1970). Effects of transportation on survival and homing ability of salmonids from the Snake River. *Bur. Comm. Fish., Biol. Lab., Prog. Rep.*

Ebel, W. J. (1971). Dissolved nitrogen concentrations in the Columbia and Snake Rivers in 1970 and their effect on chinook salmon and steelhead trout. *NOAA Tech. Rep., NMFS SSRF* **646.**

Gorham, F. P. (1898). Some physiological effects of reduced pressure on fishes. *J. Boston Soc. Med. Sci.* **3,** 50.

Gorham, F. P. (1899). The gas bubble disease in fishes and its cause. *Bull. U.S. Fish Comm.* **19,** 33–37.

Hall, F. G. (1924). The function of the swim bladder of fishes. *Biol. Bull.* **47,** 79–126.

Hughes, J. T. (1968). Grow your own lobsters commercially. *Ocean Ind.* **3,** 46–49.

Jacobs, W. (1930). Untersuchungen zuer Physilogie der Schwimmblase der Fischs. I. Uber die Gassekretion in der Schwimmblase von Physoklisten. *Z. Vergl. Physiol.* **11,** 565–629.

Koch, H. (1934). L'emission de gaz dans le visicule und Resorption in der Schwimmblase des Flassbausches. *Z. Vergl. Physiol.* **21,** 646–657.

Leham, B. (1973). Complying with supersaturated gas standard. Notes for mid-Columbia PUD's and Washington Dept. of Ecology Meeting on Revised Conceptual Plan (unpublished).

Lindroth, A. (1957). A biogenic gas supersaturation of river water. *Arch. Hydrobiol.* **53,** 589–597.

Malouf, R., Keck, R., Maurer, D., and Epifanio, C. (1972). Occurrence of gas bubble disease in three species of bivalve molluscs. *J. Fish. Res. Board Can.* **29,** 588–589.

Marcello, R. A., Jr., and Fairbanks, R. B. (1974). Gas bubble disease mortality of Atlantic menhaden, *Brevoortia tyrannus,* at a coastal power plant. Marine ecology studies related to the operation of Pilgrim Station, semiannual Rept. No. 4, 1974, pp. 1–10.

Marcello, R. A., Jr., and Strawn, R. K. (1972). The cage culture of some marine fishes in the intake and discharge canals of a steam-electric generating station, Galveston Bay, Texas. *Tex. A & M Univ., Sea Grant Publ.* No. TAMU-SG-72-206, pp. 1–267.

Marsh, M. C. (1903). A fatality among fishes in water containing an excess of dissolved air. *Trans. Am. Fish. Soc.* **32,** 192–193.

Marsh, M. C. (1904). Exopthalmia, or popeye, in fishes. *Am. Fish Cult.* August, p. 5.

Marsh, M. C., and Gorham, F. P. (1905). The gas disease in fishes. *U.S., Bur. Fish., Rep.* pp. 343–376.

Meldrim, J. W., Gilt, J. J., and Petrosky, B. R. (1974). "The Effects of Temperature and Chemical Pollutants on the Behavior of Several Estuarine Organisms," Bull. No. 11. Ichthyological Assoc.

Powers, E. B., Hopkins, F. G., Hickman, T. A., and Shipe, L. M. (1932). The relation of respiration of fishes to environment. *Ecol. Monogr.* **2,** 385–473.

Schnieder, F. (1971). "Nitrogen Supersaturation in the Columbia and Snake Rivers," EPA Reg. X, Summary Rep. USEPA, Research Triangle Park, North Carolina.

Scholander, P. J. (1957). Oxygen dissociation curves in fish blood. *Acta Physiol. Scand.* **41,** 340–344.

Scholander, P. J., and van Dam, L. (1954). Secretion of gases against high pressures in the swim bladder of deep sea fishes. I. Oxygen dissociation in blood. *Biol. Bull.* **107,** 247–259.

Stickney, A. P. (1968). Supersaturation of the coastal waters of the Gulf of Maine. *Fish. Bull.* **67,** 117–123.

Water Quality Criteria. (1972). Report prepared for the U.S. Environmental Protection Agency by the National Academy of Sciences, 1972.

Weitkamp, D. E. (1972). Dissolved gas monitoring at Grand Coulee Dam and Lake Roosevelt. Unpublished Rept. to U.S. Dept. of Interior, Bureau of Reclamation, Boise, Idaho, Seattle Marine laboratories, Seattle, Washington, pp. 1–63.

Wittenberg, J. B. (1958a). The secretion of inert gas into the swim bladder of fish. *J. Gen. Physiol.* **41,** 783–804.

Wittenberg, J. B. (1958b). Active transport of oxygen. *Biol. Bull.* **115,** 372–373.

Wyman, J. J., Scholander, P. F., Edwards, G. A., and Irving, L. (1952). On the stability of gas bubbles in sea water. *J. Mar. Res.* **11,** 47.

9

Underwater Acoustic Biotelemetry: Procedures for Obtaining Information on the Behavior and Physiology of Free-Swimming Aquatic Animals in Their Natural Environments

LEONARD C. IRELAND and JOHN W. KANWISHER

I.	Introduction	342
II.	Sound as a Medium for Underwater Telemetry	346
III.	Biological Applications of Underwater Acoustic Telemetry	349
	A. Tracking Studies	350
	B. Determining Depth	358
	C. Measuring Temperature	358
	D. Monitoring the Electrocardiogram	360
IV.	Construction of Telemetry Equipment and Equipping Animals with Transmitters	363
	A. Simple ''Pinger''	364
	B. Temperature Transmitter	365
	C. Pressure Transmitter	366
	D. Large Heartbeat Transmitter	366
	E. Small Heartbeat Transmitter	367
	F. Sonic Receiver and Hydrophone Preamplifier	368
	G. Directional Hydrophone	368
	H. Equipping Animals with Transmitters	370
V.	Conclusions and Speculations	372
	Appendix	373
	References	375

I. INTRODUCTION

The first prerequisite for obtaining a comprehensive record of the natural history of any species is the ability to maintain contact with the animals for long periods of time. In the case of animals which spend much or all of their lives in water, this has usually proven to be difficult or impossible, and our knowledge concerning the behavior and physiology of most species of aquatic organisms in their natural environment is limited. Most information on the life cycles of all but the most sedentary and accessible aquatic creatures has been derived indirectly, from fishery investigations or from laboratory studies. A brief survey of the techniques that have been used to maintain contact in the field with aquatic animals illustrates the many problems encountered in such investigations.

Man first learned about the natural history of aquatic animals by direct visual observation from above the surface of the water. Visual observations from shore or from a boat, however, provide information only on those species which live or travel within a few meters of the surface, and such observations are possible only in clear water, on calm days.

The most direct approach to studying animals underwater is to go diving. Unfortunately, even when equipped with the most advanced underwater breathing apparatus and protective suit, the diver's time beneath the surface is limited to only a few hours per day. Also, the diver soon finds that his terrestrially adapted locomotor and sensory abilities are ill-suited to gathering information in aquatic environments. The diver cannot travel great distances. His hearing is largely ineffective and nondirectional. Even in the clearest water, under the brightest sky, he can see no more than about 100 m. Underwater habitats and submersible vehicles extend the diver's time and range, but do nothing to improve the visibility.

Sonar or echo ranging has been used to monitor the movements of schools of fish past anchored boats (Cushing and Hardin-Jones, 1967; Groot and Wiley, 1965). Unfortunately, the identification of the species of animal, or individual animals, detected in this manner is virtually impossible.

Tagging and recapture studies in which animals are caught, equipped with tags which serve to identify individuals, and returned to the water have provided information concerning the movements and distribution (Carr, 1975; Hardin-Jones, 1968; Mather et al., 1967), and homing abilities of many species (Bertmar and Toft, 1969; Gunning, 1963; Tesch, 1970). One problem with such studies is that usually only a small percentage of the tagged animals are ever recaptured. Also, tagging studies often provide data more related to the distribution of commercial and sports fisheries than to the distribution of the species in question. They provide no information concerning an animal's actual travel path between the release and the recovery area.

A surface float attached by a line to a fish or other aquatic animal permits one to determine its travel path with great precision (Hasler *et al.*, 1958; Jahn, 1969; Winn *et al.*, 1964). Floats, however, produce physical drag, tend to hold the animal near the surface, and often produce irritation at the point where the line is attached to the animal's body (Stasko, 1971). For these reasons, the smallest possible floats are usually employed. The problems involved in maintaining visual contact with a small float generally restrict the use of this technique to daytime studies carried out in calm water. Further, the investigator must usually follow closely behind the animal, a procedure which may influence its behavior.

In recent years, ever increasing use has been made of telemetry to acquire information about animals in their natural habitat. Numerous telemetry studies have been performed with terrestrial animals, in situations where efficient radio transmission is possible (Craighead and Craighead, 1965; Cochran, 1972; Schneider *et al.*, 1971; Williams and Williams, 1967). Until recently, telemetry studies with aquatic animals have been relatively few because of the difficulty of propagating suitable energy through water.

Over ranges of more than a few meters, sound is the only practical form of energy for underwater telemetry (Kanwisher *et al.*, 1974b). Acoustic energy travels through water with little loss, whereas radio waves and light are rapidly absorbed. The procedures involved in acoustic telemetry are basically quite simple. An aquatic animal is equipped with a battery-powered transmitter which projects sound into the water, usually in all directions. The signal from the transmitter may serve to simply indicate the animal's position, or may be modulated to carry information concerning behavioral, physiological, or environmental variables. Ideally, the frequency or frequencies of sound projected by the transmitter should be either above or below the range of the animal's auditory sensitivity in order to minimize possible influences on its behavior. The investigator maintains contact with the animal by means of an underwater microphone or hydrophone, which may be directional. The output of the hydrophone is fed into a sonic detector or receiver. The receiver amplifies the acoustic signal and usually converts it to a tone audible to the investigator. If a directional hydrophone is used, it is possible to follow the animal by moving in the direction of maximum signal strength. A simple acoustic receiver and directional hydrophone are shown in Fig. 1. Animals equipped with acoustic transmitters are shown in Figs. 2 and 3.

Acoustic telemetry allows studies of the behavior and physiology of unrestrained aquatic animals over periods of time and in many situations in which it is impossible to obtain information by means of any other technique. Today's electronic technology allows the construction of equipment which enables one to maintain contact with an animal at ranges of over 5 km for several weeks, or which will send information such as heart rate and temperature over ranges of

Fig. 1. Sonic receiver and directional hydrophone for use in studies of the behavior and physiology of free-swimming aquatic animals. The bracket is used to attach the hydrophone to the tracking boat and allows the hydrophone to rotate 360° horizontally. The bracket also allows the hydrophone to be tilted from the water. (Photograph by L. Ireland.)

several hundred meters for several months. Acoustic telemetry has been used to obtain data from animals ranging in size from hatchling sea turtles to large tuna and sharks.

Our purpose here is to acquaint the investigator with both the potential advantages and limitations of acoustic telemetry. First, we consider sound as a medium for underwater telemetry, emphasizing those characteristics of sound in water which must be taken into account in order to select efficient equipment for a given experimental situation. We then review how acoustic telemetry has been used to obtain information from aquatic animals in the field. Next, we describe the construction of a sonic receiver, a directional hydrophone, and several types of acoustic transmitters which may be used to solve a variety of experimental problems. Finally, we indulge in a few speculations concerning future work with acoustic telemetry.

Fig. 2. A saithe or pollock (*Pollachius virens*) equipped with an acoustic transmitter. The transmitter is held in place by surgical thread. (Courtesy of SINTEF, Trondheim, Norway.)

Fig. 3. A snapping turtle (*Chelydra serpentina*) carrying an acoustic transmitter which sends information on heart rate. The transmitter is attached to four stainless steel screws driven into the animal's shell. Epoxy putty around the transmitter and on the shell helps prevent the transmitter and electrocardiogram electrodes from becoming entangled with plants or other materials. (Photograph by L. Ireland.)

II. SOUND AS A MEDIUM FOR UNDERWATER TELEMETRY

The practical range of an underwater acoustic telemetry system is determined by a large number of variables. These include the physical properties of sound in water, certain inhomogeneities in aquatic environments, the frequency and power of the transmitter, and the sensitivity and selectivity of the hydrophone and receiver.

Sound may be considered as a propagating pressure wave. As sound travels, it successively compresses and releases particles of the medium in its path. The form of the pressure change over time depends primarily upon the method of its generation. For purposes of this discussion, and for most practical purposes, acoustic transmitters may be considered to produce regular, alternate compressions and relaxations of the surrounding water, resulting in the production of sinusoidal pressure waves. A detailed discussion of all the variables affecting the propagation of sound through water is beyond the scope of this chapter, and only factors particularly relevant to acoustic telemetry are considered here. The reader is referred to Tucker and Gazey (1966) and Urick (1967) for excellent discussions of all aspects of underwater acoustics.

Consider a transmitter capable of radiating acoustic energy equally in all directions. If the surrounding medium, i.e., the water, were infinite, absolutely loss free, and uniform in all respects, then the spreading of the sound wave would be spherical, and the inverse-square law would precisely relate sound intensity to distance from the transmitter. Of course, one only rarely encounters situations in which these ideal conditions are approximated. Almost no acoustic transmitter radiates sound in an absolutely uniform manner. In practice, the pattern of sound projection of each type of transmitter must be determined experimentally. Also, no body of water is infinite, being bounded by the surface, its shores, and the bottom. Sound waves in water tend to be reflected downward from the surface, inward from the shores, and upward from the bottom. Thus, the sound waves tend to be somewhat channeled and, if this were the only additional factor involved, sound intensities would decrease more slowly than the inverse-square law would predict.

In addition to the decrease in sound intensity due to geometrical spreading, there is also loss due to absorption and the conversion of acoustic energy to heat. The amount of the loss depends upon the frequency of the acoustic signal. The loss is relatively small at low frequencies but rises rapidly with decreasing wavelength. Over the range of frequencies usually employed in underwater telemetry (20–250 kHz), the loss expressed as decibels per kilometer is approximately proportional to the square of the frequency. At 50 kHz the loss due to absorption is on the order of 12 db, relative to 1 dyne/cm² (1 μbar) at 1 m, per kilometer (Tucker and Gazey, 1966). In practice, we have found that for ranges up to several hundred meters, any frequency below 200 kHz is suitable. If a range of several kilometers is required, the frequency must usually be less than 30 kHz.

Practical acoustic telemetry equipment was made possible by advances in the miniaturization of electronic components and by the development of inexpensive piezoelectric ceramics. Piezoelectric materials change shape when a voltage source is connected to them. In acoustic transmitters this converts electrical energy to mechanical energy, generating pressure waves in the surrounding water. Conversely, such devices produce a small electric output when compressed. This allows them to be used as hydrophones, converting the acoustic energy radiated by the transmitter back into an electrical signal. The transducers employed in acoustic telemetry are usually made of lead zirconate titanate or barium titanate and are cast in the form of thin-walled cylinders or disks. Transducers of these shapes project sound in a sufficiently uniform manner for most biotelemetry applications.

Piezoelectric transducers are most efficient when they are driven at their resonant frequency. The resonant frequency of a piezoelectric cylinder or disk decreases with increasing diameter. The diameter of a cylindrical transducer with a resonant frequency of 200 kHz, which is suitable for sending signals over short distances, would be about 0.25 cm, while the diameter of a 20-kHz transducer, suitable for long-range telemetry, would be about 5.0 cm. Because of their size and weight, low-frequency transducers are difficult or impossible to use in studies with small animals.

As one increases the power applied to a piezoelectric transducer, the distance over which a transmitter can be heard also increases. Such an increase in power, however, is rarely a practical method of compensating for the increased attenuation in water of high-frequency signals. Because acoustic transmitters are powered by batteries, the maximum power which can be applied to a transducer will be determined by the size, shape, and weight of transmitter a given animal can carry, and by the desired life of the transmitter. For this reason, studies requiring the transmission of acoustic signals over long distances can usually be performed only with large animals which can carry large transmitters. Only with fish the size of large tuna (Carey *et al.*, 1971) and sharks (Standora *et al.*, 1972) has it been possible to use transmitters large enough to work efficiently at frequencies of 30 kHz or less. The transmitters employed by Carey *et al.* (1971) had a maximum range in calm, coastal salt water of about 8 km.

The sensitivity and selectivity of sonic receivers and hydrophones also partially determine the practical range of underwater transmissions. These factors are primarily a function of the state of electronic technology and are topics beyond the scope of this chapter. It should be indicated, however, that we are able to realize long ranges with acoustic telemetry primarily because extremely sensitive and selective receiving equipment is available. With current equipment, a good signal-to-noise ratio is usually obtained when the electrical input from the hydrophone to the receiver is 1 μV or greater. Since our hydrophones have a typical resistance of 1000 ohms, the amount of acoustic power that must be intercepted in order to hear this signal is only 10^{-15} W. Such a low minimum-detectable energy requirement is the key to the successful operation of long-distance acoustic telemetry links. As a working example, one of our acoustic transmitters suitable for use with small fish has an output of only 100 μW, equivalent to a sound pressure of about 32 db re 1 μbar at 1 m. A 10% efficient hydrophone must recover only 1×10^{-10} of this energy for the transmitter to be detected.

Certain inhomogeneities in aquatic environments may severely limit the range of acoustic transmissions. Dissolved chemicals, bubbles of gas, particles suspended in the water, objects on the bottom, and differences in temperature and pressure from one area of water to another absorb, reflect, refract, and otherwise interfere with acoustic signals. One consequence of these effects is that sound waves are attenuated more rapidly in salt water than in fresh. Only rarely, of course, does one have a choice concerning which kind of water to conduct experiments in. Bubbles of gas can be particularly troublesome. In extremely turbulent waters where a great deal of air is entrapped, for example near reefs, in white-water rivers, or in the water immediately below dams, an acoustic telemetry system which can routinely send information over distances of more than 1 km may have its effective range reduced to only a few meters. In situations where there is considerable attenuation of acoustic signals, radio telemetry may be used to carry out relatively short-range, short-term studies (Evans, 1971; Frank, 1968; Lonsdale and Baxter, 1968; Monan et al., 1975).

The reflection and refraction of sound waves by inhomogeneities in the water often creates a situation in which a signal from a transmitter may arrive at a hydrophone by way of several different paths, in addition to that of a straight line. These can involve reflections from the surface and the bottom. Even more complex paths are possible and usually present. Fortunately, since sound waves traveling the shortest distance through water are usually the least attenuated, multiple path effects usually do not interfere to any great degree with an investigator's ability to locate a transmitter with a directional hydrophone. Pressure waves traveling by different paths, however, can meet and combine to form waves of either higher or lower amplitude. This process can produce marked changes in sound intensity and even the momentary loss of the desired signal at the hydrophone. For this reason, frequency modulation of acoustic signals is usually superior to amplitude modulation as a means of encoding information for underwater telemetry. Multiple path effects are particularly troublesome in streams, small ponds, and laboratory tanks. In such situations, radio telemetry is often a more useful technique.

Relative motion between an acoustic transmitter and a hydrophone produces a doppler shift in the frequency of the signal. The velocity of sound in water is approximately 1500 m/sec. From this, one can calculate that a relative velocity of 1 knot (1.85 km/hr) between the transmitter and the hydrophone shifts the frequency of the signal about 0.03%. This can be a significant change when the frequency of a signal must be interpreted critically, i.e., when the signal is frequency modulated to carry information. Frequency-modulated transmitters, therefore, must be designed to provide excursions from the carrier frequency so great that these changes can not be mistaken for doppler effects.

Finally, one must consider the level of interfering background noise present in the proposed study area. Background noise can be generated by such diverse sources as wave action and aquatic animals. Man-made noise, like that from boat motors and SCUBA equipment, can also be troublesome. The intensity of background noise varies greatly from one location to another. In general, the shallow water tropics are the noisiest, particularly in the immediate vicinity of coral reefs. At Coconut Island in Hawaii the natural background noise is frequently over 100 times greater than that encountered at Friday Harbor in Puget Sound. Much of the noise off Hawaii appears to be produced by aquatic animals such as snapping shrimp and fish that graze on coral (Kanwisher et al., 1974b).

These remarks are meant to make one's ambitions more modest when considering the use of acoustic telemetry. It is simply not possible to send an acoustic signal across oceans with a transmitter of the size that can be carried by most aquatic animals. On the other hand, a small transmitter of simple design, operating at virtually any frequency, will allow an investigator to reliably locate an aquatic animal day after day in a small pond or lake. Within broad limits, we have found that the only way to determine if acoustic telemetry will aid in the solution of a particular experimental problem is to try it.

III. BIOLOGICAL APPLICATIONS OF UNDERWATER
ACOUSTIC TELEMETRY

One of the earliest experiments using acoustic telemetry was conducted by Parker S. Trefethen and James H. Johnson of the U. S. Bureau of Commercial Fisheries (now the National Marine Fisheries Service) during the winter of 1956. These biologists released an adult coho salmon (Oncorhynchus kisutch) fitted with a 132-kHz acoustic transmitter in a lake near Seattle, Washington, and followed it in an open boat equipped with directional receiving equipment. The chase lasted about 1 hr, covered a distance of a few hundred meters, and ended with the failure of the receiving gear. Fortunately, the two scientists were sufficiently encouraged by the results of the test to continue development of the equipment (Monan et al., 1975).

Surprisingly, the receiving equipment used in these early tracking studies (Trefethen, 1956; Trefethen et al., 1957) is comparable to the most sophisticated ever designed. A directional hydrophone was mounted in such a way that it could be turned in any direction beneath the surface of the water. A receiver–servo system automatically pointed the hydrophone toward the transmitter-equipped fish. Once the hydrophone was positioned toward or had ''homed'' on the transmitter, a separate echo-ranging device was used to determine the distance between the hydrophone and the animal. The range and bearing of the fish were displayed on a cathode ray tube. The depth of the fish was calculated from its range and the attitude of the hydrophone. Unfortunately, the equipment was extremely complex, expensive, and required that an ac generator be carried in the tracking boat. These factors discouraged its duplication by other scientists. The appearance of inexpensive, light-weight, battery-powered receivers a few years later made it possible for many investigators to make use of the technique. Since 1956, acoustic telemetry equipment has been used in over 200 studies.

A. Tracking Studies

The majority of studies involving underwater acoustic telemetry have been concerned simply with determining an animal's position over time. In many cases, the work was carried out or aided by organizations concerned with commercial fisheries. Johnson (1960) reported on the movements of chinook salmon (*Oncorhynchus tshawytscha*), coho salmon (*O. kisutch*), and steelhead trout (*Salmo gairdneri*) in the waters above the Bonnevile Dam in 1957. Johnson was able to plot the travel paths of 43 fish. In general, he found that all three species tended to travel along the shoreline, both in the slow moving water just above the dam as well as in currents of up to 60 cm/sec. The fish often stopped or slowed down during the night or when they encountered log rafts tied along shore.

Poddubny (1969) tracked migrating Russian sturgeon (*Acipenser güldenstadtii*) in several rivers. He was able to follow 182 fish over periods of from 2 to 181 hr. Poddubny paid particular attention to the jumping behavior of the fish. He reported that when they encountered eddies or sections of the river with a particularly complicated bottom topography, and if these areas were near steep or forested shores, some of the fish appeared disoriented. In such situations, they would frequently jump out of the water and then swim in a straight line along the shore. Poddubny suggested that this jumping behavior might allow them to orient by means of suprasurface visual landmarks when their underwater travel paths were complicated by unusual or conflicting cues. He also noted that the orientation and swimming speed of several sturgeons changed abruptly when they passed under a high-voltage power line spanning the river. The strength of the horizontal component of the magnetic field produced beneath the surface of the water by the power line was about equal to the strength of the earth's magnetic field. These observations suggest that this species may employ the natural lines of magnetic force which circle the earth as cues for orientation.

Yuen (1970) placed an acoustic transmitter in the stomach of a large skipjack tuna (*Katsuwonus pelamis*) at Kaula Bank, Hawaii, and was able to plot its daily travels for almost a week. The tuna made nightly journeys of from 25 to 106 km away from the bank and, with a single exception, returned to the bank each morning and remained there all day. Another skipjack was tracked off Penguin Bank, Hawaii for 12 hr. It also remained near the bank during the day and left the area during the night. Yuen interpreted his data as indicating that skipjacks are capable of accurate homing behavior and that they have a sense of time.

Leggett and Jones (1971) tracked 13 spawning American shad (*Alosa sapidissima*) in the Connecticut River. During the course of their work, transmitter-equipped fish made a total of 49 approaches to commercial drift gill nets. The shad were remarkably successful at avoiding the nets (see Fig. 4). Only one fish

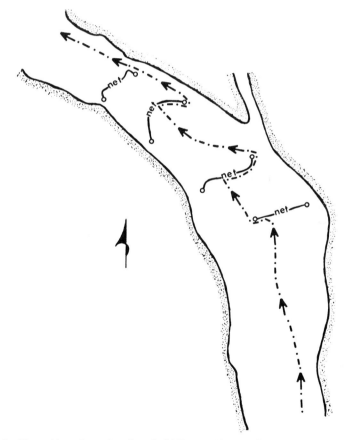

Fig. 4.   Net avoidance by an American shad (*Alosa sapidissima*) fitted with an acoustic transmitter. (From Leggett and Jones, 1971. Courtesy of Information Canada.)

was captured during the experiments. All the fish displayed similar behavior when approaching the nets. Typically, a shad swam to within 1 or 2 m of a net before appearing to sense its presence, then turned and swam parallel to it until reaching its end. The fish then again turned and continued its upriver journey. Leggett and Jones suggested that vision might play an important role in such avoidance behavior, but noted that 14 cases of net avoidance occurred when light intensities appeared inadequate to permit visual detection of the mesh. They suggested that other sensory processes, perhaps involving the lateral-line organs, are also used for net avoidance.

Working also in the Connecticut River with American shad, Dodson *et al.* (1972) found that five of the seven fish they tracked exhibited possible disorientation or "extensive meandering," which lasted for from 23 to 54 hr, when the fish were in the region of the saltwater–freshwater interface in the lower estuary. These movements appeared to result from a combination of passive drift and relatively inactive swimming. These five fish were tracked during all tidal conditions. Most of the time they remained near the leading edge of the salt water. Dodson and his associates suggested that keeping close to the interface serves to provide time for physiological adaptation of the fish to fresh water. Of the remaining two fish, one swam directly upstream without wandering, and one traveled downstream toward the sea.

Stasko *et al.* (1973) followed the coastal movements of pink salmon (*Oncorhynchus gorbuscha*) in the San Juan Channel, British Columbia. The fish were released at a location approximately 70 km south of the Fraser River, toward which they were presumably migrating. Stasko and his colleagues were able to track 11 salmon for periods of from 3 to 50 hr over distances of 2–127 km. The fish were classified as either "active" or "passive." Active fish swam more rapidly and had straighter travel paths. The tracks of the five active fish tended in the general direction of the Fraser River; those of passive salmon ended near or to the south of the release point. The active fish did not travel along the shoreline. Instead, they swam primarily along the axis of tidal currents. The fish traveled both with the northward flood and against the southward ebb currents, during the day as well as at night. The average speed of the active fish was about 2.2 km/hr. The authors suggested that the presumably inappropriate behavior of the passive fish might be due to trauma produced by handling or irritation from the transmitters.

The behavior of migrating sockeye salmon (*Oncorhynchus nerka*) entering the Skeena River estuary in British Columbia was studied by Groot *et al.* (1975). Fifteen of 18 salmon released and tracked in the lower river seemed to move passively in and out with the flood and ebb streams. Two of the fish moved upstream independent of the state of the tides, and one fish swam against both flood and ebb currents. Three additional salmon released in the ocean outside of the mouth of the river also seemed to ride the tidal flow passively. The tracks lasted for periods of from 0.6 to 33 hr and covered distances of 1–85 km. Groot and his assistants concluded that these passive movements were not an artifact and that sockeye salmon normally slow down or pause when they reach their "home river." The authors, however, offered no suggestions concerning the adaptive significance of this passive activity. The behavior of the majority of salmon in this study appears similar to that of the "passive" *O. gorbuscha* described by Stasko *et al.* (1973) and to that of *A. sapidissima* reported by Dodson *et al.* (1972). Further work will be required to determine if these passive movements are abnormalities produced by experimental manipulations or if such behavior is normally part of the animals' behavioral repertoires.

Ireland *et al.* (1976) equipped 11 hatchling green sea turtles (*Chelonia mydas*) with miniature acoustic transmitters and were able to track them at night during the animals' journey from their natal beach toward open ocean. The work was carried out off Burmuda with turtles hatched from eggs flown in from Tortuguero, Costa Rica. Because the smallest available transmitters proved too heavy for the hatchlings to carry, the transmitters were suspended from small balsa wood floats which were attached to the rear of each turtle's shell by a fine thread (see Fig. 5). The floats were almost neutrally buoyant and the turtles appeared to have little difficulty either towing them or pulling them under water. Hatchlings released on the same beach traveled seaward on similar headings. Turtles released from beaches facing in different directions displayed different travel paths. The tracks of all the turtles either approximated straight lines or took the form of gradual curves. The hatchlings maintained their headings when land was below the horizon from turtle eye level. Green sea turtle hatchlings, therefore, appear capable of accurate orientation at night in open ocean, immediately after they emerge from their nest. These results are in agreement with data collected earlier by Frick (1976) on daytime hatchling orientation.

Similar tracking experiments, in which the investigators were primarily concerned with the natural movements of their animals, have been performed with bull sharks (*Carcharhinus lucas*) (Thorson, 1971), sandbar sharks (*C. milberti*), and hammerhead sharks (*Sphyrna zygaena*) (Bass and Rascovich, 1965), Atlantic salmon (*Salmo salar*) (Elson *et al.*, 1972), chinook salmon (*Oncorhynchus tshawytscha*) (Becker, 1973; Hallock *et al.*, 1970; Trefethen and Sutherland, 1968), sockeye salmon (*O. nerka*) (Liscolm, 1973; Madison *et al.*, 1972), brown trout (*Salmo trutta*) (Holliday *et al.*, 1974), cutthroat trout (*S. clarki*) (Shepherd, 1974), rainbow trout (*S. gairdneri*) (Becker, 1973; Coutant, 1969), bluefin tuna (*Thunnus thynnus*) (Bass and Rascovich, 1965), bream (*Abramis brama*) and pike (*Esox lucius*) (Malinin, 1970a,b, 1971a,b), brown bullheads (*Ictalurus nebulosus*) (Kelso, 1974), burbots (*Lota lota*) (Malinin, 1971a,b), shad (*Alosa sapidissima*) (Dodson and Leggett, 1973), striped bass (*Morone saxatilis*) (Koo

Fig. 5. A hatchling green sea turtle (*Chelonia mydas*) shown with the acoustic transmitter and balsa wood float used to determine its seaward travel path following its departure from its natal beach. Although the float produces significant drag, it has the advantage of allowing the hatchling to rest unencumbered at the surface. (Photograph by L. Ireland.)

and Wilson, 1972), and tautogs (*Tautoga onitis*) (Olla *et al.,* 1974), as well as with eels (*Anguilla anguilla*) (Tesch, 1972, 1974), king crabs (*Paralithodes camtschatica*) (Monan and Thorne, 1973), and red-eared slider turtles (*Chrysemys scripta,* formerly *Pseudemys scripta*) (Moll and Legler, 1971).

Studies have also been performed in which aquatic animals were displaced to a location distant from their presumed home range, spawning grounds, or territory, equipped with acoustic transmitters, and followed to determine if they displayed accurate homing behavior. Hasler *et al.* (1969) captured 17 white bass (*Morone chrysops,* formerly *Roccus chrysops*) with nets on their spawning grounds along the eastern shore of Lake Mendota, Wisconsin. The fish were displaced 1.6 km west–southwest of the capture area to a mid-lake release point. Small acoustic transmitters were placed in the stomachs of each of the fish, and the animals were tracked for periods of from 4 to 11 hr over distances of from 1 to 10 km. All of the fish maintained steady courses and showed a distinct directional preference for the eastern half of the lake where their spawning grounds were located. These findings, and the results of float-tracking experiments performed with *M. chrysops* by Hasler *et al.* (1958), demonstrate that white bass are capable of accurate homing behavior. The studies indicate that the position of the sun, water currents, and wind-generated surface waves might all serve as cues for orientation. The specific cues employed by *M. chrysops* while homing, however, were not identified.

McCleave and Horrall (1970) displaced 42 adult cutthroat trout (*S. clarki*) from their spawning tributaries to several open water release sites in Yellowstone Lake, Wyoming. Each of the release sites was 2 km or more from shore. Five of the trout were anesthetized and blinded prior to release. Four control fish were also given anesthesia. All of the fish that received anesthesia were allowed time to recover from the effects of the drug before release. The fish were tracked for an average of approximately 5 hr over a mean distance of about 4.5 km. Fish displaced from the eastern side of the lake tended to travel in an easterly direction until they arrived near shore. They then chose the appropriate direction for along-shore movement to their spawning stream. Trout captured in streams on the western side of the lake behaved in a similar manner, except that their initial heading was in the opposite direction. Vision appeared to be unnecessary for accurate homing behavior. The behavior of blinded *S. clarki* was not appreciably different from that of either control fish that had received anesthesia or normal fish. In a more recent homing study conducted with *S. clarki* in Yellowstone Lake, however, McCleave and LaBar (1972) found that significantly fewer blinded trout displayed accurate homing behavior than did anosmic fish or control fish. The differences in the findings of McCleave and Horrall (1970) and McCleave and LaBar (1972) concerning the role of visual cues in the homing behavior of cutthroat trout have yet to be resolved.

The possibility that the spiny lobster (*Panulirus argus*) might display homing behavior was investigated by Herrnkind and McLean (1971). The study was carried out near a reef in Great Lameshur Bay, St. John, U. S. Virgin Islands. Five lobsters were equipped with saddle-shaped acoustic transmitters and tested in ten daylight releases. Two lobsters were blindfolded with opaque tape during two of the trials. Release sites were 200 m or more from the animals' capture sites. On all of the trials, except two, the lobsters returned to within 30 m of where they were caught. Of the two exceptions, one normal lobster moved in the homeward direction but continued on past the place where it was captured, and the second, a blindfolded animal, headed in the homeward direction but stopped when it reached the edge of a reef. The authors noted that the lobsters quickly adopted homeward bearings, indicating rapid recognition of whatever sensory cues they use for orientation. Acoustic telemetry studies concerned with the sensory basis of homing behavior have also been performed with shad (*A. sapidissima*) (Dodson and Leggett, 1974) and with coho salmon (*O. kisutch*) (Scholz *et al.,* 1973).

In the majority of tracking studies described above, contact with the animals was maintained by simply following them in a small, open boat equipped with directional receiving equipment. The investigators attempted to stay a relatively constant distance behind the animal, usually by estimating signal strength, and determined the position of the tracking boat either by reference to landmarks or by means of a sextant. This method of tracking requires both skill and patience, is limited by weather conditions and the dedication and endurance of the tracking crew, and leaves much to be desired concerning the accuracy with which an animal's position may be determined over time.

Several investigators have devised acoustic telemetry systems which in certain situations provide improved positional information and which, in some cases, are either partially or completely automated. Hallock *et al.* (1970) placed stationary acoustic receiving equipment at various points along streams and rivers in the Sacramento–San Joaquin Delta, California. Whenever a chinook salmon (*O. tshawytscha*) equipped with an acoustic transmitter passed near one of these "shore monitors," the event was recorded either on magnetic tape or on a strip chart. Trefethen *et al.* (1957) employed an echo-ranging device along with a directional hydrophone to determine both the bearing and range of transmitter-equipped fish. Kuroki *et al.* (1971) and Mitson and Storeton-West (1971) independently developed transponding acoustic transmitters suitable for use with fish. Transponding transmitters emit a sonic pulse only in response to an interrogation signal from the tracking boat or station. The time delay between the transmission of the interrogation signal and the reception of the sonic pulse from the transponder can be used to determine the distance between the transponder and the hydrophone. When used simultaneously with directional receiving equipment, both the bearing and range of the transponder can be obtained. Young *et al.* (1972) placed two remotely steerable directional hydrophones some distance apart on the bottom of Airthrey Loch, Scotland, and used them to determine the position of transmitter-equipped brown trout (*S. trutta*) by triangulation.

The most sophisticated acoustic tracking procedure reported to date was devised by Hawkins *et al.* (1974). Hawkins and his associates positioned arrays of either four or five omnidirectional hydrophones on the bottom of Lock Beag, Scotland. They determined the position of codfish (*Gadus morhua*) carrying acoustic transmitters by measuring differences in the time of arrival of sonic pulses at the hydrophones (see Fig. 6). The outputs of the hydrophones were fed to a storage oscilloscope, and delays in the arrival times of sonic pulses at the hydrophones were measured directly on the cathode ray tube of the scope (see Fig. 7). A group at SINTEF in Trondheim, Norway has developed similar tracking equipment, with the important difference that the outputs of the hydrophones are fed into a small computer and the position of the animal is recorded automatically on an X–Y plotboard (I. Mohus, personal communication).

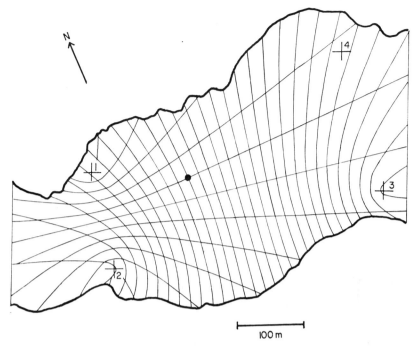

Fig. 6. Families of equal delay hyperbolas for two hydrophone pairs (no. 1 and no. 2, no. 2 and no. 3), superimposed on an outline of Loch Beag, Scotland. The spacing of the hyperbolas is at 20-msec intervals. For the fish shown, the pulse from the acoustic transmitter arrives at hydrophone no. 1, 20 msec before it arrives at hydrophone no. 2, and at hydrophone no. 2, 80 msec before it arrives at hydrophone no. 3. (From Hawkins *et al.*, 1974.)

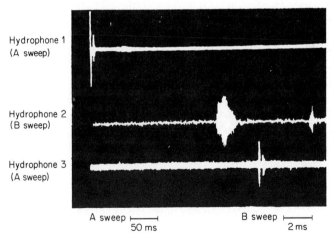

Fig. 7. Oscillogram illustrating the method of measuring differences in the time of arrival of an acoustic pulse at two hydrophones. The pulse arrives first at hydrophone no. 1 (top beam), triggering the slow time base (A sweep). The pulse arrives later at hydrophone no. 2 (lowest beam, A sweep). Greater accuracy in time measurement is obtained from the center beam, which has been delayed by a known time interval and which sweeps at a faster speed (B sweep). (From Hawkins *et al.*, 1974.)

B. Determining Depth

In the majority of tracking studies described above, the available equipment allowed only the horizontal components of the animals' movements to be determined. This shortcoming has limited the usefulness of acoustic telemetry for understanding the behavior of aquatic animals in waters where temperature, salinity, oxygen concentration, chemical composition, illumination, and currents vary with depth (Luke *et al.*, 1973).

Various types of receiving equipment allow one to determine the depth of an aquatic animal fitted with an acoustic transmitter or transponder with reasonable precision (Gardella and Stasko, 1974; Kuroki *et al.*, 1971; Trefethen *et al.*, 1957; Walker *et al.*, 1971). Also, transmitters which send data concerning the level of illumination in the vicinity of an animal provide accurate measures of depth in some situations (Gaiduk *et al.*, 1971). The easiest and most accurate method of determining depth, however, is to equip the animal with a transmitter which is capable of sensing and sending information about water pressure. The recent development of small and extremely sensitive silicon pressure transducers has made the construction of such devices possible. Several investigators have described the construction of pressure transmitters (see below). To date, however, few studies of the swimming depth of aquatic animals have been reported in the literature.

Stasko and Rommel (1974) captured five adult American eels (*Anguilla rostrata*), placed pressure-sensitive transmitters in their stomachs, and released them in Passamoquoddy Bay, New Brunswick. The transmitters projected a pulsed signal, and their pulse repetition rate varied linearly with depth. The eels were tracked for periods of from 4 to 40 hr over distances of up to 65 km. The animals made frequent dives from the surface to the bottom. At times they swam to depths of 45 m, at vertical speeds of up to 76 cm/sec. Approximately one-quarter of the eels' time was spent near the surface. The animals spent very little time near the bottom or at any constant intermediate depth. The eels were active both during the day and at night. Stasko and Rommel speculated that this pattern of diving activity might be a method of sampling water-current-generated electrical fields. These geoelectric fields may be employed by fish during ocean migrations (Rommel and McCleave, 1973; Rommel and Stasko, 1973). Such electrical currents are most intense near the surface and the bottom, and weakest at intermediate depths. A preliminary study of the swimming depth of yellowtails (*Seriola quinqueradiata*) was reported by Ichihara *et al.* (1972).

C. Measuring Temperature

Carey *et al.* (1971) used acoustic temperature transmitters to investigate thermoregulation in free-swimming bluefin tuna. Two temperature-sensitive thermistors were employed in the construction of each transmitter. Prior to each test, a transmitter and one of the thermistors was placed in a tuna's stomach. The other thermistor was led up the esophagus and out the last gill slit, so that the temperature of the water near the fish, as well as the fish's stomach temperature, could be measured. The transmitters broadcast pulsed signals. Pulse repetition rate was proportional to temperature. Stomach and water temperatures were sent for alternating 1-min periods. The tuna were captured, equipped with transmitters, and released in the ocean off the coast of Halifax, Nova Scotia. The investigators tracked the fish with a boat fitted with directional receiving equipment for periods of up to 54 hr and over distances in excess of 300 km. In general, most of the bluefins remained in water of remarkably constant temperature, usually staying near the surface or on the upper side of the thermocline. Some fish would swim down through the thermocline, but usually spent only a few minutes in the cold water before coming up again. One tuna swam from 16°C surface water into 5°C water below the thermocline immediately after release and remained there for about 4 hr (see Fig. 8). The fish then returned to 13°–14°C water on the upper side of the thermocline and remained there for most of the rest of the day. While the fish was in the cold water, its stomach temperature gradually decreased from 21° to about 18°C, and remained near 18°C after the fish returned to warm water.

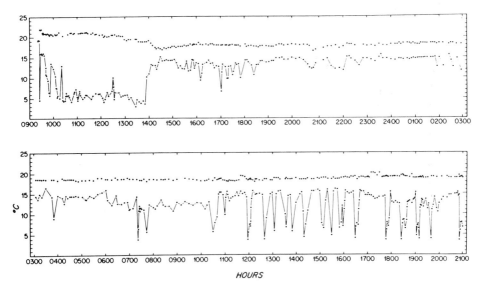

Fig. 8. Temperature record from a blue fin tuna (*Thunnus thynnus*). The upper trace shows stomach temperature, and the lower trace shows the surrounding water temperature. (From K. D. Lawson and F. G. Carey, unpublished manuscript, 1972. Courtesy of the Woods Hole Oceanographic Institution.)

Clearly, the fish was maintaining a remarkably constant deep-body temperature despite an 11°C decrease in water temperature for an extended period of time. The findings of Carey *et al.*, therefore, show that adult *T. thynnus* appear to thermoregulate during rapid changes in ambient temperature.

Using similar transmitters and tracking procedures, Carey and Lawson (1973) performed further investigations of thermoregulation in bluefins, and also investigated the possibility that bigeye tuna (*Thunnus obesus*) and dusky sharks (*Carcharhinus obscurus*) could thermoregulate. In these experiments, the bluefins were found to be capable of regulating the temperature of their epaxial muscles as well as their stomach temperature. Further, it was found that the bluefin does not have a fixed temperature setpoint. Fish captured from the same school were found to vary 5°C or so in their maximum muscle temperature, and on several occasions the stomach temperature of a fish was observed to change independently of water temperature. No evidence of an ability to thermoregulate was found in the case of either *T. obesus* or *C. obscurus*. Temperature studies with *S. quinqueradiata* have been reported by Ichihara *et al.* (1972), and several designs for acoustic temperature transmitters have been published (see below).

D. Monitoring the Electrocardiogram

While demonstrations of the use of acoustic telemetry to send electrocardiogram (ECG) information from animals moving freely in their natural environments have been reported (Baldwin, 1965), long-term studies of the ECG of free swimming animals appear to have been performed only in laboratory tanks. Wardle and Kanwisher (1974) used acoustic transmitters with a 3-week life to examine the ECG and heart rate of codfish (*G. morhua*). The cod were housed in a tank 10 m in diameter and 1 m deep. A transmitter was placed in the stomach of each fish and the active ECG electrode was placed next to the heart (see Fig. 9). The transmitter projected a continuous sonic signal. Signal frequency was shifted about 100 Hz/mV of ECG input. Inputs of 1 to 5 mV were observed. The cod were trained to race between two feeding points 8 m apart by association of underwater flashing lights with the appearance of food. During other tests, a fish was made to swim rapidly until it reached the point of exhaustion, by prodding it with a pole. Also, the fish were made to swim at slow speeds for long periods by projecting intense lights onto them. Wardle and Kanwisher found that low heart rates were characteristic of resting fish and that maximum rates were associated with exhaustion and rapid swimming. High rates continued during periods of oxygen debt repayment. Maximum heart rates were observed when the period between the recovery wave (T) and the initial wave (P) of the ECG was zero and were limited by the P to T period. The P to T period was not observed to vary in individual fish. Brief inhibition of heart rate was associated with the sudden

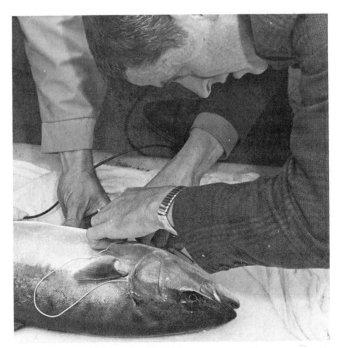

Fig. 9. Equipping a fish with an acoustic heart rate transmitter. The transmitter is located in the stomach, and the active electrode, brought out through the last gill arch, is inserted through the skin over the heart. (Courtesy of the U. S. National Marine Fisheries Service.)

introduction of novel stimuli and with maximum swimming exertion. Cardiac arrest could last for from 10 to 15 sec.

Kanwisher *et al.* (1974b) reported further examples of cardiac arrest phenomena. They found it to occur following the presentation of extremely subtle novel stimuli. A plaice (*Pleuronectes platessa*) was equipped with an acoustic ECG transmitter and allowed to settle to the sand on the bottom of a circular aquarium 18 m in diameter. The aquarium was 1.5 m deep and had opaque walls. It was mid-winter with low water temperatures, and the plaice appeared to be hibernating. In spite of its seeming lethargy, the fish reduced its heart rate in response to doors opening, the clicking of relays, and to any other sort of human activity in the vicinity. The most dramatic responses came early in the morning before local laboratory activity began. At this time, for example, if an investigator came quietly up to the tank and pushed a pencil a few centimeters over the edge, the plaice typically responded by stopping its heart for 8 or 9 sec. The results of similar experiments with *G. morhua* and *S. salar* are shown in Fig.

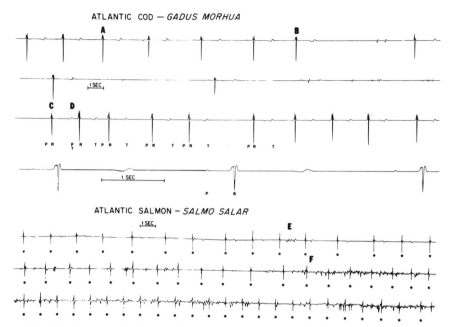

Fig. 10. Examples of electrocardiogram records from a free-swimming Atlantic cod and an Atlantic salmon. The experimenter approached the aquarium at A and looked over at B. Heart rate decreased. As the experimenter moved away, heart rate increased to the maximum rate observed (C). Note that the T wave is piled on the next P wave at D. When approached by the experimenter, the heart rate of the salmon also decreased (E). The salmon was chased with a pole beginning at F. This resulted in an accelerated ECG. The "noise" shown on the record from *S. salar* was produced by acoustic reflections from the walls of the aquarium. (From Kanwisher *et al.* 1974b. Courtesy of the U. S. National Marine Fisheries Service.)

10. In another test, a codfish which had been in captivity for more than a year and had largely habituated to the presence of people was approached with a dip net that it had not seen before. The cod stopped swimming, faced the approaching net, and extended its fins in what the investigators came to recognize as a fright response. Its heart stopped for 19 sec. Recently, we discovered that common snapping turtles (*Chelydra serpentina*) also display a reduced heart rate when confronted suddenly with novel, visual stimuli. The results of these preliminary experiments call into question the validity of many laboratory studies of the behavior and physiology of aquatic animals.

Acoustic ECG transmitters have also been used with human divers working in open ocean. Kanwisher *et al.* (1974a) equipped a group of Hawaiian SCUBA divers with both pressure and combination ECG and respiration transmitters in order to measure the physiological stresses they endured while setting fish traps at depths of 60 m or greater. These experienced divers did not follow accepted decompression procedures, often ascending to the surface more rapidly than recommended. In general, the divers' heart rates stayed in the neighborhood of 100 beats/min and their respiration rates stayed within normal limits, indicating that they experienced little stress. The low heart rates imply low cardiac outputs. Kanwisher and his colleagues suggest that such low outputs might result in the accumulation of smaller amounts of dissolved gases in the bodily tissues than might normally be expected, allowing more rapid decompression.

Gooden *et al.* (1975) equipped both amateur and experienced SCUBA divers with combination pressure and ECG transmitters. The divers then performed a survey of a coral reef. On the average, the heart rates of amateur divers were higher than those of experienced divers, and this difference was independent of swimming depth.

Other investigators besides Kanwisher *et al.* (1974a) and Gooden *et al.* (1975) have reported using transmitters capable of sensing and sending information about more than one parameter. Ferrel *et al.* (1973) designed a multichannel transmitter for work with sharks which is capable of sequentially sending data on compass heading, illumination, pressure, temperature, and swimming speed (see also Standora *et al.*, 1972). Fell *et al.* (1974) tested a multichannel unit with human divers. This transmitter is capable of monitoring heart rate, body temperature, skin temperature, and pressure. Baldwin (1965) described a transmitter capable of sending information on ECG and simultaneously providing olfactory stimulation.

IV. CONSTRUCTION OF TELEMETRY EQUIPMENT AND EQUIPPING ANIMALS WITH TRANSMITTERS

One of the reasons acoustic telemetry is not more widely used concerns the fact that commercially-built sonic receivers, hydrophones, and acoustic transmitters are expensive. A basic receiver and directional hydrophone together cost a minimum of about $1000. The prices of the simplest transmitters begin around $35, a significant amount for an item unlikely to be used more than once.

We have found that anyone with a moderate knowledge of electronics, who is willing to expend a little time and effort, can construct highly efficient equipment for less than one-quarter the commercial price. Those with no knowledge of electronics will find all the information necessary to understand the following circuit diagrams and commentary in Brophy (1972), Diefenderfer (1972), or Myers (1974). In addition to electronic theory, Myers provides many useful suggestions concerning construction techniques. An oscilloscope, a volt–ohm milliammeter, and a frequency generator are required for building the equipment described below. A digital frequency counter and a variable voltage dc power supply are useful. Most of the necessary electronic parts may be obtained locally.

Sources for hard to find components and commercially available acoustic telemetry equipment are given in the Appendix.

A. Simple "Pinger"

Figure 11 is a circuit diagram for a 50-kHz acoustic transmitter, which projects
pulses of sound at a rate of about 60/min. Pulsing the signal conserves battery
life. A transmitter of this type is usually referred to as a "pinger." The components are assembled inside a glass epoxy or stainless steel tube. Care must be
taken when soldering connections to the silvered inside or outside of the
piezoelectric transducer or to the battery. Excessive heat may damage either of
these components. When completed, the inside of the tube is filled with epoxy
casting resin. This procedure renders the transmitter completely waterproof.
Alternately, if the transmitter is to be used more than once, the electronic components can be potted in epoxy resin and the battery potted in waterproof silicone
rubber of the type used to seal aquariums. Two leads extending beyond the case
of the transmitter serve as a switch, and are soldered together in order to activate
the device. A magnetically controlled reed switch is also a convenient means of
turning on a sealed transmitter. The finished device is about 7.6 cm long and 2.0
cm in diameter, with a weight of approximately 20 gm in salt water. Pulse length
is about 500 μsec. Acoustic output is about 47 db re 1 μbar at 1 m. This gives a
range of up to 1.5 km in calm salt water when used with the receiver and

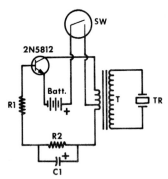

Fig. 11. Circuit diagram for a 50-kHz acoustic "pinger." C1, 10-μF, 6-V, tantalum capacitor;
R1, 680-ohm resistor; R2, 270 kohm resistor (increasing the value of R2 decreases the pulse repetition rate of the transmitter and vice versa); Batt., 4 2 V, 1000 mAh (milliampere-hours) mercury
battery; TR, Marine Resources Incorporated lead zirconate titanate cylinder, 1.65 cm o.d., 1.33 cm
i.d., 0.64 cm long, TCD-4 material; T, transformer wound on a Ferroxcube 1107P-A100-3B7 pot
core (primary, 25 turns no. 36 magnet wire, tapped at 9 turns; secondary, 220 turns no. 38 magnet
wire). (Increasing the number of turns on the transformer secondary decreases the frequency of the
transmitter and vice versa.); SW, switch. Adapted from a circuit design by K. Lawson.

directional hydrophone described below. The life of the transmitter is about 30 days.

Other designs for acoustic "pingers," or for simple transmitters which produce a continuous signal, have been published by Bass and Rascovich (1965), Henderson *et al.* (1966), Lund and Lockwood (1970), Monan *et al.* (1975), Monan and Thorne (1973), Novotny and Esterberg (1962), Rochelle (1974), Trefethen *et al.* (1957), and Young *et al.* (1972).

B. Temperature Transmitter

A circuit diagram for a 70-kHz temperature transmitter is shown in Fig. 12. Construction procedures for this device, and the other transmitters described in this chapter, are the same as for the simple "pinger." The finished transmitter is 1.4 cm in diameter and 5.0 cm long. Its weight is approximately 10 gm in salt water. The temperature-sensitive thermistor may either be located inside the transmitter or attached to waterproof leads and placed at some distant point. Temperature information in the range from 0° to 38°C is coded by a changing pulse rate. At 38°C the transmitter produces about 300 pulses/sec and at 0°C about 50 pulses/sec. Pulse length is 350 μsec. Acoustic output is 53 db re 1 μbar at 1 m. Life of the transmitter is about 6 days.

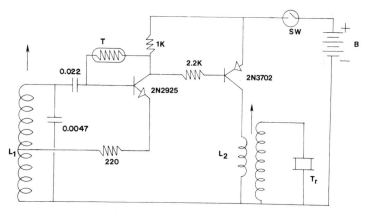

Fig. 12. Schematic for a 70-kHz acoustic temperature transmitter. T, Fenwall CA615MI thermistor; Tr, Marine Resources Incorporated 1.27 cm o.d., 1.11 cm i.d., 0.64 cm long ceramic transducer, TCD-4 material; L1, 300 turns no. 38 wire, center tapped, wound on 0.95 cm length of soda straw, tuned with 8-32 × 0.95 cm threaded ferrite slug; L2, primary, 35 turns no. 36 wire, secondary, 375 turns no. 38 wire wound on 0.95 cm length of soda straw, tuned with 8-32 × 0.95 cm threaded slug; B, 7 V, 160 mAh mercury battery; SW, switch. (From Monan *et al.*, 1975. Courtesy of the U. S. National Marine Fisheries Service.)

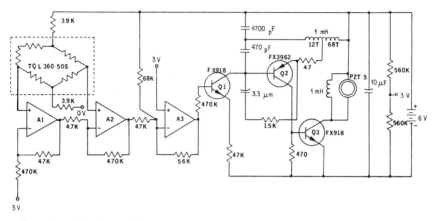

Fig. 13. Circuit diagram for a 75-kHz pressure sensing transmitter capable of determining the swimming depth of an aquatic animal. A1,A2,A3, Westinghouse WC788B; transducer, Vernitron 1.5 cm o.d., 1.34 cm i.d., 1.0 cm long. The center tapped coil is wound on a Ferroxcube 1107P-A100-3B7 pot core. Battery, 6 V, 120 mAh silver oxide. The value of the 68K resistor may have to be altered for proper operation. (From Luke *et al.*, 1973. Courtesy of Information Canada.)

C. Pressure Transmitter

A circuit diagram for a 75-kHz pressure transmitter is shown in Fig. 13. This device may be used to determine an animal's depth, or for such purposes as measuring the gas presssure in the swim bladders of large fish. The device is 1.6 cm in diameter, 7.0 cm long, and weighs about 17 gm in salt water. The pressure sensor (Kulite TQL-360-50S) is mounted at one end of the glass epoxy tube used to house the electronic components. Pressure is coded in terms of transmitter pulse rate. The device is functional at depths of from 0 to 40 m. Pulse rate at the surface is 40 pulses/min, and at 40 m 400 pulses/min. Pulse length is 300 μsec. A maximum depth of up to 70 m can be realized by substituting a Kulite TQL-360-100S pressure sensor. The transmitter has an accuracy of ± 0.35 m, and is stable over temperatures of 5°–20°C. The acoustic output of the device is about 42 db re 1 μbar at 1 m. Maximum signal range in salt water is slightly less than 1 km. Transmitter life is about 3 days. Kanwisher *et al.* (1974b) have published a schematic for a similar transmitter.

D. Large Heartbeat Transmitter

A circuit diagram for a 50-kHz ECG transmitter, suitable for use with large aquatic animals, is shown in Fig. 14. The continuous signal projected by this device is shifted about 200 Hz/mV of ECG input. The human ear can easily

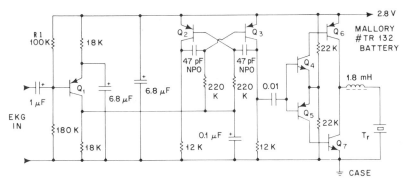

Fig. 14. Schematic for a large, 50-kHz, heartbeat transmitter. $Q_{1,2,3,5,6}$,2N5138; $Q_{4,7}$,2N5133; T_r, Vernitron transducer, PZT-4 ceramic cylinder 2.25 cm o.d., 1.93 cm i.d., 1.27 cm long; frequency deviation $\simeq$ 200 Hz/mV of EKG input. (From Kanwisher *et al.*, 1974b. Courtesy of the U. S. National Marine Fisheries Service.)

detect this change. If a permanent, pen-written record of the ECG is required, it is necessary to use a phase-locked receiver (see Kanwisher *et al.* 1974a). The transmitter is 2.5 cm in diameter, 8 cm long, and weighs 45 gm in salt water. The case is of stainless steel and serves as the indifferent electrode. Acoustic output is 42 db re 1 μbar at 1 m, giving a range in calm salt water of about 1 km. Transmitter life is 3 weeks.

In experiments with fish, it is sometimes convenient to place the transmitter in the animal's stomach. This is easily accomplished in a specimen anesthetized with MS-222. The active ECG lead is brought out under the last gill arch. It is then pushed under the skin immediately over the heart. The receiving hydrophone is held against the fish so that the transmitter can be monitored. The active electrode is then moved to different locations until an acceptable heartbeat signal is heard. The lead is then sutured in place. Most fish recover fully in a few hours. Placing transmitters in the stomach, however, may not be possible or desirable with some species (see below).

E. Small Heartbeat Transmitter

The schematic in Fig. 15 shows a smaller and less powerful 50-kHz ECG transmitter than the one described above. If resistor R1 is replaced by a thermistor, temperature will control the carrier frequency on which ECG information is superimposed. The device is 1.5 cm in diameter, 7.0 cm long, and weighs 16 gm in salt water. An acoustic output of 30 db re 1 μbar at 1 m provides a reliable signal at a range of 100 m. It will transmit for 3 weeks.

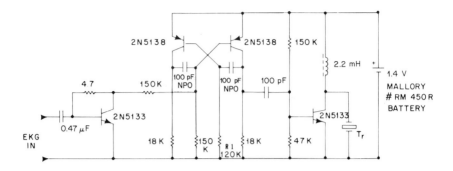

Fig. 15. Schematic for a small, 50-kHz, heartbeat transmitter. T_r, Vernitron transducer, PZT-4 ceramic cylinder 1.27 cm o.d., 1.02 cm i.d., 1.41 cm long; frequency deviation, $\simeq$ 200 Hz/mV of ECG input. (From Kanwisher *et al.*, 1974b. Courtesy of the U. S. National Marine Fisheries Service.)

F. Sonic Receiver and Hydrophone Preamplifier

Schematics for a simple beat frequency sonic receiver and a frequency-selective hydrophone preamplifier are shown in Fig. 16. Amplification within the hydrophone is important to eliminate interference from such sources as boat motor ignition. The combination works best at frequencies of from 45 to 55 kHz. A 1 μV, 50-kHz signal at the hydrophone is clearly audible at the headphones. The sensitivity of the system is about 3 db down at 45 and 55 kHz. The system's bandwidth may easily be reset. Decreasing the value of resistor R1 tunes the receiver for higher frequencies; increasing the value of R1 has the opposite effect. The hydrophone preamplifier must also be tuned for the new frequency range. This is accomplished by changing the value of capacitor C1. The proper value of C1 is determined by using the formula:

$$C1 \text{ (picofarads)} = [330 \times (50/\text{desired frequency in kHz})^2].$$

The value of resistor R2 must then be adjusted so that the preamplifier once again has a gain of 100.

G. Directional Hydrophone

Figure 17 provides all the information necessary for the construction of an inexpensive directional hydrophone. Beam width (3-db points) is 20° at 20 kHz. The beam width decreases at higher frequencies. The hydrophone can be mounted at the end of a hand-held stick or shaft, or to a rotating shaft fixed to the tracking boat. Brackets of the kind supplied with small, electric fishing motors are ideal for this purpose. The hydrophone can be used at speeds of up to several knots. If higher speeds are necessary, provision must be made for tilting the hydrophone out of the water. Alternately, a heavy-duty mount and streamlined

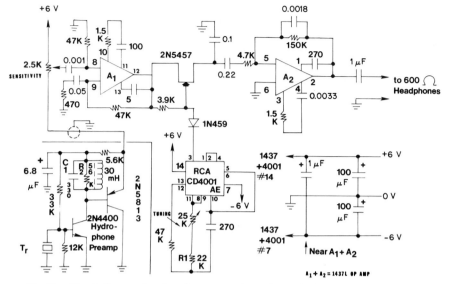

Fig. 16. Circuit diagrams for a beat frequency sonic receiver and a frequency selective (50-kHz) hydrophone preamplifier. The transducer, 2.25 cm o.d., 1.93 cm i.d., 1.27 cm long, TCD-5 material, is manufactured by Marine Resources Incorporated. Two transducers may be employed for slightly greater efficiency. Any 6-V batteries may be used. (Adapted from Kanwisher *et al.*, 1974b. Courtesy of the U. S. National Marine Fisheries Service.)

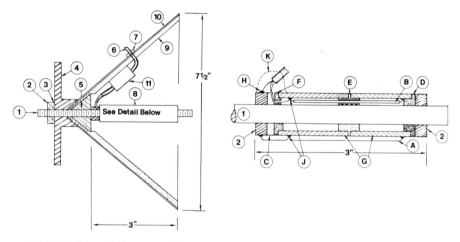

Fig. 17. Schematic for construction of a directional hydrophone with detail of preamplifier and transducer arrangements. (1) Stainless steel threaded shaft, ¼ in.; (2) stainless steel nut, ¼-20; (3) stainless steel lock washer; (4) galvanized deck flange, 1 in.; (5) brass "V" nut (custom made); (6) coaxial cable, RG58A/U; (7) rubber grommet, ¼ in.; (8) epoxy-formed coating; (9) neoprene, ¼ in.; (10) stainless steel conical reflector, 90°; (11) preamplifier. (A) Outside wire, #28; (B) inside wire, #28 insulated; (C) insulating washer, notched; (D) insulating spacer, front; (E) insulating spacer, center; (F) insulating spacer, rear; (G) ceramic transducers; (H) epoxy solder joint; (J) silver solder joint; (K) epoxy. (Adapted from Stasko and Polar, 1973. Courtesy of Information Canada.)

housing have been described which permit hydrophones of this type to be used at speeds of up to 9 knots (Stasko and Polar, 1973).

H. Equipping Animals with Transmitters

After constructing acoustic telemetry equipment, one must arrange for the animal of interest to carry the transmitter. External transmitter attachment produces drag and may produce trauma. Further, there is always the possibility that the transmitter may become entangled. Hallock *et al.* (1970) used pins and straps to hold transmitters on the backs of adult chinook salmon (*O. tshawytscha*) (see Fig. 18). Five different methods of mounting the devices were tested (see Fig. 19). They found that fastening a transmitter forward of the dorsal fin produced the best results; none of the tags were lost and none of the pins pulled out. All of these arrangements, however, produced some damage and irritation and the authors considered none of them entirely satisfactory. Numerous investigators have reported similar problems.

Stomach placement is usually accomplished by means of a hollow tube inserted in the esophagus. Stomach evacuation, however, is of major importance in controlling appetite and, therefore, feeding schedules (Windell, 1971). Also, some species have a tendency to regurgitate stomach-borne transmitters. For example, Henderson *et al.* (1966) found that about one-third of the 165 transmit-

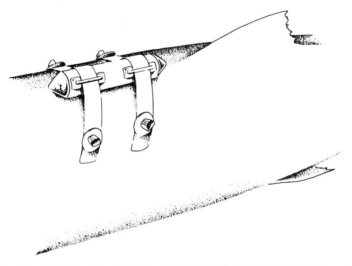

Fig. 18. Acoustic transmitter in place on the back of a chinook salmon (*Oncorhynchus tshawytscha*). The transmitter is held in place by means of straps made of mylar or nylon and plastic pins pushed through the back. (From Hallock *et al.*, 1970. Courtesy California Department of Fish and Game.)

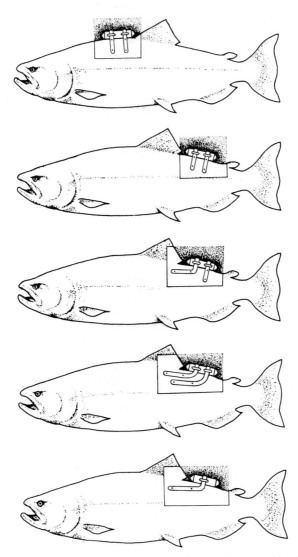

Fig. 19. Five different methods of mounting acoustic transmitters on chinook salmon (*On-corhynchus tshawytscha*). The procedure shown at the top proved best, but was not completely satisfactory (see text). (From Hallock *et al.*, 1970. Courtesy of the California Department of Fish and Game.)

ters they placed in the stomachs of white bass (*M. chrysops*) were expelled within a few days. Further, Hart and Summerfelt (1975) reported that all of three largemouth bass (*Micropterus salmoides*) and all of five flathead catfish (*Plodictis olivaris*) regurgitated transmitters within 24 hr. McCleave and Stred (1975) found that stomach-borne transmitters significantly reduced the swimming speed of Atlantic salmon smolts (*S. salar*), but that the reduction was not as great as when externally mounted transmitters were employed.

In an attempt to overcome these problems, Hart and Summerfelt (1975) developed surgical procedures for the implantation of acoustic transmitters into the peritoneal cavities of catfish (*P. olivaris*). Neither the survival nor the growth rate of the fish appeared to be affected by their procedures. The catfish were tracked for periods as long as 40 days in a large lake, and their behavior appeared entirely normal. The authors also reported using similar procedures successfully with both largemouth and striped bass (*M. saxatilis*). Such surgical procedures, however, may not be equally successful with all species. Henderson *et al.* (1966) reported a significantly lower recapture rate for white bass with transmitters implanted in the body cavity than for fish with transmitters in their stomachs or with transmitters mounted externally.

Whatever the method employed to equip an animal with a transmitter, the potential effects of the weight of the device on the animal's behavior must be taken into consideration. Attempts to compensate for increased negative buoyancy may lead to fatigue with accompanying changes in behavior and physiology. Further, some species of fish require time for buoyancy adjustments (Gallepp and Magnuson, 1972). Immediate release of such fish in a deep stratified lake would likely result in the fish sinking into the hypolimnion and dying. In less severe cases, an incorrect picture of their usual depth distribution might be obtained. One thing is certain; if a large animal will serve in one's experiments as well as a small animal, use the large animal. In the case of small animals, it may be necessary to suspend the transmitter from a float.

In summary, it appears that no one has yet devised a single "best" method of equipping aquatic animals with transmitters. We suggest that, whenever possible, members of the species to be tested in the field first be fitted with transmitters and observed in the laboratory. Both the animals' initial and long-term reactions to the devices should be noted. Such preliminary observations could result in considerable savings of both time and money.

V. CONCLUSIONS AND SPECULATIONS

We have tried to outline the possibilities and procedures for obtaining information concerning the behavior and physiology of aquatic animals by means of acoustic telemetry. We have shown that it allows investigations over periods of time, over distances, and in many environments in which it would otherwise be impossible to gain reliable data. The use of acoustic biotelemetry is expanding rapidly. The majority of studies in the area have been performed since 1970. Given the ever-increasing interest in the natural history, husbandry, and conservation of aquatic animals, the number of investigators employing acoustic telemetry equipment is likely to increase geometrically. The number of scientists currently using acoustic telemetry, however, is actually quite small. Therefore, there has been little motivation for the electronics industry to develop equipment specifically for this area. Consequently, we have been forced to improvise in our designs by using components produced for other purposes. These are occasionally what we would have developed ourselves if we could command the resources. Good examples are the COS/MOS oscillators used in electronic wrist watches, which allow the construction of extremely efficient and stable transmitters, and the recently developed lithium battery, which has a significantly higher power-to-weight ratio than any other battery currently available to the public (see Lyman, 1975). We are presently experimenting with these components. Sources for these parts are given in the Appendix.

Currently, acoustic telemetry studies must be considered labor intensive. One group of investigators usually follows and/or obtains data from one animal at a time. While automated tracking systems have been described for use in rivers and small lakes, keeping track of aquatic animals in large bodies of water is likely to remain a one-boat-to-one-animal affair for many years to come. The burgeoning state of electronic technology, however, promises rapid advances in methodology beyond the accomplishments we have cited here.

APPENDIX

As indicated in the text, acoustic telemetry equipment may be purchased already assembled, or the devices may be constructed from components available from various sources. Below are mentioned several major suppliers of acoustic telemetry equipment and sources for components which may be difficult to obtain locally.

Sonic Receivers, Hydrophones, and Acoustic Transmitters

Bayshore Systems Corporation
5406A Port Royal Road
Springfield, Virginia, 22151

Chipman Instruments
641 Charles Lane
Madison, Wisconsin, 53711

Dukane Corporation
Ultrasonics Division
St. Charles, Illinois, 60174

H. Tinsley and Company, Ltd.
Werdnee Hall, South Norwood
London, S. E. 25, England

Lawson Instruments
P. O. Box 428
Woods Hole, Massachusetts, 02543

Smith-Root, Incorporated
14014 N. E. Salmon Creek Avenue
Vancouver, Washington, 98665

Piezoelectric Transducers

Aquadyne Incorporated
P. O. Box 175
East Falmouth, Massachusetts, 02536

Gulton Industries, Incorporated
Gulton Street
Metuchen, New Jersey, 08840

Marine Resources Incorporated
755 Highways 17 and 92
Fern Park, Florida, 32730

Vernitron Piezoelectric Division
232 Forbes Road
Bedford, Ohio, 44146

Pressure Sensors

Kulite Semiconductor Products, Incorporated
1039 Hoyt Avenue
Ridgefield, New Jersey, 07657

Pot Cores (Ferroxcube)

North American Phillips Electronic Components
  Corporation
175 Scott Street
Elk Grove Village, Illinois, 60007

COS/MOS Oscillators

James Electronics
P. O. Box 822
Belmont, California, 94002

Glass Epoxy Tubing

Stevens Tubing Incorporated
128 N. Park Street
East Orange, New Jersey, 07019

Epoxy Casting Resins

Emerson and Cuming, Incorporated
Dielectric Materials Division
Canton, Massachusetts, 02021

The Dexter Corporation
Hysol Division
Olean, New York, 14760

*Miniature Electronic Components, Mercury
Batteries, and Silver-Oxide Batteries*

Newark Electronics
500 N. Pulaski Road
Chicago, Illinois, 60624

R S Electronics
12775 Lyndon
Detroit, Michigan, 48227

Lithium Batteries

Power Conversion Incorporated
70 MacQuestin Parkway S.
Mount Vernon, New York, 10550

ACKNOWLEDGMENTS

    We wish to thank all of our colleagues who kindly allowed us to use illustrations from their publications or from their unpublished work. Jane Frick, Kenneth Lawson, and David Wingate made many useful suggestions concerning this chapter. We thank Helen Poole for typing and painstakingly proofreading the manuscript.

REFERENCES

Baldwin, R. (1965). Marine biotelemetry. *BioScience* **15,** 95–97.

Bass, G. A., and Rascovich, M. (1965). A device for the sonic tracking of large fishes. *Zoologica* **50,** 75–82.

Becker, C. D. (1973). Columbia River thermal effects study: Reactor effluent problems. *J. Water Pollut. Control Fed.* **45,** 850–869.

Bertmar, G., and Toft, R. (1969). Sensory mechanisms of homing in salmonid fish. I. Introductory experiments on the olfactory sense in grilse of Baltic Salmon (*Salmo salar*). *Behaviour* **35,** 235–241.

Brophy, J. (1972). "Basic Electronics for Scientists," 2nd ed. McGraw-Hill, New York.

Carey, F. G., and Lawson, K. D. (1973). Temperature regulation in free-swimming bluefin tuna. *Comp. Biochem. Physiol.* **44,** 375–392.

Carey, F. G., Teal, J. M., Kanwisher, J. W., Lawson, K. D., and Beckett, J. S. (1971). Warm-bodied fish. *Am. Zool.* **11,** 137–145.

Carr, A. (1975). The Ascension Island green turtle colony. *Copeia* no. 3, 547–555.

Cochran, W. W. (1972). Long distance tracking of birds. *In* "Animal Orientation and Navigation" (S. R. Galler, K. Schmidt-Koenig, G. J. Jacobs, and R. E. Belleville, eds.), pp. 39–59. NASA, Washington, D.C.

Coutant, C. C. (1969). Temperature, reproduction and behavior. *Chesapeake Sci.* **10,** 261–274.

Craighead, F. C., Jr., and Craighead, J. J. (1965). Tracking grizzly bears. *BioScience* **15,** 88–92.

Cushing, D. H., and Hardin-Jones, F. R. (1967). Sea trials with modulation sector scanning sonar. *J. Cons., Explor.* **30,** 324–345.

Diefenderfer, A. J. (1972). "Principles of Electronic Instrumentation." Saunders, Philadelphia, Pennsylvania.

Dodson, J. J., and Leggett, W. C. (1973). Behavior of adult American shad (*Alosa sapidissima*) homing to the Connecticut River from Long Island Sound. *J. Fish. Res. Board Can.* **30,** 1847–1860.

Dodson, J. J., and Leggett, W. C. (1974). Role of olfaction and vision in the behavior of American shad (*Alosa sapidissima*) homing to the Connecticut River from Long Island Sound. *J. Fish. Res. Board Can.* **31,** 1607–1619.

Dodson, J. J., Leggett, W. C., and Jones, R. A. (1972). The behavior of adult American shad (*Alosa sapidissima*) during migration from salt to fresh water as observed by ultrasonic tracking techniques. *J. Fish. Res. Board Can.* **29,** 1445–1449.

Elson, P. F., Lauzier, L. M., and Zitko, V. (1972). A preliminary study of salmon movements in a polluted estuary. *In* "Marine Pollution and Sea Life" (M. Ruivo, ed.), pp. 325–330. Fishing News (Books) Ltd., New York.

Evans, W. E. (1971). Orientation behavior of delphinids: Radio telemetric studies. *Ann. N. Y. Acad. Sci.* **188,** 142–160.

Fell, R. B., Skutt, H. R., and Waterfield, A. (1974). A four-channel ultrasonic telemetry system for obtaining physiological data from ocean divers. *Biotelemetry* **1,** 50–59.

Ferrel, D. W., Nelson, D. R., Sciarrotta, T. C., Standora, E. A., and Carter, H. C. (1973). A multichannel ultrasonic marine bio-telemetry system for monitoring marine animal behaviour at sea. *Instru. Aerosp. Ind.* **19,** pp. 71–84.

Frank, T. H. (1968). Telemetering the electrocardiogram of free swimming *Salmo irideus*. *IEEE Trans. Biomed. Eng.* **15,** 111–114.

Frick, J. (1976). Orientation and behaviour of hatchling green turtles (*Chelonia mydas*) in the sea. *Anim. Behav.* **24,** 849–857.

Gaiduk, V. V., Malinin, L. K., and Poddubny, A. G. (1971). Determination of the swimming depth of fishes during the hours of daylight. *J. Ichthyol. (Engl. Transl.)* **11,** 140–143.

Gallepp, G. W., and Magnuson, J. J. (1972). Effects of negative buoyancy on the behavior of the bluegill, *Lepomis macrochirus* Rafinesque. *Trans. Am. Fish. Soc.* **101**, 507–513.

Gardella, E. S., and Stasko, A. B. (1974). A linear-array hydrophone for determining swimming depth of fish fitted with ultrasonic transmitters. *Trans. Am. Fish. Soc.* **103**, 635–637.

Gooden, B. A., Feinstein, R., and Skutt, H. R. (1975). Heart rate responses of SCUBA divers via ultrasonic telemetry. *Undersea Biomed. Res.* **2**, 11–19.

Groot, C., and Wiley, W. L. (1965). Time-lapse photography of an ASDIC echo-sounder PPI-Scope as a technique for recording fish movements during migration. *J. Fish. Res. Board Can.* **22**, 1025–1034.

Groot, C., Simpson, K., Todd, I., Murray, P. D., and Buxton, G. A. (1975). Movements of sockeye salmon (*Oncorhynchus nerka*) in the Skeena River Estuary as revealed by ultrasonic tracking. *J. Fish. Res. Board Can.* **32**, 233–242.

Gunning, G. E. (1963). The concepts of home range and homing in stream fishes. *Ergeb. Biol.* **26**, 202–215.

Hallock, R. J., Elwell, R. F., and Fry, D. H. (1970). Migrations of adult king salmon (*Oncorhynchus tshawytscha*) in the San Joaquin delta. *Calif. Dept. of Fish and Game, Fish Bull.* No. 151, 92 pp.

Hardin-Jones, F. R. (1968). "Fish Migration." St. Martin's Press, New York.

Hart, L. G., and Summerfelt, R. C. (1975). Surgical procedures for implanting ultrasonic transmitters in flathead catfish (*Pylodictis olivaris*). *Trans. Am. Fish. Soc.* **104**, 56–59.

Hasler, A. D., Horrall, R. M., Wisby, W. J., and Braemer, W. (1958). Sun-orientation and homing in fishes. *Limnol. Oceanogr.* **3**, 353–361.

Hasler, A. D., Gardella, E. S., Horrall, R. M., and Henderson, H. F. (1969). Open-water orientation of white bass, *Roccus chrysops,* as determined by ultrasonic tracking methods. *J. Fish. Res. Board Can.* **26**, 2173–2192.

Hawkins, A. D., MacLennan, D. N., Urquhart, G. G., and Robb, C. (1974). Tracking cod *Gadus morhua* L. in a Scottish sea loch. *J. Fish Biol.* **6**, 225–236.

Henderson, F. G., Hasler, A. D., and Chipman, G. G. (1966). An ultrasonic transmitter for use in studies of movements of fishes. *Trans. Am. Fish. Soc.* **95**, 350–356.

Hermkind, W. F., and McLean, R. (1971). Field studies of homing, mass emigration, and orientation in the spiny lobster, *Panulirus argus. Ann. N. Y. Acad. Sci.* **188**, 359–377.

Holliday, F. G. T., Tytler, P., and Young, A. H. (1974). Activity levels of trout (*Salmo trutta*) in Airthrey Lock, Sterling, and Loch Leven, Kinross. *Proc. R. Soc. Edinburgh* **75**, 315–331.

Ichihara, T., Soma, M., Yoshida, K., and Suzuki, K. (1972). An ultrasonic device in biotelemetry and its application in tracking a yellowtail. *Bull. Jpn. Sea Reg. Fish. Lab.* **7**, 27–48.

Ireland, L. C., Frick, J. A., and Wingate, D. B. (1976). Nighttime orientation of hatchling green sea turtles (*Chelonia mydas*) in open ocean. In preparation.

Jahn, L. A. (1969). Movements and homing of cutthroat trout (*Salmo clarki*) in Yellowstone Lake after displacement from spawning streams. *J. Fish. Res. Board Can.* **25**, 1243–1261.

Johnson, J. H. (1960). Sonic tracking of adult salmon at Bonneville Dam, 1957. *Fish. Bull.* **60**, 471–485.

Kanwisher, J., Lawson, K., and Strauss, R. (1974a). Acoustic telemetry from human divers. *Undersea Biomed. Res.* **1**, 99–109.

Kanwisher, J., Lawson, K., and Sundnes, G. (1974b). Acoustic telemetry from fish. *Fish. Bull.* **72**, 251–255.

Kelso, J. R. M. (1974). Influence of a thermal effluent on movement of brown bullhead (*Ictalurus nebulosus*) as determined by ultrasonic tracking. *J. Fish. Res. Board Can.* **31**, 1507–1513.

Koo, T. S. Y., and Wilson, J. S. (1972). Sonic tracking striped bass in Chesapeake and Delaware Canal. *Trans. Am. Fish. Soc.* **101**, 453–462.

Kuroki, T., Kawaguchi, K., Sakamuto, W., and Watanabe, H. (1971). A new telemetric apparatus to detect fish location and its surrounding water temperature. *Bull. Jpn. Soc. Sci. Fish.* **37**, 964–972.

Leggett, W. C., and Jones, R. A. (1971). Net avoidance behavior in America shad (*Alosa sapidissima*) as observed by ultrasonic tracking techniques. *J. Fish. Res. Board Can.* **28**, 1167–1171.

Liscolm, K. L. (1973). Sonic tags in sockeye salmon, *Oncorhynchus nerka,* give travel time through metropolitan waters. *Mar. Fish. Rev.* **35**, 38–41.

Lonsdale, E. M., and Baxter, G. T. (1968). Design and field tests of a radio-wave transmitter for fish tagging. *Prog. Fish Cult.* **30,**, 47–52.

Luke, D. McG., Pincock, D. G., and Stasko, A. B. (1973). Pressure-sensing ultrasonic transmitter for tracking aquatic animals. *J. Fish. Res. Board Can.* **30**, 1402–1404.

Lund, W. A., and Lockwood, R. C. (1970). Sonic tag for large decapod crustaceans. *J. Fish. Res. Board Can.* **27**, 1147–1151.

Lyman, J. (1975). Battery technology: Packaging more muscle into less space. *Electronics* **43**, 75–82.

McCleave, J. D., and Horrall, R. M. (1970). Ultrasonic tracking of homing cutthroat trout (*Salmo clarki*) in Yellowstone Lake. *J. Fish. Res. Board Can.* **27**, 715–730.

McCleave, J. D., and LaBar, G. W. (1972). Further ultrasonic tracking and tagging studies of homing cutthroat trout (*Salmo clarki*) in Yellowstone Lake. *Trans. Am. Fish. Soc.* **101**, 44–54.

McCleave, J. D., and Stred, K. A. (1975). Effect of dummy telemetry transmitters on stamina of Atlantic salmon (*Salmo salar*) smolts. *J. Fish. Res. Board Can.* **32**, 559–563.

Madison, D. M., Horrall, R. M., Stasko, A. B., and Hasler, A. D. (1972). Migratory movements of adult sockeye salmon (*Oncorhynchus nerka*) in coastal British Columbia as revealed by ultrasonic tracking. *J. Fish. Res. Board Can.* **29**, 1025–1033.

Malinin, L. K. (1970a). "The Use of Ultrasonic Transmitters in Tagging *Abramis brama* and *Esox lucius.* Report 1. The Reaction of Fish to Fishnet Panels," Transl. Ser. No. 1818. Fish. Res. Board Can., Ottawa.

Malinin, L. K. (1970b). "Use of Ultrasonic Transmitters for the Marking of Bream and pike. II. Behavior of Fish at the Mouth of Rivers," Transl. Ser. No. 2146. Fish. Res. Board Can., Ottawa.

Malinin, L. K. (1971a). "Behavior of Burbot," Transl. Ser. No. 2171. Fish. Res. Board Can., Ottawa.

Malinin, L. K. (1971b). "Home Range and Actual Paths of Fish in the River Pool of the Rybinsk Reservoir," Transl. Ser. No. 2282. Fish. Res. Board Can., Ottawa.

Mather, F. J., III., Bartlett, M. R., and Beckett, J. S. (1967). Transatlantic migrations of young bluefin tuna. *J. Fish. Res. Board Can.* **24**, 1991–1997.

Mitson, R. B., and Storeton-West, T. J. (1971). A transponding acoustic fish tag. *Radio Electron. Eng.* **41**, 483–489.

Moll, E. O., and Legler, J. M. (1971). "The Life History of a Neotropical Slider Turtle, *Pseudemys scripta* (Schoepff) in Panama," Nat. Hist. Bull. No. 11. Los Angeles County Museum.

Monan, G. E., and Thorne, D. L. (1973). Sonic tags attached to Alaska king crab. *Mar. Fish. Rev.* **35**, 18–21.

Monan, G. E., Johnson, J. H., and Esterberg, G. F. (1975). Electronic tags and related tracking techniques aid in study of migrating salmon and steelhead trout in the Columbia River basin. *Mar. Fish. Rev.* **37**, 9–15.

Myers, R. (1974). "The Radio Amateur's Handbook," 52nd ed. American Radio Relay League, Newington, Connecticut.

Novotny, A. J., and Esterberg, G. F. (1962). A 132-kilocycle sonic fish tag. *Prog. Fish Cult.* **24**, 139–141.

Olla, B. L., Bejda, A. J., and Martin, A. D. (1974). Daily activity, movements, feeding, and seasonal occurrence in the tautog, *Tautoga onitis. Fish. Bull.* **72**, 27–35.

Poddubny, A. G. (1969). Sonic tags and floats as a means of studying fish response to natural environmental changes and to fishing gears. *FAO Fish. Rep.* **62,** 793–801.

Rochelle, J. M. (1974). Design of gatable transmitter for acoustic telemetering tags. *IEEE Trans. Biomed. Eng.* **21,** 63–66.

Rommel, S. A., Jr., and McCleave, J. D. (1973). Sensitivity of American eels (*Anguilla rostrata*) and Atlantic salmon (*Salmo salar*) to weak electric and magnetic fields. *J. Fish. Res. Board Can.* **30,** 657–663.

Rommel, S. A., Jr., and Stasko, A. B. (1973). Electronavigation by eels. *Sea Front.* **19,** 219–223.

Schneider, D. G., Mech, D. L., and Tester, J. R. (1971). Movements of female raccoons and their young as determined by radio-tracking. *Anim. Behav. Monogr.* **4,** Part 1.

Scholz, A. T., Cooper, J. C., Madison, D. M., Horrall, R. M., Hasler, A. D., Dixon, A. E., and Poff, R. J. (1973). Olfactory imprinting in coho salmon: Behavioral and electrophysiological evidence. *Proc. Conf. Great Lakes Res.* **16,** 143–153.

Shepherd, B. G. (1974). Activity localization in coastal cutthroat trout (*Salmo clarki clarki*) in a small bog lake. *J. Fish. Res. Board Can.* **31,** 1246–1249.

Standora, E. A., Jr., Sciarrotta, T. C., Ferrel, D. W., Carter, H. R., and Nelson, D. R. (1972). "Development of a Multichannel Ultrasonic Telemetry System for the Study of Shark Behavior at Sea," TR-5. California State University, Long Beach Foundation.

Stasko, A. B. (1971). Review of field studies on fish orientation. *Ann. N. Y. Acad. Sci.* **188,** 12–29.

Stasko, A. B., and Polar, S. M. (1973). Hydrophone and bow-mount for tracking fish by ultrasonic telemetry. *J. Fish. Res. Board Can.* **30,** 119–121.

Stasko, A. B., and Rommel, S. A., Jr. (1974). Swimming depth of adult American eels (*Anguilla rostrata*) in a saltwater bay as determined by ultrasonic telemetry. *J. Fish. Res. Board Can.* **31,** 1148–1150.

Stasko, A. B., Horrall, R. M., Hasler, A. D., and Stasko, D. (1973). Coastal movements of mature Fraser River pink salmon (*Oncorhynchus gorbuscha*) as revealed by ultrasonic tracking. *J. Fish. Res. Board Can.* **30,** 1309–1316.

Tesch, F. W. (1970). Heimfindevermogen von Aalen (*Anguilla anguilla*) nach Beeinträchtigung des Geruchssinnes, nach Adaptation oder nach Verpflanzung in ein Nachbar-Astuar. *Mar. Biol.* **6,** 148–157.

Tesch, F. W. (1972). Versuche zur telemetrischen Verfolgung der Laichwanderung von Aalen (*Anguilla anguilla*) in der Nordsee. *Helgol. Wiss. Meeresunters.* **23,** 165–183.

Tesch, F. W. (1974). Speed and direction of silver and yellow eels, *Anguilla anguilla,* released and tracked in the open North Sea. *Ber. Dtsch. Wiss. Komm. Meeresforsch.* **23,** 181–197.

Thorson, T. B. (1971). Movement of bull sharks, *Carcharhinus leucas,* between Caribbean Sea and Lake Nicaragua demonstrated by tagging. *Copeia* No. 2, 336–338.

Trefethen, P. S. (1956). *Sonic equipment for tracking individual fish. U. S., Fish Wildl. Serv., Spec. Sci. Rep.—Fish.* **179.**

Trefethen, P. S., and Sutherland, D. F. (1968). Passage of adult chinook salmon through Brownlee Reservoir, 1960–1962. *Fish. Bull.* **67,** 35–45.

Trefethen, P. S., Dudley, J. W., and Smith, M. R. (1957). Ultrasonic tracer follows tagged fish. *Electronics* **30,** 156–160.

Tucker, D. G., and Gazey, B. K. (1966). "Applied Underwater Acoustics." Pergamon, Oxford.

Urick, R. J. (1967). "Principles of Underwater Sound for Engineers." McGraw-Hill, New York.

Walker, M. G., Mitson, R. B., and Storeton-West, T. (1971). Trials with a transponding acoustic fish tag tracked with an electronic sector scanning sonar. *Nature (London)* **229,** 196–198.

Wardle, C. S., and Kanwisher, J. W. (1974). The significance of heart rate in free-swimming cod, *Gadus morhua:* Some observations with ultra-sonic tags. *Mar. Behav. Physiol.* **2,** 311–324.

Williams, T. C., and Williams, J. M. (1967). Radio tracking of homing bats. *Science* **155,** 1435–1436.

Windell, J. T. (1971). Food analyses and rate of digestion. *In* "Methods for Assessment of Fish Production in Fresh Waters" (W. E. Richer, ed.), 2nd ed., pp. 215–248. Blackwell, Oxford.

Winn, H. E., Salmon, M., and Roberts, N. (1964). Sun-compass orientation by parrot fishes. *Z. Tierpsychol.* **21,** 798–812.

Young, A. H., Tytler, P., Holliday, F. G. T., and MacFarlane, A. (1972). A small sonic tag for measurement of locomotor behaviour in fish. *J. Fish Biol.* **4,** 57–65.

Yuen, H. S. H. (1970). Behavior of skipjack tuna, *Katsuwonus pelamis,* as determined by tracking with ultrasonic devices. *J. Fish. Res. Board Can.* **27,** 2071–2079.

Index

A

Abramis brama, tracking of, 353
Abudefduf abdominalis, predation on, 11
Acanthurus
  bahianus, social organization and, 9
  dussumieri, anemones and, 21
  nigrofuscus, social organization and, 9
  olivaceous, social organization and, 9
  triostegus
    group feeding behavior, 5
    social organization, 9
Acclimation, nematocysts and, 20
Accommodation, visual acuity and, 91–92
Acipenser güldenstadtii, tracking of, 350
Acropora, fish and, 19
Actinomycin D
  response acquisition and, 58
  response retention and, 66
Action spectrum, visual pigments and, 115–116
Acuity
  psychophysical results, 92–94
  structural consideration, 89–92
Aequidens portalagrensis, visual acuity, 90
African mouthbreeders, *see Tilapia macrocephala*
Aggression
  interspecific territorial defense and, 6–8
  mistaken identity and, 5, 8
  telencephalon ablation and, 167
Alosa sapidissima, tracking of, 351–352, 353, 355
Alpheus
  rapacida, goby and, 18, 19
  rapax, goby and, 18, 19
Amblyeleotris, 18
Amphiprion
  anemones and, 19, 20
  chrysopterus, nonsymbiotic, 21
Amyda, retina of, 248
Anemone/fish, relationships, 19–21

Anguilla
  anguilla, tracking of, 354
  rostrata, swimming depth, 358
Animals
  aquatic, difficulties of study, 342
  equipping with transmitters, 370–372
Argon, swim bladder and, 323
Aspidontus taeniatus, mimicry by, 23, 24
Astronotus ocellatus
  cornea, pigmentation of, 116
  visual acvity of, 92
Audiograms
  behavioral, 206
    criticism of, 208–209
Audition, in turtles, 249–251
Auditory electrophysiology
  responses of the eighth nerve and brain, 227–229
  responses of the inner ear
    frequency doubling effect, 225–227
    origin of saccular microphonic, 224–225
    postsynaptic potentials in auditory nerve fibers, 227
Auditory information
  analysis
    frequency discrimination experiments, 211–213
    masking experiments, 213–216
    mechanisms, 216–219
Auditory localization, 219–220
  inner ear and, 220–224
  lateral line system and, 220
Auditory nerve fibers, postsynaptic potentials in, 227
Auditory sensitivity, determinants and bandwidth, 209–211
Auditory stimuli, avoidance training and, 52–53
Auditory systems
  peripheral
    modes of stimulation, 204–206
    morphology, 201–204

Avoidance
    passive, telencephalon ablation and, 163–164
Avoidance conditioning, 49–50
    discrete trial procedure
        CS-UCS interval, 50
        inescapable shock, 53
        intertrial interval, 51–52
        prior fear conditioning, 50–51
        respondent stimulus reinforcers, 53–55
        shock intensity, 53
        species differences, 53
        stimulus modality, 52–53
    Sidman avoidance and, 55–56
    turtles and, 262–266
Avoidance learning, telencephalon and, 150,
    153–154, 162–164

B

Backgrounds
    moving, orientation to, 96
Bandwidth, critical masking, 214–215
Bass, retina of, 91
Batteries, acoustic transmitters and, 347
Behavior(s)
    species-specific, secondary reinforcement
        and, 154–157
Behavioral toxicity, 57–58
    response acquisition
        actinomycin D, 58
        ethanol, 59–63
        piracetam, 58
        scotophobin, 59
    response retention
        posttraining drug effects, 63–67
        state-dependent learning, 67–68
        steady state responding, 68–70
Benthic carnivores, guild of, 10–11
Benthic herbivores
    feeding guilds, 4–6
        aggression and interspecific territorial de-
            fense, 6–8
        social organization, 8–10
Betta splendens
    aggression, telencephalon and, 167
    agonistic behavior, reinforcement and, 170–
        171
    conditioned suppression in, 56–57
    operant conditioning of, 41–42
    reproduction, telencephalon and, 167

respondent conditioning, 36
response suppression, punishment and, 175
state-dependent learning by, 68
Black-tip shark, form discrimination by, 99
Bladder, gas volume control and, 322–323
Blennius
    corneas, 116
    pholis
        photopic spectral sensitivity, 121, 122
        spectral sensitivity curves, 118
Bloodflow, pattern, diving and, 270
Blue acara, form discrimination by, 99, 104
Bluegill sunfish, spectral discrimination by,
    124
Box salpa
    schooling, telencephalon and, 166
Brain, auditory responses of, 228–229

C

Carassius auratus, see also Goldfish
    auditory sensitivity, 210–211
    color vision in, 149
    conditioning of, 37, 38
    contrast sensitivity of, 83–84
    critical masking ratio for, 214
    frequency discrimination, 212
    reinforcement, conspecifics and, 172
    schooling, telencephalon and, 166
    spectral sensitivity curve, 118
    tonal masking in, 215
Carbon dioxide
    exchange of, 322
    lever pressing rate and, 261
Carcharhinus
    lucas, tracking of, 353
    milberti, tracking of, 353
    obscurus, thermoregulation by, 360
Caretta
    caretta, 242
        optokinetic responses, 299
        water-finding by, 301
    nestlings, migration by, 274
Carotenoids, turtle retinas and, 247
Carp
    color mixture in, 82, 126
    form discrimination by, 99, 100, 104
    photopic spectral sensitivity, 120
    saccular potentials, 226
    visual stimuli, properties, 108

Catfish
  auditory sensitivity, 206–207
  pressure sensitivity, 209
  swim bladder, ear response and, 205–206
Centropyge, feeding of, 10
Chaetodon
  avriga
    behavior, reinforcement of, 173
    cleaning symbiosis and, 13–14, 26
Chelodina longicollis, 283
Chelonia
  mydas, 242
    audition in, 249
    chemoreception by, 251
    hatchlings, tracking of, 353, 354
    learning by, 258–259
    migration by, 272, 305–309
    movements of, 238
    optokinetic responses, 299
    retina of, 246
    water-finding by, 300–301
    spectral sensitivity, 247–248
Chelonidae, members of, 242
Chelydra
  serpentina
    acoustic transmitter and, 345
    electro cardiograms, 362
    heart rate, breathing and, 270
    optokinetic drum and, 292
    visual receptors of, 247
Chemoreception, in turtles, 251
Chromatic contrast, adaptation and, 127
Chromatic vision
  color discrimination
    chromatic contrast and adaptation, 127
    color constancy, 128
    color mixture, 126
    color vision by rod system, 128
    different spectral distributions, 124–125
    psychological color space, 128
    saturation discrimination, 126–127
    wavelength discrimination function, 125–126
  spectral sensitivity, 114–116
    curves and interpretation, 116–123
Chromis, anemones and, 19
Chrysemys, 243
  avoidance conditioning, 262
  learning by, 256–257
  picta

audition in, 249
depth perception of, 285, 286, 287
homing by, 309, 310–311
learning by, 254–255
spectral sensitivity, 255
visual alarm reaction, 291
  scripta
    depth perception of, 286–287
    homing by, 309, 311
    optokinetic responses, 293–299
    tracking of, 354
    visual alarm reaction, 291
Cichlid, spectral sensitivity, 82
Circulation, turtle, 241–242
Cleaning symbiosis, feeding guilds and, 11–15
Clemmys
  guttata, depth perception of, 285, 286
  insculpta
    audition in, 249
    depth perception of, 287
Cod
  auditory sensitivity, 198, 207, 209
  directional hearing by, 223–224
Coding, spatial and temporal, 217–218
Color
  constancy, 128
  preferences, turtles and, 252
Coloration, aggression and, 5, 7, 8
Color mixture, discrimination and, 126
Color space, psychological, 128
Commensalism, measures of, 2
Competition, measures of, 2
Competitors, social organization and, 8–9
Conditioned fear, puromycin and, 65
Conditioned responses, detection of motion and, 96–97
Conditioned stimulus
  avoidance conditioning and, 50
  intensity effects, 37
  interval and, 37–38
Conditioned suppression, punishment and, 56–57
Conditioning
  classical, pan-species reinforcers and, 158–159
  instrumental
    negative reinforcement, 162–166
    positive reinforcement, 159–162
  limbic ablations and, 147, 151

Conditioning and learning
  operant, 40–41
    negative reinforcement and punishment, 49–57
    positive reinforcement, 41–49
  respondent, 35–36
  variables influencing, 36–40
Contour
  figural, discontinuities in, 102–103
  orientation, transfer effects and, 104–106
Contour discontinuities, discriminations and, 114
Corals, fish and, 19
Corneas, light absorption by, 116
Crassostrea
  gigas, gas bubble disease in, 320
  virginica, gas bubble disease in, 320
Cryptodiroidea, characteristics of, 243–244
Ctenochaetus strigosus, attacks on, 5
Curvature, discrimination and, 113–114
Cyprinus
  carpio
    actinomycin D and, 58
    conditioning of, 37
  idus, saccular otolith of, 202

D

Dascyllus, anemones and, 19, 20
Dendrochirus brachypterus, anemones and, 21
Depth, determination, telemetry and, 358
Depth perception, in turtles, 285–288
Dermochelys coriacea, migration by, 272
Diethyldithiocarbamate, response retention and, 66–67
Discriminations
  spatial vision related, 112
    constancies: size, orientation, brightness, 114
    contour discontinuities, 114
    curvature, 113–114
    figure-ground discriminations, 113
    texture and texture density, 114
    visual orientation, 113
Discrimination and classification of shapes, definitions and approach, 93–98
Discrimination learning, 46–47
  habit reversal and, 47–48
  probability learning and, 48–49

Discrimination thresholds
  contrast sensitivity, 82–83
    adapting luminance, 83–84
    spatial frequency analysis, 87–89
    spatial summation, 85–87
Divers, heart rates, 362–363
Diving
  animal studies and, 342
  by turtles, 241, 268–270
Dominant responses
  inhibition, telencephalon and, 152–153
Dopplershifts, telemetry and, 348–349
Drug effects
  posttraining
    actinomycin D, 66
    diethyldithiocarbamate, 66–67
    fluorothyl, 66
    puromycin, 63–66

E

Ecsenius
  mimicry and, 22
  bicolor, mimicry by, 22
  gravieri, mimicry by, 22
Ectoparasites, cleaning symbiosis and, 11–12
Eggs, as food, 10–11, 23
Egglaying, turtles and, 238, 275–276
Eighth nerve, responses of, 227–228
Elasmobranchs, spectral sensitivity of, 121–122
Electrocardiogram, monitoring of, 360–363
Electroencephalogram, sleep and, 266, 267
Environment, visual pigments and, 117
Eretmochelys imbricata, 242
  tortoise shell and, 283
  water-finding by, 303–304
Escape conditioning, 49
  discrete trial procedure
    CS-UCS interval, 50
    inescapable shock, 53
    intertrial interval, 51–52
    prior fear conditioning, 50–51
    respondent stimulus reinforcer contingencies, 53–55
    shock intensity, 53
    species differences, 53
    stimulus modality, 52–53
  turtles and, 262–266

Esox lucius
  orientation of, 96
  tracking of, 353
Ethanol
  response acquisition and, 59–63
  state-dependent learning and, 67–68
Ethologist, marine, field methods of, 2–4
Etroplus
  maculatus, cleaning symbiosis and, 12
  suratensis, cleaning symbiosis and, 12
Eunotosaurus africanus, turtle evolution and, 238
Eupomacentrus
  jenkinsi, territorial defense by, 6
  partitus, territorial defense in, 7–8, 27
  planifrons, territorial defense by, 6
Extinction
  reinforcement and, 43, 44–45
  telencephalon ablation and, 151–152, 164–165
Eye
  movements, orientation and, 96
  size, acuity and, 89–90

F

Far red light, sensitivity to, 120
Fear conditioning, avoidance and, 50–51
Feeding guilds
  interaction between
    cleaning symbiosis, 11–15
    parasitic feeding relationships, 15–17
  interaction within
    benthic carnivores, 10–11
    benthic herbivores, 4–10
Feeding relationships, parasitic, 15–17
Figures, parts versus whole, transfer effects, 103–104
Figure-ground, discrimination, 113
Fish, species studied, 181–186
Fish/anemone, relationships, 19–21
Flatfish, auditory sensitivity, 207
Floats, animal studies and, 343
Fluorothyl, response retention and, 66
Food, reinforcement and, 41
Forebrain, evolutionary puzzle of, 137–141
Form
  definition of, 97
  discrimination, experiments on, 98–100

Fovea, occurrence of, 91
Frequency analysis
  mechanisms, 216–217
    experimental approaches, 218–219
    spatial and temporal coding, 217–218
Frequency discrimination, experiments on, 211–213
Frequency doubling, microphonic potentials and, 225–227
Frequency modulation, telemetry and, 348–349
Fundulus heteroclitus, reproduction, telencephalon and, 168–169

G

Gadus morhua
  critical masking ratio for, 214
  electrocardiograms and, 360–361, 362
  noise masking in, 215
  tracking of, 356
Gallus domesticus, visual alarm reaction, 290
Ganglion cells, ratio to cones, 93–94
Gas, supersaturation, temperature and, 332–334
Gas bubble disease
  adaptation to supersaturation and, 320–324
  environment and, 324
  experimental induction in menhaden, 324–328
  first report of, 319
  symptomatology in menhaden, 330–332
Gas nuclei, formation of, 322
Gasterosteus aculeatus
  aggression
    reinforcement and, 172–173
    telencephalon and, 167
  color vision in, 149
  foraging, reinforcement of, 175
  reproduction, telencephalon and, 167, 168
Geochelone carbonaria, sleep in, 267
Glycogen, turtles and, 269
Glycolysis, anaerobic, turtles and, 241, 269
Gobio fluviatilis, schooling, telencephalon and, 166
Gobiosoma, cleaning by, 14
Gobius bucchichii, anemones and, 21
Goby/shrimp, relationships, 17–19
Goldfish, *see also Carassius auratus*
  amplitude-modulated signals and, 219
  auditory frequency analysis, 198

Goldfish (*continued*)
  auditory nerve responses, 228
  auditory sensitivity, 209
  avoidance training of, 53–54
    telencephalon and, 163
  brain, auditory responses, 228–229
  chromatic preadaptation by, 127
  conditioned suppression in, 56, 57
  conditioning of, 39, 40
  critical masking bandwidth, 215
  detection of motion by, 96–97
  diethyldithiocarbamate effects, 66–67
  ethanol effects on, 59–61
  flurothyl effects, 66
  form discrimination by, 99, 100
  frequency tuning curves, 216, 217
  habit reversal in, 48
  hair cell microphonic potentials in, 224–225
  lens movement in, 92
  maze learning, telencephalon and, 152, 160
  nystagmus in, 96
  operant conditioning of, 44–46
  orientation thresholds in, 95
  pain sensitivity in, 149
  passive avoidance by, 164
  photopic spectral sensitivity, 119–122, 123
  piracetam effects on, 58
  probability learning by, 48
  psychological color space, 128
  puromycin effects on, 63–66
  retina of, 91, 94
  rod system, color vision and, 128
  saturation discrimination by, 127
  scotophobin effects on, 59
  scotopic spectral sensitivity, 117
  short-term memory in, 150
  Sidman avoidance and, 55–56
  spatial and temporal coding, 217–218
  spatial frequency analysis and, 87–89
  spatial summation in, 85–87
  spectral discrimination by, 124–125
  state-dependent learning by, 67–68
  steady state responding by, 70
  stimulus polarity determination by, 222
  swim bladder, ear response and, 205–206
  transfer effects, spatial estimuli and, 101, 102–103, 104–105

  visual acuity of, 92, 93
  visual orientation and, 113
  visual stimuli
    other properties, 109, 110–111
    size, 106, 108
  wavelength discrimination function, 126
Gopherus
  agassizii, 242, 243
  polyphemus, homing by, 309, 311–313
Gourami, form discrimination by, 99
Graptemys pseudo-geographica, depth perception of, 287
Gray shark, form discrimination by, 99
Grooming, symbiosis and, 26
Grunt, auditory sensitivity, 207
Gudgeon, transfer effects, spatial stimuli and, 101, 102

H

Habit, reversal of, 47–48
Habitats, of turtles, 284
Heartbeat transmitter
  large, construction of, 366–367
  small, construction of, 367–368
Heart rate, diving and, 269–270
Helmholtz principle, visual acuity and, 92, 93, 94
Hemichromis
  bimaculatus
    aggression, telencephalon and, 167
    reproduction, telencephalon and, 167
  philander, reproduction, telencephalon and, 168
Herring, vision testing in, 81
Hibernation, turtles and, 270–272
Holocentrus rufus, critical masking ratio for, 214
Homarus americanus, gas bubble disease in, 320
Homing, by turtles, 305–313
Hydrophone
  directional, construction of, 368–370
  preamplifier, construction of, 368
  telemetry and, 343, 344, 347–348
Hydrostatic pressure, gas bubble disease and, 321
Hypercarbia, heart rate and, 269–270
Hypsoblannius, color pattern, 23

I

Ictalurus
  nebulosus
    auditory sensitivity, 210–211
    tracking of, 353
  punctatus
    auditory sensitivity, 210–211
Inner ear
  localization by
    experimental approach, 223–224
    intensity difference cues, 221–223
    time difference cues, 220–221
  morphology of, 201–204
Intensity difference cues, auditory localization and, 221–223
Intertrial interval, avoidance conditioning and, 51–52
Iodoacetate, turtles and, 269
Istiblennius striatus, cleaners and, 14

K

Kanamycin, microphonic potentials and, 224–225
Katsuwonus pelamis, tracking of, 351
Key pressing
  turtles and, 253–256
  variations, turtles and, 256–259
Kinosternon subrubrum, depth perception of, 287

L

Labrisomus kalisherae, anemones and, 21
Labroides
  dimidiatus
    cleaning by, 14
    mimic of, 23
  phthirophagus, 17
    as reinforcer, 173
    stimulation by, 14
Labroides spp., cleaning symbiosis and, 12–13
Lagodon rhumboides
  avoidance conditioning of, 52–53
  critical masking ratios for, 214
Lateral-line organ, stimulation of, 201
Lateral-line system, auditory localization and, 220

Learning
  limbic ablations and, 147–148, 159
  state-dependent, response retention and, 67–68
Leatherbacks
  body temperature, 241
  characteristics of, 242
Lemon shark
  form discrimination by, 100
  spectral sensitivity of, 121–122
Lens
  acuity and, 90
  of turtles, 246
Lepidochelys
  kempii, 242
  olibacea, 242
Lepomis
  cyanellus
    aggression, telencephalon and, 167
    learning by, 160
  macrochirus, reproduction, telencephalon and, 169
  scotopic spectral sensitivity, 116–117
Lever pressing, turtles and, 259–262
Light, water-finding by turtles and, 301–305
Limbs, turtle, 240
Limbic system
  lesions, effects of, 147
  rhinencephalon and, 146–148
  telencephalon and, 140, 144–145
Lissemys punctata, 284
Little tunny, visual acuity of, 92
Lucioperca sandra, saccular otolith of, 202–203
Luminance
  adapting, spatial vision and, 83–84
  visual acuity and, 93

M

Macaca mulatta, visual alarm reaction, 290
Macrochelys temmincki, common name, 283
Macropodus opercularis
  habit reversal in, 47–48
  maze learning, telencephalon and, 152
  reproduction, telencephalon and, 168
Malacochersus tornieri, shell of, 284

Masking
  experiments
    frequency analysis
      critical masking bandwidth, 214–215
      narrow band masking, 215–216
      wide band masking: critical masking
        ratios, 213–214
      narrow band, 215–216
      ratios
        critical, wide band masking and, 213–214
Mauthner cells, auditory localization and, 221
Maze learning, turtles and, 252
Meiacanthus
  atrodorsalis, mimics of, 22
  mimicry and, 22
  nigrolineatus, mimics of, 22
Menhaden
  gas bubble disease
    experimental induction, 324–328
    symptomatology, 330–332
Mercenaria mercenaria, gas bubble disease in,
  320
Microcanthus strigatus, visual acuity of, 92
Micropterus salmoides, equipment with trans-
    mitters, 372
Migration, turtles and, 272–275, 305, 313
Mimicry, relationships and, 21–24
Minnow
  color mixtures and, 126
  form discrimination by, 99, 100
  psychological color space, 128
  texture density discrimination by, 114
  transfer effects, spatial stimuli and, 101, 103,
    104
  visual stimulus
    other properties, 108, 109–110
    size, 107
  wavelenth discrimination function, 126
Mirror images, discrimination and, 113
Mollensia
  avoidance conditioning and, 53
  conditioning of, 37–38
Morone
  americanus, conditioning of, 40
  chrysops
    equipment with transmitters, 372
    tracking of, 354–355
  saxatilis
    equipment with transmitters, 372
    tracking of, 353

Morphine, state-dependent learning and, 68
Motion
  detection of
    conditioned responses, 96–97
    eye movements, 96
    orientation to moving backgrounds, 96
Mucus
  feeding on, 17
  nematocyst toxin and, 20, 21
Mud skipper, retina of, 91
Mullus, schooling, telencephalon and, 166
Mutualism
  cleaning and, 12
  measures of, 2
Myoglobin, turtles and, 269

                               N

Nanemys, see Clemmys
Near and far fields, sound detection and, 199–
  200
Near-field, manipulation, auditory sensitivity
  and, 206–207
Negaprion brevirostris, scotopic spectral sensitivity, 117
Nematocysts
  anemone fish and, 20–21
  discharge, inhibition of, 20–21
Neon tetra
  spectral sensitivity of, 122
  vision testing, 81
Nesting sites, method of location, 274
Nets, avoidance of, 351–352
Nitrogen
  exchange of, 322–323
  gas bubble disease and, 320
Noise
  auditory sensitivity and, 208–209
  background, telemetry and, 349
Nonspecific arousal, telencephalon and, 151–
  152

                               O

Oil globules, turtle retinas and, 247, 249
Olfaction
  nesting sites and, 274
  schooling and, 167
  telencephalon and, 149

Olfactory bulb
  functions of, 179
  telencephalon and, 145
Olfactory system, rhinencephalon and, 147
Oligoplites, 16
Oncorhynchus
  gorbuscha, tracking of, 352, 353
  kisutch, tracking of, 350, 355
  nerka, tracking of, 352–353
  tshawtscha
    equipment with transmitter, 370–371
    tracking of, 350, 353, 356
Operant conditioning, turtles and, 253
Optic tectum, optokinetic responses and, 294, 295
Optokinetic responses, turtles and, 292–299
Orientation thresholds, discrimination and, 94–95
Ouabain, microphonic potentials and, 224
Oxygen
  exchange of, 322–323
  uptake by turtles, 268–269

P

Panulirus argus, tracking of, 355
Paradise fish
  agonistic behavior, reinforcement and, 172
  maze learning by, 160
  probability learning by, 48
Paralithodes camtschatica, tracking of, 354
Parasitism, measures of, 2
Parupeneus, associations of, 11
Pecking order, generic, food supply and, 6
Perca
  corneas, 116
  fluviatilis
    photopic spectral sensitivity, 121, 122, 123
    spectral sensitivity curves, 118
Perch
  auditory localization in, 221
  form discrimination by, 99
  nystagmus in, 96
Phenergan, state-dependent learning and, 68
Photopic spectral sensitivity, models of, 122–123
Photopic vision, spectral sensitivity, 119–122
Phototaxis, nestling migration and, 275
Phoxinus
  color vision in, 149

  spectral discrimination by, 124
  telencephalon-ablated, 145
  temperature sensing in, 149
  laevis
    frequency discrimination, 212
    schooling, telencephalon and, 166
    visual acuity, 92
Pike, form discrimination by, 99
Pimephales notatus, respondent conditioning of, 35–36
Pinger, simple, construction of, 364–365
Piracetam, response acquisition and, 58
Plagiotremus
  mimicry and, 22, 23
  laudandus
    feeding by, 17
    mimicry by, 22
  townsendi, mimicry by, 22
Pleurodiroidea, characteristics of, 243
Pleuronectes platessa, electrocardiograms, 361
Plodictis olivaris, equipment with transmitters, 372
Pocillopora, fish and, 19
Pollachius virens, acoustic transmitter and, 345
Pollutants, indirect effects of, 33
Pomacentrus
  anemones and, 19
  jenkinsi, interspecific attacks of, 5
Porphyropsin
  absorption maxima, 121
  proportion of, 117, 118, 120
Posing, cleaning and, 12–13
Potassium chloride, microphonic potentials and, 224
Power plants, gas bubble disease and, 324
Pranesus insularum, scales, feeding on, 15–16, 17
Pressure, transmitter, construction of, 366
Probability learning, 48–49
Pseudemys
  avoidance conditioning, 262–266
  diving by, 268
  heart rate, breathing and, 270
  lever pressing by, 259–262
  oxygen uptake by, 269
  phototaxic response, 252
  retina, area centralis, 248–249
  spectral sensitivity, 247–248, 265

Pseudemys (continued)
  scripta
    audition in, 249
    elegans, 242, 243
    retina of, 246
Psilogobius, 18
  mainlandi, relationship with shrimp, 18
Psychological research, comparative, 176–187
Psychophysical methods, vision and, 80–82
Pterocaesio spp., scales, feeind on, 17
Punishment, conditioned suppression and, 56–57
Puromycin
  response retention and, 63–66
  steady state responding and, 70

R

Rainbow trout
  form discrimination by, 99, 100
  lens movement in, 92
Rana pipiens, visual alarm reaction, 290
Range, acoustic telemetry and, 346
Rat, dark preference, brain lesions and, 156
Recorders, marine ethology and, 4
Reflex methods, vision and, 81
Reflex rebound, optokinetic responses and, 295
Reinforcement
  conditioned, 42–43
  delay of, 44
  magnitude of, 44–46
  negative
    conditioned suppression and punishment, 56–57
    escape and avoidance conditioning, 49–56
  partial vs. continuous, 39–40
  positive
    discrimination learning, 46–49
    parameters, 41–46
  schedules of, 43–44
  telencephalon and, 140, 157
  visual, 41–42
Reinforcers
  pan-species contingent on pan-specific behavior
    classical conditioning, 158–159
    contingent on species-specific behaviors, 173–176
    instrumental conditioning-negative reinforcement, 162

instrumental conditioning-positive reinforcement, 159–162
  pan-species contingent on species-specific behaviors, 173–176
  species-specific contingent on pan-species behaviors, 170–173
  aggressive behavior, 167
  reproductive behavior, 167–170
  schooling behavior, 166–167
  types of, 41–43
Reproduction, turtles and, 275–276
Reproductive behavior, telencephalon ablation and, 167–170
Reserpine, steady state responding and, 70
Respiration, turtles, 241
Respondent stimulus reinforcer contingencies, avoidance conditioning and, 53–55
Responding, steady state, 68–70
Response, opportunity for variability, telencephalon ablation and, 162
Rete mirabili, gas exchange and, 322
Retina
  acuity and, 89, 90, 92, 93, 94
  inhibitory mechanisms in, 123
  of turtles, 246–247
  visual pigment distribution in, 119
Rheotropism, vision and, 96
Rhinencephalon
  limbic system and, 146–148
  telencephalon and, 145–146
Rhodopsin, action spectrum and, 116, 117
Ricco's law, vision and, 85
Rod system, color vision and, 128
Rudd
  photopic spectral sensitivity, 119–120, 122–123
  scotopic spectral sensitivity, 117
  visual threshold, 85

S

Saccular microphonic, origin of, 224–225
Salmo
  clarki, tracking of, 353, 355
  gairdneri, tracking of, 350, 353
  salar
    electrocardiograms, 361–362
    equipment with transmitters, 372
    tracking of, 353
  trutta, tracking of, 353, 356

Saturation, discrimination and, 126–127
Scales, feeding on, 15
Scardinius erythophthalmus
   contrast threshold of, 84
   spectral sensitivity curves, 118
Scarus spp., social organization and, 9
Schooling, telencephalon ablation and, 166–167
Sclera, of turtles, 246
Scomberoides lysan, feeding habits, 15–16
Scotophobin, response acquisition and, 59
Scotopic vision, spectral sensitivity, 116–119
Sculpin
   auditory nerve responses, 227
   frequency tuning curves, 216
Secondary reinforcement
   species-specific behaviors and, 154–157
   utilization, telencephalon and, 153–154
Seriola quinqueradiata
   swimming depth, 358
   temperature studies, 360
Shape, definition of, 97
Sharks, transmitters and, 347
Shell, turtle, composition of, 238
Shock
   inescapable, avoidance training and, 53
   intensity, avoidance training and, 53
   threshold, ethanol and, 62
Short-term memory, telencephalon and, 149–150
Shrimp, cleaning by, 14
Shrimp/goby, relationships, 17–19
Sidman avoidance, conditioning and, 55–56
Size
   discrimination of, 114
   symbionts and, 16
Skipjack tuna, visual acuity of, 92
Skull, turtle, 238–239
Sleep, turtles and, 266–268
Smaris, schooling, telencephalon and, 166
Smell, synthesis and, 137–141
Social behavior, symbiotic guidelines for research, 26–27
Social organization, benthic herbivores, 8–10
Sodium chloride, microphonic potentials and, 224
Sonar, animal studies and, 342
Sonic receiver, construction of, 368
Sound, telemetry and, 343, 346–349

Sound detection
   sensitivity
      behavioral audiograms, 206
      criticism of behavioral audiogram, 208–209
      determinants of auditory sensitivity and bandwidth, 209–211
      near-field manipulation, 206–207
      standing wave manipulation, 207
   underwater sound, 198–199
      near and far fields, 199–200
      standing waves, 200–201
Sound pressure, particle displacement and, 199
Spatial frequency analysis, vision and, 87–89
Spatial summation, contrast sensitivity and, 85–87
Species, differences, avoidance conditioning and, 53
Spectral distributions, discrimination between, 124–125
Spectral sensitivity curves, interpretation
   models of photopic sensitivity, 122–123
   photopic, 119–122
   scotopic, 116
Spherical aberration, acuity and, 90
Sphyrna zygaena, tracking of, 353
Spillway dams, gas bubble disease and, 324
Standing wave
   manipulations, auditory sensitivity and, 207
   sound detection and, 200–201
Stenotherus odoratus
   odor production by, 251
   oxygen uptake by, 269
Sticklebacks
   form discrimination by, 98, 99
      transfer effects, 104
   nest building, telencephalon and, 152
   visual stimuli, properties, 108
Stimulation
   otolithic organs, 204–206
   tactile, cleaning and, 13–15
Stimulus
   size, transfer effects and, 106–108
   visual, other properties of, 108–112
Stimulus modality, avoidance conditioning and, 52–53
Streptomycin, microphonic potentials and, 224–225
Sunfish, photopic spectral sensitivity, 121
Supersaturation
   adaptation to, 320–324

Supersaturation (*continued*)
  an environmental problem, 324
  gas, testing procedure for, 328–329
Swim bladder, auditory stimulation and, 204–
    205, 209, 210, 219, 222, 223
Symbioses
  modern views, 1–2
  research guidelines, 24–25

T

Tagging, animal studies and, 342
Tape recorders, marine ethology and, 4
Task, complexity, telencephalon and, 160
Tautoga onitis, tracking of, 354
Telemetry
  animal studies and, 343–345
  biological applications, 349–350
    depth determination, 358
    electrocardiogram monitoring, 360–363
    temperature measurement, 358–360
    tracking studies, 350–357
  equipment
    construction and use, 363–372
    sources of, 373–374
Telencephalon
  analysis of role
    critical examination of hypotheses, 148–
      154
    "secondary" reinforcement and species-
      specific behavior, 154–157
  anatomical and ontogenetic aspects, 141–145
  as rhinencephalon, 145–146
Telencephalon ablation
  behavior and reinforcement
    review of data, 158–176
    scheme for organizing data, 157
  effects of, 138, 140
Television cameras, marine ethology and, 3–4
Temperature
  fish behavior and, 327
  gas supersaturation and, 332–334
  hibernation and, 270–271
  lever pressing rate and, 261
  measurement, telemetry and, 358–360
  transmitter, construction of, 365
Temperature control, turtles, 240–241
Terrapene, 243
  carolina
    audition in, 249

  depth perception of, 285, 286, 287, 288
  homing by, 309–310
  sleep in, 267
  visual alarm reaction, 291
Territory, sharing of, 7
Testidomata, divisions of, 282–283
Testudo
  elephantopus, 243–244
  gigantea, 244
Texture, discrimination and, 114
Thunnus
  obesus, thermoregulation by, 360
  thynnus
    temperature maintenance by, 359–360
    tracking of, 353
Tilapia
  heudelotti macrocephala, scotopic spectral
    sensitivity, 117
  macrocephala
    auditory sensitivity, 210–211
    conditioning of, 39–40, 44
    critical masking ratios for, 214
    habit reversal in, 47, 48
    probability learning by, 49
    reproductive behavior, telencephalon and,
      167
    steady state responding by, 69–70
    swim bladder, ear response and, 206
  mossambica, reproduction, telencephalon and,
    167
  respondent conditioning of, 36
Time difference cues, auditory localization and,
    220–221
Toxicity, behavioral, 33–34
Tracking, telemetry and, 350–357
Training methods
  vision and
    avoidance, 82
    operant, 82
    respondant, 81–82
Transducers, acoustic telemetry and, 347
Transfer experiments
  form discrimination and, 101–102
    discontinuities in figural contour, 102–103
    orientation of principal contours, 104–106
    other stimulus properties, 108–112
    parts of figures versus whole figures, 103–
      104
    stimulus size, 106–108
Trionychidae, characteristics of, 244

Trionyx, oxygen uptake by, 269
Trionyx spinfer spinfer, 242
Trout
    transfer effects, spatial stimuli and, 101,
      105–106
    visual stimuli
      other properties, 108, 110
      size, 108
Tuna
    auditory sensitivity, 198
    temperature measurement in, 358–360
    transmitters and, 347
Turtles
    anatomy of, 238–240
    classification of, 245
    depth perception, 285–288
    evolution of, 237–238, 283–284
    habitats, 284
    learning by, 251
      avoidance and escape conditioning, 262–
        266
      key pressing techniques, 253–256
      lever pressing techniques, 259–262
      maze learning, 252–253
      operant conditioning techniques, 253
      variations of key pressing techniques,
        256–259
    major behavior patterns
      diving, 268–270
      hibernation, 270–272
      learning, 251–266
      migration, 272–275
      reproduction, 275–276
      sleep, 266–268
    migration and homing, 305–313
    optokinetic responses, 292–299
    respiration and circulation, 241–242
    sensory systems of, 244, 246
      audition, 249–251
      chemoreception, 251
      vision, 246–249
    systematics of, 242–244
    temperature control in, 240–241
    visual alarm reactions, 288–292
    water-finding behavior, 300–305
Typhlogobius, 17

U

Uca pugnax, visual alarm reaction, 290
Ultraviolet light, sensitivity to, 120–121
Umbra spp., respondent conditioning, 36

V

Vertebrates, homology of structure, 281
Vision
    psychophysical methods, 80–81
      reflex methods, 81
      training methods, 81–82
    spatial
      discrimination and classification of shapes,
        97–114
      discrimination thresholds, 82–97
    telencephalon and, 149
    in turtles, 246–249
Visual alarm reactions, turtles and, 288–292
Visual cliff, advantages of, 286
Visual orientation, discrimination and, 113
Visual pigments, absorption spectra, 115
Visual stimuli, avoidance training and, 52–53
Visual systems
    aquatic, limitations of, 79
    lesions, depth perception and, 288
Vitamins A, turtle retinas and, 246

W

Water, sound conduction in, 348
Water-finding behavior, of turtles, 300–305
Water pressure, depth determination and, 358
Wavelength
    discrimination function, 125–126
    signal intensity loss and, 346–347
Weberian ossicles, bandwidth and, 209, 210
Weber's law, vision and, 83

X

Xiphophorus
    helleri, avoidance contioning of, 52
    maculatus
      aggression, telencephalon and, 167
      reproduction, telencephalon and, 168, 169